VOTIVE OFFERINGS
TO HATHOR

VOTIVE OFFERINGS
TO HATHOR

Geraldine Pinch

GRIFFITH INSTITUTE
ASHMOLEAN MUSEUM
OXFORD
1993

This book is dedicated to my husband, Richard

ISBN 0 900416 54 8 (cased)
    0 900416 55 6 (paperback)

British Library Cataloguing-in-Publication Data: a catalogue record for this book is available from the British Library.

Typeset in Lasercomp Garamond at
Oxford University Computing Service
Printed in Great Britain at
the University Press, Cambridge

Contents

List of Illustrations

Plans

Figures

Plates

Photographs by R. Harris used by permission of the Trustees of the British
Museum and of the Victoria and Albert Museum, London, and the Visitors
of the Ashmolean Museum, Oxford

Acknowledgements

This book, a revised and updated version of my Oxford D.Phil. thesis submitted in 1984, could not have been written without the help of a great many museums. I am grateful for information or photographs received from the Anthropological Museum, Aberdeen; the Staatliche Museen, East Berlin; the Historisches Museen, Berne; the City Museum and Art Gallery, Birmingham; the Museum of Fine Arts, Boston; the City Museum and Art Gallery, Bristol; the Brooklyn Museum, New York; the Art Institute and the Oriental Institute, Chicago; Christie's; the National Museum, Dublin; the Museum and Art Gallery, Dundee; The Royal Scottish Museum, Edinburgh; the Museum and Art Gallery (Kelvingrove) and The Hunterian Museum, Glasgow; the Semitic Museum, Harvard University; the Heckscher Museum, Huntingdon, Long Island; Cliffe Castle Museum, Ilkley; the City Museum, Liverpool; the Victoria and Albert Museum, London; Manchester Grammar School; the Metropolitan Museum of Art, New York; the Carnegie Museum, Pittsburgh; Sotheby's; and the Medelhavsmuseet, Stockholm. Acknowledgements for photographs used are made in the list of Plates.

I am particularly grateful for the generous help which I received from Angela Thomas at the Museum and Art Gallery, Bolton; Luc Limme at Les Musées Royaux d'Art et d'Histoire, Brussels; Janine Bourriau at the Fitzwilliam Museum, Cambridge; Maurice Bierbrier at the British Museum, London; Mary Crawford, Shirley Strong and Patricia Spencer at the Egypt Exploration Society; Barbara Adams and Rosalind Hall at the Petrie Museum, University College, London; Rosalie David at the University Museum, Manchester; Helen Whitehouse at the Ashmolean Museum, Oxford; Helen Murray and Diana Magee at the Griffith Archives and Fiona Strachan at the Griffith Institute, Oxford; Lynne Williamson at the Pitt-Rivers Museum, Oxford and Faith Stanley at the Royal Ontario Museum, Toronto.

The late Raphael Giveon helped me with information about his finds at Serabit el-Khadim. I would also like to thank Beno Rothenberg for information about the offerings from Timna; Jadwiga Lipińska for sending photographs of an inscription from Deir el-Bahri; Deborah Sweeney for examining objects from Timna in the Museum Haaretz, Tel Aviv; Don Starr for photographing objects and copying records in the University Museum, Kyoto; Anthony Leahy for examining records in the Cairo Museum; Andrea McDowell for much assistance with the bibliography; Mrs A. Nibbi for translations from Italian; the late Professor M. O. Beshir for delivering a letter to the Khartoum Museum; Nigel Strudwick for sending a photograph of a fertility figurine excavated by him; Delwen Samuel for advice on poppy seed loaves; and Alison Roberts, Gay Robins and Lisa Leahy for stimulating discussions and moral support.

I am most grateful to my brother, Richard Harris, for taking photographs, under difficult circumstances, of material in the British Museum, the Victoria and Albert Museum and the Ashmolean Museum; and to my husband, Richard Pinch, for teaching me to use a word-processor and for his unswerving support. Above all, I wish to thank John Baines for his invaluable advice, constructive criticism and encouragement during the writing of this book.

Introduction

This book examines votive offerings presented to the goddess Hathor at Deir el-Bahri, Faras, Mirgissa, Serabit el-Khadim, Timna and Gebel Zeit. These are the only sites at which large quantities of Second Intermediate Period or New Kingdom offerings to Hathor have survived.

All of these sites are described in Part I of the book. Each chapter has accounts of the major excavations at the site, the history of the Hathor temple or shrines, and the find places and date range of the offerings. Due to its complexity, Deir el-Bahri has to be treated somewhat differently from the other locations. Publication of the Gebel Zeit excavations is not yet complete so only a preliminary assessment of this site and its artefacts can be given here.

In Part II the eleven main categories of votive offering found at the sites are described and discussed. The term 'votive offering' is used in its general sense of a 'gift to a deity' rather than in its specific sense of a 'gift in fulfilment of a vow'. Temple statues of private individuals have been left out, on the grounds that they were set up to provide bodies for the donors rather than gifts for a deity. Part II is not intended as a complete catalogue of the offerings. The quantity of material is much too great and not all of it is accessible. The categories are not treated equally. Preference is given to types of object, such as the votive textiles, about which comparatively little has been written. More space is allotted to the symbolic values of the offerings and to their functions in the Hathor cult than to their technical or stylistic features. In order to explain the significance of the offerings, it has sometimes proved necessary to discuss large amounts of comparative material. In the illustrations, preference has been given to previously unpublished material. The votive offerings from Mirgissa and Timna are very well illustrated in the relevant excavation reports, so no material from these sites is included in my illustrations.

Part III of the book treats the offerings to Hathor in the wider context of religion in daily life during the New Kingdom. It discusses the manufacture, distribution and presentation of the offerings and examines the role of the state temples in the religious life of private individuals. My main aim is to arouse interest in this neglected body of material. The study of votive offerings can provide many insights into religion and society in ancient Egypt.

I

The sites

1.1 Deir el-Bahri

1.1.1 The site

Deir el-Bahri is the name given to a natural amphitheatre in the hills of Western Thebes at the head of a narrow valley known as the Asasif. The Asasif became the most important part of the Theban necropolis when Nebhepetre᷄ Mentuhotpe of the 11th dynasty built his mortuary temple against the cliffs at Deir el-Bahri. During the 18th dynasty temples were built at this site by Amonhotpe I, Hatshepsut and Thutmose III (Plan 1). Until the reign of Hatshepsut, Deir el-Bahri and the Asasif seem to have been known as *the valley of Nebhepetre᷄* (Allam 1963.68). After the queen built her temple [hieroglyphs] the Deir el-Bahri area came to be referred to as [hieroglyphs], [hieroglyphs] or [hieroglyphs] (Otto 1952.61–2). Although Hathor was not the principal deity of any of the temples at Deir el-Bahri, she seems to have been more closely associated with the site than any other god or goddess.

The attention of early European visitors to Deir el-Bahri was chiefly focused on the imposing ruins of Djeser-Djeseru, the mortuary temple of Hatshepsut. In the 1820's J. G. Wilkinson had some of the rubble cleared away from Hatshepsut's temple and subsequently published the first detailed description of it (1835.90–8). A. Mariette tried to put a stop to illicit excavations on the site and worked on the temple of Hatshepsut for brief periods in 1858, 1862 and 1866 (1877.1–2). Mariette's excavations did not expose the whole of Djeser-Djeseru, some of which came to be buried deeper by his spoil heaps, but he did clear most of the Hathor shrine at the south end of the temple's middle colonnade (1877.23–5).

During these excavations Mariette noted the presence of 11th dynasty masonry (1877.5). These blocks came from [hieroglyphs], the mortuary temple of Nebhepetre᷄ Mentuhotpe. Between 1858 and 1860 Lord Dufferin and C. Graham excavated part of this temple while searching for antiquities. They uncovered the speos and cella and removed statues, offering tables, stelae and relief fragments, but no plan of the temple was established (Edwards 1965.17–21, pls. 9–10).

In the latter part of the 19th century several scholars dug at Deir el-Bahri, searching for intact burials (see Naville 1894.1–3; Arnold 1974.70–1), but a full excavation of Djeser-Djeseru was not attempted until 1893. In that year E. Naville, assisted chiefly by S. Clarke and H. Carter, began to excavate and record the temple on behalf of the Egypt Exploration Fund (Naville 1894–6; n.d. [1895–1908]; Clarke 1898–9). From 1903 to 1907 Naville, assisted chiefly by H. R. Hall, E. Ayrton and C. T. Currelly, undertook the first full-scale excavation of the 11th dynasty temple on behalf of the EEF (Naville & Hall 1904–6; Naville 1907a). He cleared the whole of the main part of Akh-isut, together with its north and south courts and most of its forecourt (Plan 2; Naville 1907; 1910; 1913). Naville also discovered several structures dating to the reign of Thutmose III, including a Hathor shrine built near the rear of the 11th dynasty temple (Plans 1–2).

In 1910 Carter and Lord Carnarvon worked in the Asasif, discovering the site of the valley temple of Hatshepsut and excavating part of the three causeways which ran up the valley to the temples at Deir el-Bahri (1912.28–33). In 1912 the Asasif became part of the concession of the Metropolitan Museum of Art Egyptian Expedition. The expedition, led by H. Winlock, worked its way up the valley towards Deir el-Bahri. In the winter of 1921–22 Winlock re-excavated part of the 11th dynasty temple and its north court, and the MMA expedition spent many seasons between 1922 and 1936 excavating in the vicinity of Hatshepsut's temple (Winlock 1921–4, 1926, 1928–31; Lansing 1935–6).

Between 1910 and 1937 the Antiquities Service carried out a programme of repair and restoration work on the temples of Nebhepetreʿ Mentuhotpe and Hatshepsut. In 1961 the continuing task of restoring Djeser-Djeseru was entrusted to a Polish expedition under the direction of L. Dąbrowski. The following year the Poles discovered the ruins of a third temple on the hillside between Akh-isut and Djeser-Djeseru (Plan 1). This proved to be 𓎼𓏏𓉐, a temple built in the last decade of the reign of Thutmose III (Dąbrowski 1964; 1968; Lipińska 1966; 1968a, b; 1977; 1984; Dąbrowska-Smektała 1968; Marciniak 1974; Laskowska-Kusztal 1984). The Hathor shrine excavated by Naville was part of this temple complex. In recent years Belgian, Italian, German and Austrian expeditions have all worked in the Asasif. The work of the German expedition included a detailed survey of the 11th dynasty temple, under the direction of D. Arnold (1974; 1974a; 1981).

1.1.2 The Hathor shrines

1.1.2.1 *The 11th dynasty temple (Akh-isut)*

Hathor's association with the Theban necropolis can be traced back at least as far as the First Intermediate Period (Allam 1963.58). E. Otto suggested that a 'popular cow-cult' flourished at Deir el-Bahri in a 'cave' shrine before the 11th dynasty, and that the cow goddess of the necropolis first came to be identified with Hathor, Lady of Dendara, when Nebhepetreʿ Mentuhotpe built Akh-isut (1952.51). This king used the title *Son of Hathor, Lady of Dendara* (Allam 1963.60), and he built shrines for her at Dendara (Labib Habachi 1963.22–6) and Gebelein (Robins 1990.23–4, 68–75). The 11th dynasty royal ladies buried in the temenos of Akh-isut nearly all bore the title of *ḥmt nṯr* of Hathor (Naville 1907 pls. 17, 20; 1910 pls. 11, 13; 1913 pl. 2) and Hathor, Lady of Dendara, features in some of the reliefs and inscriptions from the temple (Arnold 1974a.83, pls. 1, 5, 18, 25, 28, 44, 59). One 11th dynasty relief fragment from Deir el-Bahri shows a king, presumably Nebhepetreʿ Mentuhotpe, suckling from a goddess in cow form (Woldering 1955 pl. 23; Arnold 1974.83).

Naville suggested that some part of the 11th dynasty temple must have been set aside for the worship of Hathor (1907.63). There is Old Kingdom evidence for a

Hathor shrine being a standard part of a royal mortuary complex (Ricke 1952.28; Allam 1963.7–19; Arnold 1974.83). Naville was uncertain whether Hathor was worshipped somewhere in the rear part of the temple or in an earlier building on the site of the Hathor shrine of Thutmose III (1907.63; 1910.7). Arnold (1974.83–4) cannot identify any part of the existing structure as a Hathor shrine and proposes that Nebhepetre͑ Mentuhotpe built a separate shrine for the goddess, probably on the site later used for the platform of Hatshepsut's Hathor shrine.

Wherever Hathor may have been worshipped in the Middle Kingdom and the Second Intermediate Period, there is evidence that in the New Kingdom offerings were made to her in the main part of Akh-isut. Many of the stelae and statues found inside the 11th dynasty temple are inscribed with prayers to Hathor. These inscriptions might be taken as referring to the Hathor of the shrine built by Thutmose III, since, although this shrine was officially part of Djeser-Akhet, it was approached through Akh-isut (Plan 2; Lipińska 1977.42). Some of the broken stelae and statues recovered from Akh-isut could have been thrown onto the temple platform from the adjacent Hathor shrine of Thutmose III or from the main part of Djeser-Akhet at the time of their demolition (1.1.2.4).

Not all the references to Hathor can be explained away in this fashion. Some occur on statues from Akh-isut which range in date from Thutmose I to Hatshepsut, and therefore predate the building of Djeser-Akhet (*e.g.* New York MMA 06.1231.86, Naville 1913.5, pl. 6.3; Chicago OI 8635, Naville 1913.2, pls. 4.3, 8a; London UC 14351, Page 1976.57, fig. 63). The inscription on one late 18th dynasty statue asks Amon and Hathor for permission to remain in Akh-isut (Pittsburgh CM 2940.2, Naville 1913.2–3, pl. 9d; Patch 1990.62–3, no. 48), and one 18th dynasty stela fragment of a *waab* priest of *Hathor who is in Akh-isut* was found in the temple (1913 pl. 7.3). The text on a mid 18th dynasty statue refers both to Hathor *who is in Djeser-Akhet* and Hathor *Lady of Akh-isut* (Edinburgh RSM 1905.279.3; Naville 1913.1–2, pls. 4.1, 8f), which suggests that the donor was honouring two hypostases of Hathor, one in each temple.

Several objects found in Akh-isut suggest the presence in the temple of a cult statue of Hathor in cow form. A late 18th dynasty stela depicts a statue of *Hathor, Lady of Djeser who is in Akh-isut* in cow form suckling and protecting a king whose name is not preserved (Pl. 9, top left; 2.1.1 List 1.11). A votive cloth dedicated by a man who held several priestly offices in Akh-isut at the end of the 18th dynasty shows a statue of Hathor in cow form with Nebhepetre͑ Mentuhotpe standing beneath her head (Pl. 25b; 2.2.1, Cat. 4.9). In November 1904, a beautiful life-size calcite cow's head with glass inlays (Pl. 9, centre = London BM 42179) was found among debris on the north side of the platform of the 11th dynasty temple (Newberry Mss 1905.np; 1.1.3). Statues of Amon-Re͑ and Nebhepetre͑ Mentuhotpe dating to the end of the 18th dynasty were discovered in the speos and cella of Akh-isut (Edwards 1965 pl. 9) and Arnold suggests that these were replacements for cult statues destroyed in the Amarna period (1974a.31–2). It seems probable that the calcite head once formed part of another replacement cult statue. The cult of Hathor in Akh-isut is also attested to by a large number of small 18th dynasty votive offerings discovered in and around the 11th dynasty temple (Plan 1). Some of these offerings are datable by royal names to the period prior to the construction of the Hathor shrine of Thutmose III (1.1.3.5).

1.1.2.2 *The temple of Amonhotpe I*

While excavating to the north of Hatshepsut's temple, Carter and Carnarvon discovered mud bricks stamped with the cartouches of Amonhotpe I and Ahmose-Nefertary (1912.31–2, pl. 23). Some of these bricks had been reused in walls; others were lying in ancient refuse heaps. In 1923 the MMA expedition excavated the remains of the mud brick temple of Amonhotpe I, which was built at the northern edge of the shield-shaped forecourt of the 11th dynasty temple. An incorrect plan of this temple was published by Winlock in 1942 and copied in PM II, plans XXXIV–XXXV (for a correct plan see Thomas 1980 pl. 1). This temple appears to have been demolished during the final stages of the construction of Djeser-Djeseru (Dorman 1988.70-2). All that remained were the foundations and the lower courses of a few walls, preserved under the first ramp of Hatshepsut's temple (Winlock 1924.14–6, 1932.23–4; Gitton 1975.19–20; Arnold 1979.42, 67; Thomas 1980.77).

Nothing definite is known about the dedication of this temple. It may have been used for the royal mortuary cult but it was not Amenhotpe I's main mortuary temple (Gitton 1975.19–20). From at least as early as the 12th dynasty, the cult image of Amon of Karnak visited the Asasif and Akh-isut during the Beautiful Festival of the Wadi; a festival in which Hathor played an important role as goddess of the necropolis (Schott 1952.1, 94; Allam 1963.68–75; Arnold 1974a.33; Bietak in Bietak & Reiser-Haslauer 1978.19–20, 24–9). It has been suggested that the temple of Amonhotpe I was built to serve as an alternative, or additional, setting for this festival (Gitton 1975.19).

A small number of faience objects, such as beads, scarabs, cartouche plaques and votive menit counterpoises bearing the names of Amonhotpe I, or of members of his family, have been found at Deir el-Bahri (Fig. 4, Pl. 4; Hall in Naville 1913.13, 26; Winlock 1923.28; Hayes 1959.46, 48, 52). These might be interpreted as offerings to, or in the name of, royal ancestors, but the scholars who have examined the pieces have judged them to be contemporary with the rulers whose names they bear (Hall in Naville 1913.13–4; Winlock 1942.81; Hayes 1959.46, 48, 52; Gitton 1975.28–9; see also 1.1.3.5). The beads and scarabs, and even the cartouche plaques, might have been worn as amulets for some time before being dedicated to the goddess, but this would be most unlikely in the case of the fragile menit counterpoises (2.9.2.2). It would be natural to assume that these early 18th dynasty objects came from a Hathor shrine in the temple of Amonhotpe I, but there are objections to this hypothesis. No votive faience is said to have been found on the site of this temple or among the mounds of bricks from the temple. Most of the early 18th dynasty objects were discovered on the platform of Akh-isut or in its north court (Plans 1–2; 1.1.3.1).

Winlock proposed that a separate Hathor shrine had been built by Amonhotpe I on the site later used for Hatshepsut's Hathor shrine (1942.81). Though plausible, this solution does not account for a group of small faience objects, including a bead, a cartouche plaque and two scarabs, inscribed with the name of Ahmose (Pl. 6f; 1.1.3.1). It cannot be proved that these particular pieces were presented to Hathor during Ahmose's reign, but a contemporary tomb-painting in the Asasif which shows Ahmose-Nefertary making offerings to Hathor, Lady of Dendara, in cow form (TT 15; Carter & Carnarvon 1912.16, pl. 6; Davies 1925.14, pl. 2; Gitton 1975.11–2) suggests that the cult of Hathor at Deir el-Bahri did enjoy royal patronage under Ahmose.

It might be argued that from Ahmose to Thutmose II rulers made offerings to Hathor in a Middle Kingdom shrine, situated on the site either of Hatshepsut's or of Thutmose III's Hathor shrine. The former is more likely. No traces of an earlier structure were found beneath the Hathor shrine of Djeser-Akhet (1.1.2.4), but the area beneath the platform supporting the Hathor shrine of Djeser-Djeseru, which juts out into the north court of Akh-isut (Plan 1), has never been excavated (1.1.2.3). However, in a description of the stratigraphy of the north court of Akh-isut, Hall stated that all the votive offerings to Hathor, including the early 18th dynasty objects, were lying *above* a layer of stone chips attributable to the building work of Hatshepsut, which in turn lay directly on the 11th dynasty pavement (in Naville 1907.17). This layer of stone chips must also represent the building work of Thutmose III, which was much more extensive than Hall realised. Therefore these offerings were not dumped in the north court until *after* the construction of Djeser-Akhet. This analysis is confirmed by the fact that both here, and elsewhere at Deir el-Bahri, the early 18th dynasty offerings were found mixed in with material ranging in date from Hatshepsut to Amonhotpe III (1.1.3.5).

Either the early 18th dynasty offerings, and a few pottery objects which might date to the late Second Intermediate Period (1.1.3.5), were dedicated in a structure which was still accessible after the building of Djeser-Djeseru and Djeser-Akhet, or they were transferred to Akh-isut from a destroyed shrine. Evidence from other Hathor sites (see esp. 1.6.3) shows that the latter explanation is possible but, so long as the existence of earlier Hathor shrines is unproven, it is simplest to assume that before the construction of Djeser-Djeseru offerings were made to Hathor chiefly or solely in the main part of the 11th dynasty temple. Evidence that early 18th dynasty rulers took an interest in Akh-isut is provided by the colossal statues of himself which Amonhotpe I set up flanking the ramp to the temple platform (Hall in Naville 1907.26, pl. 25; Szafránski 1985.258–60), and by a statue of Thutmose I found inside the temple (EEF Cat. [1906].12 = London BM 1457). 18th dynasty votive stelae attest to a cult of Amonhotpe I and Ahmose-Nefertary in Akh-isut before such a cult became generally popular in the Theban necropolis (Naville 1907.60–1, pl. 25.b, d; London BM 1455).

1.1.2.3   *The temple of Hatshepsut (Djeser-Djeseru)*

Djeser-Djeseru was primarily dedicated to Amon-Reꜥ-Horakhty and to the funerary cult of Hatshepsut and her father, but shrines for Anubis and Hathor were included at either end of the middle colonnade (Plan 1). The Hathor shrine, at the south end of the colonnade, is partly rock-cut and partly built on a platform of masonry projecting into the north court of Akh-isut. It consists of two transverse halls (the

court and the hypostyle), a hall or ante-chamber with four statue niches, an outer
sanctuary with four niches and an inner sanctuary with two niches (Naville
[1901].1–6; Clarke in Naville [1908].22–5; Werbrouck 1949.119–33). The small
sanctuaries are vaulted and lined with limestone slabs. Originally they must have
contained statues, such as are shown in reliefs on the walls, of Hathor in cow form
protecting and nurturing Hatshepsut. Naville and Hall proposed that the calcite
cow's head (Pl. 9, centre) had come from Hatshepsut's Hathor shrine 'from which it
fell onto the XIth Dynasty building below' (1907.69). This is unlikely since the
head was found on the platform of the 11th dynasty temple about 20 m from the
edge of the platform of Hatshepsut's Hathor shrine. In the reliefs in this shrine,
Hathor is somtimes called Lady of Dendara (*e.g.* Naville [1901] pls. 87, 93–4, 104),
but her most common epithet is *ḥrit-tp wȝst* – 'Chieftainess of' or 'Foremost in
Thebes'. E. Brovarski (1976.69–70) suggests that Hathor Foremost in Thebes was
the name of the cult statue of the Hathor shrine in the south chapel of the Ptah
temple at Karnak, and that she was 'resident' at Deir el-Bahri only during certain
festivals when this cult statue crossed the river. The epithet Foremost in Thebes is
found on many of the 18th dynasty offerings, but it seems to have fallen out of use
at the end of the 18th dynasty to be replaced by the more specific 'Lady of
Djeseru/Djeseret' (Marciniak 1971.54–6; 1974.24).

The polygonal columns of the court have no capitals, but the hypostyle has
circular columns with elaborate Hathor sistrum capitals (von Mercklin 1962
pl. 2.8–9). It is probable that the shrine was originally fronted by these columns and
that the court was a slightly later addition (Clarke in Naville [1908].24; Tefnin
1975.140–1). The main access to the shrine seems to have been via a ramp built
along the edge of the second court of Djeser-Djeseru (Plan 1; Wysocki 1985.307).
During Hatshepsut's reign the shrine appears to have become a focus for popular
devotion to Hathor and numerous offerings were made to her there (1.1.3.1).

Some time after Hatshepsut's death, perhaps during the construction of
Djeser-Akhet, her statues were removed from Djeser-Djeseru and broken up, her
figure was erased from the temple reliefs, and her name was replaced, usually by
that of Thutmose I or II. The frequent substitution of Thutmose II's name in the
Hathor shrine, leads Z. Wysocki to propose that the construction of the shrine
began in this king's reign (1986.227–8). A desire to stress the blessing of Hathor on
the 'legitimate' Thutmosid succession seems a more likely explanation for
Thutmose II's name replacing that of Hatshepsut. Arnold suggests that Thutmose
III built Djeser-Akhet to diminish Hatshepsut's reputation by overshadowing her
temple (1974.68), while Brovarski proposes that this king constructed his Hathor
shrine 'to replace Hatshepsut's chapel in the affections of Hathor's devotees'
(1976.71). Few details are available about the two dumps of votive offerings which
may have come exclusively from the Hathor shrine of Djeser-Djeseru (1.1.3.2).
The fact that they contained model bunches of grapes, which are characteristic of
the late 18th dynasty (2.10.1), suggests that small votive offerings continued to be
made to Hathor in Djeser-Djeseru after the construction of Djeser-Akhet, but in
itself this evidence is not decisive.

After Hatshepsut's death, Djeser-Djeseru lost most of its mortuary character,
but it continued to be an important temple of Amon-Reˁ (Otto 1952.15–7). During

the Beautiful Festival of the Wadi the bark of Amon-Re⁽ seems to have visited all three of the temples at Deir el-Bahri (Schott 1952.5–7, 108–9), but the causeway of Hatshepsut's temple was the main processional route (Bietak in Bietak & Reiser-Haslauer 1978.25–8). Djeser-Djeseru was damaged in the Amarna period and restored in the early 19th dynasty under the supervision of the Vizier Paser (Naville 1907.33). Graffiti on the pillars of the middle colonnade, including drawings of Hathor, Bes and Taweret, probably date to these restorations (Niwiński 1985.211–13, figs. 12, 14, 23). On the basis of hieratic inscriptions found in a grotto in the cliff behind Djeser-Djeseru, Marciniak suggests that some kind of sanatorium existed in one of the Hathor sanctuaries at Deir el-Bahri as early as the 19th dynasty (1981; 1981a; see 3.3). In the 21st dynasty, earlier tombs under or beside Djeser-Djeseru were reused, and part of the middle colonnade seems to have become an embalmers' workshop (Naville 1894.6). From the late 22nd to the 26th dynasty burials were made in the rubbish which had accumulated over much of the structure (Naville 1895.34–5; PM I.II 643–9) but the upper terrace probably still functioned as a temple. Hathor, Lady of Djeseru, features prominently on Theban coffins of the Third Intermediate Period, so her cult probably continued at Deir el-Bahri, though by this time she was also a co-templar deity at Medinet Habu (Wente 1967.50). The Hathor shrine of Djeser-Djeseru may have fallen into disuse by the Late Period, as Naville found a 26th dynasty burial in the rubbish filling the court (1895.34–5), but the Beautiful Festival of the Wadi was still celebrated at Deir el-Bahri during this period (Bietak in Bietak & Reiser-Haslauer 1978.29). In the Ptolemaic Period, parts of Djeser-Djeseru were rebuilt or remodelled, and the cults of Imhotep and Amonhotpe son of Hapu were established there (Karkowski & Winnicki 1983; Laşkowska-Kusztal 1984). The Ptolemaic reliefs include a representation of Hathor (Naville [1906] pl. 150), indicating that the goddess was still associated with the site.

1.1.2.4 The temple of Thutmose III (Djeser-Akhet)

The temple of Djeser-Akhet was constructed on a narrow site above and between the temples of Akh-isut and Djeser-Djeseru (Plan 1). This temple may have replaced or incorporated a slightly earlier shrine known as Kha-Akhet (Meyer 1982.65; Dorman 1988.135). Djeser-Akhet was primarily dedicated to Amon and the temple played an important part in the Beautiful Festival of the Wadi (Lipińska 1977.62–3). Private statues and other objects inscribed with prayers to Hathor were found in the main part of Djeser-Akhet (Lipińska 1984.21–9, 49–53, 56), and the temple complex included a Hathor shrine. This shrine was built some 12.75 m below the level of the main structure. To accommodate the shrine, the rock face behind the north-west corner of the platform of the 11th dynasty temple was cut away, leaving a small triangular platform. The north court of Akh-isut appears to have been converted into a middle court for Djeser-Akhet, and there may have been a colonnade at the rear of the court which would have joined on to the north wall of the Hathor shrine (Lipińska 1977.47–59, figs. 33, 51). The Hathor shrine of Thutmose III therefore stood in the same relation to the main part of Djeser-Akhet as the Hathor shrine of Hatshepsut does to the main part of Djeser-Djeseru.

The structure on the triangular platform, which is paved in sandstone, has been almost totally destroyed. Its form is hard to reconstruct. A central passage, 6.5 × 2 m, was flanked by one narrow room to the north and two rooms to the south (Naville 1907.63–4; Lipińska 1977.38–45, fig. 33). J. Lipińska proposes that there were two further side rooms and some kind of vestibule with engaged Hathor mask columns, fragments of which were found in the vicinity of the shrine (1977.39–44, figs. 32–3). Some of the shrine walls were as thick as 1.44 m. Lipińska comments that:–

> In relation to rooms so narrow, the walls were indeed huge, and the entire appearance of the building is that it had been completely incorporated into the substructure of the Tuthmosis III temple platform . . . (1977.39)

Even if the shrine was incorporated into the main part of Djeser-Akhet, it was probably approached through the north upper colonnade of Akh-isut. A small flight of steps must have been provided to link the shrine to the temple platform (1977.42, fig. 31). To the rear of the central passage of the Hathor shrine was a rock-cut speos, 4.02 m long, 1.6 m wide and 2.44 m high (Plan 2; Naville 1907.37, 63–5; Lipińska 1977.38). The narrow entrance originally had a wooden door. The floor had never been paved, but the speos was lined with carved and painted sandstone slabs and the roof had a false vault. Inside, most of the space was taken up by a life-size sandstone statue of a Hathor cow, bearing the cartouche of Amonhotpe II (Pl. 41b; Naville 1907.65–6, pls. 1, 29–31; Maspero 1915.131). The reliefs show Amon and Hathor, in her cow and human forms, being adored by members of the royal family (Naville 1907.64–5, pl. 28). The epithets given to Hathor in the inscriptions are Lady of Dendara and Foremost in Thebes.

Due to the location of this Hathor shrine, its subsequent history has to be considered in relation to the histories of both Djeser-Akhet and Akh-isut. Djeser-Akhet was damaged in the Amarna period and restored in two stages, which Lipińska attributes to Horemheb and Ramesses II respectively (1977.63). The votive stelae and statues found in the temple range in date from Hatshepsut to Seti II (Lipińska 1984), while the pillars of the hypostyle hall are covered in graffiti which date mainly to the second half of the 20th dynasty (Marciniak 1974). Some of these record visits to the temple during the Beautiful Festival of the Wadi (Marciniak 1971.53–65), but most are brief, formulaic prayers to Hathor, Lady of Djeseret (Marciniak 1974.24–5; Sadek 1982; 1984). The construction of the mortuary temple of Ramesses IV blocked access to the causeways of Akh-isut and Djeser-Akhet (Bietak in Bietak & Reiser-Haslauer 1978.28). The last known reference to Djeser-Akhet occurs in an inscription in Theban Tomb 65 which describes Ramesses IX officiating at the Beautiful Festival of the Wadi (LD III.236; Lipińska 1967.28).

Huge boulders were found among the ruins of the temple, so it appears that Djeser-Akhet was destroyed, or at least badly damaged, by a rock fall (Lipińska 1977.10, pl. 13). Lipińska dates this destruction to the end of the 20th dynasty (1977.64). The temple was subsequently used as a quarry and large amounts of stone were removed or cut up and shaped into bowls on the site (1977.10–1; 1984.7–8). From the 26th dynasty onwards, burials were made in the debris above the temple (Lipińska 1967.30; 1977.11). The site was used as a rubbish heap in the Christian period, and as a dumping ground by 19th century excavators, so that the temple came to be buried under 24 m of debris (Lipińska 1977.10; 1984.7).

The history of Akh-isut from the 18th dynasty to the Third Intermediate Period seems to have been similar to that of Djeser-Akhet. In the New Kingdom, its principal deities were Amon-Reᶜ, Nebhepetreᶜ Mentuhotpe and Hathor (Naville 1907.57–65; Otto 1952.15; Arnold 1974.72–84). The temple was damaged in the Amarna Period and restored under Ramesses II (Hall in Naville 1907.14, 24, 33; 1913 pl. 35.5) and again under Siptah (1907.14, 24, 33, pl. 8; Naville 1910.12, pl. 10k). Ramessid interest is also attested to by a small number of 19th dynasty stelae (Naville 1913.4, 22, 25, pls. 6.2, 7.6, 22.8; Liverpool Cat, 1932.53; PM II 396) and statues (Naville 1913.6–8, 23, pls. 4.3–4, 9.b, 10b, 14.c; Speelers 1923.59, 64, nos. 248, 268).

The tomb of Nebhepetreᶜ Mentuhotpe is known to have been intact as late as the reign of Ramesses IX (Hall in Naville 1907.10), but some time after this Akh-isut became derelict and was used as a quarry. The reason for this may have been the same rock fall that damaged Djeser-Akhet. During the quarrying, the supporting wall of the main part of Djeser-Akhet was removed (Lipińska 1977.11). This caused a large amount of rubble to fall on Akh-isut, which would hardly have been allowed to happen if the temple had still been functioning. The quarrying may have been stopped because of further rock falls before the temple could be completely demolished. Many of the 11th dynasty tombs in the precincts of Akh-isut were reused during the 21st dynasty (PM I, 2 650–7). By the late 21st or early 22nd dynasty, burials were being made in the debris lying on the temple platform (Naville & Hall 1904.6–7; Naville 1913.1, pl. 35.3). Rubbish continued to accumulate on the site of Akh-isut and burials were occasionally made in it down to the Roman period. The temple itself was not disturbed again until the 19th century AD.

So little of the Hathor shrine of Thutmose III survives, and so few votive objects were found in it (1.1.3.1), that its history is difficult to reconstruct. The figure of Amon-Reᶜ on the rear wall of the speos was erased in the Amarna period and then beautifully restored in the late 18th or early 19th dynasty (Naville 1907.65, pl. 28f). On the rear and south walls are graffiti made by a single 19th dynasty scribe (Naville 1907.65, pl. 28), perhaps when the workmen of Ramesses II were restoring the temple. Naville mentioned that a block from the doorway to the Hathor shrine was covered in graffiti consisting of prayers to Hathor and Amon (1907.63). This block was sent to the University Museum in Tokyo and no information about the date of these graffiti is available. The presence of numerous 20th dynasty graffiti with prayers to Hathor in the hypostyle hall of Djeser-Akhet (Marciniak 1974.24–5) may mean that after the 19th dynasty visitors to Deir el-Bahri worshipped the goddess in the main part of the temple, rather than in its Hathor shrine. However, an undamaged statue of a scribe bearing the cartouches of Merenptah and Ramesses III found just outside the speos (Naville 1907.63; 1913.7, pl. 4.5) suggests that the shrine was still functioning in the early 20th dynasty.

Naville wrote that the speos had been sealed off by 'a fall of rubbish from the North which closed the shrine and saved the goddess' (1907.64). He assumed that this rock fall had taken place after the 11th dynasty temple had been partially demolished and just in time to save the speos from destruction at the hands of the quarriers. This would mean that the speos continued to be accessible for some time after the temples of Djeser-Akhet and Akh-isut fell into disuse.

The contents of the speos might be taken as confirming this view. Although the Hathor cow statue is well preserved, part of the left ear and the head of the uraeus on its brow have been broken off, and the gilding which originally covered its head has almost disappeared (Naville 1907.65, pl. 31). The flat, unfinished face of the king under the cow's head suggests that it was originally covered by a menit necklace of precious metal (1907.66), but this too is missing. Nothing of intrinsic value was discovered in the speos. With or without official approval, the priests seem to have taken everything valuable from the damaged temple before leaving. The statue itself would have been too large and heavy to move. The only other objects found in the speos were about forty crude wooden phalli (2.7.1.2; Pls. 52a, 53), and a fragmentary stela depicting a statue of a Hathor cow suckling and protecting a king (2.1.1 List 1.4). This stood just inside the door and was probably damaged in the rock fall. Naville gave the phallic objects as little publicity as possible. He may have viewed them as offerings made by ancient *fellahin* after the temple fell into disuse, rather than as part of an official cult in a temple maintained by the state.

The Hathor shrine's position (Plan 2) makes it is equally possible that the speos was sealed off by collapsing masonry when a major rock fall damaged the main part of Djeser-Akhet. Reopening the shrine may have been considered too difficult or too dangerous and this could have been a factor in the abandonment of Djeser-Akhet and Akh-isut. In this case, Naville would have found the speos exactly in the state in which it stood on a particular day in the late 20th dynasty. The contents of the shrine can also be interpreted as supporting this view. The damage to the Hathor cow statue could date to the Amarna period, when some of the reliefs in the speos were erased. The gilding and the precious necklace could have been confiscated or simply stolen by workmen sent to deface the shrine. Subsequent restoration work would not necessarily have run to regilding or to providing a new necklace of equal value.

There is no room in the speos for furniture, and the absence of small objects of any value might be explained by two factors. Firstly, no 20th dynasty ruler seems to have taken a particular interest in the cult of Hathor at Deir el-Bahri. Secondly, the economic conditions of the period may have led to few individuals being able to afford offerings of any value. In any case, the practice of dedicating small votive objects seems to have been less common in the Ramessid period than in the 18th dynasty (3.1). The presence of wooden phalli in the shrine should not be interpreted as a sign of 'moral decadence'. Such objects appear to have been a traditional offering to Hathor and 18th dynasty faience examples were found 'in the rubbish at some distance from the shrine' (Currelly in Naville 1913.31; 2.7.1.3). The speos may have been sealed off shortly after the phalli were presented to Hathor during a festival (2.7.3). As no detailed account of the nature of the 'rubbish' which blocked the entrance to the speos survives, the question of exactly when the speos of the Hathor shrine was sealed off cannot be answered with any certainty.

1.1.3 The votive offerings

Some large votive objects, such as stelae, were found inside the three temples. Groups of small offerings were discovered in at least nine areas of the site (Plan 1). Because it is often difficult to establish which shrine these offerings were originally dedicated in, I describe the material in order of excavation.

1.1.3.1 *The Egypt Exploration Fund*

When the Egypt Exploration Fund began their work on Djeser-Djeseru, the site had already been partially cleared by Mariette, and much disturbed by diggers searching for mummies. Only seven private statues and two private stelae appear to have been discovered inside the temple (PM II, 375; Brovarski 1976.58; 2.1.1), and their exact find-spots are unrecorded. Neither Mariette nor Naville mentioned finding small votive objects during their excavations of Djeser-Djeseru, but Hall wrote in a discussion of the votive offerings from the 11th dynasty temple that 'a number of similar objects were found during the excavation of the Great Temple itself' (in Naville 1913.13).

Distribution lists for the Deir el-Bahri excavations of 1892–4 now in the Egypt Exploration Society archives mention 27 typical votive offerings to Hathor, such as Hathor masks, cow plaques, and model ears and eyes, together with an unspecified number of faience beads and amulets. These objects must have come from Djeser-Djeseru, but since the seasons of 1892–4 saw the preliminary clearance of the whole temple, the date does not provide a clue to their exact provenance. As Naville was the first excavator to clear the court of the Hathor shrine of Djeser-Djeseru to floor level (Naville & Clarke 1895.34–5), the votive offerings may have come from this area.

In 1894–5, Naville excavated the northern half of the north court of Akh-isut, discovering several 11th dynasty tomb shafts close to the Hathor platform of Djeser-Djeseru (Naville & Clarke 1896.3). The EEF distribution lists for 1895 mention a group of objects sent to American museums including two stela fragments, four Hathor masks, five faience Hathor cows, two bronze cow plaques, four model ears, twelve model eyes, one eye plaque, seven menit counterpoises, and a necklace of Hathor masks and Bes pendants. The EES archives contain unpublished paintings and drawings of about 50 votive objects from Deir el-Bahri (for a selection, see Figs. 2–4, Pls. 3–5). These pictures are attributed to a Miss Carhew on the folder which contains them and are dated to 1895. This should mean that the objects illustrated by Miss Carhew all come from the excavation of Djeser-Djeseru and the part of the north court of Akh-isut nearest to Djeser-Djeseru. There is some doubt about this because two of the objects painted by Miss Carhew were distributed as late as 1905 (Boston MFA.05.239 = Pl. 3, second row, left; London V&A 676.1905 = Fig. 4, bottom right), and so could come from the excavation of Akh-isut. Either some small objects were held over for a long time, or the date given to Miss Carhew's pictures is wrong, and should perhaps be amended to 1905. Very few votive offerings were found in 1905 (see below), and the fact that not one of the objects illustrated by Miss Carhew appears in the excavation reports for Akh-isut suggests that the former explanation may be the correct one.

Akh-isut lay virtually undisturbed from the 21st dynasty to the 19th century AD, so it is not suprising that many votive objects have been recovered from it. Graham and Dufferin discovered a small group of Middle Kingdom stelae and offering tables and two 18th dynasty statues *in situ* in the speos and cella (Edwards 1965 pls. 9–12). Naville found about 35 votive stelae and about 28 private statues in a reasonable state of preservation, as well as fragments from many more. The few published references to the find-spots of individual objects (Naville 1907.63–5; Hall in Naville 1907.33, 45, 50–1) show that private statues and votive stelae were recovered from the ambulatory, the upper colonnades, and the east colonnade of the west court (Plan 2).

This information can be supplemented by the evidence of distribution lists in the EES archives. Six stela fragments were distributed after the excavations of 1903–4, which covered the north court, the north lower colonnade, and the north-east corner of the temple platform. Five stelae were distributed after the excavations of of 1904–5, which covered the ramp, the south lower and upper colonnades, the ambulatory, the north upper colonnade, the east colonnade of the west court, and a small part of the south court. Seven stelae were distributed after the excavations of 1905–6, which covered the remainder of the west and south courts, and the Hathor shrine of Thutmose III. Eleven stelae were distributed after the excavations of 1906–7, which covered the hypostyle hall, cella, and speos.

It was the usual practice for EEF excavators to ship back their finds at the end of each season and to distribute them as quickly as possible. The lists have to be used with caution, as they are not always complete, and it cannot be proved that individual objects were not held over for several years before being distributed, but they do give the impression that votive stelae and private statues were found in all parts of the 11th dynasty temple. Some of the votive offerings will have been moved from their original positions during the demolition of Akh-isut, but it is likely that large and heavy statues and stelae would have been broken up where they stood or pushed down a convenient tomb shaft.

The exact provenance of the small votive offerings from the 11th dynasty temple is hard to establish from the published accounts of the EEF excavations. Naville had little or no interest in these objects, but Hall gave several rather vague descriptions of their find-spots, of which the following is the most detailed:–

In the stone *débris* (but always close to the pavement) are found 'pockets' of small rubbish, containing the remains of votive offerings dedicated by the ancient *fellahîn* to the goddess Hathor of Deir el-Bahari. At the western end of the platform, in the (North) Court between the two temples and in the Northern Lower Colonnade was found a regular stratum of this rubbish, full of little broken offerings, nearly all of which are demonstrably of XVIIIth Dynasty date, and belong to no other period. They consist of small cows (the sacred animal of the goddess) and female figures in earthenware and blue glazed fayence, votive eyes and ears ... of bronze and fayence, small bronze plaques with roughly-incised cows on them, broken blue vases and bowls with representations of the holy cow emblazoned with stars and with spiral and lily patterns, &c., scarabs and beads, many on their original strings, and other small objects of the same kind. These votive offerings ... were undoubtedly originally devoted in the Hathor-shrines, and when these became too full were thrown down by the sacristans into the space between the two temples, which thus became a dust-heap, and on to the pavement of the XIth Dynasty temple. The layer of this dust at the western end of the latter was never cleared away (although the columns and walls of that part of the building bear records of the restorations of Ramesses II. and the devotion of Siptah under the XIXth Dynasty), and when discovered was about two feet deep. (in Naville 1907.17)

Three other sources of information on the find-spots of the small votive offerings are available – brief articles published in the annual *Archaeological Report* of the EEF, three catalogues of exhibitions which included material from Deir el-Bahri, and the EEF distribution lists. These sources do not always bear out Hall's accounts. The report for 1903–4 confirms that a large quantity of votive objects was found during this season in the north court and the north lower colonnade (Naville & Hall 1904.10–1), but the report for 1904–5 states that:–

> The interesting discovery of small votive offerings of the XVIIIth Dynasty made last year has not been repeated, only a few stray votive cows and plaques of blue faience, bronze, etc., having been found. (Naville & Hall 1905.7–8)

This is curious, because the western end of the temple platform, where Hall claimed to have found a 'regular stratum' of votive offerings 'about two feet deep', was excavated during the season of 1904–5.

The distribution lists appear to support the evidence of the annual reports on this point. Over the four excavating seasons, there was much greater variation in the number of small objects distributed than in the numbers of stelae and statues. In 1904, about 300 small votive objects and a large quantity of beads and scarabs were distributed, but in 1905 only about 25 small votive objects and a few beads were sent out to museums.

The excavation report for 1905–6 noted the 'interesting discovery' of some votive cloths, as well as the phalli from the speos of the Hathor shrine of Thutmose III, but no other finds of small votive objects (Naville & Hall 1906.5–7). However, the lists for 1906 show a slight increase in the number of small votive objects distributed. If these pieces were excavated in 1905–6 they could have come from the south or west courts. The latter is more probable, since offerings could have been thrown into the west court from the adjacent Hathor shrine (Plans 1–2). Since all but the speos was demolished to pavement level, it is unlikely that any small votive offerings remained *in situ* on the platform of this shrine and none are mentioned by Naville or Hall.

The excavation report for 1906–7 contained no references to votive objects, yet the distribution lists for 1907 show that about 100 small offerings, and an unspecified quantity of beads and scarabs, were sent out. Again the question arises whether some or all of these objects had been held over from previous seasons. In a few cases it is possible to say that they were. The British Museum entry register for 1907 records the arrival of wooden phalli from the Hathor shrine, and these were definitely discovered in the season of 1905–6. It seems unlikely that all the small objects distributed in 1907 were held over, so some offerings may have been found in the hypostyle hall, the cella, or the speos, the only parts of the temple excavated in 1906–7.

The catalogues of the three EEF exhibitions give a slightly different picture

again. The first catalogue lists a large and varied group of votive offerings
([1904]. 7–13). The second contains an equally large and diverse group of offerings,
including votive textiles ([1906]. 1–21), while the third mentions only a few small
offerings but a larger number of votive stelae, cloths and statues than the other two
([1907]. 1–14). The EEF exhibition mounted in 1905 consisted mainly of objects
found by Petrie at Serabit el-Khadim (Petrie 1905a. 1–19). Possibly the pieces found
at Deir el-Bahri in 1904–5 were held over until 1906 for this reason, but it could
equally be argued that no Deir el-Bahri material was exhibited in 1905 because not
enough had been found to make a good display.

   Two things are clear: that Naville and Hall did not publish a full account of the
exact provenance of the votive offerings, and that the latter's hypothesis about the
sacristans of the two Hathor shrines throwing objects into the north court and onto
the platform of the 11th dynasty temple requires modification. Offerings could
easily have been brought out of the Hathor shrine of Djeser-Djeseru and thrown
over the edge of the Hathor platform into the north court (Plan 1). The distance
between this Hathor platform and the platform of the 11th dynasty temple is never
less than 20 m, so it is most unlikely that any objects found in Akh-isut can have
been thrown there from Djeser-Djeseru. There may have been a direct route from
the Hathor shrine of Thutmose III to the north court, via the middle colonnade of
Djeser-Akhet (Lipińska 1977. 56–9), but it would have been easier to carry objects
from this shrine a short distance through the north upper colonnade to the edge of
the platform of Akh-isut in order to dump them in the court (Plan 1). The platform
of Akh-isut is over 5 m high, so objects are not likely to have strayed from the
north court into the 11th dynasty temple.

   According to Hall, small votive objects were found in two main areas inside
Akh-isut – at the western end of the temple platform, and in the north lower
colonnade. His reference to inscriptions of Siptah and Ramesses II indicates that by
the 'western end of the platform' he chiefly meant the west colonnade of the
ambulatory (Plan 2). Although the northern end of this colonnade is in front of the
platform of the Hathor shrine of Djeser-Akhet, it was separated from it by a high
wall (Plan 2; Naville 1910 pls. 21, 24b). While the temple was still intact, offerings
could not have been tossed or swept into this area from the Hathor shrine, but they
could of course have been carried there. To carry offerings from this shrine to the
north lower colonnade would have involved taking them the length of the temple
platform and down the ramp (Plan 2). This is, however, more plausible than
supposing that they were brought there from Hatshepsut's Hathor shrine, which
would have meant a journey half-way down the forecourt of Djeser-Djeseru and
half-way back up the forecourt of Akh-isut (Plan 1).

   The most obvious explanation is that all the offerings found inside Akh-isut
came from the Hathor shrine of Djeser-Akhet, while the material in the north court
included offerings from the Hathor shrines of Hatshepsut and Thutmose III. The
evidence of the EES archives indicates, however, that the situation is more
complicated. The votive offerings drawn by Miss Carhew in 1895 range in date
from Amonhotpe I to Amonhotpe III (Fig. 4, Pls. 3–5). Among the objects
distributed in 1895, after the excavation of part of the north court of Akh-isut, were
two votive menit counterpoises, one with the cartouches of Ahmose-Nefertary

(Pl. 4, top), and one with the cartouches of Hatshepsut. The lists for 1904 mention a cartouche plaque of Ahmose, several scarabs of Amonhotpe I, and a bead, a vase fragment and a menit counterpoise of Ahmose-Nefertary. These objects must have been found in the north court or the north lower colonnade. As already noted (1.2.2), all the votive objects in the north court seem to have been placed there after the construction of Djeser-Djeseru and Djeser-Akhet.

The lists for 1905 include cartouche plaques of Amonhotpe I, Hatshepsut, and Thutmose III, and those for 1906 include an alabaster lid with the cartouches of Hatshepsut. Most interestingly, a menit counterpoise of Ahmose-Nefertary was distributed in 1907. If this was excavated in the previous season, it must have come from the hypostyle hall, the cella, or the speos. The evidence of the EEF distribution lists and exhibition catalogues suggests that votive offerings were discovered in the rear part of the temple. Quite apart from their date, such offerings are not likely to have come from the Hathor shrine of Djeser-Akhet. It is improbable that priests would have moved superfluous offerings from this shrine into the holiest part of Akh-isut, and implausible that the workmen who demolished the shrine would have carried offerings into the hypostyle hall rather than just throw them aside (1.1.3.5). It is safest to conclude that the votive objects found in the north court come from three sources – the Hathor shrines of Djeser-Djeseru and of Djeser-Akhet, and an area of Akh-isut (probably in the hypostyle hall) dedicated to the cult of Hathor. The offerings found in the north lower colonnade and on the platform of Akh-isut could have come from this 'cult area' and/or the Hathor shrine of Djeser-Akhet.

The votive offerings discovered by the EEF at Deir el-Bahri are briefly described in the first volume of the full excavation report on the 11th dynasty temple (Hall in Naville 1907.12, 17, 21, 36). The third volume of this report contains a chapter by Naville on the best preserved stelae and statues (1913.1–9), and sections by Hall and Currelly on the cloths and the small votive objects (1913.13–8, 28–31). The EEF distribution lists, which were later copied into one register, show that material from these excavations was shared between about sixty museums. Some of the votive objects were subsequently destroyed or lost; many remain uncatalogued, and only about a quarter have been published in any form. I have been able to examine or obtain detailed information on about 70 per cent of these objects.

1.1.3.2 *Carter and Carnarvon*

In 1910 Carter and Carnarvon made trial excavations on the north and eastern perimeters of the forecourt of Djeser-Djeseru. In *Five Years' Explorations at Thebes* Carter wrote that:–

> In two places the trenches cut through the temple refuse heaps, one high upon the north side of the monument, the other at the north-east corner of the temenos. These heaps are certainly of great interest and should one day be carefully worked through, for in them are numbers of broken offerings, brought by the populace to invoke the aid and assistance of the local divinity. They consist of bronze, earthenware, blue glaze Hathor heads, cows, *menats*, model bunches of grapes, rings, balls, sistrums, sphinxes,

scarabs, scarab shaped and cowroid beads (one bearing the name of Aahmes I),
amulets such as ears, eyes and *ankhs*, dishes and bowls of pottery, some of which are of
very large dimensions. (1912.32)

Of all these votive objects, only a small selection of the pottery is illustrated in
Carter and Carnarvon's book (1912 pl. 22.1). The Carter papers in the Griffith
Institute include a group of unpublished photographs relating to these excavations.
Two are of selections of offerings from the refuse mounds (Carter Mss I.J. 204–5
= Pls. 6–7), and a third is of a cross section of one of the mounds, with small
faience objects visible among the rubble (I.J. 182). Two photographs of the general
area of the excavations show the hillside north of Djeser-Djeseru covered both by
ancient refuse mounds and by spoil heaps from Naville's excavation of this temple
(I.J. 192–3).

The mounds examined by Carter and Carnarvon were fairly close to the site of
the temple of Amonhotpe I and bricks from this temple were found nearby (Carter
& Carnarvon 1912.28–9), so it might be assumed that the offerings came from this
structure. The only closely datable object mentioned by Carter is a cowroid of
Ahmose (Pl. 6f), but the photographs in the Griffith Institute show that not all the
material he found was early 18th dynasty. Two faience fragments, one from a menit
counterpoise and one from a bowl, bear the prenomen of Hatshepsut (Pl. 7). The
position of the mounds indicates a relationship to Djeser-Djeseru. The mound at
the north-east corner would have been close to the second of the two postern gates
in the north wall of the forecourt of this temple, while the other mound was
probably close to the first postern (Plan 1).

The offerings found by Carter and Carnarvon were almost certainly dumped on
the hillside at some time after the construction of Djeser-Djeseru. It seems most
likely that they were brought there from the nearest of the Hathor shrines, that of
Djeser-Djeseru, but the cowroid of Ahmose is an obstacle to this hypothesis. The
cowroid might indicate that some of the objects in these mounds came from
Akh-isut, even though there were other dumping grounds much closer to that
temple (Plan 1; 1.1.3.3). Alternatively, it could be argued that the piece was
already old when dedicated in Djeser-Djeseru. This is not unlikely in the case of
scarabs and scaraboids (2.10.1.7), although such an explanation would be less
plausible for cartouche plaques, and unsatisfactory in the case of fragile votive
menit counterpoises.

Carter and Carnarvon seem to have removed only a small selection of votive
material from these mounds. Most of the pieces in Plate 7 have recently been
rediscovered at Highclere House, Berkshire, and are now in the collection of the
present Earl of Carnarvon (N. Reeves pers. comm. 1988). The mounds were later
cleared away by the Metropolitan Museum of Art expedition (1.1.3.3).

1.1.3.3   *The Metropolitan Museum of Art Expedition*

In the season of 1921–2 the Metropolitan Museum of Art expedition excavated the
southern half of the forecourt of the 11th dynasty temple, completely exposing the
boundary walls (Winlock 1922.21–32, figs. 6–8). To the south of the forecourt the
expedition found a large deposit of votive offerings:–

In the XVIII dynasty Deir el-Bahari was peculiarly sacred to the goddess Hathor and a shrine was built in the Mentuhotep Temple where Naville found the famous cow ... Daily devotees flocked to her chapel to beg for her favors, and on the way they bought from a hawker at some roadside booth a string of beads or a little pottery cow to offer with their prayers, and others carried a blue faience platter of fruit or flowers ... It was a very little shrine and the priests had to clear it out from time to time to make room for this never-ending stream of offerings. The old and broken ones they carried half-way across the courtyard of Mentuhotep's temple to the side doors that opened north and south, and just outside they dumped them. All over the hillside south of the courtyard we found the most astounding assortment of rubbish brought out from this chapel. (Winlock 1922.31–2)

Winlock's vague description of the offerings as lying all over the hillside is not confirmed by drawings made by other expedition members. D. Arnold, who has collated the MMA archive material relating to these excavations, notes that:–

There are two huge areas between the southern walls of the court called 'Hathor Dump' on the field map 1:400. One of these is drawn in section as a low layer of rubbish directly on the surface of Dynasty XI. (1979.28–9)

The drawings and maps published by Arnold show this 'Hathor Dump' between the brick outer walls of the forecourt of Akh-isut, beside its southern postern gate (1979 pls. 16b, 29; Plan 1).

Winlock's suggestion that the offerings found in this dump had been carried out of the Hathor shrine of Thutmose III through the 11th dynasty temple and half-way across its forecourt to the nearest gate is a plausible one. He did not state whether any of the offerings bore royal names, so it is impossible to say if any early 18th dynasty material was present. There may have been, because this dumping ground would also have been convenient for objects from Akh-isut itself.

In the season of 1922–3 the expedition again discovered numerous votive offerings when excavating part of a depression between the causeways of Djeser-Djeseru and Djeser-Akhet (Winlock 1923.28–39). Winlock's original account of these excavations is confused by the fact that, at this stage, he believed the causeway built by Thutmose III to be a northern causeway belonging to the 11th dynasty temple:–

... as the men cleared along, drawing each day nearer and near the temples, we began to find broken ex-votos from the Hathor chapels up at Deir el-Bahari. Among them were innumerable scarabs, mostly of Thutmose III, but also bearing nearly all the royal names of the XVIII dynasty, from its founder Ahmose I, and his wife Ahmose-Nofretere, down to Amonhotep III. More and more of them were found on the left-hand side of the dig. At first they seemed to lie against the sides of the Mentuhotep bank [Thutmose III causeway], but eventually pockets of dirt containing them were found deeper and deeper in the bank itself ... (1923.28)

To the south of Hatshepsut's causeway, 'within a few yards' of the temple forecourts, was a huge 'rubbish hole' (Winlock 1923.30–9, figs. 21–2). This depression seems to have been used as a dump from the reign of Hatshepsut onwards. Ostraca relating to the building of both Djeser-Djeseru and Djeser-Akhet were found in it (1923.36–8). During the latter part of Thutmose III's reign numerous statues of Hatshepsut were removed from her temple, broken up, and dumped in this hole. The north wall of the causeway of Thutmose III was subsequently built over part of this dump (1923.32–4). Winlock noted that:–

> Mixed in with all of this rubbish left by the temple builders there were thousands of ex-votos from this very shrine of Zeser-Akhet, from the Hathor shrine built just before it by Hatshepsut, and – if we are not mistaken – from a still earlier XVIII dynasty Hathor chapel which Hatshepsut's must have superseded and from which the earliest scarabs came. The inscribed scarabs already mentioned were among them. Of the little shapeless, uninscribed scarabs of brilliant blue faience which were strung up like beads and offered by myriads in the chapels, we got between three and four thousand. The ground was literally sown with such offerings which had been left for a while in the chapels, and then thrown out into the rubbish hole on the periodical cleaning days. Bits of broken blue faience platters in which food had been presented to the goddess were uncountable. Symbols of Hathor were everywhere. Sometimes she was the cow carved on plaques of limestone, copper, or faience ...; or again she was represented by the primitive symbol of a post with a woman's head atop which gave the inspiration for the Hathor-head columns of her temples ... She was a protectress, and tablets engraved with a pair of eyes or ears would assure her seeing and hearing a supplicant (1923.38).

This rubbish hole is close both to the main entrance to Hatshepsut's temple and to the gate made in the front wall of the 11th dynasty forecourt to give access to Djeser-Akhet (Plan 1). The hole may therefore have been used as a convenient dumping ground for offerings from Akh-isut, Djeser-Djeseru, and Djeser-Akhet. Prior to the construction of Djeser-Djeseru, this area lay behind an unbroken stretch of 11th dynasty wall (Arnold 1974 pl. 42). The fact that no votive offerings were found south of Thutmose III's causeway, in the vicinity of the gate which gave access to the temples of Akh-isut and Amonhotpe I, suggests that the area in front of the forecourt was not used as a dumping ground before Hatshepsut built her temple. Presumably it was the creation of an artificial valley, by the construction of a second causeway parallel to that of Akh-isut, which first made this area particularly suitable for dumping or burying objects. The early 18th dynasty material, which included a menit counterpoise of Ahmose-Nefertary (New York MMA 23.3.80; Hayes 1959.46), was found mixed in with middle and late 18th dynasty pieces. Winlock noted that the dumping was done in pockets rather than layers and found it impossible to date any piece by its position in the rubbish hole (1923.38–9). This probably means that all the dumping of offerings took place after the reign of Amonhotpe III, the latest king to be named on the votive faience (1.1.3.5).

In the season of 1923–4 the expedition cleared the whole of the forecourt of Djeser-Djeseru. According to Winlock's excavation notebook, a 'little blue material' – probably votive faience – was found in the upper layer of a hole in the south-east corner of forecourt (Plan 1; Arnold 1979.47). From 1927 to 1929, the expedition worked in the area just to the north of Djeser-Djeseru, clearing away both Naville's spoil heaps and the ancient mounds examined by Carter and Carnarvon (Winlock 1929.13–9, figs. 18–9). In a reference to one of the north postern gates of Djeser-Djeseru, Winlock wrote that 'through this gate all sorts of rubbish and sweepings had been carried out in ancient times and dumped on the hillside' (1929.14). He went on to describe this hillside as being choked 'with rubbish thrown out from the temple in the XVIII dynasty' (1929.18). Presumably, this 18th dynasty temple rubbish included votive offerings of the kinds found in this area by Carter and Carnarvon.

A remark by Winlock that votive offerings to Hathor 'permeate every level at Deir el-Bahari which was exposed during the use of the Hathor shrine in the temple' (1928.30) may imply that he found many more of these objects than he chose to mention. Winlock was comparatively uninterested in small votive objects, only three of which are illustrated in his reports (1922.35, fig. 22; 1923.38–9, figs. 33–4). It is probable that not all finds of small groups of offerings were recorded. A very large number of votive offerings from Deir el-Bahri were taken back to the Metropolitan Museum of Art. A selection of these was briefly described by W. C. Hayes in *The Scepter of Egypt* II (1959.46–8, 52, 79, 104–5, 173, 180–4, 198). Some of the offerings found by Winlock were later 'de-accessioned', many are still uncatalogued, and most remain unpublished. At the time of my doctoral research, the museum would not allow examination of this material, but it did provide information on many of the objects.

1.1.3.4   *The Polish Expedition*

During the Polish expedition's excavation of the main part of Djeser-Akhet, a number of large votive objects were found at pavement level. These consisted of three votive stelae and fragments of at least eight more; four relatively intact private statues, and fragments from about 34 others; three fragmentary offering tables, and fragments from at least three stone libation basins (Lipińska 1966.63–72; 1968.153–69; 1984; Dąbrowska-Smektała 1968.98–102). Most were discovered in a room to the north of the vestibule to the sanctuary, which the excavators named the Hall of Offerings (Lipińska 1968.149–50).

Fragments from a number of faience vessels and a quantity of beads were recovered from the debris above the temple (Lipińska 1966.96–7). These are most likely to have been thrown out of Djeser-Djeseru, since they were found mixed in with fragments from the latter temple. However, fragments of one large faience bowl and part of a faience menit counterpoise bearing the name of Hathor were found at pavement level (Lipińska 1968.170; Dąbrowska-Smektała 1968.128). These may originally have been offered in the main part of Djeser-Akhet. The votive material from this temple is supplemented by about 500 surviving graffiti, mainly written on the columns of the hypostyle hall (Marciniak 1974; Sadek 1984).

The votive objects from Djeser-Akhet have been individually described in articles (Marciniak 1965; Lipińska 1966; 1968; 1969; 1969a; Dąbrowska-Smektała 1968), and in a subsequent volume (Lipińska 1984). Most of the objects found by the Polish expedition are still in magazines at Deir el-Bahri (Lipińska 1984.8), but a few are on display at the Luxor Museum.

1.1.3.5   *The date range of the offerings*

Most of the votive stelae and textiles can be dated both by their inscriptions and by stylistic features. The private stelae from Akh-isut range in date from the 11th dynasty to the reign of Ramesses II (PM II 395–6; 2.1.6), and the textiles from the mid 18th to the early 19th dynasty (2.2.7). The date range of the stelae from Djeser-Akhet is from the mid 18th to the late 19th dynasties (PM 541; 2.1.6). Both Carter and Winlock simply dated the small votive offerings to the 18th dynasty, but Hall was more specific:–

> The majority can be dated between the reigns of Amenhetep I. and Amenhetep II., not only by their general style, and especially by the colour of the blue faïence of which they are made, but also by the fact that almost all the scarabs found among them, and all the other inscribed objects, are demonstrably of this date ... No scarabs of later date than the reign of Amenhetep II at latest were found. The characteristic scarabs, rings and *utjat*-eyes of the reign of Amenhetep III ... are represented by one broken specimen, and nothing whatever of the XIXth Dynasty was discovered. The commonest royal name is, as might have been expected, that of Hatshepsu ... (in Naville 1913.13–4).

Among the offerings found by the EEF were two rings with the prenomen of Amonhotpe III (2.9.3.2). A bowl fragment said to come from Deir el-Bahri bears the cartouche of Satamon, either the daughter of Ahmose or the eldest daughter of Amonhotpe III (2.11.3.1). A menit fragment of Baketamon (Pl. 5, second row) belongs to a daughter of Thutmose III of this name (D'Auria 1983.161–2; Troy 1986.165) rather than to the youngest daughter of Amonhotpe III. Winlock recovered scarabs of Amonhotpe III from the rubbish hole between the causeways (1923.28). One cartouche plaque of Horemheb was discovered (Hall 1913.199; London BM 41145), but none of the excavators at Deir el-Bahri found a single small object with a Ramessid cartouche. The date range of the inscribed votive faience is thus from Ahmose to Horemheb, although Hall was correct in stating that the majority belonged to the narrower date range of Amonhotpe I to Amonhotpe II.

The uninscribed votive objects, which have to be dated by stylistic or technical features, and with the aid of comparative material, present a similar picture (for details of dating see 2.3–11). A few pottery figurines and vessels (2.6.1.1–2; 2.10.1.3; 2.11.5) could date to the late Second Intermediate Period and be relics of a popular cult of Hathor, such as that which flourished at Gebel Zeit in this period (see 1.6.2–3). Some offerings are early 18th dynasty (Ahmose to Thutmose I), most are mid 18th dynasty (Thutmose II to Amonhotpe II), and a few are late 18th dynasty (Thutmose IV to Amonhotpe III). Although stelae and textiles were dedicated to Hathor again after the Amarna period, there was no comparable revival of votive faience. The only small offerings which are probably post-Amarna are the wooden phalli found in the Hathor shrine. I discuss the significance of this decline in the dedication of small objects in 3.1.

The context in which the offerings were found was rarely of much or any help in dating objects precisely. No votive stelae or private statues were found in the various dumps. It seems that such objects tended to remain inside temples for very long periods. For example, the 11th dynasty stelae and offering tables found by Graham and Dufferin had stayed in the speos and cella of Akh-isut throughout the nine hundred years or so during which the temple functioned. Large votive objects may sometimes have been moved about within a temple during restoration or rebuilding works (1.4.3) or even have been transferred from one structure to another (1.6.3), as may have been the case with a statue of Senenmut found in Djeser-Akhet (Marciniak 1965.201–7). For this reason, one cannot be absolutely certain that a statue found, for example, in Djeser-Djeseru is no earlier than the reign of Hatshepsut.

The small votive objects are less likely to have been replaced in position after major restoration or rebuilding work, so it is reasonable to assume that the offerings found inside Djeser-Djeseru (1.1.3.1) date to Hatshepsut or later. This is the only group of small votive objects which can be closely dated within the 18th dynasty by its context. All the other groups could have come from more than one Hathor shrine. The small offerings were found in three types of context – inside a temple, in a temple court, and in dumps just outside the temple precincts. It is probable that all the offerings were originally placed as close as possible to one of the cult images of Hathor, yet about 80 per cent of the small votive objects were discovered outside the temples.

At least four explanations of this fact can be offered. The small votive objects may have been ejected from the Hathor shrines:–

A. At regular intervals when the shrines became too full
B. In the Amarna period
C. During post-Amarna restorations of the temples
D. When Akh-isut and Djeser-Akhet were demolished

The variety of locations in which the offerings were found suggests that more than one of these explanations may be correct.

Explanation A was favoured by Hall (in Naville 1907.17) and Winlock (1923.31), but the manner in which votive material of different dates was found jumbled together argues against it. If objects were cleared out of the shrines and dumped on a regular basis, one would expect the excavators to have discovered traces of stratification in the refuse mounds and the rubbish hole, or to have found deposits of offerings which were all of one date. This does not seem to have been the case at Deir el-Bahri, or at other Hathor sites.

Explanation B is put forward by Arnold (1974.68–9), who proposes that the small votive objects were ejected from the shrines in an attempt to terminate the popularity of the cult of Hathor at Deir el-Bahri. To remove all the offerings from the shrines at once would have been a large task. It is doubtful whether the cult of Hathor at Deir el-Bahri, which seems to have been in decline by the reign of Amonhotpe III, would have been deemed important enough to merit such trouble. Atonists might have cleared away objects which would have been underfoot from areas, such as the speos of the Djeser-Akhet Hathor shrine, where they intended to mutilate reliefs or inscriptions, and then dumped them in the nearby north court. It is much less plausible that Atonists would also have painstakingly moved some groups of offerings within Akh-isut and carried others to at least four main dumping grounds. It should also be asked why the Atonists should remove the small votive objects and yet fail to eject or destroy stelae, cloths, and statues dedicated to Amon and Hathor.

Explanation C is my own proposal. Whether or not Akhenaten's workmen moved or threw out any of the offerings, they must have left the temples in disarray. The restorers may have been faced by disorderly piles of old, broken objects of obsolete types, and have decided to tidy them away. If most of the offerings were removed from the Hathor shrines during the post-Amarna restorations, the mixture of early, mid and late 18th dynasty material attested in the north court of Akh-isut, and in most of the dumping grounds, becomes explicable. The three types of context may be due to differing attitudes to the votive material on the part of successive groups of restorers. Perhaps during the first restoration of Akh-isut the offerings were only moved internally to little-used parts of the complex. After the building of Djeser-Akhet the north lower colonnade of Akh-isut was masked by a structure of Thutmose III (Lipińska 1977.54–5, Plan 11), and may, for this reason, have been relegated to serving as a storeroom. The ambulatory would also have been a convenient place to pile up offerings out of sight of the courts and away from the main thoroughfare (Plan 2). Later restoration pro-grammes may have employed people to dispose of the offerings carefully by carrying them to dumps out of sight beyond the enclosure walls or between the causeways. Finally, it is possible, though less likely, that offerings were simply dumped in the north court of Akh-isut to clear them out of the way as quickly as possible during restoration work.

Explanation D might seem an obvious solution to the problem, but there are several arguments against it. Firstly, Djeser-Djeseru was not demolished at the end of the New Kingdom and yet, at some point, most of the offerings seem to have been removed from its Hathor shrine. An explanation which is irrelevant for Djeser-Djeseru may also be irrelevant for Akh-isut and Djeser-Akhet. Secondly, while it is plausible that the demolishers might move offerings out of their way into the north court, or into parts of the temple which they were not quarrying, it seems unlikely that they would go to all the trouble of carrying large numbers of votive objects to dumping grounds outside the enclosure walls. Moreover, the offerings in the dumps included some small metal objects which one might expect the demolishers to have taken away for melting down. Thirdly, Hall·stated that whereas the statues and stelae were found in or above the debris representing the destruction of Akh-isut, the small votive objects in the north lower colonnade and on the temple platform were always found under it (in Naville 1907.15, 17). This indicates that they were already in the positions in which they were found before the demolition of Akh-isut and Djeser-Akhet.

Because evidence about the exact provenance of individual objects is lacking, it is unlikely that the problem can be conclusively solved. The most satisfactory single explanation is that almost all the offerings were moved during successive restorations of the temples. The most attractive composite explanation is that some of the small offerings were moved within the temples by priests, and others were ejected, for practical rather than for religious reasons, by Atonists, while the majority were removed by restorers and a few, which had remained in the shrines, were scattered during the demolition of Akh-isut and Djeser-Akhet, or stayed in place in Djeseru-Djeseru when the temple fell into disuse.

Summary

Hathor was worshipped at Deir el-Bahri at least as early as the First Intermediate Period. Hathor, Lady of Dendara, was one of the principal deities of Akh-isut, the mortuary temple of Nebehepetreʿ Mentuhotpe. There may also have been a Middle Kingdom rock-cut Hathor shrine at Deir el-Bahri. Votive offerings were dedicated to Hathor somewhere inside Akh-isut during the 18th dynasty. There is no definite evidence that offerings were made to Hathor in the temple built by Amonhotpe I. A shrine with a rock-cut sanctuary was built for Hathor, Foremost in Thebes, at the south end of the middle terrace of Djeser-Djeseru, the mortuary temple of Hatshepsut. A similar shrine was constructed just behind the platform of Akh-isut as part of Djeser-Akhet, a temple of Thutmose III. The original stone Hathor cow statue was found in the rock-cut sanctuary of this shrine. Both these shrines seem to have been focuses for popular religion, and numerous small votive offerings were dedicated in them. Akh-isut and Djeser-Akhet were both abandoned and partially dismantled by the end of the 20th dynasty. Some areas of Djeser-Djeseru continued in use until Roman times.

The date range of the large votive objects associated with Hathor is from the early 18th to the early 20th dynasties. This material includes a very unusual group of votive textiles. Many 20th dynasty votive graffiti in Djeser-Akhet contain prayers to Hathor. The date range of the votive faience from the site is from Ahmose to Amonhotpe III, but most of it belongs to the period from Amonhotpe I to Amonhotpe II. A few pottery votive objects could be as early as the late Second Intermediate Period.

Some votive offerings seem to have been found inside the Hathor shrine of Djeser-Djeseru. Votive phalli were discovered in the speos of the Hathor shrine of Djeser-Akhet. A large quantity of 18th dynasty votive material was found inside Akh-isut, and in the courtyard between this temple and Djeser-Djeseru. Greater numbers of small offerings were recovered from a series of dumps just outside the enclosure walls of the temples (Plan 1). These dumps are most likely to have been the work of post-Amarna restorers of the temples.

1.2 Faras

1.2.1 The site

Before the building of the High Dam and the creation of Lake Nasser, the site known as Faras lay between the First and Second Cataracts on the modern border of Egypt and Sudan. The floodplain at Faras seems to have been exceptionally broad (Trigger 1976.75–6). In recent times the dry bed of a second river channel could still be traced along the edge of the western desert (Mileham 1910.22; Griffith 1921.80). The area between the modern course of the Nile and the western desert has generally been referred to as Faras West, and the area on the east bank as Faras East.

Faras received comparatively little attention from early European visitors to Nubia. No excavations were undertaken there until 1909, when G. S. Mileham and D. Randall-MacIver of the Eckley B. Coxe Expedition of the University of Pennsylvania examined nine Christian churches at Faras (Mileham 1910.22–6). Although primarily concerned with the churches, Mileham also took an interest in the dynastic remains (1910.22–4). The archaeological importance of Faras West was finally established by the Oxford Expedition to Nubia, which worked at the site from 1910 to 1912. The expedition was led by F. Ll. Griffith, assisted by A. M. Blackman and C. L. Woolley. Its finds included material from the Palaeolithic to the Christian periods (Griffith 1921; 1924; 1926).

No evidence of Old Kingdom activity was discovered at Faras, but Griffith did excavate a small Middle Kingdom fort on the west bank of the western channel of the Nile (1921.80–3, pl. 16). He also examined a large C-group cemetery, which he assigned to the Middle Kingdom (1921.72–9, pls. 9–15). Woolley, who actually cleared this site, judged that it was contemporary with the 18th dynasty (1921.78). Apart from four undecorated, rock-cut tombs in the western hills (1921.94), all the New Kingdom remains examined by the expedition were close to the eastern channel of the Nile. Griffith believed that he had located three, or possibly four, New Kingdom temples in this area (1921.83–94).

The oldest of these temples was situated on the north side of an isolated outcrop of rock known locally as the *Nabindiffi* – 'The Tower of Gold'. This temple, which appears to have been dedicated to Hathor ⏝𓏤𓊑𓈖 'Lady of Ibshek', lay beneath the ruins of a mudbrick church (Mileham 1910.24, pl. 12a). Cut into the east side of the 'Hathor rock' was a 'grotto' containing a Ramessid rock stela (Fig. 5).

To the west of the 'Arab Citadel' on the 'Great Kom', inside the Meroitic fortifications known as the Enclosure (Griffith 1921 pl. 1), lay dynastic blocks which Griffith took to be the remains of a temple built by Thutmose III and dedicated to Horus of Buhen, Satis and Anukis (1921.90). At the south-west corner of the Enclosure some fragmentary sandstone blocks of Ramesses II were built into the base of a tower (Griffith 1921.89, pl. 1; 1926 pl. 23). Griffith suggested that these came either from a Ramessid addition to the Hathor temple or from a separate Ramessid temple built to the west of the Great Kom (1921.84, 89).

While excavating a large Meroitic cemetery to the north-east of the Great Kom, the expedition uncovered the remains of a substantial sandstone temple and an adjacent walled settlement built in mudbrick (1921.91–4, pl. 26). Inscribed material identified this site as *sḥtp-nṯrw*, a temple complex built for Tutankhamon by his Viceroy Huy, and known from the latter's tomb (Nina Davies & Gardiner 1926.17–8, pls. 14–5). Tutankhamon himself may have been the chief deity of this temple, but Ptah, Isis, Anukis, and Hathor were also worshipped there (Griffith 1921.93–4).

Griffith's excavations at Faras West did not exhaust the possibilities of the site. A. J. Arkell visited Faras in 1946 and worked on a C-group settlement (1950.24). In 1960 the Sudan Antiquities Service and UNESCO commissioned a more detailed survey of the site, which was carried out by W. Y. Adams, H. Å. Nordström and G. J. Verwers (Adams 1961.7–10, pl. 1; Nordström 1962.34–41; Verwers 1961.15–9; 1962.19–21). Verwers excavated the C-group settlement and a number of C-group and New Kingdom graves on the edge of the floodplain. He concluded that the latter belonged to an 18th, and possibly a 19th, dynasty agricultural population, but it remained uncertain whether this population consisted of Egyptian immigrants or Egyptianized Nubians (Verwers 1961.27–9; Säve-Söderbergh 1968.211–41; Trigger 1976.131–4).

As part of the same UNESCO campaign, a Joint Scandinavian Expedition excavated C-group and X-group burials at Faras East (Säve-Söderbergh 1962.76–105; 1963.47–69; 1968.211–41), and a Polish expedition, led by K. Michałowski, worked at Faras West from 1961 to 1964. Most of their time was spent in excavating a well-preserved 8th century AD cathedral on the Great Kom, but they also recovered parts of about 565 18th dynasty blocks (Michałowski 1962.19–24; 1965.14–38; Karkowski 1981.3p–63). J. Karkowski, a member of the Polish team, has suggested that the Thutmosid blocks come from the Southern Temple at Buhen, of which only the lower courses survive *in situ* (1972.84–9; 1981.30–6). He assumes that they were transported the 35 km from Buhen to Faras for reuse as building material during the Christian period, when Faras became the capital of the Kingdom of Nobadia (Jakobielski 1972.23–4).

The Polish expedition also recovered 22 Ramessid sandstone blocks from the south-west corner of the Meroitic fortifications, but no temple foundations were discovered in this area (Karkowski 1981.277–338). Karkowski proposes that these were brought to Faras, for reuse, from the Ramessid temple of Aksha, only 10 km to the south (1981.63–5). He therefore believes that there is definite evidence for only two New Kingdom temples at Faras, the Hathor temple and the temple of Tutankhamon. However, on the basis of a single sandstone fragment, dated on stylistic grounds to Thutmose IV, he suggests that a small temple was built 'in the time from the death of Tuthmosis III to the accession of Akhenaton' in the area later occupied by the temple complex of Tutankhamon (1981.73).

In 1964 F. Hinkel supervised the removal of some of the structures at Faras to

higher ground and the transfer of the most important objects to the Khartoum
Museum (1965.97). The site is now permanently flooded.

1.2.2   The Hathor temple

A fragment of masonry with a foundation inscription mentioning a goddess and
a queen (Fig. 5.1) indicates that the principal deity of the temple built against the
Nabindiffi was female. Three further inscriptions name the goddess as Hathor,
Lady of Ibshek (Fig. 5.4, 6, 11). Ibshek was probably the ancient name for Faras
(Griffith 1921.83, 88; Säve-Söderbergh 1960.30; Desroches Noblecourt &
Kuentz 1968.162–4; Karkowski 1981.21–4). The sanctuary of the rock-cut Small
Temple at Abu Simbel contains a statue of Hathor, Lady of Ibshek in cow form
(Desroches Noblecourt and Kuentz 1968.105–7, pls. 123–6). A similar statue may
once have stood in the semi rock-cut sanctuary at Faras.

   Neither the form nor the history of the Faras Hathor temple is easy to establish.
When Griffith and Woolley excavated the site, only the foundations and probably
the lowest courses of a few walls were found. By the time when Faras West was
surveyed, even these traces had disappeared (W. Y. Adams pers. comm. 1978).
Woolley's plan of the temple is far from clear (Plan 3); especially since the letters
used in the text to refer to the various rooms are omitted from the plate. Griffith
began his description by stating that 'we discovered and cleared the foundations of
the temple', but went on to state that the plan showed 'the walls and foundations'
(1921.84). In most of the plan the absence of doorways indicates that only
foundations remained (Plan 3). Some of the walls of the sanctuary do seem to have
survived, since these are shown in section in Woolley's plan.

   In his text, Griffith did not attempt a complete reconstruction of the form of
the Hathor temple:–

> Mr Woolley's plan ... shows the disposition of the walls and foundations,
> distinguishing the two main periods of construction so far as he could ascertain them.
> The axis of the temple was to the N.E., parallel to the present river course. Two
> parallel walls, A, must have been for an ascending approach or ramp. It passed several
> cross walls, where there may have been doorways and courts in the original
> construction, and finally reaches the N.E. wall of the main temple building G, which
> nearly coincides with the face of the rock on this side. The rock behind is almost all
> bare, but has been cut about in a remarkable way: several flights of steps are cut in it,
> and the top may perhaps have been used for sacrifice. On the right of the ramp is a
> small chamber F, in which stands a rectangular base like those for sacred barks, 80 cm.
> high, 80 cm. long and 65 cm. broad, with the usual beading and cavetto cornice at the
> top, but uninscribed. (1921.84–5)

   Griffith nowhere specified the material of the foundations and walls, but
Woolley seems to have thought that the 'rough stonework' shown on his plan was
contemporary with the second of the 'two main periods of construction' (Plan 3).
The flights of steps mentioned by Griffith are not included on the plan. Mileham
assumed that these, together with a passage through the rock, were cut in the
Christian period (1910.24), but since access to the roof is a feature of some New
Kingdom temples, the steps could have been of that date. The rear part of the

temple may have been intended to form a 'cave' for the Hathor cow, with the 'Hathor rock' taking the place of the Western Mountain at Thebes.

A separate plan of the grotto in the east face of the 'Hathor rock' shows that it was nearly square, measuring 6 + 6.40 m (Fig. 5.13). Griffith commented that:–

> The grotto resembles a small tomb, but we failed to find any pit. The floor has been cut away; the door was originally about 1.20 m high. In a niche about 80 cm high in the back wall are the remains of a seated statue, utterly defaced. (1921.87)

Carved on the north wall, to the right of the statue niche, was the rock stela of Setau, who was a viceroy of Nubia under Ramesses II (Fig. 5.11; Griffith 1921.87, pl. 24.11; Hinkel 1965.97, pl. 23a; Karkowski 1975.120–1; 1981.112–4, fig. 4). Setau is shown with his hands raised in adoration. Behind him, his wife Neferetmut holds a loop sistrum and a stem of papyrus with one hand and raises the other. The text reads:–

> The Son of Reʿ, Ramesses Meryamon, beloved of Hathor, Lady of Ibshek. Dedicated by the King's Son [of Kush], the Overseer of Southern Foreign Lands, Setau, true of voice; his sister, the Lady of the House, the Chantress of Amon, Neferetmut, [true of voice]. (Fig. 5.11)

Low down on the south wall was a graffito, consisting of the name and titles of a Ramessid scribe called Meripet (Fig. 5.12; Griffith 1921.88; Karkowski 1975.122; 1981.114–5). A small number of other New Kingdom graffiti were found in 1961 on the outside of the 'Hathor rock' and copied by the German Democratic Republic Epigraphic Expedition (Karkowski 1981.6).

Griffith felt able to propose a tentative history of the Hathor temple:–

> From all the remains we drew the conclusion that a temple, going back at least to the beginning of the New Kingdom, existed here; that probably the indefatigable Hatshepsut rebuilt it, using Egyptian limestone brought from Egypt, and that Ramesses II probably added to it in sandstone. There is no trace of later occupation of the Hathor rock until Christian times. (1921.87)

In his discussion of the grotto, Griffith rejected the idea that it had been cut as a tomb, and concluded that it had been constructed by Setau as a shrine to Ramesses II and Hathor, Lady of Ibshek (1921.87–8).

The Polish excavations did not include the 'Hathor rock', but after examining the site and some of the objects from it, Karkowski wrote an article suggesting a history of the Hathor temple slightly different from that proposed by Griffith (1975.112–23). Since that time he has revised his ideas, and the history of the Hathor temple outlined in his *Faras V* (1981) differs sharply from that proposed by Griffith. Karkowski's proposals are as follows: A modest, mudbrick structure, with a few architectural details in sandstone, was built on the 'Hathor rock' in the 'late XVII Dynasty'. This fell into disuse after the reign of Thutmose III, and was rebuilt in sandstone under Tutankhamon. The grotto was cut by Setau as a shrine to Ramesses II and Hathor, Lady of Ibshek, but the building of the temples at Abu Simbel resulted in the abandonment of the Hathor temple at Faras. The latter was dismantled and another structure was built on the 'Hathor rock' sometime between the late 19th dynasty and the Christian period (1981.68–71).

Karkowski bases his hypothesis that the temple was founded in the late 17th dynasty on the royal name scarabs and scaraboids excavated by Griffith (1981.68). These objects, which were found among small votive offerings to Hathor (1.2.3), range in date from Inyotef V (Nubkheperreʿ), Nebireyeraw (Swadjenreʿ) and Kamose (Wadjkheperreʿ), all of the 17th dynasty, to Thutmose III (Griffith 1921.86, 103, pl. 18; Karkowski 1981.92–100). The most common royal names were Amonhotpe (probably Amonhotpe I), Thutmose I, and Thutmose III. The evidence of royal name scarabs always has to be treated with caution, both because such objects might be kept for years before finding their way into a temple, and because of the complication of posthumous scarabs. Nor does the presence of a royal name scarab prove that the ruler in question controlled the territory in which it was found. Nevertheless, these scarabs do provide useful termini for the offerings, which are confirmed by the fragmentary stelae found in the temple. Only two preserve inscriptions of any length. Both are incomplete, but they are still of great value for the history of the Hathor temple.

The first inscription is on a round-topped limestone stela broken into nine fragments (Fig. 5.6; Khartoum 4452; Griffith 1921.85–6, pl. 24.6; Karkowski 1975.118–9; 1981.77–80). The bottom and much of the right-hand side are missing. The lunette contains a *shen* sign between two *wadjet* eyes; below it are four horizontal lines of inscription consisting of a *ḥtp di nsw* formula for a man whose name 𓂓𓊪𓏏𓏤𓀀 should probably be read as *kꜣ* (Karkowski 1981.79). Griffith thought that 'The stela cannot be later than the the very beginning of the New Kingdom and may be considerably earlier' (1921.86).

Karkowski at first dated this stela to the Second Intermediate Period (1975.119), but has now redated it to the 'very beginning' of the 18th dynasty (1981.80). He admits that the name of the stela owner suggests a pre-New Kingdom date, since Ka is an unusual name, recorded in Egypt only during the Middle Kingdom, and in Nubia only during the Second Intermediate Period (Ranke 1935.337; Säve-Söderbergh 1949.50). Karkowski also concedes that the rare writing of Hathor's name (Fig. 5.6) might imply a date in the Second Intermediate Period or even earlier (1981.80). The writing of the first part of the offering formula is one which was particularly common in the Second Intermediate Period, though it does occur both earlier and later (Smither 1939.34–7; Barta 1968.233). The decoration in the lunette is of a type frequently found on Middle Kingdom and Second Intermediate Period stelae, but rare on New Kingdom stelae (Smith 1976.92).

Karkowski's counter-argument is that the workmanship of the stela is too good for it to have been made in the Second Intermediate Period (1981.80). For the same reason he dismisses the idea of identifying the owner of the Faras stela with a man named Ka who is mentioned on several Second Intermediate Period monuments from Buhen dedicated by members of the family of the *sr* Sobekemheb (1981.80 n.356). Karkowski claims the workmanship of the Faras stela is 'far superior' to that of the Buhen stelae which mention Ka. This is certainly true, but stelae of a quality comparable to the Faras example were produced in Buhen during the Second Intermediate Period (*e.g.* Smith 1976 pl. 71.4). When publishing the Buhen material, H. S. Smith drew attention to striking differences in quality among objects which could all be dated to the Second Intermediate Period (1976.42), so some competent craftsmen must have been available.

The most detailed information about Ka of Buhen is on a stela dedicated by his daughter's son, Iahwoser (Khartoum 18; Säve-Söderbergh 1949.50–4). This stela has the same type of decoration in the lunette and the same writing of the offering formula as the Faras stela, but is of cruder workmanship. The offering formula is 𓏲𓏤𓈗𓆓𓏌𓏲𓆓 'for the *sr* Ka'. After this comes a brief biographical inscription which T. Säve-Söderbergh translated as follows:–

> He says 'I was a valiant servant of the ruler of Cush; I washed [my] feet in the waters of Cush in the suite of the ruler *Nḏḥ*, and I returned safe and sound [to my] family.' (1949.52)

A sandstone lintel fragment from Buhen with a partly preserved kneeling figure is also inscribed with an offering formula for Ka, this time written 𓏲𓆓𓏌𓏲𓆓 (Smith 1976.19, no.1569, pl.7.2). In a stela inscription, Sobekemheb II, the father of Ka, states that he made a *ḥwt-kꜣ* for his god Horus (Barns 1954.19–22). On another stela, Sepedhor, a younger brother of Ka, claims to have built a temple for Horus of Buhen 'to the satisfaction of the ruler of Kush' (Säve-Söderbergh 1949.54–6, fig. 2; Smith 1976.55, pl.72.1). It is generally agreed that these monuments belong to a single Egyptian family who governed Buhen on behalf of the 'Kerma rulers' in the late Second Intermediate Period (Säve-Söderbergh 1949.51–5; Barns 1952.19–22; James 1965.10–11; Smith 1976.79–80; Trigger 1976.97). Smith suggests that over several generations a temple of Horus was constructed on the site of the later Northern Temple at Buhen by members of the Sobekemheb family, and that the lintel of Ka might have been part of an addition to this temple (1976.19–20).

Faras is not far from Buhen and probably served as its agricultural supply base. The fact that Ka had a sister called Ta-ibsheki (Smith 1976.47–8) suggests a family connection with the site. The deities named in the offering formula on the Faras stela are Hathor, Lady of Ibshek, Isis(?), and Senwosret III (Fig. 5.6). Prior to the reign of Thutmose III, the only evidence for the cult of this king in Nubia comes from the monuments of the Sobekemheb family at Buhen (Smith 1976.91–2). Sobekemheb II was a *wḥmw* of Senwosret III and Ka may have inherited this office from his father.

Thus it seems likely that Ka, and perhaps other members of the Sobekemheb family, built a temple for Hathor at Faras in the late Second Intermediate Period. This would have been in mudbrick with perhaps a small rock-cut sanctuary. At this time Faras was in the territory of the 'Kerma rulers', so the temple may nominally have been dedicated on their behalf. The Sobekemheb family may also have had economic dealings with the Theban kings of the 17th dynasty. The scarab of Inyotef V found in the temple is interesting, since offerings were made during this king's reign in a Hathor shrine at the galena mining site of Gebel Zeit (Castel & Soukiassian 1985.291; 1.6.3). The offerings found at Gebel Zeit are very similar to those from Faras. It is possible that during the Second Intermediate Period Faras sometimes served as a stopping-off point for Theban trading or gold-mining expeditions.

The temple of Horus erected by the Sobekemheb family at Buhen seems to have replaced a destroyed Middle Kingdom sanctuary (Smith 1976.76–8), so there may also have been a Middle Kingdom shrine at the Hathor rock at Faras. A few small objects found in the temple area, such as a calcite kohl pot (Oxford Ash. 1912.938; Karkowski 1981.110–1, no. 17), part of a faience figurine (Pl. 8.5 = London BM 51264), and a head from a male statuette (Pl. 8.46), could date either to the Middle Kingdom or to the Second Intermediate Period, but no Middle Kingdom scarabs or stelae were recovered. In Middle Kingdom Nubia it was not customary to build temples outside fortifications (Kemp 1972.651–6; Trigger 1976.70–1), but an exception might have been made at Faras because the 'Hathor rock' itself was considered sacred. In the flat Nubian landscape, prominent natural features – such as Gebel Barkal – tended to become holy places. If the modern name 'Tower of Gold' was given to the rock because it was golden in colour, this suggests a possible reason why the ancient Egyptians associated it with Hathor.

Although he does not say so clearly, Karkowski seems to believe that the Hathor temple was founded by one of the 17th dynasty rulers whose scarabs were found at Faras – presumably Kamose (1981.68). Very little temple building seems to have been undertaken in the early stages of the reconquest of Nubia, so it is unlikely that Kamose would have constructed a new temple at Faras (James 1965.12). At Buhen, a stone doorway bearing the name and titles of Ahmose and an official called Turo seems to have been inserted into the mudbrick temple of Horus built by the Sobekemheb family (Smith 1976.55). This was probably a means of establishing it as an Egyptian state temple, and of transferring the credit for its construction to Ahmose and his official. A fragmentary stela found by Griffith suggests that something similar may have happened at Faras. One piece from the top right-hand side and a smaller piece from the bottom left-hand corner are all that remains of this round topped-limestone stela (Fig. 5.5; Khartoum 4453; Griffith 1921.85, pl. 25.5; Karkowski 1975.119; 1981.80–3, pl. 3). The very broken inscription begins with the titulary of a king Amonhotpe and continues with conventional praises of a high official, whose name is not preserved (Fig. 5.5). Griffith believed that the style of this stela, together with the absence of epithets after the nomen, indicated that the king was Amonhotpe I (1921.85). Karkowski agrees and proposes that the high official named is most likely to have been Amonhotpe I's Viceroy, Turo (1981.85). This is an attractive suggestion, since it can then be assumed that the Viceroy Turo restored or rebuilt the Hathor temple at Faras, or simply set up a stela to 'claim' it for Amonhotpe I, as he had earlier 'claimed' the temple of Horus at Buhen for Ahmose. Karkowski believes that Woolley's plan (Plan 3) is so unreliable that almost nothing about the form of the 18th dynasty Hathor temple can be deduced from it:–

> It is difficult to find any parallels between this plan and the other known Pharaonic temples ... The only feature of the structure which seems to be indisputable is the orientation towards the north, parallel to the river. In addition it can be concluded from the section ... that particular parts of the temple could have been built on two or more levels, following the slope of the rock (1981.67).

It is not correct that no parallels at all can be cited. The manner in which the sanctuary was built against the cut-away rock face is reminiscent of the Hathor sanctuary at Timna, which is fitted beneath an overhanging rock (Plan 6). The building of the temple on a slope, with the levels joined by ramps, recalls the design of the temples of Hatshepsut and Thutmose III at Deir el-Bahri (Plan 1).

Griffith noted this point of resemblance between Djeser-Djeseru and the Faras Hathor temple (1921.84), but his theory that Hatshepsut rebuilt the latter in Egyptian limestone seems to have been based on a single object found to the east of the ramp (Fig. 5.1; Griffith 1921.85, pl. 24.1; Karkowski 1975.120–2; 1981.83–4). He described the object as:–

> Limestone door-lintel with remains of two lines of inscription of goodwill of a goddess (i.e., Hathor of Abeshek) to a queen (i.e., Hatshepsut). (1921.85)

Karkowski agrees that the unnamed queen is almost certain to be Hatshepsut, but challenges Griffith's identification of the piece as a lintel (1981.84). He notes that the inscription runs from right to left, rather than from the centre outwards, as is common on lintels, and claims that, at 95 cm wide, this object is too narrow to fit any of the doorways shown on Woolley's plan. He prefers to regard it as part of a large royal dedicatory or commemorative stela, and suggests that if it is not a structural element, it cannot be used as evidence for building work by Hatshepsut. This re-identification is not altogether convincing. Some 18th dynasty lintels do have inscriptions running from right to left (e.g. Smith 1976.19, 55), and as no doors are shown on most of Woolley's plan (Plan 3), it is impossible to be certain that there were no doorways narrow enough to fit this lintel. In any case, as Karkowski has claimed that everything on Woolley's plan dates to the reign of Tutankhamon or later (1981.69–70), this line of argument is no longer open to him.

Whether this piece is a lintel or a stela fragment, it does suggest some activity at Faras on the part of Hatshepsut. The inscription seems to be part of a text in which the goddess blessed the queen in return for services performed for her (Fig. 5.1). Although Hatshepsut's daughter Neferure' is named on a glass inlay from the 'Hathor rock' (Cooney 1976.40, no. 356; Karkowski 1981.85–6), no small objects bearing the queen's name were recovered. Four scaraboids and two cartouche plaques of Thutmose III were found in the temple (Griffith 1921.86, 103, pl. 18.22–4; Karkowski 1981.98–9, nos. 36–41, pls. 6–7). During this king's reign Hathor, Lady of Ibshek, was honoured in the temple at el-Lessiya (Curto n.d. fig. 38) and in a rock-cut shrine at Qasr Ibrim (Caminos 1968.38, pl. 9). In view of this, and of the extensive building work of Hatshepsut and Thutmose III for Hathor elsewhere (1.1.2.3–4; 1.4.2), it seems likely that the Hathor temple at Faras was rebuilt in their reigns. The work was probably begun under Hatshepsut and finished in Thutmose III's sole reign, like the Southern Temple at Buhen.

Since the 'lintel' was the only piece of dressed limestone found at the site, it is unlikely that a limestone temple was ever built on the 'Hathor rock'. Under Thutmose III, the Hathor temple was probably still a mudbrick structure with some architectural elements, such as doorways, in stone. It is not certain whether this structure can be identified with the 'second main stage of construction' marked as Hatshepsut's work on Woolley's plan (Plan 3). The 'first main stage of construction', which included the ramp, is too elaborate to date to the Second Intermediate Period. Griffith dated it to the early 18th dynasty (1921.83). This is certainly possible – a split-level mudbrick temple approached by a ramp was built at Abydos under Ahmose (Ayrton *et al.* 1904.32–4) – but it seems less likely that such a project would have been undertaken in Nubia before the Egyptian reoccupation was complete. It may be that the earlier stages of the Hathor temple left little or no trace and that it is Woolley's 'first main stage of construction' which should be dated to Hatshepsut and Thutmose III.

Karkowski's belief that the temple fell into disuse after Thutmose III is based on that fact that his is the latest royal name on the scarabs found there (1981.69). He suggests that the desertion of the Hathor temple might be due to the popularity of new sanctuaries, such as the rebuilt Northern Temple at Buhen, or the hypothetical temple of Thutmose IV at Faras (1.2.1). It is true that only two of the votive offerings found at the 'Hathor rock' can be dated to a period later than the reign of Thutmose III (1.2.3). This may reflect a decline in the level of royal patronage, and in the number of small offerings made, but it is unlikely to mean that the temple was totally abandoned. Not a single Ramessid scarab was recovered from Deir el-Bahri, but we know from many other sources that the temples continued to function until the end of the New Kingdom (1.1.2).

Although in Karkowski's view the Hathor temple was deserted for about a century, he assumes that:–

> ... the stone elements however of the original temple must have been left standing in their original places, since the names of Hathor on them were destroyed by the followers of Aton. (1981.69)

This statement is founded on a remark by Griffith about a fragment from a sandstone door-jamb discovered to the east of the ramp (Fig. 5.4; 1921.85, pl. 24.4; Karkowski 1981.90–1, pl. 5.9). The inscription on this doorjamb, which reads '... 'beloved of Hathor, Lady of Ibshek, given life' was 'faint, perhaps having been cut through plaster' (Griffith 1921.85). Karkowski, who was not able to locate the door-jamb, takes this to mean that the inscription had been erased in the Amarna period and subsequently restored (1981.67, 91). There are other circumstances in which an inscription might be recut, for example when a monument was being usurped by another king, but some Nubian temples were damaged during the Amarna period (Dewachter 1971.102–3; Baines & Málek 1980.182–3), so Karkowski's suggestion is a plausible one.

Karkowski's theory that the Hathor temple was rebuilt under Tutankhamon is based partly on its orientation. A north-south orientation is rare in an independent temple, but Edfu and the temple of Nekhbet at el-Kab provide other examples of temples whose main axes are parallel with the river. The orientation may have been dictated by a desire to build against a particular part of the sacred 'Hathor rock'. The New Kingdom Hathor shrines at Timna and Gebel Zeit, which are also built against rock faces, both have an approximately north-south orientation (1.5.2; 1.6.2). Karkowski's explanation is that the Hathor temple faced towards Sehetep-netjeru only after it had been completely rebuilt to form part of that temple complex (1981.69–72). This line of argument has awkward consequences. Since the 'first main stage of construction' on Woolley's plan has a north–south orientation (Plan 3), Karkowski is obliged to identify it with Tutankhamon's rebuilding, and to assume that no trace was left of the groundplans of any earlier stages of the temple. He is also faced with a problem in dating the 'second main stage of construction' and the 'rough stonework'. He comments that:–

> Since no Pharaonic objects, which could have belonged to the time after Tutankh-amun, were found in the rubbish, it would seem probable that these structures could be post-Pharaonic. (1981.70)

Griffith noted that two objects found on the 'Hathor rock' provided proof that the temple was still functioning during the reign of Tutankhamon (1921.86). The first of these is a scarab which may bear the name of Tutankhamon's queen, Ankhesenamon, though one character is missing (Khartoum 928; 1921.104, pl. 18.25; Karkowski 1981.99, no. 42, pl. 7). The second is a sandstone basin dedicated by the wife of Tutankhamon's Viceroy, Huy (Fig. 5.9–10; Khartoum 4449; Griffith 1921.86; Karkowski 1981.89–90; 2.12.1). Karkowski uses the scarab and the bowl to argue that the Hathor temple was not only rebuilt under Tutankhamon, but rededicated to Hathor and Ankhesenamon. He also proposes that Hathor's chief epithet at Faras would have changed at this period from Lady of Ibshek to she 'who is in Sehetep-netjeru' (1981.70).

The latter title appears on a block found in the vicinity of Tutankhamon's temple in an offering formula for the Viceroy Huy (Khartoum 5196; Griffith 1921.92–4, pl. 28.19; Karkowski 1981.133–4, pl. 16). Griffith believed that this block was part of 'a low screen, such as may have run along the front of the colonnade' (1921.92), but Karkowski comments that:–

> Its lower edge and the way in which the inscription is written, seems to point to the fact that the fragment could have belonged to a balustrade of a ramp or a staircase, leading to some structure on a raised level. In the area around Tutankhamun's temple no such place has been reported. Could not this fragment have belonged to the balustrade of the ramp leading to the structure at the Hathor Rock? The hypothesis concerning the connection of the Hathor Rock and Tutankhamun's town is additionally confirmed by the find of the two stelae of Hatia . . . in the rubbish at the rock and . . . in the area of Tutankhamun's temple. (1981.70)

This last statement is rather misleading. The two stelae of the *wr* Hatia date to the end of the 18th dynasty. One depicts Hatia worshipping Ptah, Anukis, and an unnamed goddess who is probably Hathor (Khartoum 4446; Griffith 1921.94, pls. 21, 28; Karkowski 1981.137–8, pl. 17). Griffith specifically stated that this stela was found in the area of the temple of Tutankhamon (1921.94). The second stela shows Hatia adoring Ptah, while his wife, a Chantress of Hathor, shakes a sistrum before a goddess simply labelled as ⟨glyph⟩ (Khartoum 4451; Karkowski 1981.70, 87–8, pl. 4). In the Register of the Khartoum Museum the 'probable provenance' of this stela is given as Faras (1981.87). It was not mentioned by Griffith, and was presumably not found by the Oxford Expedition. This piece is most likely to have come from the temple of Tutankhamon, like the other stela of Hatia. Even if it did come from the 'Hathor rock', the stela could not be used to support Karkowski's hypothesis that the goddess was worshipped there as she *who is in Sehetep-netjeru* since it gives her no epithet at all. A reference to Hathor, Lady of Ibshek, in Horemheb's reign (Karkowski 1981.24) and her popularity under Ramesses II (Dewachter 1971.102–8) show that this epithet did not die out in Tutankhamon's reign. The inscription of Setau suggests that the goddess continued to be worshipped as Lady of Ibshek at the 'Hathor rock' long after Hathor was established as a co-templar deity in Sehetep-netjeru.

Karkowski's theory that the Hathor temple was rededicated to Hathor and Ankhesenamon is an attractive one. As he points out, the Faras temple could then be seen as equivalent to the temples dedicated to Hathor and Tiye at Sedeinga, and to Hathor and Nefertary at Abu Simbel (1981.70). It is also plausible that the temple was extensively renovated or even rebuilt during Tutankhamon's reign. This could be Woolley's 'second main stage of construction'. It is far less plausible that the temple was entirely rebuilt in sandstone, for only three dressed sandstone blocks were found at the 'Hathor rock'. These comprised the doorjamb already described, which may date to before the Amarna period, a fragment carved in low relief with a king (?) wearing an *atef* crown (Fig. 5.2; Griffith 1921.85; Karkowski 1981.91), and a smaller fragment with part of a vertical inscription, perhaps reading *to destroy* (Fig. 5.3; Griffith 1921.85; Karkowski 1981.91). If the Hathor temple had been rebuilt in stone, one would expect it to have included some columns, but no column bases were excavated by Woolley. Moreover, no dynastic blocks reused elsewhere in Faras can definitely be ascribed to the Hathor temple through their reliefs or inscriptions. Perhaps only the sanctuary was ever rebuilt in stone, while the rest of the temple continued to be of mudbrick with some stone elements. The Northern Temple at Buhen provides a parallel for this type of construction (Caminos 1974).

No 19th or 20th dynasty objects were found among the offerings, so the only direct evidence for Ramessid activity at the 'Hathor rock' comes from the grotto – the rock-cut shrine of Setau. A square rock-cut shrine was part of the Middle Kingdom Hathor temple at Serabit el-Khadim (1.4.2), so it is conceivable that the 'grotto' at Faras was cut in the Middle Kingdom or Second Intermediate Period and thus formed the oldest part of the temple. However, there is no inscriptional evidence to support such an hypothesis.

Setau was Viceroy of Nubia between years 35 and 50 of Ramesses II (Helck 1975.111–2), so the decoration of the shrine must date to this period. It is closely paralleled by two other rock-cut shrines dedicated by Setau, one at Qasr Ibrim and one at el-Kab (Drenkhahn 1975.46–8). A niche in the back wall of the Qasr Ibrim shrine contained statues of Ramesses II, Horus of Buhen, and Hathor, Lady of Ibshek (Caminos 1968.49, pl. 16). Karkowski may be right in suggesting that the single statue in the Faras niche was of Ramesses II, since the inscription on the adjacent stela consists only of the royal titulary followed by an offering formula (1981.112–4). R. Drenkhahn argues that the rock-cut shrines of Setau were private religious monuments (1975.44–8), so the shrine at Faras should probably not be seen as an addition to the Hathor temple. There is ample evidence for the popularity of the cult of Hathor, Lady of Ibshek, during the viceregency of Setau (Dewachter 1971.107–8). It seems unlikely that he would have failed to repair the Faras Hathor temple if he had found it in a ruinous state.

The absence of Ramessid stelae, statues, and small offerings at Faras is not particularly significant. Such objects are scarce in Nubian temples – none was found at Abu Simbel for example. Their place appears to have been taken by rock stelae for high officials and by graffiti for lesser officials. These are represented at Faras by the rock stela of Setau, the graffito of Meripet – an official under Ramesses II known from five other Nubian graffiti (Žaba 1974.189–92) – and the unpublished graffiti; which all suggest that the 'Hathor rock' continued to be visited as a holy place during the 19th dynasty.

Faras and its temples were probably abandoned as part of the general Egyptian withdrawal from Nubia at the end of the 20th dynasty. The only evidence for any occupation of Faras between the end of the New Kingdom and the Meroitic period is a group of sandstone blocks bearing the cartouches of Taharqa (Karkowski 1981.341–6), and Karkowski believes that these come from Buhen (1981.65). He proposes that the Faras temples were dismantled by Meroitic builders (1981.74), but he does not attempt to account for his alleged 'Post-Pharaonic' structures on the 'Hathor rock'. It might be argued that the rough stonework shown on Woolley's plan was the remains of Meroitic houses, such as those which Griffith mistook for the foundations of a Thutmosid temple (1921.90; Michałowski 1962.226). However, while Griffith may not have been very experienced at interpreting structural remains, he was certainly competent at recognising Meroitic objects. He stated that none was found at the 'Hathor rock' (1921.87). This would be odd if people of that period had lived there. Moreover, the fact that well-preserved 18th dynasty votive offerings were discovered 'at a slight depth' in this area (Griffith 1921.85) makes it unlikely that this was the site of a Meroitic settlement. During the New Kingdom brick buildings were sometimes built on rubble foundations with the lowest courses of their walls in rough stonework (A..J.Spencer 1979.120). It seems probable that the rough stonework on Woolley's plan, which in places seems to run under the 'second main stage of construction' (Plan 3), comes from dynastic structures of this type.

Since no dynastic blocks were reused in the church built on the 'Hathor rock', Karkowski may be right in saying that the temple was dismantled, or simply vandalized, in the Meroitic period. According to Mileham, burials were made on the south and west sides of the rock during the Christian period, and in modern times part of the temple/church site was reduced to a 'sort of hard mud paving' used as a threshing floor by the inhabitants of a nearby village (Mileham 1910.25).

1.2.3   The votive offerings

In his excavation report Griffith gave little detail about the find-spots of the small objects. He did record that the limestone 'lintel' and the three sandstone fragments were discovered in the vicinity of Chamber F, which also contained the base of a bark shrine (1921.85; Plan 3). Griffith went on to state that:–

In this upper part and on the west practically nothing else was found. The N.E. slope on the other hand, was composed chiefly of temple rubbish: only the space between the ramp walls was filled with clean sand; the rest, especially about the chamber B at a slight depth, abounded in potsherds and remains of bowls of glazed ware, beads, scarabs, etc. etc. (1921.85)

B is not marked on Woolley's plan, but only two chambers are shown in the lower part of the temple to the east of the ramp (Plan 3). Since the ramp is A, and Griffith intended the plan to be lettered from north to south, B is probably the more northerly of the two rooms in 'rough stone work'.

The inscribed pieces found in this area included the stelae of Ka and of the official of Amonhotpe I (Fig. 5), two stone basins, one dedicated by the wife of Huy (Fig. 5), a faience statuette base (?) (Fig. 5.7; Karkowski 1981.86–7, pl. 5), and 'about two hundred engraved scarabs and scaraboids' (Griffith 1921 pl. 18; 2.10.1.7). In addition to the potsherds, bowls and beads mentioned above, pottery and faience fertility figurines, pottery cows, gold plaques incised with cows or female figures, heads from stone statuettes, faience ears, eyes, and Hathor masks, and a variety of amulets were also recovered from the north-east slope of the temple (Pl. 8; Griffith 1921.86, 104).

In spite of his comment that 'practically nothing' was found in the upper part of the temple, Griffith noted that:–

> The chamber D produced in quick succession three of the earliest-looking scarabs ... and it is probable that it was the source of most of the earliest pieces; but this point was not observed till too late, when the digging had to be stopped. We could not bring ourselves to sacrifice the large and imposing block of brickwork, still remaining from the apse of the church ... when it threatened to fall on the men working at its base in chamber D (1921.86–7).

This reference to the apse makes it possible to identify chamber D on the plan (Plan 3).

No further detail about the context of the votive offerings was given by Griffith and only a selection of these objects seems to have been preserved. The stelae were published in line drawings (1921 pl. 24.5–7, 11 = Fig. 5), and photographs of 28 scarabs and scaraboids (1921 pl. 18), 67 small votive objects (1921 pl. 19 = Pl. 8), and nine faience bowl fragments (1921 pl. 20) were included in the excavation report. The records of the Oxford Expedition to Nubia are in the Griffith Institute, but they do not include object cards or distribution lists for the material from the 'Hathor rock'.

The large objects, and some of the scarabs and scaraboids, are in the Khartoum Museum. The majority of the small offerings brought back by Griffith were divided between the British Museum and the Ashmolean Museum, Oxford. Smaller groups of material from the Hathor temple were sent to the Pitt-Rivers Museum, Oxford, the Royal Scottish Museum, Edinburgh, and the Musées Royaux d'Art et d'Histoire, Brussels. I have been able to examine all of this material. Karkowski publishes the large objects and the scarabs and scaraboids in detail (1981.77–108, 111–4, pls. 3–10). He also gives small photographs and brief descriptions of the votive offerings in the British Museum and the Ashmolean Museum (1981.109–11), and descriptions and some drawings of the pieces in the Royal Scottish Museum (1981.111–2).

Inscribed material was rather scarce at Faras. Only three stelae have survived and the royal name faience is confined to scarabs, scaraboids, and cartouche plaques (2.10.7, 11). If this material is considered in isolation, the pattern which emerges is that offerings began in the late Second Intermediate Period and continued until the middle of the 18th dynasty, with peaks under Amonhotpe I and Thutmose I, and again under Thutmose III. After the reign of this last king the offerings appear to have stopped, with only a slight revival under Tutankhamon (1.2.2). Scarabs, scaraboids, and cartouche plaques have to be used with caution when assessing the period during which private votive offerings were made in a temple. Some may orginally have been attached to official offerings of a perishable nature, but others might have been worn as amulets for some time before being dedicated.

When the uninscribed objects are dated by style and technique, and by reference to comparative material, they give a date range from the late Middle Kingdom to the mid 18th dynasty. Some scarabs and scaraboids can be dated on stylistic grounds to the Second Intermediate Period (Karkowski 1981.102–8), including two which are of Hyksos types (1981.99–100, nos. 43–4). More significant are the kohl pot, the head of a stone statuette, and the faience figurine which could date either to the late Middle Kingdom or to the Second Intermediate Period (1.2.2). Of these, the most interesting is the faience head (Pl. 8.5; Karkowski 1981.110–11, no. 4c), since this could belong to a type of fertility figurine produced only during the Middle Kingdom and the early Second Intermediate Period (2.6.1.1). Other fertility figurines from Faras are of a type made in the late Second Intermediate Period and the early 18th dynasty (Pl. 8.14–5; 2.6.1.3). This early material is very similar to objects recovered from the Middle Kingdom/Second Intermediate Period Hathor shrine at Gebel Zeit (1.6.3). The range of mid–18th dynasty material resembles that from Deir el-Bahri, except that there is less royal-name faience. The absence of pieces in red or yellow faience, and of the new bead, amulet and jewellery types introduced in the late 18th dynasty, confirms that the small offerings at Faras stopped, or declined sharply, after the reign of Thutmose III.

The find-spots of the votive offerings reveal little about their dates. All the offerings may originally have been placed in the sanctuary, but no small objects seem to have been found there. Griffith's comment about chamber D –which is adjacent to the sanctuary – having been the source of some of the earliest scarabs (1921.86) is rather suprising, since this area of the temple was apparently rebuilt during the 'second main stage of construction'. This room may have been used during the early 18th dynasty to store offerings. When Chamber D was rebuilt, these offerings might have been moved to another part of the temple, or simply thrown out onto the north-east slope. A few small objects could easily have been left behind and preserved under the new floor, as happened at Timna (1.5.3).

The pieces found on the north-east slope of the 'Hathor rock' ranged in date from the late Middle Kingdom to the reign of Tutankhamon. Griffith does not state whether the material from the lower part of the slope had the same date range as that from the upper part, or whether the earlier objects were found under the later ones with any layers of sand between them. His comment that the offerings were found at a 'slight depth' (1921.85) could indicate that all the votive material was mixed up in a single layer. There may have been other 'dumps' of votive material just beyond the temple precincts which Griffith did not find. The presence of many intact objects, (Pl. 8) and some pieces of intrinsic value, such as the gold plaques, suggests that the small offerings were moved from the vicinity of the sanctuary to the north-east slope during one or more of the restorations of the temple, rather than ejected by Atonists or scattered by post-dynastic vandals and looters. Griffith's description fails to clarify whether most of the offerings were in chamber B, which might mean that it was built as a storeroom, or close to B, which could mean that they had been dumped out of sight behind a convenient structure. The Viceroy Setau may well have been responsible for such a clear-out of the temple. As at other sites (1.1.3.5; 1.4.3; 1.6.3), the large votive objects are likely to have stayed in the Hathor temple throughout the New Kingdom, perhaps being moved to side chambers or even incorporated in the structure during successive rebuildings. This would have made them vulnerable to vandalism in the period after the Egyptian withdrawal. Griffith noted that:–

> Unfortunately the figures and other larger objects were broken up into small fragments, and it was seldom that any two pieces could be fitted together. (1921.85)

Summary

There could have been a shrine at the 'Hathor rock' at Faras as early as the late Middle Kingdom. A shrine for Hathor, Lady of Ibshek, was probably built there by the Sobekemheb family from Buhen during the Second Intermediate Period. In the New Kingdom the rock was the site of a state-run Hathor temple. This was rebuilt several times, probably under Amonhotpe I, under Hatshepsut and Thutmose III, and under Tutankhamon. The mainly mudbrick temple was terraced, and had a semi rock-cut sanctuary. It continued in use during the 19th dynasty, when the Viceroy Setau dedicated a small rock-cut shrine to Ramesses II and Hathor, Lady of Ibshek.

The date range of the large votive objects is from the Second Intermediate Period to the 19th dynasty. The date range of the small votive objects is from the late Middle Kingdom, or Second Intermediate Period, to the mid 18th dynasty. The earlier offerings are similar to those from Gebel Zeit and the later ones to those from Deir el-Bahri, but there is less royal name faience than at either of those sites. A few votive pieces were found inside the temple near, but not in, the sanctuary. The majority had been moved to the north-east slope of the temple mound, perhaps during the 19th dynasty.

1.3 Mirgissa

1.3.1 The site

The fortified settlement known in modern times as Mirgissa was located on the west bank of the Nile, at the head of the Kabuka rapids in the Second Cataract. Mirgissa was about 50 km south of Faras and 16 km south of Buhen. Between October 1962 and January 1969 J. Vercoutter led the work of the French Archaeological Mission to the Sudan at Mirgissa. An aerial survey had revealed structures and cemeteries on the plain to the north of the Upper Fort (W. Y. Adams 1963.13). After trial excavations the French were able to divide the site into five main areas: the Upper Fort; the Fortified Town; the Open Town; the North, or Lower, Fort; and the Western Necropolis (Vercoutter 1968.269–79; 1970.9–23; Trigger 1976 fig. 21). None of these areas was completely cleared before the site was flooded during the creation of Lake Nasser.

Vercoutter established that the Upper Fort had been linked to a Middle Kingdom walled settlement with port facilities – the Fortified Town (1968.274–6; 1970.9–10). In the Second Intermediate Period or the early New Kingdom, the settlement expanded beyond its walls, so this phase was designated the Open Town (1968.274–5; 1970.11–3; Trigger 1976 fig. 21). The Western Necropolis proved to be made up of cemeteries ranging in date from the 12th to the 18th dynasties (Vercoutter 1965.69–70; 1968.276–7; 1970.15–8; 1975–6). The discovery of a substantial settlement and port attached to the Upper Fort, and of seal-impressions, scarabs and stelae bearing the name 𓐍𓈉, led Vercoutter to identify Mirgissa with the fortress and trading station of Iqen mentioned on the boundary stelae of year 8 of Senwosret III (1964.179–91; 1970.167–73).

1.3.2 The Hathor shrine

From 7–12 December 1963 the French team excavated a small mudbrick structure in the north-west corner of the inner part of the Upper Fort (Vercoutter 1964.179–80; 1965.64–6). On the evidence of the votive objects found inside, in particular five stelae depicting Hathor, Vercoutter identified the structure as a Hathor shrine (1965.65–6). On two of the stelae the goddess is described as *nbt iḳn* – 'Lady of Iqen' (Vercoutter 1970 pls. 38–9). Unlike Lady of Ibshek, the epithet 'Lady of Iqen' seems to have remained a simple indicator of place, with no currency outside Mirgissa. The shrine may not have functioned for long enough or ever have been prestigious enough for Hathor of Iqen to become closely associated with specific forms, roles or aspects of the goddess. A detailed description of the shrine and its contents by C. Karlin was published in *Mirgissa* I (Vercoutter 1970.307–62).

The shrine was a rectangular building with an approximate east–west axis (Plan 4). Its western end was formed by the inside wall of a road running round the inner part of the fort (Karlin in Vercoutter 1970 fig. 1). The shrine was divided into two unequal parts, which the excavators designated the Vestibule and the Sanctuary (1970.307–13). The vestibule was 4 × 20–40 m and the sanctuary 1.20 × 3.20 m. The walls seem to have been preserved to heights varying between 0.50 and 2 m.

The vestibule, in which hardly any objects were found (1.3.2), may have been a small open forecourt rather than an antechamber. The sanctuary, which was full of votive offerings and would have contained a cult image, is certain to have been roofed. This roof may have consisted of grass matting or reeds coated with mud, as in some of the mudbrick shrines in the 'workmen's village' at el-ʿAmarna (Kemp 1984.19; 1985.8–11; Bomann 1991.12).

The mudbrick walls of the vestibule were three courses thick and showed no traces of plaster. The narrow entrance in the east wall was reached by a short stair made up of bricks and stones of uneven size (Karlin in Vercoutter 1970.310). There seems to have been a niche in the north wall, just inside the entrance (Plan 4). There was not enough time to clear the whole of the vestibule, but exploratory trenches revealed five distinct strata, which were termed Strata 7–11 (1970.335–6; figs. 30–1). The shrine had been built on top of an earlier structure, for Stratum 7 consisted of foundations sunk into Middle Kingdom brick walls. Stratum 8 was a beaten earth floor which showed traces of combustion in the centre, around a sandstone basin sunk into the ground (Plan 4; 1970.311–2). Stratum 9, the first 'occupation level', was some 3 cm thick and included sand, which Karlin thinks was deliberately strewn on the floor of the shrine (1970.335). Stratum 10 consisted of a second beaten earth floor, also showing traces of combustion around the sandstone basin, which appears to have continued in use (1970.312). Stratum 11 was a second 'occupation level', impacted by rain after the abandonment of the shrine (1970.335). Karlin concludes that the vestibule was rebuilt or restored once during its period of use (1970.312).

The sanctuary, which was at a slightly higher level than the vestibule, was reached by a brick stair (1970.312, fig. 6). A mudbrick wall, with a wooden door in the centre, divided the sanctuary from the vestibule (1970.313). Inside, the walls retained some traces of plaster and there was a niche on each side of the door (Plan 4; 1970.313). The sanctuary was not fully paved, but several pieces of stone had been set into the earth floor just inside the doorway. Karlin suggests that these stones were placed where the priest would stand during the daily ritual (1970.313). Resting against the centre of the back wall were two bricks and a granite boulder which must have served as a base for the missing cult image (1970.313, fig. 7). Karlin notes that:–

> Le sédiment rencontré est un sable plus ou moins identique de la base au sommet, c'est-à-dire ne présentant pas les deux niveaux visibles dans le vestibule. (1970.318)

She concludes that the sanctuary was not restored at any stage in its use.

The building and restoration of the shrine are difficult to date. The excavators merely describe this structure as New Kingdom (Vercoutter 1964a.183; 1965.64; 1970.191, 307). The building itself is of little help in arriving at a more precise date.

The shrine has to be dated by its contents and by what is known of the history of Mirgissa. These two types of evidence are not always easy to reconcile.

A sondage in the vestibule revealed two Middle Kingdom 'occupation levels' below the first floor of the shrine, so a Middle Kingdom date for this structure is ruled out (1970.331–4, figs. 30–1). The simple plan of the shrine and its amateurish construction might indicate a date in the Second Intermediate Period, but there are several objections to this hypothesis. Layers of debris and rain-impacted soil were found between the Middle Kingdom 'occupation levels' and the first floor of the vestibule, suggesting a long period of decay between the abandonment of the Middle Kingdom structures and the building of the shrine on their ruins (1970.334). This would place the construction of the shrine in the late Second Intermediate Period at the earliest. Since the Upper Fort was occupied by Kerma people at this time (1970.183–4), it seems unlikely that an Egyptian community would have chosen to build a shrine there. Only two small objects which might date to the late Second Intermediate Period or the early 18th dynasty were found (1.4.3). The survival of a group of Second Intermediate Period material in the Hathor temple at Faras, in spite of its having been rebuilt several times (1.2.2–3), suggests that the scarcity of such pieces at Mirgissa is an argument against dating its Hathor shrine to the Second Intermediate Period.

During the Egyptian reconquest of Nubia the Upper Fort was repaired and re-garrisoned, probably under Ahmose or Amonhotpe I (1970.188; Trigger 1976.107–8). Mirgissa never seems to have regained the importance it enjoyed in the Middle Kingdom. Like most other Second Cataract forts, it does not appear to have been garrisoned after the reign of Thutmose III (Säve-Söderbergh 1941.193; Trigger 1976.123). There is some evidence for later government interest in Mirgissa in the form of architectural fragments with the names of Amonhotpe II and III, Ramesses I, and the Viceroy Setau (Vercoutter 1964a.183 n.2; 1968.21; 1970.192). It is probable that all this stonework came from a temple built inside or close to the Upper Fort, but because the excavations were only partial this question remains open (1970.191–2).

In reports on the New Kingdom cemetery at Mirgissa, C. Venot concludes that none of the burials was later than Thutmose III and that the majority dated to his reign (1974.27–49; in Vercoutter 1975.475–6). This suggests that at Mirgissa, as elsewhere in Lower Nubia (Adams 1964.106–7; Trigger 1976.131–7), the population enjoying a formal burial was in decline from the mid 18th dynasty. Due to the incompleteness of the excavations, and the difficulty of dating the houses which were examined (Vila in Vercoutter 1975.193–201), it is uncertain what size and type of community lived at Mirgissa during the remainder of the New Kingdom. One might assume that the Hathor shrine was erected as part of an official building programme shortly after the re-occupation of the Upper Fort and that it was used only until the end of Thutmose III's reign. However, the evidence both of the structure itself and of the objects found in it is against such an assumption.

Vercoutter tentatively suggests that the Hathor shrine was a chapel, primarily or exclusively for the use of women, which formed part of a New Kingdom temple complex dedicated to the triad of Mirgissa – Montu, Hathor, and the deified Senwosret III (1970.190–2). The shrine was quite close to the place where Sir

Henry Lyons found stelae dedicated to Senwosret III (1916.182–3; Vercoutter 1970.190–1), but no further evidence for a temple complex was discovered. The French team were able to establish very little about the New Kingdom structures in the vicinity of the shrine, but one thing is clear. Although the normal position for a Hathor shrine in a temple complex was to the south of the main structure (1.1.2.3–4), the Mirgissa shrine lay to the south of New Kingdom granaries (Karlin in Vercoutter 1970. fig. 1).

Whether the shrine was independent or part of a complex, it is difficult to accept that such a simple and crudely built structure could have been a New Kingdom *state* foundation. Some 18th dynasty state temples in Nubia were small mudbrick structures, but they all seem to have incorporated architectural features in dressed stone, many of which bear royal inscriptions (for examples see Dunham *et al.* 1967.13–4; Smith 1976.19–20). The excavators of the Hathor shrine do not believe that any structural elements were missing, so the building had never had any dressed stone, inscribed or otherwise. This suggests that the shrine was not a state foundation. This impression is strengthened by the absence of stelae or other monuments dedicated by high officials.

Almost all the offerings found in the shrine date to the period between the accession of Thutmose III and Hatshepsut and the end of the reign of Amonhotpe III (1.3.3). In terms of the design and manufacture of votive objects, the reigns of Hatshepsut, Thutmose III and Amonhotpe II seem to form a unit, so the shrine could have begun to function while Mirgissa was still garrisoned or shortly after the garrison left. There is no direct evidence that it was used by soldiers or officers of the garrison. Of the seven donors depicted on stelae from the shrine, two are priests and five are women (Vercoutter 1970 pls. 38–9). The presence of fertility figurines among the offerings (1970.350, fig. 45) relates the shrine to the concerns of family life (2.6.4). The New Kingdom cemetery at Mirgissa contained burials of women and children as well as adult males (Vercoutter 1975.422, 443; Boyaval 1981.191–206). Perhaps during the reign of Thutmose III the soldiers of the garrison began to have their families living with them. The shrine could have been built to serve such a new, mixed community.

The offerings did not, however, decline in number after the time when the garrison is thought to have been withdrawn. They seem to have reached their peak in the reigns of Thutmose IV and Amonhotpe III (1.3.3). Thus, some kind of Egyptian or Egyptianized community continued to live at Mirgissa in the late 18th dynasty. The Hathor shrine could have been built by members of this community in what had become a deserted area of the Upper Fort. The find of blocks with the cartouches of Amonhotpe III could mean that this king rebuilt or enlarged the state temple at Mirgissa (Vercoutter 1970.192). The population might have been increased by new temple personnel, and the vestibule of the Hathor shrine could have been rebuilt at this time. The contents of the shrine suggest that it served a community rather than one family, but it could still have been built at the initiative of a single family. Such a family would then have provided the clergy for the shrine and shared any income that accrued. Evidence from Deir el-Medina shows that shares in religious buildings, and the rights and incomes attached to them, could be held, bequeathed or sold by both men and women (Janssen & Pestman 1968.156–8; Allam in Lesko 1989.129–30).

The shrine may have been abandoned in the Amarna period, although one would not expect a humble, community foundation to have been attacked by Atonists. One scarab which might be Ramessid was found (1.3.3). It is possible that the Mirgissa shrine was still in use in the early 19th dynasty but that, as at Deir el-Bahri and Faras, the custom of presenting votive objects was not resumed after the Amarna period. The absence of a cult image could mean that it was stolen when the shrine was derelict. Alternatively, it may have been reverently removed when a decision was made to abandon the shrine. The Mirgissa community may have moved, or been moved, *en masse* – perhaps in the 19th dynasty – and have taken their image of Hathor with them to found a new shrine.

Because so little is known about the New Kingdom town at Mirgissa, these conclusions are tentative, but it does seem certain that this edifice was a 'community shrine' rather than a temple built and run by the state. It is comparable to some of the simpler shrines built by and for the artisans' community at Deir el-Medina (Bruyère 1952a; Valbelle 1985.325–8) and to some of the shrines in the 'workmen's villages' at el-ʿAmarna (Kemp 1985.29–50; 1987.56–70; Bomann 1991.18-24, figs.9–14), and Deir el-Ballas (Richards in Lacovara 1990.11–14, fig.3.2). That is not to say that it would have been completely independent of the state. At Deir el-Medina, wine, cakes, oil, and other commodities used in the village shrines were sometimes supplied by the state as part of the 'expenses' of the community (Janssen 1976.18; Valbelle 1985.267, 271, 319) and time was allowed off work to celebrate religious festivals (1985.318–335). A similar arrangement could have existed at Mirgissa, especially if the shrine was built before the withdrawal of the garrison. Nevertheless, as a community shrine, Mirgissa does fall into a different category from the other sites. This difference is visible in the votive offerings.

1.3.3 The votive offerings

The only objects discovered in the vestibule were three faience beads and a potsherd in the sandstone basin, and a piece of flint and a lock of hair under it (Karlin in Vercoutter 1970.312). A large group of offerings was found in the sanctuary:–

> Two flights of steps gave access to a small recess which was literally packed with small objects: beads, scarabs, amulets of glazed faience, broken vases, worked wood, basketry, stones of curious shapes and, most important, four stelae which seemed to be still *in situ* when we discovered them. However the main stela, or statue, or relief of the divinity, which must once have stood in the shrine had been removed ... The number of small monuments representing Hathor alone showed that the shrine had once been dedicated to this goddess. This was further vindicated by the objects found during the clearing of the shrine, such as the beads, amulets – a number of them in the shape of Bes the companion of Hathor – wooden counterpoises for menit necklaces, as well as small faience statuettes of 'concubines', one of them in sandstone. This last type of object, whose connexion with Hathor-worship is well-known, confirmed us in assigning the small sanctuary to the cult of Hathor. When we reached the original

ground level we found the remains of baskets and pots and a small wooden stela, which seems originally to have been quite near the place where the cult image of Hathor stood. Nearby was a vase of coarse pottery filled with small votive objects ... (Vercoutter 1965.65–6)

An inventory of these offerings by Karlin in *Mirgissa* I gives a brief description of each item (1970.335–57). Most are illustrated with a drawing and in some cases a photograph (1970.357–61, figs. 27–8, 35, 38–50, pls. 34–9). More detailed publication is planned for the inscribed material. Most of the offerings are now in the Khartoum Museum, but a few are on loan to the Institute of Papyrology and Egyptology at the University of Lille.

Karlin hardly ever discusses the dates of individual objects and Vercoutter confines himself to stating that:–

En fait tout ce que nous avons trouvé dans le sanctuaire d'Hathor: stèles, scarabées, amulettes, perles, etc. paraît dater de le XVIIIe dyn. et rien n'y est indisputablement postérieur. (1964a.183.n.2)

The only inscribed material found in the shrine was a group of five stelae (Vercoutter 1970 pls. 38–9), and some scarabs, including two of Amonhotpe III (Karlin in Vercoutter 1970.352). Apart from the scarabs, royal name faience is entirely lacking. On the basis of their style, technique, and materials, the votive objects can be divided into two uneven groups. About one fifth appear to date to the period spanning the reigns of Hatshepsut, Thutmose III and Amonhotpe II, and almost all the remainder to the late 18th dynasty. The 'early' material consists of three of the stelae, the faience fertility figurines, segmented faience balls, and some of the beads, amulets, and scaraboids. The 'late' material includes two of the stelae, a stone fertility figurine, a wooden menit counterpoise, model bunches of grapes, earrings, cornflower pendants, figures of Bes playing the tambourine, some of the scarabs, and all of the jewellery made in glass or red, yellow or black faience. Much of the jewellery was of types used in daily life and may have been the personal possessions of the donors (2.10.4).

A few pieces cannot be fitted into this neat division. The upper part of a small Middle Kingdom granite statue of a man was found in the sanctuary, but since it was lying above everything else, almost at surface level, it is likely to have strayed there from another part of the site (Karlin in Vercoutter 1970.313, fig. 37). A carnelian scarab and a glazed steatite button seal could both date to the late 17th or early 18th dynasties (1970.353, nos. 169–70), but they may have been kept for some time before being dedicated. One faience scarab is inscribed with the words *wsr m3ʿt rʿ nb* (1970.352, no. 160). If these signs were intended to write a royal name, the scarab must be 19th dynasty, which would make it the only Ramessid object from the shrine.

Some of the beads and amulets are of types used throughout the 18th dynasty, so they cannot be closely dated. Normal dating criteria do not apply to offerings such as pebbles in female or phallic shapes (2.6.3; 2.7.1), or to dried fish (1970.318, fig. 16; 2.10.1.5). In these cases the question arises whether the exact position of an object within the shrine is a useful dating criterion. An excellent series of photographs and plans shows the precise position of most of the offerings in the sandy soil which filled the sanctuary (1970 figs. 8–21), but Karlin warns against attaching too much significance to this evidence:–

> Maintenant voleurs, destruction, effondrement de brique ont perturbé les vestiges et certaines des significations que nous avons pu essayer d'attacher à nos constatations pourraient, peut-être, être contredites par la fouille d'un autre sanctuaire différemment perturbé. (1970.328)

She also believes that 'la fouille ne nous a donné qu'une mince partie de ce que les fidèles avaient offert à Hathor' (1970.328), but this may be too pessimistic a view. Some of the wooden objects had been attacked by termites, so others may have been have been completely eaten by them (1970.321–2). Damp had destroyed the stringing of all the beads and amulets and affected the paint on the stelae (1970.234). Yet, in proportion to the total number of finds, only Gebel Zeit produced more intact objects than Mirgissa. The fact that all the objects were found packed into the sanctuary, rather than scattered in the vestibule, suggests that they had not been picked over by thieves. The stelae, which would have been an obvious target for vandals, were not defaced, and three were discovered standing upright in their original position beside the base for the cult image (Karlin in Vercoutter 1970 fig. 17). Among the small objects, the damage was consistent with wear and tear in a crowded shrine, the collapse of the upper walls, and partial exposure to the weather.

One possibility which must be considered is that some offerings were cleared out of the shrine, either because they were broken or because the sanctuary had become too full. No dumps of votive material were found in the vicinity of the shrine, but as only part of the Upper Fort and its environs were excavated, their existence cannot be ruled out. There is some evidence for broken objects being removed. One piece of calcite, one of striped glass, and several faience sherds with a lotus pattern (1970.355, nos. 199–204) indicate that vessels in these materials once stood in the shrine. They may have been discarded when broken because they were used in the daily ritual and replacements were needed. Some of the offerings, including a mid 18th dynasty fertility figurine and a scarab of Amonhotpe III, were found in two pieces, one half lying on the floor and the other inside a large pottery full of both 'early' and 'late' material (1970.323, fig. 49g). It seems from this that broken offerings were left where they lay, or tidied away into a container, rather than being thrown out of the shrine.

At Deir el-Bahri the evidence suggested that, in spite of the large numbers of offerings, the Hathor shrines were not regularly cleared out (1.1.3.5). It seems unlikely that the Mirgissa shrine, which served a comparatively small and poor community, would have suffered from chronic overcrowding. The dedication of votive objects never seems to have become a standard religious practice, and the majority of the offerings would have been perishable commodities, such as beer, cakes or flowers (3.2). Thus the objects discovered in the shrine may, after all, represent a substantial proportion of those originally dedicated there.

In the top layer of the sand filling the sanctuary were numerous twigs and leaves which cannot have come there naturally, since the shrine is situated on a desert plateau (1970.318). These are probably the remains of garlands presented to the goddess, which would usually have been removed once they began to wither. Below the foliage came the layers containing the votive objects. As a general rule, the 'late' material was at a higher level than the 'early' material. For example, the stone fertility figurine, one of the scarabs of Amonhotpe III, and the scarab which may be Ramessid, were in the uppermost layer (1970 fig. 8), while most of the 'early' beads and amulets were at floor level (1970 figs. 12, 19).

There were, however, plenty of exceptions to this rule. A group of 'late' jewellery was found at a low level near the base for the cult image (1970 figs. 10–1). This area may have been kept clear of offerings in the early years of the shrine's existence, or it could have been the first resting place for votive objects, which would later have been pushed aside to make room for new ones. The contents of the jar demonstrate that offerings were moved about and that objects of different dates could end up grouped together. Given this, together with disturbance caused by collapsing walls and drifting sand, Karlin is probably right to be wary of using the exact position of an object as a principal dating criterion. Nevertheless, the objects in the Mirgissa shrine can still provide valuable evidence about the daily ritual of a Hathor shrine and the way in which offerings were presented (see 3.2).

Summary

The Mirgissa shrine was dedicated to Hathor, Lady of Iqen. It was an exceptionally well-preserved example of a simple shrine built and run by a local community. The most likely date for its construction is the reign of Thutmose III. The vestibule of the shrine may have been rebuilt under Amonhotpe III. About one-fifth of the offerings date to the period covered by the reigns of Hatshepsut, Thutmose III and Amonhotpe II, and most of the remainder to the reigns of Thutmose IV and Amonhotpe III. There is almost no royal name faience. Some of the offerings appear to be objects used in daily life rather than specially made votive pieces. All the offerings were found inside the sanctuary, some in their original positions.

1.4 Serabit el-Khadim

1.4.1 The site

Serabit el-Khadim is the modern name for a sandstone plateau, some 850 m above sea level, in the south-west of the Sinai peninsula. The ravines that cut through the plateau once contained rich turquoise deposits, which were periodically mined by the local nomadic population and by expeditions from Egypt (Petrie 1906.109–21, 154–64; Černý 1955.3–21; Rothenberg 1979.161–4). These mining expeditions began in the early Middle Kingdom and continued, with breaks in the Second Intermediate Period and the Amarna period, until the late New Kingdom (Černý 1955.38–41). At the eastern end of the plateau of Serabit el-Khadim the Egyptians set up stelae commemorating expeditions and founded a temple dedicated to Hathor ⏢𓏤𓂝𓏤 ◯ ◦◦◦.

mfkꜣt is commonly translated 'turquoise' (Harris 1961.106–10), but Middle Kingdom inscriptions mention Hathor *nbt mfkꜣt* at three sites where it is now known that the Egyptians mined for or smelted copper – Maghara, Wadi Kharit, and Bir Nasib (Černý 1955.68–72; Giveon *et al.* 1977.61–3; 1978.76–8; Rothenberg 1979.164), and a temple was built for her at Timna, where only copper was mined (1.5). *mfkꜣt* may therefore sometimes be a general term for turquoise, copper ore, malachite, or any blue-green mineral, or for the area from which such minerals came. There can be no doubt that at Serabit el-Khadim itself Hathor, Lady of Mefkat, was closely associated with turquoise.

Serabit el-Khadim was first brought to the attention of Europeans by C. Niebuhr, who visited the site in 1762 and mistook the ruined temple with its numerous freestanding stelae for a graveyard (Weill 1904.61). In spite of the remoteness and inaccessiblity of the plateau, Serabit el-Khadim was visited by many Europeans during the 19th century (1904.61–92). In 1845 C. K. MacDonald stayed there for some weeks or months. During this time he made squeezes of many of the best preserved stelae and collected about 400 fragments of Egyptian votive offerings which he donated to the British Museum in 1849 (Cooney 1972.280–5; Dyke & Uphill 1983.165–6). In 1867 the plateau of Serabit el-Khadim was surveyed and photographed by a British survey team (Wilson *et al.* 1869). A plan of the temple was drawn up by C. Wilson, many of the inscriptions were copied, and 'a few slight excavations' were made, probably at the eastern extremity of the temple. R. Campbell Thompson visited the site in 1902 and brought back some votive faience for the British Museum (1905.87–91, 131–3).

No full-scale excavation of the Hathor temple was attempted until the Egypt Exploration Fund financed an expedition to Sinai in 1904. This expedition was led by W. M. F. Petrie, whose assistants included C. T. Currelly, L. Eckenstein, and R. Weill (1906.x). During the expedition's three months at Serabit el-Khadim, numerous inscriptions were copied, the mines were surveyed, the whole of the temple was cleared, and a large quantity of votive objects was recovered.

In 1917 the EEF published *The Inscriptions of Sinai*, the first of two projected volumes by A. H. Gardiner and T. E. Peet. After a brief visit to Sinai, J. Černý extensively revised both volumes and the resulting works were published in 1952 (plates) and 1955 (text). He made his trip to Sinai as a member of a Harvard University Expedition (1952.1). Harvard sent expeditions to Serabit el-Khadim in 1927, 1930 and 1935, the first two being jointly undertaken with Catholic University, Washington DC. During the third expedition R. Starr cleared one of the mines and several quarries, some of which had been turned into shrines, and re-excavated the eastern end of the temple (Starr & Butin 1936. 3–27, pls. 1–7).

From 1967 to 1981 Israeli archaeologists, led by R. Giveon, regularly visited the plateau to carry out a programme of excavation and conservation (Giveon *et al.* 1977). Giveon found a variety of unrecorded blocks, stelae, and small objects. He died before he could complete his intended corpus of new, or unpublished, Egyptian material from Sinai.

1.4.2 The Hathor temple

There can be no doubt that the temple at Serabit el-Khadim was primarily dedicated to Hathor, Lady of Mefkat. Her name appears in dedication inscriptions all over the temple. She is shown, usually in human form, in numerous reliefs and on almost every stela. The majority of the small offerings either represent Hathor or are inscribed with her name. Serabit el-Khadim also contains more sets of Hathor mask columns than any other Egyptian temple (Petrie 1906 pls. 95, 100–4, 111; 2.3.1). Sopdu and Thoth were the most important co-templar deities.

The locally quarried sandstone from which the temple is built is of poor quality (Starr and Butin 1936.15–20). The orientation of the Hathor temple is approximately east–west. In its final form the temple was about 70 m long. The easternmost part is cut into a knoll of rock, but the rest is freestanding (Plan 5). The temple has suffered considerable damage from high winds, violent rain storms, sharp frosts, and, particularly in this century, from theft and vandalism. A few walls and columns were still standing to roof height when Petrie excavated the temple, but on the whole the structure was not in good condition. The erosion of inscriptions and reliefs by damp and by wind-driven sand made exact dating of some sections of the temple difficult or impossible.

The earliest firmly dated object found in the temple was the base of a statue dedicated by Amenemhet I (Černý 1955.84, no. 63), while the oldest structural element was a lintel of Senwosret I (1955.84, no. 64), to whose reign the oldest commemorative stela dates (1955.85, no. 66). Stelae commemorating mining expeditions were also set up under Amenemhet II, Senwosret II and Amenemhet III (1955.87–90). Černý suggested that in the early Middle Kingdom the Hathor temple consisted only of a rock-cut shrine – the 'Hathor cave' (T; for letters see Plan 5) – and some kind of vestibule, approached from the north-west by an avenue of freestanding stelae (1955.36).

During the reign of Amenemhet III, at least twenty-two stelae were erected and several officials left inscriptions in the 'Hathor cave' (1955.90–122). The portico (S) in front of the 'Hathor cave' appears to have been built or restored under Amenemhet III and IV (Petrie 1906.98; Starr & Butin 1936.6–9). Since the south door of the portico is said to have been inscribed by an official of Amenemhet II (Petrie 1906.105), Černý suggested that the so-called Sopdu rooms (U, V–W), which lie to the south of the portico (Plan 5), must have been built by that date (1955.36). The Sopdu rooms, which date in their present form to the joint reign of Hatshepsut and Thutmose III, consist of a deep rock-cut niche and two small chambers (Plan 5). It is possible that the room which Petrie called the sanctuary (Q, Plan 5) was also first constructed in the late 12th dynasty, since two inscriptions of this date are thought to have been found there (Černý 1955.36).

The portico was restored or rebuilt under Amonhotpe I (Petrie 1906.93–4; Starr & Butin 1936.9–10). The large chamber (Z), which Petrie named the Hathor Hanafiyah after the courtyard where ablutions are performed in a mosque, as well as rooms O and N (Plan 5), were built during the joint reign of Hatshepsut and Thutmose III (Petrie 1906.80–1, 86–7). The Sopdu rooms were either built or restored in their reigns. The 'Lesser Hanafiyah' (X) between the Sopdu rooms and the Hathor Hanafiyah, and the court (P), which lies between O and the sanctuary, should probably also be attributed to those rulers (Černý 1955.37).

During the sole reign of Thutmose III a pylon was built; this was presumably intended to make an imposing entrance to the temple (Petrie 1906.79–80, pl. 96). However, the temple continued to expand westwards, with a series of small, narrow rooms ranging in date from Amonhotpe II to Seti I (M–A, Plan 5; Petrie 1906.76–9; Černý 1955.38; Giveon 1978.55). These rooms should probably be seen more as symbols of the desire to please the goddess by 'making monuments' for her than as functional additions to the temple. Ramesses II inscribed rooms B and A and restored the Lesser Hanafiyah (Černý 1955.38). Merenptah repaired room J (Petrie 1906.78); Seti II usurped the pylon (1906.80); Ramesses III set up a stela in room A (1906.76; Černý 1955.186, no. 273); Ramesses IV rebuilt the sanctuary (Q) and added the porch (P; Petrie 1906.89–90, pl. 107); and Ramesses VI inscribed pillars in room O (1906.108). The dry stone wall which surrounds the temple may date to the reign of Amonhotpe III (Petrie 1906.76; Giveon 1978.55–6).

Serabit el-Khadim has been described as the oldest example of a partially rock-cut Egyptian temple (Wildung 1977.162), but the exact date and nature of the Hathor and Sopdu 'caves' have been a source of controversy. The 'Hathor cave' measures 5 × 3 m. Its roof was originally supported by a single rock pillar and later by two beams and a secondary column, probably of wood (Butin & Starr 1936.11, pl. 1). Two niches are cut in the east wall, the smaller of which retained traces of the fitments for a wooden door, and there is a third niche in the south wall (Petrie 1906.95). The walls have been badly damaged by damp (New in Lake *et al.* 1932.24–5, pls. 142–3) and most of the reliefs and inscriptions have flaked away, but on the western face of the rock pillar Amenemhet III and a group of officials are shown worshipping Hathor (Černý 1952 pl. 26; 1955.90–1, no. 83). The only objects found by Petrie in the 'Hathor cave' were two stone incense altars, and three stone offering tables dedicated by officials who served under Amenemhet III (1906.95; Černý 1955.96–7, 103–4).

Eckenstein (1914.9–13) suggested that the 'Hathor cave' was adapted from a natural cave in which a local moon deity was worshipped before the Egyptians came to Serabit el-Khadim but, after a careful examination of the 'cave', Starr declared that there were 'no indications that it was originally a natural formation' (1936.11). It is unlikely that the local nomadic population would have cut a rock shrine of this type, and the 'Hathor cave' should be accepted as a purely Egyptian structure. L. Borchardt and R. Weill believed that it was originally cut as a tomb for an expedition leader (Weill 1904.36, 46). Giveon proposed that it was intended as the tomb of an official of Amenemhet III called Ameny, whose name features prominently in the inscriptions in the 'cave' (1976.24; 1978.54). He went on to suggest that the smaller and more roughly cut 'Sopdu cave' was the original Hathor shrine, and assumed that the cult image was later transferred to the 'Hathor cave', which was 'larger and more convenient' (1978.63).

The fact that none of the surviving inscriptions in the 'Hathor cave' predates the reign of Amenemhet III does present a problem. Petrie's solution was that the 'cave' was merely enlarged and redecorated under Amenemhet III (1906.98). This seems plausible. Because of the poor state of the walls, it is not possible to be sure that there were no early 12th dynasty inscriptions. The date of the 'Hathor cave' may be in doubt, but Giveon's theory that it was cut and decorated as a tomb for Ameny should certainly be rejected. Sinai never seems to have been thought of as part of Egypt and, in the light of such texts as the 'autobiography' of Sinuhe, it is inconceivable that any Egyptian official would choose to be buried there. The 'cave' must have taken a great deal of time and trouble to cut, and thus is unlikely to have been made as a temporary resting place for a body due to be taken back to Egypt at the end of a mining season. No funerary equipment was found in the 'cave,' and it contained no niche or shaft suitable for a sarcophagus. The surviving decoration is not of a funerary nature. The presence of reliefs showing a king and his officials, and of *ḥtp di nsw* formulae for these officials and their families, does not indicate that the 'cave' was an official's tomb. Such reliefs and inscriptions occur all over the temple. Černý commented that:–

> This abnormality is very easily explained. Far away from Egypt in the heart of the Sinai the leader of the expedition was supreme, and here he had, and took advantage of, a freedom from Pharaoh's supervision, which he could never have hoped to enjoy in Egypt, to belaud himself to the full. (1955.40)

Close parallels to the form and decoration of the 'Hathor cave' are provided by a type of rock-cut shrine found in the territory of the viceroys of Nubia (1.2.2). These shrines commemorated the high officials who had them cut, but were dedicated to the reigning king and local deities. They were private foundations and did not enjoy the status of state temples, though they might be situated beside such temples, as at Faras (1.2.2). The 'Hathor cave' at Serabit el-Khadim might have been a shrine of this type which was later incorporated into the temple; in which case Giveon may have been right in saying that the 'Sopdu cave' was the original Hathor speos. There are two objections to this hypothesis. First, all the other rock-cut shrines of officials date to the New Kingdom, and second, at the analogous site of Gebel el-Silsila, a whole series of shrines was cut by leaders of quarrying expeditions (Caminos & James 1963). It is difficult to explain why there should be only one at Serabit el-Khadim.

The main alternative is to assume that the 'Hathor cave' was constructed as the speos of a partially rock-cut temple (Wildung 1977.162) and to adopt Černý's explanation for the prominence of individual officials in its reliefs and inscriptions. This might make Serabit el-Khadim the oldest surviving example of a semi rock-cut cult temple. A precedent is provided by the 11th dynasty mortuary temple at Deir el-Bahri. The cliffs at Deir el-Bahri were laboriously cut away to accommodate the hypostyle hall of this temple and the speos is inside the cliff (Plan 2). There may also have been an 11th dynasty rock-cut Hathor shrine at Deir el-Bahri (1.1.2.1). At Elephantine, a natural cleft in the rock served as a shrine to Satis at least as early as the 1st dynasty (Kaiser et al. 1977.65, fig. 1), so cave shrines were a very ancient part of Egyptian religious architecture. As a passage in the Coffin Texts seems to refer to the 'Caverns of Hathor' at Serabit el-Khadim (Spell 486, CT VI.63m), there may have been specific iconographical reasons for constructing a cave-like speos at this site (see further 2.4.6).

1.4.3 The votive offerings

MacDonald published no account of his stay at Serabit el-Khadim, so the exact find-spots of the votive objects which he discovered are unknown. The British Museum entry slips for this material simply note that it was 'found on the site of the temple of Hathor', but the fact that the inscriptions copied by MacDonald were situated along the old approach, and in room N, the sanctuary (Q), the portico (S), and the 'Hathor cave' (Černý 1952.11–5) gives an indication of the area of the temple in which he worked.

The objects he donated to the British Museum consist of a small stela and several statue fragments; small numbers of faience menit counterpoises, sistra, Hathor masks, cat figurines, beads and scarabs, and a large group of faience bracelets and numerous fragments from glass, faience, and calcite vessels. All these objects were described in some detail in the museum entry slips written by S. Birch, who also made drawings of the more interesting pieces. Most of the faience pieces which bore royal inscriptions were published by Weill (1904.219–25). In an article on MacDonald, J. D. Cooney gave a brief description of this whole group of votive objects, illustrating two of the finest pieces (1972.281–3, pl. 45), and he later published all of the glass (1976.54–7, nos. 508–72). Much of the faience found by MacDonald has deteriorated to the point where the designs and inscriptions recorded by Birch are no longer visible.

Wilson noted that the results of the 'slight excavations' of 1867 were 'a small gold ornament, a few scaribae, some broken necklaces and fragments of pottery' (1869.193). A small number of beads, scaraboids and fragments from faience vessels were presented to the British Museum by the Sinai Survey. The location of the gold ornament – the only object in precious metal recorded from this site – is unknown.

In his one published account of his brief visit to Serabit el-Khadim, Campbell Thompson did not mention the votive offerings. His description of the temple mainly concerns the portico and the 'Hathor cave' (1905.88–9), so the pieces he brought back may have come from this area. They consist of about twenty fragments from faience vessels and a few faience bracelets and menit counterpoises.

By far the largest group of offerings to come from Serabit el-Khadim was that excavated by Petrie early in 1905. He noted that:–

> Beside the multitude of large historical steles, which were inscribed with the records of expeditions, there were also many lesser monuments of kings and private persons ... These were mostly found in the sanctuary and the portico, and nearly all of them were broken ... (1906.122)

These 'lesser monuments' consisted of votive stelae (2.1.1), and statues of, or dedicated by, private individuals who were members of mining expeditions. One block statue, a sphinx, and fragments from several other statues were all inscribed in the alphabetic script now known as Proto-Sinaitic (1906.129–30, pls. 138–9, 141). These statues, whose date remains controversial (Giveon 1978a.140–3), were presumably the gifts of Asiatics. Some 12th dynasty stelae include Asiatics in their list of expedition members (Černý 1955.19; Giveon 1978a.131–5); and two New Kingdom votive stelae with prayers to Hathor written in Egyptian were set up by Asiatics in the vicinity of the temple (Černý 1952 pl. 89, no. 423; Giveon 1981.168–71).

All the small votive offerings excavated by Petrie were of Egyptian types:

> The greater part of the offerings were of glazed ware – vases, bowls, and cups; beside lesser quantities of plaques, *menats*, bracelets, wands, sistra, animals etc. These objects had all been broken up, so that not a single whole thing was found. The fragments formed a layer, two or three inches thick, over all the sanctuary and portico, and extending outside of the sanctuary on the north for a distance of some feet. (1906.138)

In addition to the 'many hundredweights' of faience fragments, Petrie found pieces of numerous calcite and glass vessels (2.11.1.2, 4).

Petrie devoted two chapters of his book *Researches in Sinai* to describing the offerings. He published photographs of many of the stelae and statues, and of a selection of each category of small votive object (1906.122–53, pls. 126–59). Most of the stelae were left at the site, but about 800 objects were brought back to England and briefly exhibited (EEF Cat. 1905) before being distributed. The Egypt Exploration Society archives contain a group of photographs of objects from Serabit el-Khadim, which are published here for the first time (Pls. 29, 39, 31 43–4, 58, 61–64). Some distribution lists written by Petrie survive in University College, London. These are not always accurate, and the lists for the stelae and statues are missing. Objects were sent to museums all over the world, but the British Museum and the Victoria and Albert Museum, London; the Ashmolean Museum; the Civic Museum and Art Gallery, Bolton; the Musées Royaux d'Art et d'Histoire, Brussels; the Museum of Fine Arts, Boston; and the Royal Ontario Museum, Toronto have the largest collections of this material. Almost all the stelae and statues, and many of the small objects with royal inscriptions, are described in Černý's edition of *The Inscriptions of Sinai* (1952; 1955).

In his report on his excavations at Serabit el-Khadim, Starr gave no details of the find-spots of votive objects, noting that:–

... no trust could be placed in the location of the minor objects that fell to our lot, for the system used by Petrie – of dumping on the areas previously cleared – hopelessly removed them from their original locations. (1936.4)

No description of these 'minor objects' was included, but to judge from the photographs published in the report (1936 pls. 12–3), they consisted of a small number of faience Hathor masks, cat and Hathor mask plaques, bracelets, menit counterpoises, beads, and vessel fragments. Some of these finds were sent to the Cairo Museum; others to the Harvard University Semitic Museum. The objects in this latter group were never catalogued and they have now 'disintegrated'. I have been able to examine, or obtain detailed information on, about 75 per cent of the small offerings from the excavations mentioned above.

More inscribed material was found at Serabit el-Khadim than at any of the other five sites. This makes the dating of most categories of votive object relatively easy. Stelae were set up by expedition leaders during the 12th dynasty, from the early 18th dynasty to the death of Amonhotpe III, and from the reign of Seti I to that of Ramesses VI. The votive stelae dedicated by individual expedition members range in date from the mid 18th dynasty to the 20th dynasty (2.1.6). The small votive offerings with 'royal name' inscriptions include Hathor mask and cat plaques, sistra, menit counterpoises, bracelets, scarabs, cartouche plaques, model throwsticks, vases, and bowls. All these pieces are New Kingdom. The rulers named are Amonhotpe I, Thutmose I, Hatshepsut, Thutmose III, Amonhotpe II, Amonhotpe III, Seti I, Ramesses II, Merenptah, Seti II, Tawosret, and Ramesses III, IV, V, and VI. The commonest royal names are Thutmose III among the 18th dynasty pieces, and Ramesses II among the Ramessid pieces. Inscribed Ramessid material outnumbers the inscribed 18th dynasty material by about four to one.

Although such a high proportion of the inscribed faience is Ramessid, the uninscribed material includes a large body of 18th dynasty beads and scaraboids and faience and glass vessels. Much of the uninscribed material can be dated by reference to pieces inscribed with royal names. For example, uninscribed vessel fragments in a distinctive pale green faience with violet inlay (e.g. Petrie 1906 pl. 147.18) can be dated to Amonhotpe III because his name occurs on menit counterpoises and dishes of this ware (e.g. Hayes 1951.235, fig. 35). Some categories of offering, such as cat figurines, beads, amulets, many of the scarabs, and most of the vessels in calcite, faience, glass, and pottery have to be dated by means of their style, technique and material. These objects extend the date range a little, since they include a few Second Intermediate Period and 'Hyksos' scarabs (Brussels MR 2029–30; London UC 35447–8; Manchester 968, 970–1). These unpublished pieces provide the only evidence that mining expeditions might have continued, presumably on an occasional basis and a much smaller scale, during the Second Intermediate Period. The complete absence of small Middle Kingdom objects suggests that ordinary expedition members did not make votive offerings inside the temple in this period, though they may have dedicated them in humbler shrines elsewhere on the plateau (see 1.6.2; 3.1).

Petrie raised the question of how many of the offerings originally dedicated inside the temple have survived. He wrote that:–

It is clear that the Bedawyn revenged themselves on the Egyptians by overthrowing and smashing all the offerings that had accumulated here during many centuries. We hoped that, as the site had been very little dug over before our clearance, we might be able to reconstruct many of these broken offerings ... Every fragment was collected, sorted over, and every possible joining was tried. The result was that very few pieces could be fitted together; for instance not a single one of a dozen sistrum-heads fitted any handle that was found. The general conclusion was forced on me that we have not more than about a third of all the glazed ware that had been broken up. What then had become of the rest? We found many hundredweights of fragments, but half a ton or more of pieces must have entirely disappeared. They could not be hidden around the temple, for the whole space is bare rock, and we turned over all the sand and earth in the neighbourhood. The only conclusion seems to be that the greater part of the pieces were scattered upon the rock around; that there they gradually disintegrated under the sun and dew and frosts, and every loose grain was blown away by the high winds which sweep the plateau. Thus the pieces have in three thousand years entirely disappeared in dust, and only those have been preserved which were hedged round by walls and stones sufficiently to keep a layer of sand and earth over them. (1906.138–9)

The find-spots of the small offerings must be examined in more detail before this conclusion can be accepted.

The offerings discovered by Petrie were spread thinly all over the floors of the portico and the sanctuary, including the unroofed part of the latter. This is unlikely to have been their original position. At least three main explanations of this state of affairs could be put forward. First, each batch of offerings may have been dedicated in the sanctuary – the 'Hathor cave' – and then moved to a nearby chamber, such as the portico (S) or the roofed part of the sanctuary (Q), to make room for new gifts. 'Hall of Offerings' might be a more appropriate name for the latter room. A second possibility is that the small offerings may have been intended to stay in the 'Hathor cave', but were cleared out and piled up in the portico and the sanctuary during one or more Ramessid restorations of the temple. In both these cases, the spreading out of the offerings could be due either to the movement of drift sand or to the actions of looters after the temple was abandoned. Thirdly, the offerings may have stayed in the 'Hathor cave' (with the portico perhaps used for the overflow) throughout the New Kingdom, only to be brought out and scattered by thieves and vandals between the late 12th century BC and the 19th century AD.

Linked to this problem, is the question of why and when some of the offerings came to be lying 'outside of the sanctuary on the north for a distance of some feet' (Petrie 1906.138). It might be assumed that these offerings had been carried there by drift sand or tossed over a crumbling wall, but this cannot be right, since the north wall of the sanctuary, which contained no doors or windows, is one of the best preserved in the whole temple. In 1905 it stood some 2.10 m high, and the front wall of the sanctuary and the north walls of the porch and the portico were also preserved to almost their original height (1906.90–4). The offerings found north of the sanctuary must therefore have been placed there deliberately. During the New Kingdom, to do this would have involved carrying the offerings through the court to the north door and back along the side of the temple (Plan 5). Once the north wall of the court had become ruinous (1906.86), it would have been possible to take a shorter route. In either case, it is most unlikely that thieves or vandals would take such trouble. The obvious conclusion is that the offerings were dumped out of sight in this spot by Egyptians, either on a regular basis to make more room in the sanctuary, or during a restoration of the temple.

If the offerings were regularly dumped, most of the 18th dynasty material should have been found outside the temple. No definite information is available on this point. The objects brought back by MacDonald, which are most likely to have come from inside the temple, were predominantly Ramessid but did include some 18th dynasty material. There is no hint in *Researches in Sinai*, or in Petrie's unpublished Sinai diary and excavation notebooks, that the offerings in the sanctuary and portico were later in date than those to the north of the sanctuary. Petrie was very interested in the votive objects and, by the standards of his day, a meticulous excavator, so it is difficult to believe that he would have failed to notice such a difference. It is safest to assume that 18th dynasty and Ramessid offerings were found mixed together both inside and outside the temple.

I would tentatively propose that the small votive offerings were kept in and/or near the 'Hathor cave' until the reign of Ramesses IV, when the sanctuary was restored and the porch was inserted between it and the portico (1906.90–1). In the course of this work, some of the offerings may have been tidied into piles in the portico and the roofed part of the sanctuary while others, which were badly broken or just in the way, were taken out of the nearest door and dumped. Deir el-Bahri provides parallels for the partial clearance of offerings from a temple (1.1.3.5).

Petrie believed that soon after the Egyptian withdrawal the offerings had been deliberately smashed by vengeful Bedouin (1906.138). If the local nomads had been as hostile as this, one might expect to find the type of defacement of inscriptions and divine images that occurred during the Midianite occupation of the Hathor temple at Timna (1.5.3). None of the temple reliefs at Serabit el-Khadim seems to have been attacked and numerous Hathor columns and large stelae were left upright and undefaced. Some of the smaller votive stelae and statues found in the sanctuary and the portico had been smashed (1906.122), but these were probably casual acts of vandalism by looters.

A higher proportion of the small offerings are badly broken than at Deir el-Bahri, Faras, or Mirgissa, but this could be due to a variety of factors. Much of the votive faience dedicated at Serabit el-Khadim had a particularly friable body, and the objects may have been damaged by being crammed together or piled on top of one another. After the abandonment of the temple, they would have been exposed to high winds, rain-storms, extremes of temperature, and collapsing masonry. They are also likely to have been picked over by looters in search of turquoise or metal objects. The temple was never deeply buried in sand, and the offerings may have been disturbed over and over again in the three thousand years between the Egyptian withdrawal and Petrie's excavations.

As Petrie suggested (1906.139), the objects lying in the shelter of a wall will have the best chance of survival. Many of the offerings dumped north of the sanctuary must have been totally destroyed. However, if the hypothesis that the dumping did not take place until the 20th dynasty is correct, the offerings which survive are probably a representative sample of what was originally dedicated in the temple. This means that, in sharp contrast with Deir el-Bahri, Faras, and Mirgissa, more offerings were made to Hathor at Serabit el-Khadim in the Ramessid period than in the 18th dynasty.

Summary

The temple at Serabit el-Khadim was a state foundation dedicated to Hathor, Lady of Mefkat. It was used by Egyptian turquoise-mining expeditions during the Middle and New Kingdoms. The unusual form of the temple is due to the geography of the site rather than to any influence from Semitic cults. The choice of a rock-cut sanctuary was probably dictated by the iconography of Hathor.

Stelae and statues were set up in the temple from the 12th dynasty onwards. The date range of the small votive offerings is from Amonhotpe I to Ramesses VI. There is a very high proportion of 'royal name' faience, especially from the Ramessid period. A few statues and stelae were dedicated by Asiatics, but none of the small votive objects are of un-Egyptian types. Some of the offerings were found in or near the sanctuary. Others were dumped just outside the temple, probably during the 20th dynasty.

1.5 Timna

1.5.1 The site

Timna is a modern name for a valley of about 70 sq km in the hills between the Arabah and Negev deserts. The site is 30 km north of the Gulf of Eilat and some 160 km north-east of Serabit el-Khadim. The harsh climate of the Timna valley has always made it unsuitable for permanent human habitation, but its rich copper deposits have been sporadically exploited over a period of six thousand years.

F. Frank explored the Timna valley between 1932 and 1934 and published descriptions of seven smelting camps (1934.191–280). In 1959 B. Rothenberg organized a survey of archaeological sites in the Arabah, and traces of numerous mining and smelting camps were discovered at Timna (1962.5–71; 1988.3–5). Between 1964 and 1970 Rothenberg directed excavations in the valley by an expedition from Tel Aviv University and the Museum Haaretz (1988.5–8). The archaeological finds suggested two main periods of mining activity : the Chalcolithic period and the Late Bronze Age–Early Iron Age.

Rothenberg was able to show that the Late Bronze Age–Early Iron Age mining and smelting camps had been established by Egyptians, who seem to have employed local Amalekite, and later Midianite, workers (1972.63–105, 180–3). The expedition also discovered several Semitic cult places, presumably used by these workers, including one on top of a striking rock formation known as 'King Solomon's Pillars' (1972.112–24). In 1969 they excavated a low mound with protruding pieces of white sandstone situated beneath the central 'pillar'. This proved to be the remains of a small Egyptian temple dedicated to Hathor, Lady of Mefkat. Two chapters on the Hathor temple and its significance were included in Rothenberg's book *Timna: Valley of the Biblical Copper Mines* (1972.125–202).

Further excavations of the mine workings and smelting camps at Timna were carried out from 1974 to 1976 (Rothenberg 1988.8–11). Some 'evidence for a short revival of Egyptian activities during the 10th century BC' was discovered at one of the smelting sites (1988.11). From 1978 to 1983 the 'New Arabah Project' carried out archaeo-metallurgical research in the southern Arabah, and evidence was found for Roman and early Islamic mining activities at Timna (1988.11–15, 17). All this research is documented in *The Egyptian Mining Temple at Timna* (Rothenberg 1988).

1.5.2 The Hathor temple

Rothenberg's identification of Timna as a Hathor shrine is supported by the presence of Hathor mask columns and by representations of Hathor among the small offerings and on a rock stela above the shrine (Rothenberg 1988.85–6, pl. 105, fig. 52). Hathor's name occurs on three pieces of votive faience (Schulman

1976.127; in Rothenberg 1988.123, 125, 141), and the epithet Lady or Mistress of Mefkat on several small objects (Schulman 1976.127; in Rothenberg 1988.118, 121, 141).

The ruins of the Hathor temple proved to be difficult to interpret, but Rothenberg distinguishes five main occupation levels, which he labels Strata I–V (1972.128–9; 1988.24–5, 270). At the lowest level, Stratum V, rock pits, flint tools and pottery dating to the late 4th millennium BC were discovered (1972.128–9, fig. 42, pl. 73; 1988.275–6). Strata IV and III represent the building and rebuilding of a New Kingdom Egyptian temple (1972.129–49; 1988.273–5). Stratum II marks the occupation of the temple by a Semitic group, probably Midianite, who turned it into a 'tent shrine' some time in the late 12th century BC (1972.150, figs. 41, 44; 1988.272–3). Stratum I was originally interpreted by Rothenberg as the remains of a Nabataean metal workshop of the 1st century AD (1972.177–9, fig. 60, pl. 71). He now attributes this occupation level to Roman squatters and dates it to some time between the late 1st and the 3rd centuries AD (1988.271, 278). Above Stratum I was a layer of drift sand which had protected the remains.

In spite of damage caused by earthquakes and rockfalls, by the Midianite occupation, and by trenches dug by the Roman squatters, Rothenberg was able to recover the basic plan of the Egyptian temple in both its phases. In its initial phase, the temple consisted of a sanctuary (called a naos by Rothenberg) and an open court (Plan 6). The court measured 9 × 7 m. It was bounded on three sides by dry-stone walling and on the fourth by the rock face of the 'pillar', in which three niches were cut (Rothenberg 1972 pl. 68; 1988.75–6, pl. 86). A naos, c. 2.70 × 1.70 m, constructed of white sandstone, stood against the rock face (1988.78–81, 114–5, pls. 87–98). According to Rothenberg:–

> Very little masonry of the original naos remained *in situ*, but two well-dressed square bases and several additional basic parts of the original structure helped in establishing some of its details. Two square pillars, bearing sculptured representations of the head of Hathor, were found in the excavation and seem to have stood on the bases. One end of the large stone architrave, parts of which were found in the excavation, had rested on the Hathor pillars, whilst the other end rested in the two niches cut for this purpose into the rock-face.
>
> A considerable number of well-dressed and also several finely ornamented architectural elements were found on the site ... testifying to the unusually high aesthetic quality of the original naos building. (1972.130)

This first temple was very badly damaged by a rockfall (Rothenberg 1988.36–9, pls. 18, 23–5), and then rebuilt. The floor of the second temple was largely made up of crushed white sandstone from the first temple (1972.131, fig. 41; 1988.35–7, 273–4, pls. 15–16). The court was enlarged to about 9 × 9 m and its walls were repaired. The entrance was slightly off centre but aligned with the sanctuary (Plan 6). In the north-east corner of the temple, a small casting installation had been set up (1988.192–8, 274, illus. 31). A stone platform, 3 × 3 m, was constructed in front of the sanctuary, perhaps as a base for a vestibule or pronaos (1988.72–3, pls. 81–3). The sanctuary itself was rebuilt, utilizing some architectural elements and a stela from the first temple (1972.131, fig. 41, pl. 68; 1988.77–83, 274 pls. 88–97).

Two large stone basins may belong to the second phase of the temple (1972.149; 1988.43–44, 274). One of these basins was found *in situ* to the west of the sanctuary, where it had been crushed by the partial collapse of the latter (1972 fig. 41; 1988.53–4, pl. 53). A basin, a Hathor column, and four stone incense altars of the type found at Serabit el-Khadim (Petrie 1906.133–4, pls. 142–3) had been utilized by the Midianites to form a row of 'standing stones' (Rothenberg 1972.150, fig. 41, pls. 72, 78; 1988.41–7, pls. 29–43). Their original positions are not known.

There is no reason to doubt that the temple at Timna was built, and rebuilt, by and for the personnel of the Egyptian copper-mining expeditions. The strong similarity between the votive faience dedicated at Serabit el-Khadim and Timna (1.5.3), the presence of several sphinxes and a statue of a goddess or queen, all carved in local stone but purely Egyptian in style (Rothenberg 1972 pls. 75, 79, 81; 1988.116–7, 268, pls. 114–5, 117), and the rock stela depicting Ramesses III before Hathor (1988 pl. 105) all suggest that the Timna temple was an Egyptian foundation. Even more convincing is the Egyptian character of the masonry, particularly the Hathor mask columns (Rothenberg 1972 pl. 78; 1988.116, 268, figs. 23.1–2, pls. 37–40, 111.4), and the fact that some of the structural elements bore hieroglyphic inscriptions (1988.115–6). Finally, there seems to have been no local culture that built and decorated comparable structures during the second millennium BC.

Giveon accepted that the Timna temple was Egyptian, but commented that:–

> ... it may be difficult to find parallels for the plan of this temple inside Egypt. The reason for this may be that the builders adapted the plan to natural conditions or influences of native traditions. (1978.25)

The absence of an exact parallel in Egypt itself may not be relevant. To judge by the peculiarities of Serabit el-Khadim (1.4.2), and the variety of plans among New Kingdom temples in Nubia, the normal rules were not always strictly applied when building outside Egypt. The dry-stone walling is of the same type used at Serabit el-Khadim. The builders were obviously adapting to local conditions, as the mud bricks normally used for enclosure walls were unavailable. The basic plan of the first phase of the temple (Plan 6) is similar to that of the Mirgissa Hathor shrine (Plan 5), and the orientation of the temple and the way in which the sanctuary is fitted beneath an overhang are reminiscent of the Faras Hathor temple (Plan 4). At both sites, a desire to build against a striking rock formation and to give the sanctuary a cave-like appearance may have been the dominant considerations. There is little need to search for signs of 'native traditions' in the plan and location of the Timna temple.

Rothenberg proposes that the temple was built under Seti I, the earliest king whose name definitely appears on votive faience from the site (1988.276). He believes that it was rebuilt under Ramesses II and 'remained in use, with periods of abandonment, re-use and frequent renovation, until the time of Ramessses V' (1988.277). A. Schulman, who wrote the catalogue of the Egyptian finds published in *The Egyptian Mining Temple at Timna*, has a different theory. He proposes that the temple was first built by Ramesses II, possibly during the period when he was co-regent with his father, and then rebuilt under Ramesses III (1988.145).

Rothenberg's main reason for dating the first phase of the temple to Seti I was a faience bracelet bearing this king's name excavated in Stratum IV (1988.86, 125, 271, fig. 31.8). Due to the many disturbances of the site, Rothenberg found it 'extremely difficult to date the ever-changing features of the Temple in relation to individual finds' (1988.270). This bracelet was an exception because it lay under a red sandstone rock beneath the White Floor of Stratum III, and therefore 'could not have infiltrated to this location from above' 1988.275).

His theory that the temple was rebuilt by Ramesses II is chiefly based on the evidence of a block from the naos with a partially erased cartouche which Giveon took to be Ramessid (Rothenberg 1972 pl. 76; 1988.52, pls. 50, 110.3, fig. 22.10). After studying a photograph of this block, K. A. Kitchen argued that the name in the partially erased cartouche was Thutmose (1976.262–4), but Schulman, who has examined the block, states that the name is Ramesses, almost certainly Ramesses II (in Rothenberg 1988.115–6). Rothenberg assumes that this block was made and decorated as part of the second naos (1988.274, 277). Schulman assumes that this block comes from the first phase of the temple (1988.115, 145). He suggests that this temple was destroyed in 'the chaotic period' at the end of the 19th dynasty, and rebuilt, using some of the original masonry, under Ramesses III (1988.145). He suggests that the rock stela showing Rameses III before Hathor was carved to commemorate this rebuilding. The naos and pronaos seem to have been partially dismantled by the Midianites when they turned the temple into a tent shrine (1988.272–4). The crucial inscribed block was among the elements of the naos found 'dumped in total disarray into a corner of the courtyard', so it is impossible to be certain of its original position.

In general, the structural remains are not of much help in dating the foundation of the Timna temple. Fine masonry is characteristic both of the 18th dynasty and of the reign of Seti I. The dry-stone enclosure wall at Serabit el-Khadim is thought to date to Amonhotpe III (1.4.2) but, since such walls were used in both phases at Timna, it would be wrong to place much weight on this. The Timna Hathor columns appear to have been quite similar to examples at Serabit el-Khadim which date to Amonhotpe III (Petrie 1906 pl. 95), but it is difficult to judge this point because of the defaced state of the former (Rothenberg 1988.45, pls. 38–9).

Most of the temple statues are also too damaged or defaced to be closely dated. Schulman suggests that a badly damaged white sandstone head from the temple is that of a queen in the role of Hathor (1988.116–7, pl. 117.1). He notes 'Traces of some sort of head-dress (crown?)' and that 'what appears to be a thin back pillar (uninscribed), reaching as far as the head, suggests that the original complete statuette was a seated figure.' (1988.117). He proposes that this was the cult statue from the naos, but claims that it cannot definitely be identified with Hathor because it has human rather than cow ears (1988.117). Hathor in full human form never has cow's ears. Cow's ears are only shown on Hathor masks (2.3.1). On numerous votive stelae from Serabit el-Khadim, Hathor, Lady of Mefkat, is depicted by a standing statue of a woman wearing a sun disc and horns with uraeus (Figs. 8–9). It is likely that the cult statue of Hathor, Lady of Mefkat, at Timna would have been of a similar type.

Schulman suggests that the damaged statue can be identified as Queen

Nefertari in the role of Hathor, and uses this to support his theory that the Timna temple was built by Ramesses II. This identification seems plausible, since the statue is similar to one of this queen found in the Hathor temple at Serabit el-Khadim (Petrie 1906.125, pl. 140). Several other fragmentary statues of queens were recovered from Serabit el-Khadim (1906.125, 129), the most notable being the head from a statuette of Queen Tiye (1906.126–7, pl. 133), who was identified with Hathor in the temple of Sedeinga (1.2.2). None of these pieces is likely to have been the cult statue at Serabit el-Khadim. Only that of Tiye would have been small enough to fit in the niche of the sanctuary there. In the Small Temple at Abu Simbel, which is dedicated to Hathor, Lady of Ibshek, and Queen Nefertari, the rock-cut cult statue depicts Hathor in cow form protecting Ramesses II (Desroches Noblecourt & Kuentz 1968.105–7, pls. 123–6). This suggests that the identification of a queen with Hathor did not go as far as using a likeness of that queen as the cult image.

Another statue fragment from the Timna temple, consisting of a base and two feet from a standing figure, has also been proposed as a cult image (Rothenberg 1988.268, pl. 116.2). A standing figure is more consistent with the known iconography of Hathor, Lady of Mefkat, than a seated one, but it is not even possible to say whether this statue is male or female. It may be a fragment of a royal statue or of a votive statue of an expedition leader.

Because the harsh climate and lack of water at Timna made copper-mining a seasonal occupation, Rothenberg assumes that the temple would not have had a permanent staff, and is likely to have been deserted for long periods (1972.53, 110; 1988.270). In these circumstances, I think it is most likely that each mining expedition brought a cult image in a portable shrine to instal in the sanctuary for the duration of their visit, just as Wenamon took an image of 'Amon of the Road' on his timber-buying expedition to Byblos. If so, the other home of this cult image may have been at Gebel Abu Hassa on the eastern frontier of Egypt. Mining expeditions seem to have assembled there, and a New Kingdom stela dedicated to Hathor, Lady of Mefkat, has been found at the site (Clédat 1919.212; Giveon 1978.66). Schulman's identification of the Timna statue with Nefertari does not therefore help to date the foundation of the temple; it only shows that Ramesses II sent an expedition to Timna, a fact already clear from the occurrence of this king's name on some of the votive faience and glass (Rothenberg 1988.144–5, 216).

The evidence of the small votive objects from Timna suggests a history for the temple slightly different from those proposed by Rothenberg or Schulman. The bracelet with the cartouches of Seti I which came from Stratum IV (Rothenberg 1988.275) does not prove that the first phase of the temple dates to that king. All it shows is that the temple was in existence under Seti I. The Hathor temple may have been founded earlier.

After the excavations of 1964–70, Rothenberg noted that two of the smelting camps at Timna – Sites 30 and 34 – seemed older than the rest (1972.65–6). These two camps, which are directly opposite the Hathor temple, were unusual in being fortified, and the pottery and smelting equipment found there was different from that in the other camps (1972.64–6, fig. 15). The first phase of Site 30 is now definitely dated by Rothenberg to the 14th century BC (1988.11). He states that the

Hathor temple cannot have been in existence at this time because no pottery of the type found at Site 30 was discovered in the temple area (1988.276). However, J. Glass in his essay on the pottery in *The Egyptian Mining Temple at Timna* states that a few sherds found in the temple were of the same type as those from Site 30 (1988.99, 113). Hardly any 18th dynasty Egyptian pottery was found in the temple at Serabit el-Khadim (2.11.5), so its scarcity at Timna does not seem a very strong argument for dating the temple later.

Only a small amount of 'royal name faience' survives from Timna (1.5.3). Most of it is Ramessid, but a few pieces might be earlier. On the votive faience from Serabit el-Khadim the epithet 'Lady (*nbt*) of Mefkat' is used on 18th dynasty pieces, but 'Mistress (*ḥnwt*) of Mefkat' on nearly all the Ramessid material. The two inscribed fragments from Timna which bear the epithet 'Lady of Mefkat' (Schulman in Rothenberg 1988 nos. 33, 221) might therefore be 18th dynasty. One small faience plaque may bear the prenomen of Amonhotpe III (1988 fig. 46.10, pl. 123.5). Schulman interprets this as a cryptographic writing of Amon, and dates it to the Ramessid period (1988.138), but similar writings have been found on scarabs from the palace of Amonhotpe III at Malqata (Hayes 1951 fig. 34). An unglazed steatite plaque appears to be inscribed with the name Amonhotpe (Rothenberg 1988 fig. 46.13), but Schulman again interprets the inscription as a cryptogram of Amon's name (1988.138). Even if Nebmaatreʿ and Amonhotpe are the correct readings, these could be royal names used as 'talismans' long after the death of the ruler in question, so their value as evidence for the date of the temple is uncertain.

Some faience pieces, such as cat figurines (1988.126, fig. 33.2, fig. 38.1), a Hathor mask (1988.118, fig. 27.1), and fish and flower bowls (1988.129–31, figs. 41.6, 9, 42), can be dated to the 18th dynasty on stylistic grounds (1.5.3). Some of the glass fragments come from vessel types with a date range from the late 18th to the mid 19th dynasties (G. Lehrer-Jacobson in Rothenberg 1988.214–5). The chemical composition and manufacturing techniques of much of the Timna glass closely resembles late 18th dynasty glass from Amarna and Malqata (R. Brill & I. Lynus Barnes in Rothenberg 1988.222). Some of the Egyptian-made pottery was similar in style and composition to late 18th dynasty material from Malqata (Glass in Rothenberg 1988.112).

From what we know of other New Kingdom Egyptian mining sites, it seems likely that Timna would have had some sort of shrine from the start of the Egyptian presence there. The dramatic rock-formation close to the early smelting camps must have been the obvious place for such a shrine. It might at first have been a 'community shrine' of the type excavated at Gebel Zeit (1.6), rather than an official foundation. Such a shrine could have consisted of a niche cut in the rock-face and a simple sanctuary of rough stonework. For all or most of the Amarna period no expeditions would have been sent to Timna. When they resumed, the simple shrine might have been rebuilt by Seti I, who added a room to the temple at Serabit el-Khadim (1.4.2). The fragmentary royal building inscriptions (1988.115–6) show that in the Ramessid period Timna was a state foundation. Frequent earthquakes and rockfalls in the Timna area made the temple very vulnerable to damage, so it would not be suprising if it had to be rebuilt under Ramesses II.

It does not seem to have been the custom at Timna to record mining expeditions by carving rock stelae, so Schulman is surely right in saying that the rock stela of Ramesses III suggests the completion of a building project. His proposal that the temple had been deliberately destroyed at the end of the 19th dynasty (1988.145) is much less plausible. The remote Timna temple is unlikely to have been affected by political upheavals in Egypt, and only two years are thought to separate the death of Tawosret, who seems to have sent an expedition to Timna, and the accession of Ramesses III (Baines & Málek 1980.36, 46). The temple may have needed repair or rebuilding after further rockfalls. Rothenberg noted that the White Floor of the second phase of the temple ran for some way under the base for the pronaos (1988.72–4). This raises the possibility that the pronaos represents a third phase of the temple, which might date to Ramesses III. The last king mentioned on the votive faience from Timna is Ramesses V (Schulman in Rothenberg 1988.144–5). No evidence was found for the temple being used by the Egyptian mining expeditions of the 22nd dynasty.

1.5.3   The votive offerings

Some ten thousand small objects were excavated in or near the Hathor temple from Strata II–IV. These finds can be divided into three main categories:–

A.   Objects in Egyptian style, most of which can be paralleled by votive material from Serabit el-Khadim. All of the faience and glass, and some of the pottery, metal, and stone pieces fall into this category.

B.   Objects in non-Egyptian styles. Most of the pottery and many of the metal offerings fall into this category.

C.   Objects which cannot be attributed with certainty to any particular culture. These include shells, pebbles, and copper miscastings in curious shapes.

The Category A objects will be discussed first.

Only a few Egyptian small objects were found in the sanctuary and the pronaos (Rothenberg 1988.73, 77). This is probably due to the fact that these structures were partially dismantled by the Midianites who set up the tent-shrine, and then badly damaged by Roman treasure-hunters who dug trenches and pits. Numerous Egyptian small objects were found in the court, particularly in Locus 107, to the west of the sanctuary (Plan 6; 1988.51–2). Some of these objects were lying under the White Floor of the second temple but most were above it.

A large group of Egyptian offerings was discovered just outside the north-east corner of the courtyard wall:–

> The Midianites when refurnishing the Egyptian Hathor temple as a Semitic desert shrine cleared votive gifts, sculptures, inscriptions and Hathor sculptures out of the temple court. Most things were simply thrown out and piled behind the temple wall, out of sight of the visitors to the renovated shrine. This explains why most of the temple gifts were found, broken and mixed up, in one thick layer in Locus 101. (Rothenberg 1972.151–2)

Also in Locus 101, 'lying right against the outside of Wall 1', was a heap of objects consisting of copper and iron ore nodules, non-Egyptian jewellery and figurines, and some Egyptian faience (1972.127 pl. 95; 1988.29, pl. 6; Plan 6).

The Egyptian offerings found in or near the temple included about 3,500 faience beads; 100 or so beads in carnelian or limestone; and about 150 fragments from glass vessels. The faience comprised 13 menit counterpoises, 11 cat figurines, 5 Hathor masks, at least 8 sistrum fragments, 43 bracelet fragments, 9 scarabs and 5 seals (some in glazed steatite), 1 cartouche plaque, 20 amulets, 5 fragments from model throwsticks, 3 fragmentary ring-stands, and 74 fragments from inscribed or decorated vessels. There were also a few gold beads, pieces from several copper loop sistra, some calcite vases, and 'numerous fragments of carved stone objects and statues' (Rothenberg 1972.166). The scarcity of royal or private stelae is suprising, particularly in view of the wide range of stelae found at Serabit el-Khadim and Gebel Zeit (1.4.3; 1.6.3; 2.1.1). The most likely explanation for this is that nearly all the Timna stelae were completely destroyed by the Midianites.

The Egyptian offerings are mentioned briefly in several of Rothenberg's articles (1969.22; 1970.32–3), and are described in his first book on Timna (1972.163, 166, 171–2), in which about 100 items are illustrated in photographs and/or line drawings (1972.164–70, figs. 48–54; pls. 80, 82–94, 98; X, XII-VI, XXI, XXV). Some of the Egyptian objects were exhibited at the British Museum in 1971 and at the Bergbau Museum, Bochum, in 1973 and published in catalogues relating to these exhibitions (Rothenberg 1971 pls. 17–27; Rothenberg 1973 pls. 44–5, 48–55). All the Egyptian objects are fully published in *The Egyptian Mining Temple at Timna* and most are illustrated there (Rothenberg 1988 pls. 19–29, 118–123, 125; figs. 27–49, 78–86). The finds from the temple are now in the Museum Haaretz, Tel Aviv.

On the basis of the inscribed faience, Rothenberg (1972.132, 171) and Schulman (1976.117, 126) date all the Egyptian faience from Timna to the Ramessid period. Only 25 pieces of votive faience inscribed with royal names were recovered from the temple, compared with nearly 500 from Serabit el-Khadim. The royal names mentioned are Seti I, Ramesses II, Merenptah, Seti II, Tawosret, and Ramesses III, IV, and V (Schulman in Rothenberg 1988.145). At Serabit el-Khadim the date range of the 'royal name' faience is from Amonhotpe I to Ramesses VI, but the Ramessid rulers seem to have dedicated a much greater quantity and a wider variety of inscribed faience than the 18th dynasty rulers did (1.4.3). Given this, and the troubled history of the Timna temple, if offerings were made at there during the 18th dynasty, one would expect only a small proportion of the surviving faience to be of that date.

Most of the non 'royal name' Timna faience can be dated to the Ramessid period by style, technique and material, but some categories provide exceptions. The evidence of comparative material from Deir el-Bahri and Serabit el-Khadim suggests that some of the cat figurines found at Timna are 18th dynasty (*e.g.* Rothenberg 1988 figs. 33.2, 4; fig. 38.1; 2.5.1). One of the Timna Hathor masks (1988 fig. 30.1) is similar to 18th dynasty pieces from Deir el-Bahri (*e.g.* Pl. 30). The fish and flower decoration on some of the faience bowls is of a type usually dated to the 18th dynasty (*e.g.* Rothenberg 1988 figs. 42–4; 2.11.3.1). The use of spiral decoration around the rim of bowls decorated with fish and flowers is characteristic only of the 18th dynasty (2.11.3.1), so the example illustrated by Rothenberg is unlikely to be Ramessid (1988 fig. 41.6). Some of the bead types common at Timna, such as the corrugated spheroids and gadrooned discs, are usually dated to the 18th dynasty (Rothenberg 1972.171–2, pls. XII-XIII; Kertesz in Rothenberg 1988.204, 208; 2.9.1). Much of the glass and some of the pottery could date to the late 18th dynasty (1.5.2). On the basis of the objects themselves, I would suggest that offerings were being made at Timna at least as early as the reign of Amonhotpe III.

Close dating by context was hardly possible at Timna. There can be little doubt that originally all the offerings were placed inside the sanctuary and/or the vestibule. It follows that few were discovered *in situ*. In theory, everything found below the White Floor should belong to Phase I of the temple and everything above it to Phase II, but Rothenberg stresses that the stratigraphy of the site was so disturbed that such assumptions can rarely be made. Some Chalcolithic objects from Stratum V were found near the surface, while Roman pottery from Stratum I had slipped down to the lowest levels. It was usually impossible to tell whether an Egyptian object originally belonged in Stratum III or Stratum IV. To illustrate the problem of 'seepage', Rothenberg notes that fragments which come from a single faience bowl were found scattered inside and outside the court in Strata II, III, IV and V (1988.270).

In his first book on Timna, Rothenberg stated that the offerings found beyond the east wall of the court were 'broken and mixed up in one thick layer' (1972.151). This sounds very similar to the situation at Faras (1.2.3) and Serabit el-Khadim (1.3.3), and to some of the dumps at Deir el-Bahri (1.1.3.2–3). Three explanations might be offered for the presence of the Timna dump. First, this area could have been regularly used by Egyptians to dump old or broken offerings during one or both phases of the temple. Second, a large quantity of broken offerings may have been dumped in this spot by Egyptian rebuilders or restorers. Third, as Rothenberg proposes, the contents of the second temple could have been thrown over the east wall by the Midianites who set up the tent shrine. In all three cases it must be assumed that the clearing out of the temple was not very thorough, and that many small items were left scattered about the court.

The first explanation is the least likely. Evidence from the other sites suggests that offerings were left in or near the sanctuary for as long as possible and that votive objects might even be preserved and replaced after extensive rebuilding work (1.2.3; 1.6.3). A remote shrine used only during copper-mining expeditions is unlikely to have suffered much from overcrowding, but badly broken objects might have been removed periodically. Many of the offerings were broken while still inside the temple, since pieces of the same object were sometimes found both inside the court and outside in the dump (Rothenberg 1988.270–1). It is likely that some offerings, especially broken ones, were cleared out of the way when the first temple was rebuilt and/or during the rebuilding or restoration work under Ramesses III. However, the date range of the 'royal name' faience found mixed together in the dump is from Seti I to Ramesses IV (1988.30). This suggests either that the offerings were all cleared out under Ramesses V, the last king known to have sent an expedition to Timna, or that Rothenberg is correct in assuming that this dump was the work of the Midianites who set up the tent-shrine.

In his more detailed account of the dump, Rothenberg states that in one area the layer of objects was much thinner and the objects were 'partly of a different character, and obviously of a much earlier period' (1988.30). Since the dump is just to one side of the entrance to the court, it is in the obvious position for the disposal of refuse from the sanctuary. Perhaps some of the offerings were placed there by Ramessid restorers, while the majority were dumped over much the same area by the Midianites.

Rothenberg dubs the pile of offerings just outside Wall I 'the hoard' (1988.29, pl. 6). He originally assumed that this hoard had been assembled by Nabatean metal-workers (1972.127, 179). The high proportion of metal objects does suggest that the hoard was gathered together by metal-workers or by treasure hunters. The hoard contained much Midianite metalwork, including a phallic figurine in bronze (1988.29, 87, 147). The Midianites themselves might have decided to melt down and recast these objects. The hoard could also have been put together by Roman treasure hunters. In either case, something must have happened to prevent the assembler of the hoard from making use of it; perhaps one of the many rock falls that damaged the temple.

Context provides only equivocal answers to the question of who presented the Category B and C offerings. About one quarter of the pottery recovered from the temple was painted Midianite ware (1988.92.4, figs. 4–13). These elaborately decorated bowls, goblets, and jugs were probably made as votive pieces (2.11.5). Some of the plain pottery from the temple area seems to have been made by the local Negev population, perhaps to be identified with the Amalekites (Glass in Rothenberg 1988.111). The non-Egyptian metal objects are mainly of copper, with some bronze, iron or tin items (P. Craddock in Rothenberg 1988.170). They consist of pins, rings, earrings, amulets with hand or 'tree of life' designs, a model snake, a model ram, and two phallic figurines (Rothenberg 1972.173–6; figs. 55–9, pls. 97, XIX–XX; 1988.147–169, figs. 53–5, 63–73). A large quantity of locally made beads of shell and mica should probably also be classed as non-Egyptian (1972.171; Kertesz in Rothenberg 1988.204).

Rothenberg assumes that some of these non-Egyptian objects were offered during the Egyptian phases of the temple:–

> In Timna, according to the evidence in the temple, the Midianites and Amalekites, the indigenous inhabitants of the area, seem to have become some kind of 'partners' not only at work but also in the worship of Hathor. (1972.183)

Serabit el-Khadim provides a parallel for such a state of affairs, but there the votive pieces known to have been donated by Asiatics are Egyptian in style (1.4.3). Alternatives to worshipping in the Hathor temple were available. Rothenberg discovered several Semitic holy places in the Timna area. On the basis of the pottery, he was able to assign two to the Midianites and one to the Amalekites (1972.112–9). In view of the religious tolerance normally displayed by the Egyptians, it seems unlikely that the Semitic workforce would have been compelled to worship in the Hathor temple by their Egyptian overseers.

The erasure of the face of the goddess on the Hathor mask columns (1972 pl. 78; 1988.44), the presence of male idols (1972 pls. XVII-III; 1988.147, figs. 53.1–2, pl. 126), and the absence of 'Astarte plaques' (see 2.6.3.2), or any other Semitic material relating to goddesses, all suggest that the Midianites who erected the tent shrine did not worship Hathor. Rothenberg concludes from the stratigraphic evidence that there was no 'period of abandonment' between the departure of the Egyptians and the conversion of the temple into a tent shrine (1988.277–8). Therefore the tent shrine was probably erected by the same group of Midianites who had previously worked with the Egyptians. If they were hostile or indifferent to Hathor at this period, it seems likely that were in earlier times too.

Inside the temple, a few sherds of Midianite and Negev-ware pottery were found below the White Floor of the second temple (1988.60, 73–4), but none is in a context where slippage can be ruled out. The same is true of the Midianite pottery and metal-work recovered from Stratum III, but the quantity of this material makes it more significant. Numerous non-Egyptian objects, including painted pottery, beads, and metal jewellery, were found in Stratum II. Many were mixed up with animal bones from sacrifices in the vicinity of the row of 'standing stones' in the western half of the court (Rothenberg 1970.33; 1988.46–7, 272). All this material can probably be assigned to the Midianite phase of the temple. However, as a few Egyptian offerings were recovered from Stratum II in this area (1988.46–7), it is possible that some of the Midianite objects were also in secondary use.

The content and stratigraphy of the dump just outside the temple is more helpful. Rothenberg mentions recovering 'copper rings' from this dump (1972.173; 1988.30). Two types of copper ring were found at Timna: large, plain ones, and smaller rings with incised decoration (1972.173–4, fig. 55; 1988.158–9). The plain rings could have been offered by Egyptians, possibly as a tithe on the copper mined by each expedition, but the decorated rings are probably Midianite votive objects. Numerous sherds of Midianite and Negev-ware pottery were found in the dump (1988.30). Some of this material could have been added to the dump during the Midianite occupation of the temple. The Midianites may have discarded votive offerings more frequently than the Egyptians did. However, Rothenberg does state that Egyptian and non-Egyptian material was found mixed together in the dump, some of it in the part thought to be earlier than the rest (1988.30). This does suggest that the local peoples made some offerings to Hathor.

Since it is difficult to know whether individual Category B objects belong to the Egyptian or the Midianite phases of the temple, I deal only briefly with the non-Egyptian material from Timna. More space is given to the Category C material because comparative evidence from Mirgissa (1.3.3) suggests that objects such as stones in phallic or feminine shapes (1988.266–9) are likely to have been gifts of Egyptians. The shells and corals found in the Timna temple (1988.260–6) can be paralleled by material from the Egyptian Hathor shrine at Gebel Zeit (1.6.3). The copper miscastings in vaguely animal shapes (Rothenberg 1972 pls. 99–100) are impossible to assign to any particular culture. The casting installation in the court, which was used by both the Egyptians and Midianites (1988.192–202), is an interesting example of a workshop for votive offerings inside a temple (3.1).

Summary

The Timna temple was an Egyptian foundation dedicated to Hathor, Lady of Mefkat. It was used by copper mining expeditions. A shrine may have existed at the site at least as early as the reign of Amonhotpe III. The temple was repaired and rebuilt several times, probably under Seti I, Ramesses II, and Ramesses III. It is of a basic Egyptian type, with the semi rock-cut sanctuary characteristic of Hathor shrines.

Hardly any votive stelae or statues have survived intact. The date range of the small Egyptian offerings is from the late 18th dynasty to the mid 20th dynasty. The 'royal name' faience is similar to that from Serabit el-Khadim, but most of the Timna offerings are Ramessid. Timna was a state-run temple at this period, but is unlikely to have had a permanent staff. The local peoples who worked with the Egyptians probably made some offerings in the temple, but there is also evidence for Midianite hostility towards the Hathor cult.

1.6 Gebel Zeit

1.6.1 The site

A site likely to prove of great importance for the study of Hathor offerings, and of popular religion in general, is Gebel Zeit. Its publication is not yet complete, so it is only possible to give a preliminary account of this shrine and its contents. Gebel Zeit is a mountainous area close to the Red Sea coast, south of Ras Gharib (Castel *et al.* 1984.46–7; Castel *et al.* 1985.16, fig. 2). It is bisected by the Wadi Kabrit. When prospecting for oil in this vicinity in 1977, P. Mey noticed galleries and semi-circular terraces on the west side of the Wadi Kabrit and was shown Egyptian objects found at the site by local people (Mey *et al.* 1980.299–300). Subsequent excavations by the Institut Français d'Archéologie Orientale, led by G. Castel, have established that the Egyptians mined galena in this area from the 12th to the 19th dynasties (Posener-Kriéger 1983.345–6; 1984.349–50; 1985.297–8; 1986.380–2; Castel & Soukiassian 1989).

On the west bank of the Wadi Kabrit, in an area designated Site 1 by the excavators, are galleries cut by the earliest Egyptian mining expeditions (1989.8–9, 139–140). Several of these were later used as living, cooking, or storage areas (Castel *et al.* 1985.22–4). There were also some rough dry-stone shelters or workshops and the remains of two shrines of different periods. Another Egyptian mining area, Site 2, was identified some four kilometres away (Castel *et al.* 1984.54–6; 1985.24–7; Castel & Soukiassian 1989a.165–7). Rough stone shelters and small shrines were discovered at this site (Posener-Kriéger 1986.382; Castel & Soukiassian 1989.51).

The appearance of Hathor on many of the stelae from Gebel Zeit (Mey *et al.* 1980 pl. 80b; Castel & Soukiassian 1985.291–3, pls. 63–4; Posener-Kriéger 1986.381) and the nature of the votive offerings found at Site 1 make it clear that she was the chief deity of the area, as at other Egyptian mining sites (1.4–5). On at least one stela (Castel & Soukiassian 1985.291, pl. 64), Hathor is called *nbt msdmt* – 'Lady of Galena', an epithet of quality equivalent to 'Lady of Mefkat'. The cult of Hathor, Lady of Galena, never seems to have become established elsewhere in Egypt.

1.6.2 The Hathor shrines

The original Hathor shrine at Site 1 consisted of a roughly levelled platform, 4 × 3 m, and a rock-cut sanctuary (Posener-Kriéger 1986.380, pl. 70a). The rectangular platform is bounded by a row of limestone blocks on the side nearest the wadi. The cave-like sanctuary at the south-east end of the platform is only 2 m long and 1.50 m wide. Its entrance was partly closed by a dry-stone wall. Possibly the shrine was sealed at the end of each expedition to protect its contents. The preliminary report on this shrine does not mention any decoration or inscriptions on the walls; nor is it stated whether the 'cave' was natural or man-made. Since there are several mines and processing areas in the immediate vicinity (1986.381), the sanctuary may well have been cut by the miners. Nothing was found inside the sanctuary, but among the objects recovered from nearby mine entrances were 'une tête de vache portant le disque entre les cornes' and 'un cobra dressé en bois ... qui semble avoir appartenu à une frise de naos' (1986.381). These pieces may have formed part of the furnishings of the rock-cut shrine.

The shrine in use during the New Kingdom stood at a higher level and in a slightly different position.

> L'accumulation des couches d'habitat et des coulées de terrain aux périodes d'abandon du site a provoqué l'élévation progressive de terrasses aménagées qui compensent, au flanc de la vallée, le pente originelle du rocher. Ainsi, sur l'emplacement fouillé, le dernier état du terrain, celui de la fin du Nouvel Empire, est une large terrasse artificielle constituée par l'accumulation des époque précédentes (Castel et al. 1984.47–8).

The best preserved feature of the shrine situated on top of this terrace was the dry-stone enclosure wall. This was made out of boulders and stones of widely differing sizes, and would have been about 1.20 m high when intact (Castel et al. 1984.48, figs. 1–2; 1985.17–8, figs. 4–5). It formed an oval enclosure about 7.7 m in diameter. The rear (north-east) stretch of the wall, which was built against the rock-face, included a small circular space in which stelae, statuettes, and other votive objects had been deposited and then covered with stones (Castel & Soukiassian 1985.285–6, figs. 1–2).

The remains of the shrine within the enclosure wall are not easy to interpret, but preliminary conclusions have been published -:

> A l'intérieur du cercle on observe un dispositif dont l'élément majeur est une pierre dressée contre laquelle un muret se retourne à angle droit. A l'opposé de cette pierre et dans alignement du muret sont implantés en équerre trois poteaux; le quatrième manque. Leurs dispositions et leurs sections (10 cm environ) font penser à un support de construction légère. L'ensemble paraît constituer une installation cohérente, ouverte du côté des poteaux et ayant pour fond la pierre dressée. (Castel et al. 1986.99–100)

The excavators suggest that major expeditions usually repaired or recon-structed the sanctuary on arrival (Castel et al. 1984.49; 1985.18). This sanctuary may have been a kiosk-like structure with wooden Hathor columns. The small enclosure in front of the sanctuary could have served as the resting place for portable shrines brought by expeditions, or as a pronaos where offerings were presented (Castel et al. 1985.18). The main enclosure wall appears to have been frequently repaired or rebuilt (Castel & Soukiassian 1984a.163). Its entrance may have been blocked at the end of each expedition to protect the shrine and its offerings. Site I was a sacred place for over six hundred years, but the structures were mostly temporary. This could be because the site was never permanently inhabited and mining expeditions were infrequent. The constant danger of rock falls might be a factor, but this did not deter the Egyptians from trying to build a permanent stone temple in a similar position at Timna (1.5.2).

Although Hathor was the chief deity of Gebel Zeit, there seem to have been several co-templar deities. The most important of these was Horus, who on two stelae is given the epithet *nb ḫ3swt* – 'Lord of the Desert Hills' (Castel & Soukiassian 1985.290–1, pls. 42, 44). A wooden figure of a crowned hawk-headed god found in the shrine area may once have served as a cult statue (Castel *et al.* 1984.52 fig. 2). Min of Koptos and Ptah, South of his Wall, are shown on other stelae from the shrine (Castel & Soukiassian 1985.288, 290, pls. 41–3).

At Site 2, some small shrines were found close to mine entrances. One consisted of a rough semi-circle of stones built against the rock face (Posener-Kriéger 1986.381). This contained a sandstone naos, stelae, vases, shells, and beads of the Second Intermediate Period (Castel & Soukiassian 1989.51). One of the stelae mentions Hathor. A second shrine took the form of two cairns with a circle of rough stonework between them (Posener-Kriéger 1986.382, pl. 70c). Inside the circle was found a stela carved with falcons, pieces of a naos, and Second Intermediate Period pottery, shells, and beads. This shrine, which was probably dedicated to Horus, Lord of the Desert Hills, was built on a bed of cinders. There are interesting parallels here with Serabit el-Khadim. At the latter site, cairns, rough stone circles, and a large bed of ashes were found on the plateau in front of the Hathor temple (Petrie 1906.99–100, 190–1, pls. 77–84). Petrie assumed that all these features were the remains of Semitic cult practices (1906.65–70, 100, 186–9), but their occurrence at Gebel Zeit shows that this need not be so. Twelve of the thirty stone circles at Serabit el-Khadim contained Middle Kingdom royal stelae, and Černý suggested that the circles 'were built round the stelae to make them more conspicuous' (1955.49–50). During the Middle Kingdom, the ordinary miners may have made individual offerings in such circle shrines rather than in the royal temple of Serabit el-Khadim, to which they probably had no access (see further 3.4).

The shrines at Site 2 seem to have been used only during the Second Intermediate Period. The history of the sacred area at Site 1 is much more complicated. The structures are not of very much help in determining the periods at which the shrines functioned. Rock-cut Hathor shrines have a wide date range. There may have been a Hathor 'cave' at Deir el-Bahri as early as the First Intermediate Period (1.1.2.1). Middle Kingdom (1.4.2), Second Intermediate Period (1.2.2), and 18th dynasty examples (1.1.2.3–4) have already been described, and rock-cut Hathor temples were still being built in the 19th dynasty (2.4.6).

The plan of the shrine built on top of the terrace is quite similar to that of the temple at Timna (Plan 6). Both had a small naos and pronaos, both are fitted against a rock face, and both have a rough stone enclosure wall. A similar enclosure wall at Serabit el-Khadim is thought to date to Amonhotpe III (1.4.2). The date of the first temple at Timna may lie between Amonhotpe III and Ramesses II (1.5.2). In contrast to Timna, not a single inscribed or decorated piece of masonry seems to have been recovered from the sacred area at Gebel Zeit. The use of roughly worked local stones of convenient size is more reminiscent of the 18th dynasty community shrine at Mirgissa (1.3.2; Plan 4), than of the state Hathor temples at Serabit el-Khadim and Timna.

1.6.3 The votive offerings

Only a selection of the votive offerings has so far been published (Mey *et al.* 1980; Castel *et al.* 1984; 1985; 1986; Castel & Soukiassian 1985; 1989a; Leclant 1984.393, figs. 35–8; Leclant & Clerc 1985.393–4, figs. 59–65; 1986.295–6, figs. 61–9; 1987.358–9, fig. 66; Posener-Kriéger 1984; 1985; 1986). The offerings found at Site I comprise stelae, faience plaques, statuettes, textiles, pottery fertility figurines, phalli, model falcons and baboons, Hathor masks, clappers, Bes, Taweret and cow pendants, uraei, amulets, scarabs, rings, beads, shells, pottery and calcite vessels, and basketware. Many of the offerings are exceptionally well preserved and both the inscribed and uninscribed votive objects provide extremely valuable evidence for the history of Site 1.

One limestone fragment appears to come from a Middle Kingdom royal commemorative stela (Castel & Soukiassian 1985.288, pl. 61). This shows a king, almost certainly Amenemhet III, offering to Min of Koptos. The main text, now lost, starts with a dating formula and probably described a mining expedition to Gebel Zeit in Year 10, or later, of Amenemhet III (1985.288). Several stelae recovered from the site show obscure kings of the Second Intermediate Period. The excavators suggest that a small, crudely carved basalt stela depicting a king before a deity (probably Ptah) may belong to one of the two late 13th dynasty kings given the prenomen Sehetepibre⟨ in the Turin Canon (Mey *et al.* 1980.304; pl. 80a). They propose that a faience stela-shaped plaque showing a king adoring Ptah and Horus records an otherwise unknown ruler of the 13th or 14th dynasties (Castel & Soukiassian 1985.290, pl. 62), and that a stela showing a King Bebi⟨nkh adoring Horus and Hathor dates to the early 17th dynasty (1985.291–2, pl. 64). The inscription on this stela states that it was made as the king's monument for the goddess (1985 pl. 64). A limestone stela fragment shows the Nomarch of Koptos, Minemhat, who was a contemporary of the 17th dynasty king, Inyotef V, before a god and goddess, almost certainly Min and Hathor (1985.290–1, pl. 63).

In contrast to Serabit el-Khadim (1.4.3), pre-New Kingdom small objects were plentiful at Gebel Zeit. This early material is dominated by pottery fertility figurines (Castel *et al.* 1984.50–2; 1985.19–20; Leclant & Clerc 1986 figs. 61–7, 69). These are of two main types; one has a date range covering the Middle Kingdom and the Second Intermediate Period (Castel *et al.* 1984.50, figs. 2–4; 2.6.1.2; Pl. 47b), and the other from the late Middle Kingdom to the early 18th dynasty (1984.51, fig. 7; 1985.20, fig. 13; 2.6.1.3; Pl. 47c). Ithyphallic pottery baboons could date to the Middle Kingdom or the Second Intermediate Period (1985.20, fig. 11; 1986.104, pl. V.11). Two types of pottery characteristic of the Second Intermediate Period – Tell el-Yahudiya ware (1984.49; 1986.104, pl. V.12) and Pan Grave Pottery (1984.49, 57; 1985.28; Castel & Soukiassian 1985.292) – were among the votive material. There were also Middle Kingdom amulets and beads; some bearing the names of Senwosret II, Amenemhet II, Senwosret III, and Amenemhet III (Leclant & Clerc 1986, fig.68; Posener-Kriéger 1986.381), and Second Intermediate Period scarabs (Castel *et al.* 1984.49; 1985.28, fig. 28).

Castel and Soukiassian conclude that:–

Ces stèles, ainsi que la masse de matériel de la Deuxième Période Intermédiaire trouvée au Gebel Zeit attestent une intense activité minière à cette èpoque ... La stèle au nom de Minemhat, nomarque de Coptos, prouve qu'à la fin de la Deuxième Période Intermédiare les expéditions venaient de Coptos, point de départ traditionnel vers la Mer Rouge et les mines du Désert Arabique. Dans l'état actuel des connaissances le Gebel Zeit est le site le plus au Nord qu'on atteignait à partir de la région thébaine. A l'appui de l'indication de la stèle, le matériel de la Deuxième Période Intermédiaire trouvé sur le site est très semblable à celui des grandes nécropoles de cette région à cette époque. Cependant, si le Gebel Zeit semble rattaché au royaume thébain à la Deuxième Période Intermédiaire et continue d'être lié à Thèbes sous la XVIIIe dynastie, il n'est théoriquement pas exclu que les expéditions soient venues du Nord au Moyen Empire et sous la XIIIe dynastie (1985.292).

One New Kingdom stela from Gebel Zeit shows a king offering wine to a goddess (Mey et al. 1980.316–7, pl. 80b). The king's name is not preserved. The crude workmanship suggests that this may be a private stela depicting a king as intermediary, rather than a commemorative stela set up by an expedition leader on behalf of his king. The New Kingdom royal names which occur on beads, scarabs, seals, or rings from Gebel Zeit are Amonhotpe I, Thutmose III, Amonhotpe III, Akhenaton, Tutankhamon, Ay, Horemheb, and Ramesses II (Mey et al. 1980.309, fig. 2.1; Castel et al. 1984.49–50). It therefore appears that, unlike Serabit el-Khadim, this site continued in use throughout the Amarna period.

The New Kingdom votive material includes early 18th dynasty scarabs and scaraboids (Mey et al 1980.310; Castel et al. 1984.51, fig. 8; 1985.19, figs. 8–9), and some of the pottery fertility figurines probably date to this time (2.6.1.3). There seem to be few mid 18th dynasty objects, but a storage area in a disused mine north of the sanctuary contained jars bearing seals of Thutmose III (Castel et al. 1984.52; 1985.23–4, figs. 18, 20), so there must have been at least one expedition during his reign. A large group of material, comprising rings, pendants, and amulets in faience of various colours, dates to the late 18th dynasty (Mey et al. 1980.304–10; Castel et al. 1984.50). At least one private stela was found which probably dates to this period (Castel & Soukiassian 1985.286, pl. 60, bottom right). The only definitely Ramessid objects are some rings of Ramesses II (Castel et al. 1984.49; Castel & Soukiassian 1985.286).

The votive objects give a clear picture of the periods during which expeditions took place, but it remains uncertain when the original shrine became inaccessible. The excavators suggest that the shrine discovered on top of the artificial terrace functioned from Amonhotpe III to Ramesses II (Castel et al. 1984.52). There may have been earlier structures in the same position but at lower levels. One reason for this uncertainty lies in the diverse find-spots of the votive offerings. Some were discovered among the stones of the enclosure wall of the second shrine (Castel & Soukiassian 1985.286; 1989a.163), and some at floor level or in a layer of drift sand inside the enclosure (Castel et al. 1986.100). Many objects, mainly of the late 18th dynasty, were concentrated close to, or just north of, the post-holes of the sanctuary (1986.100). Further votive material was recovered from levels midway down the artificial terrace (Castel et al. 1985.18, fig. 6), and from mine entrances close to the original shrine (Posener-Kriéger 1986.381). Some objects had been swept right down into the bottom of the wadi by floods or land-slips (Mey et al. 1980.302).

While some offerings seem to have been discarded when the shrines were repaired, refurbished or rebuilt, many others were carefully preserved and transferred to new structures. The deposit of votive objects found in a miniature chamber in the north-east corner of the enclosure wall contained material ranging in date from the late 12th to the late 18th dynasties (Castel & Soukiassian 1985.286–8, pl. 60). It included the stela of Amenemhet III and a faience stela of the early Second Intermediate Period (1985 pls. 61–2), which must both have been taken from the original shrine and set up again in the New Kingdom shrine. Castel and Soukiassian suggest that the stones covering the miniature chamber were a temporary measure to protect the stelae in the periods between expeditions (1985.286). The small objects in this deposit included pottery fertility figurines, wooden statuettes, votive phalli, and a ring of Amonhotpe III (1985.286, pl. 60). 'Dans le grand mur lui-même, périodiquement restauré, des groupes d'objets étaient dissimulés entre les pierres à la manière d'un dépôt de fondation ...' (1989a.163). Among the objects found in the wall were fertility figurines of the Second Intermediate Period or early 18th dynasty, and faience *wadjet* eye rings (Castel & Soukiassian 1985.286). These examples show that at Gebel Zeit votive objects cannot always be dated by the level in which they were found. They also demonstrate the care and reverence with which even small votive objects could be treated.

The royal stelae, which were presumably set up by leaders of mining expeditions, suggest that the Gebel Zeit shrine had some kind of official status, but the extreme simplicity of the structures, the absence of inscribed and decorated masonry, and the dominance of fertility figurines among the pre-New Kingdom small objects, all seem more indicative of a 'community shrine'. The stela of Amenemhet III does suggest a royal mining expedition of the type that visited Serabit el-Khadim (1.4.2), and the 'cave' shrine may have been cut out of the rock at this time. From the late Middle Kingdom onwards, the expeditions which visited Gebel Zeit must have been different in type from those sent to Sinai. They were small (Castel *et al.* 1984.56), and seem to have included no skilled artists or masons. Expeditions were probably sent to Gebel Zeit on the initiative of local rulers – minor kings or officials such as the nomarchs of Koptos – and so continued even in periods when there were no large-scale mining expeditions organized by central government. Those who sent the expeditions seem to have been content with stelae rather than building works as their monuments for the goddess.

The late Middle Kingdom and Second Intermediate Period offerings from Gebel Zeit resemble those from Faras (1.2.3), where the first Hathor shrine was probably set up by a family of local officials. Castel points out similarities between the Gebel Zeit material and objects from burials in northern Upper Egypt (1985.292). It may be even more to the point that much of this material can be paralleled by the earliest offerings to Hathor at Deir el-Bahri (1.1.3.1, 1.1.3.5). The elaborate decorative faience characteristic of the mid 18th dynasty offerings at Deir el-Bahri (1.1.3) seems to be absent from Gebel Zeit, as does the Ramessid 'royal name' faience characteristic of Serabit el-Khadim and Timna (1.4.3; 1.5.3). The range of late 18th dynasty material from Gebel Zeit is similar to that from the community shrine at Mirgissa (1.3.3). All this suggests that most expeditions to Gebel Zeit were not equipped with offerings by the central government, and that the maintenance and rebuilding of the shrines was essentially a private initiative by the miners and their leaders. The particular interest of Gebel Zeit lies in the fact that it probably represents the kind of religion practised in small, local temples. Such temples and their contents rarely survive in the Nile Valley. The votive material from Gebel Zeit is also similar to that found in household shrines, and confirms that fertility was one of the central concerns of popular religion (see further 2.6.4; 3.4).

Summary

Shrines to Hathor, Lady of Galena, were set up by Egyptian mining expeditions to Gebel Zeit on the Red Sea coast. At Site 1, the late Middle Kingdom/Second Intermediate Period shrine had a rock-cut sanctuary. When this shrine became inaccessible, a new one was built on top of a terrace of debris. The later shrine had a dry stone wall forming an oval enclosure. Post-holes mark the position of the sanctuary, and there was some kind of pronaos built in rough stone work. At Site 2, two small dry-stone circle shrines were found close to mine entrances.

The date range of the offerings extends from the late 12th to the early 19th dynasties. The site continued to be visited throughout the Second Intermediate Period. The most characteristic offerings of the Middle Kingdom and Second Intermediate Period were the pottery fertility figurines. The New Kingdom offerings consist chiefly of late 18th dynasty beads, rings, and amulets. The offerings are more similar to those from Deir el-Bahri, Faras, and Mirgissa than to the votive material from the royal mining temples at Serabit el-Khadim and Timna. The shrines at Gebel Zeit should probably be regarded as community rather than state-run foundations. They belong primarily to the sphere of popular religion.

1.7 Other sites

Small votive figurines in a variety of materials have been found in cult temples of the Early Dynastic Period and the Old Kingdom (*e.g.* Dreyer 1986 pls. 11–16, 57). No Middle Kingdom offerings of this kind have been discovered in temples in the Egyptian Nile Valley, but it was during the Middle Kingdom that private statues and stelae first seem to have been set up in cult temple areas. Votive stelae and statues have been found in almost every New Kingdom Egyptian temple, but deposits of small votive offerings are rare. The preservation of such offerings is partly a matter of chance. At several important cult centres of Hathor, such as Atfih and Gebelein, virtually nothing of the New Kingdom remains and there are few traces of votive offerings.

The New Kingdom Hathor temple at Dendara has not survived, but in 1898 Petrie came across a dump of votive material in the 18th dynasty section of the sacred animal catacombs:–

> In one of the chambers in the middle of the row there were some scraps of carved ivory under the burnt bones; among them two sistrum handles, on one of which could be read the inscription of a priestess of Hathor named Baku. From the work this is probably 18th dynasty. More certain however were the pieces of glazed ware ... These were found broken up and cast aside, amidst the bones, and are clearly pieces of the temple furniture of Tahutmes III and Amenhotep II ... (1900.28)

The 'glazed ware' included model stems of papyrus and bunches of grapes; large *ankh* signs; Hathor masks; fertility figurines; segmented balls; model throwsticks; pot-stands; and bowls decorated with fish and flowers (Fig. 6; 1900.28–9, 68). The only cartouches were those of Thutmose III and Amonhotep II (van Siclen 1985.72). Petrie suggested that the material he found had been cleared out of the sanctuary during a refurbishment of the temple under Amonhotpe III (1900.29). The offerings were dumped or buried in the catacombs and later covered by animal mummies. At some point these caught fire and most of the objects lying beneath them were destroyed or badly damaged (1900.29). Not enough of the Dendara material survives to merit a section on its own, but I refer to it for comparison throughout this book.

A roughly comparable range of New Kingdom offerings is preserved in only two temples of other deities. The first of these is the shrine of 'Sekhmet of Sahure', built during the 18th dynasty inside the southern part of the 5th dynasty mortuary temple of Sahure at Abusir (Borchardt 1910.101–2; Baines 1973.9–14). Inscriptional evidence suggests that this shrine functioned in the reign of Amonhotpe III and again from Tutankhamon to Merenptah (Borchardt 1910.121–34). The shrine was decorated with a frieze of Hathor masks (1910.102, fig. 124), and the offerings are extremely similar to those found in Hathor shrines. They include stone and wooden ear stelae (1910.128, figs. 173–4); faience bracelets; Taweret figures; model fruit, flowers and papyrus stems; model throwsticks; and bowls decorated with 'cow and marsh' scenes (1910.130–4, figs. 177–84). Some of these objects are inscribed with royal names.

The second temple is that built by Amonhotpe II for the Great Sphinx at Giza (Selim Hassan 1953; 1957). Much votive material of the New Kingdom and later was found in the vicinity of this temple, including ear stelae, and model ears (1953.41–4, figs. 30–1); hawk, lion and sphinx figurines, and hawk plaques (1953.33–55; C. Zivie 1976.246–56; Sadek 1988.23–8).

Faience ears, eyes, and fertility figurines recovered from a foundation deposit of the temple of Nekhbet built by Amonhotpe II at el-Kab (Quibell 1898.16, pl. 21; Weinstein 1973.256) suggest that small votive offerings were dedicated there. The same is true of objects relating to Hathor from a foundation deposit of the temple of Min built by Thutmose III at Koptos (Petrie 1896 pls. 14–6; Weinstein 1973.434). These include faience fertility figurines and elaborate pottery vessels (2.6.1.5; 2.11.5). Min of Koptos was a co-templar deity with Hathor at Gebel Zeit (1.6.1).

One other relevant site is Byblos. The temple of the *Baalat* referred to by Egyptians as Hathor 'Lady of Byblos' is contemporary with the Old Kingdom and contained some Egyptian objects, such as calcite vases inscribed with royal names (Montet 1928.68–75). Less well known are the deposits of offerings buried in the procella of the Temple of the Obelisks (Dunand 1950; 1958), which is thought to have been in use during the Middle Kingdom and the early part of the Second Intermediate Period (Wein 1963.21–5). These offerings included Middle Kingdom Egyptian faience figurines. Some of these – such as the fertility figurines, the Taweret figures, and the models of dwarfs, cats, and hippopotami (Dunand 1958 pls. 95, 99, 102–3, 108) – seem to provide the 'missing link' between Early Dynastic and Old Kingdom votive offerings, on the one hand, and the type of votive faience found in temples in Egypt during the New Kingdom, on the other.

Summary

Votive faience dedicated to Hathor survives from the Middle Kingdom/Second Intermediate Period Temple of the Obelisks at Byblos, and from the 18th dynasty temple at Dendara. A shrine of Sekhmet at Abusir, and foundation deposits from el-Kab and Koptos provide comparative material. The Temple of the Sphinx at Giza is the only excavated New Kingdom site where a range of small votive objects was dedicated to a male deity.

The general date range of the votive offerings to Hathor is from the late Middle Kingdom/early Second Intermediate Period to the late New Kingdom, but each of the Hathor shrines at the six sites functioned for a different period within this range. Votive objects were dedicated to the goddess in the sanctuaries of state-run temples, in popular shrines within the precincts of state-run temples, and in 'community shrines'. In all these types of sacred building, the offerings seem to have been kept in or near the sanctuary for very long periods, rather than being regularly cleared out.

Certain categories of object can be regarded as typical Hathor offerings, but few of these categories are found at all six sites. Of the six sites, Serabit el-Khadim and Timna have the most similar range of offerings. The iconography of Hathor differs from site to site. Her cow form, for example, was very prominent at Deir el-Bahri and Faras, and occurs at Serabit el-Khadim and Gebel Zeit, but is absent from Mirgissa and Timna. These differences are explored in Part Two: a detailed study of the eleven main categories of votive object.

2

The votive objects

2.1 Stelae

Almost all the stelae from Deir el-Bahri, Faras, Mirgissa, and Serabit el-Khadim have been published, so only brief descriptions of individual stelae are given here. Lists 1–3 form a catalogue of the New Kingdom votive stelae from Deir el-Bahri, Mirgissa and Serabit el-Khadim which were dedicated wholly or partly to Hathor by private individuals. Such stelae are referred to in the text as 'Hathor stelae'. No list appears for Faras, since the only stela from this site to mention Hathor dates to the Second Intermediate Period (Fig. 5.6). The 'rock stela' of the Viceroy Setau (Fig. 5.11) should be classed as an inscription relating to the statue in the rock-cut shrine. Both these pieces are fully discussed in the chapter on Faras (1.2.2). The New Kingdom stelae set up at Serabit el-Khadim by expedition leaders on behalf of the king are classed here as commemorative rather than votive (3.1; 3.3). No private stelae survive from Timna. At least ten, mainly pre-New Kingdom, Hathor stelae have been excavated at Gebel Zeit (Mey *et al.* 1980.316, pl. 80; Castel & Soukiassian 1985.291–3, pls. 33–4; Posener-Kriéger 1986.381–2). Few of these have yet been published in detail. The Gebel Zeit pieces are therefore not included in the catalogue, but I refer to them for comparison. Stelae decorated only with ears or with eyes are dealt with separately in 2.8.2 and 2.8.5.

H. M. Stewart proposes that votive stelae are those which were 'dedicated to deities by private individuals in the hope of benefits in this life or the hereafter' (1976.ix). This definition is adopted here, on the understanding that the term 'deities' can include living and deceased kings. In these lists, the stelae are grouped according to the site at which they were found. They can also be divided by compositional form into three main types:–

    A.   Stelae on which only deities are represented
    B.   Stelae with a single register on which deities and donors are shown
    C.   Stelae of more than one register on which both deities and donors are shown

This type can be subdivided into:–

    1.   Stelae with deities in the upper register and donors in the lower register/s
    2.   Stelae with deities and the principal donor/s in the upper register, and other donors in the lower register/s

Further variants of Type C are known, but they do not happen to occur at the six sites. Of the Hathor stelae which are intact, or nearly so, 8 are Type A, 18 are Type B, 4 are Type C1 and 2 are Type C2. Type C might be better represented in the Hathor material if the stelae from Deir el-Bahri were less badly damaged. The examples from the sites are discussed with a view to establishing whether Hathor stelae display any characteristics which distinguish them from votive stelae in general.

2.1.1 Lists of Hathor stelae

Abbreviations

P   provenance
M   material
T   technique
De   deity/ies
Do   donor/s
I   inscriptions
Da   date
–   information not available

early 18th dynasty   Ahmose to Thutmose I
mid 18th dynasty   Thutmose II to Amonhotpe II
late 18th dynasty   Thutmose IV to Amonhotpe III
end of 18th dynasty Tutankhamon to Horemheb

List 1: Hathor stelae from Deir el-Bahri

1) London BM 41518; Naville 1913.22, pl. 7.7; *HT* 1914 pl. 41 (Pl. 9.5)
   P   11th dynasty temple; north court?
   M   Limestone
   T   Raised relief
   De   Hathor cow in papyrus
   Do   One woman
   I   Name of donor
   Da   Early or mid 18th dynasty

2) Philadelphia 11818; Naville 1907.69–70, pl. 25f (Pl. 9.2)
   P   11th dynasty temple
   M   Limestone
   T   Raised relief
   De   Hathor cow and Amonhotpe I
   Do   A woman, her husband and his son
   I   Names and titles of deities and donors
   Da   Mid 18th dynasty

3) Destroyed in 1888; Schiaparelli 1887.154, n.1
   P   Hathor shrine of Djeser-Djeseru
   M   Stone
   T   –
   De   Hathor cow with Hatshepsut (?) under head and suckling
   Do   –
   I   Name and titles of queen and goddess?
   Da   Mid 18th dynasty

4) Location unknown; Naville 1907.65

    P   Speos of the Hathor shrine of Djeser-Akhet
    M   Stone?
    T   –
    De   Hathor cow with king under head and suckling
    Do –
    I   –
    Da Mid 18th dynasty?

5) Bolton 48.04.26; unpublished (Pl. 12a)

    P   11th dynasty temple; north court?
    M   Limestone
    T   Raised relief
    De   Hathor in human form and Min
    Do –
    I   Name and titles of deities
    Da Mid 18th dynasty?

6) New York MMA 23.3.47; Winlock 1922.38, fig. 33; Hayes 1959.173

    P   Dump south of the forecourt of the 11th dynasty temple
    M   Limestone
    T   Sunk relief
    De   Three cows in papyrus
    Do Not shown
    I   None
    Da Mid 18th dynasty?

7) Ilkley CC 7145; unpublished (Pl. 12b)

    P   11th dynasty temple
    M   Limestone
    T   Raised relief
    De   Hathor in human form
    Do A man and a woman
    I   Name and title of goddess
    Da Mid or late 18th dynasty

8) Manchester 4404; unpublished (Pl. 10)

    P   11th dynasty temple
    M   Acacia wood
    T   Painted on gesso
    De   Hathor cow in papyrus
    Do A priest and his wife
    I   Name and titles of goddess and donors, praises of Hathor, prayers for donors
    Da Late or end of the 18th dynasty

9) Location unknown (ex Mclean Museum, Greenock); PM II, 396

    P   11th dynasty temple
    M   Stone
    T   –
    De   'head of Hathor'
    Do   –
    I   Name and titles of goddess
    Da   Late or end of 18th dynasty

10) London BM 53891; *HT* 1922.9, pl. 29

    P   11th dynasty temple?
    M   Limestone
    T   Sunk relief
    De   Nebhepetreꜥ Mentuhotpe offering to Hathor in human form
    Do   –
    I   Names and titles of goddess and king and caption to offering scene
    Da   Late or end of the 18th dynasty

11) London BM 689; Naville 1907.65, pl. 25e; *HT* 1914 pl. 41 (Pl. 9.1)

    P   11th dynasty temple
    M   Limestone
    T   Sunk relief
    De   Hathor cow with king under head and suckling
    Do   –
    I   Name and titles of goddess
    Da   Late or end of 18th dynasty

12) Location unknown; Naville 1913.22, pl. 7.8 (Pl. 9.4)

    P   11th dynasty temple
    M   Limestone?
    T   Sunk relief
    De   Hathor cow 'in' mountain, a king, and a seated goddess
    Do   –
    I   Name and titles of cow
    Da   End of 18th dynasty

13) Destroyed in 1940; Naville 1907.61, pl. 26a; Liverpool 1932.53

    P   11th dynasty temple
    M   Limestone
    T   –
    De   Nebhepetreꜥ Mentuhotpe offering to Amon, Mut and Khons, Hathor in human form, and another goddess
    Do   –
    I   Name and titles of king and deities
    Da   End of 18th dynasty

14) Bristol H 520; PM II, 396 (Pl. 11)

P 11th dynasty temple
M Limestone
T Painted
De Hathor cow in shrine
Do None shown
I Illegible
Da 18th dynasty

15) Oxford Ash. E 2723; Naville 1913.23, pl. 14.7

P 11th dynasty temple
M Limestone
T Raised relief
De Hathor cow
Do None shown
I None
Da 18th dynasty

16) London BM 43144; Naville 1913.23, pls. 14.8, 22.1 (Fig. 1.1)

P 11th dynasty temple
M Limestone
T Raised relief
De Hathor mask naos sistrum
Do None shown
I –
Da 18th dynasty

17) Belfast 1911.569; PM II, 396

P 11th dynasty temple
M Stone
T –
De King offering to [goddess]
Do –
I Name and titles of Hathor
Da 18th dynasty?

18) London BM 706; Naville 1913.4, pls. 6.2; 8c; *HT* 1922 pl. 48 (Fig. 7.c)

P Upper north colonnade of 11th dynasty temple
M Black granite
T Sunk relief
De Amon, Mut and Khons, Hathor cow 'in' mountain, Hathor in human form, and nine other deities
Do One man named
I Name and titles of deities and donor, praises of deities, *ḥtp di nsw* formula, and appeals to the living
Da Late 19th dynasty; reign of Siptah?

19) Location unknown; PM I.2, 650
- P   First court of Djeser-Djeseru
- M   Limestone
- T   Sunk relief
- De   One god or deified king, the rest missing
- Do   A man, three women and a boy
- I   Praises of Hathor and other deities, prayers for life and funerary benefits
- Da   Late 19th or 20th dynasty

20) Luxor F 4093, 5619, 932; Lipińska 1984.49, fig. 167
- P   Hypostyle hall of Djeser-Akhet
- M   Sandstone
- T   Sunk relief
- De   Hathor cow 'in' mountain
- Do   One man, one woman
- I   Names and titles; the rest missing
- Da   19th dynasty?

21) Luxor F 824; Lipińska 1984.49, fig. 166
- P   North-east part of Djeser-Akhet
- M   Limestone
- T   Raised relief
- De   Hathor cow 'in' mountain
- Do   Missing
- I   Missing
- Da   Ramessid?

22) Yale Peabody Museum 6738 (fragment); Scott 1986.189, no. 118
- P   Deir el-Bahri
- M   Limestone
- T   Raised relief
- De   Hathor in human form, and god?
- Do   Missing
- I   *ḥtp di nsw* formula, most missing
- Da   Mid 18th dynasty?

List 2: Stelae from the Hathor shrine at Mirgissa

All these stelae were found in the sanctuary of the Hathor shrine.

1) Inv. no. 171; Karlin in Vercoutter 1970.320, 353, pl. 38a
- M   Limestone
- T   Raised relief
- De   Hathor in human form
- Do   One woman
- I   Names of deity and donor, *ḥtp di nsw* formula
- Da   Mid 18th dynasty

2) Inv. no. 178; Vercoutter 1965.182–3, fig. 1; Karlin in Vercoutter 1970.353, pl. 38b

    M   Wood
    T   Painted
    De   Hathor in human form
    Do   One woman
    I   Names and titles of deity and donor
    Da   Mid 18th dynasty

3) Inv. no. 172; Karlin in Vercoutter 1970.320–1, 353, pl. 39b

    M   Limestone
    T   Sunk relief
    De   Cow in papyrus
    Do   None shown?
    I   *ir n* formula
    Da   Mid 18th dynasty?

4) Inv. no. 173; Karlin in Vercoutter 1970.320–2, 353, pl. 39a

    M   Sandstone
    T   Sunk relief
    De   Senwosret III (?), Montu, and Hathor in human form
    Do   Two men and two women
    I   Names and titles of deities and donors, mainly illegible
    Da   Late 18th dynasty?

5) Inv. no. 174; Karlin in Vercoutter 1970.321, 353, pl. 38c

    M   Sandstone
    T   Painted
    De   Hathor in human form
    Do   One woman
    I   Names of deity and donor (?), mainly illegible
    Da   Late 18th dynasty

List 3: Private Hathor stelae from Serabit el-Khadim

The provenance of these stelae within the temple is not usually recorded, but most of the private stelae came from the portico (S) and the sanctuary (Q). Unless stated otherwise, the stelae remain at Serabit el-Khadim. They are all in local sandstone. Details of the type of relief are rarely available.

1) London UC 14302; Černý 1952 pl. 65a, no. 226; 1955.170 (Fig. 8)

    De   Hathor in human form
    Do   One man
    I   Name and titles of deity and donor
    Da   Early 18th dynasty?

2) Černý 1952 pl. 65, no. 227; 1955.170
    De   Hathor in human form
    Do   One man
    I   Name and titles of deity and donor
    Da   Early 18th dynasty

3) Černý 1952 pl. 67, no. 233; 1955.172
    De   Hathor in human form and Horus
    Do   One man
    I   Names and titles of deities, *ḥtp di nsw* formula
    Da   18th dynasty

4) Glasgow K 05.143a; Černý 1952 pl. 67, no. 236; 1955.172 (Fig. 8)
    De   Hathor in human form
    Do   One man
    I   Name and titles of Hathor, prayer for life benefits
    Da   18th dynasty

5) Dublin NM 1905.262; Černý 1952 pl. 68, no. 243; 1955.174 (Fig. 8)
    De   Hathor in human form
    Do   One man
    I   Name and titles of Hathor and prayer for life benefits
    Da   18th dynasty

6) Černý 1955 pl. 67, no. 234; 1955.172
    De   –
    Do   One man
    I   *ḥtp di nsw* formula, addressed to Hathor
    Da   Late 18th dynasty

7) Cairo JE 38266; Černý 1952 pl. 67, no. 235; 1955.172 (Fig. 8)
    De   Hathor in human form
    Do   One man
    I   Names and titles of deity and donor, *ḥtp di nsw* formula
    Da   Late 18th dynasty

8) Černý 1952 pl. 67, no. 237; 1955.173
    De   Hathor in human form
    Do   One man
    I   Name and titles of deity and donor
    Da   Late 18th dynasty

9) Černý 1952 pl. 69, no. 239; 1955.173
    De   Hathor in human form
    Do   Two men
    I   Title of deity, names of donors
    Da   18th dynasty?

10) Černý 1952 pl. 68, no. 242; 1955.173 (Fig. 9)

    De   Hathor in human form
    Do   Two men
    I   Name and titles of deity, the remainder illegible
    Da   18th dynasty?

11) Brussels MR E 3084; Černý 1952 pl. 88, no. 428; 1955.213 (Pl. 14a)

    De   Hathor mask column
    Do   Two men?
    I   Names of donors?
    Da   18th dynasty?

12) Brussels MR E 3086; unpublished

    De   Hathor mask column
    Do   None shown
    I   None
    Da   18th dynasty?

13) Brussels MR E 3085; unpublished

    De   Hathor mask column (on both faces of stela)
    Do   None shown
    I   None
    Da   18th dynasty?

14) Brussels MR E 2474; unpublished (Pl. 13a–b)

    De   Face A, a Hathor mask naos sistrum; Face B, a lioness-headed goddess
    Do   Face A, one woman (?); Face B, one man
    I   Titles of deities, name of female donor
    Da   18th dynasty?

15) Černý 1952 pl. 89, no. 423; 1955.212

    De   Hathor in human form
    Do   One named
    I   *ḥtp di nsw* formula, mainly illegible
    Da   Late 18th or 19th dynasty

16) Giveon 1981.168–71, fig. 1

    De   Hathor in human form
    Do   One named
    I   Name and titles of deity, prayer for life benefits
    Da   Late 18th or 19th dynasty

17) Dublin NM 1905.262; Černý 1952 pl. 69, no. 240; 1955.173 (Fig. 9)

    De   Hathor in human form
    Do   Two men
    I   Names and titles of deity and donors
    Da   19th dynasty?

18) Manchester 981; Černý 1952 pl. 75, no. 303; 1955.194–5
  De   –
  Do   One man
  I   Praises of Hathor and prayer for life benefits
  Da   19th dynasty?

19) Černý 1952 pl. 81, no. 299; 1955.194
  De   Hathor in human form
  Do   One man
  I   Title of Hathor
  Da   19th–20th dynasty

20) Černý 1952 pl. 78, no. 306; 1955.195 (Fig. 9)
  De   Hathor in human form
  Do   One man
  I   Name and titles of deity and donor
  Da   19th–20th dynasty

21) Ex Mclean Museum, Greenock; Černý 1952 pl. 76, no. 295; 1955.193 (Fig. 9)
  De   Hathor in human form
  Do   One man and two women
  I   Name and title of Hathor and *n kꜣ n* formula
  Da   20th dynasty

2.1.2 Materials and classification

Most of the votive stelae are of stone, either limestone or sandstone according to what was locally available. At Gebel Zeit 'les stèles locales sont de petites dimensions et de facture très grossière' (Castel & Soukiassian 1985.293). They are carved in poor quality limestone, sandstone, or 'évaporite' (1985.293). One elaborate Ramessid stela from Deir el-Bahri is in black granite (List 1.18). On one stela from Deir el-Bahri (Pl. 11), and one from Mirgissa (List 2.5), the design has been drawn and then painted on a flat stone surface. All the other stone stelae have carved designs and inscriptions. Most of these will originally have been painted too. A few of the Hathor stelae are double-sided (*e.g.* Pl. 13) and this is not uncommon among votive and commemorative stelae.

A few Middle Kingdom wooden funerary stelae are known from the Asasif (Hayes 1953.330–1, figs. 218–9), but wood seldom seems to have been employed for funerary stelae during the New Kingdom. It was used for votive stelae during this era. In addition to the examples cited in the lists (Lists 1.8, 2.2), two small wooden ear stelae and one wooden eye stela were found at Deir el-Bahri (Pl. 56a-b; 2.8.2.2; 2.8.5.3). Four wooden stela fragments were excavated at Mirgissa (Karlin in Vercoutter 1970.353). On the ear stelae, the design is both carved and painted, but on most wooden stelae the design is painted on a flat surface which was first given a thick coat of gesso (Pl. 10). New Kingdom votive stelae in wood have also been recovered from Deir el-Medina (*e.g.* Bruyère 1939.267–8, fig. 94; *HT* 1982 pl. 8.3), and from the shrine of Sekhmet at Abusir (Borchardt 1910.128, fig. 174). Wooden stelae were probably common, but their chances of survival are poor.

Two fragmentary Second Intermediate Period faience stelae from Gebel Zeit show a king offering to deities (Castel & Soukiassian 1985.290, pl. 60; Castel *et al.* 1986.104, pl. 5.3; 1.6.3). The better preserved of the two stelae would have been 25 to 30 cm high when intact. These are the earliest known examples of faience stelae. The excavators comment that:–

> A notre connaissance, les stèles en faïence sont rares. Cependant, au Gebel Zeit, plusieurs fragments de stèles en faïence ont été retrouvés. De petites dimensions, ces stèles pouvaient être facilement transportées avec le matériel sacré que les expéditions apportaient de la Vallée. (Castel & Soukiassian 1985.290)

A number of cow plaques from Deir el-Bahri in faience and metal (2.4.2; Pls. 35, 37), and some faience Hathor mask and cat plaques from Serabit el-Khadim (2.3.2.4; 2.5.2; Pls. 31, 43–4), might be classed as miniature Type A stelae. As with the stone or wood Type A stelae, the design on these plaques is restricted to a representation of a deity, occasionally supplemented by a brief inscription. I have classified anything in stone or wood which has one measurement of 12 cm or more as a stela, and anything under 12 cm or made of faience or metal as a plaque. This is a convenient but arbitrary division. It is not clear that the Egyptians would have regarded a faience Hathor mask plaque as being in a different category from a stone Hathor mask stela. The Type A votive stelae could be thought of as spanning everything from the largest stone pieces to the smallest metal or faience pieces; a range of size and materials matched only by the analogous Type 1 ear stelae (2.8.2, List A). The occurrence of a similar range of Type A stelae and plaques in the vicinity of the Great Sphinx at Giza (Selim Hassan 1953.234–76) shows that this phenomonen is not unique to the cult of Hathor, but it seems to have no equivalent in the sphere of funerary stelae.

2.1.3 Form of deity

There seems to have been no rigid rule that votive stelae had to be dedicated to the primary deity of the temple or shrine in which they were set up. Hathor appears with other deities on stelae from Deir el-Bahri, Mirgissa, Serabit el-Khadim and Gebel Zeit. At least five Type B votive stelae from Serabit el-Khadim were dedicated wholly to other deities (London BM 8509, unpublished; Černý 1952 nos. 276, 297, 300, 308).

Almost all the stelae dedicated to Hathor include some kind of representation of her, if only of her ears or eyes (2.8.6). On the private votive stelae in the catalogue, Hathor is shown in human form 26 times, in cow form 14 times, in various types of Hathor mask form 5 times and in lioness-headed form once. These figures give the impression that the human form of the goddess, which dominated temple iconography, and which appears on all the 'royal' commemorative stelae at Serabit el-Khadim, Timna, and Gebel Zeit, was also pre-eminent among the votive offerings. This is probably misleading. At Mirgissa, Serabit el-Khadim, and Gebel Zeit the human form of Hathor is used on a majority of the private stelae, but at

Deir el-Bahri the cow form is more common (List 1). If all the Type A plaques were included in these figures, the cow form of the goddess would be seen to dominate the votive material at Deir el-Bahri, and her Hathor mask and cat forms would figure very prominently at Serabit el-Khadim.

It is also noteworthy that the human form of the goddess appears on only one of the Type A Hathor stelae, a piece dedicated by an Asiatic at Serabit el-Khadim (List 3.16), and possibly on two gold Type A plaques from Faras (2.7.3; Pl. 8.45, 47). Where alternative forms were available, there seems to have been a strong tendency to avoid the full human form or even the animal-headed form of a deity on Type A stelae and plaques. At Giza, for example, the hawk-headed human form of the sun god appears on the Type B and C votive stelae but not on the Type A stelae and plaques. On these, the deity is depicted in sphinx or hawk form (Selim Hassan 1953.234–76; C. Zivie 1976.248–52). This may mean that Type A stelae should be regarded as a different category of object from other types of votive stela.

On a Type A stela from Deir el-Bahri, three cows are depicted standing beneath a bent papyrus stem (List 1.6), while several plaques from the same site show a pair of cows (2.4.2; Pls. 3, 37). Stelae featuring multiple animal forms of deities such as Amon (e.g. Lacau 1909 pl. 61; Munro 1962 pl. 6.3), Mertseger (e.g. Bruyère 1947 pl. 8; Tosi & Roccati 1972 nos. 500064–5), Sobek (Kuentz 1969.190–3, pl. 45; Bakry 1971.137–9), Thoth (Munro 1962 pl. 6.1–2), and Wepwawet (Munro 1962 pls. 4–5), became quite common in temples and shrines from the late 18th dynasty onwards. They do not seem to occur in a funerary context, except where a tomb became a popular shrine, as in the case of the tomb of Hapdjefa III at Asyut (Sadek 1988.40–2). Outside funerary papyri, Hathor is the only deity to appear in a multiple *human* form during the New Kingdom, but since this is in a specific group of seven (Helck 1977.1033) it is not directly comparable to the apparently limitless multiplication of the animal forms of some deities. Some of these multiple animal forms should probably be interpreted as portrayals of sacred animals kept in temples (see further 2.4.4).

On a Ramessid stela from Deir el-Bahri (List 1.18), Hathor is shown in both her cow and human forms. Since these forms are in different sub-registers (Fig. 7.c), they might be regarded as belonging to separate scenes, but on a few New Kingdom stelae two forms of the same deity are shown side by side (e.g. Bruyère 1935.113, fig. 53; HT 1939 pl. 31). Hathor is depicted more often than any other deity on stelae of this kind, and combinations can be cited of her human and cow forms (e.g. Petrie 1909 pl. 28.1), Hathor mask and cow head forms (e.g. Weigall 1906.135), and human and Hathor mask sistrum forms (Černý 1958 no. 7; HT 1970 pl. 37.2; Wildung 1974.264, fig. 15). Two forms of the goddess appear together on some plaques (e.g. Reisner 1958 no. 12819), and faience bowls (e.g. Borchardt 1910 fig. 179; Strauss 1974 fig. 17), and four forms in one statue group (Vandier 1969.159–70, fig. 5).

It is difficult to decide whether many votive stelae show a deity or the deity's manifestation in a sacred animal or a cult image or object. When Hathor is shown enclosed in a shrine (e.g. Pl. 14) or standing on a plinth (e.g. Pl. 9.1; Figs. 8–9), a statue is meant. The depiction of such statues on New Kingdom votive stelae could be due to a lingering reluctance to show living, private individuals in the presence of a deity. Alternatively, these stelae could reflect the important role played by specific royal and divine statues in New Kingdom popular religion (see further 3.3). The statue of a Hathor cow suckling and protecting a king, shown on a stela from Deir el-Bahri (Pl. 9.1), is very similar to a surviving cow statue found at the site (Pl. 41b), just as the Great Sphinx is quite accurately depicted on some votive stelae from Giza (Selim Hassan 1953 figs. 93–4, 172–4, 178–94; C. Zivie 1978 pl. 20). Such representations can probably be used as a guide to the general form, though not to the exact details, of the cult images in a particular temple. In other cases, the stelae may show cult objects or images carried in procession during festivals (*e.g.* Pl. 13a).

One notable feature of the Hathor stelae, particularly those from Deir el-Bahri, is the number on which a king is shown with the goddess (Lists 1.2–4, 10–13, 17; 2.4). Votive stelae on which kings appear can be divided into three main types. First, there are those on which the king is depicted as an intermediary offering to a deity, while the actual donors occupy the lower registers. New Kingdom examples on which a contemporary king is shown playing this kind of role are quite common, particularly from the Ramessid period (*e.g.* Selim Hassan 1953 figs. 66, 99; Černý 1958 no. 9; Bosticco 1965 no. 54; Wildung 1974 fig. 1; Stewart 1976 pl. 41; see Altenmüller 1981). Schulman suggests that stelae of this kind could commemorate the donor's attendance at a festival or temple ritual at which the king was present (Schulman 1988.3–4, 192–7). This is certainly possible at Deir el-Bahri, where kings often took part in the Beautiful Festival of the Wadi. There is evidence to link some of the votive offerings with this festival (2.2.8; 2.4.5–6; 2.6.3; 2.7.3; 2.9.2.2; 3.3). Even if the stelae do record a specific event, the role of the king is still likely to have been that of a permanent intercessor for the donor.

The 'royal stelae' from Serabit el-Khadim, on which contemporary kings appear as the primary, and expedition leaders as the secondary donors, might have been placed in this group if their texts did not classify them as commemorative rather than votive. Deceased kings can also be shown playing an intermediary role (*e.g.* HT 1922 pls. 34–6; Černý 1958 no. 11; Stewart 1976 pl. 38; Altenmüller 1981.1–7, fig. 1), as Nebhepetreʿ Mentuhotpe is on two Hathor stelae from Deir el-Bahri (List 1.10, 13).

Second, there are votive stelae on which a dead king is shown being worshipped, either alone or on apparently equal terms with other deities (*e.g.* HT 1922 pls. 32, 37–8; HT 1939 pls. 45–6; Bruyère 1940 pls. 12, 38; Černý 1958 no. 10; Stewart 1976 pl. 38). Many of these stelae should be interpreted as showing a particular cult image of a deified king, as on the stelae from the late 18th/early 19th dynasty shrine of Thutmose III at Gurob (Loat 1904.7–8, pls. 14–19). On a stela from Deir el-Bahri, Amonhotpe I is depicted as a god, seated on a throne in front of Hathor (Pl. 9.2); while on a stela from Mirgissa a king, probably Senwosret III, forms a triad with Hathor and Sopdu (Vercoutter 1970 pl. 39a).

Third, there are votive stelae which show statues of living kings as objects of worship (*e.g.* Labib Habachi 1954 pl. 34; 1969.34, fig. 21; Ramadan el-Sayed 1979; Sadek 1988.13–15). The nearest parallels to this among the Hathor stelae are the pieces from Deir el-Bahri which depict statues of Hathor in cow form suckling and protecting a king (List 1.3–4, 11). The kings shown in this way in temple reliefs and statue groups, votive cloths, and tomb paintings, may be contemporary or deceased (2.2.4; 2.4.5–6). Rather than portraying two separate deities, these stelae seem to illustrate temple statues which celebrated a particular relationship between Hathor and the king. Votive stelae from Giza which depict contemporary kings standing between the paws of the Great Sphinx provide comparative material (Selim Hassan 1953.71, figs. 62, 66–8, pl. 67).

One unusual feature of some of the Hathor stelae from Deir el-Bahri and Mirgissa, is the depiction of the goddess in a specific setting – the Western Mountain (List 1.4, 11–12, 18, 20–1), or a papyrus thicket representing the marshes of Chemmis (Lists 1.1, 6, 8; 2.3). There are some parallels on funerary stelae for the depiction of deities in a specific setting; the scene in which the sycamore-goddess offers refreshments to the deceased and their *ba* is one of the more common (*e.g.* Quibell 1896 pls. 20, 24; *HT* 1925 pl. 24; Bosticco 1965 nos. 36, 48; Moftah 1966.43–7). Parallel scenes on votive stela are scarcer, but stelae which depict Mertseger in snake form in a papyrus thicket (Bruyère 1935.107, fig. 46), Taweret in a landscape representing Gebel el-Silsila as the 'source of the Nile' (Bruyère 1952.76–8, fig. 7), or the Anukis gazelle in front of the Western Mountain (Valbelle 1981.118, fig. 276), may be cited. The predominance of animal forms in such scenes suggests that the animal form of a deity was linked with the concept of immanence.

2.1.4 The donors

Although the deity to whom a votive stela was dedicated was almost always portrayed on it in some manner, a representation of the donor was not essential. On some Type A stelae the donor is not even named (Lists 1.6, 14–5, 3.12–3), but on most of the Type B and C stelae the donors are named as well as shown. The kind of individual or group who dedicated stelae to Hathor will have varied from site to site. Since Deir el-Bahri was close to one of the biggest cities in Egypt, one might expect the greatest range of donors to be found there, but only six Hathor stelae depicting donors have survived from the site (List 1.1–2, 7–8, 19–20). This is too small a sample to draw conclusions from, but the fact that two of these stela show a woman as the principal donor (Pl. 9.2, 5) is interesting, since a high proportion of the votive textiles found there were dedicated by women (2.2.5). The men shown or named on the Deir el-Bahri stelae tend to be priests, officials or artisans associated with the temples through their work. This is also true of funerary stelae from the Deir el-Bahri temples, such as that of the High Priest of Amon and Hathor, Senenu (Brovarski 1976.59–60, pl. 11.1), and of votive stelae from the site that are dedicated to other deities.

Three of the five intact stelae from Mirgissa were dedicated by women (List 2). On another stela from this site the donors are two men who are shaven-headed, and so probably priests, and two women (Vercoutter 1970 pl. 39a). This stela, and one from Deir el-Bahri which shows the mayor of Western Thebes, Ramose, with three women and a child (List 1.19), provide the largest family groups shown on the Hathor stelae. The type of late 18th dynasty and Ramessid stelae depicting very large family groups making offerings to deities, come mainly from tomb chapels.

Such stelae are not common in temple contexts, as is indicated by their scarcity at sites such as Giza and Memphis, where a wide range of votive stelae was found, indicates. It seems natural that stelae intended for family tombs should place a greater emphasis on the 'extended family' than those dedicated in temples by small groups or individuals. However, it should be noted that some of the votive textiles from Deir el-Bahri do feature large family groups (2.2.5).

Very few of the donors at Serabit el-Khadim included their absent families on the stelae which they dedicated in the temple. During the Middle Kingdom, the inscriptions on the 'royal stelae' at this site included a full list of the personnel of each mining expedition and corporate prayers for them. Such lists do not recur in the New Kingdom, when only high officials are named on the 'royal stelae'. The New Kingdom private stelae are mainly dedicated by minor officials and artisans, who in the Middle Kingdom would have been listed on the 'royal stelae'. Of the important officials named on the 'royal stelae', only the royal scribe Sethnakhte also appears as a donor of a private stela (List 3.21). The lowest social group at Serabit el-Khadim, the ordinary miners, do not seem to be present among the stela donors.

Eleven of the private stelae from Serabit el-Khadim have a single male donor, and four have a pair of apparently unrelated male donors. Two women are shown on the stela of Sethnakhte which, to judge by its quality, was brought out from Egypt (Černý 1952 pl. 76), and a small stela has a man offering on one face and a woman offering on the other (Pl. 13). It is not necessary to assume that these women visited the site, but it is possible that priestesses sometimes served in the temple there (3.2.3). None of the private stelae from Gebel Zeit has yet been fully published, but one Second Intermediate Period example was apparently dedicated by a 'un policier' (a Medjay?) called Sobekhotpe (Posener-Kriégger 1986.381). On another stela from this site, a woman smelling a lotus – and therefore probably deceased – stands before Horus (Castel & Soukiassian 1985 pl. 60, far right).

There seem to have been no strict rules about the relative positions of deity and donor on New Kingdom votive stelae, except that private individuals are never shown in physical contact with a deity, as kings can be. The deity is normally on the left side (as viewed from the front), but this order is reversed on some stelae from Serabit el-Khadim (e.g. List 3.4–5, 8–9, 21; Fig. 8). On most of the stelae, the principal donor stands before the goddess or, more likely, a statue of her. The donors perform a variety of standard actions. On a few of the private stelae from Serabit el-Khadim, the donors stand before Hathor with their arms raised in adoration (List 3.15, 17). This pose is usually associated with adoration of kings, but it is quite common on New Kingdom votive stelae dedicated to gods or goddesses. On only one of the Hathor stelae are the donors shown kneeling in adoration (List 3.21).

The donors frequently burn incense and/or pour libations (e.g. Pls. 9, 12b, 13; Figs. 8–9), or present offerings of food or flowers (e.g. Pls. 9.2, 12b; Fig. 9). On one stela from Serabit el-Khadim, a man burns a pair of ducks in two portable altars (Fig. 8; see 2.5.5). A stela from Mirgissa depicts a woman – perhaps a priestess of Hathor – playing a tambourine before the goddess (List 2.2; Vercoutter 1970 pl. 38b). This is very unusual, but a few other New Kingdom votive stelae on which donors play musical instruments before a deity can be cited (e.g. Černý 1958 no. 7; Ziegler 1979.9), and a donor is shown playing a harp before Hathor on one of the votive textiles from Deir el-Bahri (Pl. 16b).

2.1.5 Inscriptions

An inscription has been described as an essential component of a stela (Yoyotte in Posener 1962.271). All funerary stelae may have an inscription of some kind, but this is not the case with votive stelae. Four of the Type A Hathor stelae have no inscriptions (Lists 1.6, 16; 3.12–3). Comparative material is provided by some large, uninscribed Type A stelae from other temples and shrines (*e.g.* Lacau 1909 pl. 61; Munro 1962 pl. 6; Schulman 1968.153–6; Tosi and Roccati 1972 nos. 50064–5), and by uninscribed ear stelae (2.8, List 1). All the Type B and C stelae in the catalogue are inscribed, as votive stelae of these types almost always are.

The inscriptions on the Hathor stelae tend to be brief and formulaic. On 12 of the stelae from Deir el-Bahri, 3 from Mirgissa, and 10 from Serabit el-Khadim, the surviving inscriptions consist only of the names and titles of the deities and/or the donors. Such inscriptions are usually written in short vertical columns beside the deity or the person they name. When a donor is depicted, he or she is usually named. To judge by the absence of inscriptions on some Type A stelae, it was not considered so important to name the deity, who could presumably be recognised by iconography alone. However, when a deity is named, epithets tend to be given. This is particularly common at Deir el-Bahri, where it may have been important to distinguish between the hypostases of Hathor in the various temples. No inscription on any of the votive stelae includes a speech by the deity. The kind of dialogue which features in the captions of temple reliefs does not occur. This could support the view that only statues or cult animals are represented on private votive stelae.

Elaborate inscriptions containing prayers to the goddess were obviously desirable, but they cannot have been considered necessary. When a votive stela has a brief inscription in addition to names and titles, this is normally written in horizontal lines at the bottom of the stela. On some of the cruder pieces from Serabit el-Khadim, and on one stela from Gebel Zeit, such inscriptions are squeezed in between the figures of the donors and the deity (Figs. 8–9; Castel & Soukiassian 1985 pl. 60, bottom right). Longer inscriptions may be written in horizontal or vertical columns below the main scene, sometimes with a space in the bottom right-hand corner for representations of the donors (Pl. 10; List 1.8, 19). Both short and long inscriptions consist almost entirely of standard formulae.

The only private Middle Kingdom stela found in the 11th dynasty temple at Deir el-Bahri is of an ordinary funerary type (Edwards 1965.22, pl. 10.2), but none of the New Kingdom Hathor stelae from this site have inscriptions which are purely funerary (List 1). The only possible exception is the stela of the High Priest Senenu (Brovarski 1976). This stela has been omitted here because it does not depict any deities and is funerary in type, but its inscriptions, which paraphrase chapters of the Book of the Dead, do mention Hathor (1976.59–60). At Serabit el-Khadim, all the surviving Middle Kingdom inscriptions of private individuals are funerary (Černý 1955 nos. 53, 71, 84, 93–6, 98, 103, 105–7, 112, 114, 118, 122, 136, 142, 153, 155–60, 176–70), but only one New Kingdom private stela can be classed as funerary (Černý 1952 pl. 45, no. 225 = Bolton 58.05.3). Two stelae from Deir el-Bahri (List 1.18, 22), one from Mirgissa (List 2.1), and four from Serabit el-Khadim (List 3.3, 6–7, 15), are inscribed with *ḥtp di nsw* formulae. One of the pieces from Deir el-Bahri, which is primarily dedicated to the Theban triad, has the longest and most varied inscriptions of any of the Hathor stelae, including two 'appeals to the living' and invocations and brief prayers to all the deities shown on the stela (Fig. 7.Ca; translated in Naville 1913.4). These prayers contain requests relating to the donor's' life, death and burial and to the continued presence of his *ka* in the temple – a concept more often found in the inscriptions on temple statues of private individuals than in stela texts. This stela will have been set up in the donor's lifetime, but it was intended to remain there after his death for the benefit of his *ka*. Several other stelae found at Deir el-Bahri depict offerings being made to deceased persons, or the deceased offering to Osiris, and these are clearly funerary (*e.g.* Naville 1913 pl. 7.3 = London BM 40963; 1913 pl. 6.4 = London BM 1454; Brovarski 1976 pls. 10–11 = Chicago OI 8798 & Paris Louvre 6244; Bristol 2212).

However, the inscriptions on the granite stela are not purely funerary. In the context of a New Kingdom votive stela a *ḥtp di nsw* formula need not introduce funerary prayers. On the stela from Mirgissa, the prayer is for the standard funerary benefit 'All good and pure things [on which a god lives]' (List 2.1), but on stelae from Serabit el-Khadim, the *ḥtp di nsw* formula introduces requests for 'life, prosperity, health, skill (*spd ḥr*), favour, and love for the *ka* of ... ' or 'favour, love and skill' or, more specifically 'favour, love and skill in the presence of the sovereign' (Figs. 8–9, nos. 234, 233, 235). A similar formula was present on a fragmentary stela from Deir el-Bahri (List 1.22). These requests related to the donors' earthly lives. Lists of similar 'life benefits' occur on votive cloths from Deir el-Bahri (2.2.6; Pl. 25), and on some New Kingdom votive stelae from other sites (*e.g.* Bruyère 1952a.34; Černý 1958 no. 3; Labib Habachi 1969.34, fig. 21; Romano 1979 fig. 49), but they are not very common. The earliest are on temple stelae of the mid 18th dynasty, the period when funerary motifs began to disappear from the lunettes, and when votive stelae of Types A and C were introduced.

On a stela from Serabit el-Khadim lacking the introductory formula, the donor requests 'A good life, favour and love' (Fig. 8, no. 236), and on another stela from this site Hathor is invoked 'that she may give life and skill' (Fig. 9, no. 243). The latter text should probably be taken as an abbreviation of the standard invocation formula 'Giving praise to X, making obeisance to X, that he/she may give ... ' (Stewart 1976.ix). This formula begins an inscription on a stela from Serabit el-Khadim requesting a group of life benefits which Černý translated as 'a happy lifetime, a body of joy, and pleasure of heart in the course of the day ... ' (1955.195, no. 303). It is also found on two of the more elaborate Hathor stelae from Deir el-Bahri (List 1.8, 19). The text on the wooden stela is now mainly illegible (Pl. 10), but the presence of $\bigwedge\!\!\!\!\!\!\!\overset{\varphi}{}$ – 'skill' or 'intelligence', indicates a list of 'life benefits'. In the second column, the words $\overset{\frown}{\square}\!\!\!\!\int\!\!\!\int\!\!\!\overset{\circ}{\vee}$ – 'old age and a good burial' are just legible, so the benefits requested may have covered the life, death, burial, and afterlife of the donor. Parts of the other stela are broken and not all the text is legible. It is clear that Hathor and Anubis are asked to bestow the standard list of 'life benefits' – 'life, prosperity, health, skill, favour, and love' and 'a good lifespan upon earth'. The donor then requests funerary benefits, including a place among the retinue of Hathor and Anubis. The formula $n\ k\beta\ n$ – 'for the ka of' is used by itself on one stela from Serabit el-Khadim (Fig. 9, no. 295). This need not imply a funerary prayer because it occurs in three other inscriptions from the site which request 'life benefits' (Fig. 8, nos. 234, 236; Giveon 1981 fig. 1). An introductory formula that is found only in votive inscriptions is $ir\ n$ – 'dedicated by' (Stewart 1976.ix; 2.8.2.3). This begins the otherwise illegible inscription on a stela from Mirgissa (Vercoutter 1970 pl. 39b).

2.1.6 Date range

The date range of the Hathor stelae varies from site to site. At Deir el-Bahri, most of the stelae date between the reign of Hatshepsut and the end of the 18th dynasty (List 1). Only four of the twenty-two Hathor stelae appear to be Ramessid. Much the same proportion of 18th dynasty to Ramessid material is found in other stelae and stela fragments from this site. The only stela from the Faras temple which names Hathor dates to the Second Intermediate Period (1.2.2). At Mirgissa, the surviving stelae were all mid or late 18th dynasty (List 2). Most rulers from Hatshepsut to Ramesses VI dedicated stelae at Serabit el-Khadim (1.4.2–3). The New Kingdom private stelae cover much the same date range, with the addition of two pieces which might be early 18th dynasty (List 3.1–2). 'Royal name' faience recovered from the temple shows that there were expeditions to Serabit el-Khadim during the early 18th dynasty (1.4.3). Private stelae were dedicated at Gebel Zeit as early as the Second Intermediate Period, and continued to be set up there until the late 18th or early 19th dynasty.

It is not possible to discuss here the dating of each of the 48 Hathor stelae. Standard dating criteria have been used. The Type A stelae are the hardest to date, but comparisons with other types of votive object, such as the faience Hathor mask or cat plaques which bear royal names (2.3.2.4; 2.5.2), can be helpful. I know of no Type A stela which is definitely earlier than the mid 18th dynasty. The examples from Deir el-Bahri and Serabit el-Khadim are probably all 18th dynasty, but Ramessid specimens are known from other sites (*e.g.* Hayes 1959.384–6, fig. 242; Tosi & Roccati 1972 nos. 50064–5; PM 1.2.714). Simple Type B votive stelae, showing donors before statues of Min, occur as early as the 13th dynasty (*e.g.* Simpson 1974 pls. 25.2, 71.2; Malaise 1981.279–81). The earliest example from the six sites is the 17th dynasty stela from Gebel Zeit which depicts a nomarch of Koptos before statues of Min and Hathor (Castel & Soukiassian 1985.290–1, pl. 63). Type B votive stelae continued to be dedicated throughout the New Kingdom, as the examples from Serabit el-Khadim show (Figs. 8–9). The more elaborate Type C, which was introduced in the mid 18th dynasty, did not supersede Types A and B.

Summary

Type A stelae are exclusively votive. Types B and C also occur as funerary stelae. The Hathor stelae do not display any unique characteristics, but they do have some unusual features. One of these is the wide range of materials used for the Type A stelae and plaques. Stelae of Types B and C depicting other deities have been recovered from Deir el-Bahri, Mirgissa, Serabit el-Khadim, and Gebel Zeit, but all the Type A stelae and plaques from these sites show Hathor alone. Type A stelae and plaques rarely depict the full human form of the goddess. This suggests that they are objects of lower status than the more elaborate types of stelae. None of the forms of Hathor is unique to her, but the richness and complexity of her iconography has few parallels. This is reflected in the variety of forms on the stelae. All these forms should probably be interpreted as showing cult statues, cult objects, or sacred animals. Kings are frequently shown as deities or intermediaries on votive stelae from Deir el-Bahri. This may be because several rulers provided facilities for popular religion at this site (see 3.2.4; 3.4). The importance of statue cults in popular religion is very apparent from the stelae.

The only uncommon feature of the people who dedicated the Hathor stelae is the high proportion of female donors at Deir el-Bahri and Mirgissa. With the possible exception of the woman playing the tambourine (List 2.2), the actions performed are not unique to the cult of Hathor. None of the donors is shown presenting objects that correspond with the small votive offerings found at the six sites. In spite of the diversity of these sites, the inscriptions on the Hathor stelae show little variety. None of the formulae used is specific to Hathor, and the prayers are largely restricted to generalised requests that could be made to almost any deity. Although Hathor can be associated with burial and the afterlife, funerary prayers do not dominate the inscriptions. In the 18th dynasty it became acceptable to record prayers relating to the earthly life of a private individual even in the very formal context of a stela dedicated in a state temple. This could be seen either as a stage in the development of personal piety or as marking a change in the relationship between popular religion and the state cults (see further 3.4).

2.2 Textiles

A number of New Kingdom drawings and paintings on linen, described by Hall and Currelly as votive cloths (in Naville 1913.15–16, 30), were found in the vicinity of the 11th dynasty temple at Deir el-Bahri. The catalogue which follows includes all the votive textiles known to have been excavated at Deir el-Bahri and some cloths and shirts acquired in Luxor which most probably came from Deir el-Bahri. I have adopted the system devised by K. Parlasca (1966.153–4), and used by the *Topographical Bibliography* (II, 399–400), of classifying the textiles according to the form of Hathor shown on them.

2.2.1 Catalogue of votive Hathor textiles

Abbreviations

P   provenance
S   size (width × height, without fringes)
M   material
T   technique
B   type of borders
F   details of form of Hathor and her context
Do   donors
I   inscriptions
Da   date (see 2.1.1 for terms used)

Type 1 : Cloths and shirts showing Hathor in human form

1) Cloth: Boston MFA E42.8.1 (07.538); unpublished (Fig. 12)
    P   11th dynasty temple, Deir el-Bahri: EEF excavations
    S   30 × 16.5 cm (upper half only)
    M   Very coarse linen with looped fringe at top and one long knotted fringe
    T   Design painted in black, white, yellow and red
    B   3 red and yellow linear borders
    F   Holding a *wȝs* sceptre
    Do   1 woman (censing?)
    I   Name and title of Hathor, *ir n* formula
    Da   Mid 18th dynasty

2) Cloth: London BM 43216; Naville 1907.62; Hall and Currelly in Naville
    1913.15, pl. 31.4 (Pl. 15)
    P   11th dynasty temple, Deir el-Bahri: EEF excavations
    S   21 × 20 cm
    M   Coarse linen with looped fringe at top and one long and one short fringe
    T   Yellow background; design painted in black, white, red, blue, and green
    B   4 red and black linear borders
    F   Seated on a throne on a dais, holding an *ꜥnḫ* sign and a *wȝs* sceptre
    Do   A woman censing and libating
    I   Name and title of Hathor, *ir n* formula
    Da   Mid 18th dynasty

3) Sleeveless shirt: Boston MFA E52.28 (18040); de Rustafjaell 1909.51–2, pl. 26;
    (Pl. 17)
    P   Bought in Luxor
    S   28 × 23 cm

M   Coarse linen with long fringe on bottom
T   White background; design painted in black, red, blue, and yellow
B   3 black and red linear borders and a petal frieze
F   Seated on a throne holding and ꜥnḫ sign and a papyrus sceptre
Do   None shown, but 3 women named
I   Name and title of Hathor, ir n formula
Da   End of 18th dynasty

4) Cloth: London BM 65348; unpublished (Pl. 16a)

P   Luxor; bought from the Mond collection
S   33 × 18 cm
M   Fine linen with looped fringe at top and 1 long and 1 short fringe
T   White background; design painted in black, red, yellow, green, blue, and brown
B   3 linear borders – red and black; petal frieze at top
F   Seated on a throne, holding an ꜥnḫ sign and a wꜣs sceptre
Do   3 women, 1 libating (?), 1 offering papyrus, and 1 a basket of fruit
I   Name and titles of Hathor, ir n formula
Da   End of 18th dynasty

5) Cloth: Toronto ROM 910.16.1; Currelly in Naville 1913 pl. 31; Parlasca 1966.154, pl. 54.2 (Fig. 10a)

P   11th dynasty temple, Deir el-Bahri: EEF excavations
S   36 × 29 cm
M   Coarse linen. Looped fringe on top threaded with cord and 1 short fringe
T   White background; design painted in black, red, green, and blue
B   4 linear borders – red and black; petal frieze at top
F   Seated on a throne, holding an ꜥnḫ sign
Do   A priest holding a portable altar, a woman offering bunches of grapes, a boy offering grapes and papyrus, and a girl offering grapes
I   Name and titles of Hathor, ir n formula
Da   End of the 18th dynasty

6) Cloth: Location unknown; de Rustafjaell 1906.240, pl. 2; 1913.51, pl. 26 (Pl. 16b)

P   Ancient rubbish mound, Deir el-Bahri
S   60 × 30 cm
M   Linen with looped fringe on top, 1 short and 1 long side fringe
T   White background; design painted in several colours
B   3 linear borders; petal frieze surmounted by band of chequered pattern
F   Seated on a throne on a dais, holding an ꜥnḫ sign and a papyrus sceptre
Do   9 in 2 registers. Upper register: a priest playing a harp and 4 women carrying loaves and jars. Lower register: 3 priests and a boy offering papyrus
I   Names and titles of Hathor and of the donors
Da   End of the 18th dynasty

7) Cloth: Location unknown; de Rustafjaell 1913.52; not illustrated

   P   Ancient rubbish mound, Deir el-Bahri
   S   18 × 18 cm
   M   Linen
   T   Design painted
   B   ?
   F   Seated on a throne
   Do   A man and a woman offering
   I   ?
   Da   18th dynasty?

8) Cloth: Location unknown; de Rustafjaell 1913.52; not illustrated

   P   Ancient rubbish mound, Deir el-Bahri
   S   19 × 14 cm
   M   Linen
   T   Design painted
   B   ?
   F   Standing, holding a sceptre
   Do   None shown?
   I   'An inscription'
   Da   18th dynasty?

9) Sleeveless shirt: Berlin E 17606; Roeder 1924.340

   P   Bought in Luxor
   S   *c.* 18 × 20 (max) cm
   M   Very coarse linen with long fringe at bottom
   T   Design drawn in black
   B   None
   F   Seated in a chair
   Do   1 woman adoring
   I   Name and title of Hathor, *ir n* formula
   Da   Ramessid? (Drawing may be modern)

Type 2: Cloths showing Hathor in cow form

1) Cloth: Toronto ROM 910.16.4; unpublished (Pl. 26a)

   P   11th dynasty temple; Deir el-Bahri: EEF excavations
   S   32 × 21 cm
   M   Coarse linen, with 1 long, and 1 short fringe, and 3 rows of small blue beads woven into each end of the cloth
   T   Design drawn in black
   B   None
   F   Standing on baseline with a calf
   Do   None shown or named
   I   Name and title of Hathor in hieratic
   Da   Mid 18th dynasty

2)   Cloth: Location unknown: Currelly in Naville 1913 pl. 31.1 (Fig. 10b)

    P   11th dynasty temple, Deir el-Bahri: EEF excavations

    S   *c*. 30 × 10 cm

    M   Linen, with long knotted fringe at bottom and looped fringe at top (part only)

    T   Design drawn?

    B   None?

    F   Standing on baseline; wearing a menit-necklace

    Do   A woman censing and libating, and her female child offering a pot

    I   Partly in hieratic: royal names and titles, name and titles of Hathor

    Da   Mid 18th dynasty

3)   Cloth: Location unknown; Currelly in Naville 1913 pl. 31.2 (Fig. 11a)

    P   11th dynasty temple, Deir el-Bahri: EEF excavations

    S   *c*. 22 × 20 cm

    M   Linen with looped fringe at top, and 1 long and 1 short fringe

    T   Design painted?

    B   3 linear borders and a petal frieze

    F   Standing on a plinth; wearing a lotus necklace

    Do   8 in 2 registers. Upper register: a priest and 2 women offering papyrus. Lower register: 2 priests and 2 women offering papyrus, 1 woman offering a grape vine

    I   Name and titles of Hathor, *ir n* formula

    Da   Late or end of the 18th dynasty

4)   Cloth: Location unknown; Currelly in Naville 1913 pl. 30.2 (Fig. 11.b)

    P   11th dynasty temple; Deir el-Bahri: EEF excavations

    S   *c*. 30 × 20 cm

    M   Linen. No fringes shown – cloth incomplete?

    T   Design painted?

    B   None?

    F   Forequarters projecting from a shrine in a bark on a pool. A figure of a king standing beneath the cow's chin, another kneeling at the rear of the shrine

    Do   A woman holding a portable altar or censer, a priest offering papyrus, 1 woman offering a loaf, and 1 woman offering papyrus (?)

    I   Epithets of Hathor?

    Da   Late or end of the 18th dynasty

5)   Cloth: Location unknown; Hall in Burlington Cat. 1922.39; Oppenheimer Cat. 1936.15; not illustrated

    P   Deir el-Bahri: EEF excavations?

    S   80 × 19 cm

    M   Linen 'with fringe'

    T   White background; design painted in black, red, blue, and yellow

    Do   10 women 'worshipping the cow of Hathor with clapping and cymbals'

I   Name and title of Hathor, names of donors
Da   Late or end of the 18th dynasty?

6)   Cloth: Location unknown; de Rustafjaell 1913.51; not illustrated
P   Ancient rubbish mound, Deir el-Bahri
S   55 × 28 cm
M   2 pieces of linen, joined in the centre
T   Design painted
B   ?
F   The head and shoulders projecting from a canopied shrine
Do   On the left, a man, a woman, and a child adoring. On the right, upper register – a man, a woman, and a child adoring; lower register – a man and 3 women offering
I   '... remains of an inscription'
Da   Late or end of the 18th dynasty?

7)   Cloth: London V&A 468.1906; Wace 1927.29 (Pl. 18a)
P   11th dynasty temple, Deir el-Bahri: EEF excavations
S   30 × 25 cm (central portion only)
M   Linen, no fringes preserved
T   White background; design painted in black, red, pink, blue, and green.
B   Petal frieze at top, other edges not preserved
F   Standing in a canopied shrine
Do   1 priest censing
I   Name of Hathor; *ir n* formula (mainly illegible)
Da   End of the 18th dynasty?

Type 3: Cloths and shirts showing Hathor in cow form in the context of the Western Mountain

1)   Cloth: Toronto ROM 910.16.5; Currelly in Naville 1913 pl. 30.1 (Pl. 21a)
P   11th dynasty temple, Deir el-Bahri: EEF excavations
S   36 × 29 cm (only one end preserved)
M   Coarse linen with looped fringe at top threaded with cord
T   White background; design painted in black, red, pink, blue, and green
B   3 broad red and black linear borders, and a petal frieze
F   Head projecting from mountainside; papyrus umbel behind. In front of Hathor a stela with a 'cow and mountain' motif, flanked by 2 'Osirid' statues
Do   1 woman holding a portable altar
I   Name and titles of Hathor, *ir n* formula
Da   Late or end of the 18th dynasty

2)   Cloth: Toronto ROM 910.16.3; Parlasca 1966.153–54, pl.155.1
P   11th dynasty temple, Deir el-Bahri: EEF excavations
S   46 × 24 cm

M   Fine linen with looped fringe at top and 1 long fringe
T   White background; design painted in black, red, blue, and green
B   3 red and black linear borders, and a petal frieze
F   Forequarters projecting from mountainside, with a papyrus thicket behind
Do   A priest holding a portable altar, a woman and a second priest offering
     papyrus, a second woman offering a grape vine, a third woman adoring.
I   Name and title of Hathor, *ir n* formula
Da   Late or end of the 18th dynasty

3)   Cloth: Berlin E 17578; Scharff 1923.30, pl. 31; Capart 1942.44, pl. 59.

P   Deir el-Bahri
S   *c.* 78 × 40 cm
M   Fine linen with looped fringe at top, and 1 long fringe
T   White background; design painted in black, red, blue, green, and yellow
B   4 red and black linear borders, and petal frieze
F   Head and shoulders projecting from mountainside, with grape-vine behind
Do   1 woman censing and libating, and a second offering papyrus
I   Name and titles of Hathor, 2 *ir n* formulae
Da   Late or end of the 18th dynasty

4)   Short-sleeved shirt: Boston MFA 52.29 (18041); de Rustafjaell 1909.51–2,
     pl. 26 (Pl. 19)

P   Bought in Luxor
S   33 × 25 cm (without sleeves)
M   Coarse linen
T   White background; design painted in red, black, blue, and yellow
B   Black and red bands on sleeves, floral collar
F   Head and shoulders projecting from mountainside
Do   1 woman holding a portable altar or censer
I   Name and title of Hathor, *ir n* formula (partly illegible)
Da   Late or end of the 18th dynasty?

5)   Cloth: London BM 43215; Naville 1907.62; Hall in Naville 1913.15 (Pl. 18b)

P   11th dynasty temple, Deir el-Bahri: EEF excavations
S   49 × 19–22 cm (one end missing)
M   Coarse linen with looped fringe at top
T   White background; design painted in black, red, pink, blue, green, and
     yellow
B   3 red and black linear borders
F   Forequarters projecting from mountainside, with papyrus thicket behind
Do   6 women offering papyrus
I   Name and titles of Hathor, names of donors
Da   End of the 18th or early 19th dynasty

6)   Long-sleeved shirt: London BM 43071; unpublished (Pl. 20)

P   Bought in Luxor
S   35 × 20 cm

M   Coarse linen
T   White background; design painted in black, yellow, red, blue, and green
B   Single green line
F   Cow, wearing sistrum-necklace, standing in front (?) of the mountain
Do   None shown, 1 woman named
I   Name and titles of Hathor (twice), *ir n* formula
Da   19th dynasty?

Type 4: Cloths showing Hathor in cow form in the context of a papyrus thicket

1)   Cloth: London BM 47805; Hall in Naville 1913.16 (Pl. 23)

P   11th dynasty temple, Deir el-Bahri: EEF excavations
S   19 × 19 cm (one end missing)
M   Coarse linen, no surviving fringes
T   White background; design painted in black, red, brown, green, blue,
      and yellow
B   3 red and blue linear borders
F   Standing in a bark on a sled in a papyrus thicket
Do   1 woman censing and libating
I   Name and titles of Hathor, *ir n* formula (name lost)
Da   Mid 18th dynasty

2)   Cloth: Berlin E 17579; unpublished (Pl. 22a)

P   11th dynasty temple, Deir el-Bahri; EEF excavations
S   —
M   Linen, with looped fringe at top, and 1 long fringe
T   White background; design painted in black, red, blue, green, and yellow
B   4 black linear borders
F   Standing among papyrus in a bark, with a grape vine above
Do   1 man censing and offering a bouquet, a woman offering grapes
I   Name and titles of Hathor, 2 *ir n* formulae
Da   Mid 18th dynasty

3)   Cloth: New York MMA 07.230.23; Hayes 1959.167 (Pl. 22b)

P   11th dynasty temple, Deir el-Bahri: EEF excavations
S   25 × 14 cm
M   Coarse linen with 1 short fringe, and 1 long knotted fringe
T   Design painted in black, white, red, blue, and green
B   4 red, white, and black linear borders
F   Standing in a bark on a pedestal in a papyrus thicket
Do   A woman censing and libating, and 2 other women
I   Name and titles of Hathor, *ir n* formula
Da   Mid 18th dynasty

4)   Cloth: Location unknown; de Rustafjaell 1906.242, fig. 3; 1913.51

P   Ancient rubbish mound, Deir el-Bahri
S   50 × 27 (max) cm

M   Linen with 1 long and 1 short fringe
T   White background; design painted in several colours
B   4 linear borders
F   Standing in canopied bark-shrine in a papyrus thicket
Do   7 in all. A priest censing and libating, a woman carrying a jar (?), and a priest offering (grapes?). Behind them: upper register, a priest and a woman offering papyrus; lower register, 2 women carrying jars (and loaves?)
I   Name and title of Hathor, names of donors (mainly illegible on photograph)
Da   Late or end of the 18th dynasty

5)   Cloth: Toronto ROM 910.16.2; Currelly in Naville 1913 pl. 30.3 (Pl. 24)
   P   11th dynasty temple, Deir el-Bahri: EEF excavations
   S   31 × 20 cm. (Only one end preserved)
   M   Coarse linen with 1 long fringe
   T   White background; design painted in black, red, yellow, green, and blue
   B   Petal frieze, surmounted by patterned band (very faded). Other edges not preserved
   F   Standing in a bark on a pedestal in a papyrus thicket
   Do   A priest holding a portable altar or censer, foot of a second donor
   I   A few traces of name and title of Hathor
   Da   Late or end of the 18th dynasty

6)   Cloth: Location unknown; de Rustafjaell 1913.52, not illustrated
   P   Ancient rubbish mound, Deir el-Bahri
   S   28 × 21 cm
   M   Linen
   T   Design painted
   B   ?
   F   Standing in a papyrus thicket
   Do   'Several', arranged in two registers
   I   ?
   Da   Late or end of the 18th dynasty

7)   Cloth: Toronto ROM 910.16.6; unpublished (Pl. 21b)
   P   11th dynasty temple, Deir el-Bahri: EEF excavations
   S   31 × 20 cm
   M   Coarse linen with looped fringe at top and 1 long fringe
   T   White background; design painted in black, red, blue, green, and yellow
   B   2 red and black linear borders, and petal frieze surmounted by grape-vine pattern
   F   Standing on plinth (?) in a papyrus thicket
   Do   1 woman censing (and libating?), a priest and a woman offering.
   I   Name and title of Hathor, *ir n* formula (mainly illegible).
   Da   End of the 18th dynasty.

8) Cloth: St Petersburg, Hermitage 2400; Golénischeff 1891.352–3; Parlasca
    1966.154, pl. 55.2 (Pl. 25a)

    P   Bought in Luxor in 1860
    S   44 × 27 cm
    M   Fine linen with 1 long side fringe
    T   Yellow background; design painted in black, red, pink, yellow, brown,
         blue, and green
    B   4 red and black linear borders
    F   Standing on a plinth on a sled in a papyrus thicket
    Do   1 woman censing
    I   Title of Hathor, invocation of Hathor, and prayer for donor
    Da   End of the 18th dynasty

9) Cloth: Huntington, Long Island HM 59.294; de Rustafjaell 1906.241, fig. 1;
    1909.47–50, pl. 25; 1913.50, pl. 39; Naville 1907.61 (Pl. 25b)

    P   Ancient rubbish mound, Deir el-Bahri
    S   55 × 30 cm
    M   Fine linen with 1 looped fringe at top threaded with cord, and 1 long side
         fringe
    T   White background; design painted in black, red, brown, yellow, green,
         and blue
    B   Single black line, and petal frieze
    F   Standing in a canopied bark on a plinth in a papyrus thicket with a figure
         of Nebhepetreᶜ Mentuhotpe under the chin, (and another suckling ?)
    Do   A priest adoring, a woman carrying papyrus and a jar, and 3 priests and 2
         women carrying papyrus and grapes
    I   Name and titles of Hathor, royal name and titles, invocation formula, and
         prayer for donor(s)
    Da   End of the 18th dynasty

10) Cloth: Brussels MR E2541 (cannot now be located); Speelers 1923.46; not
    illustrated

    P   11th dynasty temple, Deir el-Bahri: EEF excavations
    S   25 × 20 cm
    M   Linen
    T   Design painted
    B   ?
    F   Standing in a bark in a papyrus thicket
    Do   1 woman censing
    I   Name and title of Hathor, *ir n* formula
    Da   18th dynasty

11) Cloth: Location unknown; de Rustafjaell 1913.52; not illustrated

    P   Ancient rubbish mound, Deir el-Bahri
    S   28 × 30 cm
    M   Linen

T   Design painted
B   ?
F   Standing in a papyrus thicket
Do   A woman offering
I   Name of donor
Da   18th dynasty?

Type 5 : Cloths and shirts on which more than one form of Hathor is shown

1)   Cloth: Location unknown; de Rustafjaell 1913.51, not illustrated
     P   Ancient rubbish mound, Deir el-Bahri
     S   35 × 30 cm
     M   Linen
     T   Design painted
     B   ?
     F   Hathor in human form, seated, and in cow form standing in a papyrus
          thicket
     Do   A man and a woman offering
     I   ?
     Da   Late or end of the 18th dynasty?

2)   Short-sleeved shirt: Berlin SM 17568; Roeder 1924.340 (Pl. 14b)
     P   Deir el-Bahri
     S   c. 18 × 16 cm (without sleeves)
     M   Linen
     T   White background; design painted in black, red, blue, green, and yellow
     B   Linear border on 3 sides, petal frieze across shoulders and sleeves, and
          floral collar
     F   Hathor in cow form standing in papyrus thicket, and in Hathor-mask form
     Do   1 woman kneeling to adore
     I   Name and title of Hathor, *ir n* formula
     Da   End of the 18th or early 19th dynasty

2.2.2 Provenance

Unpainted votive textiles have recently been excavated at Gebel Zeit (Posener-Kriéger 1985.298, pl. 65; 1986.381). Some were discovered *in situ* in a deposit of votive offerings within the enclosure wall of the New Kingdom Hathor shrine (Castel & Soukiassian 1989a pl. 60). The provenance of the Gebel Zeit textiles is not in doubt, but Parlasca suggested that the Hathor cloths published in the first and third volumes of *The XIth Dynasty Temple at Deir el-Bahri* were bought rather than excavated and that they came not from a Hathor shrine but from tombs (1966.155). His reasons for classifying these cloths as funerary are discussed in 2.2.8, but the provenance of the Deir el-Bahri votive textiles must be examined in detail before further comment can be made on them.

No votive textiles are mentioned in the reports, exhibition catalogues, or distribution lists for the excavations of 1903–4 and 1904–5 at the 11th dynasty temple. However, in the preliminary report for the season of 1905–6, Hall and Naville wrote that:–

> Of the smaller objects, a number of XVIIIth Dynasty scarabs were found in the tomb-dromos (?) at the western end of the temple and in the southern court a fine earthenware vase with the rope-network by which it was suspended from the roof still perfect. The votive cloths with representations of the worship of Hathor are also a notable find. (1907.6)

This fails to make clear whether the cloths were found in the south court, or in the west peristyle court which contains the tomb-dromos (Plan 2). Votive textiles were included in the exhibitions of finds from Deir el-Bahri held in 1906 and 1907 (EEF Cat. [1906].18; 1907.13) and in the distribution lists for both these years. This raises the possibility that some textiles were discovered in the hypostyle hall, the cella, or the speos (Plan 2), all of which were excavated in the season of 1906–7. No further information on the exact provenance of the votive textiles is available in the excavation records.

In the first volume of the full excavation report, Naville wrote that:–

> We have found several specimens of cloth on which Hathor is seen issuing from her sanctuary and coming down to the river among the papyrus plants. Most of those found are in a bad state and the drawing is hardly recognisable, except one or two quite good ones. (1907.61)

He went on to specify that 'the two good cloths mentioned as found by us are in the British Museum, Nos. 43215, 43216' (1907.61; Cat. 3.5; 1.2). In the third volume of the full excavation report, both Hall and Currelly briefly discussed the votive textiles, and seven were illustrated in line drawings by Currelly (in Naville 1913.15–6, 30, pls. 30–1 = Figs. 10–11).

Hall noted that:–

> Some fine specimens of these votive cloths seem to have been found here by natives in past years. Those found during the course of the present excavations are of a smaller type, on which only the cow and the devoter appear, often the cow alone. (in Naville 1913.15)

The only cloths which Hall described in detail were the two already mentioned by Naville and London BM 47805 (Cat. 4.1). Currelly commented that:–

> I illustrate a class of votive offering which, I believe, has … been found only near this temple, viz., the painted picture on linen cloth … The subject is always a votive scene, where a man, usually accompanied by his wife and family, makes an offering to Hathor. The goddess is usually represented in her cow form, sometimes in a boat, sometimes just appearing from the Deir el-Bahari cliff. In a few examples she is represented in her human form. (in Naville 1913.30)

Both Naville and Hall stated unequivocally that they had found votive textiles during their excavations and there is no reason to disbelieve them. Their vagueness about the exact provenance of the Hathor textiles is of little significance, because they were equally vague about the provenance of most types of votive object (1.1.3.1). However, a comparison of the textiles distributed by the EEF with the accounts given in the excavation reports does raise some queries.

Naville's use of the phrase 'several specimens' (1907.61) implied that only a few textiles had been discovered, but 18 are listed as distributed by the EEF. The more important finds were despatched individually, sometimes direct from Egypt, and not always recorded in the distribution register. In a transaction not recorded in the EEF archives, a votive cloth (Cat. 4.2) was sent to Berlin; this suggests that 18 must only be taken as a minimum number. Seven of the 18 cloths are intact (Cat. 1.2, 5; 2.3; 3.2; 4.2–3), and on all but one (4.3) the paintwork is well preserved. This does not agree with Naville's remark that only two 'quite good ones' were found (1907.61), but since he was writing before the final season of excavations, it could be assumed that most of the 'good' cloths were found in the rear part of the 11th dynasty temple during the winter of 1906–7.

More puzzling is the discrepancy between the descriptions of the cloths given by Hall and by Currelly. Hall's comments that the cloths found during the excavations were small and simple, showing the Hathor cow and a single donor, or the cow alone, are not supported by the examples illustrated by Currelly. Of the textiles distributed by the EEF, just three have a single donor (Cat. 1.1–2; 4.1) and only one depicts a cow alone (Cat. 2.1). It is also curious that Hall mentioned only the three cloths in the British Museum (Cat. 1.2; 3.5; 4.1), when larger, more complex, and better preserved cloths – such as the outstanding example allocated to the Oppenheimer Collection (2.5) – had been distributed by the EEF. Currelly's description does fit both the examples illustrated by him and the range of cloths distributed, but it should be noted that he never claimed specifically to be describing textiles excavated by the EEF.

There are two possible explanations for these discrepancies. The first assumes simple carelessness. Hall wrote his report on the small votive objects some years after excavations at Deir el-Bahri had ended. His memory of the range of cloths found may have been at fault, especially as he was at the site for only three weeks during the final season (Naville 1907a.177). In 1913, Hall was working at the British Museum and Currelly at the Royal Ontario Museum, Toronto; so they may not have had any opportunity to compare notes. Hall stated that he had illustrated his chapter 'chiefly from the objects in the British Museum and Oxford' (in Naville 1913.21, n.1). This would explain why he described only the three cloths in the British Museum. The Royal Ontario Museum had received six of the finest cloths from Deir el-Bahri (Cat. 1.5; 2.1; 3.1–2; 4.5, 7), so Currelly had a wider range of votive textiles to draw on.

The second explanation is that some of the textiles distributed by the EEF were bought locally rather than excavated, and that in their reports Naville and Hall restricted themselves to describing cloths which had actually been discovered by them. Of relevance here is Hall's remark that 'some fine specimens' had been found at Deir el-Bahri 'by natives in years past' (in Naville 1913.15). He went on to note that these cloths were in the collection of an R. de Rustafjaell. Naville had already described a cloth showing a priest and his family worshipping Hathor and Nebhepetreᶜ Mentuhotpe (Cat. 4.9) that was 'evidently found in the neighbourhood of this temple' and which belonged to de Rustafjaell (1907.61). This cloth was published by de Rustafjaell in his book *The Light of Egypt*

(1909.47–52, pl. 25 = Pl. 25b) and, with two other cloths (Cat. 1.6; 4.4), in an article in *The Connoisseur* (1906.241–3, figs. 1–3). He claimed that these textiles came from the 11th dynasty temple at Deir el-Bahri (1906.242). This claim is supported by the fact that two of the cloths (Cat. 1.6; 4.9) were dedicated by a man named Tjanefer, who is known from inscriptions on stelae found at Deir el-Bahri to have been a priest of Hathor, Nebhepetre' Mentuhotpe, and Amon-Re' in Akh-isut (Naville 1907.61; Hall 1925.237). The 1913 sale catalogue of the de Rustafjaell collection lists these three cloths and six other textiles (Cat. 1.7–8; 2.6; 4.6, 12; 5.1) as 'found in a mound of debris on the site of the Temple of Hathor at Thebes' (de Rustafjaell Cat. 1913.50–1).

Hall's reference to 'past years' gave the impression that the textiles belonging to de Rustafjaell had been found some time before the excavation of the 11th dynasty temple, but de Rustafjaell himself stated that he 'came across' the cloths in Thebes in the summer of 1905 (1906.242). It seems likely that the 'natives' who found this group of cloths were Naville's own workmen, doing some illicit digging on the site of the 11th dynasty temple between seasons. The fact that one of the cloths distributed by the EEF and published by Currelly (Cat. 1.5) was dedicated by the priest Tjanefer strongly suggests that it came from the same place as the two cloths of this man in the de Rustafjaell collection (Cat. 1.6; 4.9). This could have happened if Naville had found out about the illicit digging and managed to recover a few specimens from the 'natives'. Alternatively, in the course of his excavations Naville may have discovered more cloths close to the spot where the illicit digging had taken place.

In 1906, de Rustafjaell bought in Luxor two linen shirts decorated with paintings of Hathor (1909.52; Cat. 1.3; 3.4). On one of the shirts, Hathor is given the epithet Lady of Djeser (Pl. 17), which on an 18th dynasty object is a firm indication that the piece comes from Deir el-Bahri. The same year in Luxor, the British Museum acquired a shirt with a painting of a Hathor cow (Cat. 3.6), and the Berlin Museum bought a cloth and a shirt both decorated with Hathor cows (Cat. 3.3; 5.2). All these textiles were said to come from Deir el-Bahri. It is possible either that Naville's workmen had kept back some of their finds of 1905 to sell at a later date, or that they found a second, smaller group of textiles during illicit digging in the summer of 1906.

A cloth now in St Petersburg (Cat. 4.8) was bought in Luxor in 1860, which suggests that it could have come from the speos or cella of the 11th dynasty temple, which were partially excavated by Graham and Dufferin between 1858 and 1860 (1.1.1). Another possible provenance would be the temple of Djeser-Djeseru, which Mariette began to clear in 1858 (1.1.1). Although there is only direct evidence for votive textiles from Akh-isut, they were probably offered in the other temples at Deir el-Bahri too. Any cloths found in the west (peristyle) court of the 11th dynasty temple could have been thrown there from the adjacent Hathor shrine of Djeser-Akhet (Plan 2). No textiles seem to have been recovered from the dumps of votive material (1.1.3.1–3), which may mean that, like stelae and statues, the votive textiles stayed in the shrines long after the small 18th dynasty offerings had been removed.

2.2.3 Size, material, technique and borders

One of the votive cloths is square (Cat. 1.7). Most of the others are rectangular. In contrast to the votive stelae, nearly all the cloths are wider than they are tall, some considerably so (Cat. 1.6; 2.2, 5; 3.3). The width of the cloths varies from 18 to 80 cm. A few of the cloths taper towards one end (Cat. 3.1–2, 5; 4.4, 9), but this is might be due to faulty weaving. The shirts (Cat. 1.3, 9; 3.4, 6; 5.2) range in height from 17.5 to 35 cm. The smallest of them would have to be regarded as baby clothes (de Rustafjaell 1909.51), or as miniatures, analogous perhaps to the model vases found in some tombs or to the model tools placed in foundation deposits. All the shirts consist of a doubled-over rectangle of cloth, hemmed at the bottom, partly sewn up at the sides, and given a 'key-hole' neck opening with drawstring ties. Two of the shirts are sleeveless (Pl. 17; Cat 1.9), two have elbow length sleeves (Pls. 14b, 19), and one has long narrow sleeves with drawstrings at the wrists (Pl. 20). The construction of these garments is identical to that of surviving full-size New Kingdom shirts (e.g. Hayes 1959.187, fig. 103; R. Hall 1986.36–7).

All the cloths and shirts are made of coarse to medium quality undyed linen of the standard 'tabby' weave (Walton & Eastwood 1983.12). This differentiates the votive textiles from the painted funerary cloths from Deir el-Medina (2.2.8), which tend to be made of fine linen of the quality often used to wrap mummies (e.g. Parlasca 1966 pl. 54.1). None of the votive textiles seems to have had any 'linen marks'. All the cloths appear to have been specially woven, rather than adapted from other uses or cut from rolls of linen. The shirts are all in coarser grades of linen than normally seem to have been used to make garments for Egyptians of the 'middle' and 'upper' classes. Garments are turned 'right way out' after they are finished, but two of the shirts are painted on the 'wrong side' (Cat.3.4, 5.2). This suggests that they were specially made to be painted and were never worn (but see 2.2.8).

One of the votive cloths (Cat. 2.1) is unusual for two reasons. First, it is taller than it is wide and the design is parallel to the sides of the cloth (Pl. 26a). Second, it has three evenly spaced, vertical rows of blue faience ring beads woven into the cloth on either side of the image of a Hathor cow. Beads of this type were used to string menit necklaces and thousands were found among the votive offerings at Deir el-Bahri (2.9.1–2). A rectangular piece of linen from Deir el-Bahri (London V&A 1907.730) also has beads woven into the fabric (Pl. 26b). One end of the cloth is missing. It is now about 35 × 25 cm. The cloth is of 'tabby' weave, except for an openwork panel in the centre which consists only of 'ends'. This piece never seems to have had a drawn or painted design. On the right (as seen from the front) side of the cloth there are four vertical columns of blue ring beads, while on the left side two columns of beads survive. Another fragment of linen (London V&A 1907.729), which measures 10 × 18 cm, has a double horizontal row of faience ring beads. Below this a single horizontal row of beads, mainly of blue faience but including two made of amethyst (Pl. 27b). 'Lady of Amethyst' is one of Hathor's epithets (Allam 1963.80–1). Two small pieces of cloth woven with faience beads were illustrated by Hall (in Naville 1913 pl. 27.6). Similar cloth fragments with beads from these excavations are now in the University Museum, Kyoto (Kyoto 579), and the Pitt-Rivers Museum, Oxford (PR 1904.35.84 = Pl. 27a).

Though beadwork nets were worn over dresses (Riefstahl 1944.14; R. Hall 1986.64–5), ancient Egyptian textiles with beads woven into the fabric are extremely rare (Eastwood 1983 pers. comm.). Significantly, the closest comparative material comes from Gebel Zeit, where small pieces of coarse linen cloth were used to wrap the pottery fertility figurines found in or near the Hathor shrines (Castel & Soukiassian 1985 pl. 60; Castel & Soukiassian 1985a.164; Posener-Kriéger 1985.298, pl. 65; 2.6.1.2–3).

> Die Statuetten waren in eine Art Mantel eingewickelt: ein quadratisches oder rechteckiges Leinentuch, das mit farbigen Wollfäden oder Perlenreihen geschmückt ist und an deren Fransen Perlen, Amulete und Skarabäen befestigt sind. (Castel *et al.* 1985.19)

All the votive cloths have one or more fringes, though none has them on all four sides. On 15 specimens the starting border (top edge) is finished with a long fringe which has been looped over and sewn down. In three cases, parts of a cord threaded through this fringe survive (Cat. 1.5; 3.1; 4.9). All the cloths with looped fringes probably had such cords originally. The top few rows of these cloths are woven with additional threads, presumably to strengthen them to take the strain of suspension from a cord (Eastwood pers. comm. 1983). Two of the shirts have a long warp fringe at the bottom (Cat. 1.3, 9), a feature also found on some full-size New Kingdom shirts (Hayes 1959.187). Three of the cloths, one with a short unlooped fringe at the top (Cat. 3.3), and two whose other edges are missing (Cat. 2.2; 3.5), have long fringes at the bottom. Of the remaining cloths for which information is available, three have a looped fringe at the top, one long and one short side fringe and a selvedge at the bottom (Cat. 1.4, 6; 2.3); six have a looped fringe at the top, one long side fringe and two selvedges (Cat. 1.5; 3.2–3; 4.2, 4, 9); and one has a long side fringe and two selvedges (Cat. 4.8).

The cloth with six rows of beads has a badly preserved loop fringe on the starting border, a long fringe at the bottom, a short side fringe, and a selvedge from which several uneven loops threaded with faience beads hang down (Pl. 26a). The fragment of cloth in the Pitt-Rivers Museum (Pl. 27a) and London V&A 1907.729 (Pl. 27b) have blue faience beads threaded on their knotted fringes. London V&A 1907.730 has one plain short fringe, and a long fringe threaded with faience ring beads and reed 'packet beads' (Pl. 26b) of a type found strung to make votive necklaces at Deir el-Bahri (Pl. 57c; 2.9.1). The cloth now in Kyoto (UM 579) is also decorated with 'packet beads'. The only cloth from Gebel Zeit so far illustrated (Posener-Kriéger 1985 pl. 65), has a long fringe decorated with ring and cylinder beads.

On one shirt (Cat. 1.9), and one cloth (Cat. 2.1), a design without a border has been drawn in black with a reed pen directly on to the linen. Some parts of these designs were blocked in in black, but no colours were added. The same technique was used on two Ramessid funerary cloths from Deir el-Medina (Bruyère 1930.86–7, fig. 41.1; 1939.227, fig. 116), and on shrouds of the Third Intermediate Period (Parlasca 1966.155–7; Abdalla 1988 pls. 21–3). The crudity of the design on the shirt, the fact that Hathor holds nothing in her hands and is seated on a chair not a throne, and the placing of her nipples as if the torso is shown from the front, all suggest that the drawing could be a modern forgery. However, the hieroglyphic inscription seems authentic, and the shirt is certainly ancient. There is no reason to doubt the authenticity of the cloth (Pl. 26a), especially as its drawing is accompanied by an hieratic inscription. The absence of borders, and the presence of hieratic characters in the inscription of a cloth of unknown location illustrated by Currelly (Fig. 10b), suggest that its design was drawn rather than painted.

On one cloth (Cat. 1.1), the design was drawn in outline directly on the surface of the linen and then partly filled in with white, red, and yellow paint (Fig. 12). A comparable technique occurs on a fragmentary leather hanging from Deir el-Bahri (Pl. 54; 2.7.2). On the remaining votive textiles for which detailed information is available, the technique is the same as that employed on most wooden stelae. First, the front of the cloth or shirt was given a thin coat of gesso, yellow in two cases (Cat. 1.2; 4.8), and white in the rest, which stiffened the linen and provided a smooth surface. The design was drawn in black, or partly in black, partly in red, and then painted in a minimum of four colours; after which the outlines were retouched. On most of the votive textiles, blocks of bright colour are used and the effect resembles that of a painted stela. On a few specimens (*e.g.* Pls. 16a, 18a–b, 25a–b), the wider range of colours and more subtle brushwork is reminiscent of the type of painting found on good quality funerary papyri. Only three of the cloths (Pls. 18a, 25a–b), and one of the shirts (Pl. 14b), represent high quality workmanship. The funerary cloths from Deir el-Medina tend to be better painted than the votive textiles from Deir el-Bahri.

On all the painted Hathor cloths, and on most of the painted funerary cloths, the design is delimited by a rectangular, linear border. This border usually consists of three thick lines, of which the innermost is a different colour from the outer two. Red and black on a white background is the most common combination, but red and blue (Cat. 4.1) and red and yellow (Cat. 1.1) also occur. I know of only one stela with a border of this type – a 20th dynasty false-door stela (Ranke 1951 fig. 25) – but they do occur on New Kingdom painted wooden boxes (Baker 1966.122, 146, figs. 169, 225, pl. 9; Bresciani 1975.55, pl. 30); on a painted wooden table top (Baker 1966.154, fig. 239), and on paintings of Tutankhamon with various deities mounted on a box made of papyrus pith (1966.100–1, fig. 127). This type of border seems to represent the inlaid strips, or 'stringing,' common on New Kingdom Egyptian furniture.

On ten cloths, the top border is surmounted or replaced by a lotus-petal frieze (Cat. 1.3–6; 2.3; 3.1–3; 4.5, 7, 9). The lotus petals can be blue, white, or white with a blue spot. Two of the cloths have a band of black and white checks above the lotus-petal frieze (Cat. 1.6; 4.7). The same may have been true of a third cloth which is badly faded (Cat. 4.5). The lotus-petal frieze might be considered analogous to a *kheker* frieze, but it seems mainly to have been employed on furniture (Baker 1966.91, 87, 103, 130, 137, pl. 9). It is also used to decorate the cornice of a Hathor shrine at Deir el-Bahri depicted in a tomb painting dating to the end of the 18th dynasty (Davies 1933.65–6, pl. 54). The combination of lotus-petal frieze and check pattern is found as a top border to scenes on a painted chest of Tutankhamon (Edwards 1972 no. 21), and as a decorative motif on several alabaster vessels from this king's tomb (Desroches Noblecourt 1963 pls. 24, 40a; 42;

Edwards 1972 nos. 4–5). The check pattern border may be derived from furniture inlays in ivory and ebony.

The shirts have a variety of borders. On the long-sleeved shirt (Cat. 3.6), the painted scene is edged on three sides by a single green line, and by a single black line at the bottom. Similar single, coloured lines are the usual form of border for most stelae. Two of the shirts (Cat. 1.3; 5.2) have three black and red linear borders and a lotus-petal frieze at the top which, on the example with short sleeves, extends to the end of each sleeve (Pl. 14b). On both these shirts an elaborate floral collar is painted round the neck-opening, below the frieze (pls. 14b, 17). Another shirt (Cat. 3.4), which is not so well preserved, appears to have no borders but is painted with a floral collar. Collars of this type, in real flowers or faience imitations, were characteristic of the latter part of the 18th dynasty (Hayes 1959.319–22, figs. 202–3). Their incorporation into the designs on the shirts might be compared with the very elaborate decoration of the neckline of Tutankhamon's 'dalmatic' (Desroches Noblecourt 1963.270, fig. 172; R. Hall 1986.41–3).

2.2.4 Form of deity

Hathor appears on all the painted cloths from Deir el-Bahri which I have been able to trace, but this type of offering may not have been unique to the goddess. Hall wrote that on some of the cloths found 'in years past':–

> We see the devotees represented, sometimes with their families, offering to the Holy Cow or to the solitary figure of the deified king [Nebhepetreᶜ Mentuhotpe], sometimes to both. (in Naville 1913.15)

None of the published cloths from the de Rustafjaell Collection is dedicated to Nebhepetreᶜ Mentuhotpe alone, but one of them does depict a statue group of Hathor in cow form with this king (Cat. 4.9, Pl. 25b). This demonstrates that there were cloths celebrating a joint cult of Hathor and the founder of the 11th dynasty temple. The five votive shirts, which probably come from Deir el-Bahri, are all dedicated solely to Hathor and no examples from other sites are known.

If the method used for dividing the votive stelae (2.1) is applied to the textiles, 2 cloths and 2 shirts can be classified as Type A (only deity shown), 22 cloths and 3 shirts are Type B (deity and donor in single register), and 5 cloths are Type C (deity with donors on more than one register). If Hall was correct in claiming that the cloths excavated by the EEF often showed a 'cow alone' (in Naville 1913.15), the original proportion of Type A cloths must have been higher. For reasons which will become apparent, this method of classification is not as suitable for the votive textiles as it is for the votive stelae. This is why I mainly use Parlasca's system, which is based on the iconography of the goddess. Hathor is represented in her human form on 8 cloths and 2 shirts, and in her cow form on 22 cloths and 3 shirts; so the cow form is even more dominant than it is on the votive stelae from Deir el-Bahri (2.1.3).

Type 1 (Figs. 10a, 12; Pls. 15–17)

Seven cloths and two shirts show Hathor in her standard human form, wearing the disc and horns headdress. On the cloths for which colour information is available, her dress and the sun disc are red, and the horns are blue. Her hair may be black or blue, and is sometimes bound with red ribbons, while her jewellery is usually green. On one of these textiles the goddess is standing (Cat. 1.8), but on the remainder she is seated on a throne, normally on a dais. In these cases it is difficult to tell whether a statue is intended. As on all the stelae from the six sites which show Hathor in human form, the goddess is not given any kind of background. There is nothing unusual about these portrayals and they resemble closely those found on painted stelae.

Type 2 (Figs. 10b, 11a-b; Pls. 18a, 26a)

On seven cloths Hathor is shown in cow form in no specific location (for the iconography of the cows on the textiles of Types 3–5 see 2.4.3.2). The Type 2 cloths do not form a very cohesive group and this is a weakness in Parlasca's classification. On two of the cloths (Cat. 2.1–2), the Hathor cow stands on a baseline with a table of offerings in front of her. On one, the cow has a calf with its own baseline (Pl. 26a; see further 2.4.5; 2.4.7). On two of these cloths (Cat. 2.3, 5), the cow stands on a tall plinth, so these can probably be classed as representations of statues. The same is true of three other Type 2 cloths on which the Hathor cow is depicted 'in' an elaborate shrine (Cat. 2.4, 6–7).

On one of the latter, the shrine has a lotus column and is hung with red fabric patterned in blue and yellow (Pl. 18a). Only the central part of this cloth survives, and there may originally have been a papyrus thicket behind the shrine, since similar shrines are shown on two Type 4 cloths (Cat. 4.4, 9). The 'tent or shrine' shown on a cloth from the de Rustafjaell Collection (Cat. 2.6) was presumably of the same kind. On this cloth, only the head and shoulders of the cow were painted, a practice usually restricted to the 'cow and mountain' motif. This treatment can probably be interpreted as showing the contents of a closed shrine. The same applies to the cow on the third cloth (Fig. 11b), whose head and forequarters project from a bark shrine. One figure of a king stands beneath this cow's head and a second kneels at the rear of the bark. A third figure suckling, as in a similar scene in the temple of Ramesses II at Abydos (Zayed 1962 fig. 5), should probably be envisaged inside the shrine. The rectangle of water under the bark could be interpreted as the Nile or as a sacred lake or pool, though the 11th dynasty temple does not seem to have had a lake. In either case, some specific festival during which a bark of the goddess took to water may be alluded to (see further 2.2.8). Alternatively, the water could indicate a marsh setting and this cloth might belong in Type 4.

Type 3 (Pls. 18b, 19–20, 21a)

On four cloths and two shirts, Hathor is shown in cow form in the context of the Western Mountain. The mountain slope is usually painted pink or reddish-brown with a scattering of red pebbles. Sometimes only the head (Cat. 3.1, 3–4), or the head and forequarters (Cat. 3.2, 5), project from the mountainside. Such scenes are normally described as depicting the cow emerging from the Western Mountain, but it is equally possible that she should be interpreted as standing in a cave just inside the mountain, as the cow statue does in the artificial cave forming the speos of the Hathor shrine of Djeser-Akhet (Pl. 41b). On one shirt, the Hathor cow stands on a platform-like extension of the mountainside (Pl. 20). Similar 'platforms' are occasionally found in 'cow and mountain' scenes in funerary papyryi, tomb paintings and coffins (Allen 1923.11).

On two of the cloths, a stylised papyrus thicket is painted behind the cow (Cat. 3.2, 5), and on a third a single stem of papyrus entwined with convolvulus is shown in the same position (Pl. 21a). The 'cow and mountain' and 'cow and marsh' motifs are sometimes combined in tomb paintings and funerary vignettes (2.4.6), but I know of no examples on votive stelae. One Type 3 cloth (Cat. 3.3) is unique in showing a grapevine rather than papyrus behind the cow. A second grapevine is painted in the opposite corner, overhanging two wine jars (see further 2.2.8; 2.4.6). Another Type 3 cloth (Cat. 3.1) is very unusual in depicting the Hathor cow and the mountainside enclosed in a shrine, in front of which stands a table of offerings and a stela with a 'cow and mountain' motif flanked by Osirid statues (Pl. 21a). 'Cow and mountain' stelae were recovered from the Hathor shrines of Djeser-Djeseru and Djeser-Akhet (2.1, List 1.3–4). The painting on this cloth may be a schematic representation of the speos of one of these two Hathor shrines, or perhaps of a shrine within the 11th dynasty temple. The ramp of the latter temple was flanked by Osirid statues of Nebhepetre' Mentuhotpe and Amonhotpe I that were the focus of a popular cult (Naville 1907.60–1; Szafrański 1985). The Hathor cow on this cloth is clearly a statue; probably all the 'cow and mountain' scenes on the Type 3 textiles should be seen as referring to specific divine images at Deir el-Bahri.

Type 4 (Pls. 21b, 22–6)

On 11 cloths Hathor is shown in cow form in the context of a papyrus thicket. This the most common of the five types of votive textile. On the Type 4 cloths for which detailed information is available, the cow always stands on some kind of base, so these may all be representations of divine images. On one cloth the base is a bark with a prow ending in a stylised papyrus umbel (Cat. 4.2), on four it is a bark on a plinth (Cat. 4.1, 3, 5, 10) and on four a plinth on a sled (Cat. 4.7–8). One cloth shows the Hathor cow standing 'in' a shrine, hung with red cloth patterned in blue and yellow, and garlanded with lotus petals. The shrine rests in a bark on a plinth (Cat. 4.9 = Pl. 25b). A less well preserved cloth depicts a draped and garlanded shrine in a bark on a sled (Cat. 4.4). The prow of this bark appears to end in a head, probably of Amon-Re', wearing a cap with a double plume. In a relief in the speos of the Hathor shrine of Djeser-Akhet, a statue of a cow suckling and protecting a king stands 'in' a draped shrine very similar to those shown on the two cloths (Naville 1907 pl. 28c). The red fabric, with its hexagonal pattern, should probably be envisaged as draped over a wooden shrine containing a Hathor cow statue, like the linen veil with bronze rosettes found draped over the second shrine in Tutankhamon's burial chamber (Desroches Noblecourt 1963.71, fig. 34; Reeves 1990.100–01).

The papyrus thickets on these cloths tend to be painted in greater detail than those on the Type 3 cloths. On one badly faded cloth, some of the papyrus umbels seem to be shown from above (Cat. 4.5 = Pl. 24), a feature which can be paralleled in a few New Kingdom tomb paintings and funerary vignettes (Keimer 1956.232, figs. 21–2). The papyrus stems are entwined with convolvulus on two of the cloths (Cat. 4.2, 4). Convolvulus is usually shown only on plucked stems or papyrus columns. It is difficult to say whether the single stem of entwined papyrus shown on each side of a shrine (Cat. 4.4) should be interpreted as part of a thicket, as papyriform columns, or as offerings. Although 'cow and marsh' scenes should be understood as showing Hathor within a papyrus thicket (2.4.5), the cow is normally painted in front of the papyrus. However, one Type 4 cloth provides a rare example of a Hathor cow behind stems of papyrus (Cat. 4.2). It is equally unusual in having a grape-vine above the deity and donors (Pl. 22a). The only comparative material which can be cited for this is the grapevine and 'cow and mountain' scene on another cloth from Deir el-Bahri (Cat. 3.3).

Another cloth is unusual in having a tree with green foliage and blue fruits or flowers painted behind the donor (Cat. 4.1 = Pl. 23). Hall suggested that it was a persea (in Naville 1913.16), but it looks more like a sycamore, a tree closely associated with Hathor (Bonnet 1952.84–6). Hathor, Lady of the Southern Sycamore, can be shown as a cow in a papyrus thicket (*e.g.* Petrie 1909 pl. 28.1), and the scene of the tree-goddess nourishing the dead from a sycamore tree can be combined with the 'cow and mountain' motif in funerary contexts (2.4.5).

One Type 4 cloth shows a statue group of Hathor in cow form with a figure of Nebhepetreꜥ Mentuhotpe standing beneath her head (Cat. 4.9 = Pl. 25b). Although this detail is not visible in the available photographs, de Rustafjaell stated that on the damaged part of the cloth there was another figure of the king suckling (1909.50). A king standing beneath the head of a Hathor cow is quite common on votive stelae and in tomb paintings (2.4.6), but very few private monuments show a king suckling from a Hathor cow (2.4.5). The fact that only two of the votive textiles depict a king (Fig. 11b; Pl. 25b) is in contrast to the votive stelae from Deir el-Bahri (2.1.3). On both cloths, the king is shown in a dependent position rather than as a co-equal deity. No kings appear as inter-mediaries on the textiles.

Type 5 (Pl. 14b)

Another type has to be added to Parlasca's four to accommodate textiles which show Hathor in more than one form. On one cloth from the de Rustafjaell Collection (Cat. 5.1), the goddess apparently appeared in the same register as a woman seated on a throne and as a cow in a papyrus thicket (de Rustafjaell Cat. 1913.51). One shirt depicts Hathor in cow form in a papyrus thicket (Cat. 5.2). Above, painted partly on the inside back and partly on the front of the shirt, is a Hathor mask with scroll wig and pole neck (Pl. 14b). Combinations of various forms of Hathor on stelae have already been cited (2.1.3).

2.2.5   The donors

In discussing the donors of the textiles, it is helpful to use both Parlasca's system of classification (Types 1–5), and that devised for the votive stelae (Types A–C; see 2.1). As with the votive stelae, it was clearly not essential for the donor to be shown on a votive textile. One Type 2/A cloth does not even name its donor (Cat. 2.1). On most of the textiles, the donors are shown and named. Among both the stelae and the textiles, Type B is by far the most common. However, whereas the Type B votive stelae show only one or two donors standing before the deity, up to ten donors are shown in this position on the Type B cloths, which are much wider than they are long. Nor do all the Type C textiles correspond exactly with the Type C stelae. Two of the cloths from the de Rustafjaell collection showed Hathor in the upper register and the donors in the lower, and can be classified as Type C.1 (Cat. 4.11; 5.1). Two cloths depict the deity on one side while the donors are arranged in two registers on the other, so that the goddess is drawn on a much larger scale than the humans (Cat. 1.6; 2.3 = Pl. 16b, Fig. 11a). This layout is more reminiscent of a relief or wall painting than of a stela. Another cloth (Cat. 4.4), which has the goddess on one side, the principal donors standing before her, and the other donors arranged in two registers behind them, might be seen as an adaptation of Type C.2 to an object which is wider than it is high. A further cloth from the de Rustafjaell collection (Cat. 2.6), which showed the goddess and three donors in an upper register, four donors in a lower register on the right, and three more donors on the left, has no exact parallel.

There are several striking differences between the donors on the Hathor stelae and the donors of the painted textiles. First, whereas only 4 of the 48 Hathor stelae were dedicated by more than two donors, 14 out of the 35 votive textiles name and/or show more than two donors. Some depict whole families, the largest of which has nine members (Cat. 1.6). One has a group of ten, apparently unrelated, women (Cat. 2.5). Second, to judge from their shaven heads and simple costumes, *all* the adult males shown on the votive textiles are priests. The artisans and officials who form the bulk of the donors of the votive stelae do not feature on the textiles at all. Third, the female donors outnumber the male by 74 to 30. No intact cloth has a single male donor, but 12 cloths and all 5 shirts are dedicated by women alone. On two cloths (Cat. 2.4 = Fig. 11b; 4.7 = Pl. 21b), a woman is the principal donor even though men are also shown.

In order to demonstrate how unusual these figures are, they may be compared with those obtained from three groups of New Kingdom votive stelae from other sites. On 24 votive stelae from the vicinity of the Great Sphinx at Giza, 35 men and 6 women are shown; 20 of these stelae are dedicated by men alone and none by women (Selim Hassan 1953.234–76). On 17 votive stelae from the temple of Ptah at Memphis, 25 men and 7 women are depicted; 11 of these stelae are dedicated by men alone and 2 by women (Petrie 1909.7, pls. 10–14). On a group of 73 votive stelae from Qantir, mainly dedicated to royal statue cults, 69 men and 14 women appear (Habachi 1952.519–44). Only 5 of these stelae were dedicated by women. On the Hathor stelae from the six sites, male donors do far outnumber female ones, but this is may be mainly due to the amount of material from Serabit el-Khadim material. It is difficult to compare the votive textiles with the votive stelae from Deir el-Bahri, because so few of the latter have survived intact. The existing Hathor stelae from this site have a higher proportion of female donors than is usual, but not as high as the votive textiles (see further 2.2.8; 3.2.3).

Some of the actions and offerings of the donors on the votive textiles also differ from those shown on the Hathor stelae. On both types of object, the donors almost always stand rather than kneel. On only five textiles are donors shown with both arms raised in adoration (Cat. 1.9; 3.2; 4.2, 9; 5.1), but many donors hold an offering in their right hand and raise their left in adoration, a combination rare on stelae. As on the Hathor stelae, the principal donor is often shown burning incense, or burning incense and pouring a libation. On a few cloths the principal donor burns food offerings on a portable altar (Cat. 1.5; 3.1–2, 4; see 2.5.5). There is no discernible difference between the actions and offerings of male and female principal donors.

The remaining donors usually carry offerings such as bouquets, loaves, jars, stems of papyrus – often entwined with convolvulus – and bunches of grapes. These last two types of offering do not occur on the Hathor stelae. Papyrus bound with convolvulus is sometimes offered to Hathor in temple reliefs (*e.g.* Desroches Noblecourt and Kuentz 1968 pls. 110–12). It is quite a common offering to deities and deceased relatives on New Kingdom funerary stelae (*e.g.* Bruyère 1924 pl. 10; 1926.129, figs. 88–9), but it is rarely shown on votive stelae (see further 2.2.8). L. Manniche has suggested that this plant might be black bryony rather than convolvulus (1989.161). Grapes are also an unusual offering, but model bunches of grapes were among the votive objects found at Deir el-Bahri, Mirgissa, Serabit el-Khadim, and Gebel Zeit (2.10.1.1).

As on the Hathor stelae, a table or stand piled with offerings of food and flowers is usually shown between deity and donors, but two cloths are unusual in having offerings placed behind the donors (Cat. 1.6; 3.3). The jar-stand, basket and lotus bouquet (Pl. 16b), and the wine jars (Cat. 3.3), were probably put in to fill up space after the required number of donors had been painted. On one of these cloths, more columns for inscription were provided than were used (Cat. 3.3). On another specimen the last donor is crammed onto the edge of the cloth, overlapping the border (Fig. 10a). This indicates that some cloths must have been supplied from stock with the figures and names of the donors added as required.

On one cloth (Cat. 1.4), grapevines are shown between the donors but not held by them, perhaps so that both offerings of grapes and papyrus and the gesture of adoration could be included (Pl. 16a). Another cloth (Cat. 2.4 = Fig. 11b) is unusual in depicting a trussed and beheaded bullock, a type of sacrifice common in temple reliefs but not normally found on private monuments. Two other cloths show donors performing uncommon actions (Cat. 1.6; 2.5). On the first of these, the priest Tjanefer as *Chief Singer of Hathor* stands before the goddess playing a tall harp (Pl. 16b). This is, I believe, the only surviving New Kingdom example of a harpist before Hathor. Equally unusual, to judge from Hall's description, was a cloth (Cat. 2.5) which showed ten women wearing red dresses and 'depicted with considerable abandon ... worshipping the cow of Hathor with song and clashing of cymbals' (in Burlington Cat. 1922.39; see further 2.2.8). Perhaps these 'cymbals' were in fact the type of tambourine shown being played before Hathor on one stela from Mirgissa (Vercoutter 1970 pl. 38b).

2.2.6 Inscriptions

The inscriptions on the votive textiles tend to be even briefer than those on the votive stelae from the six sites. They consist chiefly of names. In only one case is the inscription laid out in horizontal columns below the scene (Cat. 3.6). One inscription is in hieratic (Pl. 26a) and one uses some hieratic signs (Fig. 10b). The rest are in hieroglyphs. Many are very poorly written. The inscriptions on the textiles display less variety than those on the Hathor stelae. The goddess is named, and given at least one epithet, on all the votive textiles for which detailed information is available. The donors are usually named, but titles are scarce. One male and one female principal donor bear priestly titles (Cat. 1.6; 3.3; 4.9). The only other title used is *nbt pr* – 'Mistress of a Household', which is applied to many of the women. On the cloths which depict families, the relationship of each person to the principal donor is usually stated, even if this means that there is no space to write out their names. On most of the textiles, the name of the principal donor is prefaced by an *ir n* formula. On one cloth, such formulae introduce the names of at least the first three out of the nine donors (Cat. 1.6), and on two cloths it is used for both the donors shown (Cat. 3.3; 4.2).

Only three textiles have continuous inscriptions of any length. A cloth drawn by Currelly (Cat. 2.2) has a curious inscription, which uses some hieratic signs, changes direction several times, and includes a triple royal titulary (Fig. 10b). It has not been possible to check Currelly's copy against the original, so only a tentative translation can be offered:–

> The Perfect God, Menkheperreᶜ, given life eternally, (in his) true name[1], like Reᶜ every day. The Perfect God, Menkheperreᶜ, given life, beloved of Hathor, Lady of Dendara. The Perfect God, Menkheperkareᶜ[2], ... Ruler[3], beloved of Hathor, Lady of Dendara. Dedicated by Ramesuneferet[4] (and) her daughter Mutnisu, called Heqaniwety[5] ...

[1] Or possibly 'in the name of Maat' or even 'the nursling of Maat'. I can find no equivalent to this phrase in other titularies of Thutmose III. Due to the seemingly erratic changes of direction, it is not entirely clear to which titulary the phrases in the middle of the inscription belong.

[2] The reading of this cartouche is doubtful. It might be ᶜAkheperkareᶜ, but Menkheperkareᶜ, a variant prenomen of Thutmose III mainly used during his joint reign with Hatshepsut (Uphill 1961.250; Meyer 1982.25–6), is equally likely. This variant is found in Djeser-Djeseru, where both forms can occur in one inscription (*e.g.* Naville [1906] pl. 130).

[3] I cannot read the sign immediately under the cartouche. 𓏏𓏏 and 𓏏𓏏 are epithets sometimes found in this position in the titularies of Thutmose III (Gauthier 1912.260–2), though not written on their sides. *mꜣꜥ ḫrw* is a possible reading, but it would be very odd in this context, even if this cartouche were that of Thutmose I.

⁴Perhaps a variant writing of the name ⊙[hieroglyphs], which is attested in the 18th dynasty (Ranke 1935.218, no. 5).

⁵ The last few signs, which do not all face in the same direction, may be part of the daughter's name, perhaps a peculiar writing of [hieroglyphs] 'to magnify'.

This inscription gives the impression of having been badly put together from formulae appropriate to a royal rather than a private context. A cartouche of 'The Perfect God, Nebhepetreꜥ' occurs on one cloth (Pl. 25b), but there it identifies the king beneath the head of the Hathor cow. The cartouches on this cloth might be taken to imply a scene of a king protected by and suckling from the Hathor cow, or to indicate a desire to use Thutmose III – and perhaps Thutmose I – as intermediaries.

The second of the cloths with longer inscriptions (Cat. 4.8) has a prayer for 'life benefits' beginning with an invocation formula (Pl. 25a):–

Hail to you, who shines as Gold¹, the Horus Eye ² upon the head of Reꜥ, may you³ give life, prosperity, health, skill, favour, and love for the ka of the Mistress of a Household, Mutemwiya.

¹ Or 'who rises as the Golden One'

² [hieroglyphs] is more usual in references to Hathor's role as the Solar Eye (Wb. I.107).

³ Reading [hieroglyph] for [hieroglyph] and [hieroglyph] for [hieroglyph].

The third cloth (Cat. 4.9) also has a prayer for 'life benefits' (Pl. 25b):–

Giving praise to the Lord¹ of the Two Lands, making obeisance to the Foremost in Thebes, that she may give life, prosperity, health, skill, favour, and love for the ka² of the Chief Singer of Hathor, Tjanefer, his sister³, the Mistress of a Household, Mernubet, her mother Sen, his son Huy, his son … ⁴, his son of his body whom he loves⁵, Ma[hu]ia, his daughter, whom he loves, Tenitimentet.

¹ If [hieroglyph] here is read as *Lord*, it must refer to Nebhepetreꜥ Mentuhotpe, but one would not expect the king's title to come before Hathor's. Since the inscription continues 'may she give', *nb* should probably be read as *nbt*.

² As *kꜣ* is in the singular, the prayer might be for the principal donor only, but perhaps it should be taken to include the others.

³ 'Sister' probably means wife both here and on another cloth where Mernubet appears with Tjanefer (Cat. 1.5), but on a third cloth the same Tjanefer is shown with a woman called Hathory (or Nebet-Hathory) and a different set of children (Cat. 1.6).

⁴ The name was not written in.

⁵ Or 'his son, of his body, who loves', if D. Franke is right in maintaining that this phrase is a priestly title referring to the child or children who were to carry out their parents' burial rites (1983.309–10).

2.2.7 Date range

Although the art of drawing on linen goes back to Predynastic times (Peck 1978.18–9), examples are scarce before the Third Intermediate Period. Some royal burials of the 17th and 18th dynasties included linen sheets decorated with spells and vignettes from the Book of the Dead (Abdalla 1988.163). Apart from the Deir el-Bahri material, I have been able to find only three New Kingdom paintings of deities on small pieces of linen. One almost intact cloth dating to Ramesses II which shows a couple adoring Taweret, was recovered from a house at Deir el-Medina (Cairo JE 43983; Anthes 1943.60, pl. 18a). Fragments from two painted cloths were found in tombs at this site. One depicts the same couple as on the intact cloth, again adoring Taweret (Bruyère 1930.23; Anthes 1946.60). The other, which bears the cartouche of Ramesses III, shows a row of people worshipping Hathor in cow form and Amonhotpe I (Bruyère 1928.38).

At least fifteen cloths with paintings or drawings of a deceased person, and sometimes of relatives making offerings to them, have been found in tombs at Deir el-Medina (Roeder 1924.340; Bruyère 1927.11, 31–2, figs. 3, 16; 1929.42, pls. 2–3; 1929a.86–7, fig. 41.1–3; 1930.25, 109, figs. 9, 37; 1934.97, fig. 63; 1939.227, fig. 116; Lansing 1945.201–3; Parlasca 1966.153–5; PM I², 747–8). The subject matter of these cloths is purely funerary, but in terms of material, technique, and style they are very similar to the votive textiles. The date range of these funerary cloths is from the end of the 18th dynasty to the 20th dynasty. Since some of them can be precisely dated by reference to the tomb owners, they provide useful comparative material for the votive textiles.

The main criteria for dating the votive textiles differ somewhat from those generally used to date stelae. Material and technique do not assist very much. All the votive textiles for which detailed information is available share the same weave, and the types of fringe do not seem to form a date sequence. Cloths on which the design is drawn need not be older than those on which it is painted, both techniques occurring on Ramessid funerary cloths. The mid 18th dynasty textiles do seem to use a more limited range of colours than the later specimens. Stylistic features are important in dating. To take just one example, the relaxed, fluidly drawn figures on a cloth of Tjanefer (Pl. 25b) obviously belong to the immediate post-Amarna period. The fact that another cloth of this donor has stiff, badly proportioned figures (Pl. 16b) is a warning against relying entirely on style for dating.

The type of border can be a decisive dating factor. The lotus-petal frieze does not seem to have been used before the late 18th dynasty. It occurs on 19th, but not 20th, dynasty funerary cloths. The only funerary cloth to have a combined lotus-petal frieze and check pattern border can be dated, by reference to the tomb owner, to the reign of Horemheb (Bruyère 1929.42). This combination is also found on objects from Tutankhamon's tomb (2.2.3), so cloths bearing it probably date to the end of the 18th dynasty.

Through comparison with closely datable tomb-paintings, coffins and funerary papyri, some details of the 'cow and mountain' and 'cow and marsh' scenes can be indicators of date. The 'cow and mountain' scene first appears in tombs at the end of the 18th dynasty (2.4.6). The practice of showing the Hathor cow standing in front of, rather than against or projecting from, the Western Mountain does not seem to occur before the mid 19th dynasty, which suggests a Ramessid date for one of the shirts (Cat. 3.6 = Pl. 20). The position of the donors in relation to Hathor can be of some help in giving a tentative date to cloths for which little information is available. Specimens with the donors arranged in several registers are unlikely to be earlier than the late 18th dynasty. As the male donors on the cloths are priests, their costumes are less helpful in dating than those of the male donors on the Hathor stelae. The clothes and hairstyles of the female donors are usually a vital factor in dating. The six cloths on which the women have simple hairstyles and wear plain sheath dresses (Cat. 1.1–2; 2.2; 4.1–3) are not likely to be much later than Amonhotpe II.

The orthography of the inscriptions and the formulae used in them are not often helpful. The epithet given to Hathor can be important, since 'Lady of Dendara' was not used at Deir el-Bahri after the mid 18th dynasty, while 'Lady of Djeser' did not come into use until the late 18th dynasty. Partly because of the high proportion of women, the identity of the donor usually provides no assistance, but the priest Tjanefer is known from other monuments to have lived at the end of the 18th dynasty (Naville 1907.61; Hall 1925.237; PM II, 395). This fixes the date of his three cloths (Cat. 1.5–6; 4.9), which in turn helps to date other cloths with similar features.

A date range from the mid 18th to the 19th dynasty emerges for votive textiles with paintings or drawings. Only a small number of cloths survive from the mid 18th dynasty. One of these (Cat. 1.2) has a pair of *wadjet* eyes at the centre top of the cloth corresponding to the lunette of a stela (Pl. 15). This suggests that the cloths, like the votive stelae, developed from funerary stelae during the mid 18th dynasty. Painted textiles were offered at Deir el-Bahri in the late 18th dynasty, but seem to have been most common at the end of the dynasty. Only a few specimens can be assigned to the 19th dynasty. This parallels the scarcity of Ramessid stelae at Deir el-Bahri (2.1.6).

The date range of the small textiles decorated with beads seems to be different. From the reports so far published, it appears that the beaded textiles from Gebel Zeit were found wrapping examples of a type of fertility figurine common in the Second Intermediate Period and early 18th dynasty (see further 2.6.1.3). If they were also found with the Middle Kingdom type of fertility figurine (2.6.1.2), this might push their date range back still further. However, the issue is complicated by the fact that textiles may sometimes have been used to wrap old offerings as part of a restoration programme. The evidence of stelae from the site, suggests that some expeditions to Gebel Zeit set out from the Theban area (Castel *et al.* 1985.28; Castel & Soukiassian 1985.292; 1.6). The Gebel Zeit textiles may even have come from the same workshop that made the unpainted textiles found at Deir el-Bahri. The latter probably date to the first half of the 18th dynasty, but it is possible that some of them, such as the example with amethyst beads (Pl. 27b), are as early as the late Second Intermediate Period.

2.2.8 Functions

Parlasca's scheme for dividing up the Hathor cloths is a convenient one, but the four types are contemporary with one another and there is no evidence that they had differing functions. The Type A votive textiles, which can feature the human form of Hathor (Cat. 1.3, 8), and which are all inscribed, do not seem to form a group apart as the Type A stelae and plaques do (2.1.2–3). The cloths and the shirts might be viewed as separate categories of object, but they share the same range of scenes and inscriptions. The conventions governing drawing on linen seem to have been slightly different from those for painting on linen. The absence of borders on the line drawings provides one example of this. The most meaningful distinction appears to be between textiles which depict a deity, and those which show a deceased person.

Parlasca does not accept that such a distinction can be made. Searching for forerunners to the mummy portraits of the Graeco-Roman Period, Parlasca turns to the cloths from Deir el-Medina which show deceased persons. One of these cloths was found *in situ* tied to the breast of an anthropoid coffin (Bruyère 1929.42, pl. 2). After describing these cloths, Parlasca states that:–

> Es liegt deshalb nahe, dass auch die Hathortücher aus dem benachtbarten Deir el-Bahari eine sepulkrale Zweckbestimmung hatten. Die auf ihnen befindlichen Weihinschriften an diese als Herrin der Nekropole lassen es immerhin möglich erscheinen. Zuverlässige Beobachtungen der Fundumstände liegen gerade bei den aus regulären Grabungen stammenden Stücken dieser Gruppe nicht vor. (1966.155)

Several objections can be raised against this suggestion. First, there are very few New Kingdom private tombs at Deir el-Bahri from which such cloths could have come. Second, Naville and Hall both specifically stated that some cloths were found in the 11th dynasty temple (2.2.2). Third, the recently found cloths from Gebel Zeit now prove that textiles were dedicated in Hathor shrines. Fourth, the painted textiles themselves provide evidence that they are votive rather than funerary objects. On all the painted textiles which are definitely or probably from Deir el-Bahri, living donors are shown worshipping Hathor. No funerary prayers are included in the inscriptions, and two of the cloths have prayers for 'life benefits' (Cat. 4.8–9). This is in contrast to the cloths from Deir el-Medina listed by Parlasca, which are mostly inscribed with funerary prayers for persons who are given the title of 'Osiris' and/or the epithet 'true of voice'.

It is somewhat misleading to say that Hathor is named on the textiles from Deir el-Bahri as 'Herrin der Nekropole'. The three main epithets of place given to Hathor on the textiles: 'Lady of Dendara' (Cat. 1.1–2; 4.2); 'Foremost in Thebes' (Cat. 1.1–2, 6; 3.6; 4.1, 3–4, 9); and 'Lady of Djeser' (Cat. 1.3; 3.4–5) have no particular funerary connotations. All appear on votive stelae from the 11th dynasty temple. The epithets 'Lady of the West' (Cat. 1.4; 3.3) and 'She of the West' (Cat. 1.5; 4.8) can be epithets of quality, linked to Hathor's funerary aspect, but at Deir el-Bahri they could be simple epithets of place. The specifically funerary epithet 'Foremost in the Necropolis' does not occur on the votive textiles. The 'cow and mountain' motif, found on six of the textiles (Cat. 3.1–6), is primarily funerary in its symbolism, but it appears on stelae from the Hathor shrines at Deir el-Bahri (2.1, List 1.3–4, 11–2, 18, 20–1).

Parlasca does not cite the cloths from Deir el-Medina which show donors worshipping deities. On the Taweret cloth found in a house, the inscription consists of names and titles and an *ir n* formula (Anthes 1943 pl. 18a). This formula is usually found on votive, rather than funerary objects (2.1.5), so the cloth was probably kept in a household shrine. Parallels for such a usage are provided by statues, stelae, offering tables, and basins dedicated to Taweret recovered from houses at Deir el-Medina (Bruyère 1952.72–82). When publishing this piece, R. Anthes suggested that the other fragment of cloth on which Taweret is adored by the same couple, was also intended as a votive object, although its provenance was a tomb (1943.40). As it was only a fragment, and as it was not found in association with the burial of donors but in a later tomb (Bruyère 1930.23), nothing much can be deduced from its find-spot.

The third cloth (Bruyère 1928.38) does seem to indicate that textiles depicting deities might be placed in New Kingdom tombs. I have not been able to trace this cloth, and its inscriptions have not been published, but the combination of Hathor in cow form and Amonhotpe I found on this piece is familiar from wall-paintings, statue groups, and stelae in tomb chapels at Deir el-Medina (2.4.6). This cloth should probably be regarded as analogous to the New Kingdom tomb chapel stelae which depict people worshipping funerary deities, or honouring deceased relatives and funerary deities. Most of the Deir el-Medina cloths are similar to the common type of funerary stela on which the deceased is shown with a table of offerings, or with relatives making offerings, so it is not suprising that other kinds of tomb stelae should have their counterparts on linen. The shrouds with paintings or drawings of deities, including Amonhotpe I, which first occur in the Third Intermediate Period (Parlasca 1966.154–7, pls. 56–7; Abdalla 1988.158–61), may well have developed from funerary cloths like the one showing Hathor with Amonhotpe I.

The five types of votive textile from Deir el-Bahri can be seem as analogous to the Hathor stelae from the site, but whereas stone and wooden stelae are clearly the same category of object made in different materials, the textiles cannot simply be regarded as 'linen stelae'. Some distinctive features, such as the tendency to be wider than they are tall and their decorative fringes, arise from the manufacturing process. Others must be deliberate divergences from the rules which governed the design of stelae. For example, the kinds of border used link the textiles with items of furniture rather than with stelae.

Several aspects of the portrayal of deity and donors distinguish the Hathor textiles from the Hathor stelae. Among the most striking is the preponderance of female donors. It might be argued that few women were able to afford stone stelae, and that they offered textiles because these were cheaper; J. Yoyotte suggests that the textiles were 'substituts prolétarians des stèle de pierre' (1960.61). However, stone Hathor stelae dedicated by women are known (*e.g.* 2.1 Lists 1.1; 3.1–2, 4), and the priest Tjanefer provides an example of a man of substance offering both cloths (Cat. 1.5–6; 4.9), and stelae (Naville 1907 pl. 26b = London UC 14390; Hall 1925.237 = London BM 56921). This suggests that textiles were regarded as a separate category of offering rather than as inferior substitutes for stone stelae.

One explanation for the high proportion of female donors might be that cloth was particularly associated with women, but in the New Kingdom the introduction of the vertical loom meant that weaving was no longer chiefly 'woman's work' (Hall 1986.15–19). It is also noteworthy that more men than women are depicted on the Deir el-Medina funerary cloths. De Rustafjaell believed that the shirts, which all have female donors, were baby clothes dedicated to Hathor in anticipation of, or gratitude for, a safe delivery (1909.52). If the shirts are baby clothes, they might also have been offered by women wishing to conceive, rather as barren women in India offer model cradles at local shrines (Crooke 1896.97; O'Malley 1935.100). The fact that one of the inscriptions on the shirts names a woman and her two daughters may argue against this hypothesis (Cat.1.3), though it could be assumed that she was praying for a son. The shirts might just be the Egyptian equivalent of a christening robe, but some are too small to have been worn even by a baby, and in scenes on ostraca which appear to depict celebrations after a safe birth, the child is naked (*e.g.* Vandier d'Abbadie 1937 pl. 51).

Women certainly did pray to Hathor for children (2.6.5), but the inscriptions on the shirts give no hint of the reasons for which they were offered. Nor are the forms of Hathor used on the shirts of very much help. The 'cow and marsh' motif, derived from the image of Hathor suckling the infant Horus in the marshes of Chemmis (2.4.5), would be appropriate to prayers related to childbirth. The 'cow and mountain' motif belongs to the imagery of the daily death and rebirth of the sun god (2.4.6). Its funerary connotations might seem inappropriate to prayers related to childbirth. However, on objects from Deir el-Bahri, the 'cow and mountain' motif may sometimes simply depict the image of the goddess in one of the rock-cut shrines, with no particular symbolic value attached.

The votive cloths which show large family groups are not likely to be connected with prayers for the birth of children, and two cloths are inscribed with prayers for the general welfare of the donors (2.2.6). The remaining inscriptions convey nothing of the nature of the requests made to the goddess, a reticence characteristic of inscribed votive offerings of all kinds (3.3). In most cases, the prayers are likely to have been for the general blessing of the goddess on the donor's life and afterlife. Given that the shirts are so similar to the cloths in their borders, scenes, and inscriptions, it seems unlikely that the former should be offered only to reinforce one, specific type of prayer, while the latter were not. A possible interpretation of the shirts is that, as miniature garments, they in some way represented the body of the donor, and that, by offering a shirt, the donor was placing her body under the protection of Hathor. In Spell 61 of the Coffin Texts, the deceased is protected by wearing the 'cast-off garment of Hathor' (Hall 1985.239). R. Hall has pointed out that the garments worn by dead people are usually turned inside-out (1985.239), as are two of the shirts from Deir el-Bahri (2.2.3). She suggests that this custom might be linked with birth as well as death (240–1).

In the absence of any definite evidence to link the shirts with either birth or funerary customs, it seems most likely that they were model raiments for Hathor herself, or actual garments for cult images of the goddess in human form. The way in which a Hathor mask is painted inside the neck-opening of one of the shirts

(Pl. 14b) suggests that the goddess was thought of as wearing this garment. The Deir el-Bahri Hathor shrines may each have contained the standard type of small anthropomorphous cult image, as well as a large stone cow statue. This explanation is also consistent with the use of the small textiles to wrap figurines.

One notable fact about the women depicted on the votive textiles is the number whose names are linked with Hathor. These include [hieroglyphs] (Cat. 1.1); [hieroglyphs] (Cat. 1.2); [hieroglyphs] (Cat. 1.4–5; 2.5; 3.6; 4.9); [hieroglyphs] (Cat. 1.6); [hieroglyphs] (Cat. 3.4); and variants of [hieroglyphs] (Cat. 1.4–5; 2.5; 3.6; 4.9). This raises the possibility that many of the female donors were connected with the cult of Hathor. Priests are distinguishable by their dress, but this is not necessarily true of priestesses. Only one woman is given a priestly title – 'Singer of Hathor' (Cat. 3.3), but then only Tjanefer of the men is given a priestly title (2.2.5). On the evidence of the titles of the 11th dynasty royal ladies buried in Akh-isut, Naville suggested that a 'college of Hathor priestesses' existed at Deir el-Bahri during the Middle Kingdom (1910.7). There may have been a similar institution in the New Kingdom. Alternatively, some of the donors, both male and female, could have belonged to some kind of religious corporation with semi-lay, semi-priestly status, which participated actively in festivals of the goddess (3.2.3).

Several of the votive textiles may allude to festivals. The Hathor sanctuaries at Deir el-Bahri seem to have contained portable images of the goddess in cow form (Naville [1901] pls. 88–9; PM II, 350). The draped shrines shown on some of the cloths (Cat. 2.6–7; 4.4, 9) may be portable shrines used during festivals. The bark shrine on another cloth (Fig. 11b) is certainly not depicted in the context of a sanctuary. Possibly it represents the bark of Hathor, Foremost in Thebes, crossing the river from Karnak to Deir el-Bahri (Brovarski 1976.70–1). The cloth on which ten women dressed in red sang and played the cymbals before Hathor 'with considerable abandon' (Cat. 2.5; Hall in Burlington Cat. 1922.39), sounds as if it depicted a rite in the cult of Hathor. Music and dancing were a feature of Hathor festivals in general (Hickman 1956.122; Wild 1963.69–70), but the description of the women resembles 18th dynasty tomb paintings of the 'Dancing Troupe of Hathor' who sang, danced, and played during the Beautiful Festival of the Wadi (Davies 1930.40–1, pl. 41; Schott 1952.44–5; 2.6.3.1). The two cloths which show grapevines above Hathor (Cat. 3.3; 4.2) may also be linked with this festival. During the Beautiful Festival of the Wadi, Hathor was worshipped as 'Lady of Drunkenness'. Both ritual drunkenness and music seem to have been used to break down the boundaries between the living and the dead (Brunner 1954.82–3; Altenmüller 1978.21–3). Thus the image of the cow in the vine arbour may allude to Hathor's aspect of mediator between life and death.

On most of the Hathor stelae, the donors are shown performing actions which belong to a standard offering sequence, but on some of the votive textiles the donors present more unusual offerings (2.2.5) which may have been appropriate at specific festivals. It is tempting to see the cloths on which papyrus stems are offered as alluding to the ancient ceremony of 'Shaking papyrus for Hathor' (Montet 1957; Harpur 1980; Troy.74–5, fig. 48), but papyrus stems and bunches of grapes were offered to deities, and to deceased relatives, during the Beautiful Festival of the

Wadi (Schott 1952.51–4). Ramessid graffiti in Djeser-Akhet and, in smaller numbers, in Akh-isut (1.1.2.1, 4) show that many people visited the Deir el-Bahri temples during this festival. In spite of the funerary aspect of the festival, the prayers of these visitors seem mainly to have been concerned with daily life (Marciniak 1971.53–65).

An unusual erotic scene on a leather hanging from Deir el-Bahri (Pl. 54) may represent a fertility rite (2.7.2). It is possible that some of the cloths with female donors, particularly the examples with groups of women (*e.g.* Pls. 16a, 18b, 22b), could allude to fertility festivals in which women were the main participators. Such cloths might have been dedicated on taking part in such a festival, or as a substitute for participating in person. In the latter case, stelae at Abydos whose purpose was to enable the donors to participate in the mysteries of Osiris (Simpson 1974.3), would provide comparative material. Such interpretations must remain speculative, but many of the textiles do give the impression of recording a particular event. Possibly, linen was considered a more suitable medium than stone for representations of specific events, or specific types of event.

Nothing is known for certain about whether or how the painted textiles were displayed in temples. Votive statues and stelae seem to have been set up all over the temples at Deir el-Bahri, wherever there was a convenient space, but this may not have been true of the votive textiles. The fact that the borders used on the cloths relate them to items of furniture rather than to stelae, suggests that they may have been regarded as temple furnishings. The cloths which had been stiffened with gesso would need to have lain or hung flat to avoid their paintwork cracking. Cords are preserved threaded through the looped fringes at the top of some of the cloths (*e.g.* Pls. 21a, 25b). One funerary cloth was tied to a coffin with such cords at top and bottom, and Parlasca uses this as an argument for the Hathor cloths being funerary (1966.155). Other uses can be suggested for the cords. Naville wrote of the large calcite shrine in the 'tomb dromos' of Akh-isut (Plan 2) that:–

All round the shrine in a line were holes for pegs or hooks, which were either for offerings or rather for garments. For we also found in the shrine heaps of mummy cloth. (1910.4)

The calcite pronaos in the hypostyle hall (Plan 2), whose upper part is not preserved, had similar holes for pegs from which votive cloths could have hung. It is equally possible that the painted textiles were normally stored in chests and only brought out during festivals to adorn the temple or the portable shrines, or to be carried, attached to poles, as festival banners. This might explain why it was desirable to offer both stelae and cloths, and would make it more understandable that the painted cloths should be an offering restricted to people associated with the cult of Hathor at Deir el-Bahri.

Not all the painted cloths can have been banners, since some have no means of attaching a cord. These specimens may have served as altar mats, or coverings for sacred objects. The remarkable state of preservation of many of the cloths suggests that they might have been used only once before being rolled up and stored. If the shirts were not garments for cult images, they too could have been hung up on shrine walls. The unpainted cloths woven with beads (Pls. 26b, 27a–b) were probably used to wrap votive or cult objects. At Gebel Zeit, they seem to have been used only to wrap, or serve as dresses for, pottery fertility figurines (2.2.3; 2.6.4). Similar fertility figurines were among the offerings at Deir el-Bahri (*e.g.* Pls. 1, 47a), so these may once have been 'dressed' in linen. At Deir el-Bahri, textiles could have been used to wrap other types of fertility figurine, or perhaps any small sacred figure. The pendant of Weret-Hekau suckling the king from the small gold shrine of Tutankhamon, was decorated with bead necklaces and wrapped in linen (Eaton-Krauss & Graefe 1985 pl. 6). Some of the longer textiles from Deir el-Bahri are similar in shape to the fringed linen scarves found wrapped around the necks of statuettes of deities in this king's tomb (*e.g.* Desroches Noblecourt 1963.85, 221, figs. 43, 131–2). Necklaces of faience beads were the most common offering to Hathor at Deir el-Bahri (2.9.2.1), so scarves decorated with beads may also have been presented to the goddess.

Summary

Thirty linen cloths and five linen shirts decorated with paintings or line-drawings come from Deir el-Bahri. Some of the cloths were definitely excavated in the 11th dynasty temple. These textiles range in date from the mid 18th to the early 19th dynasty. Most of the textiles have designs painted in several colours, but on a few the design is drawn in ink. All of these decorated textiles bear representations of Hathor, most of which should be interpreted as cult images. The cow form of the goddess is more common than the human form. It features in both 'cow and marsh' and 'cow and mountain' scenes. Occasionally, the goddess is accompanied by a deceased king.

The inscriptions on the textiles are mainly confined to names and titles, but some request 'life benefits.' Women were the donors of the majority of the textiles. All the male donors shown are priests. Some of the cloths probably depict specific shrines and/or specific festivals. All the Deir el-Bahri textiles are votive rather than funerary. The cloths are not just linen versions of stelae. They have features in common with tomb paintings, and with decorated items of furniture. The cloths may have served as festival banners, or as temple furnishings. The shirts may have been symbolic or actual garments for cult images. Smaller textiles woven with beads have been found at Gebel Zeit and Deir el-Bahri. At Gebel Zeit, such cloths were used to wrap late Second Intermediate Period/early 18th dynasty fertility figurines.

2.3 Hathor masks

All the types of offering from the six sites which consist of, or incorporate, Hathor masks are described in this chapter. The iconography of the Hathor mask presents many problems. Because there is no standard work on this topic, it is necessary to explain the terminology which I use.

2.3.1 Terminology

Bat symbol – an emblem or image of Bat, goddess of the 7th Egyptian nome. C. Aldred described it as 'the cow-eared face of a woman wearing in-curving horns on her head and a trapezoidal panel of beads falling below her chin' (1971.146). The trapezoidal panel is usually striped, and is fringed at the bottom with a row of drop beads (*e.g.* Bourriau 1988.147 no. 156). It can be flanked by plain, shorter strips (*e.g.* Aldred 1971 pls. 26, 34), or by loops (*e.g.* A. Wilkinson 1971.34, fig. 23, pl. 1a). In the latter case, the panel resembles the lower part of the *tyet* (girdle-tie) (Aldred 1971.175). Norman de Garis Davies suggested that origins of the Bat symbol might lie in the elaborate collars worn by sacred cattle in the Old Kingdom (1920.69). The Bat symbol had a profound influence on the iconography of Hathor. From the 12th dynasty onwards it could be used as an image or emblem of Hathor (Fischer 1962.12–4).

Hathor mask – A flat, cow-eared face, which may or may not be framed with a wig (*e.g.* Pls. 28–9). When the head of Hathor is used on its own, it usually differs in many respects from the type of head shown on the full human form of the goddess. The most important differences are the 'frontal' presentation and the use of cow rather than human ears. I use the term 'Hathor mask' when a head of the goddess is reduced to a flattened face, with no indication of the depth or roundness of the skull. Describing an example forming part of a Late Period statue, E. Russmann comments that:–

> In fact the [Hathor] head, although modelled in the round is conceived two dimensionally and handled with the same conventions usually applied to Egyptian representations of the full face in relief. This is quite deliberate, for it is not really the head of the goddess that is depicted but her symbol ... (1973.35).

A more neutral term, such as 'cow-eared mask', might be preferred to 'Hathor mask', because other goddesses can be associated with this symbol.

Bifrontal mask – Two cow-eared masks (not heads) back to back. The bifrontal Hathor mask may be derived from the Bat symbol, since in the Pyramid Texts this goddess is referred to as 𓃾𓂝𓊹𓏥𓏤𓏤𓂋𓏭𓊹 – 'Bat with her two faces' (PT 1096b).

Scroll wig – The 'Hathoric' wig, in which the the tresses on either side of the face are curled up and inwards around a roundel (*e.g.* Pl. 32c–d). This wig was combined with the Hathor mask at least as early as the 12th dynasty. The scroll wig is attested on figures of 12th dynasty queens and court ladies, so this may be an instance of royal fashion influencing the representation of deities. However, because similar hairstyles were worn by several Near Eastern goddesses from the late third millennium BC onwards, some scholars have argued that the scroll wig is Mesopotamian in origin (Pritchard 1943.40–1; Brunner-Traut 1956.27). Whatever its origins, the scroll wig came to be associated with the Hathor mask, rather than with Hathor in her full human form.

Tripartite wig – The long, straight-ended wig, divided into three tresses (e.g. Pl. 30c,d). During the 18th dynasty this wig, which is worn by many goddesses in their human forms, began to be used on Hathor masks. Among the offerings from the six sites it is more common than the scroll wig. On both the scroll and the tripartite wig the hair may be bound with ribbons. On painted examples the ribbons are red.

Semi-circle – A semi-circle in the centre of the brow (e.g. Pl. 31). This appears on both two and three-dimensional Hathor masks from the 12th dynasty onwards. The details of the semi-circle, which can be painted black or blue, differ from piece to piece. The main variants are: ⌣ ▬ ▬ ▬ . This object has been variously interpreted as a fillet (Brunner-Traut 1956.28) and as a piece of jewellery (Giveon 1975.37). Its occurrence on the forehead of a painted wooden statuette of a 12th dynasty lady who wears a tripartite wig (New York MMA 19.3.1; Lansing 1920.16, 18, fig. 8) suggests an origin in Middle Kingdom fashions, but the blue or black colouring argues against the jewellery theory. R. Anderson has described the semi-circle as a 'stylised fringe' (1976.51), which would fit with its colouring and could be seen as analogous to the fringe sometimes shown on the Bat symbol (e.g. A. Wilkinson 1971 pl. 1a). On Hathor masks with wigs, the semi-circle might be interpreted as the natural hair shown protruding from under the wig.

Podium – A low, circular headdress base (e.g. Pls. 28, 33). This has also been referred to as a cornice (Petrie 1906.146), a *kalathos* (Strauss 1974.41), an abacus (Brunner-Traut 1956.27; Russmann 1973.35), a modius (Aldred 1971.232; Ziegler 1979.34), and a platform crown (Troy 1986.120). The podium can be plain red or yellow, or blue-green with vertical black stripes. The plain and the striped podia were probably different in origin, but by the New Kingdom they seem to be used interchangeably. In the New Kingdom the red or gold podium is a common base for the crowns and headdresses of goddesses and royal ladies. The striped podium can also be used in this way, but it is most common on Hathor masks by itself. When it occurs on a model Hathor mask, it is conceived two-dimensionally and so comes out looking like a cavetto cornice. Some scholars identify the podium with the abacus of a Hathor mask capital (Brunner-Traut 1956.27; Russmann 1973.35), even though the abacus of such capitals rarely rests directly on the head of the goddess.

Troy suggests that the striped, blue-green podium represents a reed or papyrus crown (1986.121–2), but Anderson proposes that the striped podium is a stylised fringe (1976.41). If it is a fringe, it could be traced back to the fringe on some Old

Kingdom Bat symbols, which in turn is probably derived from the fringe across the forehead of a cow. On Middle Kingdom Bat symbols, the fringe is usually reduced to a narrow strip, sometimes striped, sometimes not. When the scroll wig began to be combined with the cow-eared mask, this strip could have been reinterpreted as a low reed diadem, and perhaps incorporated into the design of Hathor capitals to serve as an abacus.

Loop crown – A podium, usually surmounted or encircled by a row of loops. Headdresses of this type appear on a few plaques from Serabit el-Khadim (*e.g.* Pls. 30b, 31, left) and on faience bowls (*e.g.* Borchardt 1910 fig. 179). Petrie interpreted the loop crown as a cornice surmounted by a row of uraei (1906.147). Model sistra of the Late Period often incorporate a striped podium topped by uraei (*e.g.* Anderson 1976.47–50, figs. 80–2; Ziegler 1979 figs. 23, 34, 36, 40, 43, 51, 54, 66). In three dimensions the shape of the podium was very different from that of a cavetto cornice, but in two dimensions the resemblance would have been close, so the two objects may have come to be equated. The podia surrounded by loops might represent the crown encircled by uraei worn by queens from Tiy onwards (Troy 1986.57, fig. 34).

On some plaques from Serabit el-Khadim the loops do not closely resemble uraei (Pl. 31 left), so other explanations have to be considered. Several 18th and 19th dynasty Theban tombs contain friezes of Hathor masks wearing striped podia surmounted by tall feathers which are painted alternately blue and green (*e.g.* Davies 1948 pls. 7, 26; Abdul-Qader Muhammed 1966.51–2, 169). These feather crowns resemble those sometimes worn by Bes figures (*e.g.* Bonnet 1952.102, fig. 34) and, less closely, the crown of Anukis. In the earliest of these friezes, that in the tomb of Senenmut (TT 71), each Hathor mask has a striped podium surmounted by two loops painted with curved bands of red and blue edged with white (W. S. Smith 1965 pl. 103). These loops are reminiscent of a pair of loops, one red and one blue, which replace the usual incurving horns on a 12th dynasty Bat symbol (Aldred 1971.191, pl. 34). The loops might be identified with the double plume of the 𓎤𓊽𓋞 symbol (Blackman 1914.2; 1953 pls. 9, 19; Staehelin 1978.78–9), or with stylised petals of the type used in petal friezes, and shown encircling the crowns of royal ladies from Ahmose-Nefertary onwards (Troy 1986.75–6, figs. 49–50). Perhaps such loops were originally a decorative treatment of the incurving horns of the Bat symbol, causing these to be reinterpreted as feathers or petals.

Triangle crown – A podium, usually striped, surmounted by roughly triangular projections. It is uncertain whether the triangle crown, which appears on a few bowls (*e.g.* Karkowski 1981 pl. 11.1a), should be regarded as separate from the loop crown. A kiosk shown in a 12th dynasty tomb at Meir has columns which terminate in a Hathor mask surmounted by a blue lotus (Blackman 1953 pl. 11). This raises the possibility that the triangles could be lotus petals. Alternatively, they could represent the triangular calices of a papyrus umbel. This is suggested by mirror handles of the Middle and early New Kingdoms, which are shaped like stalks of papyrus and incorporate a Hathor mask with a striped podium below the umbel (*e.g. Egyptian mythology* 1968.24). On some mirror handles a papyrus umbel seems to take the place of the podium (*e.g.* Vandier d'Abbadie 1972 no. 754), and on the Hathor mask columns in Djeser-Djeseru striped podia are flanked by papyrus umbels (von Mercklin 1962 pl. 1.8–9).

Naos – A rectangular structure, usually flanked by volutes, surmounted by a cornice and containing a central recess (*e.g.* Pls. 27d, 32a). This structure is often interpreted as a shrine, though some scholars identify it as a temple gateway (*e.g.* Daumas 1970.66; Nagy 1977.49; Ziegler 1979.32). The central recess is frequently occupied by one or more uraei. The volutes may have developed from the incurving horns of the Bat symbol (Ziegler 1979.33). The naos usually rests on a podium, but on a few Hathor mask plaques (*e.g.* Pl. 31, top centre) characteristics of the striped podium and the naos seem to be combined in one headdress.

Pole neck – An elongated neck, trapezoidal in shape and often decorated with horizontal bands. Some Hathor masks have necks of normal length, which can be adorned with necklaces, but on many examples the neck is elongated into a trapezoid whose lower end may be shown resting on a plinth (*e.g.* Pl. 31, 32c–d). Such necks have been described as poles (Petrie 1906.147), beards (Reisner 1955.23), columns (Russmann 1973.35), and handles (Anderson 1976.55). Their shape and their decoration suggest that they are related to the striped, trapezoidal panel of the Bat symbol. Probably this striped panel was later combined with, or reinterpreted as, a pole or column.

Hathor masks, sistra and columns – There is a tendency to refer to all types of Hathor mask, and even to the Bat symbol, as sistra. Such a broad usage of this term hinders attempts to define loop and naos sistra and the contexts in which they occur. The Bat symbol was combined with a naos as early as the late Old Kingdom and Hathor mask naos sistra are known from the Middle Kingdom onwards, but the Hathor mask loop sistra are not shown before the 18th dynasty (Ziegler 1984.959–60). Objects can confidently be identified as sistra only when they include the major components of the loop or the naos sistra as shown in temple reliefs and tomb paintings. Surviving functional and model sistra of the Late Period also provide information about these components (Ziegler 1979.31–40).

Loop sistra should consist of a long handle, a bifrontal Hathor mask, and the loop itself. On functional specimens, the loop is pierced, and rattles, sometimes in the form of snakes, are inserted. A naos sistrum should consist of a long handle, a bifrontal Hathor mask, and a naos with volutes. The rattles strung across the central recess are not usually shown on model naos sistra. If these criteria are strictly applied, only a small number of objects from the six sites can be classified as models or representations of sistra.

Columns whose capitals incorporate cow-eared masks are sometimes referred to as sistrum columns, but this is misleading. A relief in a prince's tomb at Giza shows that the Bat symbol was utilised as a capital at least as early as the 4th dynasty (Borchardt 1897.168; Selim Hassan 1943.140, fig. 81), well before the cow-eared mask first appears on sistra. The earliest surviving columns to incorporate Hathor mask naos sistra are those in the Hathor shrine of Djeser-Djeseru (von Mercklin 1962 pl. 1.8–9). Sistrum columns were by no means common during the New

Kingdom. 'Cow-eared mask columns' would be the best term, since such columns are found in the temples of other goddesses, such as Anukis (Kaiser 1970.110, pl. 62c) and Nekhbet (Jéquier 1924 pl. 27).

When a bifrontal mask is not surmounted by a loop or a naos, but does have a long circular, square or octagonal neck, preferably resting on a base, it can be identified as a Hathor column. Such columns usually terminate in a podium, but this is not sufficient evidence, since podia are a component of most sistra and of several types of headdress. The plaques which show Hathor masks with pole necks (*e.g.* Pl. 31, left) are more problematical. They could represent columns or, as Petrie suggested (1906.147), Hathor masks mounted on carrying poles. It is not clear whether the two would have had the same symbolic value (2.3.4). When a piece is not surmounted by a loop or a naos and has a short neck, or no neck at all, I refer to it as a Hathor mask.

2.3.2 Votive Hathor masks, columns, and sistra

The offerings from the six sites which consist of, or incorporate, Hathor masks are described in this section. They are divided according to the material from which they are made. The faience and glazed steatite pieces are subdivided into five main types of object.

1 *Stone* (Pl. 27c)

Among the objects found by the EEF during their excavation of the 11th dynasty temple at Deir el-Bahri were two large sandstone Hathor masks (Edinburgh RSM 1906.442.6; Dundee 66.186), which probably come from the facade of the Hathor shrine of Djeser-Akhet (1.1.2.3), and two smaller bifrontal limestone Hathor masks (London BM 4100; Philadelphia UM E 11816). The first of these measures 13 × 9.4 cm. It is crudely carved and not very well preserved (Pl. 27c). No ears are visible, but each mask has a striated scroll wig and the remains of a striped podium. Below the chins is a wide piece of stone shaped roughly like a plinth. This is incomplete, but the mounting does not allow the break to be examined. If it is a plinth, this object is a Hathor mask rather than the top of a votive column. Alternatively, the stone below the chins might be interpreted as the top of a *djed* column. A few 18th dynasty examples of such columns surmounted by Hathor mask or sistrum capitals are known (*e.g.* von Mercklin 1962 pl. 3.10).

The other bifrontal mask was described by Naville as 'Small limestone Hathor column-capital ... Probably votive' (1913.24). The piece is incomplete, since the neck is broken just below the bead collar (1913 pl. 16.3). Both masks have a tripartite wig, surmounted by a striped podium and a naos with a single uraeus in the central recess. On each side, a stem of papyrus is carved in the join between the masks, with a uraeus in a recess above the umbel. This piece should probably be classified as a miniature Hathor sistrum column. It closely resembles the Hathor sistrum columns of Djeser-Djeseru.

A bifrontal steatite Hathor mask, which shows no trace of glazing, was found by Petrie at Serabit el-Khadim (1906 pl. 151.11 = London UC 35346). The present height of this piece is 10.7 cm. Each of the masks has a striated tripartite wig surmounted by a striped podium. One is much better carved than the other. The masks have a circular, elongated neck which is broken about half-way down. Petrie described this object as a sistrum (1906.146–7), but it should probably be regarded as a miniature Hathor column. Such votive stone columns are rare, but a few probable examples can be cited (Edinburgh RSM 1964.109; von Mercklin 1962 fig. 30). Similar columns are incorporated in some sistrophorous statues (*e.g.* Vandier 1958 pl. 150).

2 *Wood* (Pl. 1, Fig. 1)

Winlock discovered a miniature wooden Hathor column at Deir el-Bahri (1923.38–9, fig. 34). It consists of a bifrontal mask, with tripartite wig and podium, surmounting a circular column which is pegged into a base in the form of a double staircase (Cairo JE 47740; Grdseloff 1940.196–7, fig. 3). Below one of the masks is a brief inscription reading:–

> Hathor, Lady of Dendara. May she give vitality and life[1] to the *ka* of [...].

> [1] Perhaps a mistake for 𓊽𓋹 – 'a good life'.

The EEF also found some wooden Hathor masks at Deir el-Bahri. Four were published by Hall and Currelly (in Naville 1913.14, 23; Fig. 1.4; Pl. 1, top right). Two of these are now in the British Museum (London BM 41098, 47797), and one is in Brussels (MR 1905.710). I have been unable to trace the fourth. Brussels MR 1905.710 (Pl. 1, top, far right) is made of acacia, has a few traces of red paint, and is 12.8 cm high. It comprises a bifrontal Hathor mask with tripartite wig and very low podium. This surmounts a circular column which ends in a peg – perhaps for attachment to a double stair. London BM 41098 (Pl. 1. next right) is also made of acacia and is 12.9 cm high. The bifrontal mask has a tripartite wig, a striped podium, and a yellow-painted naos (Anderson 1976.62). The elongated neck is painted with horizontal black stripes and terminates in a peg. This suggests that it should be interpreted as a miniature Hathor sistrum column rather than as a model sistrum.

The piece whose location is unknown (Pl. 1, top centre) was larger and better carved than MR 1905.710 and BM 41098. Presumably, it too was bifrontal. The visible mask has a tripartite wig and a headdress which might either be a tall podium or a naos. The details would originally have been painted in. The elongated neck is broken off just below the bottom of the wig, which makes it difficult to decide whether this object was a model sistrum or a miniature sistrum column. London BM 47797 (Fig. 1.4) is even more problematical. It is crudely carved in a dark wood which Hall identified as ebony (in Naville 1913.14), and retains its original height of 20.3 cm. In his drawing, Currelly showed a scroll wig surmounted by a sun disc and horns (Fig. 1.4), but on examination, the headdress proves to consist of a plain roughly shaped rectangle, which might just be intended for a podium (Anderson 1976.62–3). Painted details may have been visible when the piece was first excavated. The bulbous handle resembles the shape of the papyrus stem handles common on Hathor mask mirrors (*e.g.* Bourriau 1988 no. 185). London BM 47797 does not seem to be a model sistrum, but it was not free-standing or attached to a base, as one would expect with a miniature column.

Some clues to the date of these objects are available. The use of the epithet Lady of Dendara suggests that Cairo JE 47740 is not later than the mid 18th dynasty. These wooden pieces are similar in many respects to columns and masks shown on plaques from Serabit el-Khadim (Pl. 31), several of which are inscribed with the names of Hatshepsut or Thutmose III (2.3.2.4). Comparative material is scarce. Both functional and model sistra could be made in wood (*e.g.* Hickmann 1949.90–1; Bruyère 1952b.51, fig. 36; Anderson 1976.62; Ziegler 1979.53–4). A wooden Hathor mask said to come from Kom el-Ahmar could have been part of a naos sistrum, a naos-sistrum column, or a miniature shrine (Tutundjian 1986). It is surmounted by a naos with uraeus and volutes and the chin rests on a papyrus umbel (1986.73, pl. 1). A few wooden 'cow-eared mask' columns which are probably votive can be cited (*e.g.* Anderson 1976.62, fig. 119; George 1978.28–9, fig. 6; Valbelle 1982.236, pl. 5). A miniature wooden shrine with cow-eared mask columns, dedicated to Khnum, Satet, and Anukis, was found in a house at Deir el-Medina (Donadoni 1988 pl. 215). There seems to be no exact parallel for the base in the shape of a double stair on the wooden column which was excavated by Winlock. However, part of a model staircase, made in limestone, and inscribed with a prayer to Hathor, was discovered in the 11th dynasty temple (Fig. 7d; Naville 1913.22, pl. 5.2). It is possible that a stone Hathor column once stood on this base.

3 *Metal*

The EEF distribution lists mention a 'copper Hathor head' and a 'bronze Hathor plaque' from the 11th dynasty temple, but I have not been able to obtain information on these objects. Hayes noted that among the offerings found by Winlock at Deir el-Bahri:–

> The characteristic full-face human head of the goddess, with its massive head-dress and projecting cow's ears, occurs twice on an oblong strip of copper and once on a tiny silver plaque ... (1959.173)

The strips of copper are menit counterpoises which are described in 2.3.3.2. The silver plaque (New York MMA 23.3.137), which measures 2.5 × 1.4 cm, is pentagonal in shape and pierced for suspension. This, and the copper and bronze examples found by the EEF, are analogous to the metal Hathor cow plaques from Deir el-Bahri and Faras (2.4.2.1).

A tiny gold Hathor mask, only 0.4 cm high, was excavated by Griffith at Faras (London BM 51271; Karkowski 1981.109–10, no. 14). The mask, which is surmounted by a striped podium, is wigless and no ears are shown. It is not pierced. Perhaps it may be regarded as an inlay, comparable with the much larger golden Hathor masks from the caskets of Sathathoriunet (Winlock 1934 fig. 3) and Mereret (Aldred 1971 pl. 46). Metal Hathor masks of any kind are rare from the New Kingdom, but a few gold Hathor mask pendants can be cited (*e.g.* Petrie 1914 pl. 30; Dunand 1938 pl. 126).

4 *Faience and glazed steatite*

Hathor masks in these materials were recovered from five out of the six sites. Hall
noted that at Deir el-Bahri 'Her human face with cow's ears ... occurs of course
constantly' (in Naville 1913.14), and the EEF distribution lists include 64 'glazed
Hathor heads'. Carter mentioned finding 'blue glaze Hathor heads' (Carter &
Carnarvon 1912.32) and seven are illustrated in one of his photographs (Pl. 6c, h).
Hayes described only one faience Hathor mask excavated by Winlock at Deir
el-Bahri (1959.173). Griffith discovered at least eight faience or glazed steatite
Hathor masks at Faras, seven of which are illustrated in his report (Pl. 8.29, 61–6).
At Serabit el-Khadim MacDonald found four faience Hathor masks (London BM
12872–5) and five fragments from faience Hathor mask plaques (London BM
12866–7, 12878–9, 13071), Campbell Thompson discovered one faience Hathor
mask (London BM 38180), and Petrie excavated about 100 faience Hathor masks
and plaques (1906.146–8, pls. 151–3). Rothenberg reports finding five 'Hathor
heads in glazed pottery' at Timna (1972.166; pls. X, 80, 86–9; 1988 pl. 118.3,
figs. 27.1–2, 4, 30.1–2). At Gebel Zeit, Hathor masks were among the most
frequently encountered amulets (Castel *et al.* 1984.50; 1985.20). The objects noted
above can be divided into four main categories:–

A. Unifrontal, modelled Hathor masks (Pls. 6, 8, 27–8)

Pieces of this type have a flat back and a single Hathor mask modelled on the front.
They were made in open moulds. Carter illustrated four examples which obviously
come from the same mould (Pl. 6c). These masks are 2–6 cm high and tend to be of
poor workmanship. The 22 examples from Deir el-Bahri which I have been able to
examine, or obtain detailed information on, are all made of faience (Bolton 48.04.9;
Brussels MR E 727, 2461; Carnegie Museum 2940.12b; Ilkley 7096.1–3; London
BM 41054, 41088 = Pl. 28a, bottom right, 41093, 41095–6, 41702, 41735; Oxford
Ash. E 2741–2; PR 1906.45.14–5 = Pl. 28a, top; Toronto ROM 907.18.166–7,
169 = Pl. 27d, 188). They can be turquoise, light or dark blue, or light blue with
details in dark blue. The features, including the cow's ears, are often barely visible
under the glaze. All but one (Toronto ROM 907.18.188) have wigs. The scroll wig
is rather more common than the tripartite. Most of these masks have a striped
podium, but one (Pl. 27d) is surmounted by a naos. They can have elongated or
short necks. Some of these masks are pierced through the podium or have a loop
attached to the top of the head or to the flat back.
     Five of the Hathor masks illustrated by Griffith are probably unifrontal
(Pl. 8.61–3, 65–6, location unknown; Karkowski 1981.109). Nos. 63 and 65 on this
plate may have come from the same mould. Both have the scroll wig and a striped
podium. A similar piece, 1.3 cm high, is now in the Pitt-Rivers Museum
(unnumbered). It is made in glazed steatite and is pierced through the podium. Nos.
61–2 and 66 on Griffith's plate, which clearly came from a single mould, are very
crude, but include the scroll wig and the podium.
     Petrie noted that at Serabit el-Khadim –'Some small glazed heads of Hat.Hor
were also offered, which are single faced, and without a long handle' (1906.147).
He illustrated three examples (1906 pl. 151.12 & 15, [location unknown],

13 = Manchester 885). One of these does have an elongated neck which might be interpreted as a pole or column (1906 pl. 151.15). Fragments from three unifrontal masks were found at Timna (Rothenberg 1988.118–19, figs. 27.4, 30.1–2). One fragment comprises only part of a striated wig and a possible cow's ear (1988 fig. 27.4). On the second, which is 3 cm high, the goddess has a wig and a striated podium (1988 fig. 30.2). Two further fragments form part of a face which would have been about 5.5 cm high when intact (1988 fig. 30.1). This wigless mask is in blue-green faience with details picked out in black. Schulman notes that 'Something was affixed to the chin at its lower edge and set in a little from the front' (in Rothenberg 1988.119). He suggests that 'this mask was part of a composite piece and that the head-dress (now lost) was made separately' (1988.119).

Small, unifrontal Hathor masks, or moulds for making them, are quite common at New Kingdom settlement sites (*e.g.* Petrie 1912 pl. 45; Reisner 1955 pl. 5; Herrmann 1990.32–3, nos. 38–41). Most such masks are pierced, or fitted with loops, so they may have been designed to be worn as amulets.

B. Bifrontal modelled Hathor masks, columns, and sistra (Pls. 28–30, Fig. 6)

Petrie stated that sistra were not common at Serabit el-Khadim (1906.146). He was able to illustrate only seven bifrontal faience masks which he believed to have been components of model sistra (1906 pl. 151.4–10; Pl. 29). He suggested that the inscribed faience 'handles' shown in the same plate (1906 pl. 151.16–20) belonged to Hathor masks like these, though none of them fitted together. Three of the bifrontal masks terminate in podia, and so cannot be classified as sistra (1906 pl. 151.4–5,9; Pl. 29, top row, first and third from left = Bolton 68.05.42a–b; bottom row, centre, location unknown). Bolton 68.05.42a is broken off just below the chin and now measures 8.4 × 6.4 cm. It is made of light blue faience with the details picked out in dark blue. This piece is too heavy to have been supported by a slender faience handle. Since Petrie's plates maintain the relative scales of the objects, the piece of unknown location must have measured at least 10 × 8 cm. Bolton 68.05.42b is broken at chin level and now measures 4.7 × 4.5 cm. It is made of pale green faience with the details picked out in black. These large bifrontal masks should probably be regarded as the capitals of miniature Hathor columns. A square faience 'handle' from Serabit el-Khadim inscribed with the prenomen of Thutmose III (Oxford Ash. E 4462a) may be a component of such a column. Sistrum handles are normally circular, not rectangular, and the lower end of this piece is vertically pierced, perhaps for attachment to a base.

One fragment from a bifrontal Hathor mask was excavated at Timna (Rothenberg 1988.118, fig. 27.2) and Naville found at least eight examples at Deir el-Bahri (1913 pls. 24.1–3, 25.2; Kyoto UM 580; London BM 41087, 41089–90; Liverpool 13.10.04.13–14; Toronto ROM 907.18.168 = Pl. 28b, 839). The largest of these is 6.6 cm (London BM 41089). All of them are broken off at chin level or just above the bottom of the wig. None is pierced, or has loops for suspension. Most of these pieces are in plain blue faience, but ROM 907.18.168 is in bright blue with the eyebrows and the rims of the eyes inlaid in pale blue. On one side, the ribbons binding the wig are inlaid in violet. The eyes of this unusually elaborate piece must also once have been inlaid (Pl. 28b). Other faience objects inlaid in this manner are datable by their inscriptions to Amonhotpe III (2.10.2.2). Small bifrontal masks terminating in podia (*e.g.* Reisner 1958 nos. 1266971, 1266978, 1266986) are quite rare at New Kingdom sites. The only New Kingdom parallels I can find for the larger examples are a piece from among the Hathor offerings at Dendara (Fig. 6.4), and an elaborate mask from Aswan, which probably represents Anukis (Delange in IFAO Cat. 1981.236–7, no. 257).

Other bifrontal Hathor masks from Deir el-Bahri, Serabit el-Khadim, and Timna seem to have been components of model sistra. One badly damaged example with a scroll wig, illustrated by Petrie (1906 pl. 151.7, location unknown), has a projection to one side of its low podium which looks like the wall of a naos. A fragment from the upper part of a faience naos was found by Petrie (1906 pl. 151.10), so it is clear that model naos sistra were offered at this site. Another bifrontal mask illustrated by Petrie was probably a component of such a model (Pl. 29, top right = London V&A 712.1905). It is very well modelled in light green faience, with its scroll wigs, semi-circles, and facial features all marked in dark turquoise. The neck is broken away and there are two square depressions in the top of the head which are probably the bases for the walls of a naos. The piece now measures 7.4 × 9 cm.

A similar, but smaller and less well made bifrontal mask comes from Deir el-Bahri (London V&A 683.1905). This has a hole beneath the chin for the insertion of a handle and a square depression in the surviving half of its podium for the wall of a naos. It might be argued that these masks were from loop sistra, but Hathor masks with wigs are uncommon on loop sistra and the depressions would be narrower if they were for a loop rather than a naos. The discovery at Timna of a faience naos bearing a royal name shows that model naos sistra were also dedicated at this site (Rothenberg 1972 pls. 82–3; 1988.118, pl. 119.1, fig. 28.1). Two other fragments from Timna may also belong to naos sistra (Schulman in Rothenberg 1988.118–9). An 8 cm high fragment from a large bifrontal Hathor mask with a long striated wig is also likely to have formed part of naos sistrum (1988.118, pl. 118.3, fig. 27.1). This piece has a hole in the neck for the insertion of a handle.

Petrie believed that one wigless bifrontal mask had formed part of a naos sistrum (1906.146; Pl. 29, bottom row, second left; location unknown), but the outward curve of the surviving projection suggests a loop rather than a naos. Other wigless bifrontal masks from Serabit el-Khadim have clear remains of loops above their podia (Pl. 29, top row, second left, location unknown; London BM 38181; Cairo CG 37655; Hickmann 1949.91, fig. 37). A very similar mask, which preserves its loop to about a quarter of its original height, was found by Naville at Deir el-Bahri (London V&A 682.1905). Two more damaged masks from the same site (London V&A 1210.1904; Pl. 6c, Carnarvon collection) look as if they might have come from the same mould as V&A 682.1905. Three other wigless masks from Deir el-Bahri (London BM 41086, 43145 = Pl. 30a; Oxford Ash. E 2740 = Naville 1913 pl. 24.3, left) are almost certainly components of loop sistra. Anderson proposes that the examples in the British Museum are from naos sistra (1976.68–9), but the shape of the depressions in their podia and their similarity to the loop sistra noted above, suggests otherwise. These nine masks range in height between 4 and

6 cm. Most are in plain blue faience, but BM 43145 has the details picked out in
dark blue. London BM 41086 has a hole beneath the chin, presumably for the
insertion of a handle in some other material. A large wigless, bifrontal Hathor mask
in green faience from Gebel Zeit (Castel *et al.* 1986.100, pl. 5.14) probably formed
part of a loop sistrum, and the fragmentary wigless Hathor mask from Timna
(Rothenberg 1972 pls. X, 80; 1988 fig. 30.1) may have come from a composite loop
sistrum in which two unifrontal masks were fixed back to back.

Some bronze fragments from Timna have been identified as parts of a loop
sistrum (1972.166, fig. 50; 1988.151). Fragments from the pierced loop of a faience
sistrum were found by Petrie at Serabit el-Khadim (London V&A 720 1905 =
Pl. 30c). The arc is decorated with fans, and with wings which could come from a
vulture or a winged disc. Each side has a Meret figure. The two Merets represent
Upper and Lower Egypt. They are often associated with Hathor and have been
called 'the personification of the priestess as singer' (Troy 1986.87). This
interesting object seems to be the only surviving New Kingdom example of a loop
sistrum with the type of elaborate decoration common on metal sistra of the Late
Period (*e.g.* Anderson 1976.40–5, figs. 70–4; Ziegler 1979.55–8, fig. 67).

At least twelve 'sistrum handles' inscribed with royal names were found at
Serabit el-Khadim. Five of these were illustrated by Petrie (1906 Pl. 151.103.16–
19 = Bolton 68.05.45, 48, 14, 47; 20, location unknown). He discovered six
fragments from other inscribed 'handles' at the same site (London UC 4,
unnumbered; V&A 698.1905; 709.1905). Two similar 'handle' fragments were
excavated at Timna (Rothenberg 1972 pl. 86; 1988.118, fig. 29.4–5) and Naville
found two uninscribed fragments from such 'handles' at Deir el-Bahri (London BM
43176; 47765).

The examples which are almost intact range from 8 to 12 cm high. Some are
round and flare out slightly towards the bottom, while others (*e.g.* Bolton 68.05.47;
Oxford Ash. E 4462a) are straight and rectangular. As already noted, some of these
objects may be components of miniature Hathor columns rather than sistrum
handles. Most have a vertical column of inscription on both back and front. This
usually consists of the name and titles of a royal person, who is described as
'beloved of Hathor' (Pl. 29). Such inscriptions are common on faience sistra of the
Late Period (*e.g.* Hickmann 1949 pls. 60–1; Ziegler 1979.40–4, 51–2). Alternatively,
this formula, which is also found on menit counterpoises (2.9.2.2), could be
translated as 'that which is beloved of' the king and the goddess, referring to the
offering itself (Bianchi 1979.18). One piece from Serabit el-Khadim has a titulary of
Ramesses III in one column and a *ḥtp di nsw* formula for an unnamed person –
perhaps an expedition leader – in the other (Bolton 68.05.46). *Ḥtp di nsw* formulae,
usually for high ranking priests or priestesses, occur on some Third Intermediate or
Late Period sistra (*e.g.* Ziegler 1979.55–6). One fragmentary faience sistrum handle
from Serabit el-Khadim, decorated with a dot and scale pattern (London V&A
709.1905), has an inscription mentioning a high priest of Heliopolis, who may have
been the donor of this object. One ivory sistrum handle from among the offerings
at Dendara was inscribed with the name of a priestess of Hathor (Petrie 1900.28).

New Kingdom amulets in the form of sistra are rare, but a glazed steatite
example, only 1 cm high, was excavated by Griffith at Faras (London BM

51362 = Pls. 8.29, 60a, bottom left). One faience sistrum amulet was found by Carter and Carnarvon at Deir el-Bahri (Pl. 6h, Carnarvon Collection).

Middle Kingdom royal stelae at Serabit el-Khadim mention the presentation of sistra to the goddess (Černý 1955.114). A 12th dynasty bifrontal Hathor mask from Thebes may have been a royal gift of this kind (Bourriau 1988.132, no. 127). The mask, which is inscribed with the titulary of Senwosret I, is in glazed steatite with eyes inlaid in bronze, calcite and obsidian. Holes in the podium and below the chin suggest that this mask formed part of a naos sistrum. I can cite only two comparable New Kingdom large faience or glass Hathor mask sistra (Feucht 1986.152, no. 351; Wildung *et al.* 1985.59–60, no. 43), and these are unprovenanced and fragmentary. Surviving wooden loop sistra (*e.g.* Petrie 1924.26; Anderson 1976.51, fig. 88; Ziegler 1979.54, no. 64), and representations of loop and naos sistra in tomb-paintings and temple reliefs show that, except in the Amarna period, there was relatively little change in the form and decoration of sistra during the New Kingdom. The inscribed 'handles' from Serabit el-Khadim suggest that faience sistra and miniature columns were occasional offerings at this site from the early 18th to the early 20th dynasty. The rulers named are Amonhotpe I (Bolton 68.05.45), Ahmose-Nefertary (Bolton 68.05.48), Thutmose III (Oxford Ash. E 4462a), Amonhotpe III (Toronto ROM 906.16.101), Ramesses II (Bolton 68.05.14, 43), Merenptah (London BM 38182), Seti II (Bolton 68.05.47; London BM 41838), and Ramesses III (Bolton 68.05.46).

C. Flat, shaped Hathor masks (Pls. 28a, 30c–d, 31)

At Serabit el-Khadim 'Another type of tablet had the Hat.hor head cut in outline, the flat surface being painted' (Petrie 1906.147–8). Petrie excavated fragments of about 40 of these flat, Hathor-mask shaped plaques, and illustrated six (1906 pl. 153.1–5). MacDonald had earlier found pieces of four such masks in the temple area (London BM 12872–5). The 25 flat Hathor masks from Serabit el-Khadim which I have been able to examine or obtain detailed information on are between 0.5 and 1 cm thick. When intact, they would have ranged in height from 12 to 20 cm. They are all in pale green faience and most have an almost identical Hathor mask drawn in black on each side (Bolton 68.05.39 = Pl. 31 bottom, centre; Liverpool 49.05.6; London BM 12872–5, 43146, 41839 = Pl. 30c; UC 35348; Manchester 882; Oxford Ash. E 3350–1, 3353, 4464.b, f, 4465.a–c; Sydney 15749, 15751, 15752; Toronto ROM 906.16.93, 98, 99 = Pl. 30d).

These objects can be subdivided into two types: masks with scroll wigs, which end in a long pole neck, and masks with tripartite wigs, which end at the bottom of the wig. The pole necks have usually snapped off, but one mask with a scroll wig has a hole under the chin for the insertion of a handle in some other material (Petrie 1906 pl. 153.3 = Oxford Ash. E 3350–1). The most common headdress is the striped podium, but the loop crown (*e.g.* London BM 41840; Manchester 882; Oxford Ash. E 3353) and a podium encircled by loops (London BM 41839 = Pl. 30c; Oxford Ash. E 4465c; Toronto ROM 906.16.93) also occur. The form of the faience naos illustrated by Petrie suggests that it does not belong to the Hathor mask shown with it (1906 pl. 153.3, upper & lower). It may have come from a model naos sistrum.

A few flat, shaped Hathor masks were found at Deir el-Bahri, but they are smaller and of lower quality than the pieces from Serabit el-Khadim. One specimen, which is broken at the neck and now 4.9 cm high, has a crude Hathor mask with a scroll wig and striped podium on each side (London BM 41091 = Pl. 28a, bottom left). Two similar pieces, which would have been about 5 cm high when intact, are unifrontal (London V&A 1211.1904; Toronto ROM 907.18.170). A more elaborate example 5 cm high, has a Hathor mask with a striated tripartite wig and a naos painted on one side only (Edinburgh RSM 1904.134.13). The only comparative material which I can find for these flat, shaped masks is an unprovenanced piece in the Cairo Museum (Reisner 1958 pl. 5, no. 12669). The flat masks from Serabit el-Khadim have much in common with the Hathor mask plaques from the site, some of which definitely date to the early and mid 18th dynasty (see below). The podium encircled by uraei was first worn by Queen Tiye (G. Robins, pers. comm. 1983), so if the podium with loops in front is interpreted as showing this headdress, the plaques on which it occurs will probably not be earlier than the reign of Amonhotpe III.

D. Hathor mask plaques (Pls. 2, 31)

MacDonald brought back fragments of five oblong Hathor mask plaques from Serabit el-Khadim (London BM 12866–7, 12878–9, 13071), and Petrie excavated about 50 such fragments, of which he illustrated 11 (1906 Pl. 152.1–11). Another two plaques were found during the third Harvard Expedition (Starr & Butin 1936 pl. 13 nos. 68, 93). The 33 oblong plaques which I have been able to examine, or obtain detailed information on, are 0.5–1 cm thick and 12–20 cm high (Bolton 68.05.7; Bristol 3276; Brussels MR 2091–3; Edinburgh RSM 1905.284.19; London BM 12866–7, 12878–9, 13071; UC 35347; V&A 715.1905; Liverpool 49.05.7; Manchester 875, 881; Oxford Ash. E 3354, 3355–6, 4463, 4464.a–e, g–h; Sydney 15753 & 15748; Toronto ROM 906.16.94–6). They are all in green faience. Most are glazed on both sides, and about half are decorated in black on both sides. One plaque has a linear border (London BM 12866).

The Hathor masks shown on these plaques may wear the scroll or the tripartite wig. They all have pole necks, which usually rest on plinths. The striped podium is the most common headdress, but the loop crown (e.g. Pl. 31, left) and the podium encircled by loops (Oxford Ash. 4464.a) also appear. Several of the masks are surmounted by what appears to be a naos (e.g. Pl. 31, centre and right). One example has a naos topped by a row of uraei (Manchester 875). On several plaques the pole neck is flanked by lotus buds (Pl. 31; Starr & Butin 1936 pl. 13.68 [photographed upside down]; Oxford Ash. E 3356, 4464.g). In a few cases the plaques have an inscription, written on either side of the pole neck (Petrie 1906 pl. 152.5, 9–11 [location unknown]). Petrie found one plaque inscribed with the cartouche of Amonhotpe I, two with that of Hatshepsut, and five with that of Thutmose III (1906.149). On one of these plaques the name of Hathor is written below that of Thutmose III (Edinburgh RSM 1905.284.19) and on another (Starr & Butin 1936 pl. 13.93) a king, whose name is lost, is described as 'beloved of Hathor, Lady of Mefkat'. These inscriptions indicate a date range from the early to the mid 18th dynasty. As noted above, the podium with loops in front may extend the date range to the late 18th dynasty. The absence of any examples with Ramessid inscriptions suggests that these objects were only offered during the 18th dynasty.

These oblong Hathor plaques appear to be unique to Serabit el-Khadim. The closest parallel being the faience cat plaques from the same site (2.5.2). A broken faience plaque from Deir el-Bahri is decorated with an ear and a *wadjet* eye and below them something which might be the top of the podium of a Hathor mask (Pl. 2, top, centre = London BM 41079). The only other pieces from Deir el-Bahri that can be classed as Hathor plaques are one fragment which might come from an oblong plaque (Liverpool 13.10.04.17), and a small, pierced faience oval incised with two Bat symbols with curious projections between their horns (Pl. 2 top, centre).

2.3.3   Objects decorated with Hathor masks

1   *Vessels*

A. Stone

A sandstone basin carved on the outside with a Hathor mask was recovered from Djeser-Akhet (Lipińska 1966.72; 1984.56, No. 79). The bowl, which was found in nine pieces, is 62 cm in diameter. It has an inscription consisting of an offering formula for a *waab*-priest and chief sculptor and his wife, who are shown on either side of the Hathor mask kneeling with their arms raised in adoration. Another sandstone fragment from this temple, inscribed with a *ḥtp di nsw* formula addressed to Hathor, Lady of Djeser and showing a high official called Amoneminet (see 2.3.3.3) kneeling in adoration (Lipińska 1968.169, pl. 13.22; 1984.56, No. 80), is likely to have come from a basin carved with a Hathor mask. The inscription includes a cartouche of Ramesses II. The general date range for such bowls is from the late 18th dynasty to the end of the Late Period (2.11.1.1).

B. Faience (Pls. 3, 32a–c, 45c–d)

One green faience Hathor mask from Serabit el-Khadim could come from a vessel or have formed part of a composite sistrum (Toronto ROM 906.16.89). Fragments from faience 'marsh' bowls were recovered from five of the six sites (2.11.3). Hathor masks or sistra are among the rarer decorative motifs on these bowls (Strauss 1974.20; Milward in Brovarski 1982.141), but a few examples have been found at Deir el-Bahri, Faras, and Serabit el-Khadim. In most cases the Hathor mask is on the inside of the bowl, while the outside has lotus petal decoration. There is considerable variety in the depictions of Hathor on such bowls. Hall noted that at Deir el-Bahri 'Both the cow and the [Hathor] head appear very often on the fine votive bowls' (in Naville 1913.15), but I have traced only eight examples with Hathor masks or sistra from this site. A fragment from a large bowl decorated with a Hathor mask with a striated wig bound with ribbons was among the objects from the 1892–5 excavations illustrated by Miss Carhew (Pl. 3, centre). Two bowl fragments from the 1904–7 excavations, each bearing the upper right-hand side of a Hathor mask, were published by Hall (in Naville 1913 pl. 26.3, upper = London V&A 668.1905; lower = London BM 43148). One has a striated wig and a podium, while the other wears a striped podium with volutes. Two further fragments from Deir el-Bahri also show Hathor masks with tripartite wigs and podia (London V&A 667.1905; Strauss 1974 fig. 37). A piece from a very small bowl has a Hathor mask with a striped podium, a dark tripartite wig, and a pole neck from which two lotus buds appear to grow (Manchester E 4347). On another fragment from a small bowl, the Hathor mask has a striated wig and is surmounted by a naos (Pl. 32a = Brussels MR E 718). A piece from a much larger bowl has a mask with a pole neck and a striated scroll wig but no headdress (London BM 41018).

Griffith illustrated one bowl fragment showing a Hathor mask with a striated wig and a triangle crown (1921 pl. 20a, location unknown). Four other bowl fragments with Hathor masks survive from this site. A piece from a large bowl has a badly drawn mask with a very tall striped podium (Pl. 32b, right = London BM 51252). A smaller fragment shows part of a mask with a striated scroll wig and a pole neck (Pl. 32b, left = London BM 51254). The third piece has a striped podium and striated wig, and the fourth a dark wig and no headdress (Oxford Ash. 1912.941a–b; Karkowski 1981 pls. 11.b, 12.b). Petrie did not mention or illustrate any bowls with Hathor masks from Serabit el-Khadim, but the Ashmolean Museum has three small fragments from these excavations decorated with Hathor masks with striped wigs and podia (in Boxes E 4457 & 4457.3).

The appearance of these bowls can be reconstructed by reference to a small number of intact or nearly intact examples from other New Kingdom sites (e.g. Boulos 1906.2, fig. 6; Borchardt 1910.131–2, figs. 179–80; Scamuzzi 1963 pl. 55; Strauss 1974.20, figs. 16–8). Most have a patterned rectangle in the centre representing water and marsh flora. Hathor masks with pole necks are shown rising from this water. Some bowls have two Hathor masks opposite each other. On a small bowl from Nag el-Kelebat there are four masks, one for each side of the rectangle of water (Boulos 1906 fig. 6). A bowl from the sanctuary of Sekhmet at Abusir depicts a Hathor cow and a Hathor mask in a marsh setting (Borchardt 1910 fig. 179). For the date range and function of these bowls, see 2.11.3.

The Royal Ontario Museum has a fragment of a shallow faience bowl from Deir el-Bahri which has a Hathor mask drawn on the exterior (907.18.217 = Pl. 32c). The mask has a striated scroll wig and striped podium and was flanked by bouquets. The inside of the fragment is undecorated. This piece seems to reproduce in faience the type of votive stone basin which has one or more Hathor masks carved on the exterior. Another faience fragment from Deir el-Bahri, which has an inscription containing prayers to Hathor and the figure of a priest adoring (Naville 1913 pl. 26.5 = Oxford Ash. 2745), probably comes from such a bowl. Some faience fragments excavated by Rothenberg at Timna (1972 pl. 91) may have formed part of a bowl with a Hathor mask flanked by cats drawn on the exterior (2.5.4). The closest parallels are two small faience bowls from the sanctuary of Sekhmet at Abusir, one of which has a seated figure of Sekhmet on the exterior and the other a man adoring Amon in ram form (Borchardt 1910.133, fig. 181).

A type of object that appears to be unique to Serabit el-Khadim is the circular faience jar or bowl stand decorated with Hathor masks, or with Hathor masks and a pair of cats (2.5.4; 2.11.2). Petrie illustrated only one example (1906 pl. 150.16), but I have traced three other ring-stand fragments with Hathor masks (Pls. 32d,

45c–d). Two wear the scroll wig and one the tripartite wig. All three have a podium. For the motif of the Hathor mask flanked by cats, see 2.5.4–5.

C. Pottery (Fig. 1; Pls. 1, 33a–b)

Naville and Hall mentioned finding pottery vessels decorated with Hathor masks at Deir el-Bahri and illustrated ten examples (1913.25, pls. 23–4, 32; Fig. 1, Pl. 1). At least 11 fragments from such vessels were distributed by the EEF. The ten examples which I have been able to examine come from three different types of vessel. Four are redware sherds between 5 and 9 cm high. These have Hathor masks just below the pot rim which are quite well modelled in low relief (London BM 41000, 47679, 49250 = Pl. 33a; Oxford Ash. E 2716). Three of these sherds show traces of paint, the faces being yellow, the tripartite wigs blue, and the features picked out in black. Hall illustrated one sherd which is probably of this type (Fig. 1.2, location unknown) that has breasts below the Hathor mask.

Five grey sherds between 3.6 and 11.5 cm high have very crude Hathor masks modelled in high relief (London BM 40998–9 = Pl. 1.1, bottom left, 43150– 1 = Fig. 1.5, 35, 43152). The wig can be scroll or tripartite, but none of these pieces has cow's ears or a recognizable headdress. Two have the features and the stripes of the wig picked out in black, and two are carelessly painted in blue and yellow. Tall necked jars decorated with modelled Hathor masks seem to have been quite common during the Second Intermediate Period and 18th dynasty, at least in the Theban area (Guidotti 1978.105–18; Hope in Brovarski 1982.86–7). A redware sherd with a Hathor mask in low relief that comes an 18th dynasty tomb at Deir el-Medina and another found near the mortuary temple of Thutmose IV (Guidotti 1978.110, figs. 12–3) are very similar to the redware sherds from Deir el-Bahri. These pieces seem to be forerunners of the very large blue-painted jars with modelled Hathor masks produced in the late 18th dynasty and the Amarna period (*e.g.* Hayes 1959.247–8, fig. 150; Guidotti 1978.112–5; Wildung *et al.* 1985.60, no. 42).

Hall and Naville also recovered some tall pottery vessels decorated with projecting flowers and Hathor masks (1913.25). A bifrontal mask from such a vase is now in the British Museum (47680 = Pl. 33b, left). It is 5 cm high, and has a very elongated neck and a striped podium. Traces of blue, black and yellow paint remain. Hall suggested that this pottery imitated metal temple vessels with rims decorated with flowers, Hathor masks, cows, cats etc. (in Naville 1913.15; see further 2.5.4; 2.11.5).

2 *Jewellery decorated with Hathor masks* (Fig. 3; Pls. 33c, 60a)

Some of the small faience Hathor masks are pierced or have loops for suspension and may have been strung by themselves or as part of votive necklaces or bracelets (2.9.2.1). A square, vertically pierced, seal carved with a Hathor mask was found by Naville at Deir el-Bahri (Boston MFA 06.2493; G. Spalinger in Brovarski 1982.253, no. 358). The seal, which is 1.4 × 1 cm, is made in glazed steatite. It has the name Amonhotpe – probably Amonhotpe I – inscribed on its base. A similar Hathor mask seal from Deir el-Bahri drawn by Miss Carhew has a floral design on its base (Fig. 3, top left). At Faras, Griffith excavated two pierced Hathor mask scaraboids which are made in glazed steatite. They each have a scroll wig and a podium (London BM 51326 = Pl. 60a, bottom right, 51346). The first has an *ʿnḫ* and a *nb* on the base, and the second has a *nfr* and a ⨍ sign. Hathor mask scarabs and seals seem to be confined to the early and mid 18th dynasty (Brunton & Engelbach 1927 pl. 21; Hayes 1959.126), although Hathor masks, Bat symbols and sistra are found on the bases of scarabs and scaraboids throughout the New Kingdom (Hornung & Staehelin 1976.324–5; Thomas 1981 pl. 31).

Menit necklaces were dedicated at Deir el-Bahri, Mirgissa, Serabit el-Khadim, and Timna (2.9.2.2). The counterpoises sometimes show Hathor masks or heads. This is the case with an unusual pair of bronze menit counterpoises found by Winlock at Deir el-Bahri (New York MMA 23.3.137; Hayes 1959.173, 182). Each counterpoise is 5.3 cm long and pierced twice at the top and once at the bottom of the stem. Both have a floral design of standard type on their discs. In the middle of each stem is a crudely incised Hathor mask loop sistrum and below this a wigless mask with a striped podium. On one counterpoise the reverse side is plain, but the other has the floral design on both sides of its disc. Double counterpoises were originally standard on menit necklaces (Aldred 1971.45, 227), so these objects are likely to have been attached to the same miniature necklace.

Some menit counterpoises of the reign of Amonhotpe III and later terminate in a head of Hathor in profile (2.9.2.2). One wooden counterpoise of this type was excavated at Mirgissa (Karlin in Vercoutter 1970 Inv. no. 3, fig. 40). This poorly carved piece is 15.4 cm long. The Hathor head has a tripartite wig and the disc and horns headdress. The disc is painted red, the horns are blue, and the details of the face are picked out in black. Petrie found two fragments from similar counterpoises in faience at Serabit el-Khadim (1906.149). One of these is in the British Museum (41837 = 1906 pl. 148.13). It is made in green faience and is now 9 cm long. On one side, the goddess is named as Hathor, Mistress of Mefkat. On the other, is the top of a cartouche, probably that of Merenptah. Hathor wears a broad collar, a striated tripartite wig, and a podium. She does not have cow's ears, since this is the head of the human form of the goddess, or of a queen in the role of the goddess, rather than a Hathor mask. One faience fragment illustrated by Miss Carhew (Fig. 3, bottom) might possibly come from the stem of a menit counterpoise. Only the end of an inscription naming the goddess and the disc and horns of Hathor survive.

One other category of jewellery is Hathor mask rings. Although he did not mention them in his report, Petrie found at least seven blue faience rings at Serabit el-Khadim with bezels consisting of a Hathor mask (London UC 30064–6 = Pl. 33c, 35456a–d). On each of these crude rings, the Hathor mask has a scroll wig and podium. The British Museum has one blue faience ring from Deir el-Bahri with a bezel in the form of a Hathor mask with tripartite wig and podium (47703). Faience Hathor mask rings are suprisingly rare. One example now in Liverpool may have come from el-ʿAmarna (56.21.383; Boyce in Kemp 1989.161, fig. 8.1). The Haskell Museum, Chicago has two unprovenanced examples (Allen 1923.214), while the Metropolitan Museum of Art has a Ramessid example bought at Deir el-Ballas (Hayes 1959.397). One Hathor mask ring was found in the tomb of an early 19th

dynasty prince or high official at Gurob (Brunton & Engelbach 1927 pl. 31.17).
Few faience rings are thought to have been made before the time of Amonhotpe III
(Boyce in Kemp 1989.160). The Hathor-mask rings from Deir el-Bahri and Serabit
el-Khadim may date to this king's reign.

3 *Stelae, textiles, and statues with Hathor masks* (Figs. 1, 18; Pls. 13–14)

Five stelae which fall into this category have already been noted (2.1 Lists 1.16;
3.11–4). On the example from Deir el-Bahri, the Hathor mask is surmounted by a
naos and flanked by stems of papyrus (Fig. 1.1). It is unusual in showing a falcon
rather than a uraeus in the naos. Further falcons perch on top of the papyrus
umbels. Two of the stelae from Serabit el-Khadim are carved with Hathor mask
columns or Hathor masks mounted on poles, each mask having a scroll wig and a
podium (Brussels MR E 3085–6). On the first of these, the mask is flanked by lotus
buds, as on some of the faience plaques (*e.g.* Pl. 31). The third of the Serabit
el-Khadim stelae has a woman adoring a Hathor mask sistrum (Pl. 13a). The fourth
stela shows two men adoring a Hathor mask which is unusual in combining a scroll
wig with the incurving horns of the Bat symbol, and in having an elongated neck of
plaited hair (Pl. 14). Two Hathor masks on a votive faience bowl from Abydos
which bears the cartouche of Ahmose-Nefertary provide further examples of these
rare plaited necks (Strauss 1974 fig. 18). Such necks might be derived from the
beard or ruff of early Bat symbols (*e.g.* Allam 1963 pl. 2; A. Wilkinson 1971 pl. 1a)
or from the 'Hathor lock' which was sometimes substituted for a papyrus stem in
mirror handles (*e.g.* Garstang 1901 pl. 14.12; Staehelin 1978.81). A sandstone
fragment incised with part of a Hathor mask wearing a striped podium with
volutes, was found by the second Harvard Expedition to Serabit el-Khadim
(Leibovitch 1934.3, fig. 4). It may come from a small stela, though the light incision
could indicate that it was an ostracon.

Although never common, Hathor mask stelae occur from the reign of
Hatshepsut to the end of the New Kingdom. Most of the surviving examples are
Ramessid (Vandier 1966.76–84; Wildung 1974.258–68, figs. 1–16). Many of these
stelae come from the temple and votive shrines of Deir el-Medina. Hathor masks on
plinths, Hathor mask columns, and Hathor mask naos sistra are all shown being
adored by donors. The mask, sistrum, or column is usually identified in the
inscription as Hathor, but is sometimes associated with other deities, such as
Anukis (Valbelle 1985.330). A shirt from Deir el-Bahri is the only surviving New
Kingdom votive textile to depict a Hathor mask (2.2, Cat.5.2). The mask has a
pole neck, and a scroll wig painted blue with red ribbons (Pl. 14b).

Four private statues from Deir el-Bahri and one from Serabit el-Khadim
incorporate Hathor emblems. Although private temple statues have been excluded
from this study on the ground that they are primarily funerary rather than votive,
this particular type of statue can provide valuable evidence on the cult of Hathor.
Such statues have been termed 'sistrophorous' (Clère 1969.1–2), but some examples
incorporate Hathor masks or columns rather than sistra.

A granite statue of Senenmut recovered from Djeser-Akhet shows him
kneeling and holding out a Hathor mask surmounted by a naos and terminating in a

tyet symbol (Marciniak 1965.201–7, pls. 21–3; Lipińska 1984.21, No. 17). This unusual combination is found on three 'sistrophorous' statues of Senenmut from other temples (Benson & Gourlay 1899 pl. 12; Vandier 1958 pl. 155; Meyer 1982.80–1). Another statue from Djeser-Akhet depicts a kneeling man holding a Hathor mask naos sistrum (Dąbrowska-Smektała 1968.98, pl. 4; Lipińska 1984.31, No. 23). This small statue probably dates to the early 19th dynasty and is said to be made of porphyry. A badly damaged 19th dynasty statue found in Akh-isut depicts a kneeling Chiselbearer of Amon holding a Hathor mask (Naville 1913.23, pl. 14.6 = Philadelphia UM 11783).

A limestone pseudo-block statue recovered from Djeser-Akhet is that of Amoneminet, a high official under Ramesses II (Fig. 18; Lipińska 1966.67, pl. 1; 1969.41–9; 1969a.28–30; 1984.21–4, No. 18; Romano 1979.148–9, figs. 120–1 = Luxor J 141). A Hathor mask naos sistrum is carved as if leaning against the knees and one hand is cupped in front of the mouth, so this can be classified as a 'begging statue' (for other examples see London BM 501; Borchardt 1930 pl. 155; Strasbourg Cat. 1953 pl. 35; Vandier 1958 pls. 128, 154; Bjorkman 1971 pl. 5). An 'intermediary' inscription on this statue is translated and discussed in 3.2.3.

The example from Serabit el-Khadim is a crude sandstone block-statue of a Chief of Medjayu (Butin 1932.196, pl. 25; Leibovitch 1934.1–7, figs. 5–7; Černý 1955.203, no. 369, fig. 16 = Cairo JE 53833). Carved in low relief on the knees is a Hathor mask, surmounted by a naos and terminating in the trapezoidal panel characteristic of the Bat symbol. Both this statue and the Hathor emblem stelae from Serabit el-Khadim give the impression of having been made by inferior craftsmen with imperfect knowledge of the approved iconography of Hathor.

The statues of Senenmut are the earliest known 'sistrophorous statues' (Clère 1969.1–2). He may have invented or popularized this statue type, which continued throughout the New Kingdom and into the Late Period (Russmann 1973). H. Bonnet suggested that 'sistrophorous' and naophorous statues represented persons who were privileged to carry images or cult objects of deities in festival processions (1961.95). Some such statues are inscribed with a 'protection formulae' in which the statue owner claims to protect the image of the deity in return for divine patronage (Ranke 1943.107; Otto 1948.456–7; see further 3.2.3).

2.3.4 Symbolic value and functions

One indication that it is worthwhile to make distinctions between the various types of object which incorporate a Hathor mask is the clear difference in status between the loop (*sḫmt*) and the naos (*sššt*) sistrum. During the New Kingdom, loop sistra do not appear on votive plaques or bowls, or as part of 'sistrophorous' statues, and they are not shown being adored on stelae or in tomb paintings or temple reliefs. There are a few examples of loop-sistrum amulets (*e.g.* Pl. 60a), but miniature forms of other instruments, such as the adze or the aegis, were used as amulets. Although the incorporation of a cow-eared mask associates the loop sistrum with Hathor, there is no evidence that it was regarded as a form of her. The loop sistra among the offerings appear to be models or functional examples of a cult instrument, but this is not necessarily the case with the naos sistra.

A 12th dynasty text from Serabit el-Khadim records that a wooden naos sistrum was among the gifts which the leaders of an expedition offered to Hathor on behalf of the king (Černý 1952 pl. 37, no. 112, line 4; 1955.114). From the New Kingdom onwards, the naos sistrum appears as part of 'sistrophorous' statues, usually with the name of the goddess inscribed on the handle (*e.g.* Romano 1979 fig. 120). The naos sistrum also occurs on New Kingdom votive bowls, plaques and stelae (2.3.3). Some of the stelae show Hathor mask naos sistra as big, or bigger than, the donors who adore or make offerings to them (*e.g.* Wildung 1974.259, figs. 1, 4, 15). The sistrum is usually accompanied by an inscription consisting of the name and epithets of Hathor. On a stela from Deir el-Medina whose upper register shows a woman adoring a goddess in human form and a naos sistrum flanked by cats, both the goddess and the sistrum are give captions naming them as (Hathor) Nebet-Hetepet (Černý 1958 no. 7; Wildung 1974.263 fig. 12). Either Hathor was considered to have a naos sistrum form, or the naos sistrum was an emblem which conveyed the idea of a goddess present within her sanctuary. An 18th dynasty block from Serabit el-Khadim shows a naos sistrum holding out *ankh* signs (Černý 1952 no. 202; Wildung 1974 fig. 2), but the rarity of this image in New Kingdom temple reliefs suggests that the naos sistrum did not enjoy the status of the human or even of the cow form of Hathor.

The status of the Hathor column is even more ambiguous. Cow-eared mask columns seem to have been strictly confined to religious architecture and furnishings, but when they were a functional part of a structure it is unlikely that they were regarded as representations of a deity on a par with cult images or other types of temple statue. However, there is some evidence for non-structural Hathor columns, such as one found by Petrie in the middle of an open court at Serabit el-Khadim (1906.86), which might have been the objects of a cult. Given the New Kingdom practice of visitors making offerings to colossal statues and figures in reliefs in the outer areas of temples (Yoyotte 1960.42–4), it is also possible that some cow-eared mask columns on the facades of Hathor shrines became the objects of unofficial cults. A few 'sistrophorous' statues (*e.g.* Vandier 1958 pl. 150; Clère 1969 pl. 1.3) and votive stelae (*e.g.* Wildung 1974.259, 261 figs. 3, 6) feature Hathor columns. One such stelae depicts a cow-eared mask column, labelled as Hathor, adored by a priest and his wife (London BM 744 = 1974 fig. 6). This, with the evidence of the wooden column from Deir el-Bahri inscribed with the name of Hathor, Lady of Dendara, suggests that a Hathor column could sometimes be a form of the goddess. I cannot find an example of such a form in a New Kingdom temple relief, but a Late Period relief in the temple of Opet at Karnak shows a king offering to a Hathor column surmounted by a sun disc which stands on a tall plinth (Varille 1955.112–3, pl. 25).

The Hathor mask itself seems was used as a decorative motif and was quite a common amulet. Large Hathor masks sometimes form part of 'sistrophorous' statues (*e.g.* Bruyère 1952 pl. 2; Vandier 1958 pl. 128.6; Hornemann T no. 1027). A stela from Deir el-Medina depicts a Hathor mask flanked by bouquets with a man adoring and four women bringing offerings (Wildung 1974.263 fig. 10). An ostracon from the same site shows a man presenting a lotus bud to a Hathor mask, identified as Hathor, Foremost in Thebes, rising from a blue lotus (1974.261 fig. 7;

IFAO Cat. 1981 no. 280). These pieces suggest that a simple Hathor mask can sometimes be a form of the goddess. I have found no New Kingdom temple reliefs in which a King offers to a Hathor mask, though the temple of Nekhbet built by Amonhotpe III at el-Kab has a Hathor mask frieze (Badawy 1968 fig. 144, pl. 35). The Hathor mask does occur quite frequently in the reliefs of the Graeco-Roman temple of Dendara, where a giant Hathor mask on the outside of the rear wall was a focus for popular devotion (Derchain 1972.11).

The problem of classifying the Hathor masks with pole necks shown on faience plaques from Serabit el-Khadim has already been noted (2.3.1). Petrie's suggestion that they represent a Hathor mask mounted on a carrying pole for display at festivals, would certainly help to explain the prominence of the Hathor mask at this site. Such a mask on a pole might be analogous to the cult of the $wḥ$ symbol in the temple of Hathor at Cusae (Blackman 1914.2). A scene in Theban Tomb 216 depicts a festival of Satis and Anukis at Deir el-Medina during which a giant sistrum was carried in procession (Valbelle 1985.330). There must have been similar festivals and processions linked to Hathor shrines. It is also possible that the Hathor mask with a pole neck shown on the Serabit el-Khadim plaques represents a sacred standard carried by each mining expedition to protect them on their journey to and from the temple.

It is sometimes difficult to distinguish between the various classes of object, particularly in the case of naos sistra and naos sistrum columns. Often more may be implied than is shown. For example, Hathor masks with volutes should perhaps be interpreted as naos sistra even if no naos is shown. The fact that both Hathor masks and Hathor mask naos sistra are depicted on the faience plaques from Serabit el-Khadim (Pl. 31) could be used to argue that the mask and the naos sistrum were used interchangeably, but such evidence does not prove that they were inter-changeable in all circumstances. Here, as with Egyptian iconography in general, it is safest to assume that there were rules, however hard they may be to discern.

In an article on sistra, B. George distinguishes between model Hathor columns and Hathor sistra, but comes to the conclusion that there was little difference between their symbolic values (1978.30). This may be a question partly of context and partly of period. When naos sistra came to be incorporated into the design of columns in the 18th dynasty, it is natural that a transfer of symbolism from Hathor column to sistra – and perhaps vice versa – should have taken place. They may also each have retained older and distinct symbolic values.

On the basis of the sistra and menits found at Serabit el-Khadim, Giveon referred to Hathor being worshipped in Sinai as a goddess of music (1978.68–73). It is not clear that naos sistra should be regarded as musical instruments, but Hathor's association with music and dance is undeniable. The association is not so much with music and dance in the abstract as with their role in worship and festivals, particularly in relation to fertility (2.6.3–4). It is significant here that Hathor Nebet-Hetepet, an epithet which may mean either 'The Lady of the Vulva' or 'Lady of the Uterus' is commonly depicted as a naos sistrum (Vandier 1966.76–82). The epithet 'Hand of Atum', which is sometimes given to Hathor Nebet-Hetepet, refers to her sexual union with the Creator (2.7.3). This has led to suggestions that Hathor in naos sistrum form embodies the female creative principle (Derchain 1972.45–8), and that the sistrum handle can be regarded as a phallic symbol (Westendorf 1967.145). There is some evidence that requests relating to fertility were made to Hathor Nebet-Hetepet (2.6.3), and it may be no coincidence that the only naos sistrum at Serabit el-Khadim to be identified with [Hathor] Nebet-Hetepet is adored by a woman (Pl. 14a).

It is not certain whether the Hathor mask or the Hathor column had any sexual symbolism, but it is noteworthy that several Near Eastern goddesses with strong associations with fertility are shown with cow's ears and wearing scroll wigs and podia both on clay and metal plaques from Syria and Palestine and on Second Intermediate Period scarabs and Ramessid stelae from Egypt (2.6.2). E. Hermsen sees the Hathor column as a 'Tree of Life' symbol linked, like the *djed* column, with the fertility of the soil and the annual death and regeneration of vegetation (1981.51). The tree with which Hathor is most closely identified – the sycamore – did not grow very tall or large-trunked in Egypt, so a link between tree and column cannot be automatically assumed. Hathor columns and masks appear to be associated with marsh flora. This undergoes little seasonal change and so is unlikely to symbolize crop regeneration.

Some votive plaques and stelae show Hathor masks and columns flanked by lotus buds (*e.g.* Pl. 31). Hathor columns can have blue lotus capitals, Hathor masks on bowls have lotus buds attached to their pole necks, and an ostracon depicts a Hathor mask above a blue lotus. In some of these instances, the Hathor mask seems to replace an open blue lotus, which is often shown between two buds. This can be equated with the primeval lotus from which the infant Sun God was born, and therefore symbolizes Hathor's role as the mother of Re' (Strauss 1974.70–3, 84–5). If the 'double stair' used as a base on a votive Hathor column from Deir el-Bahri can be identified with the primeval mound, which is sometimes shown in this shape (*e.g.* Clark 1978.39, 171, figs. 2, 27), this would provide a link between the Hathor column and the emergence of the Creator from the primeval waters.

On several votive stelae, Hathor mask columns or sistra are shown flanked by papyrus (*e.g.* Fig. 1.8; Wildung 1974.261 figs. 4, 6). A papyrus stem formed part of the *wh* symbol (Staehelin 1978.78–9), and the combination of papyrus umbels and Hathor masks on capitals has already been mentioned (2.3.1). Naos sistra, as well as Hathor mask mirrors, can have papyriform handles (*e.g.* Davies 1920.69–70, pl. 1; Tutundjian 1986.77, pl. 1). It has been suggested that the word *sšš't* is onomatopoeic and imitates the rustling of papyrus (Junker 1940.79). Connections have been made between the offering of both papyrus and sistra and the myth of Horus in Chemmis (Gutbub 1962.54–5). Giveon wrote that:–

> The name would seem to recall an ancient festival on which papyrus was pulled and the noise of the pulling and of the waving of the plants was conceived of as music which recalled the days when Hathor guarded her child Horus in the papyrus thicket of Chemmis. The presentation of a sistrum to Hathor or to a king is therefore not so much of a musical signifance as a wish for protection – as Horus was protected – and for long life. (1978a.108–9)

If the naos sistrum does evoke the suckling of Horus in Chemmis, the significance may not be restricted to asking the protection of the goddess, since this image has connotations of birth, rebirth, and revitalization (see 2.4.5).

Some scholars have seen the two faces of the bifrontal Hathor mask as symbolizing Hathor's double role as a goddess of birth and death (Daumas 1970.73; Hermsen 1981.49), while George suggests that they express her position as the mediator of life and death (1978.30). This might explain why, in the 'cow and mountain' motif, the Hathor cow who stands on the threshold of the realm of the dead sometimes wears a loop sistrum or a Bat symbol around her neck (*e.g.* Pl. 20). A funerary significance for the loop sistrum is suggested by its occasional inclusion among burial goods (*e.g.* Quibell 1908 pl. 50; Petrie & Brunton 1924.26; Hickmann 1949.90–1), by the fact that some late 18th dynasty *shabtis* hold a pair of loop sistra (Hayes 1959.325), and by scenes from the Beautiful Festival of the Wadi in Theban tombs in which the tomb owner is offered menits and loop sistra by his female relatives to revitalize his *ka* (Schott 1953.110–12).

The tomb friezes in which Hathor masks alternate with seated figures of Anubis in his full animal form (Abdul-Qader Muhammed 1966.51–2, 169) suggest that the mask could also be associated with Hathor's role as goddess of the necropolis. Hathor mask pilasters are occasionally found in New Kingdom tombs (von Mercklin 1962.10–3; Haeny 1977.1039). Hermsen argues for a funerary significance for the miniature wooden Hathor column found at Deir el-Bahri (1981.51). He proposes that the double stair which forms the base can be identified with the Western Mountain, and that this object can therefore be linked with Hathor's role in the nightly death and daily rebirth of the sun. The inscription (2.3.2.2) might then be interpreted as a request for revitalization of the *ka* in the afterlife. I know of no evidence for the Western Mountain being shown in this fashion, but the double stair might represent 𓏺𓄿𓇇𓊹𓈖𓍼𓂋 – 'The Beautiful Western Stair', which seems to have been the route from the mortuary temple of Seti I to the Valley of the Kings via 'The Peak' (Spiegelberg 1898.9). This might support Hermsen's hypothesis, but the funerary aspect should not be overemphasized. Royal texts suggest that the presentation of sistra and menit necklaces, and the wearing of a Bat necklace during the Sed Festival, were thought to bestow a long earthly life and renewed vitality on the king (Wente in Wilson 1969.83–92; Staehelin 1982.53). The inscription on the wooden column could then relate to the earthly life of the donor.

Some scholars have seen the bifrontal mask as symbolizing the dual nature of Hathor, who is both gentle and benevolent and fierce and destructive (Brunner 1955.7–9; Bleeker 1973.61–2). Since the sistrum could be an instrument of pacification (Gardiner 1916.100–3; Brunner 1955.1955.5–11; Gutbub 1962.59), offerings of sistra may have been intended to pacify the dangerous and destructive aspect of Hathor and evoke her benevolent and creative one. The dangerous feline forms of the goddess described in the myth of the 'Distant Goddess' were prominent at Serabit el-Khadim and Timna (see further 2.5.5), which might explain the high number of sistra at these sites. It is not certain whether the Hathor column and the Hathor mask also had connotations of pacification. The sistrum can be an attribute of Hathor, who is sometimes shown presenting sistra to Amon-Reꜥ (Bonnet 1952.718). P. Derchain has suggested that in the incident of the presentation of sistra and menit necklaces to the angry king in the story of Sinuhe, the queen and princesses are playing the role of Hathor pacifying Reᶜ (1970.79–83). In 'The Contendings of Horus and Seth', Hathor 'pacifies' Reᶜ by displaying her genitals (2.6.3). The word 'pacify' may be misleading here, since the text implies that the Sun God is sexually aroused by Hathor's display, but his arousal banishes the negative and restores his positive aspect. This leads back to the union of the phallus of Reᶜ-Atum with Hathor, Lady of the Vulva, (2.7.3) and the sexual symbolism of the sistrum. W. Westendorf suggests that in the scenes on the small gold shrine of Tutankhamon in which the queen presents sistra to the king, the royal pair are re-enacting the creative sexual union of Hathor and Reᶜ-Atum (1967.145; 1977.296–8).

Derchain links the idea of Hathor as the female creative principle to representations of her with four faces, which he sees as emphasizing the cosmic aspect of the goddess (1972.45–8). His evidence for 'Hathor Quadrifrons' all comes from the Late and Graeco-Roman periods, but columns with four Hathor masks at Serabit el-Khadim (von Mercklin 1962 figs. 19–20), and a faience bowl decorated with four Hathor columns (Boulos 1906 fig. 6) seem to provide 18th dynasty examples. The practice of showing four Hathor masks may have arisen from a desire to decorate all four sides of a capital or to create a symmetrical pattern on a bowl and have acquired a symbolic value subsequently. It is difficult to judge whether the bifrontal mask was thought to be facing east and west, the directions associated with life and the afterlife, or south and north, which might express various aspects of the union of Upper and Lower Egypt.

There is some late evidence that 'Hathor Quadrifrons' was regarded as the 'The Mistress of the Four Quarters of Heaven' (Derchain 1972.45–6). Borchardt suggested that naos sistra were thought to support the four 'corners' of heaven, citing a Late Period pendant which shows Shu separating Geb and Nut and a pair of naos sistra holding them apart (1897.55, fig. 86). This concept of the 'corners' of heaven probably became attached to the naos sistrum after it began to be incorporated in Hathor columns. A double stair (or step pyramid) is the determinative for words associated with ascending or high places. Yet another possible explanation for the form of the miniature wooden column base from Deir el-Bahri is that it represents this hieroglyph. If so, the column should be thought of as supporting the sky and symbolizing Hathor's cosmic aspect. There is also the myth of the Divine Cow carrying Reᶜ-Atum up into the heavens (2.4.6). Hathor in her cow and human forms bears the sun disc between her horns. Hathor mask mirrors, and the relief in the temple of Opet showing a Hathor column terminating in sun disc and horns (Varille 1955 pl. 25), suggest that Hathor masks and columns might also be associated with supporting the Sun God. Not only was Hathor identified with the 'Sky Cow', she was also the fierce uraeus or 'Eye' on the brow of Reᶜ (Clark 1978.218–30). To show Hathor with two or four faces may have evoked the image of the Solar Eye which could look in all directions at once to protect the Sun God – and also perhaps the donor of the mask or column – from his enemies. Finally, the occurrence of a Hathor mask, sistrum, or column in place of the human form of the goddess may sometimes be due to decorum, rather than to a desire to evoke a specific aspect of the goddess.

Summary

Objects consisting of, or including, a cow-eared Hathor face are often referred to as sistra, but it is important to be more precise. This material can be divided into at least four types: loop sistra, naos sistra, Hathor masks, and Hathor mask columns. Most of these Hathor objects were strongly influenced by the iconography of the goddess Bat. There is evidence for Hathor being worshipped in naos-sistrum form and, less commonly, in Hathor column and Hathor mask forms. The two types of sistra, the masks, and the columns were sometimes used interchangeably as Hathor symbols, but each had a separate function and set of symbolic values.

The 18th dynasty Hathor shrines at Deir el-Bahri and the Hathor shrine at Timna incorporate Hathor columns. The Hathor temple at Serabit el-Khadim contains an exceptional number of Hathor columns, ranging in date from the early Middle Kingdom to the 20th dynasty. Model sistra, Hathor masks, and columns are prominent among the small offerings from this site. 18th dynasty faience plaques from Serabit el-Khadim which show Hathor masks mounted on carrying poles suggest that cult objects of this kind existed at the temple. Parts of model loop or naos sistra were also found at Deir el-Bahri, Timna, and Gebel Zeit. Faience Hathor masks have been recovered from Deir el-Bahri, Faras, Serabit el-Khadim, and Timna. Other types of votive object decorated with Hathor masks, sistra, or columns include stelae, faience bowls, pottery jars, menit counterpoises, and rings.

No single interpretation is valid for all these offerings. The bifrontal mask of the goddess may allude to the double nature of Hathor or to her presence on the boundary between the worlds of the living and the dead. Sistra can be associated with pacifying a deity, with revitalizing the *ka*, and with the protection of Horus in Chemmis. The naos sistrum can be linked to sexual symbolism, and the Hathor mask to rebirth. The Hathor column is associated with Hathor's cosmic aspect and her protective role. The concept of pacifying the 'Distant Goddess' may have been particularly relevant at Serabit el-Khadim, and that of Hathor as mediator between life and death at Deir el-Bahri. Ideally, the meaning of each Hathor mask, column, or sistrum needs to be considered individually, according to its context.

2.4 Cows

At Deir el-Bahri:–

> The commonest offering of all was a figure of a Hathor-cow, either in the round or in relief, incised, or in outline, on a plaque pierced for suspension. The figurines in the round are of wood, rough clay baked or unbaked, and of fine blue faïence. (Hall, in Naville 1913.14)

A wide range of objects decorated with cows was also found at this site. A range of cow figurines, plaques, and vessels was discovered at Faras, but cow objects were scarce at Serabit el-Khadim and Gebel Zeit. Only one cow object was recovered from Mirgissa and none from Timna.

2.4.1 Cow figurines

1 *Stone* (Pl. 34a)

A limestone cow from Deir el-Bahri is unusually large for a private votive object and should probably be classed as a statuette. It is 25.5 cm long and would originally have stood about 15 cm high (Brussels MR E 2517 = Pl. 34a). The base, most of the legs and the infill between them are missing. The horns have been broken off. A deep hole between them was probably for the fitment of a sun disc in metal or gilded wood. There may have been a figure standing beneath the cow's head, but the statuette is too broken for this to be certain. The cow is not very well carved. It is painted yellow with carelessly executed cross-shaped markings in blue. There is evidence for temple statues in cow form from the 11th dynasty onwards (2.4.5–6). The cow's head found near the Middle Kingdom shrine at Gebel Zeit (Posener-Kriéger 1986.381) may have formed part of an early cult statue of this type. The earliest closely datable large statue of a Hathor cow with a private person is of the 20th dynasty (2.4.6). A limestone cow's head said to come from Deir el-Bahri (Cambridge Fitz. E28–1937) could have been part of such a statue group. This piece probably dates to the late New Kingdom.

The EEF also found a small, badly damaged, unpainted stone cow at Deir el-Bahri (Brussels MR E 2447). This is only 4 cm long. As the body is pierced horizontally in two places, this cow may have been a pendant. Petrie excavated several bovine animals carved in calcite at Serabit el-Khadim (1906.137), but they are hollow and appear to have been used as containers (see 2.4.3.1).

2 *Wood*

Hall mentioned finding wooden cows at Deir el-Bahri and noted that 'The wooden cows are often much larger than the pottery ones' (in Naville 1913.14). No wooden cows were illustrated in the excavation report or included in the distribution lists. Either Hall's large cows were in too fragile a state to be brought back for distribution or his memory was at fault. The only example I have traced is a small cow, about 2.7 cm long (Brussels MR E 2460). This is made in a dark, unidentified wood and was originally gilded all over. A loop is fitted to the back of the neck; thus although it is modelled in the round, this cow should perhaps be classed as a pendant. I know of no directly comparable pieces, but objects in gilded wood have a poor chance of survival compared to those in stone or faience.

3 *Faience* (Pls. 34–5)

The EEF distribution lists for Deir el-Bahri mention 45 'glaze cows', but some of these will have been pendants rather than figurines. Carter stated that he found 'blue glaze cows' at this site (1912.32). Hayes described only one faience cow figurine excavated there by Winlock (1959.163). None of the 30 faience cow figurines from Deir el-Bahri which I have been able to examine, or obtain detailed information on, is intact (Brussels MR E 723–4; Glasgow K 04.164.k; London BM 41046, 41048–9, 41051–2, 41699, 43155, 47600, 47700, 58908 = Pl. 35a, 58909–10; V&A 1227.1904; Manchester 1458–9; New York MMA 05.4.34, 112; Oxford PR 1906.45.8; Toronto ROM 907.18.155–7, 158 = Pl. 35b, 159–61, 162 = Pl. 34c, 164 = Pl. 34b). The surviving fragments vary considerably in size and quality. Most of the figurines would have been 3–6 cm long when intact, but a few would have been between 10 and 15 cm long and up to 10 cm high (*e.g.* Glasgow K 04.164.k; London BM 41046,41049, 58908 = Pl. 35a; Toronto ROM 907.18.158, 164 = Pl. 34b). As far as can be judged from the fragments, all the cows were shown standing, probably on oval bases of the type found on three almost intact specimens (London V&A 1227.1904; Toronto ROM 907.18.162 = Pl. 34c; Naville 1913 pl. 27.1). Each pair of legs is modelled as one unit and the base is sometimes joined to the stomach and the legs by a flat infill. In one case the infill is incised with vertical lines, which might represent papyrus (Glasgow K 04.164.k). Most of the smaller cows are of poor quality. Some of the larger ones are well modelled, but they are highly stylized.

All the figurines are in bright turquoise-blue faience. On the smaller cows, the markings are rendered by uneven patches in dark blue (*e.g.* Oxford PR 1906.45.8), but the larger specimens can have cross (*e.g.* Pl. 35b; London BM 41048, 58906–7), rosette (*e.g.* Pl. 34b; Glasgow 04.164.k), or diamond (*e.g.* Pl. 35a; London BM 41046) markings in dark blue or purple-black. On one cow the markings are inlaid (Pl. 35a), a technique also found on some vessels from Deir el-Bahri (2.11.2). The hooves, the tip of the tail, and the details of the face are usually picked out in dark blue, and three of the cows have *wadjet* eyes (Pl. 35a–b; London BM 41049). Six of the surviving heads have the remains of a sun disc between their horns, and it is probable that all the cows would have had one originally. One specimen has a sun disc and double, curved plumes (London BM 41049). Two of the cows have holes for the fitment of horns and sun disc in another material (Pl. 35a; London 41048). On four, the lines around the neck could indicate a collar (Brussels MR E 274; Manchester 1459; Toronto ROM 907.18.159–60). Hall noted that some faience cows from Deir el-Bahri had 'the name of the goddess in black' (in Naville 1913.14). The only inscribed example I have traced has ⟨hieroglyphs⟩ – 'Hathor, Lady of Heaven' written on one flank (London BM 41052).

At Serabit el-Khadim, Petrie found a few faience fragments which may come from bovine figurines (1906 pl. 153.9, 13–4 = Manchester 913, 910, 912). A spotted head and torso might belong to a cow, but look more like a dog (Pl. 42a, top right). Two damaged heads are described on their museum cards as belonging to a cow and a calf. The first has a prominent dewlap and is probably a bull or an ox (1906 pl. 153.14). The second (1906 pl. 153.9) could be a calf or a short-horned cow. The latter is not normally associated with Hathor, who has lyriform horns.

I have not been able to find any other New Kingdom examples of standing cows modelled in the round in faience. Few New Kingdom faience figurines of any kind can compare in size and quality with the best of the cows from Deir el-Bahri. Faience figurines of animals were deposited in temples during the Early Dynastic Period (e.g. Petrie 1903 pls. 6–8; Riefstahl 1968 nos. 2–4; Seipel 1983 nos. 9–12), and the Old Kingdom (Dreyer 1986.24–38), and a large group of late Middle Kingdom faience figurines has survived in the 'Temple of the Obelisks' at Byblos (1.6). Several of these represent bovine animals, but they are seated and short-horned (Dunand 1950 pl. 55). A few small faience pieces showing a cow suckling a calf are known from Middle Kingdom and Second Intermediate Period Egypt (e.g. Keel 1980 fig. 35). In their size and elaborate decoration, the forty hippopotamus figurines from Byblos (Dunand 1950 pls. 99–101; 1958.742–5) provide closer comparative material for the larger faience cows from Deir el-Bahri. This might suggest a date in the early 18th dynasty for these cows, but the use of inlays and of fitments in other materials seems more characteristic of the late 18th dynasty. Moreover, the absence of faience cow figurines from Faras, which had a high proportion of early 18th dynasty material, could indicate that such figurines were not a common offering until the mid 18th dynasty. As with most categories of votive object, it is not safe to assume that the cruder examples are later than the better quality pieces. The faience cow figurines probably have a date range from the middle of the 18th dynasty to the Amarna period.

4 Pottery (Fig. 1; Pls. 1, 8, 36)

The EEF distribution lists for Deir el-Bahri mention 54 'clay' or 'pottery' cows. None of the 34 pottery cows from this site which I have been able to examine is intact (Bolton 48.04.10, 14,16; Bristol 4754.a–b; Brussels MR E 743–5, 4432.a–c; Glasgow K 07.792.z; Ilkley 7079; London BM 40991, 40995 = Pl. 36a, 40996–7, 41428; Manchester 1236, 1460; Oxford Ash. E 861–5, 866 = Pl. 36c, 868, 2718–21; PR 1906.45.6–7 = Pl. 36b). These fragments show less variety in size and quality than is found among the faience cows. One figurine now in the British Museum is 13.2 cm long (40995 = Pl. 36a). This, and another example of about the same length, were illustrated by Hall (Pl. 1.1). The remaining cows are 4–8 cm long. They are all shown standing. In the cruder examples the legs are reduced to two thick pillars. Some of these pieces were clearly freestanding, but others were attached to the rims of circular vessels or to the bottom of bowls (see 2.4.3.1). When the legs are missing – as they usually are – it is difficult to distinguish the free-standing examples, so all the pottery cows are described here whether or not they may have come from vessels.

The large figurine in the British Museum is well modelled (Pl. 36a), but most of the pottery cows are very crude (*e.g.* Fig. 1.20–3, 26–34). Some are in grey and some in red ware, but all were originally painted. The main colour can be white, yellow, or red, and the markings dark blue or black. These markings are rendered by uneven patches, rather than by the crosses, diamonds, and rosettes found on the faience figurines. However, one piece (London BM 41428) has incised triangular markings similar to those shown on a cow drawn on one of the votive cloths (Pl. 26a). The udder and the ears are not usually modelled and the tail is not always indicated. Prominence is given to the sun disc and horns. Some cows have a uraeus attached to their disc (*e.g.* Oxford Ash. E 861, 864, 867, 2721). One figurine is extremely unusual in having a head at each end (Oxford Ash. E 866 = Pl. 36c). This piece, which might be compared with the double sphinx known as the Aker (see 2.5.5), could be seen as analogous to the bifrontal Hathor mask form of the goddess.

Griffith stated that 'rude figures of cows' were 'abundant' at Faras (1921.86), but he illustrated only two examples (Pl. 8.19, 21). One of these appears to be well modelled, shows traces of paint, and would have been about 15 cm long. The other is smaller and cruder. The British Museum has a very similar pottery cow from Faras (London BM 51268 = Pl. 36d), 9 cm long and made in a coarse red ware. It is possible that both these smaller cows were from the rims of pots, but Griffith did not mention finding any vessels of this type.

New Kingdom animal figurines in pottery are not very common, and cows are particularly rare. Perhaps because of the importance of cattle in C-group culture, clay cows are found in Middle and New Kingdom settlement sites in Nubia (*e.g.* Steindorff 1935 pl. 73). Only figurines with a sun disc between long horns can be identified as divine cows. One example was found in a workmen's village at Abydos that dates to Ahmose (Ayrton *et al.* 1904 pl. 58.15). It may have been dedicated in a community shrine, or at a household altar. There are few dating criteria for the pottery cows from Deir el-Bahri and Faras, but they, like the faience cow figurines, are probably all 18th dynasty.

2.4.2 Plaques and pendants

1 *Metal* (Pls. 2, 6, 37)

The EEF distribution lists for Deir el-Bahri mention 11 metal cow plaques, one of which was illustrated in the excavation report (Naville 1913 pl. 24.5). Winlock found 21 such plaques at this site (Hayes 1959.173), but none of them has been published in detail. The cow plaques were described as bronze by Hall (in Naville 1913.16), and as copper by Hayes (1959.173). The eight metal plaques from Deir el-Bahri which I have been able to examine, or obtain detailed information on, appear to be made of bronze (Brussels MR E 712, 2441; London BM 17806 = Pl. 37b, 17807, 41062 = Pl. 37a; Oxford Ash. E 2731; PR 1904.35.108; Pittsburgh

CM 2940.14). They are 4–6 cm long, and all but one are roughly rectangular. The exception is a plaque which approximately follows the outline of the cow (London BM 17086 = Pl. 37b). Hayes mentioned that two of the metal plaques found by Winlock were oval (1959.173). The plaques excavated by Naville are of poor workmanship, with uneven edges and the cow figures crudely incised or stamped on one side only. All are pierced with one or two holes. In a letter written in January 1904, Hall noted that:–

> Some of the scarabs are on their original strings, with metal tags with the sacred eyes and Cow of Hathor on them; beads etc. strung with them. (EES Archives)

Two of the plaques found by Naville (London BM 41062 = Pl. 37a, top left; Oxford Ash. E 2731) and two discovered by Winlock (Hayes 1959.173) depict a pair of cows facing each other. The remainder each show one cow. The cows are all in a standing posture. Markings are not indicated, but the udder is sometimes shown (*e.g.* Pl. 37b). One of the cows is completely unadorned (Oxford PR 1904.35.108), but the others have a sun disc between the horns. On three of the plaques the cows wear lotus collars (Pl. 37b; Oxford Ash. E 2731; Pittsburgh CM 2940–14). No background is indicated, but one specimen has a *wadjet* eye above the cow (London BM 17087), and another, a pair of ordinary eyes (Craig Patch 1990.52–3). The cows on the plaques excavated by Winlock are 'sometimes accompanied by a small table of offerings or by a large pair of human eyes' (Hayes 1959.173).

Griffith mentioned finding 'Pieces of thick gold foil, some stamped with a cow' at Faras (1921.86). None was illustrated in his report and I have been able to trace only one probable example (London BM 50250, catalogued as Meroitic – almost certainly in error). This rectangular gold plaque, 3 cm long, is crudely stamped with a cow-like animal.

Flat, openwork cow pendants made in bronze or copper were also recovered from Deir el-Bahri. One was illustrated by Carter (Pl. 6A), and four are mentioned in the EEF distribution lists. Hall illustrated one of these (Pl. 2, top right), which is now in the British Museum (41061 = Pl. 37a, bottom right). This cow, which is 3.4 cm long, stands on a baseline and has a sun disc between its horns. It is fitted with one loop below the baseline and one in the centre of the back. Winlock found four similar cow pendants ' ... cut out of copper sheeting and equipped with tubes or holes by means of which they could have been suspended from cords' (Hayes 1959.173). Like the metal plaques, these objects were probably strung with scarabs, beads and other small objects to form votive necklaces.

There is some comparative material for these metal cow plaques. Three examples bought in the Asasif by G. J. Chester in 1886 are almost certain to have come from one of the Hathor shrines at Deir el-Bahri (Oxford Ash. E 1886.91, 874–5). Their provenance might have been a spoil heap from Mariette's excavation of Djeser-Djeseru (1.1.1), or the dump of votive offerings between the causeways of Hatshepsut and Thutmose III (1.1.3.3). None of the cows on these plaques has a sun disc, but two wear lotus collars. The Ashmolean Museum has two unprovenanced metal cow plaques (1878.480; 1927.1289); on one the cow has a sun disc with uraeus and a lotus collar. Eleven metal cow plaques in the Cairo Museum have been published (Reisner 1907 pl. 19, nos. 12243–53; 1958. pl. 10, no. 12819). These all show a single standing cow. Most of these cows have a sun disc and five wear lotus collars. Qurna is the provenance given for one plaque which shows a cow beside a table of offerings (1907 no. 12250). This, and most of the others, probably came from Deir el-Bahri. However, the provenance of one plaque, which shows Hathor in both cow and human form, is given as Gebelein (1958 pl. 10), the site of a Hathor temple at least as early as the 3rd Dynasty (Allam 1963.97–8; Donadoni Roveri in Robins 1990.23–4). Though rare, objects of this type are not confined to the cult of Hathor. Small copper plaques incised with hawks were among the offerings found in the vicinity of the Great Sphinx at Giza (Selim Hassan 1953.35, fig. 18).

To judge by their absence from domestic sites, cow plaques were not worn as amulets in daily life. I know of only one case where cow plaques were apparently included among funerary equipment. Three gold cow plaques are said to have come from the burial of three minor wives of Thutmose III (Winlock 1948.28–9, pl. 13). Two of these plaques show an identical cow with sun disc and uraeus and seem to have been stamped with the same die. The third has a hatched body and wears a sun disc and a narrow collar. Three stems of papyrus are shown behind this cow, a stand of offerings in front of her, and a *wadjet* eye above her. All three plaques were pierced but showed 'absolutely no trace of wear' (1948.29). Winlock stressed the similarity of these pieces to the bronze cow plaques from Deir el-Bahri. The gold examples from Faras suggest that cow plaques in this metal were also dedicated at Deir el-Bahri. As the provenance of much of the material alleged to be from this tomb is uncertain, the three gold plaques may in fact have come from Deir el-Bahri.

I can find no exact parallels for the bronze or copper cow pendants, which seem to be peculiar to Deir el-Bahri. They should not be confused with a funerary amulet, common from the Third Intermediate Period onwards, which consists of a seated cow wearing a 'saddle-cloth' (*e.g.* Reisner 1958 pls. 15–6). R. Williams classified an openwork gold pendant of unknown provenance that depicts a standing cow, as a Late Period funerary amulet (1924.162, pl. 27.107a–b), but it could be a New Kingdom votive offering. If the three gold cow plaques are from the tomb of the three royal ladies, this would prove that objects of this type were made during the reign of Thutmose III. Their date range probably covers the early and mid 18th dynasty. The metal pendants have much in common with the metal cow plaques, but they also have faience and glass counterparts, which probably range in date from the mid to the late 18th dynasty (2.4.2.2).

2 *Glazed steatite, faience, and glass* (Fig. 2; Pls. 1–2, 35c–d, 37a)

Only nine cow plaques or pendants in this group of materials are mentioned in the EEF distribution lists for Deir el-Bahri, but these lists do not always distinguish between cow figurines, pendants, and plaques. I have traced 19 plaques (Bolton 90.07.5; Brussels MR E 722 = Pl. 35c, 2446; Dublin NM 519.04; Edinburgh RSM 1904.134.15; Glasgow K 04.164.j; London BM 41053, 41055, 41057–60, 41732 = Pl. 37a, 43156–7; V&A 1226.1904; Toronto ROM 907.18.129, 132, 257 = Pl. 35d), and 10 whole or fragmentary pendants (Brussels MR E 721, 2447, 2449; London

BM 41054 = Pls. 1, bottom left, 37a; 41699, 43155, 61632; Manchester 1457; Oxford Ash. E 2762; Toronto ROM 907.18.163). Miss Carhew drew one cow plaque and one cow pendant (Fig. 2). Winlock found about 15 faience or glazed steatite plaques at Deir el-Bahri, only one of which has been published (Hayes 1959.173).

Faience is the most common material for these plaques, but Naville recovered some glazed steatite examples (e.g. London BM 41058; V&A 1226.1904). The plaques are mainly rectangular, 2–5 cm long, and pierced for suspension. One small plaque is slightly higher at one end, to accommodate the tall horns of the Hathor cow (Brussels MR E 2446). One of the steatite pieces (London BM 41060 = Pl. 1 top right) measures 9 × 4.2. When intact, a faience plaque shaped like a stela (Brussels MR E 722 = Pl. 35c) would have measured about 10 × 6 cm. Neither of these pieces is pierced and they might both be classed as small Type A stelae. Three fragments which are hard to classify consist of the head and shoulders of a cow in high relief against a flat, roughly cow-shaped plaque (Edinburgh 1904.134.15; Glasgow 04.164.k; London BM 41053). These plaques would have been 6–8 cm long and were probably too heavy to have been threaded on votive necklaces.

On the rectangular plaques, the figure of the cow may be incised, drawn in dark blue, or modelled in high relief. The design is normally on one face only, but a steatite plaque has a cow incised on both faces (London V&A 1226.1904). Miss Carhew illustrated a plaque with a design on both faces (Fig. 2, bottom left). On one fragmentary faience plaque, the cow is drawn in purplish-black, but parts of her lotus flower necklace, her uraeus, and the table of offerings in front of her were once inlaid (Toronto ROM 907.18.257 = Pl. 35d), presumably with faience of a different colour, as on one of the cow figurines (Pl. 35a).

Two of the plaques show a pair of cows facing each other (London BM 41059 = Pl. 2, centre; Toronto 907.18.29 = Naville 1913 pl. 27.1, bottom left). The remainder each have a single cow. A few cows have markings in the form of irregular patches, and two have incised decoration (London BM 41058; V&A 1226.1904) that might represent the type of 'saddle-cloth' sometimes worn by Hathor in cow form. Almost all have a sun disc between their horns, sometimes with a uraeus (e.g. Pl. 35d) or a double plume (e.g. London BM 43156). The cows may wear lotus flower collars (e.g. Pl. 35d; London BM 41058), simple, tight-fitting collars (e.g. Pl. 35c; Brussels MR E 2446), or menit necklaces (e.g. London BM 43156).

The design often consists only of a cow, but on two plaques the cow stands on a base line which curves up into a papyrus umbel at the front (Fig. 2; Pl. 2, second row from top). This should probably be interpreted as showing a cow standing in a bark in a papyrus thicket. One of these plaques has a piece of vegetation (perhaps papyrus bound with convolvulus) arching over the cow (Fig. 2). Another plaque depicts a cow with a papyrus thicket behind her (Pl. 1, top right = London BM 43156). The stela-shaped plaque, which has a winged disc in its lunette, is unusual in showing the papyrus in front of the cow's body (Pl. 35c). On one of the two plaques with a pair of cows, there is a large lotus between the cows (Pl. 2, centre). On the other plaque, there is a table of offerings in the same position (Naville 1913 pl. 27.1). This plaque shows the cows standing on a plinth or mat, so they may be statues. This is almost certainly the case on a plaque which shows a woman offering a loaf and pouring a libation to a Hathor cow standing on a plinth (London BM 41732 = Pl. 37a, bottom left). Although this piece would only have measured about 2.3 × 3 cm when intact, its iconography is comparable to that of the stone Hathor stelae (*e.g.* Pl. 9). One of the plaques depicting a cow and papyrus has a *nfr* sign in front of the cow (London BM 43156). The inlaid piece has the remains of an inscription (Pl. 35d). Beside the cow's head is the bottom of a text which must have consisted of her name and an epithet, either Foremost in Thebes or Lady of Dendara. Below the lotus collar is written *ꜥꜣt* – 'Great One' (?).

Closely related to the plaques are the cow-shaped pendants. Most of these are in faience of light blue, dark blue, green, or light blue with details in dark blue, but one (Brussels MR E 2449) is made of dark blue glass. The intact pendants are 2.2–3.1 cm long. These objects were made in open moulds and therefore have flat backs. Naville illustrated a pair of these pendants which look as if they came from the same mould (Pl. 1, bottom left). In some cases the area between the legs, stomach and base line has been cut away (*e.g.* Fig. 2, top right). Some of the pendants are pierced horizontally and others have a loop attached to the back of the neck. The intact cows all have a sun disc between their horns and two wear lotus collars (London BM 41054 = Pl. 37a, top right; Brussels MR E 721). One cow pendant of this type was found at Gebel Zeit (Mey 1980.307, fig. 13.1).

There is a small body of comparative material for the faience and steatite cow plaques. Six examples in the Cairo Museum have been published (Reisner 1907 pl. 19, nos. 12236–42). Three of these show a standing cow with sun disc and lotus collar, two have a cow and a pair of *wadjet* eyes, and one has a cow between two lotus plants. Five are unprovenanced, but the sixth is said to come from Saqqara, and so may be funerary. The British Museum has a miniature faience stela showing Hathor, Lady of Dendara, in cow form (54819) that is very similar to the miniature stela from Deir el-Bahri (Pl. 35c). This piece came from Asyut, where the cult of Hathor is attested in the tombs of the nomarchs (Allam 1963.95–6). A small plaque in blue glass crudely incised with a cow was bought by the British Museum from the Nash Collection in 1920, and is said to come from Deir el-Bahri (54930; Cooney 1976.8, no. 68). Cooney tentatively dated this piece to the 'late Dynastic Period', but if it is from Deir el-Bahri an 18th dynasty date is more probable.

The costume and hairstyle of the woman shown on BM 41732 indicate a mid 18th dynasty date for this object (Pl. 37a). The use of glazed steatite suggests an early 18th dynasty date for some of the plaques, but the elaborate inlaid piece (Pl. 35d) and the glass example (London BM 54930) are more likely to be late 18th dynasty. There is no evidence that cow plaques continued to be made during or after the Amarna period. I have been able to find only one, rather unusual piece of comparative material for the faience and glass cow pendants. A 19th dynasty stela from Deir el-Medina names the royal scribe Ramose and shows one of his servants adoring Hathor in cow form. Instead of being carved, the goddess is represented by a flat, openwork blue faience cow set into the stone (Brunner & Brunner-Traut 1981.100–1, pl. 2). This cow was broken before it was set into the stela, so it was probably already old (1981.100). It must be emphasized that the cow pendants cannot have been made as inlays, because they are pierced or fitted with loops. Hall referred briefly to the fact that 'glaze' votive cows were found strung with beads and scarabs, and perhaps (his wording is not clear) with faience Hathor masks and menit counterpoises (in Naville 1913.14).

2.4.3 Objects decorated with cows

1 *Vessels* (Fig. 1, Pls. 1, 8, 38–9)

Petrie noted that among the calcite vases at Serabit el-Khadim there were many 'in the forms of figures of the god Bes or the cow of Hat.hor' (1906.137). He illustrated one fragment which definitely comes from a cow vessel (1906 pl. 144.8) and three which may do so (1906 pl. 144.2–3, 10). The Ashmolean Museum has fragments from at least eight such vessels, some of which show traces of red paint (E 1911.411–2, 417a–d, & in Box E 4454). Three bear the cartouches of Merenptah, crudely carved and inlaid with a blue pigment (Oxford Ash.411–2, 417a). A surviving head has holes drilled for the insertion of horns (Oxford Ash. 417d). The largest of the vessels stood 20 cm high at the shoulder and would have been about 35 cm long. On one, a calcite stopper is fitted in a hole in the middle of the back. These objects were probably containers for precious unguents (Leeds 1922.2; see further 2.11.1.2). One of the fragments which may come from a cow vase, bears the cartouches of Ahmose-Nefertary (Petrie 1906 pl. 144.2), so these vessels may range in date from the early 18th to as late as the 20th dynasty. The closest comparative material is provided by the elaborate alabaster figure vases from the tomb of Tutankhamon (*e.g.* Desroches Noblecourt 1963 fig. 35, pl. 44; Edwards 1972 no. 4). The Serabit el-Khadim vessels were probably royal rather than private gifts to Hathor.

A fragment from a crudely painted red-ware vessel in the shape of a cow was excavated by Naville at Deir el-Bahri (Oxford Ash. E 854 = Pl. 38c). When intact, this object would have been about 20 cm long. The handle on its back suggests that it was used as a ewer. This was probably the function of a similar red-ware vessel from Serabit el-Khadim, of which only the well-modelled head remains (Oxford Ash. E 2444 = Pl. 38d). Cow-shaped vases are rare, although one was recovered from an 18th dynasty tomb at Deir el-Medina (Bruyère 1928.7–8, fig. 5e), but pottery vessels in the form of goats and gazelles seem to have been popular in the first half of the 18th dynasty (Bourriau in Brovarski 1982.101).

Hall noted that at Deir el-Bahri:—

> The sacred cow occurs also in the round as an ornament on the edge of vases of coarse earthenware, the curious vessels resembling the Greek *kernoi*, of which many fragments have been found. These were certainly votive. Round the edge of a large bowl were perched numerous small model vases, often of sack-like form, and usually alternating with the rude figures of the cow … Another form was a hollow ring on which vases and cows larger than those on the bowls were placed. The pottery was sometimes left unpainted, sometimes painted with red, blue, and yellow stripes. (in Naville 1913.15)

An intact pottery ring decorated with cows and miniature vases (Fig. 1.16) and two bowl fragments with cows astride the rims were illustrated in the excavation report

(Pl. 1.1, bottom right = London BM 40989–90). Many of the 54 pottery cows excavated by Naville may have come from such vessels (2.4.1.4). On the better preserved of the two bowl fragments in the British Museum (Pl. 38a) the cow is 7 cm long, has a disc and uraeus, and is painted white with blue patches.

Pottery rings and bowls decorated with miniature vases have been found in burials ranging in date from the late Middle Kingdom to the early 18th dynasty (2.11.5), but there seem to be no exact Egyptian parallels in pottery for the vessels whose rims are decorated with model cows. It is likely that these imitate the type of metal bowls and chalices, shown in New Kingdom temple reliefs and tombs scenes, whose rims have projecting lotus flowers, miniature vases, and Hathor masks or cats or cows (*e.g.* Davies 1923.18–9 pl. 54; Calverley & Broome 1935 pl. 11). A group of 18th dynasty bronze bowls, hidden in modern times in the forecourt of Theban tomb 100, all have a cow figurine in the centre (Cairo JE 34738–9; New York MMA 30.8.17; Winlock 1936.147–8, figs. 1–4; Hayes 1959.205–6). A similar, but unprovenanced bowl (Paris ML E3163; G. Spalinger in Brovarski 1982 no. 108, 121–2) has an inscription reading:–

Hathor, Lady of the West. Dedicated by the Mistress of a Household Neferether.

The use of an *ir n* formula indicates that this is a votive object. Bowls of this type are shown in reliefs in or from Djeser-Djeseru (Naville [1904] pl. 90; Keimer 1956.226–7, fig. 12). Winlock suggested that the bronze bowls found outside Tomb 100 came from the Hathor shrines at Deir el-Bahri (1936.155). Equivalent bowls in pottery have been recovered from 18th dynasty burials at Hu (Petrie 1901.12, pl. 35.103) and Deir el-Ballas (G. Spalinger in Brovarski 1982.122). Another pottery bowl with a cow in the middle has recently been excavated in the vicinity of a 'community shrine' at Deir el-Ballas (J. Richards in Lacovara 1990.13–14). Some of the pottery cows from Deir el-Bahri may originally have been attached to the centre of shallow bowls. An example now in Glasgow stands on what looks like a boss from the middle of a bowl (Glasgow K 07.79.792a).

Pottery jars decorated with Hathor masks in relief have already been described (2.3.3.1). Two sherds from Deir el-Bahari show that similar jars with projecting cow's heads were made (London BM 40992–3). One of these is of red ware, measures 6 × 4.3 cm, and has a cow's head with sun disc. The head is crudely modelled and painted black and white. The other sherd, which is of drab ware and measures 6.5 × 4 cm, has an unpainted cow's head decorated with incised dots. The only piece of pottery from the Hathor temple at Faras illustrated by Griffith was a sherd with cow's head projecting from below the rim (Pl. 8.20 = Oxford Ash. E 1912.950). This cream sherd measures 6.5 × 8 cm. A few traces of black paint are visible. The cow has a disc and uraeus and *wadjet* eyes (Pl. 38b). The closest parallels to these jars are provided by two complex pottery vessels with projecting cows from a foundation deposit in the temple of Thutmose III at Koptos (Petrie 1896 pl. 14.29, 7 = Oxford Ash. E 4291–2).

Hall stated that the Hathor cow appeared 'very often' as a motif on the faience bowls decorated with marsh flora which were common at Deir el-Bahri (in Naville 1913.14). However, although I have examined about 250 fragments of 'marsh bowls' from this site, I have found only six examples with cows (Glasgow K

04.164.e; London BM 41019–21 = Naville 1913 pl. 27.2; Munich ÄS 2931; Toronto ROM 907.18.212). The thickness of these fragments varies from 0.3–1.5 cm, which suggests that they come from six different bowls. They are all in bright turquoise blue faience, with the decoration in dark blue or purple black, and a lotus petal pattern on the exterior. Two of the cows have irregular patches (Munich ÄS 2931; Toronto ROM 907.18.212), two have crossed shaped markings (London BM 41020–1), one has patches and crosses (London BM 41019), and one has inlaid diamond-shaped markings (Glasgow K 04.164.e). On the only fragment on which the head is preserved, the cow has a *wadjet* eye and a disc and uraeus. This and another specimen wear lotus-flower necklaces (Naville 1913 pl. 27.2, top right). Four of the fragments show vertical lines behind or in front of the cow, perhaps indicating papyrus (1913 pl. 27.2; Munich ÄS 2931), and one has a lotus plant beside the cow (Glasgow K 04.164.e).

Winlock excavated 'uncountable' numbers of faience bowl fragments at Deir el-Bahri, but no examples decorated with cows have been published. Griffith did not mention finding fragments with cows at Faras and there were definitely none at Mirgissa or Timna. Petrie illustrated one bowl fragment from Serabit el-Khadim which shows a cow, wearing a lotus bud necklace, and standing beside a lotus plant (Pl. 39). I have examined over 750 faience bowl fragments from this site, but have found only one other piece with a cow (Oxford Ash. in Box E 4457). This shows the head of a cow who is licking the hand of a seated figure; a scene paralleled on a pectoral of Amenemhet III found at Byblos (Jidejian 1968 pl. 61), and in several reliefs from the Hathor shrine of Djeser-Djeseru (Naville [1901] pls. 87, 94, 96; PM II, 350).

There is a small body of comparative material for 'marsh bowls' with cows. One bowl from the sanctuary of Sekhmet at Abusir (Borchardt 1910.130–1, fig. 179) and one from an 18th dynasty burial at Qau (Brunton *et al.* 1930.41, pl. 35) show a cow, with lotus necklace and cross-shaped markings, together with Hathor masks and lotus plants. One unprovenanced bowl fragment has a cow next to a lotus bud (Strauss 1974.44–5, pl. 8). Two other bowls, one from Abusir (Borchardt 1910 fig. 180) and one unprovenanced (London BM 35120), are decorated with a cow in a papyrus thicket. Although the cow has been claimed to be an important motif on these 'marsh bowls' (Strauss 1974.78–9), it is certainly not a common one. The date range of this group of comparative material covers most of the New Kingdom, but to judge by their shape and colour, and by the degree of stylization in their design, the 'marsh bowls' with cows from Deir el-Bahri and Serabit el-Khadim were all 18th dynasty (see further 2.11.3.1).

2 *Jewellery*

The plaques and pendants might be counted as jewellery decorated with cows, but the only other example is an object from Deir el-Bahri, painted by Miss Carhew, which could be a ring bezel, or the underside of a seal (EES Archives). This is in bright blue faience and has incised decoration in the form of a Hathor cow standing in a bark in a papyrus thicket. Some rings with this motif, ranging in date from the late 18th to the 19th dynasties, are known from other sites (*e.g.* Schäfer 1910.47, fig. 33; Bruyère 1929.66; Borchardt & Ricke 1980.301, 307). A cow in a papyrus thicket also occurs on the bases of a few 18th and 19th dynasty scarabs (Hornung & Staehelin 1976.95).

3 *Stelae, textiles, ostraca, and statues* (Figs. 10–11, 18; Pls. 9–11, 18–26, 40–1)

Thirteen stelae with representations of Hathor cows were found at Deir el-Bahri and one at Mirgissa (2.1, Lists 1–2). Four of these stelae have the 'cow and marsh' motif and eight the 'cow and mountain' motif (2.1.3). One small stela depicts a group of three cows (Winlock 1922.38), while each of the rest has a single cow. All the cows wear a sun disc and uraeus, and five also have the double, curved plume. One has a lotus flower necklace, four wear menit necklaces, and the group of three cows have *ankh* signs round their necks. On the only stela on which the paint is well preserved, the cow is painted pinkish-white with diamond-shaped markings in dark blue (Pl. 10).

The 26 votive textiles which depict Hathor cows have already been described in detail (2.2.4). None of these objects shows more than a single cow, although one has a cow and a calf (Pl. 26a). All the cows on the textiles have a red sun disc between their horns, sometimes surmounted by a pair of straight or curved feathers in blue or green. Where the details of the head are visible, the cow usually has a *wadjet* eye. Most of the cows have green menit necklaces, but one is said to wear a garland around its neck (Cat.2.5), two wear tight-fitting collars (Cat.2.2; 3.1), two wear loop sistra (Cat.3.6; 4.8), and one has a lotus collar (Cat.2.3). Four of the cows have no markings (Cat.2.1,4; 3.6; 4.3). Three have naturalistic, uneven patches (Cat.3.1,4; 4.1), while others have stylized rosette (Cat.2.3,7; 3.5; 4.4), or cross-shaped (Cat.3.2; 4.8–9; 5.2) markings. These markings are always dark blue or black. The ground colour may be yellow, reddish-brown, or pinkish-white. The cow drawn in ink (Cat.2.1) has triangular markings reminiscent of the triangular designs on some votive faience from Deir el-Bahri (Fig. 1). Six of the textiles have the 'cow and mountain' motif and 13 the 'cow and marsh' motif (2.2.4).

Figured ostraca from Deir el-Bahri are rare, but Naville found two examples with Hathor cows and one with the goddess in cow headed form. One of these ostraca is incomplete and now measures 8.4 × 2.2 cm (Dublin NM 1904.537). On it is part of a drawing in black ink of a cow and a lotus plant (Dublin Cat. 1911 no. 385). The second ostracon is larger, 20 × 12.5 cm, and much more elaborate (Brussels MR E 1232; Werbrouck 1953.97–8; fig. 10). The drawing, which is again in black ink, is divided into three registers. The bottom register has stands of offerings, the middle register shows people adoring a cow, and the top register has more offerings and offering bearers. These are all very sketchily rendered and the composition might be interpreted as a preliminary drawing for a relief or wall painting (Werbrouck 1953.97) but, given its provenance, it is probably votive. A few Ramessid ostraca, mainly from Deir el-Medina, with drawings of, and sometimes prayers to, Hathor in cow form can be cited (*e.g.* Vandier d'Abbadie 1933 pl. 95, no. 2732; Peterson 1973.33–4, pl. 21; Peck 1978.122, no. 53; Page 1982.8–9, pl. 10). The Deir el-Bahri pieces probably also date to the Ramessid

Period, when most visitors left behind graffiti rather than the standardized votive offerings of the 18th dynasty (3.3).

The third ostracon measures 23 × 20.5 cm. The design is executed in black, red, white, and green (Toronto ROM 907.18.15 = Pl. 41a). It shows the priest Panedjem adoring Hathor, Lady of Djesert, who appears as a cow-headed woman wearing the disc and horns headdress with a curved double plume. Behind the priest are a man carrying a lotus (?) and a woman with a loop sistrum. The hieroglyphic inscription consists of the name and titles of deity and donors. In its iconography and inscription this piece is comparable with the Hathor stelae from Deir el-Bahri, though none of the stelae bears the rare cow-headed form of Hathor. This form does not occur on private monuments until the Ramessid Period and then usually only in tree-goddess scenes. The style, the name of the priest, and the costumes of the donors, suggest a 20th dynasty date for this ostracon.

Two 19th dynasty 'intermediary statues' from Deir el-Bahri incorporate Hathor cows. The statue of Amoneminet from Djeser-Akhet has already been mentioned (2.3.3.3). On top of the Hathor mask naos sistrum resting against the knees is a figure of Hathor in cow form with Ramesses II kneeling beneath her head (Fig. 18). This feature appears to be a unique. A block statue of the Royal Butler Tjau from Akh-isut is unique in having the frontal head of a cow with wig and sun disc incised on its knees (London BM 1459 = Pl. 40; Naville 1913.7–8). In Naville's excavation report the statue is wrongly drawn with a standard Hathor mask on the knees (1913 pl. 9a). A front view of a cow's head is sometimes found in New Kingdom tomb paintings, where it seems to be a condensed version of the 'cow and mountain' motif (Keimer 1956.251, fig. 44). The cow's head on the statue of Tjau may have the same implications.

2.4.4 The identity of the votive cows

The cows shown on the votive stelae and textiles are almost always identified as Hathor by an accompanying text, but such inscriptions are scarce among the small votive objects. One faience cow figurine has an inscription naming Hathor, Lady of Heaven (London BM 41052), and a faience cow plaque has the remains of a text which probably included the name and epithet of the goddess (Pl. 35d). It is useful to have even this much textual evidence, since the presence of two or more cows on some objects raises the question of whether all the votive cows are direct representations of Hathor. The plaques which show a pair of cows facing each other (*e.g.* Pls. 2, centre, 37a, top left) can be paralleled by votive stelae with an inscription naming a single deity but showing a pair of animals facing each other (*e.g.* Tosi & Roccati 1972 nos. 50053, 50056). These should probably be regarded as having a double scene in which the same deity is shown twice.

The small stela with the three cows standing side by side under a curving papyrus stem (Winlock 1922.38, fig. 33) is more problematic. Since three is the first plural number, the stela may be intended to convey the idea of multiple cows rather than a specific group of three. Although this piece appears to be unique among Hathor stelae, it should be seen in the context of Type A and B votive stelae from other sites depicting groups of rams, jackals, crocodiles, snakes, geese, ibises, and hawks (Munro 1962.48–58, pls. 4–6; Kuentz 1969.190–3, pl. 1). It is uncertain whether such stelae portray a deity directly or as manifest in a group of sacred animals.

This question is relevant to Hathor, because sacred cattle, referred to as ⸱⸱⸱⸱, are known to have been kept at some of her temples (Bonnet 1952.403). Burials of cows have been found within the temple precincts at Dendara and Deir el-Bahri (Petrie 1900.48; Naville 1907.46, 50), though it cannot be proved that these were *tjentet* cows. The title 'Herdsman of the *tjentet* cows' is known from Middle Kingdom texts at Dendara and Meir (Petrie 1900.47; Blackman 1914.2, 8, pl. 15). In the Hathor shrine of Djeser-Djeseru the goddess in cow form is once given the caption 'Hathor of the *tjentet* cows' (Naville [1901] pl. 105). The same epithet may occur on one of the votive Hathor stelae from Deir el-Bahri (Scott 1986.189, no.118).

In Spell 542 of the Coffin Texts, the deceased claims that 'I am one of your *tjentet* cows, o Hathor, my lady' (*CT* VI.137g). This is one of a group of spells in which the deceased plays various roles in the entourage of Hathor (Drioton 1958.188–90). The desire to identify with the sacred cattle of Hathor in order to enter the afterlife under the protection of the goddess could be a motive for offering figurines or plaques representing *tjentet* cows. Scenes of cows being milked figure prominently on the 11th dynasty shrines and sarcophagi of the royal Hathor priestesses who were buried within the temple of Nebhepetre' Mentuhotpe (Naville 1907 pls. 20, 22–3; 1910 pl. 17; 1913 pl. 2). A similar scene is found in the chapel built by this king at Dendara (Labib Habachi 1963.25, fig. 7), and a few fragments of a milking scene survive from his Hathor shrine at Gebelein (Robins 1990.74, no. 19). It is likely that these are representations of the sacred cattle of Hathor.

All the cows in the milking scenes have naturalistic markings, some are short-horned, and none wears a a sun disc, uraeus, or any kind of necklace. These attributes are usually found on even the most crudely modelled or drawn votive cows. Thus it seems unlikely that the votive cows can be identified with the *tjentet* cows, unless the New Kingdom brought a change in the way these sacred cattle were depicted. New Kingdom references to the *tjentet* cows are very rare, and there are no certain representations of them. However, a 'Controller of the young cows of Amon in Djeser-Djeseru' is known from the time of Amonhotpe II (Brovarski 1976.68,) and an unfinished painting in a 21st dynasty Theban tomb provides a tantalizing piece of evidence (Theban Tomb 68; Nina Davies 1944.64, pl. 7). A priest of Amon and his wife are shown making offerings to three cows tethered in stalls (Fig. 13a). Behind the couple are 'paintings of store-houses containing Amun barks and statues' (1944.64), which suggests that the cows are in the same category as divine statues. Each cow has a sun disc and uraeus, and two have the double plume. The inscription was never filled in, so that this scene cannot definitely be linked with the *tjentet* cows or with Deir el-Bahri, but it does show that living cows closely identified with Hathor were worshipped somewhere in Thebes. Thus it remains possible that some of the votive offerings depict sacred cows of Hathor.

During the New Kingdom, another group of cows that can be associated with

Hathor came into prominence in funerary religion. This is the group of seven cows and a bull who appear in one of the vignettes to Chapter 148 of the Book of the Dead (Allen 1974.139–41). They also occur on funerary stelae and coffins and in tomb paintings and temple reliefs (Foucart 1924 pls. 21–2; Ramadan el-Sayed 1980 nos. 1–35). These cows are often shown recumbent, which is the standard posture for Mehet-weret in cow form, but not for Hathor. They are, however, sometimes depicted standing. Each of them wears a 'saddle-cloth' (which often has the hexagonal pattern shown on the drapes of shrines containing images of Hathor in cow form), a sun disc, a double curved plume, and a menit necklace (1980.372–3, figs. 1–4). All are long-horned and each has a different combination of hide colour and markings. The fourth cow – 'She of Chemmis' – has the cross-shaped markings found on many representations of Hathor in cow form.

The main functions of the seven cows seem to have been to nourish and protect the deceased (1980.373–4; 2.4.5). Their attributes closely resemble those of Hathor in cow form, and some scholars have seen these cows as a sevenfold form of the goddess, analogous to her sevenfold human form (Ramadan el-Sayed 1980.385–6). The seven cows are occasionally reduced to four or even two (1980.375, 385), so it is a possible that the pair of cows shown on some plaques could stand for the group of seven. However, none of the votive objects features cows with a bull and there is no evidence that this specific group is represented among the offerings.

Many of the cows on the stelae and textiles clearly represent statues of the goddess. The broken state of most of the figurines and the lack of detail on plaques make it difficult to tell whether they show statues, but this hypothesis would help to explain the extreme stylization of some of these pieces. For example, the diamond-shaped markings on two of the models (Pl. 35a; London BM 58908) and on a cow on a bowl fragment (Glasgow K 04.164.e) are paralleled on a stela which appears to show a cow statue (Pl. 10) and on a life-size stone cow statue from the Hathor temple at Deir el-Medina (Vandier 1969.180, 182, pl. 9). There was almost certainly a cult image of Hathor in cow form in each of the temples at Deir el-Bahri (1.1.2) and in the Hathor temple at Faras (1.2.2). A relief in Djeser-Djeseru shows a statue of Hathor in cow form, suckling and protecting a king, being dragged in procession (PM II, 350). This suggests that movable statues of this type were displayed during festivals. The prominence of the cow among the votive offerings at Deir el-Bahri and Faras may be explained by the presence of renowned images of Hathor in cow form at these sites. This does not exclude the possibility that the votive cows were donated to evoke a particular aspect of Hathor, since the statues themselves may have embodied such aspects.

There is a striking similarity between the votive cows and the role of the cow in temple iconography. It is therefore necessary to examine the relationship between the Hathor cow and the king before discussing the possible symbolic values of the votive cows. This is most conveniently done by concentrating on the 'cow and marsh' and 'cow and mountain' motifs.

2.4.5 The 'cow and marsh' motif

From the early 18th dynasty onwards, Hathor is often shown in a marsh setting. The 'cow and marsh' motif should perhaps be divided into the 'cow and lotus' and 'cow and papyrus' motifs, because two divine cows and two mythical marshes appear to be involved. The 'cow and lotus' motif may relate to Mehet-weret, the divine cow born from or personifying the primeval waters of the Nun. She could be thought of as the mother of Reꞌ-Atum (Hornung 1982.96). Since Reꞌ-Atum was also said to be born from the primeval lotus, the cow and the lotus have been seen as complementary symbols of birth and rebirth (Barguet 1953.104; Strauss 1974.84–5). The 'cow and papyrus' motif relates to the suckling and protection of the infant Horus in the marshes of Chemmis by the *iḥt* cow. This cow can be identified with a variety of goddesses, but most commonly in the New Kingdom with Hathor. Desroches Noblecourt and Kuentz have argued that these two myths fused and that the two divine cows and divine children came to be almost interchangeable (1968.112–4). In the New Kingdom Hathor is often identified with Mehet-weret. A painting of a recumbent cow on a shrine from a Theban tomb provides an interesting example of this. In the text by the scene, the cow is referred to as Mehet-weret, but the counterpoise of her menit necklace is inscribed 'Hathor, Foremost in Thebes' (Ramsès le Grand Cat. 1976.194, pl. 45).

The concept of Mehet-weret as the mother of Reꞌ was somewhat nebulous, but the myth of the divine cow suckling Horus in the marshes of Chemmis was often given direct visual expression. The idea of the king as the nursling of the divine cow is at least as old as the Old Kingdom, since he is described in the Pyramid Texts as 'The Calf of Gold' and is told 'Your mother is the great, wild cow who lives in el-Kab. She will nurse you.' (PT 729a). The earliest temple relief to show a king being suckled by a cow in a papyrus thicket is at el-Kab and dates to Amonhotpe I (Capart 1954 pl. 44a). There are two Middle Kingdom representations of a cow suckling a king, the fragmentary 11th dynasty relief from Deir el-Bahri (Woldering 1955 pl. 23) and the pectoral of Amenemhet III from Byblos (Jidejian 1968 pl. 61), but neither of these has a marsh setting. The statue from the speos of the Hathor shrine at Djeser-Akhet shows a Hathor cow in a papyrus thicket suckling one figure of the king while another stands beneath her head, originally encircled by her menit necklace (Pl. 41b). Two similar statues survive, one showing Horemheb suckling from Anat in cow form (Brunner 1964 pl. 24b) and one Ramesses II suckling from an unnamed cow (Zayed 1962 fig. 1).

As well as the example at el-Kab, reliefs showing a king suckling from a cow in a papyrus thicket have survived at Serabit el-Khadim (Černý 1952 pl. 81; Giveon 1978 fig. 24) and at Dendara (Chassinat 1934.77–8, pl. 87). Reliefs that depict a statue group of a cow standing in a bark shrine suckling and protecting the king are rather more common (e.g Naville [1901] pls. 104–5; 1907 pl. 28; Jéquier 1924 pl. 14; Chassinat 1935 pls. 132–4; Zayed 1962 fig. 5; PM II, 110, 350). The royal birth scenes at Deir el-Bahri and Luxor provide related material, since both Hatshepsut and her *ka*, and Amonhotpe III and his *ka*, are shown suckling from a pair of unnamed cows (Naville [1896] pl. 53; Brunner 1964 pls. 11–2).

Texts in the Hathor shrine of Djeser-Djeseru make it clear that the suckling of the king is to be equated with the suckling of Horus in Chemmis (*Urk*. IV, 235–40). In one scene (Naville [1901] pl. 94) the cow says:–

> I inhabited Chemmis as the protection of my Horus ... I am your mother, sweet of milk. (I) have suckled your person with (my) breast(s), they[1] enter you as life and power.

> [1] 'They' could refer to the teats of the goddess or to the milk from them. $\overline{}$ might be a miswriting for $\|\frown$.

In another of the texts from this shrine (Naville [1901] pl. 96), the significance of the Hathor cow licking the king's hand is clarified:–

> Said by Hathor, Foremost in Thebes, the *Ḥsɜt* cow, the divine mother, the lady of heaven, the mistress of the gods, who protects her Horus, who licks the Horus she has borne ... 'I have endowed your person with life and power, as I did for Horus in the nest of Chemmis.'

The idea that the milk of the divine cow imparts 'life and power' is found in other 'suckling texts'. The use of the word $\overline{}\triangledown$ in one of the Deir el-Bahri inscriptions suggests that it may have been adapted from a text that described the suckling of the king by a goddess in human form. Although the image of the king being suckled by a cow is closely associated with the myth of Horus in Chemmis, it is not clear whether its symbolic value differed greatly, or at all, from that of the suckling scenes which feature a goddess in human or animal-headed human form. J. Leclant suggested that drinking the divine milk was an important part of the coronation of an Egyptian king and that it marked the change in his status from human to divine (1959.60–71). The milk of the sacred cows kept in temples may have been used to represent the divine milk. In a relief in the 11th dynasty shrine from Dendara, Nebhepetreᶜ Mentuhotpe 'shakes papyrus for Hathor' in the top register, while below he is offered the milk of a cow who stands before him suckling her male calf (Labib Habachi 1963 fig. 7). In front of this group, the king is shown with Hathor in human form holding an *ankh* to his nose. This scene may well represent a real ceremony (1963.25). Such a ceremony might have been performed not just at the coronation, but at regular intervals during the king's reign in order to renew his vitality and power.

The relevance of the suckling scenes to the living king is clear, but their role in royal funerary religion is less well documented. Desroches Noblecourt and Kuentz argued that Chemmis could be identified with the primeval marsh and was the place where the king would be reborn from the divine cow and revitalized by her milk (1968.110–8). The reference in the Pyramid Texts to the king being nursed by the 'great wild cow' suggests funerary implications, but this image does not occur in the decoration of royal tombs. However, a pendant showing a king suckled by Weret-Hekau in cobra form was found inside the small gold shrine from the tomb of Tutankhamon (Eaton-Krauss & Graefe 1985 pls. 6–7). Some scholars relate this shrine to coronation rituals (Bosse-Griffiths 1973), others to the regeneration of the king in the afterlife (Westendorf 1967). In a unique scene in the tomb of Thutmose

III, the king is shown suckling from Isis as a tree-goddess (Peck 1978 no. 42). The tree-goddess can also be identified with Nut or Hathor, and is sometimes depicted with a cow's head, pouring out liquid and offering food to the deceased (*e.g.* Quibell 1898 pls. 20, 24; Bosticco 1965 no. 48; Moftah 1966).

There is, then, some evidence to link suckling scenes with the king's afterlife, but it should be recalled that the king is normally identified with Horus in life rather than in death. Since the dead king was incorporated in the solar cycle, the idea of the divine cow as the mother of the Sun God is of direct relevance to royal funerary religion (Hornung 1982.98). Mehet-weret was associated both with the primeval waters and with the sky. In her cow of the sky aspect she 'swallowed' the sun each evening and gave birth to it again each morning.

The image of a king suckled by a cow appears very rarely on private monuments. A statue group of a cow suckling Seti I in a bark shrine is shown in the tomb of the vizier Paser, who was responsible for restoration work at Deir el-Bahri (TT 106; LD 173a). One of the votive cloths may show Nebhepetre𓍿 Mentuhotpe suckling from a cow in a bark shrine in a papyrus thicket (Pl. 25b; 2.2.4). Another votive cloth has Hathor in cow form with a calf (Pl. 26a). A few temple reliefs depict a cow in a bark shrine, or in a bark in a papyrus thicket, with a king standing beneath her head, encircled by her menit necklace (*e.g.* Bruyère 1952a.66–7, pl. 36; Tosi & Roccati 1972 no. 50204). Similar scenes are occasionally found in private tombs and tomb chapels (*e.g.* Bruyère 1924.46–7, pl. 12; Vandier 1969.167, fig. 3.1). The simple 'cow and marsh' motif is more common. It was by no means confined to the Theban area, as its occurrence on stelae from Mirgissa (Vercoutter 1970 pl. 39b), Memphis (Petrie 1909 pl. 28.21), Qantir (Labib Habachi 1952 pl. 36b), and the workmen's village at el-ᶜAmarna (Peet & Woolley 1933 pl. 35) demonstrates. As well as being found on the textiles, vessels, rings, and scarabs already described (2.4.2–3), the 'cow and marsh' motif appears on the disc of menit counterpoises (2.9.2.4). It seems that it was not appropriate to depict the king suckling on private monuments, but every representation of a cow with papyrus may evoke such a scene.

The donors of the votive stelae, textiles, figurines, plaques, and bowls could have had various reasons for wishing to evoke the image of Hathor in Chemmis. First, this aspect of Hathor would have been relevant to mothers of young children. Hathor in cow form seems to have been regarded as a protector of children, probably because she protected the infant Horus in the marshes of Chemmis. Middle or early New Kingdom spells identify a mother and her sick child with Isis or Hathor and the infant Horus (Erman 1901.38–40). In one such spell, the child is referred to as gaining strength through suckling from the divine cow (Borghouts 1978.44). It may be relevant here that Taweret, who was also a protector of young children and nursing mothers, is sometimes shown as a hippopotamus standing in a papyrus thicket (*e.g.* Oxford Ash. 1893.141; Brunton et al. 1930 pl. 33).

In magical texts, the process of identifying with deities went beyond what was permissible in a religious context (3.3). It is therefore worth noting that in a Ramessid graffito in Djeser-Akhet a visitor refers to himself as born of the *iḥt* cow (Marciniak 1974.24–5, no. 12). This suggests that in prayers a private individual might claim a filial relationship with Hathor analogous to that of the king. In votive inscriptions, Hathor is frequently asked for 'life, prosperity, health', the equivalent for a private person of the qualities of 'life, stability, power' bestowed on the king by drinking the divine milk. Obviously this request is a very general one, addressed to the goddess in all her forms, but it does raise the question of whether any private individuals were permitted to share the king's privilege of drinking the milk of the sacred cows of Hathor.

As noted above (2.4.4), the shrines and sarcophagi of the 11th dynasty royal ladies are decorated with scenes of milch cows and their calves – which are always male. The paintings on the shrine of Kemsit, show the royal lady being offered milk, while in a separate scene a servant milks a black and white cow who stands with her calf in a papyrus thicket (Naville 1913 pl. 2). The papyrus can hardly be dismissed as a background detail, since none of the other scenes on the shrine is given a background. It suggests that the milk of this cow might be equated with the milk of the divine cow in Chemmis. The only comparable New Kingdom piece which I have found is a stela from Giza showing the Great Sphinx in the upper register, and a priest adoring and a woman milking a cow with lyriform horns and sun disc in the lower register (Selim Hassan 1953 pl. 65). The accompanying inscription is mainly illegible on the published photograph, but Hathor appears to be mentioned.

The fact that Kemsit, like most of the other women in the temple, was a priestess of Hathor, may be more relevant here than her status as royal wife or concubine. It is possible that priests and priestesses of Hathor enjoyed the privilege of drinking the milk of the sacred cows, perhaps after it had been offered to the goddess. Such a privilege is unlikely to have been shared, unless we imagine the temple staff selling sacred milk to visitors. However, in many cultures it was and is customary for donors to dedicate food and drink to a deity and then consume part of it in the temple (*e.g.* O'Malley 1935.99). The possibility that temple visitors offered milk to Hathor in faience 'marsh' bowls, thereby transforming it into divine milk, is discussed in 2.11.3.2. The hypothesis that private individuals actually drank 'divine milk' is, and must remain, highly speculative.

There is evidence that people could drink the milk in the afterlife. The scene on the shrine of Kemsit could be interpreted as taking place in the afterlife. One of the main functions of the group of seven cows and a bull which is shown in funerary contexts was to nourish the deceased. They are sometimes referred to as providing the standard bread and beer (Ramadan el-Sayed 1980.373), but the name of the fourth cow – 'She of Chemmis' – suggests the idea of the deceased being suckled. Different methods of nourishing the deceased seem to be used interchangeably in funerary contexts. The tree-goddess usually pours out liquid from a jar for the deceased, but one 18th dynasty painting shows a private individual suckling from a tree-goddess, just as the king does (Wenig 1967.36, pl. 48). In Spell 148 of the Book of the Dead the deceased is referred to as having 'come into being' under the buttocks of the seven cows, which further suggests the idea of the deceased being reborn from the divine cow (Allen 1936.12; 1974.139). A 21st dynasty coffin shows a Hathor cow licking a calf (Devéria 1896 pl. 3), which may perhaps be identified with the deceased. On another coffin of the same date Hathor, Lady of Djeseret, is shown standing in front of the Western Mountain while the *ba* of the deceased suckles from her (Allen 1923.11–2). Both these non-royal coffins come from Deir el-Bahri. These examples indicate that the king's privilege of being suckled and licked by the divine cow was gradually extended to the non-royal dead. This idea probably existed long before it became· permissible to show it on private monuments.

2.4.6 The 'cow and mountain' motif

The 'cow and mountain' motif did not enjoy an iconographic status comparable to that of the 'cow and marsh' motif. It is not found in temple reliefs and is not included in the tomb decoration of any New Kingdom rulers, but it does occur in the tombs of some Ramessid queens (*e.g.* PM I², 758, 768). Hathor is occasionally shown in cow form in early 18th dynasty Theban tombs (*e.g.* Davies 1925 pl. 2), but the 'cow and mountain' motif does not appear in tomb decoration until after the Amarna period – the earliest examples being those in the tomb of Neferhotep, of the reign of Ay (Theban Tomb 49; Davies 1933.65–6, pls. 54, 60). The motif is found in at least 32 Ramessid tombs in the Theban necropolis (Abdul Qader-Muhammed 1966.238–40; Vandier 1969.169) and in a few tombs from other sites, such as Boggaᶜ (Hermann 1935.13), Qubbet el-Hawa (Cecil 1903 pl. 4), and Bahriya Oasis (van Siclen 1981 fig. 13). The 'cow and mountain' motif serves as a vignette to chapter 186 of the Book of the Dead (*e.g.* Fig. 13b; Naville 1888 pl. 212; Allen 1974.209–10). It also occurs on shabti boxes (*e.g.* Bruyère 1930 fig. 142), and is common on Theban coffins of the Third Intermediate Period (*e.g.* Boeser 1918 pls. 6, 8; Keimer 1956 figs. 9–10; Starck 1977 fig. 2; Goff 1979 figs. 145, 147; Brunner-Traut 1981 pl. 110).

The motif appears first at Deir el-Bahri, where it features on votive stelae and textiles from the mid or late 18th dynasty onwards. It is quite common on votive and funerary stelae of the 19th–21st dynasties from the Theban area (*e.g.* Lacau 1909 pl. 61; Bruyère 1926 fig. 8; Nagel 1938 fig. 108; HT 1982 pl. 84.2). Examples from elsewhere in Egypt (*e.g.* Goff 1979 fig. 155) are scarce.

The funerary significance of this motif is emphasized by the way in which the red desert hillside can be shown dotted with small tombs or dominated by one large tomb. In tomb paintings, the 'cow and mountain' are sometimes shown as the destination of the funerary procession (Abdul Qader Muhammed 1966.239). The identification of the mountain with that of the Theban necropolis is strengthened by the frequent use of the epithet Lady of Djeser for the cow and by the occasional substitution of Mertseger, the goddess who personified the 'Peak', for Hathor (*e.g.* Bruyère 1930 fig. 142; Downes 1974 fig. 28). The motif's association with the Perfect West, the realm of the dead, is made plain by the even more frequent use of epithets relating to the West for the cow, and by the occasional presence of the goddess of the West or her symbol in front of the cow (*e.g.* Bruyère 1930 fig. 142; Starck 1977 fig. 2).

The cow may be shown on a plinth against or in front of the mountainside, standing half inside the mountain, or with only her head showing. The analogous 'cow and marsh' motif suggests that the Hathor cow should be understood as standing at least partially inside an opening in the mountainside. She is positioned on the threshold of the realm of the dead, but she is not necessarily emerging into the realm of the living. Although the 'cow and mountain' motif seems to have originated at Deir el-Bahri, 'Hathor caves', whose shape suggests a cavern of the underworld, were created at other sites such as Faras and Gebel Zeit. This suggests that any striking cliff or rock formation might be identified as an entrance to the other world, and therefore as a holy place of Hathor.

On three of the votive textiles from Deir el-Bahri (Pls. 18b, 21a; Parlasca 1966 pl. 55.1), in most of the funerary vignettes (*e.g.* Fig. 13b), and in a few tomb paintings (*e.g.* Davies 1933 pl. 60; Keimer 1956 fig. 4) a clump of papyrus is shown behind the cow. Sometimes a clump is suggested by just one or two stems. On coffins a combination of the 'cow and mountain' and 'cow and marsh' motifs may be indicated in a more abstract way by the presence of a large bowl of lotuses in front of the cow and mountain (*e.g.* Nagel 1938.204, fig. 178; Keimer 1956.225, figs. 9–10; Starck 1977 fig. 2; Brunner-Traut 1981 pl. 110). Whether the marsh is identified with Chemmis, with the Nun, or, as H. Frankfort suggested, with the 'Field of Rushes', the home of the transfigured dead (1948.110–1), the message conveyed by the image remains similar. Hathor in cow form eased the transition from life, through death, to the afterlife and formed a point of contact between the living and the dead, especially during the Beautiful Festival of the Wadi.

The earliest surviving example of the combination of marsh and mountain motifs appears to be the statue of the Hathor cow in a papyrus thicket which was placed inside the Western Mountain in the rock-cut speos of the Hathor shrine of Djeser-Akhet (Pl. 41b). In this statue, and on three stelae from Deir el-Bahri (2.1, List 1.3–4, 11), the king appears both standing under the head of the cow and suckling from her udder. It was more common to show the king only under the head, in front of or encircled by the cow's menit necklace. Statue groups of this type stood in the sanctuaries of a number of Ramessid temples (*e.g.* Bruyère 1935.272, fig. 139; 1952b.15–6, fig. 87; Desroches Noblecourt & Kuentz 1968. 105–7, pls. 123–6). 'Cow and mountain' scenes with a figure of a king standing under the cow's chin, or just in front of her, are found in a number of private Ramessid tombs (*e.g.* Davies 1933 pl. 54; Hermann 1935 pl. 6b–c; Černý 1949.47; Bruyère 1953.31, fig. 5; Abdul Qader Muhammed 1966 pl. 11). Similar scenes are occasionally found on private stelae (*e.g.* HT 1925 pl. 31). Either a dead and deified king or the contemporary ruler could be shown, Amonhotpe I being the most common in the former class, and Ramesses II in the latter. On private monuments, the cow's menit necklace rarely encircles the king, presumably to avoid obscuring the face, but the king should still be understood as linked to the goddess by her life-giving necklace.

During the New Kingdom, kings were sometimes depicted standing or kneeling under the heads of deities in animal or semi-animal form, such as Renenutet (*e.g.* Säve-Söderbergh 1957 pl. 42) or the Great Sphinx (Selim Hassan 1953.71, fig. 62, pl. 67). Such statues may embody the idea that to stand in the shadow of a deity was to be under his or her protection (Assmann 1978.31). Some scholars have seen a special significance in the encircling of the king with the menit necklace of the goddess. In their discussion of the statue of Hathor in cow form with Ramesses II at Abu Simbel, Desroches Noblecourt and Kuentz identify the 'Caverns of Hathor' with the source of the Nile, and see the king as playing the role of Shu or Thoth in drawing forth (symbolized by the linking with the necklace) and transforming the destructive flood waters into the life-giving inundation – personified by the cow (1968.114–8). Whatever the merits of this theory in relation to Abu Simbel, it cannot be generally applied to 'cow and mountain' scenes and it would be particularly inappropriate to the Theban necropolis, where this motif seems to have originated. A. Hermann interpreted the gesture of encircling the king with the menit necklace as symbolizing the intimate relationship between the goddess and the king, who is accepted as her son, but is also the 'Bull of his mother' (1959.21–2). Leclant associated the gesture with the role of the divine cow as the nourisher and rejuvenator of the king (1961.272).

The images of the king encircled by the menit necklace and of him suckling seem so closely linked that where the first is shown the second can probably be inferred. In speeches in temple texts (2.4.5), the divine cow stresses that she both suckles and protects Horus. The Djeser-Akhet statue (Pl. 41b) could be seen as illustrating this double function. In the context of the Western Mountain, this suckling and protection would relate to the afterlife, and the combination of mountain and papyrus on private monuments probably alludes to the cycle of death and rebirth. The figures of kings suckling or standing beneath the cow's chin are often painted black (e.g. Pls. 25b, 41b), a colour that symbolizes rejuvenation and rebirth.

In some vignettes of the Book of the Dead, the cow in the Western Mountain is identified as Mehet-weret, the mother of the Sun God, rather than, or as well as, Hathor (Fig. 13b; Naville 1888 pl. 212; Allen 1974.209–10). In these vignettes a female torso may be shown 'emerging' from the mountainside to receive the sun disc in its arms and the text refers to Hathor, Lady of the West 'who enfolds Reʿ' (1974.210). Thus, the 'cow and mountain' motif can be associated with the daily death and rebirth of the sun, and specificallly with the concept of the sun god 'joining' his mother and entering the underworld to be regenerated in the waters of Nun (Hornung 1979.194–8; 1982.99–100).

The 'cow and mountain' motif can be reduced to a cow's head shown frontally against the mountainside, as in some Ramessid tombs at Deir el-Medina (e.g. Bruyère 1925 pl. 21; 1926.101, fig. 69; Keimer 1956.251, fig. 44). It is probable that the cows' heads in gilded or painted wood recovered from the tombs of Amonhotpe II (Daressy 1902.163, pl. 34), Thutmose IV (Newberry 1904.15, pl. 5), and Tutankhamon (Carter 1933.46, pl. 4b; Edwards 1972 no. 12) are three-dimensional equivalents to these paintings. E. Hornung suggests that the frontal cow's head was an image which could symbolize the whole solar cycle (1979.194–5, 198), so it may have been included in royal tombs as part of the process of identifying the dead king with the 'dying' sun.

The funerary couch in the form of a pair of divine cows found in the tomb of Tutankhamon also belongs to this category, and relates to the myth of the aging Reʿ being carried to the heavens on the back, or between the horns, of the divine cow (Carter 1933.112–3, pl. 18; Säve-Söderbergh 1957.4, pl. 3; Edwards 1972 no. 13; Hornung 1982.98–9). In this myth, the cow is identified with Nut or Mehet-weret and the effect of the journey is to rejuvenate Reʿ, so he is sometimes shown as a child riding on the back or head of the cow (Caminos 1974.39, pl. 41; Hornung 1982.100, fig. 10). In royal funerary religion, the divine cow plays an important role in the transition of the king from life through death to rebirth. This raises the question of whether the divine cow was expected to perform similar services for the non-royal deceased.

In Chapter 186 of the Book of the Dead, Hathor is described as the 'ferryboat of the favoured ones' (Fig. 13b). In a variant spell, the Hathor cow pronounces a speech welcoming the righteous dead and promising them a safe journey to the place of judgement (Allen 1974.209–10). In a similar text accompanying a 'cow and mountain' scene with king in a tomb of the end of the 18th dynasty, the cow urges the tomb owner to hurry to join his relatives in the West. She is also described as taking the righteous to the place of judgement (Theban Tomb 341; Davies 1948 pl. 27). In scenes on some Third Intermediate Period coffins, the sarcophagus is shown being dragged to the tomb by what appears to be a pair of Hathor cows, instead of a pair of oxen (*e.g.* Boeser 1918 pl. 6). This motif may allude to the idea of Hathor conveying the deceased to judgement. It could also be the explanation for a scene on a 21st dynasty coffin in which the deceased and his *ba* are shown riding on the back of a Hathor cow (1918 pl. 8). As with the scene of the *ba* suckling (Allen 1923.11), this idea may have originated long before its earliest surviving attestation.

Many passages in the Book of the Dead relate to the idea of the deceased becoming part of the solar cycle and some identify the deceased with Reᶜ-Atum (Frankfort 1948.105–11). The name of one of the seven cows includes the phrase 'who carries the god', which may allude to the myth of the divine cow carrying the sun god up into the heavens (Ramadan el-Sayed 1980.360). This suggests that the functions of the divine cow were divided up among the group of seven cows who assisted the non-royal dead in the afterlife. So the coffin scene (Boeser 1918 pl. 8) might be interpreted as the deceased in the role of Reᶜ-Atum being carried to the heavens by the divine cow.

A type of temple statue which occurs from the late New Kingdom onwards shows a private individual standing or kneeling under the head of a Hathor cow (*e.g.* Borchardt 1925 nos. 676, 784). A stone cow's head from Deir el-Bahri which might come from such a statue group has already been noted (2.4.1.1). The earliest of these statues, which is probably from Memphis and dates to the 20th dynasty, depicts a captain of archers and his wife kneeling beneath the head of Hathor, Lady of the Southern Sycamore, in cow form (Vandier 1969 pl. 10). The inscriptions consist of *ḥtp di nsw* formulae addressed to Hathor and Ptah, asking for a range of standard life and funerary benefits. In New Kingdom funerary religion there are many instances of imagery which once belonged exclusively to the king being taken over by private persons. This phenomonen is rarer in non-funerary religion, but this temple statue provides one example. Some of the votive objects from Deir el-Bahri can be regarded as forerunners of this type of statue group.

Summary

The cow form of Hathor dominates the votive offerings at Deir el-Bahri and was also important at Faras. Elaborate faience models of Hathor cows are virtually exclusive to Deir el-Bahri. Pottery cows and metal and faience cow plaques of the types found at Deir el-Bahri and Faras are also rare. The Hathor cow appears on many of the stelae and textiles from Deir el-Bahri, sometimes in a shrine or bark shrine, sometimes in the setting of a marsh or of the Western Mountain. A living or a deceased king can be shown standing beneath the cow's head and sometimes suckling from her udder. All this imagery is taken from the iconography of temple reliefs or statue groups and can be related to royal rituals and royal funerary religion.

On private monuments, the combination of the 'cow and marsh' and 'cow and mountain' motifs seems to promise that through the benevolence of the divine cow the deceased will be guided past the perils of the underworld and achieve regeneration. Although the king's presence in these scenes may be due to the fact that the 'cow and mountain' motif is based on a standard royal statue group, this need not imply that his figure was without symbolic meaning. This image of the transfigured king may have acted as a symbol of the protective love of the divine cow for humanity and as an assurance that her protection and succour would be extended to all the righteous dead. Hathor seems to embody a continuity between life and death, particularly when she is shown standing in the Western Mountain of the necropolis, the entrance to the realm of the dead, surrounded by the papyrus that evokes the creation and the renewal of life.

Among the offerings from the six sites, the 'cow and mountain' motif is restricted to stelae and textiles from Deir el-Bahri. Since objects of these types were intended to remain in the temples long after the deaths of their donors, it is not suprising that they should use funerary imagery, whether or not the prayers inscribed on them relate mainly to the earthly life of the donors. The smaller offerings were probably thought of as less permanent and are therefore more likely to relate to daily life. The 'cow and marsh' motif might be associated with birth, or with Hathor's ability to bestow renewed vigour and a long life. This could be linked with a specific ritual of drinking the milk of sacred cows. Since Hathor protected Horus in the marshes, the motif could also have been chosen by anyone seeking to place themselves under the protection of the goddess. This protection should probably be thought of as functioning both in life and in death, so that the funerary implications of the 'cow and marsh' motif need not be rejected. To most people, the cow may simply have seemed the most approachable and benevolent of the forms of Hathor.

2.5 Cats

Representations of animals of the cat family (*felidae*) were recovered from all six sites, but they were most prominent at Serabit el-Khadim and Timna. These pieces may be divided into three main groups: cat figurines; cat plaques; and other offerings decorated with *felidae*.

2.5.1 Figurines (Pl. 42)

Faience figurines of animals of the cat family were discovered at Deir el-Bahri, Serabit el-Khadim and Timna. Such figurines are not mentioned by Hall or Currelly, but two headless examples (London V&A 674.1905 = Pl. 42b, 675.1905) and two feline heads (Oxford PR 1906.45.9; Toronto ROM 907.18.151 = Pl. 42c) were distributed by the EEF. MacDonald brought back fragments of four cat figurines from Serabit el-Khadim (London BM ER 310–12, 361). Petrie excavated at least 18 figurines at this site, six of which are illustrated in his report (1906.148, pl. 153.6–11). At Timna, the excavators found one almost intact cat figurine (Rothenberg 1972 pl. 94; 1988.126 pl. 118.6, fig. 38.1), and six definite (1988.126–7, fig. 33.1–2, 4–5, 38.2, 4), and four possible (1988.126, figs. 33.3, 38.3, 5), fragments of feline figurines.

The cat figurines seem to have been 4–9 cm high and 4–8 cm long. They are made in blue or green faience with the coat markings and other details in black. The 21 examples from Serabit el-Khadim which I have been able to examine are all of rather poor workmanship (London BM ER 310–12, 361; Manchester 915–26a–b, 927, 931–3; Oxford Ash. 1911.614). The two headless figurines from Deir el-Bahri are of better quality. One piece from this site (London V&A 674.1905) and five from Serabit el-Khadim (London BM 361; Manchester 915, 918, 921 = Pl. 42a, bottom left, 925) were manufactured in open moulds and so have flat backs. The rest are modelled in the round. All the figurines seem to have had shallow, oval bases. One figurine from Deir el-Bahri (London V&A 674.1905) has a square mounting hole in the bottom of its base. None is pierced or fitted with loops for suspension, so they are figurines rather than amulets.

Most of the cats are sitting on their haunches, with the front legs straight and the tail tucked behind the back right leg. This posture is standard in Egyptian art from the First Intermediate Period onwards and is particularly common among the bronze cats of the Late and Graeco-Roman Periods (de Morant 1937.36–9; Langton & Langton 1940.1–2, 19). On figurines of this type, the head usually faces forwards, but in a few cases it is at right angles to the body (*e.g.* Pl. 42a, bottom left). This posture is found mainly in pairs of cats (2.5.4), so these pieces may belong to pairs. A few figurines show recumbent cats (London BM 310; Manchester 924 = Pl. 42a, top right, 925). On the only intact example, the head is at a right angle to the body, but this is common with recumbent cats from the 12th dynasty onwards (Langton & Langton 1940.18). It has been suggested that this posture originated with lions rather than with cats (Winlock 1948.30–1; Aldred 1972.214–5).

A variety of coat markings are shown on the figurines. An example from Deir el-Bahri has random black patches (Pl. 42b), comparable with those on some cow figurines from the same site. One figurine from Deir el-Bahri (London V&A 674.1905), six from Serabit el-Khadim (Manchester 915, 917–20, 931, 933), and the best preserved Timna cat (Rothenberg 1972 pl. 94) have a dark line along the spine and small spots on the body. Of the remaining body fragments from Serabit el-Khadim, two are marked with spots and dashes (Manchester 921, 923), three have stripes (Manchester 924, 926–7), and one is plain (Manchester 925). In two cases, the cats appear to be wearing collars (Manchester 915, 922 = Petrie 1906 pl. 153.8, 10). The range of coat patterns suggests that several species of *felidae* are represented. Petrie proposed that two of the figurines from Serabit el-Khadim were cheetahs (1906 pl. 153.6, 8) and that the rest were serval cats (1906.148). It is uncertain whether cheetahs (which are not *felidae*) were known to the Egyptians. The damaged heads of these pieces make any identification speculative. It is more likely that the figurines represent two species – *Leptailurus serval* (*e.g.* Petrie 1906 pl. 153.10; Rothenberg 1988 fig. 33.2) and *Felis libyca* (*e.g.* Pls. 42a, top right, 42c; Rothenberg 1988 fig. 33.1, 38.1).

Amulets in cat form were produced in Egypt from the First Intermediate Period down to Roman times (*e.g.* Brunton *et al.* 1928 pl. 96; Herrmann 1985.67; Herrmann 1990.40–1, nos. 67–8). They were most common during the Third Intermediate and Late Periods (Langton & Langton 1940.2–3, 13–8, pls. 4–6). Cat figurines are comparatively scarce before the 22nd dynasty. Most New Kingdom examples, which may be made in green, red, or yellow faience, have plain coats, represent *Felis chaus* or *Felis libyca*, and are no more than 4 cm high. Though inferior in quality, the figurines from Deir el-Bahri, Serabit el-Khadim, and Timna are stylistically closer to the elaborately marked faience figurines of crouching or stalking cats found in some Middle Kingdom tombs (*e.g.* Hayes 1953.223–4, fig. 140; Kemp & Merrillees 1980.143–4, pls. 15–16; Bourriau 1988.117, No. 108). Comparative material is also provided by a group of late Middle Kingdom faience cats from the Temple of the Obelisks at Byblos (Dunand 1958.750–1, nos. 15228–35).

Petrie (1906.148) assigned all the cat figurines to the mid 18th dynasty on the grounds of their affinity with the cat plaques, some of which are datable by their inscriptions to the reigns of Hatshepsut and Thutmose III. The model serval cats are unlikely to be earlier than the 18th dynasty, since this species is not attested from Egypt before the New Kingdom (Baldwin 1975.431; Störk 1980.369). The first known occurrence of the motif of a pair of seated cats with bodies in profile and heads shown full face is in a tomb dating to Amonhotpe III (Theban Tomb 48; Hermann 1937.73, pl. 8), so figurines with this posture (*e.g.* Pl. 42a, bottom left) may be of this approximate date or later. The careless workmanship of some of the figurines could suggest a Ramessid date. Schulman assumes that all the cat figurines from Timna are Ramessid, but some, especially those which represent *Felis libyca*, could be 18th dynasty.

2.5.2 Cat plaques (Pls. 43–4)

Petrie excavated fragments from at least 21 faience cat plaques at Serabit el-Khadim, 14 of which were illustrated in his report (1906.148, pl. 154). The third Harvard Expedition found at least one cat plaque at this site (Starr & Butin 1936 pl. 13 no 92). Rothenberg initially stated that at Timna cats 'appear as drawings on flat tablets' (1972.166) but no such cat plaque is included in the full publication of the Timna offerings (1988.91–268).

The 20 cat plaques which I have been able to examine, or obtain detailed information on, range in height between 9 and 15 cm (Bolton 68.05.37; Bristol H 3279; Brussels MR 1982; London BM 41842; V&A 708.1905, 714.1905; Manchester 928–9, 934–8; Oxford Ash. E 3343–6; Sydney 15745–6; Toronto ROM 906.16.31). Most are rectangular, but some have rounded tops (*e.g.* Pl. 43, top right = Toronto ROM 906.16.31; Pl. 44, centre top). They are all made in blue or green faience, and some are glazed on both faces. In contrast to the Hathor mask plaques (2.3.2.4), none has a design on both faces. The designs are always in black and the drawings of the cats are often lively and well executed.

The design usually consists of a cat seated on a plinth, facing to the right. In two cases, the plinth takes the form of a *serekh* (Petrie 1906 pl. 154.6, 13 = Bristol H 3279). One fragment is unusual in showing a left-facing cat between two papyrus umbels (Pl. 43, top centre). The *felidae* depicted on the plaques can be divided into two main groups. The first group comprises animals with rounded heads and short ears, evenly spotted coats, and striped haunches and tails (*e.g.* Pl. 43, top right, middle right = Sydney 15745, bottom right = Oxford Ash. E 3344; Pl. 44, top right = Brussels MR 1982, bottom right = London V&A 714.1905). One has a ruff (Pl. 44, bottom right), a detail sometimes found in cats drawn on ostraca or in papyri (*e.g.* Peck 1978 pls. 76, 78, XIII). The animals on these plaques, which in outline resemble the cats carved on New Kingdom stelae (*e.g.* Tosi & Roccati 1972 pls. 284–5), are probably the common *Felis libyca*. Another plaque (Pl. 43, centre bottom) might belong in this group or could represent the sandy-coated *Felis chaus*.

The second group comprises animals with tall ears, small, pointed heads on long necks, and coats with thinner spots and no stripes (*e.g.* Pl. 43, top left = Bristol H 3279; Pl. 44, top left = Bolton 68.05.37; Petrie 1906 pl. 154.8–10). These have been identified as *Leptailurus serval* (Petrie 1906.148; Baldwin 1975.431; Giveon 1971.51–3; 1978.65). On some of these plaques the cat appears to be wearing a collar.

Five plaques depicting *Felis libyca* bear fragmentary royal inscriptions. Two have the prenomen of Hatshepsut (Pl. 44, top centre; Petrie 1906 pl. 154.6). On the second of these, the queen has the epithet 'beloved of Hathor, Lady of Mefkat' (London V&A 708.1905). Two cat plaques bear the cartouche of Thutmose III (Pl. 43, top right = Toronto ROM 906.16.31; Petrie 1906 pl. 154.2). The fifth plaque, which is very similar in style to one of the Thutmose III plaques, bears traces of the epithet *nb t3wy* (Pl. 44, top right). On the basis of these inscriptions, Petrie dated all the plaques to the mid 18th dynasty (1906.148). One of the analogous Hathor mask plaques from Serabit el-Khadim bore a cartouche of Amonhotpe I (2.3.2.4), so it is possible that some cat plaques date to the early 18th dynasty.

There is little comparative material from other sites to provide help with dating. A faience plaque showing a pair of cats sitting in a window above a false door is unprovenanced and said to date to the 18th or 19th dynasties (Hermann 1937.73, pl. 9c). The few surviving stelae which show cats as the object of adoration are Ramessid. Since none of these cats can be associated directly with Hathor (2.5.5), this may not be relevant to the dating of the cat plaques. It is safest to assume that all the cat plaques are 18th dynasty, but the examples with serval cats – none of which is inscribed – could be slightly later than the pieces which show *Felis libyca*.

2.5.3 Objects decorated with a single feline (Figs. 1–3; Pls. 3, 8)

One marsh bowl fragment from Deir el-Bahri, drawn by Miss Carhew, shows the head of a cat next to a lotus bud (Pl. 3, top left). A bowl from Timna provides the only other example of a cat as a motif on the interior of a faience bowl (2.5.4). A Hathor mask and a pair of cats flanked by papyrus sometimes appear on the exterior of the faience ring-stands on which bowls were placed (2.5.4; Pl. 45) and on pottery vessels (*e.g.* Bruyère 1939.113, fig. 49; 1939b.101–2 figs. 36–7). Two rim fragments from pottery bowls from Deir el-Bahri each have a crudely modelled animal seated on or astride the rim (Fig. 1.32, 34). One of these animals could be a cow (Fig. 1.34); however, it is looking back over its shoulder, a posture well attested for cats (2.5.4–5) but found in cows only when they are accompanied by a calf. The other animal (Fig. 1.32) is almost certainly a recumbent cat, shown with the head at a right angle to the body. One faience bowl fragment from Serabit el-Khadim has a seated feline animal – perhaps a lion – astride the rim (London BM 13294).

One cat scaraboid from Deir el-Bahri was illustrated by Miss Carhew (Fig. 3, third row) and Naville found a crude, glazed steatite scaraboid in the form of a recumbent cat during the 1903–4 season (Dublin NM 1904.530). A similar faience specimen, now in Boston, may also have come from this site (MFA 1906.2498; Spalinger in Brovarski 1982 no. 378). One steatite feline scaraboid was excavated at Faras (Oxford Ash. 1912.958 = Pl. 8.35). This piece, which is 1.8 cm long and vertically pierced, has a floral design on its base. The recumbent animal, with its neatly spotted coat, rounded head, and small ears, could be a leopard. Feline scaraboids were never very common. Most examples date to the Second Intermediate Period and early 18th dynasty (*e.g.* Brunton & Engelbach 1927 pl. 26; Langton & Langton 1940.49–50, pl. 14; Hornung & Staehelin 1976.119–21; Matouk 1978.96–7).

At Mirgissa, two faience rings decorated with cats were found in the sanctuary (Karlin in Vercoutter (1970.346). One of these rings is of bright blue faience and has a walking cat attached to the shank (1970 no. 106). The other is in red faience and has a seated cat (head lost) as a bezel (1970 no. 107). Only a few comparable rings survive, all dating to the late 18th dynasty (Langton & Langton 1940.46, pl. 14). The red faience of one of the rings confirms a late 18th dynasty date. These cat rings might be seen as analogous to the Hathor mask rings (2.3.3.2, Pl. 33c).

The Victoria and Albert Museum has a head of a leopard or lioness, made in dark blue frit (678.1905), which comes from Serabit el-Khadim. The head, which is about 3 cm long, is vertically pierced and its flat back is incised with two *wadjet* eyes. Miss Carhew drew two very similar examples from the 1892–5 EEF excavations at Deir el-Bahri (Fig. 2). Feline heads of this kind are shown on some Middle Kingdom apotropaic and magical wands (*e.g.* Bourriau 1988.115, no. 104a, with references; P. Lacovara in D'Auria *et al.* 1988.127-8, no.59). They have been classed as apotropaic amulets (Petrie 1914.13; Aldred 1972.191–2) or as symbols of rebirth (Hornung & Staehelin 1976.129–30). They were incorporated into Middle Kingdom jewellery (*e.g.* Wilkinson 1971.81–2, pl. 13) and faience examples have been recovered from 18th dynasty burials (*e.g.* Petrie 1891 pl. 26.18).

Three amulets in the form of feline goddesses were found at Timna (Rothenberg 1988.140, pl. 118.1, figs. 47.4, 48.7–8, 12). Two faience amulets are badly damaged, but it is clear that they depict a lioness-headed goddess wearing a sun disc (1988.140, fig. 47.1, fig. 48.7). A gypsum amulet, 3.8 cm high, shows a female deity standing, with her head facing to the right, and holding a sceptre (Rothenberg 1972 pl. 92; 1988.140, pl. 118.1, fig. 48.8). The head is very worn 'but the outline clearly suggests a feline visage' (Schulman in Rothenberg 1988.140). Schulman proposes that Sekhmet is the 'most probable identification' for all three amulets (1988.140). Other possibilities are Tefenet or Hathor, Lady of Mefkat, who appears in lioness-headed form on a stela from Serabit el-Khadim (Pl. 13b). A fragment of a faience plaque from Deir el-Bahri also appears to show a lioness-headed form of Hathor (Pl. 3, top left). Cat amulets were found at Gebel Zeit (Castel *et al.* 1985.19) but are not so far published.

2.5.4 Objects decorated with a pair of felines (Pls. 32, 45)

A faience naos from Serabit el-Khadim, which may have formed part of a model naos sistrum, has a seated cat, facing outwards, on either side of the central recess (Petrie 1906.148, pl. 153.3). Petrie also found several fragments from faience ring-stands decorated with the motif of a Hathor mask flanked by cats (1906.145–6, 148). He illustrated one example, on which half of a Hathor mask, some stems of papyrus, and a cat looking back over its shoulder are preserved (1906 pl. 150.16, location unknown). The cat has large ears, a ruff, rosette-like markings, and a tail which seems to terminate in a flower. I have traced five unpublished fragments which probably come from ring-stands with this type of decoration (Bolton 68.05.22.6 = Pl. 32d, 7 = Pl. 45a; Toronto ROM 906.16.90 = Pl. 45d, 91 = Pl. 45b, 103 = Pl. 45c).

On one of these pieces, only a Hathor mask survives (Pl. 32d; 2.3.3.1). On two others, only a single cat and the extreme right-hand edge of the Hathor mask are preserved (Pl. 45a–b). Each of these ring-stands shows a semi-recumbent cat with the body in profile and the head shown from the front. Neither of the cats is spotted. They both have a stem of papyrus arching over them. Traces of an inscription ending in ◊⌀ (*mry*?) are visible to the right of one of the cats (Pl. 45b). The two other ring-stand fragments also have a single cat with the body in profile and the head shown from the front, but more of the Hathor mask is preserved (Pl. 45c–d). On one, the badly drawn cat is spotted (Pl. 45c). Only the head, shoulders, and front leg are left of the cat on the second fragment, but it appears to be plain coated (Pl. 45d).

Three fragments of a faience bowl from Timna show part of a spotted cat looking back over its shoulder (Rothenberg 1972 pl. 91; 1988 fig. 38.6). The cat's tail seems to terminate in a lotus bud. Schulman suggests that the cat is depicted in a papyrus thicket (in Rothenberg 1988.131). This is possible but, as the cat is looking backwards, it is probably another example of the motif of a Hathor mask flanked by cats. Schulman states that the design is on the interior of the bowl, but the photograph makes it look like an exterior design.

The earliest precisely datable occurrence of the motif of a Hathor mask or sistrum flanked by cats is on a bowl from el-ʿAmarna which bears the cartouches of Amonhotpe III (Cairo CG 18459; Vandier 1966.78, pl. 3; Martin 1974.88–9). The motif is found on pottery (e.g. Bruyère 1937.113, fig. 49; 1939.104, figs. 36–7) and metal vessels (e.g. Calverley & Broome 1935 pl. 11; Schott 1952.790, fig. 8; Hayes 1959.359, fig. 225), clappers (e.g. Hayes 1959.316), scarab bases (e.g. Hornung & Staehelin 1976.120), and stelae (e.g. Wildung 1974 figs. 11–12, 15–16) from the late 18th dynasty to the end of the New Kingdom. It is also found on objects and in temple reliefs of the Third Intermediate and Late Periods (Vandier 1966.76–9; Troy 1986.111, fig. 75). A pair of cats without a Hathor mask occurs on a few Ramessid stelae from Deir el-Medina (e.g. Oxford Ash. 1961.232 = Holden in Brovarski 1982, no. 411; Tosi & Roccati 1972. no. 50053), and above the false door in a few mid and late 18th dynasty tombs (e.g. Hermann 1937.73, fig. 3, pl. 8). On two kohl containers, one thought to date to Thutmose III (Bourriau in Brovarski 1982.220, no. 267) and the other to Thutmose IV (Hayes 1959.192–3, fig. 108), a Hathor mask or a Bat symbol is shown between a seated cat and a figure of Taweret. The combination of a seated cat with Taweret is found on apotropaic wands of the Middle Kingdom (e.g. Altenmüller 1965 figs. 9, 12–13). In these cases the cat is always the same size as the Hathor mask or Taweret and its head is shown in profile, looking forwards. The earliest closely datable occurrence of a pair of cats looking backwards over their shoulders is in a tomb of the reign of Amonhotpe II (TT 93; Hermann 1937.73, fig. 3). As already noted (2.5.1), the earliest known two-dimensional representation of cats with the bodies in profile and the heads seen from the front is from a tomb dating to Amonhotpe III.

In view of all this, the objects with cats looking backwards are probably no earlier than Amonhotpe II, and those with cats whose heads are shown from the front are no earlier than Amonhotpe III. Petrie apparently stated that some of the faience ring-stands with the Hathor mask and cats motif dated to Seti II (1906.145–6). This is curious, because no ring-stands are ascribed to Seti II in Petrie's own list of objects from Serabit el-Khadim with royal inscriptions (1906.149) – though the British Museum does have an undecorated ring-stand with the cartouches of Seti II (London BM 41775). Comparison of the cats on the 18th dynasty plaques with the stiffly drawn and poorly detailed animals on four of the ring-stands (Pl. 45) suggests that a general Ramessid date is possible for the latter. The lively drawing on the ring-stand illustrated by Petrie (1906 pl. 150.16) and on the bowl from Timna (Rothenberg 1972 pl. 91; 1988 fig. 38.6) could point to a late 18th dynasty date for these pieces.

2.5.5 Symbolic value and functions

The Egyptians kept at least three species of cat. The large striped and spotted *Felis libyca* and the smaller sandy-coated *Felis chaus* could interbreed and were probably the ancestors of *Felis cattus* (Scott 1958.1–3; Abou-Ghazi 1963.16; Baldwin 1975.429–30). Cats may have been used as hunting animals in the marshes as early as the 5th dynasty (Scott 1958.3–4). There is a possible 11th dynasty representation of a pet cat (Arkell 1962.158), but cats were rarely shown in a domestic context before the 18th dynasty. Examinations of skeletons have revealed that serval cats were imported into Egypt from sub-Saharan Africa from the 18th dynasty onwards (Baldwin 1975.431; Störk 1980.369).

Feline deities existed in Egypt from an early period, but few can definitely be associated with cats before the 22nd dynasty (Bonnet 1952.81). Bastet, for example, was depicted during the Old, Middle, and New Kingdoms as a woman with the head of a lioness (Vandier 1966.80). Hathor was occasionally shown in this way in New Kingdom temple reliefs (*e.g.* Gayet 1894 pl. 21).

References to Hathor as a cat occur in New Kingdom funerary texts (Abou-Ghazi 1963.10–1), but this would not in itself prove that there was a cult of Hathor in cat form. Nor is the presence of feline scaraboids at Deir el-Bahri and Faras, and of cat rings at Mirgissa, necessarily evidence that Hathor was worshipped there in feline form. These objects may fall into the category of personal jewellery donated to the goddess (2.9.4). The evidence of the cat figurines from Serabit el-Khadim and Timna, which seem to have been specially made as votive objects, cannot however be dismissed in this way. Late Period cat figurines sometimes have inscriptions which identify them with a goddess – usually Bastet (*e.g.* Langton & Langton 1940.31, pl. 10) – but I know of no inscribed New Kingdom examples.

The only New Kingdom stone stelae linking Hathor with cats are those which show a Hathor mask or sistrum flanked by cats (*e.g.* Wildung 1974.263–4, figs. 11–2,15–6). In these cases it is not clear whether it is the mask alone or the mask and the cats which can be associated with Hathor. However, the faience plaques from Serabit el-Khadim, which might be classified as miniature Type A stelae, do imply a cult of Hathor in cat form. One of the cat plaques names Hatshepsut as 'beloved of Hathor, Lady of Mefkat' (Petrie 1906 pl. 154.6). This suggests that the cat shown *is* Hathor, Lady of Mefkat, and such was Petrie's opinion (1906.148). Thus, the plaques dating to Hatshepsut and Thutmose III are probably the oldest surviving representations of any Egyptian goddess in full feline form.

It might be objected that the models and plaques represent cats sacred to Hathor, rather than the goddess herself, but none of these animals is described as the cat *of* Hathor. It is unlikely that large numbers of sacred cats inhabited the desert temples of Serabit el-Khadim and Timna, although it is possible that one cat, in whom the goddess manifested herself, was kept at the former. However, the fact that almost all the cats sit on plinths (Pls. 43–4) suggests that statues of cats are being depicted. No cats appear in temple reliefs at Serabit el-Khadim, even in minor scenes on lintels or pillars. I know of no relief from any site or period which shows a king offering to a goddess in cat – as opposed to cat-headed – form. Thus, the cat form of Hathor never seems to have been accorded the status of her other full animal form, the cow. Nevertheless, the cat figurines dedicated in the Temple of the Obelisks at Byblos hint that the association between Hathor and the cat goes back at least as far as the Middle Kingdom.

The next question is what symbolic values can be attached to Hathor in cat form and to the motif of the Hathor mask flanked by cats. In the Litany of Reᶜ, one of the forms of the god is 'The Great Cat' (Piankoff 1955.55–6, fig. 17; Hornung 1976.107, 115). Reᶜ is identified in the Coffin Texts with the cat who killed the Apophis serpent under a persea tree at Heliopolis and this scene is illustrated in a standard vignette for Chapter 17 of The Book of the Dead (Naville 1888 pl. 30; Allen 1974.27). It has been proposed that the cats wielding knives which appear on Middle Kingdom apotropaic wands represent the sun god in this role (Abou-Ghazi 1963.9; Altenmüller 1965.174–5, figs. 9, 13). 'The Great Cat' and 'The Beautiful Cat' who are shown being adored on a Ramessid stela from Deir el-Medina may both be forms of Reᶜ (Holden in Brovarski 1982.201–2; Te Velde 1982.133).

In some illustrations the cat beheading Apophis appears to be female, and H. Te Velde remarks that:–

> The idea is that not only Re himself, but also his daughter can defeat Apophis. Goddesses associated with cats are commonly given the epithets 'daughter of Re' and 'eye of Re'. In the vignette of BD 17 it is always one tom-cat (or she-cat) that poses as conqueror. It may be imagined however, that Re and his daughter fought the battle together. (1982.133)

The cats on the apotropaic wands could then be interpreted as helpers and protectors of Reᶜ, rather than as the god himself. The female cats who are adored on two Ramessid stelae from Deir el-Medina (Tosi & Roccati 1972 nos. 50053, 50056) might be identified with any of the goddesses who bear the epithet 'Eye of Reᶜ'.

The Solar Eye, who is the first-born daughter of Reᶜ, is the central character in the myth of the 'Distant Goddess', which H. Junker pieced together from temple texts of the Graeco-Roman Period (1911). This eye may be shown either as an ordinary eye or as a *wadjet* eye (2.8.6). It is also identified with the fierce uraeus serpent who spat fire at the enemies of the sun god or the king (Yoyotte in Posener 1962.291; Giveon 1978a.106). In the temple texts, the Solar Eye, who is usually named as Hathor or Tefenet, is described as living in the Nubian desert in the form of a ferocious lioness. The myth tells how Reᶜ wants his daughter back to fight against his enemies and how he sends Thoth and Shu to fetch her. The lioness is persuaded, by means of music and dancing and by promises of a beautiful temple with daily offerings of flesh and wine, to return home.

An earlier version of the same story seems to be contained in the myth of Onuris (Junker 1917). A late version is found in a demotic papyrus in which Thoth in ape form is sent to Nubia to fetch back the Solar Eye who is living in the desert in the form of an 'Ethiopian cat' (Spiegelberg 1917; West 1969; Tait 1974). In this version, Thoth is threatened by Tefenet in her dangerous lioness form but persuades her to return to Egypt to defeat the enemies of Reᶜ, who are identified as the chaos serpents. Once in Egypt, Tefenet transforms herself into a series of gentle and benevolent deities who include Mut, Lady of Isheru, and Hathor, Lady of the Southern Sycamore. A fragment of papyrus gives part of a 19th dynasty version of this story (Posener 1954.47–8) and several Ramessid ostraca showing an ape with a cat have been interpreted as illustrations of Thoth and the Ethiopian cat (Brunner-Traut 1956.91–2, pl. 33).

The character of the Distant Goddess closely resembles that of the Solar Eye in the Middle or New Kingdom text of the myth of the Destruction of Mankind (Piankoff & Rambova 1955.27–9; Hornung 1982.1–31). In this myth, Reꜥ summons Hathor, the Solar Eye, and sends her down as Sekhmet to destroy mankind. When Reꜥ repents, he has to make Sekhmet drunk to stop the slaughter and transform her back into the gentle Hathor. In a text at Philae, Hathor, the Eye of Reꜥ, is referred to as gracious or peaceful (ḥtp) as Bastet, and raging (nšn) as Sekhmet (Junker 1911.32). As early as the 12th dynasty, the king is described as Bastet when he is protecting dutiful subjects and Sekhmet when he is punishing rebels (Posener 1976.26–7, 29). In both cases, Sekhmet and Bastet are used to express the dual nature fierce and gentle – of a single entity. It is possible that this contrast was expressed visually by the images of the lioness and the cat from the 12th dynasty onwards. In the demotic version of the Distant Goddess, the lioness form of Tefenet seems to be purely destructive, dangerous even to the gods, but the cat form is a powerful protector against the forces of chaos. This is consistent with the role of the Great Cat in funerary texts as the slayer of Apophis and with the presence of cats on apotropaic wands.

It is not certain to what species the 'Ethiopian cat' of the demotic version of the the Distant Goddess would belong, but *Leptailurus serval* seems the most likely candidate among African *felidae*. The serval was never a native of Sinai or the Negev, so its occurrence on plaques and as figurines at these sites takes on an added significance. Giveon suggested that all the cats at both these sites represent Hathor-Tefenet as the benevolent aspect of the Solar Eye (1978a.106–7). The hypothesis that Hathor was identified with Tefenet at Serabit el-Khadim receives support from the fact that a vase whose inscription describes Ramesses II as 'beloved of Tefenet, Lady of Heaven' was found at this site (Petrie 1906 pl. 146.9). This is the only instance of a goddess other than Hathor being named on a faience object from Serabit el-Khadim. However, two other goddesses who can be identified with the Solar Eye – Mehyt and Wadjet – are shown in lioness-headed form in a temple relief and on a royal stela at Serabit el-Khadim (Černý 1952 pls. 62, no. 191, 65a, no. 203).

If the serval cats from Serabit el-Khadim and Timna all represent the Distant Goddess, the question arises of whether the models and drawings of *Felis libyca* had a different significance. The cats on the wands, and in most of the illustrations of the beheading of Apophis, appear to belong to this species. Thus, *Felis libyca* was particularly associated with the Great Cat and his/her battle with Apophis, rather than with the Distant Goddess. However, a few Ramessid funerary vignettes show a feline animal with rather long ears, which might be a serval cat, slaying Apophis (*e.g.* Rossiter 1984.89, no.15), while some of the Ramessid ostraca which may illustrate the myth of the Distant Goddess depict an animal which resembles *Felis libyca* rather than *Leptailurus serval* (*e.g.* Brunner-Traut 1956 pl. 33). This suggests that even if the two species originally had distinct symbolic associations, they came to be used interchangeably.

Various interpretations of the myth of the Distant Goddess have been advanced. Te Velde links it with the menstrual cycle (1982.136), and would presumably equate the lioness form of the goddess with women during the dangerous 'impurity' of menstruation. Derchain proposes that the kittens held between the breasts of some New Kingdom statuettes of naked girls and the cats shown under women's chairs in some New Kingdom tomb scenes can have erotic connotations (1975.69; 1976.9). Te Velde uses this to argue that a cat can be an 'erotic signal that this woman is not hampered by a menstrual period' (1982.136).

Other scholars equate the return of the Distant Goddess with the coming of the inundation, and match the lioness and cat forms with the negative (destructive) and positive (irrigating) powers of the flood (Desroches Noblecourt & Kuentz 1968.110–1; Germond 1981.226–8; Chappaz 1983.11–2). Alternatively, the Distant Goddess has been seen as embodying the dual nature of the sun – Sekhmet being identified with the oppressive effects of heat, such as drought and pestilence, and Bastet with gentle, fructifying warmth (Shorter 1937.129; Scott 1958.5). All these speculative interpretations have their attractions, but none of them seems very relevant to the mining expeditions which worshipped Hathor at Serabit el-Khadim and Timna. At these sites the dual nature of the Distant Goddess might have been associated with the double nature of the desert, which was arid and dangerous, but contained great wealth in the form of its minerals. It is necessary to examine the motif of the Hathor mask flanked by cats, which has also been linked with the myth of the Distant Goddess, before any conclusion can be drawn.

This motif is only rarely accompanied by an inscription. On an ebony clapper, perhaps of the late 18th dynasty, the group is captioned Mut, Lady of Isheru (Hayes 1959.316), while on two Ramessid stelae from Deir el-Medina it is identified with Nebet-Hetepet (Černý 1958 no. 7) or Hathor Nebet-Hetepet (*HT* 1970 pl. 37.2; Wildung 1974 figs. 11–2). A relief in the rock-cut temple of Hathor, Lady of the Two Braziers, at el-Bebeit shows Merenptah 'Playing sistra for his mother', while a naos sistrum flanked by cats stands on the table between the king and the goddess (Sourouzian 1983.216, pl. 56). On a 22nd dynasty ring (Vandier 1966.83) and in a 30th dynasty relief at Bubastis (Vandier 1964.115–6, fig. 12b), the group is labelled as Bastet. In a relief in the Roman period Birth House at Dendara a group consisting of a Hathor mask naos sistrum column flanked by a cat and a frog is identified as Hathor, Lady of Dendara (Daumas 1959.115, pl. 59). In all these cases, only one name is attached to the whole group.

From the Late Period onwards, inscriptions refer to a composite deity, Sekhmet-Bastet-Nebet-Hetepet (Vandier 1964.102–3). This suggests that these three deities could represent the three stages in the myth of the pacification of the Distant Goddess. The concept of the sistrum as an instrument of pacification has already been noted (2.3.4), and Hathor Nebet-Hetepet is frequently shown as a naos sistrum or as a woman wearing a naos on her head (Vandier 1964.141–3). It is possible that the stela from Serabit el-Khadim with a lioness-headed goddess on one face and a Hathor mask naos sistrum captioned [Nebet]-Hetepet on the other

(Pl. 13a–b) shows the destructive aspect of the Distant Goddess being pacified and the pacific aspect being adored. Hathor, Lady of the Two Braziers, is described in Papyrus Jumilhac as transforming herself into Sekhmet to destroy Sethian enemies by fire (Sourouzian 1983.220). It is noteworthy that a high proportion of the private stelae at Serabit el-Khadim show the donors making burnt offerings to the goddess; sometimes of wildfowl, creatures associated with the forces of chaos, in a pair of braziers (Pl. 13b; Figs. 8–9).

Mut, Lady of Isheru, is specifically identified with the pacific aspect of the Distant Goddess after her return to Egypt and she is one of the goddesses who can have a naos sistrum form (Te Velde 1989). Cups decorated with a Hathor mask or sistrum between two cats are shown beside the sacred bark or shrine of Mut in several temple reliefs (Calverley & Broome 1935 pl. 11; Schott 1952.790, fig. 8; Troy 1986.111, fig. 75). Such vessels may have been used to make offerings of intoxicating liquors (Brunner 1954.81; Te Velde 1982.135). The myth of the Destruction of Mankind demonstrates that the destructive power of the Solar Eye can be nullified by drunkenness, so these vessels may have been symbolic instruments of pacification, like the sistrum (Hornung & Staehelin 1976.120; Ziegler 1984.960). The bowl fragment with a cat on its rim from Deir el-Bahri (Fig. 1.32) may come from a crude pottery version of such metal vessels. It is probably significant that at Serabit el-Khadim and Timna the motif of the Hathor mask flanked by cats occurs only on sistra, bowls, or jar stands (2.5.4). This motif might then be interpreted as combining the two benevolent aspects of the Solar Eye – the fierce but protective cat and the gentle and gracious goddess into whom the cat is transformed when she returns to Egypt. It would then have to be assumed that two cats are shown rather than one to match the double face of the Hathor mask, or simply out of a desire for symmetry. A pair of animals facing towards each other and representing one deity is quite common in New Kingdom iconography (e.g. Tosi & Roccati 1972 nos.50053, 50056).

J. Vandier had a different interpretation of the motif of the Hathor mask or sistrum flanked by cats. He connected the sistrum with Hathor Nebet-Hetepet in her role as the 'Hand of Atum' and the cats with Shu and Tefenet (1966.81–2). This epithet has been seen as identifying Hathor with the feminine creative principle (2.3.4) and it implies that Hathor Nebet-Hetepet could be the mother of Shu and Tefenet, the children of Re^c-Atum (Vandier 1964.60–1; 1966.81). Vandier drew attention to a relief in the temple of Hibis which, among a series of cult objects, shows a Hathor mask naos sistrum flanked by cats – whose papyriform handle is crossed or clutched by a hand, and a second naos sistrum whose handle is replaced by an arm and a hand holding, or crossed by, a phallus of exaggerated length (1964.115; 1966 fig. 12a). These groups seem to link the Hathor sistrum flanked by cats with the conception of Shu and Tefenet, although a more general association with conception may be intended. The occurrence of a similar group in the Birth House at Dendara might seem to support Vandier's hypothesis. However, the combination of a frog and a cat (not two cats as Vandier states) is unlikely to show Shu and Tefenet. This group may instead represent three deities associated with conception and birth – Hathor in sistrum form, Heqet in frog form, and Bastet in cat form. At Dendara, the group would be linked with the birth of Horus or Ihy rather than with the conception of Shu and Tefenet.

Bruyère suggested that the motif of a Hathor mask flanked by cats and papyrus evoked the suckling and protection of Horus in the marshes of Chemmis (1939a.104). The cats shown with marsh flora (2.5.3–4; Pls. 2, 43, 45) all seem to be *Felis libyca* or *Felis chaus*, both species used in fowling in the marshes. It has been suggested that tomb scenes which show hunting in the marshes relate to the sexual union of the tomb owner and his wife in the afterlife (Westendorf 1967.142–3; Derchain 1976.8–10; Robins 1988.62–3), so that cats in a marsh setting could have both erotic and funerary connotations. It might be noted in this context that plants of the papyrus family have the same effect on some cats as catmint (Sacase 1986.119; personal observation), the smell or taste of it causing them to roll on the ground in a manner similar to a cat ready to mate. The Egyptians may have observed this phenomonen.

The bases of some New Kingdom scarabs have a design consisting of an open blue lotus flanked by cats (Hornung & Staehelin 1976.120). As already noted (2.3.3.1), a Hathor mask or sistrum can sometimes be flanked by lotus buds. The cats with tails which appear to end in lotus buds could evoke this image. E. Hornung and E. Staehelin propose that this group, in all its variants, alludes to the birth of the creator from the primeval lotus/divine mother and is thus a symbol of rebirth (1976.120).

Even if Vandier's identification of the pair of cats as Shu and Tefenet is correct, the motif may still have connotations of rebirth. There is no doubt that when Tefenet was identified as the Solar Eye, she could be shown in cat form, but Vandier admitted that there was less evidence for Shu taking feline form. However, he pointed out that Shu was also credited with slaying the Apophis serpent and may therefore have been identified with the 'Great Cat' (1966.81). He went on to propose that the image of a pair of cats was derived from the spotted lions of the horizon, who can be named as the paired souls of Reʿ and Osiris or as Shu and Tefenet (1966.82). The lions of the horizon have a spatial and temporal symbolic value because they can personify both East and West and Yesterday and Tomorrow (De Wit 1951.107–8; Westendorf 1966.18–20, pls. 6–7; Rössker-Köhler 1980.1082). Like the Aker, a double-bodied sphinx with whom they could be equated (Clark 1959.153–5, figs. 19–20), the lions guarded the eastern and western gates of the underworld. They are shown in a vignette to chapter 17 of the Book of the Dead supporting the rising sun, while in variants on this scene the sun disc is placed between the horns of the Divine Cow, who can be identified with Hathor (Hornung 1982.99–100, fig. 9). The lions of the horizon belong to the imagery of the death and rebirth of the sun and therefore to funerary religion and the symbolism of rebirth.

In jewellery at least, sphinxes, lions, and cats seem to have been used interchangeably from the Second Intermediate Period onwards (Winlock 1948.30–1). The pair of cats seated above the false door in some New Kingdom tombs (2.5.4) may be relevant to Vandier's argument, since sphinxes and lions can also be shown in this position (Hermann 1937.68–74, pls. 8–9; Hofman 1985 figs. 1–3). Hornung and Staehelin propose that, in keeping with their presence above the false door, the cats, lions, or sphinxes played a mediating role between the realms of the living and the dead (1976.120–1). Like the lunette of a stela, the window above a false door might be seen as representing the arch of the sky (Westendorf 1966.35–49). In this case, the pair of felines could be interpreted as the lions of the horizon. However, details of the posture of the felines shown above false doors argue against such an identification. The lions of the horizon always face away from each other, as their spatial and temporal symbolism demands. In contrast, the bodies of the cats seated above false doors are always turned towards each other. In one tomb, the cats glance back over their shoulders (Hermann 1937.73, fig. 3), but in some examples the cats look at each other (*e.g.* 1937 pl. 9c) or their heads are shown frontally (*e.g.* 1937 pl. 8a; Peck 1978 no. 131). The same variety of postures is found in the motif of the Hathor mask flanked by cats (2.5.4). This suggests that, although there may have been some confusion between the two, the motifs of the Hathor mask flanked by cats and of the sun flanked by lions are separate in origin.

After discussing the lions of the horizon, Westendorf proposes that the image of the 'Himmels-Raubkatze' is older than that of the Divine Cow and links the two as forms of Hathor (1966.12–3). This is disputable, but it is true that funerary statuettes of lions or panthers supporting a king and the lion beds in royal tombs do suggest that feline animals could play a role in the king's transition to the afterlife comparable with that of the Divine Cow (1966.53–6). There is no clear visual evidence that a cat could replace a lion or panther in this context, but the possibility should be borne in mind. The cats above the false doors might be interpreted as Hathor in cat form – shown twice and often full-face like the Hathor mask – on the threshold of the realm of the dead. Attention should be drawn here to the female 'Great Cat of Lapis Lazuli' to whom funerary prayers are addressed in Papyrus Skrine (Blackman 1918 pl. 6). Since Lady of Lapis-Lazuli is an epithet of Hathor at Serabit el-Khadim (Černý 1952 pl. 44, no. 102), this cat may have been a form of Hathor.

Summary

Objects depicting feline animals have been found at all six sites. Faience cat figurines were recovered from Deir el-Bahri, Serabit el-Khadim, and Timna. These range in date from the 18th dynasty to the Ramessid Period. Eighteenth dynasty faience plaques showing a single seated cat are a type of object unique to Serabit el-Khadim. Faience bowls and stands decorated with cats or with the motif of a Hathor mask flanked by cats occurred at Deir el-Bahri, Serabit el-Khadim, and Timna. There is extensive comparative material for this motif. At least two species are represented in the votive material: *felis libyca* and *leptailurus serval*. The cat plaques should probably be interpreted as showing a statue of Hathor, Lady of Mefkat, in cat form. These are the earliest representations of an Egyptian goddess in cat form.

There is a wide range of possible symbolic associations for Hathor in cat form. At Deir el-Bahri, the cat form should perhaps be seen as an alternative to the cow form, both being associated with birth, death and rebirth. The Distant Goddess appears as a cat only outside Egypt. This may help to explain the importance of the cat form at temples beyond Egyptian territory, such as Serabit el-Khadim and Timna. During the New Kingdom, most of Nubia seems to have been considered part of Egypt, and this could be why the cat form is not prominent at Faras or Mirgissa. It is the linked concepts of the Solar Eye in cat form who fights the enemies of Re᷐ and the Great Cat who slays the chaos serpent which seem most relevant to Serabit el-Khadim and Timna. Egyptian representations of the desert sometimes show it peopled by monsters such as gryphons and winged serpents, indicating that it was regarded as on the edge of, or even part of, the realm of Chaos (Yoyotte in Posener 1962.62–3). It would not be suprising if the mining expeditions in such hostile territory wished to evoke Hathor in the form of the fierce but protective cat who fought the enemies of divine order, and therefore of Egypt.

2.6 Fertility figurines

Nude female figurines in stone, faience, or pottery were recovered from Deir el-Bahri, Faras, Mirgissa, Serabit el-Khadim, and Gebel Zeit. Examples are also known from related sites such as Dendara and Koptos. I argue in this chapter that 'fertility figurine' is a more appropriate term for these objects than the commonly used 'Concubines du mort' or 'Beischläferin'. Six distinct classes of fertility figurines are represented among the votive offerings. They belong to a linked sequence spanning the Middle and New Kingdoms. These types need to be treated as a group. Therefore, each of them is described briefly before examples from the Hathor sites are discussed. Lists of all the provenanced examples of Types 1–6 which I have traced follow at the end of this chapter. I hope to provide a much fuller treatment of this material in a future publication.

2.6.1 The main types of Middle and New Kingdom fertility figurines

1 *Type 1* (Pls. 8, 46a)

Type 1 figurines may be made of stone, wood, ivory, or faience. They are always modelled in the round and most are of good workmanship. Their height varies between 10 and 20 cm. The limestone and wooden figurines are usually painted yellow, with the hair and other details in black. On the faience figurines the details are picked out in dark on light blue.

The Type 1 figurines all represent women with small breasts, high waists, flat stomachs and buttocks, and plump thighs. With the exception of a few wooden pieces whose inclusion in this category is doubtful (*e.g.* Breasted 1948 pl. 89b–c), these figurines have no feet. Their legs are rounded off just below the knee, so that they are not self-supporting. The arms usually hang at the sides with the hands flat against the thighs, but a few specimens hold a child on their left hip (*e.g.* Keimer 1948 pl. 28; Pavlov 1949 pl. 143; Hayes 1953.221, fig. 136).

Some of the faience figurines (*e.g.* Lansing 1934 fig. 29; Keimer 1948 pl. 14) and one ivory example (Muscarella 1974 pl. 170) wear patterned dresses with thin straps, similar to those painted on the wooden 'paddle dolls' found in Upper and Middle Egyptian tombs of the late Middle Kingdom, Second Intermediate Period, and early 18th dynasty (*e.g.* Garstang 1907 fig. 150; Keimer 1948 fig. 17, pl. 17). More often, the Type 1 figurines are nude. Their bodies are adorned by jewellery, such as cowrie shell girdles and strings of beads which cross over the torso, and by markings which could represent body painting, scarification, or tattooing. These marks consist of diamonds made up of dots, or diagonal lines on the thighs, or crosses about the waist and hips. The nipples, navel, and pubic triangle are usually marked in dark blue and the vulva is sometimes indicated.

None of the Type 1 figurines wears a head-dress, but at least five kinds of hairstyle can be distinguished:–

A. On some faience and wooden examples the hair appears to be cropped and the dark area is pierced with holes (*e.g.* Keimer 1948 pl. 14.2; D'Auria *et al.* 1988.28, no. 52). This could represent short curly hair, or the holes may have been for the insertion of strands of real or artificial hair, as on some wooden fertility figurines of the Late Period (*e.g.* London BM 59047). The similarity of these figures to the 'paddle dolls', which have long, full wigs of artificial hair, favours the latter interpretation.

B. On some stone, wood and faience figurines the common long tripartite wig is worn (*e.g.* Pl. 46a; Keimer 1948 pl. 12.1; Wildung *et al.* 1985.40–2, no. 28b).

C. Some stone and faience examples have the 'Hathoric' scroll wig (*e.g.* Desroches Noblecourt 1953 fig. 5; Bourriau 1988.125, no. 119).

D. Some figurines of stone, wood, and ivory have an unusual hairstyle in which a thick lock of hair – sometimes crimped or braided – falls to shoulder level, or just above, on either side of the face. The back of the head appears to be partially shaven and the remaining hair is divided into three long, thin plaits (*e.g.* Desroches Noblecourt 1953 pl. 4, fig. 14; Bourriau 1988 no. 118). The Type 1 figurines with children all have this hairstyle.

E. A few wood and ivory figurines (*e.g.* Muscarella 1974 pl. 170) wear a braided wig ending in four points, one on each side of the face and two at the back.

Most of the surviving Type 1 figurines come from tombs, but at least four rather crude examples were found in a domestic context at Kahun (Pl. 46a; List 1). Of the pieces which can be dated by their context, none is earlier than the 12th dynasty or later than the Second Intermediate Period. No Type 1 figurines have been recovered from temples in Egypt itself, but eight Type 1b and 1c figurines were found with other votive faience in the Temple of the Obelisks in Byblos (Dunand 1958.764, pl. 95). A faience head from Faras may come from a Type 1b or 1c figurine (Pl. 8.5 = London BM 51264; Karkowski 1981.109–10.4c). This head, which is 2.5 cm high, is broken at chin level and the nose is chipped. The faience has faded to a greyish-white. A similar broken-off faience head from Faras, which is only 1.4 cm high, might also come from a Type 1 figurine (Pl. 8.27 = London BM 51363; Karkowski 1981.109–10.4b). Without the bodies, this identification must remain speculative, but the discovery of Middle Kingdom and Second Intermediate Period pottery fertility figurines at Gebel Zeit (2.6.1.2–3) makes it more plausible. One 'figure féminine en calcaire', which might be of Type 1, was found near the Middle Kingdom shrine at this site (Posener-Kriéger 1986.381).

2 *Type 2* (Pl. 46c)

Type 2 figurines are modelled in the round in clay and are always of crude workmanship. Intact examples vary in height from 10 to 25 cm. The figurines can be attenuated in form, with long spindly legs tapering down to rudimentary feet. They cannot stand unsupported. These figurines all show nude women with small breasts, slim waists, flat stomachs, fairly broad hips, and very prominent buttocks.

The elongated arms hang at the sides with the hands flat against the thighs. A few Type 2 figurines have a child clinging to their back (*e.g.* Petrie 1927 pl. 52.399; Castel *et al.* 1985.20, fig. 12; 1986 pl. 1V.10). Type 2 figurines with children can sometimes be in a kneeling or sitting position (Castel *et al.* 1984.50–1, fig. 3).

Most of these figurines have crudely modelled necklaces and incised bracelets and girdles. A few also have silver loop earrings (*e.g.* Peterson & George 1982 fig. 30; Morenz 1958 pl. 13). Some examples from Gebel Zeit have necklaces of faience beads and scarabs (Castel *et al.* 1985.18). The pubic triangle is always marked by dots or deeply incised lines, and the vulva is sometimes indicated. The navel, the nipples, and dimples above the buttocks are marked by shallow depressions, which are often emphasized by an outer ring of dots (*e.g.* Pl. 46c; Bruyère 1939.130 fig. 50). Sometimes the whole breast is circled with dots (*e.g.* Posener-Kriéger 1986 pl. 71a). These dots are often filled in with mud. One example from Gebel Zeit has zig-zag markings down the front of both thighs (Cairo JE 97943).

The face is usually reduced to a 'beak nose' and slits for eyes and eyebrows. The mouth is occasionally shown. The coiffures of the Type 2 figurines can be very elaborate, but they all appear to be variations on the hairstyle of the Type 1d figurines. The hair is held back by a fillet, which is occasionally surmounted by an object which might represent a perfume cone or a top-knot (*e.g.* Bruyère 1939.124, fig. 47; Brunner-Traut 1955.25, pl. 10; Castel *et al.* 1986 pl. 4.9). A heavy lock of hair hangs on either side of the face, and three slender plaits, sometimes covered by ribbons flowing from the fillet (Desroches Noblecourt 1953 fig. 10), are shown at the back. On a few examples these plaits hang close together, but usually they are widely spaced and the head appears to be partially shaven.

Many of the surviving Type 2 figurines come from Middle Kingdom and Second Intermediate Period burials, but they have been found in domestic contexts at Badari and Koptos (List 2). At Gebel Zeit about 150 pottery fertility figurines were recovered from the sacred area at Site 1. These included numerous Type 2 figurines, as well as body fragments which could belong to Type 2 (Mey *et al.* 1980.310–12, nos. 43–5, fig. 3, pl. 81; Castel *et al.* 1984.50, figs. 2–4; 1985.20, figs. 10, 12; 1986.100, 104, pl. 4; Posener-Kriéger 1986.381, pl. 71a). On two of these examples the hairstyle is particularly elaborate and appears to incorporate a head-dress (Mey *et al.* 1980 no. 43, fig. 3; Castel et al. 1984.51, fig. 6; 1986 pl. IV.9). This hairstyle can be paralleled by examples from tombs at Esna (*e.g.* Downes 1974.86 fig. 50). On another Type 2 head from Gebel Zeit, the tresses are decorated with dots, and faience ring beads have been pressed into the clay to emphasize the fringe or fillet (Castel *et al.* 1984.50, fig. 4). Strands of artificial hair seem to be attached to the back of the fillet, linking this Type 2 head with the hairstyle of the Type 3 figurines (see Pl. 46d; 2.6.1.3).

A complete figurine with a simpler hairstyle includes a female child clinging to the woman's back (Castel *et al.* 1986 pl. 4. 10). Another Type 2 figurine from this site also has a female child on its back (Cairo JE 97943). Early Dynastic female figurines occasionally have a child in this position (*e.g.* Dreyer 1986 pl. 15). Some New Kingdom reliefs show women, usually foreigners but sometimes Egyptians, carrying babies in slings on their backs (Malek & Miles 1989.227–8, figs. 1–3;

Janssen & Janssen 1990.20–1, fig. 10). A Type 2 figurine with decorated tresses is shown seated with a child in her arms (Castel *et al.* 1984.50 fig. 3). A number of headless bodies might have come from Type 2 figurines (*e.g.* Mey *et al.* 1980.315, nos. 52–3, fig. 5.1), including one with a child on its back (1980 pl. 81b). The excavators note that one female figurine is carrying two children, one on her back and the other in front of her (Castel *et al.*1984.51), but they do not say which type this figurine belongs to. Where it is possible to tell the sex, the children appear to be female.

Desroches Noblecourt suggests that figurines of my Type 2 may have originated in provincial cemeteries in the First Intermediate Period (1953.8), but none of the examples datable from tomb groups is earlier than the 12th dynasty. Type 2 figurines have been recovered from Second Intermediate Period burials (List 2), but there are no definite New Kingdom examples. The later figurines tend to be less steatopygous than the earlier ones, and to have less elaborate body decoration. The pieces from Gebel Zeit, which provide the only examples of Type 2 figurines from a sacred context, range in date from the late Middle Kingdom to the late Second Intermediate Period.

3 *Type 3* (Pls. 1, 8, 46d, 47–8; Fig. 1)

The Type 3 figurines are modelled in the round in clay and are always of crude workmanship. Intact examples vary in height from 12 to 28 cm. Their physique closely resembles that of the Type 2 figurines, although the buttocks tend to be less prominent. Most have long straight legs that taper down to rudimentary feet, but seated and kneeling examples suckling children are known (*e.g.* Pl. 47b; Downes 1974 fig. 48). Other Type 3 figurines carry a child on the back (*e.g.* Peterson & George 1982.42–3), or in the arms (*e.g.* Pl. 48b centre; Hayes 1959 fig. 6).

None of these figurines has clothes marked on the body, but one example with a female child from a 17th dynasty Theban tomb was wrapped in strips of linen (Hayes 1959.17, fig. 6) and many Type 3 figurines from Gebel Zeit were found wrapped in pieces of cloth decorated with beads and coloured threads (Castel *et al.* 1985.19–20, fig. 13; Posener-Kriéger 1985.298, pl. 65; 2.2.3). Type 3 figurines mostly have the same kinds of jewellery as those of Type 2. One Type 3 figurine from Faras appears to wear the crescent moon amulet associated with breast-feeding children (Pl. 48a, top left; Brunner-Traut 1970a; Janssen & Janssen 1990.19, figs. 7–8). This amulet may also be intended on other figurines of Types 2 and 3 which have only a simple crescent at the neck (*e.g.* Pl. 46c). Most Type 3 figurines have pierced ears. Silver earrings survive on the linen-wrapped example from Thebes (Hayes 1959.17 fig. 6) and metal hoop earrings on several examples from Gebel Zeit (Castel *et al.* 1985.19; Castel & Soukiassian 1989a pl. 13a). Faience jewellery is preserved on many Type 3 figurines from Gebel Zeit (Castel *et al.* 1985.19–20, fig. 13).

The pubic triangle is always incised, and the vulva is sometimes indicated. The navel and, less often, the nipples and dimples are marked by shallow depressions, occasionally surrounded by a circle of dots. The depressions are sometimes filled with mud (*e.g.* Pl. 49a, right). The heads of Type 3 figurines are curiously flattened and the features are reduced to a beak nose and slits for eyes and eyebrows. The mouth is hardly ever marked in. The face is surmounted by a fringe or fillet and a convex disc pierced with three to six holes. Intact examples demonstrate that these holes were threaded with long strands of artificial hair weighted with mud pellets (*e.g.* Pl. 46d; Hornemann ST 837; Hayes 1959.17, fig. 6; Castel *et al.* 1985.19, fig. 7; Leclant & Clerc 1986 figs. 62–3, 65). These 'wigs', which are very similar to those attached to 'paddle dolls' (*e.g.* Keimer 1948 pl. 17), represent an elaborate hairstyle of numerous plaits perhaps derived from Nubian fashions.

Many Type 3 figurines come from burials, but they have been found in domestic contexts at several sites (List 3), and occur as votive offerings at Deir el-Bahri, Faras, and Gebel Zeit. Hall stated that 'numerous nude female figures of baked clay and of blue faience' were found at Deir el-Bahri, and that the pottery figures were more numerous than the faience ones (in Naville 1913.14,16). He illustrated fragments from four Type 3 figurines (Pl. 1, bottom right and centre; Fig. 1.8–9). In the EEF distribution lists, the faience figurines outnumber the pottery examples by about three to one, but it may be that only a small proportion of the pottery figurines was brought back to England. The lists do not distinguish between the various types of pottery figurine, nor do they always specify the exact number sent to a museum. At least 16 pottery figurines are mentioned, 11 of which were sent to America. I have been able to examine 14 fragments of Type 3 figurines from Deir el-Bahri (Brussels MR E 746, 2439, 25115 (4); Liverpool 13.10.04.32; London BM 41104, 41105 = Pl. 48a centre, 41106 = Pl. 49a right; Oxford Ash. E 2714–5, 2727; PR 1906.45.15 = Pl. 47a). Neither Carter nor Winlock specifically mentioned finding figures of this type at Deir el-Bahri, but Winlock's remark when describing the offerings that Hathor 'was a goddess of joy to whom those who were disappointed in love had merely to make an appropriate gift ... ' (1923.38) could be a discreet reference to sexually explicit figurines or to votive phalli.

At Faras, Griffith found 'Abundant fragments of nude female figures or dolls with curious head-dresses ... ' (1921.86). He illustrated four Type 3 fragments in his report (Pl. 8.13–4 = London BM 51269–70; 15–6 = Oxford Ash. GN 1912.949). I have traced 11 fragments of Type 3 figurines from Faras (Brussels MR E 3602.1–6; London BM 51269–70 = Pl. 48a, upper; Oxford Ash. 1912.949 (3) = Pl. 48b). Four other pieces of pottery figures from Faras were sent to the Royal Scottish Museum, Edinburgh (1912.522), but these do not survive. One of the Faras figurines consists of a head and torso with one arm holding a child to the figure's left breast (Pl. 48b, centre). Since no Type 2 heads have survived from Deir el-Bahri or Faras, the crude pottery body fragments from these sites probably belong to Type 3, but the possibilty that Type 2 figurines were dedicated here cannot be ruled out.

At Gebel Zeit, Type 3 figurines were found in various parts of the sacred area at Site I, including mine entrances close to the Middle Kingdom/Second Intermediate Period shrine (Posener-Kriéger 1986.299) and in between the stones of the enclosure wall of the New Kingdom shrine (Castel & Soukiassian 1985.286; 1.6.3). Nine Type 3 figurines from Gebel Zeit have so far been published. Six of these consist only of a head and shoulders or head and torso

(Mey *et al.* 1980.311–2, nos. 46–8, fig. 3.2; Leclant & Clerc 1985 fig. 61; 1986 fig. 69). One of these fragments, which is 4.5 cm high, has the remains of linen threads dangling from the holes in its disc (Mey *et al.* 1980.312, no. 47). On three other heads an intact mass of artificial hair, consisting of linen thread weighted with mud pellets, is suspended from the disc (Castel *et al.* 1986 pl. 4.8 = Pl. 46d; Leclant & Clerc 1985 fig. 61; 1986 fig. 69). On another head, the mud pellets are replaced by shells and faience beads (1986 fig. 61). On one intact Type 3 figurine from Gebel Zeit the wig falls to hip level (Castel *et al.* 1985.19, fig. 7). Another, on which the wig is nearly as long, has a necklace of faience beads (Leclant & Clerc 1986 figs. 64–5). A third intact figurine has metal earrings and bracelets, and several necklaces of faience beads, one with a small scarab attached (Castel *et al.* 1985.20 fig. 13; Castel & Soukiassian 1989a pl. 13a). A fourth has copper earrings and bracelets, and a girdle made up of a double string of faience beads (personal observation, Cairo Museum). Numerous body fragments from Gebel Zeit are also likely to have come from Type 3 figurines (Mey *et al.* 1980.312–4). The excavators state that both types of fertility figurine from Gebel Zeit could carry children (Castel *et al.* 1985.20), but no Type 3 figures with children have been published so far.

The figurines from Deir el-Bahri and Faras do not differ significantly from those found in funerary or domestic contexts at other sites (List 3). The Gebel Zeit examples with metal and bead jewellery may seem unusual, but the votive objects are exceptionally well preserved at this site. Gebel Zeit is the only place where fertility figurines have been found wrapped in decorative cloths, but very similar textiles were discovered at Deir el-Bahri, where they may have been used for the same purpose (2.2.3, 8). The general date range of this type of figurine is from the Middle Kingdom to the early 18th dynasty. There are four main differences between the New Kingdom examples and those dated by context to the Middle Kingdom or the Second Intermediate Period. The earlier pieces tend to be taller and more steatopygous, to have more elaborate body decorations – such as circles of dots around the navel – and to have smaller discs sloping back almost on a level with the fringe, rather than rising above it.

If these dating criteria are applied, almost all the pieces from Deir el-Bahri can be assigned to the 18th dynasty. The only piece which might be earlier is a headless example (Pl. 49a, right). This figurine is markedly steatopygous and has some dotted body decoration, although this is more carelessly applied than on most Middle Kingdom or Second Intermediate Period examples. A few Type 3 figurines from Faras are probably 18th dynasty (*e.g.* Pls. 48a, top right; 48b, right), but the discs on some examples (*e.g.* Pls. 48a, left; 48b, centre) and the steatopygous physique of others (*e.g.* Pl. 48b, left; Brussels MR E 3602) suggest an earlier date, probably in the Second Intermediate Period. On the basis of disc shape, three of the Type 3 heads from Gebel Zeit probably date to the Middle Kingdom or Second Intermediate Period (Mey *et al.* 1980 nos. 46, 48; Castel *et al.* 1986 pl. IV.8), and three to the early 18th dynasty (Mey *et al.* 1980 no. 47; Castel *et al.* 1986 pl. V.11; Leclant & Clerc 1986 figs. 61, 69). Of the intact figures from this site, one has the body shape and markings of the early examples (Castel *et al.* 1985.19, fig. 7a), while the others are probably 18th dynasty.

4 *Type 4* (Pls. 1, 8, 49, 51a–b)

Type 4 figurines are made of pottery. Most were shaped in open moulds, and so have flat backs. The height varies from 10 to 22 cm. The faces are sometimes of delicate workmanship (*e.g.* Pls. 49b, 51b, left). Some specimens show traces of yellow paint on the body, black on the hair, and red on the headdress (Petrie 1927 pl. 52.423; Bruyère 1939.141). The figurines can be unnaturally elongated (*e.g.* Petrie 1927 pl. 52.423). They all depict women with small breasts, slim waists and hips, and flat stomachs. The feet are rudimentary and the figurines cannot stand unsupported. The rim on some examples gives the impression of a woman lying on a bed, but this is in fact only part of the process of manufacture. Petrie illustrated a Type 4 figurine lying on a pottery model of a bed (1909 pl. 31), but elsewhere he stated that the figure and the bed were not found together (1927.8). Bruyère described both the Type 4 and the Type 6 figurines from Deir el-Medina as lying on beds (1939.140). It is likely that some Type 4 figurines were once accompanied by separate models of beds. A child figurine may have completed the set, as with a few Type 6a figurines (2.6.2.6).

The Type 4 figurines can be subdivided according to the position of the arms:

A. Figures on which the elongated arms hang at the sides (*e.g.* Pls. 49a, 51a);
B. Figures on which the right arm hangs at the side, but the left is folded across the breast (*e.g.* Pls. 49b, 51b, left).

In the latter type, the left hand often appears to be holding something. Where the object is identifiable, it is usually a lotus or a menit (Bruyère 1939.141). On similar figurines used as mirror-handles, a kitten or a bird is sometimes held between the breasts (*e.g.* Aldred 1972.164–7; Derchain 1976.9).

None of the Type 4 figurines wears clothing and some have no jewellery. A specimen from Faras has a delicately modelled broad collar (Pl. 49b). The line of dots around the hips on this and other figurines represents a girdle. The pubic triangle is sometimes crudely incised and the navel and nipples are indicated by shallow depressions (*e.g.* Pl. 49a,left).

The facial features are modelled in conventional Egyptian style. The ears are hidden by a tapering lock of crimped or braided hair which hangs on either side of the face. On the rare Type 4 figurines which are worked on both sides, the back of the head appears to be partially shaven and the remaining hair is gathered into one long plait (*e.g.* Bruyère 1939 pl. 43). The hair or wig is partially covered by a kerchief, which Bruyère identified with 'la coiffure symbolique de la Reine Teti-Sheri, inspirée du vautour de la mère divine Maut' (1939.139). This is usually surmounted by a tall circular diadem (e.g. 1939 fig. 58). In some cases this diadem dips at the front and is pierced with holes (*e.g.* Pls. 49a, 51b, left). On one unprovenanced specimen, these holes are still threaded with strands of artificial hair weighted with mud pellets (Bresciani 1975 pl. 12). Another Type 4 figurine has a high convex disc (Spiegelberg *et al.* 1908 fig. 11), like those of some Type 3 figurines. This suggests that Type 4 developed from Type 3.

Type 4 is the rarest of the six main types. A few have been found in tombs, but the majority come from domestic contexts, in particular from houses at Deir el-Medina (List 4). They also occur as votive offerings at Deir el-Bahri and Faras. Hall illustrated one Type 4 figurine from Deir el-Bahri (Pl. 1, bottom centre = London BM 41107) and I have been able to trace three other examples from the EEF excavations at this site (Oxford Ash. E 871 = 51b, left; PR 1906.45.12, 13 = Pl. 51a). One faience figurine from Deir el-Bahri (London V&A 686.1905) could be classified either as a Type 4a or a Type 5 (2.6.1.5). A Type 4a figurine formerly in the Hilton-Price collection was also said to have come from Deir el-Bahri (Cat. 1911.160, pl. 58). Neither Carter nor Winlock mentioned finding figurines of this kind at Deir el-Bahri.

Griffith illustrated one highly detailed and almost intact example from Faras (Pls. 8.8, 49b = London BM 51263) and a headless body which may have come from such a figurine (Pl. 8.12, location unknown). The intact figurine holds a lotus flower between the breasts. The headdress and necklace are worked in fine detail but the girdle is marked in with a careless row of dots. I have not traced any other Type 4 figurines from this site, but there probably were more among the 'abundant fragments' of pottery figurines excavated by Griffith.

One might expect the 'debased' Type 3 figurines to have developed from the 'refined' Type 4, but the reverse appears to be the case. The delicate faces of some Type 4 figurines from Deir el-Bahri and Faras resemble those of late 17th and early 18th dynasty royal statues (e.g. Aldred 1972 nos. 2, 8–9) and the type was probably introduced at that time. On the early figurines, the girdle and the details of the body are crudely incised, as in Type 3. Their headdress resembles that of the later Type 3 figurines, and is always pierced for the insertion of hair.

One Type 4 figurine from Deir el-Bahri (Pl. 51a) has a less delicately modelled face and no incised body decoration. The headdress, which has become more like a diadem, is still pierced. This piece probably dates to the mid 18th dynasty, like the unprovenanced example with intact hair (Bresciani 1975 pl. 12). Bruyère published no detailed information about the date of the houses in which Type 4 figurines were found at Deir el-Medina. Many of the examples he illustrated (1939.139, fig. 58, pls. 43–4) seem to represent a third stage in the development of Type 4. Their elongated bodies resemble those of Type 6a and they wear tall diadems that are not usually pierced. These figures probably date from the end of the 18th dynasty onwards; none was excavated at Deir el-Bahri or Faras. The two arm positions occur throughout the date range of Type 4.

5 *Type 5* (Fig. 6; Pls. 1, 6, 8, 50, 51b–c)

Type 5 figurines may be of faience or pottery. Most were shaped in open moulds and thus are worked on one side only. A rim was sometimes left around the figure (e.g. Pl. 50b). The faience examples may be bright blue, dark blue, green, or light blue with the details picked out in dark blue. Most of the pottery specimens show traces of yellow paint on the body. The largest Type 5 figurines would have been about 10 cm high when intact (Bolton 48.04.19; Brussels MR E 725; Cambridge Fitz. 55.1907), but most are between 3 and 6 cm high. The smallest specimen I have examined is only 2.3 cm high (Pl. 50b, right). Some figurines from Faras that are almost as small are pierced for suspension (London BM 51361; Oxford PR 1912.89.218–20).

The Type 5 figurines depict nude women with elongated forms. They have slim waists, flat stomachs, and almost flat chests. The legs end in large, poorly modelled feet, but the figurines are not self-supporting. The arms always hang at the sides. A few have girdles and/or broad collars, but on the whole these figurines are characterized by lack of ornament. The nipples and the pubic triangle are occasionally marked (*e.g.* Pl. 51c). The details of the face are often worn away, but they always seem to be modelled in conventional Egyptian style. All the figurines wear a long wig which is usually straight-ended, but sometimes tapered like that worn by Type 4. A few have a kerchief over the tapered wig (*e.g.* Pls. 1, bottom left; 51b, right), again linking them with the Type 4 figures. On two Type 5 figurines from Deir el-Bahri, which are unusual in being worked on both sides, a standard tripartite wig is worn (Cambridge Fitz. 55.1907; London BM 41734), but on a third the back of the head is partially shaven and the hair is divided into three plaits (Bolton 48.04.19), as in Type 1d.

Type 5 figurines are comparatively rare from domestic contexts. No faience and only a few pottery examples have been recovered from burials (List 5). Almost all the surviving Type 5 figurines come from temples. Type 5 might almost be called the 'Deir el-Bahri' type. The EEF distribution lists for Deir el-Bahri include at least 67 faience Type 5 figurines, of which I have been able to examine or obtain detailed information on 19 (Bolton 48.04.3, 19; Brussels MR E 716, 725; Cambridge Fitz. 55.1907; Ilkley· 7096(3); Liverpool 13.10.04.14–6; London BM 41008, 41044, 41734; V&A 1209.1904a–b, 672, 686.1905; Oxford PR 1906.45.11 = Pl. 51c). Carter did not mention finding faience figurines at Deir el-Bahri, but one is included in a photograph of objects from his excavations (Pl. 6d). Hayes stated that 'a number of small doll-like figures in blue faience' were discovered by Winlock at Deir el-Bahri. He described them as follows:—

> Crudely formed in one-piece moulds, open at the back, they represent for the most part slender young women, nude except for their long, black tripartite coiffures and the narrow bead girdles about their hips . . . ' (1959.163)

Griffith illustrated six less detailed, faience Type 5 figurines from Faras (Pl. 8.1, 10, 17 = location unknown; 8–9, 11 = London BM 51263, 51262, 51259). I have been able to trace 18 examples from this site (Edinburgh RSM 1912.555–8; London BM 51259–62, 51361 = Pl. 50b; Oxford Ash. 1912.943 (3), 1 = Pl. 51b, right; PR 1912.89.214–20). Four similar but cruder faience figurines were found in the sanctuary at Mirgissa (Karlin in Vercoutter 1970 nos. 145–8, fig. 45). One Type 5 figurine from Gebel Zeit has been published (Leclant & Clerc 1985 fig.62). Small faience Type 5 figurines were among the votive offerings at Dendara (Fig. 6) and and formed part of temple foundation deposits of Thutmose III at Koptos (Petrie 1896 pl. 15) and Amonhotpe II at el-Kab (Quibell 1898c pl. 21).

The majority of these figurines seem to have been made specifically as votive offerings. The very small pierced figurines may originally have been strung on votive necklaces with beads, scaraboids, and other faience objects (2.9.2.1). Some of the larger, more elaborate specimens (*e.g.* Pl. 1, bottom left; Pls. 51b–c; London V&A 686.1905) show some affinities with Type 4 and may be earlier than the simpler specimens. The latter seem chiefly to date to the reigns of Hatshepsut,

Thutmose III, and Amonhotpe II. One Type 5 figurine recovered from the workman's village at el-ʿAmarna and another from Deir el-Medina (List 5) have affinities with Type 6a.

6 Type 6

Type 6 figurines are linked by their association with beds. They may be divided into three main categories:–

A. Detached figures

This group consists of nude figurines placed on model beds. Both figurine and bed are usually made of pottery, but the British Museum does has one limestone 'set' (London BM 5595). Few measurements are available for this type, but they seem to vary in height between 10 and 20 cm. The figurines are slender and flat-chested with elongated limbs. On intact examples, the legs end in rudimentary feet. A long straight wig is always worn, usually surmounted by a cone. Some examples have a narrow black girdle and most wear large circular earrings. The figurines are usually lying down with their arms at their sides, but Bruyère found one at Deir el-Medina which is sitting up and suckling a male child (1939.142 fig. 60). A broken pottery figurine of a male child from Sawama is thought to have belonged beside a Type 6a figurine on the bed found with them (Bourriau & Millard 1971.33–4, pl. 17).

The bed is not always preserved with the figurine and this can make it difficult to distinguish between pottery Type 5 figurines and Type 6a. However, Type 6a is generally larger and has the characteristic cone and earrings. Some of these figurines have been found in burials and in temple refuse, but the majority come from houses at el-ʿAmarna and Deir el-Medina (List 6). Most, perhaps all, date from the late 18th to the early 19th dynasty. This type is not represented at any of the Hathor sites. Elaborate pottery model beds decorated with Bes figures and marsh scenes which are thought to date to the Ramessid Period have been found in temple areas (Abder-Raziq 1985.9–11, pl. 4.2).

B. Figures attached to beds and slabs (Pl. 51d)

This group consists of figurines attached to model beds or to slabs probably representing beds. The most common materials are limestone or pottery, but there are a few faience examples (*e.g.* Pl. 51d). Most are between 10 and 20 cm long, but one stone specimen from Deir Rifa is about 33 cm long (Petrie 1907.23, pl. 27b). Both stone and pottery examples tend to be elaborately painted, the central figure being yellow or red, with the hair and the details of the body in black. The woman is normally lying on her back in the centre of the bed or slab with her arms at her sides. Occasionally the head is in profile (*e.g.* Breasted 1948 pl. 93a).

Type 6b figurines are slender and flat-chested with elongated limbs. None wears any clothing, but an example from Mirgissa appears to have tattoos on both thighs (Karlin in Vercoutter 1970.350), perhaps of Bes, as on some Type 6c figurines (*e.g.* Pinch 1983 pl. 6). Some have a thin black girdle around the hips and one example has a broad collar painted in red (London UC 7722; A. Thomas 1981.82). A few have large round earrings (*e.g.* Brussels MR E 2590; Manchester E 913) like those worn by Type 6a. The figures all wear a long heavy wig, which may be bound with red ribbons and is occasionally surmounted by a white cone (*e.g.* Manchester E 913). Especially when the head is in profile, part of the wig may be tucked behind the left shoulder, which evokes a suckling scene even though no child is shown.

Some of the pottery examples lie on model beds, but slabs without legs are more common. These may be either rectangular or rounded at the head end, but most have a footboard. On a few stone examples, the figure is flanked by green plants with blue leaves (*e.g.* Petrie 1907 pls. 27b, f). These plants have been identified as palm fronds (A. Thomas 1981.82–3), but papyrus entwined with convolvulus is another possibility (Pinch 1983.407). Other figures are occasionally shown on the bed or slab. On a pottery example, a crouching girl arranges the hair of the recumbent woman (Derchain 1975.65–6), while on a limestone slab a small clothed female figure, probably an attendant, is painted in the bottom right-hand corner (London UC 16758). On another limestone example an attendant with a mirror is painted on the footboard and figures of Taweret and Bes (?) on the headboard (Boston MFA 72.739; D'Auria *et al.* 1988.137, no.74).

Type 6b has been recovered from tombs and houses (List 6). It is less common in a temple context, and where examples are found in temple refuse they might have come from houses in the temple area. However, Type 6b is represented among the votive offerings at two Hathor sites. A single example from the Mirgissa shrine is in crudely modelled and painted limestone and is 10.7 cm long (Karlin in Vercoutter 1970.350). The woman lies with her arms at her sides on a slab which is rounded at the head end and has a footboard.

Petrie stated that he found 'some' female figurines at Serabit el-Khadim but he illustrated only one example (1906.147, pl. 151. 14 = Cambridge Fitz. E FG 10). I have not been able to trace any others from Petrie's excavations, but Giveon found a very similar piece in the 'sanctuary' (Q) at Serabit el-Khadim (1983 pers. comm.). The example now in the Fitzwilliam Museum is made in faience and is only 7.3 cm long. It consists of a nude woman lying on a slab which is rounded at the head end and has a footboard (Pl. 51d). There is no jewellery, but wig, features, nipples, and pubic triangle are all picked out in dark blue. Giveon believed that this piece was Asiatic in character and that the figure should be interpreted as standing in a shrine (1983 pers. comm.). Its proportions are rather un-Egyptian and it bears some resemblance to the metal and pottery 'Astarte plaques' made in Syria and Palestine (see 2.6.2). However, on an Asiatic plaque the scroll wig could be expected and the woman has her hands at her sides, a posture common in Egypt but very rare among Astarte plaques and figurines. The slab, with its rounded head and footboard, can be paralleled on many Type 6b–c figurines from Egypt, so it is probably safe to regard the Serabit el-Khadim example as a Type 6b fertility figurine.

Type 6b seems to have been introduced in the late 18th dynasty and continues into the Ramessid period. It is difficult to distinguish between 18th dynasty and Ramessid figurines (Petrie 1890.37–8). The Mirgissa figurine closely resembles stone Type 6b figurines from Gurob datable by their context to the late 18th dynasty (Thomas 1981 pl. 54). The Serabit el-Khadim piece is much harder to place and could have been made any time between the late 18th dynasty and the end of the New Kingdom.

C. Figures with children attached to beds and slabs (Pl. 46b)

This group consists of female figures with a child attached to a model bed or to a slab representing a bed. They may be in pottery or limestone and the length varies between 10 and 25 cm. The physique, the range of jewellery, and the kind of wig worn are all identical with Type 6b. Two specimens have figures of Bes tattooed (?) on their thighs (London BM 2371 = Pinch 1983 pl. 6; EEF Cat. [1922]. 10). The posture of the principal figure varies according to that of the child. Mostly, the child lies at the woman's side, usually on her right (*e.g.* Pl. 46b). The child's face is often level with the woman's thighs. Her fingers may touch the child's head (*e.g.* Honroth 1910 fig. 8) or its upraised hand (*e.g.* Bruyère 1939 pl. 44b, right). Alternatively, the child may be suckling at the woman's left breast (*e.g.* Petrie 1890 pl. 18). When the child is suckling, the woman's wig may be tucked behind her left shoulder (*e.g.* Brunton 1927 pl. 47. 33), or her head may be turned to the left with all her hair, which is longer than usual, flowing over the right shoulder (*e.g.* Holscher 1954 pl. 6; Thomas 1981.82, no. 708, pl. 54).

The children painted or modelled on the beds or slabs are naked, hairless and long-limbed. It is not often possible to distinguish the sex, but in one case the child is definitely male (Pinch 1983 pl. 6), and in another probably female (Kestner Cat. no. 157). The custom of representing children as miniature adults makes it difficult to assess how old they are, but they should probably be interpreted as babies. Red, or red and black, snakes may be painted on either side of the woman and child (Pl. 46b). Some of these figurines are decorated with papyrus bound with convolvulus or bryony (*e.g.* Pinch 1983 pl. 6). There may also be subsidiary figures, clothed attendants (*e.g.* Brunton 1927 pl. 25.20), or nude male dancers (1927.17). All these features can be paralleled on ostraca from Deir el-Medina which show women with young children (Pinch 1983.406–10).

Type 6c, which is not represented at the Hathor sites, has been found in burials and houses and a few examples have been recovered from temple refuse (List 6). None appears to be earlier than the late 18th dynasty and they continue into the Ramessid Period. Some, especially those with the head in profile, may be as late as the Third Intermediate Period (List 6).

2.6.2 Related material

1 *Pebbles*

Among the objects found in the sanctuary of the Hathor shrine at Mirgissa were pebbles from the Nile (Vercoutter 1970, figs. 27–8). Karlin comments that:–

> Ces objets, aux formes étranges ... nous ont paru, dans la majorité des cas, évoquer par leurs formes mamellaires quelque déesse de fécondité ou quelque Vénus stéatopyge de façon si frappante que nous n'avons jamais considéré ces pierres comme venues là par hasard; leur dessin, leur densité en cet endroit précis ne permettaient pas d'équivoque. On honorait, on suppliait Hathor, déesse de l'amour ... (1970.329)

Strangely shaped pebbles and fossils resembling mother-and-child figurines or large breasted women were also found in the temple at Timna (Rothenberg 1988.266, pl. 155).

The material from Mirgissa and Timna finds one early parallel in pebbles from the courtyard and surrounding area of the temple of Satet at Aswan. These pebbles are mainly phallic in shape, but some resemble pregnant women or nursing mothers (Dreyer 1986 pl. 57). They are thought to have been offered during the late Old Kingdom (1986.153). Stones from Deir el-Medina, which may have been dedicated in community or household shrines, provide comparative material of the New Kingdom. The natural shapes of these stones resemble pregnant women and they are painted to accentuate this resemblance, with a lotus flower in place of the genitals (Keimer 1940.8–9, pl. 7). These pebbles might be viewed as 'images' of Hathor in her role as Divine Mother (2.6.4). Goddesses are almost never shown as pregnant in Egyptian iconography, but these pebbles presumably fall outside the normal conventions. Alternatively, the pebbles may be seen as a type of fertility figurine.

2 *Metal plaques* (Pl. 8)

The offerings at Faras included some small oval plaques cut from sheet gold, one of which was said to stamped with a 'nude female' (Pl. 8.47; Griffith 1921.104). This is reminiscent of the gold Astarte plaques dedicated in temples in Syria and Palestine from the 18th century BC onwards (Gray 1964.230). On these plaques a naked goddess, often wearing the scroll wig and sometimes a podium, is shown full-face, holding up animals or flowers, or touching her breasts or stomach (*e.g.* Pritchard 1943 nos. 5–8; Maxwell-Hyslop 1971.138–9, pls. 106–7; Negbi 1976.96–101, pls. 53–4). I have not been able to trace the plaque from Faras and the photograph is poor, but the figure's arms are at her side and the head is in profile. This piece therefore has little in common with the Astarte plaques, and it is doubtful whether it should be grouped with the fertility figurines. Another small gold plaque illustrated by Griffith (Pl. 8.45) appears to be stamped with a figure of Hathor wearing the disc and horns headdress. This suggests that, rather than showing a nude female, the first plaque probably depicts Hathor in human form wearing a tight-fitting dress.

3 *Models of the breasts and genitals* (Pls. 33b, 52b–c)

Some Astarte plaques show only a head and a schematized female torso (*e.g.* Maxwell-Hyslop 1971.139–40, pls. 104–5; Negbi 1976 pls. 52–3). Similar plaques in pottery have been found in Egypt in tombs (*e.g.* Randall-Maciver 1899 pl. 43; Petrie 1907 pl. 13.156; Michałowski *et al.* 1950 pl. 24), and houses (*e.g.* Petrie 1927 pl. 53; Bruyère 1939.143, pl. 45; Brussels 4644). Most of these plaques do not include a head, but one example from Abydos has a head with the distinctive pierced disc of a Type 3 figurine (Craig Patch 1990.36–7, no. 25b). On this plaque, the genital area is modelled in unusual detail and includes a semi-circular fold and a small, round knob. D. Craig Patch suggests that this plaque is 'a very rare representation of a woman giving birth ...' (1990.37). The plaque could also be interpreted as a detailed representation of the labia and clitoris, but this would be even rarer. The general date range for the pottery plaques is from the Second Intermediate Period to the late New Kingdom.

Models of female breasts and genitals were among the votive offerings at Deir el-Bahri. Hall noted that 'The breasts occur as an amulet, either separately or together on a plaque' (in Naville 1913.16). I have traced only one example, a small oval plaque in dark blue frit (London BM 41100 = Pl. 33b, right). This has a pair of breasts in relief and is pierced for suspension. Pottery vases decorated with breasts were also found at Deir el-Bahri (*e.g.* Pl. 52c; see 2.11.5).

The British Museum has two simple faience models of female genitals from this site. One of these pieces is 1.7 cm long (London BM 47766 = Pl. 52b) and the other 1.9 cm (London BM 47767). Both these objects show the pubic triangle with only a slit to represent the vulva. Similar pottery models of the female genitals have been found in houses at Deir el-Medina (Bruyère 1939 pls. 43, 45), but I know of no exact parallels for the faience models from Deir el-Bahri.

2.6.3 Theories about the functions of the figurines

Two points should be apparent from the preceding sections. Firstly, in spite of their differences, the six types are interlinked and so a hypothesis that can be applied to the whole group is preferable to a hypothesis that fits only one or some of the types. Secondly, although many scholars have described these objects as funerary, none of the types is found exclusively in a funerary context. The approximate figures for provenanced examples of Types 1–6 are 220 from tombs, 227 from settlement sites, and 321 from temples or shrines (Lists 1–6). A hypothesis relating only to a funerary context cannot completely explain the functions of any of the six types, still less this group of objects as a whole. With these two points in mind, I now review a range of existing theories about the functions of the figurines with these two points in mind.

1 *Dancing girls*

Winlock interpreted figurines of my Type 1 as models of Nubian dancing girls placed in tombs '... in order that their spirits might while away the time of the Theban grandees in the tedious hours of eternity' (1932.36). Descriptions of these figurines as servants, whose function was to entertain the deceased male with dancing and sexual pleasures, still appear in museum and sale catalogues. The fact that such figures have also been found in female burials (List 1) is an obstacle to this hypothesis, but Hayes got round this by suggesting that the figurines might be buried with women to act as their maid-servants in the afterlife (1953.221). The identification of Type 1 as servant figures seems possible in a funerary context, but unconvincing for the examples found in houses or temples.

Apart from their nudity, there is nothing to link Type 1 with the 'servant class', and young girls of any social status can be shown nude. There is no definite evidence that Type 1 figurines represent Nubian slaves. The hairstyles of Types 1a–c were worn by Middle Kingdom court ladies, and the less common hairstyle of Type 1d occurs on the daughters of officials on a few Middle Kingdom and Second Intermediate Period statuettes and stelae (*e.g.* Fischer 1974.121, figs. 10–11; Simpson 1974 pls. 21, 65, 76) and in 18th dynasty tomb paintings (*e.g.* Davies 1923 pl. 2). Most of the jewellery shown on the figurines appears to be Egyptian. Cowrie shell girdles could be Nubian in origin, but examples have been found in the burials of 12th dynasty royal ladies (Aldred 1971.191, 196, pls. 35, 45). Patterned dresses are not confined to servant girl figures or offering bearers; a few statues of the wives or daughters of high officials have brightly coloured patterns, perhaps representing beadwork nets, painted on their dresses (*e.g.* Riefstahl 1944.12, fig. 11; Hayes 1953.330 fig. 218; D'Auria et al. 1988.78-9). Patterned dresses rather similar to those on 'paddle dolls' and some Type 1 figurines appear in some Old Kingdom representations of the *ḫnr*, a troupe of women who sing, dance, and play clappers, usually in the context of a religious ceremony. They are also worn by the wife of a priest of Hathor in a Middle Kingdom tomb scene at Meir (Blackman 1953 pl. 12), by a Hathor priestess on an 11th dynasty Theban funerary stela (Hayes 1953.331, fig. 219), and by members of the *ḫnr* of Hathor depicted in 18th dynasty Theban tombs (Davies 1930 pl. 41). It is possible that the textiles decorated with beads and coloured threads found wrapped around Type 3 figurines at Gebel Zeit were meant to imitate such dresses. The cross-over bands shown on the chests of some Type 1 figurines (*e.g.* Keimer 1948 pl. 12.1) are sometimes called 'Libyan bands' (Staehelin 1966.130-2), but they too are worn by women of the *ḫnr* (Nord in Simpson & Davis 1981.137).

None of the Type 1 figurines is painted black or has obviously Nubian features. The steatopygous physique of many of the Type 2 and 3 figurines has led to suggestions that they represent Nubians, or are derived from Nubian fertility figurines (Bruyère 1939.117-8; Desroches Noblecourt 1953.18). The crude workmanship of these figurines should not be allowed to obscure the fact that their physique is basically Egyptian. They lack the very broad hips which are a distinctive feature of the female figurines found in C-group burials or settlement sites (*e.g.* Bruyère 1939 fig. 44; Keimer 1948.35-40, figs. 32-7). Slender hips but rather large or prominent buttocks were part of the Egyptian ideal feminine figure from the Old to the New Kingdoms, something which tends to be overlooked because statues are usually viewed from the front.

The hairstyle of the Type 3 figurines might be Nubian, and some scholars have proposed that the curious pierced disc of this type is Nubian in origin (Bruyère 1939.134-5; Hayes 1959.17). There is some evidence for a Nubian connection. Type 2 figurines have been found in Pan Grave burials and houses (List 2) and some of the worshippers at Gebel Zeit seem to have been Medjay (3.2.3). However, W. F. Albright pointed out that discoid head-dresses are found on female figurines from Second Millennium sites all over the ancient Near East and eastern Mediterranean, and concluded that Type 3 was derived from Syrian prototypes (1939.110-2). The possibility of foreign influence on the Middle Kingdom types of fertility figurine cannot be examined in detail here because of the vast amount of comparative material which would have to be discussed. I hope to explore this question in a future study of fertility figurines.

One link between my Types 1-3 and the C-group figurines should be noted. The circles of dots found on many Type 2 and a few Type 3 figurines, and the diagonal lines and diamond shapes shown on some Type 1 and 2 figurines, can all be paralleled on C-group fertility figurines (Keimer 1948.37-8, figs. 30-7). This need not mean that the Egyptian figurines represent Nubians, since three 11th dynasty mummies of light-skinned women with tattoos on their thighs, stomachs, and shoulders were recovered from the precincts of Akh-isut (Daressy 1893.166; Winlock 1923.11, 26; Keimer 1948.8–15, figs. 8–11, pls. 1–9). A fashion for tattoos, and Nubian hairstyles, may have been introduced into Egypt from Nubia at this time, perhaps because some of Nebhepetre⁽ Mentuhotpe's 'harim' seem to have been Nubian (Naville 1907.50, 55, pl. 23; 1913.9, pl. 2).

Two of the mummies with diamond-shaped tattoos (Keimer 1948 pls. 6–9) were found in the north court of the 11th dynasty temple by Winlock, who identified them as 'dancing girls' (1923.26). This identification was not based on the evidence of titles, since the only objects recovered from these disturbed burials were a battered gold ornament, and an uninscribed wooden jewel box (1926.5–6, figs. 1–2). The burial of these two women in such a favoured site suggests that they may have been court ladies rather than lowly slave girls and that they, like the majority of the women buried in Akh-isut, are likely to have been priestesses of Hathor. This was certainly the case with the third mummy, who is named on her coffin as the priestess of Hathor, Amonet (Daressy 1893.166; 1913.99–100; Keimer 1948.8–13, pls. 1–5). This priestess, who has tattoos in the form of patterns of dots and diagonal lines, was buried in an elaborately painted wooden coffin (1948 pl. 1). Her example shows that tattooing does not necessarily imply a low social status.

It is tempting to see such tattoos as the mark of a devotee of Hathor, but there is no definite evidence for this. In the case of the mummy of Amonet, it is not necessary to reject any association with dancing because of her priestly title. Dances to promote fertility, rejuvenation, and rebirth were part of the cult of Hathor (Hickman 1956.122; Wild 1963.69–70; Wente 1969.86–89; Nord in Simpson and Davis 1981.141–2). I know of no representations of Hathor priestesses dancing nude, but in one Middle Kingdom Theban tomb members of a ḫnr troupe dance bare-chested at a funeral (Davies 192a pl. 23A). If nude dancing was performed in temples, perhaps in allusion to Hathor's arousing and placating the Sun God by displaying her genitals, decorum would prevent its being shown in temple iconography. One hint of erotic dances associated with the cult of Hathor comes in the form of the painted leather hanging from Deir el-Bahri which shows a naked, dancing dwarf with an enormous phallus (Pl. 54; 2.7.2). Lion-masked dwarf figures were linked with ḫnr dancers as early as the 5th dynasty (Wild 1963.76–7; Wente 1979.86–7). In one of the stories in Papyrus Westcar, four goddesses disguise themselves as dancing girls to act as midwives to the woman who is destined to give birth to three kings. They are described as holding out sistra and menit necklaces to the woman's husband (Sethe 1924.33). This implies that they were dancers who took part in Hathor rituals, not just entertainers. If it was customary for such Hathor dancers to act as midwives, this might provide one reason for the fertility figurines to resemble dancers.

Bruyère suggested that figurines of my Types 1–3 might represent dancers on the grounds that the dance was a traditional preliminary to sexual intercourse and an important part of African fertility rites (1939.127). The major drawback to this hypothesis is the rudimentary nature of the feet on Types 2–3 and their total absence on Type 1. Bruyère's explanation is that the feet were omitted to prevent the dancers from 'leaving' the tomb, and that figurines of Types 2–3 were deliberately broken for the same reason (1939.129–30). There is no definite evidence for the ritual breaking of votive offerings in Egypt (3.2.2), and numerous intact figurines from burials can be cited (*e.g.* 1939 figs. 47, 50; Desroches Noblecourt 1953 figs. 9–10; Hayes 1959 fig. 6). Bourriau compares the absence of feet on my Type I figurines to 'the mutilation of hieroglyphs depicting living beings in some funerary inscriptions of the XIIIth Dynasty' and comments that:–

> If the figures, like the hieroglyphs, could be animated by magic, then their freedom of
> movement had to be controlled, otherwise they might harm the deceased, at the very
> least by running away and destroying the magic. (1988.119)

There is more evidence for Type I figurines being involved in magical rites than for the other types (Pinch, forthcoming), but they are not exclusively funerary objects and the faience animals often found with them are never mutilated. It could be argued that male fear of the power of female sexuality caused the figurines to be treated differently from other objects.

Keimer proposed that the feet were omitted from Type 1 to emphasize the female's passive sexual role (1948.102), although such passivity cannot be taken for granted in ancient Egypt (Manniche 1977.20–3). It is equally probable that the feet could be omitted because only the parts of the female body related to sex, childbirth, and child rearing are emphasized. This is suggested by the pottery plaques with no heads or arms but prominently marked breasts and pubic triangles (2.6.2.3; Bruyère 1939.299, fig. 167). The 'paddle dolls' also usually have no legs or arms, but the genitals are often shown below the dress (*e.g.* Keimer 1948, fig. 17, pl. 17; Bourriau 1988 no. 121). These figures have elaborately styled long flowing hair, perhaps because long hair was a symbol of femininity with erotic connotations (Derchain 1975.66–9). Like Types 4–6, figurines of Types 1–3 should perhaps be interpreted as lying down. This, and the fact that some of the figurines hold children, suggest that while it is quite possible that the figurines depict *ḥnr* dancers, they are not shown in the act of dancing.

2 *Male Sexuality*

Various scholars have argued that the sole purpose of some or all types of fertility figurine was to provide a sexual partner for the deceased male in the afterlife (*e.g.* Wiedemann 1913.169–72; Kees 1926.299–300; Petrie 1927.9). The main obstacle to this theory is the occurrence of the figurines in female burials, houses, and temples (Lists 1–6).

Instead of seeing them as permanent sexual partners for the deceased, Desroches Noblecourt links my Types 1–3 with a ritual to revive the virility of the deceased male (1953.15–33). She compares the crosses on some Type 1d figurines with those shown on female mourners in a few New Kingdom tomb scenes (1953.25–33, figs. 11–2, pls. 2–3). She suggests that these were temporary marks worn by women officiating in a rite, analogous to the 'Opening of the Mouth' ceremony, to revive and perpetuate the procreative powers of the deceased. She proposes that this rite was based on the myth of Isis and Nephthys reviving the sexual powers of the dead Osiris so that Horus could be conceived (1953.42–3). She very reasonably attributes the scarcity of scenes which might represent this rite to Egyptian reticence about the depiction of sexual matters in temple or funerary art. As S. Morenz pointed out, sexual pleasures in the afterlife are mentioned in New Kingdom funerary texts but are never illustrated in funerary vignettes (1958.140).

The resemblance between the mourners in the tomb scenes and the figurines of Types 1–3 is not close. The former are not nude and the crosses are on the upper parts of their bodies rather than around their hips (1953 pls. 2–3), though this could be attributed to decorum. The fact that the mourners always wear a bag wig, rather than than any of the hairstyles depicted on the figurines, is harder to explain. The figurines resemble the *ḫnr* troupe who sometimes danced and sang at funerals (Altenmüller 1978.21–2; Nord in Simpson & Davis 1981.140–2) more closely than they do the mourners who play the roles of Isis and Nephthys. Desroches Noblecourt's theory cannot serve as a complete explanation even for the Type 1 figurines because they occur in female burials, houses, and temples. She herself proposes a completely different explanation for the Type 1d figurines which carry children, even though they too are marked with crosses (1953.34–42). Since there is no difference in physique, hairstyle, or ornaments between the Type 1d figurines with and without children, a single explanation which would cover both groups seems preferable.

3 The Divine Mother

Like Desroches Noblecourt, W. Helck believes that the figurines which suckle or hold children had a different function from those without children (1971.62). He admits that the former might be associated with fertility, but sees the latter as charms to ensure sexual fulfilment for women, with no particular stress on conception (1971.284; 1975a.684–6). He proposes that the practice of using such charms in life and in the afterlife was a survival from a hypothetical 'golden age' when women enjoyed great social and sexual freedom and were not dominated by men or valued only as childbearers. There is no clear evidence that such a state of affairs ever existed in Egypt and Helck is mistaken in linking the figurines exclusively with women, since some have been found in male burials (Lists 1–4).

Helck's hypothesis about the fertility figurines is linked to the theory that one great 'mother goddess' was worshipped throughout the Ancient Near East during the matriarchal age. G. Hornblower suggested that all the figurines represented the mother goddess, who in Egypt was chiefly identified with Hathor (1929.40). He saw my Types 1–3 as the direct descendants of the female figurines found in some Predynastic burials (*e.g.* 1929 pl. 8; Ucko 1968), and proposed that they portrayed Hathor in her dual aspect as bestower of fertility and protector of the dead (1929.40–1). Historians of comparative religion agree on three main characteristics of a mother goddess: a connection with the earth; frequent representation naked; and a reputation as the bestower of fertility (Bleeker 1973a.38).

The first of these certainly does not apply to Hathor and the second is doubtful. Egyptian goddesses are not normally shown without clothing, but Hathor can be identified with Nut, who is nude when personifying the sky. A few Hyksos scarabs show a nude goddess with a scroll wig and cow's ears (*e.g.* Newberry 1907 pl. 25;

Hornblower 1922 pl. 21.14–5), but this is probably a case of the iconography of an Asiatic goddess being combined with that of Hathor because of a similarity in their functions. Hathor displays her genitals to the sun god in the Contendings of Horus and Seth and may appear naked in the Middle Kingdom story of the Herdsman and the Goddess (Goedicke 1970.257–8) and in the myth of Seth and the 'Seed Goddess' which is found in several magical texts (van Dijk 1986.33, 40), but these are clearly exceptional events. There is comparatively little evidence from before the Graeco-Roman Period to link Hathor with the general fertility of animals and crops, but she was certainly a bestower of human fertility. In New Kingdom material she often takes the role, more generally associated with Isis, of the mother of the divine child (2.4.5). Hathor may therefore be said to share some of the characteristics of a mother goddess, but her nature is too complex for this term to be an adequate description of her.

The question remains of whether any of the fertility figurines represent Hathor. Beautiful flowing hair was an attribute of Hathor, 'Lady of the Tresses' (Posener 1986.113), but only Types 1b–c and some Type 5 and 6 figurines have hairstyles that are characteristic of Hathor in temple iconography. With the possible exception of the 'diadem' found on late Type 4 figurines, none of the headdresses corresponds with those worn by the goddess. The figurines reflect changing fashions in female hairstyles and jewellery far more than is the case with representations of goddesses. Hathor in human form can be shown suckling, but she is never depicted lying down in temple or funerary art. It seems unlikely that private persons would have been encouraged to offer nude figurines of a goddess in state temples when such representations were not permitted in temple iconography.

This does not rule out the hypothesis that the figurines could represent a goddess in a less direct manner. Desroches Noblecourt links some of the figurines to a rite in which female mourners played the roles of Isis and Nephthys (2.6.3.2). Morenz argued that they might represent women who, in the crisis of birth, identified themselves with Isis or Hathor, or any of the goddesses who bore the epithet Divine Mother (1958.141). Such identifications are common in funerary and medical texts, and there is some evidence for their occurrence in religion in daily life, particularly in the cult of Hathor (2.4.5–6; 3.3). Bruyère suggested that the figurines found at Deir el-Medina might relate to women identifying with Hathor and Isis, but that they embodied something divine – 'le grand principe de la génération' – without representing a specific deity (1939.125, 137–9). The hypothesis that Hathor could embody the feminine creative principle has already been mentioned (2.3.4).

The reverence and care with which old fertility figurines seem to have been treated at Gebel Zeit (1.6.3) could suggest something approaching divine status for them. The fact that fertility figurines (mainly of Type 6a) were common at el-ʿAmarna, even in the central city, might be seen as an argument against their representing a goddess. However, this site provides the clearest New Kingdom evidence of the role of the figurines in religion in daily life, since many examples were found in rooms with household altars. A cupboard in one such altar contained a stela depicting a woman and boy worshipping Taweret, two model beds, and a Type 6a figurine (Peet & Woolley 1923.24–5, pl. 12). Taweret is closely linked with the nourishment and protection of young children (2.10.1.9). Model hippopotami have been found next to Type 1 figurines in some Middle Kingdom burials (*e.g.* Winlock 1923.20; Lansing 1934.30; Keimer 1948.18–9). Bruyère noted that the association of Hathor with a hippopotamus deity and with dwarf figures such as Bes could be traced back to the groups of clay female figurines, hippopotami, and dwarfs found in some Predynastic burials (1939.93, 123–5).

Taweret figures brandishing knives are painted in the genital area of some 'paddle dolls' (*e.g.* Keimer 1948 pl. 17; Berlin Catalogue no. 453; London BM 6459) and Taweret holding a protective *s3* sign is painted on the headboard of one Type 6b figurine (D'Auria *et al.* 1988 no.74). Similar figures appear among the protectors of the infant sun god on Middle Kingdom apotropaic wands (*e.g.* Altenmüller 1965 figs. 9, 11–3). Texts on such wands identify human mothers and babies with the Divine Mother and her child (1965.66–9). Since the 'paddle dolls' are a type of fertility figurine, this supports Morenz's view that such figurines can be associated with the Divine Mother, even though they are not direct representations of her.

A group of objects found together in the shaft of a 13th dynasty tomb under the Ramesseum confirms that the Middle Kingdom fertility figurines belong in the context of protective rites for mothers and children. A box from the shaft contained papyri, one of which was a collection of spells connected with pregnancy, childbirth, and the protection of young children. Surrounding the box were objects including a wooden figurine of a female Bes dancer holding snake wands, a metal snake wand, three ivory apotropaic wands, part of a different type of ivory wand decorated with lions, a pair of ivory hand-shaped clappers, baboon and lion figurines, a 'paddle doll', and five Type 1 fertility figurines (Quibell 1898.3, pl. 3; Bourriau 1988.110–1). It seems likely that this was the tomb of a doctor/magician. Possibly such people were called upon to pronounce spells which would invest the fertility figurines with magical power. Most of the figurines in this group can be equated with the protective figures that appear on the apotropaic wands, so perhaps the female figurines can be equated with the woman who were to be protected. Some of the jewellery shown on Middle Kingdom figurines, such as cowrie-shell girdles and crescent moon amulets, is known to be linked to the protection of women's fertility and ability to rear children. The tattoos or body-paintings on figurines of Types 1–3 should probably also be interpreted as protective charms. Such charms may have been in common use, but they are unlikely to appear in 'official' art, since they imply a reliance on private magic rather than on the religion of the state cults.

4 *Conception*

Some scholars have assumed that the main purpose of placing 'wife figures' in tombs was to enable deceased men to beget children in the afterlife (Wiedemann 1913.169; Bonnet 1952.94). A link between the figurines in burials and the conception of children is partially accepted by Desroches Noblecourt, who proposes that the Type 1 figurines which carry children are only 'pseudo-concubines' (1953.43–4). Her argument is based on the brief inscriptions found on two Type 1d figurines with children. One of these has an inscription on the left thigh which reads 'May a birth be given to your daughter Seh' (Berlin 14517; Schott 1930.23; Desroches Noblecourt 1953.34–6, fig. 14). The other has an inscription on both thighs which could be translated as 'An offering which the king gives for the *ka* of Khonsu: a birth for Tita' (Paris Louvre E 8000; Desroches Noblecourt 1953.37–40, pl. 4).

The provenance of these two figures is not known, but Desroches Noblecourt plausibly suggests that they would have been placed in or near family tombs, and that their inscriptions are direct appeals to a dead father or ancestor (1953.35–40). More tentatively, she proposes that the figurines united with the virile *ka* of the deceased to cause the donor to conceive and the ancestor to be reborn as his own child and grandchild (1953.40–2). She further suggests that the action of dedicating such a figurine at the ancestral tomb might have been a standard part of the rites of marriage (1953.40). If this were so, one would expect the figurines to be far more common than they are.

Some figurines of Types 1–3 have been found in the outer areas of tombs (*e.g.* Carter 1912.32; Winlock 1923.20; Lansing 1934.40; Michałowski 1950.198). This placing supports the idea that they were votive offerings to the dead rather than part of the funerary equipment. This seems less likely in the case of figurines found near the body in intact single burials (*e.g.* Petrie 1912.36; Scharff 1926.95; Brunton 1927.17, pls. 13, 25; Bruyère 1937.97; Hayes 1959.16–7; Downes 1974.88), but it should be noted that a letter to the dead written on a bowl was found in such a tomb at Qaw el-Kebir (Gardiner & Sethe 1928.3) and must have been placed there at the time of the burial. Evidence that dead relatives could be appealed to for children is provided by a First Intermediate Period letter to the dead from Dendara (Gardiner 1930.20). This letter, written by a man to his deceased father, includes the phrase 'Cause that there be born to me a healthy male child' (1930.20, pl. 10). This plea should be seen in the context of the letters to the dead as a whole, which contain appeals for the deceased to use their influence to solve a wide range of family problems (Grieshammer 1975.863–70). The letter does not imply that the *ka* of the deceased was supposed to beget the child. The hypothesis that the *ka* of an ancestor was being asked to beget a child with the aid of the figurines cannot in any case apply to examples found in female burials or in temples.

The idea that some of the figurines were votive offerings to the dead remains very plausible. They could have been dedicated in order to reinforce prayers to male or female ancestors to use their influence. Nor is it necessary to assume that people prayed only to their own ancestors. At Deir el-Medina all the villagers venerated the spirits of distinguished craftsmen and officials (Bruyère 1939.151–67; Demarée 1983.279–90). Desroches Noblecourt cites the parallel of the modern Egyptian practice of peasant women praying for children and making offerings at the tombs of local sheikhs (1953.35). A further possibility is that female figurines were sometimes placed in or near tombs after being used in a magical rite to protect or promote fertility. The purpose would then have been to perpetuate the rite by drawing on the *heka*, the magical power, possessed by the dead (Pinch, forthcoming).

5 Childbirth and purification

Desroches Noblecourt argues that the Type 1 figurines cannot symbolize fertility because they depict slender young girls, who are not shown pregnant and have no matronly characteristics (1953.18). This argument is seriously weakened by the fact that the figurines shown with children have exactly the same physique. At Gebel Zeit, where about one in twelve of the Type 2 and 3 figurines has a child, the excavators stress that in the examples with and without children 'le corps féminin y est traité de la même facon, les figurines ont été trouvées dans les mêmes strates. Les deux modèles se complètent sans opposer' (Castel *et al.* 1984.52). The figurines holding children on their hips or backs might represent young nurses rather than mothers, but the same physique occurs on figurines where the child is suckling. The Egyptians were reticent about depicting pregnancy and Egyptian conventions of beauty did not allow for a maturer type of female figure. This is obvious from groups consisting of a man with his wife and mother, in which the two ladies are almost invariably shown with the same youthful figure. Some of the pebbles at Mirgissa and Timna, which are not of course subject to normal artistic conventions, can be interpreted as showing pregnant women or large-breasted nursing mothers (2.6.2.1). A Type 3 plaque/figurine which may show a child being born has already been described (2.6.2.3).

Like Desroches Noblecourt, Bruyère linked the figurines with a desire to perpetuate the family line. He believed that the examples found in houses at Deir el-Medina were kept there as charms to ensure the birth of children and thereby the continuity of the family. He plausibly identified the bed or slab of my Type 6 figurines with the *mshnt* – 'the birth couch' (1939.137–9, 142–3). An object from a house at Deir el-Medina, which looks like a female ancestor bust, but which is labelled Hathor, Lady of the Vulva (Berlin Catalogue no.783; Friedman 1985 pl. 5.1), demonstrates a link between the goddess and ancestor cults. At this site, ancestor busts and *akh ikr* stelae were sometimes found in niches in the walls of the room that also contained the bed-like household altar and wall-paintings of Bes and Taweret, or head-rests decorated with figures of these deities (Friedman 1985.83; Valbelle 1985.118, 261). It is possible that some of the fertility figurines from houses were offered to the male and female ancestors depicted in the busts and stelae in the hope that their spirits would help to ensure that children continued to be born into the family.

Brunner-Traut uses comparative material from Deir el-Medina to suggest that my Types 1d and 2 represent women who had successfully given birth (1955.27). She compares the hairstyles of these figurines with those of the mothers or wet-nurses shown suckling children in a *Wochenlaube* or birth arbour on New Kingdom ostraca and in wall paintings from houses. She then cites medical texts to show that the hair was bound up in a special way during childbirth, and perhaps during the period of pollution which followed it (1953.25–7, figs. 1–5). Type 3 and 4 figurines also feature an unusual hairstyle in which the hair is constrained by some kind of fillet or diadem. Brunner-Traut's attractive argument is somewhat weakened by the fact that the Type 1 and 2 figurines and the birth arbour scenes are not contemporary and by the occurrence of this 'special' hairstyle on girls (not matrons) portrayed in family groups on stelae from Abydos and in Theban tomb paintings (2.6.1.1). It is tempting to equate this hairstyle with the cult of Hathor and see it as analogous to the partially shaven head of an *is* of the goddess (see 3.2.3), but there is no definite evidence that it was more than a fashion – probably one adopted only by women of marriageable or childbearing age.

The birth arbour scenes can be divided into two main types: those which show a nude or semi-nude woman with bound-up hair sitting on a stool and and suckling a child (*e.g.* Vandier d'Abbadie 1959 pl. 120); and those which show a clothed or nude woman sitting on a bed with a child in her lap or lying beside her (*e.g.* 1959 pl. 51). Brunner-Traut suggests that the latter depict some kind of celebration when the mother and baby had been purified at the end of a period of isolation in the birth arbour (1955.24). J. Vandier d'Abbadie briefly noted a similarity between the ostraca of this kind and my Type 6 figurines (1946.85). So marked is this similarity that all the details found on the more elaborate Type 6b–c figurines, such as papyrus bound with convolvulus, snakes, mirrors, and dancing dwarfs, can be paralleled in the birth arbour scenes (Pinch 1983.406–10). This suggests that even when no child is shown, all the Type 6 figurines can be associated with motherhood, and particularly with the mother and child surviving the dangers of childbirth and the period of maximum vulnerability which came after it.

Brunner-Traut has been criticised for failing to recognize an erotic element in many of the ostraca which she classes as *Wochenlaube* scenes (Kemp 1979.52). A. Hermann saw the ostraca and figurines that show a woman sitting or reclining on a bed as reflecting the imagery of New Kingdom love poetry and representing women awaiting their lovers (1959.161), while Keimer saw this material as evidence for prostitution (1948.99). To both, the frequent presence of a child on the bed was no obstacle to an erotic interpretation. This interpretation might seem to be supported by scenes in the Turin Erotic Papyrus where the female participant, wearing nothing but a girdle, jewellery, and a full wig, is depicted in some settings which have elements in common with the birth arbour scenes, such as an arbour entwined with convolvulus and a dwarfish attendant (Omlin 1975 pls. 4–5, 12). However, the artist of this papyrus was probably parodying the respectable birth arbour scenes for comic effect. The provenance of these scenes is enough to establish their respectability. The paintings were usually found in the room which contained the household altar (Vandier d'Abbadie 1938.27; Bruyère 1939.131–2; Kemp 1979.52–3) and some of the ostraca were recovered from tombs (Bruyère 1939.144; Peterson 1973.38–41).

Nevertheless, an erotic element in the ostraca and figurines need not be ruled out. Both seem to be primarily concerned with the successful production of children and this means that they were associated with sex as well as with pregnancy and birth. There is no reason to suppose that Egyptian married couples rigidly separated a desire for children from the desire for sexual pleasure. All six types of figurine probably represent ideals of female sexuality. This may make the figurines erotic, but it does not link them with 'immorality'.

Bonnet believed that the New Kingdom figurines were kept in houses as charms to ensure a successful sex life, including the birth of healthy children, and that they were sometimes placed in male or female burials – perhaps of those who had died childless – to continue that function in the afterlife (1952.94). This seems very plausible. Far more of the New Kingdom figurines come from a domestic than a funerary context (Lists 3–6) and they seem to belong primarily to the sphere of religion in daily life. The same may have been true in earlier periods, even though many of the surviving Middle Kingdom and Second Intermediate Period figurines come from burials. Some figurines may in any case have been votive offerings to the dead rather than pieces of funerary equipment. Bonnet, who appreciated the variety of contexts in which fertility figurines are found, also noted that they might be offered in temples to goddesses associated with childbirth (1952.94). I now examine this point in relation to the examples from the Hathor shrines.

2.6.4 Fertility figurines as votive objects

No Middle Kingdom or Second Intermediate Period fertility figurines have been found in temples in the Egyptian Nile valley or Delta. The fact that burials with grave goods were made in disused mines at Gebel Zeit (Posener-Kriéger 1986.381–2) suggests that this site was thought of as being in Egypt, because otherwise the bodies would have been taken back to the Nile valley for burial. The range of Middle Kingdom and Second Intermediate Period objects found at Gebel Zeit is different from that known from temples of this time in the rest of Egypt (1.6; 3.4). This could be because Gebel Zeit was so remote from official control, or because it was a community rather than a state-run shrine. The votive material from the first Hathor shrine has much in common with objects recovered from household shrines of the Middle Kingdom and Second Intermediate Period at sites such as Kahun (Bourriau 1988.110–11, 123). Pottery fertility figurines have been described as the most characteristic offering made in the first Hathor shrine at Gebel Zeit (Castel *et al.* 1985.18). This suggests that, while official interest may have centred on Hathor as Lady of Galena, the ordinary miners saw Hathor primarily as a fertility goddess.

During the New Kingdom, fertility figurines were left as offerings in community shrines and at shrines within state-run temples. They are not a very common votive offering at this period, so it is improbable that their dedication was a standard practice at puberty or marriage. Of the 320 examples from temple areas, only 13 were found in or near temples primarily dedicated to a god (Lists 1–6). The pieces from Koptos are probably a special case, since they were found with objects associated with Hathor, who was a co-templar deity with Min (Petrie 1894.11). The figurines discovered in temple areas at Armant, Hermopolis, and Memphis may also have been offered to co-templar goddesses, but they do raise the possibility that fertility figurines might be dedicated in any local temple. The absence of such figurines from among the extensive range of votive objects from Giza and Abusir does, however, suggest a degree of specialization among the shrines which were a focus for popular devotion.

Out of the 321 temple examples, 305 come from Hathor shrines, so it is not suprising that Types 3–5 have been described as 'Hathoric figures' (Hall in Naville 1913.14). The absence of any figurines dedicated to Isis may be due to the lack of well preserved New Kingdom temples of Isis. Fertility figurines were certainly dedicated to her in the Graeco-Roman Period (Polaczek-Zdanowicz 1975.149; Myśliwiec 1988). The example from a temple of Nekhbet at el-Kab (Quibell 1898.29, pl. 21) supports Bonnet's suggestion that they might be dedicated to any goddess associated with childbirth (1952.94). This should probably be extended to any goddess associated with conception, childbirth, and the protection of nursing mothers and young children.

Hathor fulfils all these criteria. She appears to have been the goddess of sexual love. Appeals to the Golden One to grant a lover his beloved are found in New Kingdom love poetry (Hermann 1959.14–28, 100–11) and temple graffiti (Marciniak 1974 no. 29). An intermediary text from Deir el-Bahri exhorts women visiting the temple to pray to the Golden One for 'A good child (of) this house, happiness, and a good (*nfr*) husband' (Fig. 17B; 3.2.3). In this context *nfr* may primarily mean virile and the happiness referred to be that of sexual satisfaction culminating in the conception of a child. In a Late Period hymn at Medinet Habu, men and women pray to Hathor for the gift of children (Schott 1950.82). During the Graeco-Roman Period a Hathor ritual took place at Edfu on the 30th of Athyr to ensure the fertility of women (Alliot 1949.226). Hathor is prominent in the reliefs portraying the divine conception and birth of Hatshepsut and Amonhotpe III (Brunner 1964.179; Troy 1986.55–6) and in the Birth Houses of Graeco-Roman temple complexes (Daumas 1958.380–7). In P. Leiden I 348, she is regarded as the protector of all women in childbirth. The worried father in Spell 31 sends to Hathor, Lady of Dendara, for an amulet in order that 'she may cause to give birth the one who is to give birth' (Borghouts 1971.29), while in Spell 28 the woman in labour identifies herself with Hathor giving birth to the Divine Child (1971.28). Hathor's role as the cow who suckles and protects the Divine Child has already been examined (2.4.5). In her sevenfold human form Hathor announced the fate of newborn children (Helck 1977.1033).

Hathor's prominent role as a protector of the dead is linked by shared imagery to her role as the helper of women in childbirth and the protector and nourisher of young children. Songs and dances invoking Hathor seem to have been performed for actual births, for the symbolic rebirth and revitalization of the king at his jubilee, and at funerals and festivals associated with the rebirth of the dead (Wente 1969; Altenmüller 1978.22–2; Nord in Simpson & Davis 1981.141–2). The wooden hand-shaped clappers found at Gebel Zeit (Castel *et al.* 1985.20) suggest either that such songs and dances were performed there or that the clappers and the figurines might be magical substitutes for the performance of such rites. Hathor was a goddess both of birth and rebirth, so objects used as birth charms in daily life might also be placed in tombs to ensure a successful rebirth. Funerary material tends to dominate our view of Egyptian culture, so it is important to realize that the funerary function and symbolism of such objects is secondary. They belong primarily to the domestic sphere.

A funerary interpretation for the fertility figurines found in temples is possible, especially at Deir el-Bahri, but a link with the problems and concerns of daily life is more likely. Bonnet suggested that female figurines were dedicated in temples by childless women anxious to conceive, and that the model phalli found at Deir el-Bahri (2.7.1) were offered by childless men for the same reason (1952.94, 590). This assumption would mean that the examples from Serabit el-Khadim and Gebel Zeit were proof of the presence of women at these sites. Women may sometimes have accompanied mining expeditions or have been among the possible permanent staff of the Serabit el-Khadim temple (3.2.3), but the occurrence of fertility figurines in intact male burials suggests that these objects were not used only by women. When an official or artisan had the opportunity to visit a distant Hathor temple, he probably offered a figurine on behalf of himself and his family. The motivation to do so may have been stronger in periods when it was not the practice to make such offerings to deities in state-run temples in Egypt proper. For men away from home for long periods, the figurines could also have served as a symbolic link with family life.

At sites within Egypt, the majority of the votive figurines were probably dedicated by women (3.1), but childless couples may have visited temples together. The demotic story of Setna relates how his childless wife sleeps in a temple (probably of Osiris) in the hope of a favourable dream from the deity (Griffith 1900.142–4; Lichtheim 1980.138). The Ptolemaic 'Bes Chambers' at Saqqara seem to have been designed for this purpose (Ballod 1913.81–2; 2.7.2). Incubation was customary at Deir el-Bahri in the Graeco-Roman Period (Otto 1952.61), where some inscriptions record requests to the deified Amonhotpe son of Hapu for the conception and birth of children (Wildung 1977.95–100; Karkowski & Winnicki 1983.102). On the basis of some Ramessid inscriptions in a grotto in the cliffs, Marciniak suggests that incubation may have been practised at Deir el-Bahri during the New Kingdom (1981; 1981a). If so, the probably Ramessid votive phalli are more likely to be relics of such a practice than the 18th dynasty fertility figurines (2.7.3). In the story of Setna, and in the New Kingdom tale of the Doomed Prince, the childless couple sleep together to conceive a child after receiving a sign from the deity (Griffith 1900.144; Gardiner 1932.1; Lichtheim 1976.200), so presumably Hathor was asked to grant that sexual intercourse resulted in conception rather than to provide a child by any miraculous method. Since some of the fertility figurines nurse female children (e.g. Pl. 47b), the prayers will have been for daughters as well as sons. This is an indication of the comparatively high status of women in Egypt.

Another possibility is that some of the figurines were offered by, or on behalf of, pregnant women to avert a miscarriage and bring them safely through childbirth. Morenz suggested that a Type 2 figurine which has an iron ring around its legs might be a charm against miscarriage (1958.140, pl. 13). Some of the figurines may have been used in magical rites before being left in a temple so that the power of the deity would reinforce or perpetuate the spell. Alternatively, the figurines might have been dedicated after a safe delivery of a child, in fulfilment of a vow to the goddess

It is probably a mistake to try to narrow down the functions of the figurines too far. Couples or individuals may have offered them to reinforce Hathoric rites, or prayers to Hathor about any or all of the stages from the conception to the rearing of a child. The term 'fertility' should be understood in this broad sense. The figurines are more likely to have been offered in anticipation than after the event. This was the case with the two inscribed Type 1 examples (2.6.3) and it seems to have been the standard practice in Egypt (3.3). The inscribed Type 1 examples were offered to the dead, rather than to a deity, and this probably reflects a general pattern in Middle Kingdom religious and magical practices. However, the occurrence of Middle Kingdom fertility figurines in temples and shrines outside Egypt proper shows that people chose to offer such objects to a deity when they had the opportunity to do so. Small votive offerings may not have been permitted or encouraged in state temples within Egypt during the Middle Kingdom, but that changed in the New Kingdom.

Desroches Noblecourt proposed that my Type 2 figurines were cheap imitations of Type 1, made for poorer people (1953.8). The pottery figurines from Deir el-Bahri, Faras, and Gebel Zeit might be looked on as the offerings of the very poorest worshippers, but this would almost certainly be wrong. One Type 3 figurine belonged to the owner of an elaborately painted *rishi* coffin (Hayes 1959.16, 31), indicating that the deceased was a man of some wealth and status. At Esna, examples of Types 2–3 were found in the burials of minor officials (Downes 1974.86–9). All six types seem to have been owned by artisans and officials. Expense was probably not the main factor when choosing between my Types 1 and 2 or 3 and 4. Some donors might have felt that the overt sexuality of Type 3 would make it more effective than the refined Type 4. The cruder specimens, which are comparable in many ways with Early Dynastic and Old Kingdom votive figurines, may have been thought of as more traditional and therefore more powerful.

Egyptians of all ranks wanted children to work their land or inherit their professions and offices, care for them in old age, and carry out their funerary rites. High rates of infant mortality and of women dying in childbirth made human fertility an almost obsessive concern. In the cause of fertility, things which in other contexts might have been considered obscene – such as the Herms of classical Greece or the Priapic figures of ancient Rome – became socially acceptable, even in societies which were usually reticent in public about sexual matters. However, in Egypt there were constraints which operated in temples. In temple contexts there appears to have been a greater reticence about female sexuality than about male sexuality. This may be why many of the fertility figurines at Gebel Zeit were found wrapped in linen. These pieces of linen could be interpreted as dresses, as veils, or as protective wrappings. If they are dresses, comparable to those we know to have been placed on cult images, it is wrong to view all the figurines as nude. If they are veils, their purpose could have been to cover up the dangerous power of female sexuality, which was perhaps only to be revealed during certain mysteries. If they are protective wrappings, part of their function may still have been to prevent the inappropriate exposure of sacred objects. It is interesting that the only known wrapped example from a tomb was found inside a 17th dynasty coffin next to the mummy's head (Hayes 1959.16, 31). Whether it was considered necessary to wrap figurines may thus have depended on the prestige of the context in which they were to be placed. Wrapping could also be a custom that was only introduced in the late Second Intermediate Period, when more refined types of figurine were developing.

The way in which wrapped fertility figurines were found among the stones of the enclosure wall of the New Kingdom shrine at Gebel Zeit 'a la manière d'un dépôt de fondation' (Castel & Soukiassian 1985.286) shows how closely these figurines were associated with the functions of the shrine. The presence of Type 5 fertility figurines in 18th dynasty temple foundation deposits at Koptos and el-Kab (List 5) suggests that the fertility aspect of some goddesses was officially recognized in the New Kingdom. However, it is noteworthy that the Type 5 figurines, which almost all come from temples, conform to the conventions of Egyptian art and are less overtly sexual than the other types. This may be an example of a practice which originally belonged to the stratum of folk religion changing under the influence of state religion in the context of the facilities provided for popular worship in some New Kingdom state-run temples.

Summary

Fertility figurine seems the most appropriate term for the nude female figurines which occur from Predynastic to Graeco-Roman times. Six types of fertility figurine form a sequence spanning the Middle and New Kingdoms. Types 2 and 3 do not comply with the normal conventions of Egyptian art. In all six types, the woman usually wears nothing but jewellery and has an elaborate wig or hairstyle. The emphasis on sexual characteristics is stronger in the earlier figurines than in the later ones. Type 6 figurines lie on beds. Five out of the six types can be accompanied by children, so most of the figurines can be associated with the production and rearing of children rather than simply with sexuality.

Fertility figurines have been found in three contexts; houses, burials, and temples. More examples with an exact provenance come from temples than from tombs or houses. The figurines belong primarily to the sphere of magical and religious practices to promote and protect fertility in daily life. The term fertility covers the whole process from the conception of children to their successful rearing. The figurines were sometimes offered to, or placed in the vicinity of, higher powers such as the spirits of the dead or deities associated with fertility. All six types have been found in temples or shrines of Hathor, the goddess most closely associated with all aspects of fertility. The figures could also be included in the funerary equipment of both males and females to ensure the fertility of the deceased in the afterlife and/or to assist their rebirth.

2.6.5 Lists of provenanced fertility figurines of Types 1–6

Basic details of provenanced fertility figurines of my Types 1–6 are given in tabular form in these lists. Unprovenanced figurines are usually assumed to have come from burials, but the lists demonstrate that this need not be so. For reasons of space, only one reference is given for each figurine or group of figurines. List 3a includes both headless pottery figurines and examples where the excavators did not describe the headdresses which distinguish Types 2 and 3. Pending the full excavation report, most of the figurines from Gebel Zeit have to be placed in list 3a. The lists are subdivided into three contexts; funerary, domestic, and temple. Within the lists it is not always possible to distinguish between figurines which were grave goods and those which were votive offerings to the dead. Information on the sex of tomb or grave owners is often unavailable or unreliable. The current EES excavations at Kom Rabiᶜa, Memphis, are likely to increase the number of figurines from a domestic context.

Abbreviations

A	Adult burial
C	Child burial
M	Male burial
F	Female burial
MK	Middle Kingdom
SIP	Second Intermediate Period
NK	New Kingdom
TIP	Third Intermediate Period
e.	early
l.	late
' '	approximate number
+	at least this number

List 1: Type 1

Tomb site	Details	Date	Quantity	Subtype	Reference
Abusir	–	MK	1	a	(1)
Abydos	M?	MK	1	–	(2)
	–	MK	1	d	(3)
	–	MK	1	d	(4)
Esna	–	MK	1	d	(5)
	–	SIP	1	d	(5)
	–	SIP	1	–	(5)
Hawara	FC	12 D	1	b	(6)
Deir el-Bersha	–	12 D	1	a	(7)
el-Matariya	–	l.MK	1	c	(8)
el-Lisht	–	MK	1	a	(9)
	F?	12 D	1	c	(10)
	F?	12 D	3	a	(10)
	–	MK	'32'	a–d	(11)
Quban	C?	12 D	1	d	(12)
Theban area	–	MK	1	d	(13)
	–	MK	8	a–d	(14)
Deir el-Bahri	M	12 D	1	c	(15)
	–	MK	2	b–c	(16)
Draᶜ Abu el-Nagaᶜ	–	MK	1	a	(17)
Ramesseum	–	l.MK	1	c	(18)
	–	l.MK	1	d	(18)
	–	l.MK	3	–	(18)

Town

Kahun	–	MK	2	b	(19)
	–	MK	2	–	(20)

Temple

Byblos	Pro-cella,	MK	3	c	(21)
	Temple of	MK	1	d	(21)
	the Obelisks	MK	4	–	(21)
Faras	(1.2.3)	SIP	2	–	(22)
Gebel Zeit	(1.6.3)	MK	1	–	(23)

References

1) Cairo CG 29133; Keimer 1948.22, pl. 14
2) Randall-MacIver & Mace 1902.87, pl. 43
3) Garstang 1901.13, pl. 17
4) Müller 1964.59, pl. 93
5) Downes 1974.85–7, figs. 49, 51–2
6) London UC 30094; Petrie 1912.36, pl. 30
7) D'Auria *et al.* 1988.124, no.52
8) Bourriau 1988 no. 119
9) Keimer 1948.24, pl. 14
10) Lansing 1934.30, figs. 28–9
11) Hayes 1953.221, fig. 136
12) Firth 1927.49,59, pl. 27e
13) Buhl 1974.44–5
14) Hayes 1953.221, fig. 136
15) Winlock 1923.20, fig. 15
16) Carter & Carnarvon 1912.32, pl. 44; Hayes 1953.221; Niwínski 1985.198
17) Keimer 1948.18–9
18) Quibell 1896.3, pl. 3
19) London UC 16725–6
20) London UC 16723–4; Petrie 1927.59–40, pl. 52, 390–1
21) Dunand 1950/1958.763, pl. 99
22) Griffith 1921 pl. 19.5, 27
23) Posener-Kriéger 1986.381

List 2: Type 2

Tomb sites	Details	Date	Quantity	Reference
Abydos	–	SIP	4	(1–2)
Edfu	–	MK	'10'	(3)
Esna	–	MK	1	(4)
	M?	SIP	1	(4)
	–	SIP	1	(4)
Hu	Pan Graves	SIP	2	(5)
Theban area	–	MK	1	(6)
Qurna	–	MK	1	(7)

Town

Badari	Pan Grave hut	SIP	1	(8)
Koptos	In house	SIP?	1	(9)

Temple

Gebel Zeit	(1.6.3)	l.MK/ SIP	12+	(10)

Without context

Gebelein	–	MK?	2	(2 & 11)
Koptos	–	SIP	1	(12)

References

1) Peet 1914.63–4, pl. 14.
2) Bruyère 1939.124, 130, figs. 47, 50
3) Bruyère *et al.* 1937.129 pl. 34; Michałowski *et al.* 1950.49, 55, 291–310, pls. 24–5
4) Downes 1974.86, 88, figs. 50, 56
5) Oxford Ash. E 1919; Petrie 1901.53, pl. 26
6) Berlin SM 9508; Hornemann T 836
7) Hilton-Price Cat. 1911.161, pl. 26
8) Brunton *et al.* 1930.7, pls. 9–10
9) Fayolle 1958.81
10) Mey *et al.* 1980.310–14, fig. 5, pl. 81; Castel *et al.* 1984.50–1, figs. 2–4; 1985.19–20, figs. 10, 12; 1986.106, pl. 4.7, 9, 10; Posener-Kriéger 1986.381, pl. 71a
11) Oxford Ash. E 1890.330
12) Hayes 1959.18, fig. 6

List 3: Type 3

Tomb sites	Details	Date	Quantity	Reference
Abusir el-Meleq	F	18 D	1	(1)
Abydos	–	SIP	1	(2)
	–	SIP?	2	(3)
Aniba	–	18 D	1	(4)
Balabish	–	18 D	1	(5)
Deir el-Ballas	–	18 D	1	(6)
Dendara	M	MK	1	(7)
Edfu	–	MK	'20'	(8)
Esna	M?	MK	2	(9)
	M?	SIP	1	(9)
	–	SIP	3	(9)
Thebes (Qurna)	M	SIP	1	(10)

Town

Abydos	In houses	18 D	2 +	(11)
Deir el-Medina	Village	18 D?	5 +	(12)
Memphis	Kom Rabiʿa	SIP	1	(13)
Thebes (Karnak)	Artisans' houses	SIP?	2 +	(14)

Temple

Deir el-Bahri	(1.1.3)	18 D	25 +	(15)
Faras	(1.2.3)	SIP/ 18 D	11 +	(16)
Gebel Zeit	(1.6.3)	SIP/ 18 D	12 +	(17)

Without context

Abydos	–	SIP	2	(18)
Hierakonpolis	–	SIP?	1	(10)
Koptos	–	18 D?	1	(3)

References

1) Berlin SM 18742; Scharff 1926.95, pl. 71
2) Peet 1914.63–4, pl. 14.2
3) Bruyère 1939.133, fig. 53
4) Steindorff 1937.85–6, pl. 46
5) Wainwright 1920.56, pl. 19.3
6) Lacovara 1990.9
7) Petrie 1900 pl. 21
8) Henné 1925.24, pl. 27; Bruyère et al. 1937.129, pl. 34; Michałowski et al. 1938.105–13, pls. 34–5; 1939.135, fig. 54; 1950.198, pl. 23
9) Downes 1974.88–9, figs. 49–50
10) Hayes 1959.16–7, fig. 6
11) Ayrton et al. 1904.54, pl. 58
12) Bruyère 1939 pl. 45; Valbelle & Bonnet 1982.390
13) Bourriau, personal communication 1991
14) Vergnieux 1982.390
15) Hall in Naville 1913.16, pls. 24, 32
16) Griffith 1921.86 pl. 19
17) Mey et al. 1980.311–15, fig. 3; Castel et al. 1984.49–51, fig. 7; 1985.19–20, figs. 7, 13; 1986.104, pl. 4; Castel & Soukiassian 1989.164 pl. 13.1; Leclant & Clerc 1985.393, fig. 61; 1986.295–6, figs. 61, 64–5, 69; Posener-Kriéger 1985.297–8; pl. 65
18) Craig Patch 1990.36–7, nos. 25b–c

List 3a: Type 2 or 3 figurines

Tomb sites	Details	Date	Quantity	Reference
Abydos	–	SIP	3	(1)
	–	SIP	1	(2)
Aniba	–	18 D	1	(3)
Deir el-Medina	FC	18 D	1	(4)
Edfu	–	MK	'30'	(5)
Esna	–	MK	2	(6)
	–	SIP	6	(6)
Hu	–	12 D	1	(7)
Thebes	–	MK	2	(8)
(Qurna)				

Town				
Deir el-Ballas	Houses	18 D	2	(9)
Hierakonpolis	Street	18 D	1	(10)
Koptos	In houses	SIP?	2 +	(11)

Temple				
Armant	Temple refuse	18 D?	1	(12)
Gebel Zeit	(1.6.3)	MK/SIP 18 D	128 +	(13)

References

1) Randall-MacIver & Mace 1901.80, pls. 44, 48, 50
2) Peet 1914.63–4, pl. 46
3) Steindorff 1937.85–6, pl. 46
4) Bruyère 1937a.164–6, fig. 86
5) Michałowski *et al.* 1938.105–11, pl. 35; 1950.198–210, pls. 23–4
6) Downes 1974.88–9, figs. 55–7
7) Petrie 1901.44, pl. 26
8) Petrie 1909b.3, 13, pl. 31
9) Lacovara 1990.7, fig. 5.2
10) B. Adams 1974.14, pls. 7–8
11) Fayolle 1958.81
12) Mond & Myers 1940.99, pl. 26
13) Mey *et al.* 1980.311–15, fig. 3; Posener-Kriéger 1985.297–8; 1986.381; Leclant & Clerc 1986 figs. 66–67

List 4: Type 4

Tomb site	Details	Date	Quantity	Subtype	Reference
Sawama	–	18 D	1	a	(1)
Theban area	FC	e. 18 D	1	b	(2)

		18 D?	1	a	(3)
	—	18 D	1	a	(3)
Zawiyet el-Aryan	2 A	18 D	1	a	(4)
	2 A	18 D	1	a	(4)

Town

el-ʿAmarna	Main city, in house	l. 18 D	1	a	(5)
Deir el-Medina	In houses	NK	60 +	a,b	(6)

Temple

Deir el-Bahri	(1.1.3)	18 D	3 +	a	(7)
		18 D	2 +	b	(7)
Deir el-Medina	North of Temple area	18/19 D	2 +	—	(8)
Faras	(1.1.4)	18 D	1 +	a	(9)
		18 D	1 +	b	(9)

References

1) Bourriau & Millard 1971.33, pl. 17
2) Spiegelberg 1908.11–2, fig. 11; Horneman T 942
3) Petrie 1909b.12, pls. 20, 31; 1927 pl. 52.423
4) Dunham 1978.54–5, pl. 40
5) Pendlebury 1951.140, pl. 79
6) Bruyère 1939.139, fig. 58, pls. 43–4
7) Hilton-Price 1911.160, pl. 58; Hall in Naville 1913.16, pl. 24.2
8) Bruyère 1953.90
9) Griffith 1921.86, pl. 19.12, 8

List 5: Type 5

Tomb sites	Details	Date	Quantity	Reference
Zawiyet el-Aryan	—	18 D	1	(1)
	2 A	18 D	4	(1)
	2 A	18 D	1	(1)
	—	18 D	1	(1)

Town

el-ʿAmarna	Workmen's village bedroom	l. 18th D	1	(2)
Deir el-Medina		18 D	1	(3)
Memphis	Kom Rabiʿa	NK	1	(4)

Temple

Deir el-Bahri	(1.3.1–3)	18 D	70 +	(5)
Dendara	Temple refuse	18 D	1 +	(6)
Faras	(1.2.3)	18 D	18 +	(7)
Gebel Zeit	NK shrine	18 D	1	(8)
el-Kab	Foundation deposit	Amonhotpe II	1	(9)
Koptos	Foundation deposit	Thutmose III	3	(10)
Mirgissa	(1.1.3)	18 D	4	(11)

References

1) Dunham 1978.53–5, pl. 40
2) Peet & Woolley 1923.73
3) Bruyère 1939 pl. 44, second row, right
4) Jeffreys & Malek 1988.19
5) Hall in Naville 1913.14, 16, pl. 24.2; Hayes 1959.163
6) Petrie 1900.28, pl. 23.16
7) Griffith 1921.86, pl. 19.1–2, 9–11, 17
8) Leclant & Clerc 1985.393, fig. 62
9) Quibell 1898.29, pl. 21
10) Petrie 1894.11; 1896.pl. 15
11) Karlin in Vercoutter 1970.350, fig. 45

List 6: Type 6

Tomb site	Details	Date	Quantity	Subtype	Reference
Deir el-Balah (Palestine)	–	19 D	1	b?	(1)
Deir el-Medina	3 A & 1 FC	18 D	3	a	(2)
	FC	18 D	1	b	(3)
	–	NK	10 +	a–c	(4)
Deir Rifa	–	18/19 D	1	b	(5)
Edfu	–	NK	10 +	b,c	(6)
Gurob	FC	18 D	1	c	(7)
	C	18 D?	1	c	(7)
	–	NK	2	b,c	(7)
Kahun	12 A & 2 C	18 D?	1	a	(8)
Riqqa	–	18 D	1	b	(9)
Sawama	–	18 D	1	a	(10)
	–	18 D	2	c	(11)
Sidmant	–	18 D	1	b	(12)
Thebes	Ramesseum	NK	1	b	(13)
Thebes	Tomb refuse	NK	1	b	(14)

Town

el-ʿAmarna	Workmen's village	l.18 D	6	a	(15)
	In workshop	l.18 D	1	a	(16)
	North suburb	l.18 D	22 +	a–b	(17)

	Main city	l.18 D	40 +	a	(18)
Aswan	In houses	NK–TIP	3 +	b,c	(19)
Deir el-Balah	Workshop	19 D	1	b	(1)
(Palestine)					
Deir el-Medina	In houses	NK	50 +	a–c	(20)
Edfu	In house	NK	1	b	(21)
Gurob	In houses	18–19 D	5 +	b–c	(22)
Heliopolis	In house	l.NK–TIP	1	c	(23)
Medinet Habu	In houses	l.NK–TIP	3 +	b–c	(24)
Memphis	Kom Rabiʿa	NK	'8'	b	(25)

Temple

Armant	Temple refuse	NK	1	c	(26)
Deir el-Medina	Temple refuse	NK	2 +	–	(27)
Hermopolis	Temple refuse	NK	1	a	(28)
Memphis	Temple refuse	l.NK–TIP	7	b–c	(29)
Mirgissa	(1.3.3)	18 D	1	b	(30)
Serabit el-Khadim	(1.4.3)	NK	2 +	b	(31)

References

1) T. Dothan in Rainey 1987.131
2) Bruyère 1937.97, fig. 41
3) Bruyère 1937a.124
4) Bruyère 1930.12, fig. 4; 1939.109; Valbelle & Bonnet 1976.341, fig. 9
5) Petrie 1891 pl. 27.12
6) Michałowski *et al.* 1950.207–9, pl. 25
7) Brunton & Engelbach 1927.17, pls. 13, 25, 47
8) Petrie 1907.23, pls. 27.b, f
9) Engelbach 1915.19, pl. 22.6.
10) Bourriau & Millard 1971.33–4, pl. 17
11) Breasted 1948, pl. 93c; Bourriau & Millard 1971.33–4, fig. 19
12) Petrie 1904.52, pl. 40
13) Brussels MR E 295
14) N. Strudwick, personal communication, 1990. No. 253a.121
15) Peet & Woolley 1923.69, 73–4, 78, 87, pls. 12, 23
16) P. Rose in Kemp 1989.90
17) Frankfort & Pendlebury 1933.31, 34–6, 44–5, 54, 57, 68, 78–97
18) Pendlebury 1951.118, 121, 135–6, 140, pls. 78, 109; Borchardt & Ricke 1980.32, 55, 66, 68–9, 134, 137, 152, 159, 164, 169, 175–6, 182, 191, 203, 206, 209, 217, 220, 233, 246, 251, 258, 260, 308
19) Honroth 1910.30–2, fig. 8; Kaiser *et al.* 1988 pl. 58d
20) Bruyère 1939.137–9, fig. 59, pl. 44
21) Alliot 1932.21, pl. 15
22) Petrie 1890.37–8, pl. 18.32–3, 37; A. Thomas 1981.82–3, pls. 54–5
23) Abdel-Aziz Saleh 1991.310, pl. 43.9
24) Holscher 1954.11–13, fig. 12, pl. 6h
25) Jeffreys *et al.* 1986.7
26) Mond & Myers 1940.176, pl. 26
27) Bruyère 1953.35–6

28) Roeder 1931.110, pl. 25e
29) Anthes 1965.127–8, pl. 49
30) Karlin in Vercoutter 1970.350
31) Petrie 1906.147, pl. 151.14; Giveon, personal communication, 1983

2.7 Phallic objects

Phallic objects of various kinds were among the offerings at Deir el-Bahri, Mirgissa, Timna, and Gebel Zeit. They are described below, grouped according to their material, along with comparable pieces from other sites. Such comparative material appears to be rare. It has to be borne in mind that excavators have tended to suppress or ignore phallic objects, or to assign them automatically to a very late period, when they could be explained as examples of foreign influence. Many museums have been reticent about displaying, or even cataloguing, phallic objects.

2.7.1 Votive phalli

1 *Stone*

No votive phalli are mentioned in Winlock's accounts of his finds at Deir el-Bahri, but four phallic objects from these excavations entered the Cairo Museum in 1923 (Martin 1987.79). All four were from a 'rubbish hole' in Hatshepsut's causeway. One of these objects is a stone phallus, 11 cm long (Cairo JE 47735).

Among the pebbles found in the sanctuary at Mirgissa (2.6.2.1), was one naturally shaped like a phallus (Karlin in Vercoutter 1970.329, 354, no. 191, fig. 27). It is about 3 cm long and shows traces of red paint. On one long sandstone pebble found in the temple at Timna, a groove has been added at the tip to emphasize its phallic shape (Rothenberg 1988.268, pl. 155.9). Some of the quartz pebbles from the Timna temple 'have the shape of small figurines, sometimes of phallic character' (1988.268). Rothenberg illustrates a carved stone phallus from the temple area (1988.317, fig. 92.5), but no dimensions or details are given.

Phallic pebbles were among the Old Kingdom votive material recovered from the courtyard of the temple of Satet at Aswan (Dreyer 1986.153 pl. 57). Carved stone phalli have occasionally been found among New Kingdom material (*e.g.* Barguet & Leclant 1954.47, fig. 80; Bruyère 1957.4), but most of them probably come from broken statues of ithyphallic deities. Deir el-Medina provides one definite example in the form of a stone phallus attached to a plinth (Bruyère 1927.39–40; 1952.15–6). This object, which was found in the vicinity of the Hathor temple, is inscribed with a prayer to the goddess on behalf of the 19th dynasty Scribe of the Necropolis, Ramose (2.7.3). Post New Kingdom votive stone phalli have been discovered in the area of the sacred animal necropolis at Saqqara (Martin 1981 pls. 26–8).

2 *Wood* (Pls. 52a, 53)

In his excavation report, Naville briefly mentioned that some wooden phalli were found in the speos of the Hathor shrine of Djeser-Akhet (1907.65), but neither he nor Hall described or illustrated any of them. Currelly noted the existence of:–

... many basketsfull of roughly-carved wooden phalli that had been placed on the
floor around the statue. A few of the same had been found in the rubbish at some
distance from the shrine. (in Naville 1913.31)

In a letter published by Hornblower (1926.81), Currelly gave more details about
the position of the phalli in the Hathor shrine:

So the phalli were lying about on the floor, many of them not covered up by the
rubbish, and a few found after the rubbish was removed ... There was no kind of
order; they had simply been dropped around. There was practically no dust in the
place, except where it came down from the front. I could trace no order whatever in
the laying out of these objects.

The EEF distribution lists mention only three wooden phalli from Deir
el-Bahri, two of which were sent to Kyoto (UM 586) and one to a Roman Catholic
seminary in Chicago. However, the British Museum has 19 wooden phalli from
these excavations (41171–3, 47776–86, 48107–10, 49473–4), and Currelly took 21
examples to the Royal Ontario Museum (unnumbered). 19 of the latter were
illustrated in an article by Hornblower (Pl. 53), who also acquired five wooden
phalli from the shrine which he left to the Ashmolean Museum (1926.400,
401 = Pl. 52a, 402a–c). At least two wooden phalli were found by Winlock at Deir
el-Bahri (Cairo JE 47734a–b; Martin 1987.76). A photograph of the deposit of
votive stelae and statues within the enclosure wall of the New Kingdom Hathor
shrine at Gebel Zeit shows several objects which might be wooden phalli (Castel &
Soukiassian 1985 pl. 60), but none has so far been mentioned in the excavation
report.

The examples from Deir el-Bahri which I have been able to examine in the
British Museum and the Ashmolean Museum range in length between 5.7 and 30
cm; most are 12–20 cm long. The standard of workmanship can be low and most
appear to be made of acacia, a wood which is full of knots and prone to splitting.
One example consists of a twig bound with straw (London BM 41171). Traces of
red paint survive on several of the phalli (London BM 41172, 47786, 48110; Oxford
Ash. 1926.400–1). Of the examples in the Royal Ontario Museum, five show traces
of a white gesso undercoat, one is painted with red and blue bands over white
gesso, two are red, and three are yellow (F. Stanley pers. comm. 1982). Phalli on
statues or reliefs of ithyphallic deities are painted red, the normal masculine flesh
colour. The blue bands might just represent swollen veins but the yellow examples
are harder to account for.

The wooden phalli display varying degrees of stylization. The simplest
examples consist of a shaft with a round tip (e.g. Oxford Ash. 1926.402a–c). Out of
context, these objects could not definitely be identified as phalli. Usually, a single
deep groove separates the shaft from the bulbous glans (Pl. 52a; Manniche 1987.48,
fig. 39) and the meatus is sometimes shown (e.g. London BM 41172, 48107; Oxford
Ash. 1926.401). The single groove may indicate that these objects all represent a
circumcised penis, and the cross-shaped mark on the underside of one example
(Pl. 52a) might be a circumcision scar. The bottom end of the shaft is usually flat,
but one piece has a glans at each end (London BM 47786), and on another the
scrotum is included (Pl. 53, bottom left). On one example in the Royal Ontario

Museum (Pl. 53, bottom centre) and one in the British Museum (48110), the shaft terminates in a tenon which must have been used to attach the phallus to a wooden base.

A wooden phallus from the forecourt of a Ramessid votive chapel at Deir el-Medina (Bruyère 1929.69) is the only piece of comparative material which I can find. The speos of the Hathor shrine of Djeser-Akhet was sealed off near the end of the 20th dynasty, so the phalli found inside it cannot be later than this date (1.1.2.4). Since the narrow speos was damaged and then restored in the Amarna Period, the wooden phalli from the shrine are unlikely to be earlier than the end of the 18th dynasty. They may not have been in the shrine for very long when it was sealed off (1.1.2.4), in which case they would date to the late 20th dynasty. The examples found outside the shrine could, however, belong to an earlier period. The deposit of votive objects at Gebel Zeit which may contain phalli was probably put together at the end of the 18th dynasty (Castel & Soukiassian 1985.288). Nothing is likely to have been added to it after the reign of Ramesses II.

Among the objects excavated by Naville at Deir el-Bahri were two extremely crude wooden statuettes (Kyoto UM 563; London BM 47798). Both of these have a roughly carved head, a virtually rectangular body, small holes for the attachment of arms, and a much larger hole at the bottom of the body, probably for the insertion of an erect penis. The statuette in the British Museum is about 14 cm high. Very similar statuettes have been found in domestic contexts at Edfu (Alliot 1932.23, pl. 19) and Aswan (Honroth 1909.32–3), where the excavators assigned them to the Graeco-Roman Period or later on grounds of their crudity. However, the wooden phalli from Deir el-Bahri demonstrate that crude phallic objects can date to the New Kingdom, and these statuettes may do so too.

3 *Faience* (Pl. 52b)

Currelly noted that 'a few phalli' made in blue faience were found at Deir el-Bahri (in Naville 1913.29–30). None is mentioned in the EEF distribution lists, but the British Museum has eight examples from these excavations (41727, 47768 = Pl. 52b, right; 47769–74). These consist of slender rods of bright blue faience. The only intact example is 8.7 cm long (London BM 41727). The glans is shown as a bulbous tip separated from the shaft by one, two, or three grooves. The examples with two or more grooves may represent uncircumcised penises.

These faience examples were not found inside the speos of the Hathor shrine of Djeser-Akhet like the wooden phalli. They must have come from one, or several, of the deposits of votive offerings discovered by Naville in the vicinity of Akh-isut. One faience phallus, 5.4 cm long, was found by Winlock in a 'rubbish hole' in Hatshepsut's causeway (Cairo JdE 47735; Martin 1987.76). These objects are probably 18th dynasty, like virtually all the votive faience from this site. One faience fragment that might be part of a votive phallus was found at Timna (Rothenberg 1988.268, 306, fig. 30.6).

Early Dynastic votive faience from Abydos includes some objects identified as baskets which could, however, be phalli (Dreyer 1986 pl. 63). The Cairo Museum has two small, blue faience phalli from Gebelein which are probably New Kingdom

(JE 29778a–b; Martin 1987.72). Other possible New Kingdom comparative material consists of some faience objects from the tombs of Amonhotpe II and Thutmose IV; these are said to be snake amulets, but they bear a strong resemblance to the phalli from Deir el-Bahri (*e.g.* Daressy 1902. nos. 24564–5, pl. 30; Carter & Newberry 1904.130–2). Phallic amulets in faience are known from the Graeco-Roman Period (*e.g.* Petrie 1914.11, pl. 16; Hornblower 1927), but they include the scrotum and lack the extreme stylization of the Deir el-Bahri pieces. The discovery of a phallic figurine in a Middle Kingdom burial at Lisht (Riefstahl 1972.137) provides additional evidence that phallic objects were made in Egypt long before the Graeco-Roman Period.

4 *Pottery*

There is a single possible example of a pottery phallus from Deir el-Bahri. This consists of a red-ware tube which swells at one end into a cone shape (London BM 47775). I know of no definite New Kingdom parallels. The Cairo Museum has two 'votive phalli in pottery' of unknown date (Martin 1987.72; Cairo CG 6221-2). A red-painted pottery phallus was found in debris close to the royal tomb at el-ʿAmarna, but the excavators assigned it to the Roman or the Byzantine Period (Martin 1974.368–9, no. 398, pl. 53). Several examples which may date to the Roman Period were recovered from houses at Edfu (Bruyère 1937.105).

An ithyphallic pottery baboon figurine is among the material from the EEF excavations at Deir el-Bahri now in the British Museum (London BM 47682). This crude figurine is 8 cm high and shows traces of red paint. A baboon's head (London BM 43153) probably comes from a similar figurine. A phallic figurine in pottery found by the Metropolitan Museum of Art Expedition at Deir el-Bahri may be of this type (Cairo JdE 58765). A number of ithyphallic pottery baboon figurines were discovered at Gebel Zeit (Mey *et al.* 1980.104, no. 55, fig. 5; Castel *et al.* 1984.52, fig. 1; 1985.20, fig. 11; 1986.104, pl. 5.11). One figurine, 7 cm high, is described as a baboon with 'une main (ou patte) levée vers la tête, l'autre posée sur son organe génital' (1980.314). For baboon figures as votive offerings, see 2.10.1.3.

5 *Other*

D. Reese notes that five Terebra shells and three turriculate gastropod fossils found at Timna 'resemble the phallus' and suggests that this was the reason why they were brought to the temple as votive offerings (in Rothenberg 1988.264–5, pls. 153.7, 154.11).

Two non-Egyptian bronze phallic figurines were recovered from the temple at Timna (Rothenberg 1988.147, pl. 126.6, fig. 53.1–2). These probably represent the deity worshipped in the Midianite tent shrine, but it is possible that they were dedicated while the temple was still under Egyptian control (1988.277).

2.7.2 The phallic element in Egyptian religion

If phallicism is defined as 'Worship of the reproductive powers of nature symbolized by the organs of sex' (Hartland, in Hastings 1917.815), then such an element is present in Egyptian religion, but it is usually linked with specific deities. The phallus of Osiris is frequently mentioned in texts and Plutarch claimed that images of it were worshipped in temples in Egypt (Griffiths 1970.135). In funerary texts, the male member of the deceased was identified with that of a god, sometimes Osiris, Reʿ, or Min (Behrens 1982.1018), but most often by the baboon god Baba, whose phallic aspect is emphasized from the Pyramid Texts onwards (Derchain 1952.33–6).

Spell 397 of the Coffin Texts mentions that the phallus of Baba begets human children and calves (*CT* V, 92), which illustrates an Egyptian use of phallic symbolism in connection with both human and animal fertility. In Egypt the earth was personified by a god rather than a goddess, so it is not suprising to find that the imagery associated with crop fertility is predominantly masculine. Greek and Roman writers, seeking parallels with their own religions, stressed this association of phallic symbolism with crop fertility in Egypt. The Osirian festival known as the Pamylia was at least partly an agricultural rite (Bonnet 1952.580; Griffiths 1982.659–60). It was described by Herodotus, who equated the Pamylia with Greek Dionysian rites:

> In other ways the Egyptian method of celebrating the festival of Dionysus is much the same as the Greek, except that the Egyptians have no choric dance. Instead of the phallus they have puppets, about 18 inches high; the genitals of these figures are made almost as big as the rest of their bodies, and they are pulled up and down by strings as the women carry them round the villages. Flutes lead the procession and the women as they follow sing a hymn to Dionysus. (Herodotus II.48; Selincourt 1972.149).

Plutarch linked the Pamylia with his theory about the efflux of Osiris as the source of life-giving moisture and symbol of the inundation (Plutarch XII.36; Griffiths 1970.173–5; Hani 1976.372–7).

In the cases of the sun god and of Min, it can be life-giving fire which flows from the phallus (Goodenough 1956.169; van Dijk 1979–80.11–14; 1986.40), an image possibly inspired by the form and associations of the fire-drill (Westendorf 1977.148). The phallus of Min seems to have symbolized the creation of new life by sexual means and, as with the ithyphallic form of Amon-Reʿ, he bestowed fecundity on humans, animals and crops (Hornblower 1927.151; Gauthier 1931.37–8, 132–41). The crude wooden statuettes described above (2.7.1.2) have been tentatively identified as Min figures (Shorter 1930.236). The ithyphallic Min of Koptos was a co-templar deity with Hathor at Gebel Zeit (1.6.1). Min of Koptos and Hathor, Lady of Dendara are shown together on 18th dynasty votive stelae from Deir el-Bahri (Pl. 12a) and Dendara (Bosticco 1965 fig. 26), and objects associated with the cult of Hathor appear in a foundation deposit in the temple of Min at Koptos (1.7). Min and Hathor may have been worshipped together as the embodiments of creative power through male and female sexuality. In the context of fertility rites, the same kind of offerings may have been appropriate for both of them. However, there is no firm evidence that the wooden statuettes are meant to depict Min, or any other god, and they may be no more than generalized symbols of virility or fertility.

Another deity who can be shown with an erect penis is Bes (*e.g.* Ballod 1913.80–1; Romano 1980.46, fig. 6; Bourriau 1988.112, no. 98). He is associated with Hathor much more often than Min is, though as an attendant rather than as an equal (Altenmüller 1975.722). Bes has been seen by some scholars as a bestower or protector of virility as well as fertility (Bonnet 1952.591; Derchain in Martin 1981.168–9). The 'Bes Chambers' at Saqqara may provide evidence for both these aspects. In these rooms, which probably dated to the Ptolemaic Period, large nude figures of Bes accompanied by nude females were painted on the walls (Quibell 1907 pls. 26–9; Keimer 1948 pl. 25) and phallic figurines lay on the floors (Quibell 1907.13). These rooms may have been slept in by infertile women or couples who desired the assistance of Bes in conceiving a child (2.6.4). It is also possible that impotent men came to this shrine to pray to Bes for healing.

Graeco-Roman terracotta groups of Bes figures carrying a giant phallus (Weber 1914.104–10, pls. 12–4; Martin 1981.29, pl. 23) probably depict priests dressed up as Bes to take part in a specific phallic rite. B. Stricker suggested that this rite was the Pamylia, during which the phallus of Osiris made the earth fertile (1956.40). Derchain agrees with this identification, but argues that such groups should be linked with regeneration rites for the dead and continuity of the family line through re-enactments of the resurrection of Osiris and the conception of Horus (in Martin 1981.170). This would give them a similar function to that postulated for Middle Kingdom fertility figurines by Desroches Noblecourt (2.6.4), but, unlike the figurines, phallic objects of this or any other kind are only rarely found in tombs.

Most of the phallic material relating to Bes dates to the Graeco-Roman Period, and some scholars have seen in it the influence of the satyrs of Greek Dionysian myth and ritual (Stricker 1956.36–40; Dasen 1988.272, 275). It is more probable that the Greeks adopted Bes because his qualities reminded them of their own phallic deities. Stricker believed that a Graeco-Egyptian relief which depicts Bes dancing naked with a huge penis protruding backwards through his legs was based on a Greek prototype (1956.12, pl. 3), but similar figures occur on a Meroitic block from Faras (Michałowski 1965.42–3, fig. 13) and in a painting on a piece of leather found by Winlock in one of the dumps of 18th dynasty votive material at Deir el-Bahri (New York MMA 31.3.98 = Pl. 54; Hayes 1959.167; Fischer 1974.118–9). The surviving corner of this fragment is reinforced and has a leather tie 'by means of which it was, presumably, suspended on the temple wall' (Hayes 1959.167). The hanging shows two kneeling girls, one only partially preserved, playing harps in a vine arbour. Between them is a nude, dancing figure with a large, backward-pointing penis. Although the head is missing, comparison with the Graeco-Egyptian relief (Stricker 1956 pl. 3) suggests that this is Bes. The dancer wields a scourge made up of strands of knotted rope or leather. In an upper register are traces of a standing, male figure in a long kilt and the bottom of another scourge.

This hanging provides a link between the phallic aspect of Bes and the cult of Hathor, but in its fragmentary state it is difficult to interpret. One Old Kingdom relief (HT 1927 pl. 17; Janssen & Janssen 1990.63–5, fig. 27) appears to show a person masked like Bes and carrying a whip, presiding over some kind of ritual. W. Stevenson Smith thought that this, and fragments showing a lion-masked man and female dancers from the mortuary temple of Sahure, 'perhaps represent the games and dances of a festival such as we find celebrated at the feast of Hathor of Cusae in the Middle Kingdom' (1949.210). The scene has also been interpreted as a 'fecundity or harvest ritual' (Janssen & Janssen 1990.65) or a circumcision rite (Capart 1931.73–5; Jesi 1958.172–3). B. de Rachewiltz compared this Bes priest with the masked scourge-wielding figures common in African initiation rites connected with puberty (1964.47–8). It seems likely that an object from a Hathor shrine would depict female rather than male puberty rites, and there is no definite evidence for religious celebrations of puberty in Egypt. One alternative, would be to view the dance shown on the hanging as a male equivalent to Hathor displaying her genitals to restore the benevolence of the Sun God by arousing his sexuality (2.6.4.). In the myth of the 'Distant Goddess', music and dancing are used to pacify Hathor in her dangerous aspect and to evoke her creative one (Junker 1911.5). The small Ptolemaic temple of Hathor at Philae contains reliefs showing (clothed) Bes figures dancing and playing musical instruments to celebrate the return of the goddess (Daumas 1969.9–17, pl. 5). The hanging might then depict a comic erotic dance performed to placate Hathor, but this explanation does not really account for the scourges.

Bes has some features in common with the Mesopotamian deity La-tarak, who protected buildings and people against hostile forces, and is shown wearing a lion's pelt and wielding a scourge (Black & Green 1992.116, fig. 94). Another parallel is that between the scene on the leather hanging and accounts of the Roman festival of the Lupercalia, during which young men, naked except for goat-skin girdles, ran through the streets wielding leather scourges (Michels 1953.35–59). The main purpose of this festival was probably to purify the city and to protect its boundaries by driving out evil spirits, especially those of the recently dead. Apotropaic displays of the genitals and the cracking of whips to ward off evil or danger are common to many cultures (Hartland in Hastings 1917.830). Phallic amulets were frequently used to protect people and places in ancient Greece and Rome (Johns 1982.62–75) and in Graeco-Roman Egypt (Behrens 1982.1018; Dasen 1988.275). The dance on the hanging could thus be apotropaic. If so, its purpose could still have been to banish Hathor's dangerous aspect.

The Lupercalia was also a fertility rite, since barren women hoped to conceive after being touched by the scourges of the officiants (Michels 1953.47, 59; Johns 1982.50). The deity venerated during the Lupercalia seems to have been Faunus. Faunus has much in common with the Egyptian Bes. He was a half-human, half-animal, fecundity deity with both female and group forms (1982.48,50). It is tempting to see Bes's scourge as a phallic symbol and the hanging as depicting a scene from a fertility festival presided over by Hathor and her attendant Bes. Due to the scarcity of comparative material or textual evidence, such a conclusion must remain speculative, but it can be borne in mind when considering the symbolic value of the phallic objects dedicated to Hathor.

2.7.3   Phallic offerings and the cult of Hathor

One inscribed phallus dedicated to Hathor survives (Bruyère 1952.15–6; Černý 1973.325). Its cryptically written text is hard to interpret and can be treated only briefly here. The inscription consists of two sentences of obscure praise of Hathor, each followed by a brief, almost equally obscure, request to the goddess by the scribe Ramose. These requests read ⟨𓊪𓏤𓏜𓋴𓂝⟩ ⟨𓏠𓂋𓀀𓉐⟩ and ⟨𓊪𓏤𓏠𓂋𓈖𓂋⟩ 𓂋𓏤𓉐. Černý translated the first as 'cause me to receive a compensation of (thy) house (as a rewarded) one' and the second as 'create a duration in thy house as a rewarded one' (1973.325). He did not give detailed reasons for his translation and stated that 'The rendering of the whole is rather doubtful'.

Bruyère translated the first request as 'fais que j'obtienne les faveurs des servantes de ton temple' and interpreted the second as 'fais que demeure (se perpétue) dans la maison de la déesse (gynécée) avec moi (littéralement: que se prolonge ma descendance dans mon harem)' (1952.16). His interpretation was based on the facts that Ramose's wife was a Singer of Hathor, and that several other female members of his household bore the same title. He suggested that because of this, Ramose's home could be regarded as a house of the goddess and that the inscription on the phallus was a prayer for the sexual favours of the Singers of Hathor and the gift of children by them. In spite of his 'harim', Ramose seems to have remained childless, so it would not be suprising to find him making offerings to Hathor in her aspect as fertility goddess.

Bruyère's interpretation is attractive, but it arises more from the nature of the object and the identity of the donor than from the text itself. An alternative translation of the first request would be:–

Grant that I receive the revenues[1] of your temple[2].

[1] There is no determinative to indicate that *bꜣkw* means 'female servants' here and no real justification for stretching it to mean 'the favours of the servants'.
[2] Bruyère assumed that the 𓂋 was part of the writing of the suffix and that 𓉐 was an error (1952.16). Another possibility is that 𓏠𓂋 writes the second person singular suffix, as 𓂋 appears to do in the second request, and that 𓉐 should be emended to *nb(t).i*.

The second request is harder to translate because it appears to lack a subject:–

Cause to be established in your temple with me.[1]

[1] One would expect 'Cause me to be established in your temple' and it may be possible to get this sense by translating 'Cause being established in your temple to be in my possession'. Bruyère proposed that the subject of the second request was the *bꜣkw* (1952.16), which could give the translation 'Cause them (the revenues) to be established in your temple with me'.

Thus, this inscription may contain only a standard type of request for the *ka* of the donor to dwell in a temple, sharing in the offerings of the goddess. This would leave the problem of why a prayer of the kind usually found on temple statues should be inscribed on the base of a phallus. It might be argued that the phallus was a symbol of the male donor or of the regeneration which he hoped to enjoy in the temple, but if either of these explanations were correct, one would expect such objects to be common in shrines and temples. The translation of this text must therefore remain uncertain and it does not provide much help in interpreting the phallic material from other sites.

Another isolated piece of evidence is the description of a festival in the Ptolemaic calendar of Hathor festivals at Edfu (Alliot 1949.223–4). On the 5th of Paophi there was a festival, which seems to have been chiefly in honour of Nun, during which Hathor was presented with the phallus of her father – *bȝḥ pw n srwd wnnt* 'It is the phallus that makes what exists flourish' (1949.216, col.6). The phallus of Hathor's father is presumably that of Reᶜ-Atum, who emerged from Nun. The epithet Hand of Atum is sometimes given to Hathor, especially when she is identified with Iusᶜas or Nebet-Hetepet (Vandier 1964.60–1; 2.3.4). This epithet refers to the masturbation of Reᶜ-Atum, which resulted in the birth of Shu and Tefenet (Clark 1959.42–3; Baines 1970.396–7), but the hand of the creator god has been reinterpreted as a goddess. J.van Dijk suggests that Hathor can also be identified with the 'seed', the semen, of the sun god (1986.40–2). If Hathor can be seen as the female creative principle, the consort as well as the daughter of Reᶜ-Atum (Derchain 1972.45–8), then the presentation of a phallus to Hathor during the Edfu festival might evoke or re-enact the first creative union of Reᶜ-Atum and Hathor, Lady of the Vulva – probably to promote fertility in people, animals, and crops.

It is doubtful whether the presentation of phalli at Deir el-Bahri and Mirgissa can be seen as a purely agricultural rite. Both these sites are on the edge of the desert and neither of them was the principal temple or shrine of a community dependent on agriculture. Nor does such an explanation easily fit the phallic material from the desert sites of Timna and Gebel Zeit. There are two other possibilities. First, the phalli may have been presented by men seeking a cure for impotence. The presentation of models of specific parts of the body in gratitude for healing seems to be a Graeco-Roman phenomenen (Johns 1982.57–9). However, it is not implausible that Hathor, the Hand of Atum, who sexually stimulated her father/consort should have been appealed to about this sort of sexual problem. The phalli could then have been offered in anticipation of a cure for male sexual problems.

Second, the phalli may have been offered by people who wanted to have children. Hornblower commented that:–

> There can be little doubt that these offerings point to a popular belief in Hat.hor as a fertility goddess and are symbols of prayers for the bearing of children, with perhaps a direct aphrodisiac intention, made and sold by the priests to poor devotees. (1926.81)

Bonnet expressed a similar view:–

> Sie werden vermutlich von kinderlosen Männern zur Stärkung ihrer Zeugungskraft geweiht sein. (1952.590)

While the man would have to take responsibility for impotence, it is less likely that he would admit to being the sterile partner in a childless couple. Because of this, an image of the female genitals or body would probably have been a more common choice of offering for a childless couple than a phallus. Although the Egyptians were fully aware of the male's role in conception (Manniche 1977.19–20), the fact that women bear the children makes them a more obvious fertility symbol.

It is not necessary to assume that phalli were always dedicated by men. At the Pamylia it was the women of the community who paraded the phallic statuettes (2.7.2). Comparisons might be made with the Greek fertility festival of Haloa, when women ate phallus-shaped loaves and sprinkled model phalli with water (Johns 1982.42, pl. 5); with the Roman practice of having a bride touch the phallus of a statue of Priapus; or with the presentation of phallic offerings by women to certain Christian saints with a reputation for curing barrenness (Hartland in Hastings 1917.818). In these examples the women are involved with a male supernatural being, but if Hathor embodied female sexuality, there seems no reason why female donors should not have presented phalli to symbolize the divine union which brought general fertility. Fertility rites as part of religion in daily life were probably mainly the preserve of women (3.2.3). Hathor is most closely linked with phallic symbolism in her role as the Hand of Atum, and the phallic offerings at Deir el-Bahri and Mirgissa seem to fit best into the context of this myth. It might be objected that sexual symbolism is inappropriate to the cow form of the goddess which dominates at Deir el-Bahri, but Hathor in cow form could be given the epithet of Lady of the Vulva (e.g. Petrie 1909 pl. 28.22; Vandier 1964.79–80, 117, fig. 12b). Satet was worshipped as the consort of the creator and fertility god Khnum, and has many aspects in common with Hathor, so the phallic pebbles from Aswan may also be linked to the celebration of a divine union.

The question remains of why the wooden phalli were the only small votive offerings found in the speos around the Hathor cow statue. The faience phalli excavated by Naville indicate that phallic offerings were made to Hathor in the 18th dynasty, but their numbers are very small. If phalli had always been the main offering in the Hathor shrine of Djeser-Akhet, one would expect a far greater quantity to have been recovered from the dumps of 18th dynasty votive material. Likewise, very few wooden phalli were found outside the speos, though this may be due to the poor chances of survival of wooden objects exposed to the weather. The ones inside the speos covered its floor and would have made it very difficult to approach or walk round the cult statue. It seems most probable that these phalli were presented during a particular festival and that they would normally have remained in the shrine for only a short time before being removed by priests to an outer area, or perhaps distributed to people to place in their homes as fertility charms.

The newly married, the childless, or simply any woman or couple seeking extra 'insurance' for their sex life, might have used such a festival to make appropriate offerings to the goddess who presided over conception and birth. The festival may have celebrated the creation myth of the union of Reᶜ-Atum with Hathor, the Hand of Atum, and have been similar to the festival of the presentation of the phallus to Hathor at Edfu. Alternatively, the presentation of phalli could have taken place in the context of the Beautiful Festival of the Wadi when Amon-Ra, who has an ithyphallic form, visited and 'slept with' Hathor in the temples at Deir el-Bahri (1.1.2). Couples, or women on behalf of couples, probably invoked a blessing on their sex lives by identifying with the divine couple. By the 20th dynasty or even earlier, it is possible that women or couples slept in or near the Djeser-Akhet

Hathor shrine on a festival night in the hope of a favourable dream from the goddess. The few wooden phalli outside the shrines might be the remains of earlier celebrations of such a festival. The scarcity of the 18th dynasty phalli could suggest that mass presentation was a Ramessid custom, but the pebbles from Aswan show that the tradition of offering phallic objects to a goddess was ancient. Mining expeditions to Gebel Zeit and Timna may have brought votive phalli with them, or gathered phallic pebbles in the desert, in order to celebrate a fertility festival for Hathor.

Due to the lack of inscribed material, the exact votive function of the phalli must remain uncertain, but two further points can be made. First, while Hornblower was probably right to assume that the phalli were made in temple workshops, it is unlikely that they were donated only by 'poor devotees' (1926.81). There is some evidence that the 20th dynasty visitors to the Hathor shrines were less well off than those of the 18th dynasty (3.1), but they still included minor officials, artisans, soldiers, and priests, who cannot be classified as poor. Since fertility figurines of the crudest types have been found in the houses and burials of artisans and officials (2.6.4), it is quite probable that wooden phalli were offered by people in these social groups. Second, in his discussion of Late Period and Graeco-Roman phallic objects from Saqqara, Derchain argues that these were a new development, and that at earlier periods sexual matters were expressed in religious art in a discreet symbolic code, decipherable only by the cultured elite (in Martin 1981.169). This may be true of funerary art, but the phallic offerings demonstrate that it was permissible to be sexually explicit in a religious context during the New Kingdom.

Summary

The floor of the sanctuary of the Hathor shrine of Djeser-Akhet at Deir el-Bahri was covered with wooden phalli. These probably date to the 20th dynasty. Small amounts of phallic material were found elsewhere at Deir el-Bahri and at Mirgissa, Timna, and Gebel Zeit. Some Old and New Kingdom comparative material can be cited, so that phallic objects are not a purely Graeco-Roman phenomenon.

In Egyptian religion, phallic symbolism is strongly associated with crop and animal fertility. Bes, who is linked with human fertility, appears in an ithyphallic form on a votive hanging from Deir el-Bahri. Displays of the sexual organs can be apotropaic, but this hanging could depict a fertility rite connected with Hathor. Women were involved in phallic rites to promote general fecundity, so the phallic offerings are not necessarily the gifts of men. The phalli in the shrine at Djeser-Akhet were probably presented during a specific festival, perhaps one celebrating the union of Hathor, the Hand of Atum, with the masculine creator deity. Their purpose might have been to ensure fertility by identifying the sexual life of the donor with that of the divine couple.

2.8 Ears and eyes

Offerings consisting of, or decorated with, ears and/or eyes were recovered from Deir el-Bahri, Faras, and Serabit el-Khadim. An extensive body of comparative material has to be discussed in order to clarify the function of these offerings.

2.8.1 Model ears

1 *Stone* (Pls. 8, 55a)

Naville found one intricately carved limestone ear at Deir el-Bahri (London BM 47527 = Pl. 55a, centre). This is 5 cm high, has a coating of white gesso, and is pierced through the lobe. There is no sign of its ever having been attached to anything. One ear excavated by Griffith at Faras appears to be made of limestone (Pls. 8.6, 55a, left = London BM 51257). It is 5.5 cm high and shows no traces of paint or of having been attached. Bruyère found three stone model ears at Deir el-Medina, one in a dump of 19th dynasty votive material (1930.68, fig. 20.9), and two in the court of a 19th dynasty funerary chapel (1952.61, fig. 120). The latter were painted blue. He suggested that they might once have been attached to a stela or lintel on either side of a relief of a deity (1952.61). Statuette-stelae with ears are known from other sites (*e.g.* Schulman 1981 pl. 1).

2 *Wood* (Pls. 1, 56c)

Naville excavated one wooden model ear at Deir el-Bahri (Hall in Naville 1913.16, 25). This is 13.7 cm high and is crudely carved in coarse wood (London BM 41077 = Pls. 1, bottom left, 56c). The ear hole is represented by a deep hole which appears to be drilled. There are no traces of paint and no signs that the ear was ever attached to anything. The Louvre has four comparable wooden ears of unknown provenance (Leca 1971.304, fig. 81; Vandier 1973.109).

3 *Faience and glazed steatite* (Pls. 2, 6, 8, 55a–b)

Hall stated that 'blue glaze' model ears were common at Deir el-Bahri (in Naville 1913.16), and at least 48 examples are mentioned in the EEF distribution lists. Carter also found 'blue glaze' ears; three are illustrated in one of his photographs (Pl. 6B). Hayes noted that 'many supplicants' presented ear or eye plaques at Deir el-Bahri and that these often consist 'simply of the ears themselves, moulded of faience' (1959.173–4). He did not say how many faience ears Winlock found at the site. Griffith discovered at least three faience ear models at Faras (1921.86; Pl. 8.3 = Oxford Ash. 1912.945, 4 = London BM 51256, 7 = location unknown) and Petrie recovered one damaged faience ear from the temple at Serabit el-Khadim (1906 pl. 155. = Oxford Ash. E 3357).

The 29 faience ears which I have been able to examine, or obtain detailed information on, range in height between 1.5 and 5.5 cm (Bristol H 3158; Brussels MR E 726; Edinburgh RSM 1904.134.10; Liverpool 13.10.1904.25; London BM 41070, 41071 = Pls. 2.2, 55b, right, 41072–4, 41075 = Pl. 55b, left, 41076, 51256–7 = Pl. 55a, right; Manchester 1461a–c, 4197; Manchester GS unnumbered; New York MMA 05.4.36, 38; Oxford Ash. E 2734–6, 3357, 1912.945; Oxford PR unnumbered, 2; Pittsburgh CM 2940.10; Toronto ROM 907.18.185–6). Some are left and some right ears, but I have not identified any that obviously form a pair. All appear to have been made in open moulds. The colour is usually bright blue, but one piece from Deir el-Bahri (Pittsburgh CM 2940.10) and the examples from Faras and Serabit el-Khadim are green. Some are quite elaborately modelled (*e.g.* Pl. 55a, right), but others consist of a flat ear shape with a few details marked in dark blue (*e.g.* Pl. 55b, right) or crudely incised (*e.g.* Pl. 55b, left). The three examples photographed by Carter (Pl. 6B) and 13 of the pieces listed above have one or two holes in the upper part, presumably for suspension on votive necklaces (2.9.2.1). One of the models is pierced through the lobe (London BM 41072), as are many of the ears shown on ear stelae (*e.g.* Figs. 14–5).

There is a small body of comparative material for the faience ears. The Cairo Museum has a few unprovenanced examples (Reisner 1958 nos. 12822–4), and the British Museum has an unprovenanced glass ear (Cooney 1976.18, no. 181), as well as a blue frit example, thought to come from el-ʿAmarna, which is attached to a base (1976.39, no. 344). A few faience ears were found in the vicinity of the Great Sphinx at Giza (Selim Hassan 1953.43–4, fig. 31; C. Zivie 1976.252), and two were recovered from a temple foundation deposit at el-Kab (Quibell 1898 pl. 21). An 18th dynasty 'Hathor stela' found in the mortuary temple of Thutmose IV at Thebes has two ear-shaped depressions, probably for the insertion of faience ears (Petrie 1897.4, pl. 1.3), so some of the flat ear models may have been made for inlaying in stelae.

The model ears from Giza can only be dated in relation to the ear stelae from this site, which range in date from Amonhotpe II to Ramesses II (Selim Hassan 1953.43–4; C. Zivie 1976.246–52). The examples from el-Kab definitely date to Amonhotpe II, while the piece from el-ʿAmarna obviously belongs in or near the Amarna Period. The ears from the foundation deposit at el-Kab are of a very simple, carelessly executed type and it may be that the more elaborate examples from Deir el-Bahri and Faras are earlier.

4 *Metal*

The British Museum has a roughly ear-shaped piece of sheet bronze from Deir el-Bahri (41066 = Naville 1913 pl. 24.4, second right). This is pierced at the top and crudely incised with an ear. Hayes stated that some of the votive ears found by Winlock at this site were 'cut out and beaten to shape from sections of sheet copper' (1959.174). These objects could be classed either as models or as plaques, comparable to the metal eye plaques from Deir el-Bahri (*e.g.* Pl. 55c–d).

2.8.2 Ear plaques and stelae

1 *Faience plaques* (Pl. 2)

It is difficult to draw a line between ear or eye plaques and ear or ear and eye stelae, but I classify the faience and metal pieces as plaques and the wood and stone pieces as stelae. The British Museum has a fragment, 3.9 × 3.1 cm, of a rectangular blue faience plaque (41079 = Pl. 2, top centre). On one face of this plaque a *wadjet* eye is marked in dark blue, and on the other are a *wadjet* eye and an ear above what is probably the striped podium of a Hathor mask. Faience ear plaques are rare, though Petrie published an unprovenanced example with five ears (1914 pl. 1.5). Another with eight ears, and bearing the cartouche of Thutmose III (?), was found in the vicinity of Medinet Habu (PM I, 2.778). Further comparative material is provided by faience eye plaques from Deir el-Bahri (*e.g.* Pl. 56d) and by stone ear and eye stelae, such as an unprovenanced example in the Strasbourg Museum which is carved with one ear above a pair of *wadjet* eyes (Strasbourg Cat. 1973 pl. 14).

2 *Wooden ear stelae* (Pl. 56a)

Naville found one wooden ear stela or plaque at Deir el-Bahri (Brussels MR E 2440 = Pl. 56a). It measures 5.4 × 9.5 cm and has two pairs of ears carved in low relief. There are no traces of paint. Winlock excavated a wooden ear stela or plaque only 3.7 × 5.4 cm high at Deir el-Bahri (New York MMA 23.3.167; Hayes 1959.174). This piece, which has a round top and is pierced horizontally, is carved with a pair of ears in low relief. Three wooden ear stelae were found in the sanctuary of Sekhmet at Abusir (List 1.29–31), and a fragmentary example was recovered from a house at Deir el-Medina (Bruyère 1939.204, fig. 94).

3 *Stone ear stelae* (Pl. 14a)

The EEF distribution lists for Deir el-Bahri mention a 'limestone fragment with three ears in relief', which probably formed part of an ear stela. A small sandstone stela from Serabit el-Khadim carved with two ears, two eyes, and donors adoring a Hathor mask (Pl. 14a) has already been described (2.1.3; 2.3.3.3).

I have been able to trace 86 published ear stelae from other sites. The details of these stelae are given in tabular form at the end of this chapter (Lists 1–4). The stelae may be divided into four main types:–

    1) Stelae with one or more ears (Fig. 14)
    2) Stelae with one or more ears and a deity or deities (Fig. 14)
    3) Stelae with one or more ears and a donor or donors (Fig. 14)
    4) Stelae with one or more ears and a deity/ies and donor/s (Figs. 14–5)

The stelae range in height from about 10 to 50 cm. The Type 1 ear stelae, particularly the uninscribed examples, tend to be the smallest. On four stelae all the ears are painted red (Lists 1.27, 29, 37; 4.18), while others have ears of several different colours, such as red and blue (List 1.33); red, green and blue (Bruyère 1939.204; List 3.5); red, black and blue (List 4.27), or blue, yellow and green (List 4.20). The number of ears shown ranges between one and 376, although the majority have from two to ten. On all four types of stela the ears are frequently arranged in pairs, but when single ears are shown they usually 'face' right.

Thirteen deities are represented or named on the stelae. About half the stelae are probably or certainly dedicated to Ptah. Only four name or depict Hathor (Lists 1.36; 2.7; 3.5; 4.28). On Types 2 and 4 a preference for the animal or semi-animal forms of deities is apparent. Two deified royal persons, Ramesses II and Ahmose-Nefertary, figure on the ear stelae (List 4.1–3, 21, 26). On two stelae, an unnamed king is shown ritually clubbing an enemy (Lists 2.10; 4.31). On stelae of Types 2 and 4, the most common position for the ears is immediately above or behind the deity. Type 3 is unusual among New Kingdom votive stelae in showing the donors but not the deity. The fact that the donors stand or kneel with arms raised in adoration (*e.g.* Fig. 14) implies the presence of a deity even though none is directly represented. On Type 4, the donors adore the deity or deities and make standard offerings to them. A few of the ear stelae were dedicated by important persons, such as the 19th dynasty vizier, Rahotep (List 4.1), but most of the donors named are minor priests and officials or artisans.

Nineteen stelae of Type 1 and six of Type 2 are uninscribed. Another 19 ear stelae are inscribed only with names and titles. On 16 stelae, the name and epithets of the deity are given and the donor is named in an *ir n* formula inscribed across the bottom. This formula occurs on other types of New Kingdom votive stela (*e.g.* Petrie 1909 pls. 14.33–4, 16.42; Tosi & Roccati 1972.33–4, 69), but it is not common on Hathor stelae (2.1.5). When the donors were priests or officials or their wives, the stelae were not literally 'made by' them. Preferable translations are 'made for' or 'done on behalf of', which would fit with the variant formula *ir n wḏꜣ n* 'done for the prosperity of' (List 1.20). These formulae probably refer to the setting up of a stela and the prayers and offerings which accompanied this act, as well as to the commissioning and making of the object itself. Thus, it might be best to translate *ir n* as 'dedicated by/on behalf of X'. The formula does not normally include any specific request, and perhaps it should always be understood as 'dedicated for the continuing prosperity of X'. *Ḥtp di nsw* formulae are found on only six of the stelae (Lists 1.19; 2.5; 3.4; 4.1, 9, 28). Some Type 4 ear stelae from Deir el-Medina have elaborate inscriptions incorporating hymns and penitential prayers (List 4.22–3, 25), but brief impersonal inscriptions are more characteristic of ear stelae.

Most of the ear stelae are from state temples. The fragmentary example from a house at Deir el-Medina (Bruyère 1939.204) suggests that they might also be set up in household shrines. Only two are thought to come from a funerary context (Lists 1.27; 2.3), and these may be from old tombs reused as shrines (Sadek 1987.24–5). The largest group of ear stelae comes from under the foundations of a part of the temple of Ptah at Memphis which dates to Ramesses II (Petrie 1909.7; Sadek 1987.19–20). Ear stelae seem to have been most popular from the mid to the late 18th dynasty, although they continued to be made until the end of the Late Period.

Further comparative material is provided by a few other types of private monument decorated with ears. Bruyère found fragments of two lintels at Deir el-Medina which have ears carved on either side of a relief of a deity (1952.36, 61). During the excavation of a small temple built by Ramesses II at Memphis, a rectangular crenellated stone basin and three small model towers, two in faience and one in limestone, were discovered (Anthes 1959 fig. 6; 1965.72, fig. 77, pl. 25). Each of these objects is thought to represent a temple enclosure wall (Jacquet 1958.161) and all are decorated with ears. The Petrie Collection has a similar 'ear tower' said to come from Haraga (Stewart 1983 no. 126, pl. 41).

2.8.3 The functions of the ear stelae and votive ears

There has been much more discussion of the ear stelae than of the ear models, but most scholars have assumed that their functions must be essentially the same. Wilkinson seems to have been the first to propose that the ear stelae were thank-offerings for the cure of ear diseases (1878.358). If it had been customary to present an image of an organ or part of the body that had been cured, one would expect to find numerous anatomical models in popular shrines. A wide range of such models was discovered in a cache near an Early Dynastic tomb (no. 3518) at Saqqara (Emery 1970.10–11, pl. 16.1), but these date to the Graeco-Roman Period and could be due to the influence of foreign customs.

Of New Kingdom sites, Deir el-Bahri has by far the widest range of anatomical models with ears, eyes, phalli, vulvae, and breasts, but these last three categories are explained by Hathor's association with conception and childbirth. No models of other parts of the body were found at sites such as Giza and Memphis that are rich in ear stelae, and none of the texts on the ear stelae refers to requests for healing of any kind. It might have been a breach of 'decorum' to mention physical sickness, or indeed any individual problem, in the formal context of a temple stela (3.3). However, some of the inscriptions on ear stelae specifically ask for standard life or funerary benefits, which argues against a narrowly medical interpretation.

Some scholars have raised the possibility that the ears embody a desire to hear in the afterlife, and particularly to be in the presence of and hear a deity (Devéria 1896.156; Bruyère 1925.87; Bonnet 1952.205). Requests for the restoration of the faculties of sight and hearing are frequent in funerary texts (Blok 1928.131), but this theory is based chiefly on the inscriptions of two ear and eye stelae from Deir el-Medina (List 4.24–5).

These inscriptions, which include requests to see but not to hear, are discussed in 2.8.6. Here it need only be stressed that this hypothesis depends on the ears shown being human. There are several reasons for thinking that they are not.

First, there is the large number of ears, up to 376 (List 3.4), shown on some of the stelae. It is difficult to see why people wishing to be, or having been, cured of deafness, should portray more than their own two ears. If the ears represent the faculty of hearing, this multiplication might be understandable. Egyptian deities could be thought of as having numerous ears and eyes; the Harris Magical Papyrus mentions a form of Khnum with 77 ears and 77 eyes (Lange 1927.59–60; Wagner & Quaegebeur 1973.56). There is also a parallel in the votive stelae showing multiple animal forms of a deity (2.1.3).

The appearance of the ears might be seen as an argument against their being divine, since ears of human shape are shown on stelae dedicated to deities such as

Thoth and Sekhmet who have no human-headed forms. However, the animal forms of deities were not necessarily taken literally; in offering scenes no attempt is made to suit the offerings to the limitations of an ibis's beak or the tastes of a lioness. If the ears are regarded as signifying a divine quality of hearing prayer, rather than as the ears of the specific deity shown, their standard human form becomes even more understandable. One indication that the ears are divine is their diverse colouring on some of the more elaborate stelae. Blue, green, and black are all colours that occur for the skin of gods, but which would be inappropriate for mortals (Yoyotte in Posener 1962.49–50).

The position and arrangement of the ears also provide useful clues. The marked preference for right ears may be explained by the fact that they face in the same direction as the ear visible on the deity (e.g. Figs. 14–15). On the single ear stelae on which a deity is depicted facing left, it is left ears that are shown. A stela from Memphis has a pair of ears inside the shrine of Ptah (List 4.6), a position in which it would surely be presumptuous to place the ears of a donor. In the case of the basin and model towers from Memphis (Anthes 1959 fig. 6, pl. 25), it would seem odd for the donor's ears to be shown on the enclosure wall of a temple, but natural for the ears to represent the god within listening to the prayers of visitors outside. One Memphite stela shows ears on plinths with a jar stand between them and a sun disc and uraei above them (Fig. 14). At the very least, these must be cult objects. The way in which the donors on Type 3 are shown in postures of adoration suggests that the ears on these stelae represented the person or particular quality of a deity.

On the ear stelae, the deities are named more often than the donors. A model ear from Giza is incribed in hieratic with the name of Horakhty, which probably identifies it as the ear of this god (Selim Hassan 1953.44, fig. 31.6). A link between the deities shown and the ears is provided by the divine epithet sḏm nḫt 'the one who hears prayer'. Schulman suggests that this epithet should be translated '(the pair of ears) who hears petitions' (1980.165; 1988.59, 79–80). The epithet occurs on eight of the ear stelae (Lists 1.16, 32–3, 36; 2.5; 4.10, 19, 24) and the similar epithet sḏm sprt 'the one who hears petitions' on two more (List 1.21, 4.1). On the offering basin from Memphis, Ptah is described as sḏm snmḫ 'hearing the supplicant', and the text of a stela from Thebes (List 2.11) contains the phrase 〔hieroglyphs〕 〔hieroglyphs〕 'I am calling you, Mut, Lady of Heaven, that [you] may hear my petitions.'

The epithet sḏm nḫt occurs as early as the 13th dynasty in relation to the deified official Heqaib (Labib Habachi 1985.78–9). Hathor, Nebet-Hetepet, Haroeris, Ptah, and Thoth are the deities given epithets relating to the hearing of prayers on the New Kingdom ear stelae. Amon-Reᶜ and Reshep also have such epithets in the texts of stelae without ears (Erman 1911 pl. 16; Tosi & Roccati 1972.104; Schulman 1980.166; 1988.113). Hathor, Amon, Horus, Thoth, and Reᶜ also occur in New Kingdom personal names composed with the element a god hears (Giveon 1982.39–40). The epithet sḏm nḫt was applied to the deified Ahmose-Nefertary (List 4.26) and to statues of Thutmose III (Otto 1952.27; Nims 1971.108), Thutmose IV (Davies 1923 pl. 21), Ramesses II (Yoyotte 1960.45; Labib Habachi 1969.34, 43),

Ramesses IV (Nims 1971.108), and Ptolemy VIII Euergertes II (Barguet 1962.233; Nims 1971.108).

This epithet is common in inscriptions in the Eastern Temple at Karnak (Barguet 1962.220–42). The oldest part of this temple contains a badly damaged naos which C. Nims identified with the monument referred to in a building inscription of Thutmose III in which the king stated that he had built a 'proper place of hearing' for Amon-Reʿ at Karnak (1969.70). A *waab*-priest and doorkeeper of Amon of the Hearing Ear, who must have been attached to this shrine, is known from a late 18th dynasty stela (Labib Habachi 1972.67–85). The Eastern Temple was partially rebuilt under Ramesses II, who was worshipped there as 'Ramesses Meryamon who hears prayers at the Upper Gateway of the Temple of Amon-Reʿ' (Nims 1971.108). A Ptah of the Hearing Ear is referred to in a Theban tomb (Holmberg 1946.74) and on a stela fragment from Deir el-Medina (Tosi & Roccati 1972.131). The inscriptions on the offering basin from Memphis state that prayers were made to Ptah at the enclosure wall of his temple (Jacquet 1958.161). All these references to the 'hearing ear' of deities support the hypothesis that the ears depicted on the stelae are divine. Schulman suggests that ear stelae always relate to a specific cult statue and that the epithets connected with the hearing of prayers are the names of such statues (1980.164–5; 1988.59–60). This hypothesis is consistent with the dominant role of statue cults on votive stelae in general (2.1.3), but it should probably be extended to include specific sacred animals.

A. Erman suggested that the ear stelae were set up in fulfilment of a vow by people who had had prayers, of any type, answered by a deity (1934.53). However, several of the stelae inscriptions specifically request future benefits. For example, the vizier Rahotep asks for 'life, prosperity, health, favour, skill, and love' (List 4.1), while the sculptor Ptahmose asks for permission for his *ka* to dwell in the temple of Ptah after his death (List 3.4). These texts suggest that ear stelae were dedicated in the hope or anticipation that prayers would be heard, rather than as thank-offerings.

Petrie wrote that:–

> One view is that they are the ears of the god, to receive the prayer; the other view is that the ears are put on to encourage hearing by sympathetic magic. Now it is difficult to see the use of a tablet with only an ear, and no figure or inscriptions ... for promoting a petition not recorded; but if regarded as the ear of the god, and prayed into, it might be thought to retain the prayer for the attention of the god. (1909.7)

Selim Hassan agreed with Petrie:–

> ... it is most probable that we should regard the ears as the actual substitutes for the ears of the god. Thus the devotee would make a pilgrimage to a sacred spot, dedicate an ear-tablet to the god of the same, and make his prayer or petition orally into the ear ... (1953.41)

One flaw in Petrie's argument is that the uninscribed Type 1 ear stelae can be paralleled by numerous uninscribed Type A votive stelae and plaques, on which only a deity is depicted. It is obvious from this that it was not considered necessary to show the donor, or to record the petition or even the donor's name. If the ears were 'actual substitutes' for those of the deity, they would seem superfluous on stelae of Types 2 and 4, which depict the deity complete with ears. Most visits to a temple probably included an oral prayer, and praying 'into' the ears on an ear stela might be natural enough, but the idea of donors posing in front of eye stelae for the deity to 'fix' an image of them seems rather less plausible. The existence of stelae with both ears and eyes makes it desirable that any explanation of the ear stelae should also fit the eye stelae.

The hypothesis that the ears were 'put on to encourage hearing by sympathetic magic' could easily be adapted to fit the eye stelae and plaques. H. Blok argued that:–

> Bref, les stèles dites à oreilles, comme les scarabées, les plaques apotropéiques et les autres menus objets de ce genre qui portent le même emblème, se rattachent à la croyance populaire et purement magique, qui s'efforce d'exercer une force coercitive sur la volonté divine ... (1928.135)

One might not expect votive objects to be associated with magic, but the ear stelae may be a case in which a rigid distinction between religion and magic is unhelpful. A desire to try all possible means to attain the granting of a prayer up to, and probably including, magical coercion, does not necessarily imply impiety (3.3). The large number of ears on some stelae could be seen as supporting Blok's view, since a belief in the value of repetition is often found in conjunction with sympathetic magic.

However, it would probably be wrong to lay too much stress on the magical aspect of the ear stelae. The addition of ears can hardly have been thought to be an infallible method, because otherwise all votive stelae would have them. The donors probably held a variety of views on the way in which the ears would help them. Some may have hoped that the ears on their stela would at least compel the deity to hear them, but it seems unlikely that the vizier Rahotep would have thought of himself as forcing the statue of his deified royal master to answer his prayers by setting up an ear stela. In his case, the ears might be seen as illustrating the epithet 'the one who listens to prayers' and, as Bonnet suggested (1952.205), be an expression of trust in divine attention or mercy. It therefore seems safest to describe the ears as encouraging, rather than compelling, the deity to hear a prayer. Ear stelae form only a small proportion of New Kingdom votive stelae. It is probable that they were mainly dedicated in shrines founded or run as places where the ordinary Egyptian could come to pray (see 3.3). In this case, the ears on the stelae and plaques and the model ears might be seen as embodying and invoking a divine quality particular to the manifestation of the deity worshipped at the shrine where they were offered.

2.8.4 Model eyes

1 *'Simple' eyes* (Pls. 2, 6, 55b)

Hall stated that the eye 'in its simple form' was a common votive offering at Deir el-Bahri (in Naville 1913.16). The EEF distribution lists mention 30 'blue glaze' eyes from these excavations, but this is only a minimum figure. For example, the

Royal Ontario Museum is listed as receiving two eye models but in fact has seven, and there are likely to have been some faience models among the 17 'eyes and eye plaques' sent to American university museums. Carter also found 'blue glaze' eyes at Deir el-Bahri and a single example appears in one of his photographs (Pl. 6.1). Winlock excavated eye plaques at Deir el-Bahri, but apparently no model eyes. Griffith did not include model eyes in his brief list of finds from the Hathor temple at Faras, but the Pitt-Rivers Museum has two examples from his excavations there.

The 27 examples which I have been able to examine, or obtain detailed information on, vary in width between 1.2 and 4.4 cm (Bolton 48.04.18; Bristol H 3157; Brussels MR 720, 2472; Edinburgh RSM 1904.134.9; London BM 41067, 41068 = Pl.55b, centre, 41069–70; Manchester UM 1456a–c; Oxford Ash. E 2737–9; PR unnumbered, 6; Toronto ROM 907.18.179, 180–2, 184, 840). One specimen from Deir el-Bahri is in glazed steatite, but the rest are faience. The eyes are all almond-shaped. The iris and the rim of the eye are usually marked in dark blue or purple-black on a light background (Pls. 2, 6), occasionally on both faces (*e.g.* London BM 41070; Oxford Ash. E 2739). Sometimes both the iris and the pupil are indicated (*e.g.* Pl. 55b). The details of the eye can also be incised (*e.g.* Brussels MR E 720; Oxford Ash. E 2738; Toronto ROM 907.179, 840), or modelled in low relief (*e.g.* Pl. 55b; Oxford Ash. E 2738). Sixteen of the models listed above are pierced in one corner; one example (Manchester UM 14564) retains part of the leather cord on which it was threaded (see 2.9.2.1).

Simple model eyes of this kind are rare. Petrie published some unprovenanced examples in green faience, which he assigned to the 22nd dynasty (1914 pl. 1a–b). The only provenanced comparative material that I can trace is a faience eye found, along with faience ears, in a foundation deposit of Amonhotpe II at el-Kab (Quibell 1898 pl. 21). This suggests a mid 18th dynasty date for some or all of the model eyes, although it must be borne in mind that eyes appear on a few Ramessid ear stelae (List 4.23–5).

2 *Wadjet* eyes (Fig. 4; Pls. 2, 8, 55b)

The EEF distribution lists do not usually distinguish between ordinary and 'sacred' eyes, but Naville found a few unusual *wadjet* eyes at Deir el-Bahri. One consists of a thick, flat eye shape in light blue faience, 5 cm wide, with a *wadjet* eye drawn in dark blue on both sides (London BM 41081 = Pls. 2, centre right, 55b, top). The British Museum also has an oval piece of faience, 2.3 cm wide, with a *wadjet* eye in low relief on one side (41082) and fragments from two *wadjet* eyes, one in blue and one in violet faience, which would have been about 3 cm long when intact (43183, 43206). Hall illustrated an intact example of this kind of *wadjet* eye (Pl. 2, top left, location unknown). A model similar to London BM 43183 and 43206 was recovered from the foundation deposit of Amonhotpe II at el-Kab (Quibell 1898 pl. 21). Small *wadjet* eyes of this type continued to be made in the 19th dynasty (*e.g.* Herrmann 1990.33–7). They are quite different from the large, flat, openwork *wadjet* eyes used as funerary amulets (Petrie 1914 pls. 24–5). The *wadjet* eye motif also occurs on the back of panther-head amulets from Deir el-Bahri (Fig. 2, top left; 2.5.3).

A few faience *wadjet* eye beads, 1–1.5 cm in width, and pierced longitud-inally, were found at Deir el-Bahri (*e.g.* Ilkley CC 7010; London BM 41700, 41711, 42169–70). Hall illustrated an example strung with scarabs on its original leather cord (Pl. 2, top centre = London BM 41134; see 2.9.2.1). *Wadjet* eye scaraboids, made in faience or glazed steatite and pierced for suspension, were excavated at Deir el-Bahri (*e.g.* Bolton 48.04.4; Boston MFA 06.2499; Liverpool 13.10.1904.31a–b); Faras (*e.g.* Oxford Ash. 1912.961a–b = Pl. 8.26, 28; PR unnumbered, 9), and Serabit el-Khadim (London UC unnumbered, 10). One example from Deir el-Bahri bears the prenomen of Thutmose III (Fig. 4, third row, location unknown) and another from Faras the nomen of an Amonhotpe, probably Amonhotpe I (Griffith 1921 pl. 18.23). Faience *wadjet* eye rings were recovered from Mirgissa (Karlin in Vercoutter 1970.345), Serabit el-Khadim (London UC 35466a–k, 35467a–b), and Gebel Zeit (Castel *et al.* 1984.50–1 fig. 5; Castel & Soukiassian 1985.286). All these objects belong to common types of New Kingdom jewellery. Horus was one of the deities of Gebel Zeit, so eye objects found there could relate to him, but nearly all the small votive offerings from this site do seem to be dedicated to Hathor rather than to her co-templar deities.

2.8.5 Eye plaques and stelae

1 *Faience and glazed steatite* (Pls. 2, 56d)

Naville found several faience eye plaques at Deir el-Bahri. A rectangular blue faience fragment, now 1.5 × 2 cm, has a 'simple' eye incised and marked in purple-black on both sides (Toronto ROM 907.18.183). This probably once showed a pair of eyes. The Pitt-Rivers Museum has a fragment, now 3.5 × 4 cm, from a rounded faience plaque in light blue faience (Pl. 56d = Oxford PR 1906.45.5). It has three pairs of eyes with eyebrows, marked in dark blue on each side. The British Museum has fragments of three similar faience plaques decorated with *wadjet* eyes. The largest of these is 10 × 11.6 cm and has three *wadjet* eyes carelessly incised on one face (41027 = Naville 1913 pl. 27.2, right). The second fragment is from a rounded plaque with a linear border and a pair of *wadjet* eyes on one face. The third fragment is similar, but only one *wadjet* eye remains (41080 = Naville 1913 pl. 27.2, left). The EEF distribution lists also mention two glazed steatite plaques incised with *wadjet* eyes, one of which is probably New York MMA 05.4.92. Winlock apparently found one faience and one glazed steatite eye plaque at Deir el-Bahri, but the type of eye is not specified (Hayes 1959.173). I know of no exact parallels for these pieces, but the Cairo Museum has an unprovenanced faience plaque with a cow incised on one face and a *wadjet* eye on the other (Reisner 1907 no. 12236, pl. 19). The ear plaques and stelae provide comparative material.

2 *Metal* (Pl. 55c–d, Fig. 2)

Eight metal eye plaques are mentioned in the EEF distribution lists for Deir el-Bahri, but I have been able to trace 11 (London BM 41064–5 = Naville 1913 pl. 24.4, 41713 = 1913 pl. 24.4, 43213, 48406; Manchester 1462; Oxford Ash. E 2732–3; PR 1904.35.104 = Pl. 55c, 1906.45.3–5 = Pl. 55d), six of which are not in the list. Winlock found 20 metal plaques incised with 'one or two eyes' at Deir el-Bahri (Hayes 1959.173). These have not been published in detail. The plaques which I have examined vary in width between about 3 and 5 cm. Their metal has variously been described as bronze (Hall in Naville 1913.16, 25) and copper (Hayes 1959.173). Most have the appearance of bronze. The plaques may be rectangular or roughly follow the shape of a pair of eyes. An example drawn by Miss Carhew consists of two simple eyes joined together (Fig. 2, centre). Four of the plaques are in repoussé work (*e.g.* Pl. 55d, bottom), while on the remainder the eyes are incised. With both techniques, the design is on one face only. All the plaques are pierced with one or more holes for suspension.

One of the plaques is decorated with a single 'simple' eye (Naville 1913 pl. 24.4, left) and four have pairs of such eyes, with eyebrows (Pl. 55d, bottom; 1913 pl. 24.4, next left; Manchester 1462). On BM 43213, the eyes look like the hieroglyph 𓁹. Hall commented that a 'common device' on the metal plaques was '𓁹 𓂀, often with the sign 𓊽 between' (in Naville 1913.16). Four of the plaques have, or had when complete, a pair of *wadjet* eyes (Pl. 55c; London BM 48406; Oxford Ash. E 2732–3), and one has what could either be a *nfr* or a nose between the *wadjet* eyes (1913 pl. 24.4, lower).

The Ashmolean Museum has six metal eye plaques, bought by G. J. Chester in the Asasif and the Theban area during 1886–7, which are likely to have come from Deir el-Bahri (1886.874, 876, 952–3, 1887.2592–3; see also 2.4.2.1). Two of these are decorated with 'simple' eyes (1886.874, 952); each of the others has a pair of *wadjet* eyes. There is one unprovenanced metal plaque with a 'simple' eye in the same museum (1927.1290), while the Cairo Museum has several unprovenanced examples incised with *wadjet* eyes (Reisner 1907 pl. 14). The absence of examples from other sites suggests that this might have been a type of offering peculiar to Deir el-Bahri.

3 *Wood* (Pl. 56b)

A pair of *wadjet* eyes is a common motif in the lunettes of early New Kingdom stelae, but I know of only one stela whose entire decoration consists of *wadjet* eyes. This was found by Naville at Deir el-Bahri and is now in the Pitt-Rivers Museum (unnumbered = Pl. 56b). It is made of acacia and measures 11.5 × 7.2 cm. The stela has a red linear border and four pairs of *wadjet* eyes painted in black and white directly onto the wood. There is no inscription. The wooden Type 1 ear stelae provide the closest parallel to this stela (2.8.2.2).

2.8.6 The functions of the eye stelae, plaques, and model eyes

There appear to be no stone eye stelae, but there are three Ramessid stelae from Deir el-Medina which show ears and 'simple' eyes (List 4.23–5), as well as the small ear and eye stela from Serabit el-Khadim (Pl. 14a) and one unprovenanced stela with an ear and a pair of *wadjet* eyes (List 1.38). The stelae from Deir el-Medina have been much discussed. Hypotheses about the meaning of votive eyes tend to be based on the evidence of their texts.

Wilkinson suggested that the votive eyes were dedicated to deities by people who had been cured of blindness (1878.358). Most of the arguments against the votive ears' having been dedicated by people cured of deafness (2.8.3) apply to this hypothesis too. However, Hathor can be linked with the cure of blindness, for in the myth of the 'Contendings of Horus and Seth' she restores the sight of Horus with milk (Ratié 1986.179). Moreover, while there is no textual evidence for ear stelae being associated with cures for deafness, the case of the ear and eye stelae is rather different. Two of the ear and eye stelae are inscribed with penitential prayers which include the words 'He has caused me to see darkness by day' (List 4.23, 25). This phrase, which also occurs in a prayer to Amon on an 18th dynasty Theban ostracon (Posener 1975.200–1, pl. 20), on a Ramessid ear stela from Deir el-Medina (List 4.22), and on a few Ramessid stelae from the same site which have no ears (*e.g.* Tosi & Roccati 1972.81, 85), has been interpreted as referring to actual blindness (Gunn 1916.88–9; de Meulenaere 1948.256–7; Janssen 1980.136) or as nystagmus, blurred vision (Miller 1991.19–21), inflicted as a divine punishment. This would appear to support Wilkinson's hypothesis, but the phrase has also been interpreted as alluding to spiritual blindness, a sense of being cut off from a god by sin (*e.g.* Assmann 1969.236; Brunner 1975.830–1; Manniche 1978.17). When this phrase occurs in a tomb inscription relating to Tutankhamon and the Viceroy Huy (de Meulenaere 1948.256), it seems most likely to be a metaphor for the misery caused by royal displeasure.

When sight is requested in penitential prayers, it is specifically in terms of seeing a deity, in phrases such as $\mathbb{N}\mathbb{N}\mathbb{N}\mathbb{N}\mathbb{N}\mathbb{N}\mathbb{N}$ 'Make illumination for me that I may see you' (Tosi & Roccati 1972.81, 85–6; Assmann 1975.361, no. 157, see also nos. 160, 166, 168). This could support the view that it is spiritual rather than physical blindness which is referred to in these texts. On one of the ear and eye stelae, the donor asks that his eyes 'may see Amon every day' (List 4.25). Thus the eyes on this stela might be taken as those of the donor, although similar requests occur on other stelae without eyes (*e.g.* Erman 1911.1089, pl. 16; Tosi & Roccati 1972.91) and in prayers written on ostraca (Posener 1975.202, 206). It is not clear whether such requests refer to seeing visions of the deity, perhaps as a mark of divine forgiveness, or to being in the presence of the deity in the afterlife. On another ear and eye stela, the donor praises Haroeris 'that he may give to me eyes to see the way to go' (List 4.24 = Fig. 15b). Bonnet used this stela to argue that:–

... wenn auf Stelen dieser Art neben den Ohren zuweilen auch Augen dargestellt sind, so werden diese gewiss nichts anders sein als ein magisches Unterpfand für die Augen, die der Stifter in dem danebenstehenden Gebet für seinen Wandel in Jenseits erbittet. (1952.205)

The restoration of the deceased's senses was an important part of funerary rites, and prayers inscribed in New Kingdom tombs sometimes explicitly refer to the restoration of sight and hearing (*e.g. Urk.*IV,901). Bruyère used such texts to support the hypothesis that the eyes and ears were symbolic of the donor's desire or hope of seeing and hearing in the afterlife (1925.87–8). However, it seems clear that the ears on ear stelae are divine rather than human. A case can be made out for the eyes on these stelae being divine too.

Hall suggested that the votive ears and eyes from Deir el-Bahri might be 'pictorial supplications to the deity to hear petitions and watch over the safety of the devotee' (in Naville 1913.16). Hayes proposed that the eye and ear plaques found by Winlock were dedicated by temple visitors to 'assure their being seen and heard by the great tutelary goddess' (1959.173). If so, the eyes must be those of the deity to whom they are dedicated, or must symbolize a particular quality of that deity or of her or his cult statues.

As with the ears, the number of eyes – four on three of the stelae (*e.g.* Fig. 15b) and at least six on a faience plaque (Pl. 56d) – suggests that they may be divine rather than human. The position of the eyes is of some help. On two of the stelae, right ears and eyes are arranged in a column behind the deity (List 4.23–24), which supports the hypothesis that they are divine. The Serabit el-Khadim stela has a pair of eyes above the Hathor mask, a left eye and ear to her left side and a right eye and ear to her right (Pl. 14a). Since the goddess is shown frontally, this arrangement is consistent with the eyes belonging to her. On another stela (List 4.25), four right ears are shown above the shrine of Ptah and two left eyes above a table of offerings on the donor's side. This could be seen as supporting the hypothesis that the eyes are human, but they are not close to the donor and their position may be dictated by the decision to fit in a ⊔, which probably represents the 'perfect *ka*' of Ptah, referred to on ear stelae from Memphis (Lists 1.19, 22; 4.12) and Deir el-Medina (List 4.27).

As far as appearance goes, the 'simple' eyes on the stela could belong either to humans or to deities in human form. However, it is noteworthy that among the votive objects at Deir el-Bahri 'simple' and *wadjet* eyes seem to be used interchangeably. Both appear as models (*e.g.* Pl. 55b) and on metal and faience plaques (*e.g.* Pl. 55c). A wooden stela with four pairs of *wadjet* eyes provides a parallel for the Type 1 ear stelae (Pl. 56b). The faience plaque from Deir el-Bahri (Pl. 2, top, centre) and an unprovenanced stela now in Strasbourg (List 1.38) show that ears could be combined with *wadjet* eyes, as well as with 'simple' eyes. The *wadjet* eye is a very common amulet (Bonnet 1952.280), and the *wadjet* eye beads, scaraboids and rings found at the five sites could be regarded as commonplace amuletic objects with no particular association with Hathor. However, the *wadjet* eye plaques and stela and the more elaborate models clearly do not fall into this category. Such eyes might be used in an abstract way to convey the power of sight in the afterlife, but they would surely never represent the eyes of a living donor. It is most likely that the *wadjet* eyes on the votive objects are divine. Hathor in cow form often has *wadjet* eyes (*e.g.* Pls. 20, 25a, 55a–b). In the Graeco-Roman Period at least, her epithet 'Eye of the Sun' can be written either with a ⬙ or a 𓂀 (Junker 1911.19–23).

Given that 'simple' and *wadjet* eyes are used interchangeably in a votive context, it should follow that the 'simple' eyes are also divine. There is some textual evidence for this. On one ear and eye stela, the deity is addressed as 'the one who hears prayers' (Fig. 15b), and on another the deity is exhorted to hear the donor (List 4.23). There is an analogous passage in the text of a third ear and eye stela which may be translated as 'Be merciful to me, behold me, that you may be merciful' (List 4.25). This suggests that the eyes are those of the deity who is to look mercifully upon the donor. The presence of the eyes cannot therefore be used to settle the argument over whether the donors are suffering from spiritual or physical blindness.

In view of the legal metaphors used in some New Kingdom prayers (Fecht 1965.39–41), the eyes might be there to encourage the deity to read as well as hear the donor's petition. Alternatively, a prayer to a deity to look at a donor may always have had the extended meaning of 'look favourably upon', as implied in the sentence quoted above. Hall could also have been right in proposing that the eyes were to encourage the deity to watch over, in the sense of protect, the donor. This last hypothesis is particularly appropriate to Hathor in her protective, all-seeing Solar Eye aspect (see 2.5.5). *Wadjet* eye rings may have been placed in the enclosure wall at Gebel Zeit (1.6.3) in order to put the whole shrine under the guardianship of the Solar Eye, who defeated the enemies of the Sun God and the king and, by extension, of all Egyptians. The model ears and eyes and the ear or eye plaques and stelae seem to have been the product of an increasing desire for, or confidence in, individual contact with deities. Such personal piety is usually ascribed to the Ramessid Period, but these 18th dynasty offerings suggest an earlier date for the phenomenon.

Summary

Model ears were found at Deir el-Bahri, Faras, and Serabit el-Khadim. Ear stelae and plaques were recovered from Deir el-Bahri and Serabit el-Khadim. New Kingdom ear stelae dedicated to other deities have been found at a variety of sites and were particularly common at Memphis and Giza. Such stelae usually come from popular shrines within state-run temples. Stelae showing both ears and eyes are much rarer, while eye stelae and plaques are virtually exclusive to Deir el-Bahri. Model eyes were found at Deir el-Bahri and Faras, but very little comparative material can be cited. Model *wadjet* eyes are much more widespread.

The ears and the eyes do not represent those of sick people. The ears shown on ear stelae are those of the deities (as manifested in statues or sacred animals) shown or named on the stelae. Ordinary eyes and *wadjet* eyes are used interchangeably on the stelae and plaques; both should be interpreted as divine. The texts on the ear stelae are similar to those found on other votive stelae and contain the same generalized prayers. The multiple ears shown on many of the stelae are probably a form of sympathetic magic, but the main purpose of these stelae was to encourage or beseech the deity to listen to the donors' prayers. Model ears will have served the same purpose. The function of the eye stelae and model eyes was to encourage the deity to read the petition of the donor, or to look favourably or protectively upon them. The eye may be prominent in the votive offerings to Hathor in part because of her role as the protective Solar Eye.

2.8.7 Lists of Ear Stelae

In these lists the ear stelae are divided into four main types (see 2.8.2.3).

For reasons of space, only one reference is given for each stela. I have included only New Kingdom ear stelae of which I could obtain full details. A number of ear stelae were excavated at Memphis by the University of Pennsylvania Expedition but most of these have never been individually published (Schulman 1963). For further unpublished ear stelae see Schulman 1988.109–13.

Type 1: Stelae with one or more ears

	Number of ears	Deity named	Donors named	Type of text	Date	Provenance
1)	2	-	-	-	18 D	Near Sphinx, Giza
2)	2	-	-	-	18 D	"
3)	1	Horakhty	1 man	Divine name & *ir n* formula	19 D	"
4)	2	Horakhty	-	Divine name	18 D	"
5)	2	Horakhty	-	Divine name & *ir n* formula	18 D	"
6)	1	-	-	-	18 D	West hall, temple of Ptah Memphis
7)	1	-	-	-	18 D	"
8)	1	-	-	-	18 D	"
9)	2	-	-	-	18 D	"
10)	18+	-	-	-	18 D	"
11)	10	-	-	-	18 D	"
12)	13	-	-	-	18 D	"
13)	2	-	-	-	18 D	"
14)	1	Ptah	-	Divine name & epithets	18 D	"
15)	72+	Ptah	-	Praises of deity	18 D	"
16)	2	Ptah	1 man	Divine name & epithets, *ir n* formula	18 D	"
17)	4	Ptah	-	Divine name & epithets	18 D	"
18)	5	Ptah	-	Divine name	18 D	"
19)	6	Ptah	1 man	Praises of deity and *ḥtp di nsw* formula	18 D	"
20)	6+	Ptah?	1 woman	*ir n wdꜣ* formula	18 D	"
21)	8	Ptah	1 man	Divine name & epithets, *ir n* formula	18 D	"
22)	42	Ptah	1 man	Praises of deity, *ir n* formula	18 D	"
23)	1	-	-	-	18 D	South of Ptah temple, Memphis
24)	2	-	-	-	18 D	Memphis
25)	2	-	-	-	18 D	"
26)	6	-	-	-	18 D	"
27)	4	-	-	-	18 D	Saqqara
28)	12+	-	-	-	18 D	Sekhmet shrine, Abusir

29)	2	-	-	-	18 D	"
30)	6	Sekhmet	1 man	Divine name & epithets, *ir n* formula	18 D	"
31)	4	Sekhmet	1 man	Divine name & epithets, *ir n* formula	18 D	"
32)	4	Nebet-Hetepet	1 man	Divine name & epithets, *ir n* formula	19 D	Deir el-Medina
33)	6 +	-	1 man	Divine epithets, *ir n* formula	19 D	Temple, Deir el-Medina
34)	2	Amon-Reᶜ	1 man	Divine name & epithets, *ir n* formula	19 D	Thebes
35)	2	Amon-Reᶜ	1 man	Divine name & epithets, name of donor	18 D	"
36)	6	Hathor	1 man	Divine name & epithets, *ir n* formula	18 D	"
37)	2	Isis	1 man	Divine name & epithets, *ir n* formula	18 D?	-
38)	1 & 2 eyes	-	-	-	18 D?	-
39)	1	-	-	-	NK	Heliopolis

References

1) Selim Hassan 1953.41–4, fig. 31.11
2) Selim Hassan 1953.41–4,
3) Selim Hassan 1953.10, figs. 6,30
4) Selim Hassan 1953.43, fig. 31.8
5) Selim Hassan 1953.42, fig. 30.1
6) Petrie 1909.7, pl. 10.5
7) Petrie 1909.7, pl. 10.6
8) Petrie 1909.7, pl. 10.8
9) Petrie 1909.7, pl. 10.7
10) Petrie 1909.7, pl. 13.26
11) Petrie 1909.7, pl. 13.27
12) Petrie 1909.7, pl. 10.28
13) Petrie 1909.7, pl. 10.11
14) Petrie 1909.7, pl. 10.9
15) Petrie 1909.7, pl. 9.48
16) Petrie 1909.7, pl. 10.10
17) Petrie 1909.7, pl. 11.17
18) Petrie 1909.7, pl. 11.18
19) Petrie 1909.7, pl. 12.23
20) Petrie 1909.7, pl. 12.24
21) Petrie 1909.7, pl. 12.25
22) Petrie 1909.7, pl. 13.30 fig. 31.12
23) Petrie in Engelbach 1915.33, pl. 55
24) Stewart 1976.38
25) Stewart 1976.38
26) Bruyère 1925.85
27) Unpublished: Oxford Ash. 1892.1923
28) Borchardt 1910.128, fig. 174
29) Borchardt 1910.128, fig. 174
30) Borchardt 1910.128, fig. 174
31) Borchardt 1910.128, fig. 174
32) Tosi & Roccati 1972.59,270
33) Bruyère 1953.43, fig. 53
34) Erman 1934.145, fig. 53
35) Devéria 1896.156
36) Černý 1958 no. 16
37) Unpublished: Birmingham CM W 72
38) Strasbourg Catalogue 1973.54, pl. 14
39) Abdel-Aziz Saleh 1983.69, pl. 63b.

Type 2: Stelae with one or more ears and a representation of a deity or deities

	Number of ears	Deity named	Donors named	Type of text	Date	Provenance
1)	2	Sphinx	-	-	19 D	Near the Sphinx, Giza
2)	1	2 hawks	-	-	19 D	"
3)	1	Sphinx	-	-	18 D	Giza
4)	2	Sphinx	-	*ir n* formula	18 D	Giza area
5)	2	Ptah	1 man	Divine name & epithets, *ḥtp di nsw*	18 D	West Hall, Temple of Ptah, Memphis
6)	6	Ptah	1 man	Divine name & epithets, donor's name	18 D	"
7)	2	Hathor, cow & human	-	Divine name & epithets	19 D	Temple of Merenptah, Memphis
8)	2	Ptah	-	-	19 D	Memphis
9)	1	Hawk	-	-	19 D	"
10)	4	Ptah & king	-	-	18 D	"
11)	2	Mut	1 man	Invocation & praises of deity	18 D	Thebes?

References

1) Selim Hassan 1953.43, fig. 31.9
2) Selim Hassan 1953.43, fig. 31.4
3) Holden in Simpson 1982.416
4) Kamal 1910.117
5) Petrie 1909.7, pl. 11.15
6) Petrie 1909.7, pl. 12.22
7) Petrie 1909.12, pl. 28.21
8) Blok 1928.125, pl. 8.2
9) Schulman 1964.275
10) Petrie 1909 pl. 8.2
11) Hodjash & Berlev 1982.112–4, no. 56

Type 3: Stelae with one or more ears and a representation of the donor(s)

	Number of ears	Deity named	Donors named	Type of text	Date	Provenance
1)	2	Ptah	1 man	Divine name & epithets, *ir n* formula	18 D	West Hall, Temple of Ptah, Memphis
2)	3	Ptah	1 man	Divine name & epithets	18 D	"
3)	4	Ptah	2 men	Divine name & epithets, donors' names	18 D	"
4)	376	Ptah	1 man	Long *ḥtp di nsw* formula, praises of deity	18 D	"
5)	7+	Hathor	1 man	Divine name & epithets, *ir n* formula	19 D	Deir el-Medina

References

1) Petrie 1909.7, pl. 10.12
2) Petrie 1909.7, pl. 11.16
3) Petrie 1909.7, pl. 12.21

4) Petrie 1909.7, pl. 9.49
5) Bruyère 1925.83–4, pl. 2.2

Type 4: Stelae with one or more ears and representations of deity and donor(s)

	Number of ears	Deity named	Donors named	Type of text	Date	Provenance
1)	4	Statue of Ramesses II	2 men	Divine name & epithets, donors' names & titles, *ḥtp dì nsw* formula	19 D	Qantir
2)	6	Amon-Reʿ Ptah, statue of Ramesses II	2 men, 3 women	Divine names & epithets, donors' names	19 D	"
3)	2	Statue of Ramesses II	1 man, woman & child	Illegible	19 D	"
4)	31	Horakhty	1 man	Divine name & epithets, *ir n formula*	18 D	Near Sphinx at Giza
5)	2	Sphinx	1 man	*ir n* formula	18 D	Giza
6)	2	Ptah	1 man	Illegible	18 D	West Hall, Ptah temple, Memphis
7)	2	Ptah	1 man	Divine name & epithets	18 D	"
8)	6 +	Ptah	1 man	Divine epithets, donor's name	18 D	"
9)	5 +	Ptah, Sekhmet	1 man, 1 woman	Praise of deities, *ḥtp dì nsw* formula	18 D	"
10)	44 +	Ptah?	1 man	Illegible	18 D	"
11)	10	Ptah	1 man	Donor's name & titles	18 D	South of Ptah temple, Memphis
12)	6 +	Ptah	1 man	Divine name & epithet	18 D	Memphis
13)	2	Ptah	2 men	Donors' names	19 D	Memphis
14)	2	Ptah	1 man	Donor's name & title	18 D	Memphis?
15)	7	Ptah	1 man	Praise of deity	20 D	Memphis
16)	1	Sekhmet	1 man	Divine name & epithet	18 D	Sekhmet shrine, Abusir
17)	3	Thoth?	1 man	Illegible	18 D	Hermopolis
18)	6 +	Osiris? in bark	6 men	Donors' names	19 D	Abydos
19)	3 +	Thoth (baboon)	1 man, 1 boy	Divine name & praises of deity	19 D	Deir el-Medina
20)	6	Amon-Re' (2 rams)	1 man	Divine name & epithets, *ir n* formula	19 D	"
21)	2	Ahmose-Nefertary	1 man, boy, girl	Divine name & epithets, names of donors	19 D	"

22)	4	Sopdu	1 man, 2 women 1 child	Divine name & epithets, penitential prayer	19 D	"
23)	4 + 4 eyes	Khonsu	1 man,	Divine name & epithets, penitential prayer	19 D	"
24)	2 + 4 eyes	Haroeris	1 man	Divine name & epithets, praise of deity	19 D	Deir el-Medina?
25)	4 + 2 eyes	Ptah	1 man	Divine name & epithets, penitential prayers	19 D	"
26)	4	Ahmose-Nefertary	2 men, 1 woman	Divine names & epithets, names of donors	19 D	"
27)	7	Ptah	1 man	Divine name & epithets, hymn to *ka* of deity	19 D	"
28)	2	Hathor (cow)	1 woman	Divine name & epithets, donor's name, *ḥtp di nsw* for donor's husband	18 D	Mortuary temple of Thutmose IV, Thebes
29)	2	Sphinx	1 man	*ir n* formula	19 D	Thebes
30)	2	Amon-Reᶜ (ithy-phallic)	1 man	Divine name & epithets	18 D	Thebes
31)	2 +	Ptah & king	1 man	Donor's name	20 D	Memphis?

References

1) Labib Habachi 1969.34, fig. 21
2) Labib Habachi 1954.536, pl. 34
3) Labib Habachi 1954.534, pl. 32
4) Selim Hassan 1953.44, fig. 31.5
5) C. Zivie 1976.246–7
6) Petrie 1909.7, pl. 10.13
7) Petrie 1909.7, pl. 10.14
8) Petrie 1909.7, pl. 11.19
9) Petrie 1909.7, pl. 11.20
10) Petrie 1909.7, pl. 13.29
11) Petrie in Engelbach 1915.33, pl. 55
12) Blok 1928 pl. 9.2
13) Blok 1928 pl. 8.1
14) Budge 1909.304–5
15) Bruyère 1925.85
16) Borchardt 1910.128, fig. 173

17) Roeder 1959.302, pl. 70
18) Stewart 1976.40, pl. 31.2
19) Bruyère 1952b.79, fig. 159
20) Bruyère 1925.82–3, pl. 2.1
21) Tosi & Roccati 1972.71, 275
22) Tosi & Roccati 1972.86, 282
23) Tosi & Roccati 1972.87, 283
24) *HT* 1914.12, pl. 43
25) *HT* 1970.36, pl. 31
26) Leca 1971.304, fig. 81
27) *HT* 1982.31–2, pl. 73
28) Petrie 1897.4, pl. 1.3
29) Hayes 11959.384
30) *HT* 1914.12, pl. 43
31) Schulman 1988.26–7, fig. 11

2.9 Jewellery

Jewellery formed a substantial proportion of the votive offerings at each of the six sites.

2.9.1 Beads

In this book it is not possible to do more than indicate the range of beads found at each site. The types referred to below are all illustrated in Fig. 16.

1 *Deir el-Bahri* (Fig. 4; Pls. 2, 6, 57)

Hall noted that at Deir el-Bahri:–

> Innumerable loose beads were found, so many that, coupled with the fact that they are often unfinished and that unperforated drops and sticks of glaze occur, it has been surmised that a factory of blue glaze may have existed on the spot, in the temple. (in Naville 1913.17)

In a description of the clearing of the floor of the 11th dynasty temple, Currelly commented that:–

> The most numerous objects were of blue glaze – tubular beads, disc beads, spherical beads, and fragments of bowls. The moment we dug into this layer quantities of beads were found, as if thousands of necklaces, dedicated to the Cow-goddess had been swept out by the priests with the dust ... (in Naville 1913.28)

Among the blue faience beads, ring, disc, and cylinder types are the most common, but barrel, crumb, spheroid, corrugated spheroid, lentoid, bell and gadrooned beads, as well as drop pendants were all found in quantity (Hall & Currelly in Naville 1913.17, 25–6, 28–9). Hall noted the presence of a few 'blue glass and glass paste spherical beads' (1913.17; Pl. 2. top left). Currelly mentioned 'a certain number of dull green beads' decorated with spiral designs in 'manganese purple' (1913.29). A spherical bead inscribed with the name and titles of Hatshepsut which was thought to be made of rock crystal has now been shown to be a very early example of clear glass (Reeves 1986). One shell disc bead was illustrated in the excavation report (Pl. 2, bottom left). The British Museum has two carnelian beads inscribed with the name of Ahmose-Nefertary (London BM 26291–2; Hall 1913.36–7) and a cowroid bead inscribed with the name of Hatshepsut (41704) from these excavations. Miss Carhew drew a spherical bead inscribed with a titulary of Hatshepsut, 'beloved of Hathor, Foremost in Thebes' (Fig. 4, third row, left). All the types just listed were in use during the early and mid 18th dynasty, although some – like the ring, disc, and cylinder beads – have a much wider date range. A type of bead which may be unique to Deir el-Bahri consists of a piece of reed folded into a packet and attached to votive textiles (*e.g.* Pl. 26b) or made up into necklaces (Pl. 57c = Oxford PR 1904.35.83).

Carter mentioned finding only 'scarab shaped and cowroid beads' – one of which bore the prenomen of Ahmose (Pl. 6F) – at Deir el-Bahri (1912.32). Winlock gave little detail about the beads which he recovered, but he noted that:-

> Of the little, shapeless, uninscribed scarabs of brilliant blue faience which were strung up like beads and offered by myriads in the chapels, we got between three and four thousand. (1923.38)

These small uninscribed scaraboids, of which Naville also found a few examples (*e.g.* Glasgow K 06.164 c; Kyoto UM GN 578), should probably be classed as beads rather than amulets. Hayes mentioned that Winlock had also excavated reed beads at this site (1959.184). The segmented faience balls found at Deir el-Bahri by Naville, Carter, and Winlock are described in 2.9.2.1.

2 *Faras*

Griffith briefly noted finding 'many beads of different materials' at Faras, and added that faience 'beads, plain scarabs and pendants' occurred 'in profusion' (1921.86). Among the collections of beads from this site in the British, Ashmolean, and Pitt-Rivers Museums are examples in blue or green faience and a smaller quantity in glazed steatite, limestone, carnelian, and silver. Spheroids and ring and segmented ring beads are the most common, but cylinder, disc, barrel, bell, corrugated spheroids, gadrooned beads and drop pendants also occur. Most of the closely datable types belong to the first half of the 18th dynasty, but some, particularly those in glazed steatite and carnelian, could be earlier.

3 *Mirgissa*

Large numbers of beads in blue, green, yellow, or red faience and a smaller quantity in glass, carnelian, ostrich shell, and limestone were recovered from the sanctuary (Karlin in Vercoutter 1970.325–7). Ring and segmented ring beads were the most common, but bell, cylinder, disc, and spheroid beads were numerous; lentoid, spiral and gadrooned beads and drop pendants were also found (1970.335–9, fig. 35). This range of types and materials covers the mid and late 18th dynasty.

4 *Serabit el-Khadim*

MacDonald donated 70 faience ring and disc beads from Serabit el-Khadim to the British Museum (ER 362). In his description of the Hathor temple at this site Petrie noted that:–

> Large quantities of beads were found amid the broken offerings, about half a hundredweight. (1906.152)

This indicates that Petrie recovered thousands of beads. Most of these beads were in green or blue faience, but there were also a few specimens in black or yellow faience, gold, carnelian, and glass. Ring, disc and cylinder beads were the most common, but spheroids, corrugated spheroids, crumb and gadrooned beads were also numerous (1906 pl. 159). Petrie illustrated one rock crystal barrel bead (1906 pl. 155.14) and some unusual beads which are 'of black and green faience, and seem as if made to imitate plaiting with coloured straws' (1906.152, pl. 159 top row). There were also small, plain, scarabs of the type found at Deir el-Bahri and Faras (1906 pl. 159 fifth row). Most of these beads appear to be 18th dynasty, but some could be Ramessid.

5 *Timna*

5409 beads and 48 pendants were found in or close to the Hathor temple at Timna (Kertesz in Rothenberg 1988.203). This figure includes small pebbles and Red Sea shells pierced for stringing (Rothenberg 1972.171). The majority of the beads appear to be of Egyptian origin. Blue or green faience was by far the most common material. Other substances used were white, black, or yellow faience, glass, mica, limestone, carnelian, onyx, copper, and gold (Kertesz in Rothenberg 1988.203). Disc and ring beads were the most numerous, but barrel, tubular, spheroid and gadrooned beads also occurred (Rothenberg 1972.171–2, pls. XII, 98; 1988 pl. 19–20, figs. 78–81). Some of the glass beads are decorated in the 'eye spot' or 'composite coil' techniques (1988.206). Kertesz points out that none of the comparative material for the glass beads can be dated earlier than the 19th dynasty (1988.206–7). Most of the other bead types have a date range that covers the whole of the New Kingdom.

6 *Gebel Zeit*

A very large number of beads has been found at Gebel Zeit. The small selection so far published includes ring and disc beads in blue and red faience (Mey *et al.* 1980.308–9, fig. 2.1,pl. 80; Castel *et al.* 1986.100). Blue ring beads, cylinder beads, and small plain scarabs were found attached to textiles or forming necklaces and girdles for fertility figurines (Castel & Soukiassian 1985a pl. 13a; Castel *et al.* 1985.20 fig. 13; 2.2.3; 2.6.1.2–3). Some of the miniature jewellery on the figurines was apparently made from pierced shell fragments or from palm leaves (1985.19). This palm leaf jewellery sounds similar to the reed packet-beads from Deir el-Bahri.

2.9.2 The uses of the beads

1 *Votive necklaces* (Fig. 6, Pls. 2, 6, 8, 57)

Most writers have assumed that the majority of the beads were used in votive necklaces. Illustrations of such necklaces are included in the excavation reports of Vercoutter (1970 fig. 42) and Petrie (1906 pl. 159), but these are hypothetical reconstructions, based on guesswork. Kertesz notes that at Timna 'Only rarely were groups of beads found strung together in necklaces' and gives no description of these necklaces (in Rothenberg 1988.203).

At Deir el-Bahri some necklaces were found intact or partially intact. Currelly noted beads 'still joined by the original linen thread' (in Naville 1913.28), but Hall stated that 'the strings are sometimes of plaited leather' (1913.17). Leather is used in the intact necklaces which I have been able to examine or obtain detailed information on (Bolton 48.04.20; Dublin NM 1904.521; Kyoto UM GN 578;

London BM 41126–33, 41134 = Pl. 2, top centre, 41715; Oxford PR 1904. 35.87 = Pl. 57d).

Some types of bead, such as the reed 'packets' (Pl. 57c) or the faience crumb beads (Naville 1913 pl. 27.6; Kyoto UM GN 578), are strung by themselves. Hall commented that 'the discoid beads were often elaborately strung so as to present their faces rather than their edges' (in Naville 1913.17, pl. 27.6). Several museums have necklaces of disc beads from Deir el-Bahri restrung in this manner (e.g. Edinburgh RSM 1904.134.6; London BM 47728–9; Oxford PR 1904.35.82 = Pl. 57b). Cylinder beads can be strung with ring beads (e.g. Dublin NM 1904.521), with segmented ring beads, spheroids and corrugated spheroids (Naville 1913 pl. 28.8 = London BM 41126), or by themselves (1913 pl. 27.6; Ilkley CC GN 7007).

Rectangular faience plaques were sometimes used as spacers. The Victoria and Albert Museum has two fine examples decorated with warriors drawing bows (680.1905.a–b). Hall mentioned that:–

> The ends of necklaces were usually formed by large hollow balls of faïence ... with segmental decoration in dark and light blue. Before the present excavations, the purpose of the balls of this kind which had been discovered elsewhere was unknown ... We see, however, from the specimens actually found at the end of necklaces here, what their real purpose was. (in Naville 1913.17)

The British Museum has a necklace of reed, disc, and segmented ring beads which retains a segmented ball at each end (41715). Balls of this type were excavated by Carter (Pl. 6L) and Winlock (Hayes 1959.179, 181, fig. 100) at Deir el-Bahri, by Griffith at Faras (1921.86; Pls. 8.22; 57a = London BM 51255), and by Vercoutter at Mirgissa (1970.340, no. 9). There were also examples among the votive offerings at Dendara (Fig. 6.8–9).

Balls of this type may have been made as early as the 11th dynasty. Bourriau suggests that during the Middle Kingdom they were worn strung together in necklaces, or singly on cords around the neck, or attached to the hair (1988.132–3, no. 128). A segmented ball found in a foundation deposit of Thutmose III at Koptos (Petrie 1896 pl. 15.63) provides the latest known closely datable example.

According to Hall:–

> The votive cows, heads of Hathor, and so forth, are of the same glaze and faïence as these scarabs, plaques and *menats*, and were always found with them. Further, the scarabs were often found strung with these votive objects and with beads of the same glazed faïence to form a necklace to be presented to the goddess. (in Naville 1913.14)

The metal cow plaques are known to have been strung on such necklaces (2.4.2.1); it is probable that small pierced ear and eye models and plaques, and Type 5 fertility figurines were also offered in this fashion.

Some necklaces from Deir el-Bahri seem to consist of random collections of scarabs and amulets (e.g. Pls. 2, 57d; see 2.10.2). The necklaces strung with amulets are usually too small for an adult neck, but it would probably be wrong to reclassify them as bracelets. They could have been worn by babies to protect them in infancy, and dedicated in gratitude for their survival. However, it seems more likely that size was unimportant because such jewellery was not intended for human wear. Some of the tiny necklaces (*e.g.* Kyoto UM GN578) may once have decorated fertility figurines, as on examples from Gebel Zeit (Castel *et al.* 1985.19–20, fig. 13; 2.6.1.3), or any type of small image of the goddess. Other necklaces may have been dedicated as purely symbolic jewellery for the goddess. 'Miniaturization' is a common feature of votive objects in many cultures (3.2.2).

2 *Menit necklaces*

Menit counterpoises were found at Deir el-Bahri, Mirgissa, Serabit el-Khadim, and Timna. Karlin proposes that many of the ring, spheroid, and cylinder beads from Mirgissa were originally strung on menit necklaces (in Vercoutter 1970.325). Petrie made the same suggestion about beads from Serabit el-Khadim (1906.152). The type of stringing shown on menit necklaces in temple reliefs and tomb paintings, and on a few temple statues (*e.g.* Pl. 40), is preserved on a specimen from Malqata (Hayes 1959.252–3, fig. 153). These necklaces have two long strings of large beads attached to dozens of shorter strings of small faience ring beads. These form a weighty mass which would have rattled when shaken.

Some menit necklaces made as votive rather than ritual objects seem to have been strung in a simpler fashion. A faience example from a foundation deposit of Thutmose III at Koptos had a single string with spheroid and cylinder beads and fish-shaped pendants (Petrie 1896 pl. 14). A complete faience menit necklace from Deir el-Bahri was sent to Brussels (MR E 2470). This is no longer intact, but a drawing on the catalogue card shows that it was strung with a single row of spheroid, corrugated spheroid, and ring beads. The counterpoises found at the four sites are described below, divided according to material. The significance of menit necklaces as votive offerings is discussed in 2.9.4.

A. Wood (Pls. 1, 59b)

Eight wooden menit counterpoises are listed in the EEF distribution lists for Deir el-Bahri, and Winlock found at least one wooden counterpoise at this site (Hayes 1959.184). One almost intact wooden counterpoise and the disc of another were recovered from the sanctuary at Mirgissa (Vercoutter 1970 figs. 40–1). The four examples from Deir el-Bahri which I have been able to examine are between 8.3 and 13.4 cm long (Bolton 48.04.21; Brussels MR E 711 = Pl. 59b, left; London BM 41099 = Pl. 1 top row, far left; Oxford PR unnumbered). Each is pierced with two holes at the top of the stem, as are two other wooden counterpoises illustrated by Hall (Pl. 1, top left).

Hall commented of the counterpoises that 'the wooden ones are very roughly made, and have little ornament but one or two stripes of red paint' (in Naville 1913.16). London BM 41099 has horizontal red stripes on both sides but Bolton 48.04.21 and the example found by Winlock are painted solid red. Hayes suggested that this was to imitate copper (1959.184). No paint is preserved on the specimen in the Pitt-Rivers Museum, but Brussels MR E 711 has a lotus flower pattern on either side of the disc and a linear border on both sides of the stem painted in black (Pl. 59b, left). Decoration of this kind is almost always found on the metal examples shown in New Kingdom paintings. The wooden disc from Mirgissa is incised with a similar pattern and shows traces of blue paint (Vercoutter 1970 fig. 41). The intact counterpoise from Mirgissa, which terminates in a Hathor head, has been described in 2.3.3.2. This is painted in red, blue, and black. A wooden fragment from Gurob with the head of a queen or goddess in profile probably came from such a counterpoise (London UC 16759; Thomas 1981.87, no. 751, pl. 57). I know of no plain wooden counterpoises from other sites, except one possible example from Deir el-Medina (Bruyère 1939 pl. 42).

B. Metal

Most functional menit necklaces seem to have had metal counterpoises, but the only examples to be recovered from any of the six sites were the pair of miniature copper counterpoises found by Winlock at Deir el-Bahri (New York MMA 23.3.137; Hayes 1959.173, 182). These are incised with lotus flower patterns, Hathor masks, and Hathor mask loop sistra (see 2.3.3.2).

C. Faience (Fig. 6; Pls. 4–5, 7, 58, 59b)

Only 13 faience menit counterpoises are mentioned in the EEF distribution lists for Deir el-Bahri, but I have been able to trace 44 intact or fragmentary examples from this site (Aberdeen 890; Boston MFA 05.239; Bristol 3154–6; Brussels MR E 715a–c, 2470 = Pl. 59b, right; Dublin NM 1904.540.04; Glasgow K O4.164.d, f; Ilkley 7002 & unnumbered in Box 96; Liverpool 13.10.04.18; London BM 43243, 47691, 47762–4, 48090; V&A 1217.1904, 685.1905; New York MMA 05.4.95, 113, 07.230.29; Oxford Ash. E 2725–30 = Naville 1913 pl. 27.3, 2744–5; Toronto ROM 907.18.134–6, 137 = 1913 pl. 27.1, bottom right, 138–45). Miss Carhew illustrated about a dozen examples from the EEF excavations (Pls. 4–5). Carter mentioned finding faience menit counterpoises at Deir el-Bahri and illustrated two fragments (Pl. 7, top left). Four examples excavated at this site by Winlock are described by Hayes (1959.45, 48, 52, 79). Karlin suggests that two faience fragments found at Mirgissa come from menit counterpoises (in Vercoutter 1970.339), but they look more like portions of the kind of faience throwstick discovered among offerings to Hathor at other sites (see 2.10.10). MacDonald brought back seven fragmentary counterpoises from Serabit el-Khadim (London BM 12877–8, 13073, 13258, 13281, 13301, ER 360). Petrie excavated about 50 such fragments at this site (1906.142, 149, pl. 148; Pl. 58). Rothenberg discovered pieces from 15 counterpoises at Timna (1972.163–4, pl. XXI, figs. 48, 51; 1988.119–121, pls. 120–1, figs. 29, 32–3).

Few of the counterpoises are complete, but they seem to have ranged in length from about 10–20 cm. Originally, all menit necklaces seem to have had double counterpoises, but, as Hayes noted:–

> In votive *menyets* of the New Kingdom the two counterpoises are usually combined into one, with, however, a groove running around the outside edge to suggest two elements placed together ... (1959.45)

The examples which have this groove (*e.g.* Pl. 5 bottom left) tend to be about twice as thick as the ones without it. One counterpoise from Serabit el-Khadim is pierced through the disc (Bolton 68.05.20), probably so that it could be tied to its pair.

Most are pierced with two holes at the top of the stem (Pl. 58). In a few cases, the holes do not go right through (*e.g.* Petrie 1906 pl. 148.7) or are missing altogether (Brussels MR E 715; London BM 41831). Some have holes which would be too small for any but the finest thread, and many are too thin and fragile to bear a mass of ring beads or even a single strand of beads. This suggests that these objects should be classed as representations of menit necklaces, rather than as parts of actual necklaces. The counterpoise could stand for the whole necklace.

Two of the counterpoises from Serabit el-Khadim terminate in a head of Hathor (2.3.3.2), but the remainder are the standard shape. A few examples from Deir el-Bahri are in plain blue faience (*e.g.* London V&A 1217.1904), but the majority are decorated and inscribed in dark blue on light blue or in black on green. Most, but not all, of the early 18th dynasty pieces are decorated on one side only (Petrie 1906.142). All the later ones are decorated on both sides. On a small group of counterpoises from Deir el-Bahri (London BM 43243) and Serabit el-Khadim (Bolton 68.05.19; London BM 13258; V&A 702.1905 = Pl. 58, third from right), the design is inlaid in mauve or light blue on a pale green ground. Two of these are dateable by their inscriptions to Amonhotpe III.

The decoration on the disc always consists of variations on a rosette pattern made up of lotus buds, flowers, or petals (Pls. 4–5, 58). In some highly stylized examples, the pattern comes to resemble a spider's web (*e.g.* Rothenberg 1972 pl. XXI; Toronto ROM 907.18.136). The stem nearly always has a linear border containing a single column of inscription. These inscriptions consist of royal titularies, in which the contemporary ruler, or a royal lady, is usually described as 'beloved of Hathor' (Pls. 4–5, 58). On a counterpoise from Deir el-Bahri, painted by Miss Carhew (Pl. 4, bottom left), the word *ḥtpwt* 'offerings' is written on the back of the disc and the inscription on the stem of another example may also refer to making offerings (Pl. 5, top right). The royal names appearing on the counterpoises are Ahmose-Nefertary, Amonhotpe I, Thutmose I, Thutmose II, Hatshepsut, Thutmose III, and Baketamon at Deir el-Bahri (Pls. 4–5; Naville 1913.26, pl. 27.3); Amonhotpe I, Ahmose-Nefertary, Thutmose I, (Queen) Ahmose Meryamon, Hatshepsut, Neferureʿ, Thutmose III, Thutmose IV, Amonhotpe III, Ramesses II, Merenptah, Seti II, Tawosret, and Ramesses IV at Serabit el-Khadim (Pl. 58; Petrie 1906 pl. 148); and Ramesses II, Seti II, and Ramesses IV at Timna (Schulman in Rothenberg 1988.119–20).

In nearly all cases, the counterpoises will be contemporary with the ruler or royal lady whose name they bear. This is clearly so in the case of two counterpoises from Deir el-Bahri, the first of which has Hatshepsut's cartouche on one side and Thutmose III's on the other (Toronto ROM 907.18.143), and the second Thutmose III's cartouche on one side and his daughter Baketamon's on the other (Boston MFA 05.239 = Pl. 3, second row; D'Auria 1983.161–2, fig. 1). The only doubtful case is Ahmose-Nefertary, because of the popularity of her cult at Thebes throughout the New Kingdom. Even this doubt affects only objects from Deir el-Bahri.

The design of the votive counterpoises does not seem to have changed very much during the New Kingdom, although Ramessid examples tend to have longer inscriptions and more stylized patterns on their discs than the 18th dynasty pieces.

From the reign of Amonhotpe III onwards, some complex metal counterpoises appear. These can have discs decorated with the 'cow and marsh' motif and stems terminating in the head of a goddess in profile (*e.g.* Barguet 1954 fig. 3; Hayes 1959.269; Holden in Simpson 1982 no. 418; Wildung 1985.98, no. 79). The examples from Mirgissa and Serabit el-Khadim which terminate in Hathor heads seem to be influenced by counterpoises of this type. A faience fragment from Deir el-Bahri which has the disc and horns and part of the profile of Hathor in relief (London V&A 679.1905) may come from such a counterpoise. During the Late Period, elaborate faience counterpoises seem to have been in common use as amulets (Germond 1981.324). Apart from the Deir el-Bahri, Serabit el-Khadim, and Timna pieces, one example from the Thutmose III foundation deposit at Koptos (Petrie 1896 pl. 14; 1.7), and another among the offerings at Dendara (Fig. 6, top left; 1.7), very few New Kingdom faience counterpoises have survived.

3 *Beadwork* (Pl. 2)

Two fragments from Deir el-Bahri and one from Faras indicate the presence of objects in beadwork. Hall illustrated a fragment in which dark ring beads are used in diamond patterns on a light background (Pl. 2, centre right). It is possible that this and the bead 'tassel' shown next to it, come from a bead apron. In this case, they might be funerary rather than votive (Aldred 1971.178, pl. 9). The Faras fragment consists of white, yellow, blue, and green ring beads cemented together to form a diamond shape (Oxford Ash. 1912.953). It has a loop on the back and may have been worn as a pendant or attached to a piece of clothing. The textiles from Deir el-Bahri and Gebel Zeit which have beads woven into their fabric or used to decorate their fringes have already been described (2.2.3; Pls. 26–7). A small basket with blue faience beads woven into it was among the offerings at Gebel Zeit (Cairo JE 98138).

4 *'Bead loaves'* (Pl. 59a)

Hall noted that at Deir el-Bahri:

> A peculiar use for broken cylindrical beads was found by sticking them into circular cakes of mud, flat above and rounded below (having been made in a pot), which were a common votive offering of the poorest. There can be little doubt that these objects are intended to represent loaves of bread. (in Naville 1913.17)

Four fragments from such 'bead loaves' are mentioned in the EEF distribution lists. The British Museum has two unlisted 'loaves' (41520a = Pl. 59a, 41520b = Naville 1913 pl. 22.9, right). Miss Carhew painted what appears to be a an almost square example (EEF Archives). One of the pieces in the British Museum preserves its original dimensions and is 13.6 cm wide and 5.6 cm deep. An example in Manchester is now 9.9 cm wide and 4.3 cm deep (Naville 1913 pl. 22.9, bottom).

These objects do not seem to occur at other Egyptian sites. If they are model cakes or loaves, the blue beads might represent poppy seed decoration, although the opium poppy was probably introduced into Egypt only during the 18th dynasty (Germer 1985.45). The objects might be seen as model seed cases, but the square example is against this. Among the Ashante of Ghana clay 'cakes', very similar to the

the Egyptian ones, were used until recent times as moulds for tubular glass beads (*e.g.* London Museum of Mankind 1934.10.21–2). The clay 'loaves' from Deir el-Bahri may simply be a method of manufacturing beads. They could still be votive objects, but the offering would consist of the beads while the 'loaf' would be of no more significance in itself than the leather thong of a necklace. However, a Type 2 pottery fertility figurine from Gebel Zeit has blue ring beads pressed into its wig (Castel *et al.* 1984.50 fig. 4), showing that pottery votive objects were sometimes decorated with beads. The possibility that these 'loaves' were votive objects in their own right remains open.

2.9.3 Other types of jewellery

1 *Bracelets*

A. Faience (Pl. 61)

Rigid bracelets in blue or green faience were found at most of the Hathor sites, but they were common only at Serabit el-Khadim and Timna. These bracelets can be rectangular, round, or triangular in section. Twenty-two plain bracelet fragments are mentioned in the EEF distribution lists for Deir el-Bahri. The two which I have examined are both rectangular in section (London V&A 1212.1904; Oxford Ash. E 2757). The Pitt-Rivers Museum has one fragment from a plain 'rectangular' bracelet from Faras (unnumbered), and three such fragments were found in the sanctuary at Mirgissa (Karlin in Vercoutter 1970.348). MacDonald brought back 29 inscribed bracelet fragments from Serabit el-Khadim (London BM 13193, 13197– 204, 13209, 13218, 13223, 13228, 13240, 13242–3, 13248, 13250–1, 13256, 13261, 13264–5, 13275, 13280, 13291, 13309–10). Petrie found at least 184 inscribed fragments at this site and an unspecified number of plain fragments (1906.144, pl. 149). I have been able to examine 104 of the inscribed fragments. The Harvard Expedition recovered pieces of two inscribed bracelets (Starr & Butin 1936 pl. 12.1–2). Nineteen inscribed bracelet fragments and 26 plain fragments were excavated at Timna (Rothenberg 1972.163–7, figs. 49, 51; 1988.121–5, pls. 121–2, figs. 34–7).

The most common bracelet type among the Serabit el-Khadim material is the 'rectangular' (Petrie 1906.143, pl. 149.1–13). These bracelets are 2–4 cm wide and have inscriptions in dark blue or black, usually within a linear border (*e.g.* Pl. 61, bottom row). These inscriptions consist of the titularies of contemporary rulers, who may be referred to as 'Beloved of Hathor, Mistress of Mefkat' (*e.g.* Bolton 68.05.22; Brussels MR E 2014; Liverpool 49.05.2, Manchester UM 899; Toronto ROM 906.16.51, 57, 61–2, 64, 68, 71). Seti I, Ramesses II, Merneptah, Seti II, Tawosret, Ramesses III, IV, V, and VI are all named on 'rectangular' bracelets from Serabit el-Khadim. The names of Seti I, Ramesses II, Ramesses IV, Ramesses V, and possibly Merenptah appear on bracelet fragments from Timna which have either rectangular or roughly oval sections (1988.122–3, 125, figs. 31, 34–6).

Petrie noted that:–

A different class of armlet is the narrow bangle, of which the thickness is only a little

more or less than the breadth. These are either rounded or triangular in section.
(1906.143)

The 'round' bracelets are smaller than the 'rectangular' type; some would have been
no more than 6–8 cm in diameter. The inscriptions are similar, but tend to be
briefer and to have no border. Ramesses II, III, and V are named on 'round'
bracelets from Serabit el-Khadim (Petrie 1906 pl. 149.14, 19–20). A few 'round'
bracelets are decorated with patterns in black, consisting of stripes (*e.g.* Oxford Ash.
1911.614), or dots and triangles (*e.g.* Bolton 68.05.36; London BM 13309–10). The
bracelets with triangular sections are sometimes inscribed on one face (Pl. 61, top
right; London BM 13240, 41799; Manchester 904). Ramesses II, Seti II, Tawosret,
and Ramesses III are named on such bracelets from Serabit el-Khadim (*e.g.* Petrie
1906 pl. 149.15–18). Tawosret is also named on a bracelet with a roughly triangular
section from Timna (Rothenberg 1988.122, fig. 34.3). These bracelets can also be
decorated on one or both faces with dots (*e.g.* 1906 pl. 149.24, 28), triangles (*e.g.*
1906 pl. 149.22, 26), or dots and triangles (*e.g.* London BM 41796, 49080; V&A
711.905 = 1906 pl. 149.23, 25, 27).

'Rectangular' faience bracelets were among the offerings at the shrine of
Sekhmet at Abusir (Borchardt 1910.133, fig. 183). They have been found in private
burials of the mid and late 18th dynasty (*e.g.* Daressy 1902.26, pl. 8, no. 24062;
Steindorff 1937.112; Hayes 1959.181, 185, fig. 100) and in royal tombs of the same
period (*e.g.* Daressy 1902.26–8. 153–4, 293, pl. 30; Carter & Newberry 1904.119–
21; Davis 1912 pl. 3.3; Winlock 1948.34). They do not seem to occur in domestic
contexts and should probably be classified as votive and funerary 'model' bracelets.
Plain or patterned 'triangular' bracelets in electrum, alabaster, or wood are also
known from 18th dynasty royal burials (*e.g.* Daressy 1904.28; Vernier 1927.41–2,
fig. 42; A. Wilkinson 1971.107). One faience example in the Cairo Museum is said
to come from the Valley of the Kings (CG 24982; Daressy 1904.301). 'Rectangular'
faience bracelets with an inlaid titulary were found among debris from the tomb of
Amonhotpe III (Wallis 1900 pl. 2; Hayes 1959.243). The custom of inscribing
faience funerary or votive bracelets may have begun in his reign.

B. Other materials

Seven fragments from bone 'rectangular' bracelets and one in ostrich shell were
recovered from the sanctuary at Mirgissa (Karlin in Vercoutter 1970.348,
nos. 126–7). Similar bracelets have been found in some New Kingdom burials in
Nubia (*e.g.* Griffith 1921.42, pl. 39; Steindorff 1935.59–60; 1937.112, pl. 58). One
fragment of a 'rectangular' bracelet in blue and white striped glass was excavated at
Mirgissa (Karlin in Vercoutter 1970.318, no. 125). Comparable bracelets have been
found in the tomb of Amonhotpe II (Daressy 1902.207–8) and at el-ʿAmarna
(Cooney 1978.91, no. 966). The glass bracelet and a glass vase (2.11.4) were
probably the most valuable of the small offerings found at Mirgissa. One piece of a
green glass bracelet or ring stand with an impressed pattern was excavated at Timna
(Rothenberg 1972.171; 1988.216). A few copper or bronze bracelets were found at
this site (1988.167, fig. 74), but they are unlikely to have been Egyptian offerings.

2 Rings (Fig. 4; Pl. 33b)

Finger rings were found at Deir el-Bahri, Mirgissa, Serabit el-Khadim, and Gebel Zeit. The EEF distribution lists mention only two rings from Naville's excavations. One, in green faience, is said to have been sent to the Royal Ontario Museum, but the museum can find no trace of it. The other, also in green faience, is in the Victoria and Albert Museum (676.1905). Its broken bezel consists of a cartouche with the *prenomen* of Amonhotpe III (Fig. 4, bottom right). The Victoria and Albert Museum also has a ring in dark blue glass, with a square bezel incised with a hawk-headed deity and a jumble of hieroglyphs, which is said to come from Deir el-Bahri. The British Museum has two faience rings from Deir el-Bahri, the Hathor mask ring (2.3.3.2), and another ring with a cartouche of Amonhotpe III (41730). A possible 'cow and marsh' motif faience ring has been noted in 2.4.3.2.

Two intact plain faience rings, one green and one yellow (Vercoutter 1970 fig. 43), and 27 fragments in blue, red, yellow, green, and black, were found at Mirgissa (Karlin in Vercoutter 1970.346–7). There were also two plain rings in blue glass, a fragment of another, and a ring in patterned glass (1970.347–8). The more elaborate faience rings included the two cat rings (2.5.3), and the seven *wadjet* eye rings (2.8.4.2). Others had bezels in the form of an ape or a cartouche with a double plume, or had bezels incised with a lotus pattern or Thoth in ape form (1970.346–7).

Petrie did not mention or illustrate any rings from Serabit el-Khadim, but the Petrie Collection has fragments of 38 identifiable faience rings from this site. The eight Hathor mask rings (*e.g.* Pl. 33b) and the 11 *wadjet* eye rings have already been noted (2.3.3.2; 2.8.4.2). Of the remainder, two have bezels in the form of ibexes (London UC 35461a–b), three in the form of uraei (35476a–b, 35470), and one in the form of Bes (35465). Two have a floral pattern incised on the bezel (35462, 35471), two have the Neith emblem (35472a–b), and eight have cartouches: three of Amonhotpe III (35457–9), two of Seti I (35460, 35468), and three of Ramesses II (35463a–b, 35469). Most of the rings from these three sites are of types common from the late 18th dynasty onwards (Hayes 1959.250, 396–7; A. Wilkinson 1971.130, 134). Metal rings were among the commonest non-Egyptian objects at Timna (Rothenberg 1988.158–166, figs. 63–73). Royal name faience rings of Akhenaten, Tutankhamon, Ay, and Horemheb were excavated at Gebel Zeit (Castel *et al.* 1984.49–50). Ramessid faience rings were found on the floor of the sanctuary there (Posener-Kriéger 1985.298; Castel *et al.* 1986.100) and faience *wadjet* eye rings in the enclosure wall (Castel *et al.* 1984.51 fig. 5; Castel & Soukiassian 1985.286).

3 Earrings

No earrings were found at Deir el-Bahri or Faras. One intact blue faience penannular earring with triangular ridging was recovered from the Hathor sanctuary at Mirgissa (Karlin in Vercoutter 1970.316, fig. 43). The Petrie Collection has the remains of a similar pair from Serabit el-Khadim (unnumbered). Earrings of this type were worn in the mid and late 18th dynasty (Hayes 1959.185–6, fig. 102; Cooney 1978.93–4). Various faience studs from Mirgissa (Karlin in Vercoutter 1970.349, nos. 128–43, fig. 47) may be earrings of a type worn towards the end of the 18th dynasty (Aldred 1971.143–4, pl. 68). Non-Egyptian copper and bronze earrings were excavated at Timna (Rothenberg 1972.173–4, fig. 155; 1988.148–9, fig. 55). Silver or copper earrings are sometimes worn by fertility figurines of Types 2 and 3 (2.6.1.2–3).

4 *Miscellaneous* (Fig. 2; Pl. 2)

The excavators of Timna have identified a fragment from a narrow band of sheet gold incised with a triangular pattern as part of an Egyptian headdress (Rothenberg 1972.166, 170, fig. 54.11; 1988.211, fig. 84.132). If this is correct, the piece would be the only surviving example of a headdress from any of the six sites. This would probably have been a royal gift. Eight gold leaves or petals found in the Timna temple might also have formed part of a headdress (Kertesz in Rothenberg 1988.211).

Rosettes might be classified as jewellery. Thirteen blue faience rosettes are mentioned in the EEF distribution lists. One example from the 1892–5 excavations was drawn by Miss Carhew (Fig. 2). Hayes stated that the Metropolitan Museum of Art has 78 rosettes of the 18th dynasty, 'largely from the foundation deposits and rubbish pits associated with the temple of Hat-shepsut at Deir el-Bahri' (1959.186–7). The rosettes from Deir el-Bahri which I have been able to examine, or obtain detailed information on, vary in diameter between 1.4 and 2.8 cm (Bolton 48.04.12 = Pl. 2, centre, third row from bottom; Edinburgh RSM 1904.134.16, 1906.382; Glasgow 04.164.m; Kyoto UM 578 (4); London BM 47697; V&A 687.1905; New York MMA 05.4.42–3; Oxford Ash. E 2769). They are in light blue faience and are either pierced (*e.g.* Fig. 2) or have a loop attached to the back. Six examples illustrated by Hall have alternating petals in dark and light blue faience (Pl. 2, centre, location unknown). Hayes remarked of the rosettes in the Metropolitan Museum of Art that 'the details are sometimes picked out in black, green and yellow overglazes' and that 'one of the examples from Deir el-Bahri appears to be of silver' (1959.187). He pointed out that from the mid 18th dynasty such rosettes were used 'in the decoration of garments, temple draperies, funerary palls and the like' (1959.186). It is possible that some of the rosettes from Deir el-Bahri were originally sewn on to veils used to cover shrines or on to scaled-down votive veils.

It is difficult to decide whether many of the small faience objects pierced or fitted with loops should be classed as pendants or amulets. Some, such as the trefoils found at Deir el-Bahri (Pl. 2, top centre) and Serabit el-Khadim (Petrie 1906 pl. 155.8), or the leaves from Mirgissa (Karlin in Vercoutter 1970.343, fig. 35), Serabit el-Khadim (Petrie 1906 pl. 159), and Gebel Zeit (Mey *et al.* 1980.305, fig. 1) probably never had a specific symbolic value. Since it is difficult to be sure of this, I describe most of the small objects which were originally strung on necklaces under the category of amulets (2.10).

2.9.4 Jewellery as votive offerings

When a piece of jewellery is of a common New Kingdom type thought to have been worn in daily life, or shows signs of wear, it was probably a personal possession of the donor. If amulets are excluded, comparatively little of the jewellery from the five sites meets these criteria. Mirgissa has the highest proportion of objects which were probably worn by the donors, such as the earrings and some of the bracelets and rings. Faience rings may fall into a special category, since Hayes proposed that they were mainly 'distributed as favors on the occasions of festivals, banquets and the like' and worn only once (1959.250). The occasional presence of faience rings in temple foundation deposits suggests that they were sometimes made as votive objects (Boyce in Kemp 1989.161).

After describing the jewellery found at Mirgissa Karlin states that:–

> Tous ces objets, d'usage essentiellement féminin, consacraient bien le sanctuaire à la déesse femme qu'est Hathor. (in Vercoutter 1970.327)

However, many types of 18th dynasty jewellery, such as penannular and stud earrings and faience finger rings, seem to have been worn by both sexes (A. Wilkinson 1971.121–34; Eaton-Krauss in Simpson 1982.277, 298–300). There is no justification for seeing the Mirgissa jewellery as 'essentially feminine'.

Most of the jewellery found at the six sites seems to have been specially made for votive purposes. This is particularly true of the necklaces and the faience bracelets. By presenting a necklace, each donor adorned the goddess, a privilege mentioned in Spell 484 of the Coffin Texts, which refers to the deceased tying an ornament on Hathor (CT VI,55; Drioton 1958.189–90). Ritual presentation of bracelets to Hathor is recorded in the Graeco-Roman temples of Edfu and Dendara, where it is said to 'rejoice the heart of the goddess' (Amer in Daumas 1986.18–20). Since the gift was a standard one, there is no need to assume that the faience and reed necklaces were the offerings of people who could not afford jewellery in precious metals. The offerings may originally have included precious jewellery which was 'recycled' by the priests, or looted when the sites fell into disuse, but the presence of simple faience bracelets in royal tombs is one of many indications that in religious contexts the intrinsic value of objects could be of little or no importance. The faience bracelets and necklaces can be seen as substitutes for 'real' jewellery, because of their material and of their size. This substitution was not necessarily dictated by economic considerations. It seems to have been the act of presenting jewellery which was significant, rather than the quality of the gift itself (see further 3.2.1).

The cartouches on the menit counterpoises and bracelets raise the question of whether they were royal rather than private gifts. Private individuals wore rings, cartouche pendants, and scarabs inscribed with royal names as amulets (2.10.1.11). Paintings in 18th dynasty tombs sometimes show chantresses holding menits whose counterpoises are inscribed with the titulary of the reigning king (e.g. Davies 1948.50–1, pl. 12; Nina Davies 1963 pl. 41). The bracelets and menit counterpoises found at Serabit el-Khadim and Timna were probably made in government workshops and may have been offered in the name of the king on behalf of each mining expedition. This would make them corporate rather than individual votive offerings. Alternatively, members of such expeditions might have been equipped with suitable votive offerings as part of their 'wages', which they would then dedicate individually (3.1). The kings named on the bracelets, counterpoises, and other types of object such as sistra and Hathor mask and cat plaques, might have been thought to act as intermediaries. The fact that queens and princesses are named on faience menit counterpoises (*e.g.* Pls. 4–5) is additional evidence for the involvement of royal ladies in the cult of Hathor.

It is not clear how much of the votive jewellery is specifically linked to the symbolism of Hathor. Discussing the beads from Deir el-Bahri, Currelly commented that:–

> The best of the beads are of the colour of Sinai turquoise, from which the colouring was doubtless copied. Hathor is frequently called the goddess who loves the turquoise … I think from this we may conclude that the colour of the turquoise, as well as the stone itself, was especially associated with the worship of the goddess … (in Naville 1913.28)

'The Field of Turquoise' is one of the names for the dwelling place of the blessed dead, and for this reason Giveon linked the colour turquoise with Hathor's funerary aspect (1978a.110). It is striking that not a single object made of turquoise has been recovered from the temple at Serabit el-Khadim. It is conceivable that at this site turquoise-coloured faience jewellery served as a kind of substitute for the turquoise which was being removed from Hathor's domain. However, turquoise blue is too common a colour of 18th dynasty faience for much symbolic significance to be read into it. At sites where offerings continued to be made in the late 18th dynasty, objects in red, yellow, and black faience were dedicated to Hathor.

The necklaces of reed 'packet' beads (*e.g.* Pl. 57c) could be linked with the 'cow and marsh' motif. The faience beads from Serabit el-Khadim, which Petrie described as imitating plaited straw (1906.152), may rather imitate plaited or folded reeds. At Deir el-Bahri, conditions are ideal for the preservation of fragile objects. One cannot be sure that reed necklaces were never worn in daily life, so that it is uncertain how closely they were associated with Hathor rites. The remaining beads are all of kinds which have also been found in domestic and/or funerary contexts.

The inscribed faience bracelets are unusual, but this rarity is almost certainly an accident of preservation. It is clear that these objects could be funerary as well as votive. If more pieces survived from Ramessid royal tombs, there would probably be a large body of comparative material. Two categories of jewellery – the Hathor mask rings and the menit necklaces – do have a particular association with the goddess. It is possible that Hathor mask rings were distributed and worn during Hathor festivals before being dedicated in the shrines, although if this were the case one might expect these rings to be more common than they are.

Menit necklaces were associated with the cult of Hathor from at least as early as the 6th dynasty (Allam 1963.28–30; Staehelin 1982.125–7). From the late 18th dynasty onwards the menit necklace could be a personification of Hathor and related goddesses (Baines 1985.58–9). Menit necklaces were frequently used in Hathor rituals, being carried by Hathor priestesses and by singers and dancers of the *ḥnr* (Nord in Simpson & Davies 1981.141–4). Menit necklaces as gifts for the goddess are specifically mentioned on a royal stela dating to Amenemhet III at Serabit el-Khadim (Černý 1952 pl. 27, no. 112; 1955.114). To judge by the other gifts listed on this stela, these menit necklaces are likely to have been made in precious metal or gilded wood. In the New Kingdom, either it became customary for expeditions to offer numerous faience models instead of a few precious necklaces, or the expedition leaders continued to make, unrecorded, offerings of valuable necklaces which have not survived, while ordinary expedition members participated by dedicating faience counterpoises. An unprovenanced New Kingdom stela in Geneva (MAH 9312; Chappaz 1983 figs. 9–10) is unusual in showing a menit necklace on the offering table between the male donor and Hathor Nebet-Hetepet. This demonstrates that it was permissible for 'ordinary' people to dedicate menit necklaces to Hathor. It also confirms that they were not offered only by women.

Menit necklaces had a wide range of symbolic values (Staehelin 1982.52–3), several of which could have made them appropriate votive offerings. Like sistra, they were instruments of propitiation and can be associated with the pacification of the 'Distant Goddess' (Giveon 1978.68–73; Germond 1981.264–5; Chappaz 1983.11). As a cult object of Hathor, the menit necklace can be linked with the pacification of the Sun God by this goddess. This myth seems to be alluded to in the story of Sinuhe, when the queen and princesses pacify the angry king by singing and holding out their menit necklaces, sistra, and flails (Gardiner 1916.100–3). The ⸗𓏏𓎡𓏏𓎡𓏴 can be a cult object of Hathor. It has been suggested that a string of light and dark blue cones excavated at Deir el-Bahri (Pl. 2, left) came from such a sacred flail (Davies 1923.24). It is generally agreed that in the story of Sinuhe the king is identified with Reʿ, and the queen, as well as the princesses, with Hathor, but there has been some controversy over whether Hathor plays the role of mother, consort, or daughter (see Brunner 1955.5–11; Westendorf 1967.145; 1977.296–8; Derchain 1970.79–83). In Egyptian religion these roles need not be mutually exclusive.

Barguet argued that the symbolism of the menit was linked to Hathor's role as the mother or nurse of the Divine Child (1953.103–11). He pointed out the similarity between the shape of the menit counterpoise and that of the wooden fertility figurines known as 'paddle dolls' and concluded that the counterpoise represents a stylised female body, specifically that of Hathor. If so, the lotus on the disc might symbolize the female genitals (1953.104). This identification could link the act of Hathor pacifying Reʿ by holding out her menit necklace with the myth of Hathor pacifying the Sun God by displaying her genitals (2.3.4). Barguet connected the 'Hathor lotus' on the counterpoise disc with the primeval lotus which contained the Divine Child, but pointed out that the lotus is sometimes replaced by the cow and marsh motif which evokes the suckling of Horus by Hathor in the marshes of Chemmis (1953.104).

This led Barguet to propose that the menit counterpoise was a symbol of both birth and rebirth. He drew attention to a painting of a menit necklace in which the counterpoise is replaced by a scarab – the prime symbol of rebirth (1953.108). In his discussion of the scenes on the small golden shrine of Tutankhamon, Westendorf suggests that a wordplay between 𓄹𓏤𓊪 and 𓄹𓏤𓄙 'thighs/womb' is implied and that the queen presenting a menit necklace to the king symbolizes the sexual union of the king – here identified with the Sun God – with the goddess from whom he will be born again as his own son (1967.145). Hermann saw the encircling of the king by a menit necklace as symbolic of the mystic union between king and goddess, but he was not specific about the nature of that union (1959.24, 31). The cow whose necklace encircles the king is often shown in the context of the Western Mountain of the Theban necropolis, the entrance to the realm of the dead (2.4.6–7). This suggests that the necklace was instrumental in the king's transition to the afterlife, where he would be nourished by the milk of the divine cow.

The gestures of presenting a menit necklace to the king or encircling him with such a necklace were relevant to more than just the king's afterlife. Leclant has emphasized the presence of menit necklaces in all types of suckling scenes and has linked them with the concept of the living king being invigorated or rejuvenated by drinking 'divine milk' (1951.251–84; 2.5.5). Texts accompanying scenes of a goddess holding out her menit necklace to a king usually refer to his receiving renewed life and vigour. This probably means that a kind of divine energy emanated from the menit (Desroches Noblecourt & Kuentz 1968.181–4). In one scene from the small golden shrine of Tutankhamon, the queen presents a menit necklace which is a personification of a goddess holding out *ankh* signs to the king (Troy 1986.101, fig. 70).

How far is any of this relevant to private persons and to menit necklaces that were presented to Hathor rather than to a god or a king? In some 18th dynasty Theban tombs, scenes from the Beautiful Festival of the Wadi show the tomb owner being presented with menit necklaces, as well as other cult objects of Hathor and Amon-Reᶜ, by female relatives or by priestesses of Hathor (*e.g.* Nina Davies & Gardiner 1915.94–6, pls. 19–20; Davies 1923.23–5, pls. 53–4; 1930.40–1, pl. 39; 1943.60–1, pl. 63). In the accompanying texts, the tomb owner is promised a variety of benefits, from renewed vigour and a long life on earth, to regeneration and an eternity spent in the retinue of the gods (Schott 1953.110–12). The women presenting the necklaces appear to play the role of Hathor, bestowing on the tomb owner gifts comparable to those which the king acquires from the menit necklace of the goddess (Nina Davies & Gardiner 1915.94–6). Thus, an originally royal privilege may here be taken over by private persons in funerary religion. This annexation could be seen as analogous to the way in which it became possible to show a private person standing beneath the head of a Hathor cow (2.4.6). These people are not shown encircled by the cow's necklace, but some kind of protective union is implied.

Bruyère suggested that the type of temple statue which holds a Hathor mask and a menit necklace (*e.g.* Pl. 40) depicts the owner in the role of Ihy, who is often shown offering a sistrum and sometimes a menit necklace to his mother Hathor (1952.83–6). Some of these statue owners bear the priestly title of *ihy* (Moret 1919.164–5; Barucq & Daumas 1980.438; see further 3.2.3). In Chapter 47 of the Book of the Dead, the deceased is said to be in Hathor's entourage, either as Ihy himself or as an *ihy* priest (Allen 1975.51). A funerary interpretation of offerings to Hathor is always possible, but there is no definite evidence to link the votive menits specifically with Ihy.

Since the menit counterpoise may have erotic connotations and can be decorated with the imagery of Chemmis, it might be seen as belonging to the group of offerings to Hathor which relate to fertility. However, this interpretation is less likely to apply to the royal name counterpoises from Serabit el-Khadim and Timna. The inscription on the private stela which shows a menit necklace being offered to Hathor Nebet-Hetepet (Chappaz 1983 figs. 9–10), is a *ḥtp di nsw* formula requesting the standard list of 'life benefits' (2.1.5). The presentation of menit counterpoises could have been intended to evoke Hathor in her benevolent aspect as the goddess who bestows life and vigour with her necklace. P. Germond notes that some Late Period faience counterpoises are inscribed with the common *di ʿnḫ n* formula and suggests that by wearing such an amulet the owner pacified, and placed themself under the protection of, the goddess named on the counterpoise (1981.323–5). The presentation of menit necklaces at Serabit el-Khadim and Timna – and perhaps also at the other sites – may well have served this double purpose. As with many other categories of votive object, the menit counterpoises offered to Hathor evidently had more than one meaning.

Summary

Faience beads were the most common type of object found at each of the six sites. Other materials used for beads include carnelian, amethyst, shell, and glass. Reed packet beads and mud 'loaves' studded with blue ring beads are unique to Deir el-Bahri. Some beads were used to decorate votive textiles and fertility figurines. Most of the beads were originally strung on menit necklaces or on leather thongs with plaques and amulets. Wood or faience menit counterpoises were excavated at Deir el-Bahri, Mirgissa, Timna, and Serabit el-Khadim. The faience examples usually bear contemporary royal names, as do many of the faience votive bracelets found at Serabit el-Khadim and Timna. Rings were not a very common offering, but unusual faience Hathor mask rings were discovered at Deir el-Bahri and Serabit el-Khadim. Earrings were offered at Mirgissa and Timna.

Only the Mirgissa shrine had a high proportion of jewellery which might have been the personal ornaments of the donors. Nearly all the jewellery from the Hathor sites consists of specially made votive pieces. The faience menit counterpoises and bracelets could have been official rather than private gifts. Precious materials rarely seem to have been used in votive jewellery; symbolic value was more important. Menit necklaces were associated with the cult of Hathor from the Old Kingdom onwards. The menit counterpoise can symbolize propitiation of a deity, protection by a deity, revitalization for living or dead individuals, and the promise of rebirth.

2.10 Amulets

The small objects described in this chapter consist of pendants, scaraboids, models, and figurines of types that are usually classified as amuletic. At Deir el-Bahri, some amulets were found strung on leather cords with other small votive objects (*e.g.* Pls. 2, 57d). At the remaining sites, there was little or no indication of the manner in which the amulets were presented to Hathor. The amulets are grouped according to type.

2.10.1 Types of amulet

1 *Plant forms* (Figs. 2, 6; Pls. 2, 6, 8, 57a)

Stylised plant forms, corresponding to common New Kingdom bead types, were found in small numbers at all six sites. Pendants in faience and carnelian perhaps representing pomegranates occurred at Deir el-Bahri (*e.g.* London BM 43188, 47513), Faras (*e.g.* Pl. 8.56; Oxford PR unnumbered, 5), Mirgissa (Vercoutter 1970 fig. 35, centre, left), Serabit el-Khadim (Petrie 1906 pl. 159, third row), and Gebel Zeit (Mey *et al.* 1980 fig. 1). Some palmettes in blue or green faience were recovered from Deir el-Bahri (*e.g.* London BM 47698, 41165; Pl. 2, top centre) and Gebel Zeit (Castel *et al.* 1984.50). Daisy beads in white and yellow faience featured at Serabit el-Khadim (Petrie 1906 pl. 159, second row) and Timna (Rothenberg 1972.172; 1988.205). A few cornflower pendants in blue and green faience were found at Deir el-Bahri (*e.g.* Edinburgh KSM 1901.547.43; London V&A 658.1905), Mirgissa (Karlin in Vercoutter 1970.342, no. 48), Serabit el-Khadim (*e.g.* London UC 35416a–d), and Gebel Zeit (Mey *et al.* 1980 fig. 1). At Mirgissa and Gebel Zeit, the small faience pendants included a number which seem to be derived from plant forms, but which cannot be identified specifically (Karlin in Vercoutter 1970.343, fig. 36; Castel *et al.*1984.50).

Hall noted finding 'models of persea fruit' at Deir el-Bahri and he illustrated two (in Naville 1913.17; Pl. 2, top right, second row). The British Museum has five such blue faience models from these excavations (41147, 43180, 44923–5). They are all hollow and the largest is 4.2 cm high. Several very similar models were excavated at Faras (*e.g.* London BM 51265–6 = Pl. 57a). Yellow faience mandragora or persea fruit pendants were found at Gebel Zeit (Castel *et al.* 1984.50). Hall also mentioned finding 'bunches of dark grapes' (in Naville 1913.17). I have traced fragments of seven such bunches in dark purple-blue faience from this site (Ilkley 7095; London BM 41168, 43179, 47883; New York MMA 07.230.34; Oxford Ash. E 2760–1). One example in the British Museum is almost intact and measures 4.9 × 3.9 cm (47883), while another must have come from a bunch about 10 cm high (43179). Carter also found 'model bunches of grapes' at Deir el-Bahri (1912.32). Two bunches, 6–7 cm high and pierced for suspension, were recovered from Mirgissa (Karlin in Vercoutter 1970.340, nos. 8–9, fig. 46). Petrie illustrated two small pendants in the form of bunches of grapes from Serabit el-Khadim (1906 pl. 159, second row; London UC 35394) and similar pieces were recovered from Gebel Zeit (Mey *et al.* 1980.305–7, fig. 1; Castel *et al.* 1984.50).

Currelly stated that:–

> We were for a long time puzzled by a large number of flat pieces of glaze about two inches long, and of the general form of a willow leaf, but with a broken base. These, I later found out, were set in clay models of the lower part of a lotus and formed a mass of blue petals on the top. (in Naville 1913.29)

I have not been able to trace any of these clay and faience models, but the British Museum has two small faience flowers which could be lotuses (47710–1), as well as a miniature lotiform chalice, 3 cm high, (41026) from Deir el-Bahri. Carter found a faience flower and a model lotus bud (Pl. 6.j–k) at this site. A similar faience lotus bud was among the 18th dynasty offerings at Dendara (Fig. 6.14), and examples have been recovered from 18th dynasty royal tombs (*e.g.* Daressy 1902 pl. 30; Carter & Newberry 1904 pl. 26). Two unusual faience pendants from Serabit el-Khadim show a lotus leaf on water (Petrie 1906 pl. 155.6 = Oxford Ash. E 3359; London UC 35351). Five lotus leaf (London UC 353964a–f) and six lotus flower pendants (London UC 35365–6, 35423a–d) were recovered from this site. Green faience lotus flowers and papyrus amulets were among the offerings at Gebel Zeit (Mey *et al.* 1980.305–7 fig. 1; Castel *et al.* 1984.50). Petrie illustrated two miniature papyriform columns from Serabit el-Khadim (1906 pl. 155.17 = London UC 35357–8). The Petrie Collection has two other fragments of such faience columns from these excavations (35359–60). One carnelian lotus bud pendant (Rothenberg 1988.210, fig. 83.112) and three faience lotus flower pendants were found at Timna (1988.211, fig. 84.119–21).

Many of the fruit and flower forms may have been used in jewellery for decorative rather than amuletic purposes. It is possible that some of the faience models were dedicated as permanent substitutes for daily offerings of fruit and flowers. Except in funerary contexts, this does not seem to have been a common practice in Egypt, but the wooden bouquets from household altars at Deir el-Medina provide one example (Bruyère 1939.210–11, fig. 100). Winlock suggested that fruit and flowers were offered in the 'marsh bowls' found at Deir el-Bahri (1942.81). Hall noted that:–

> Interesting relics of the XVIIIth Dynasty are the shells found in the deposit of votive offerings. The fruits comprise dûm, date, fig and nutmeg. The last must have come from the East, and it, with several of the shells, may well be relics of Hatshepsu's expedition to Punt. (in Naville 1913.18)

The British Museum has a nutmeg, a fig, a date stone, a dom palm fruit, an ear of emmer (41468–72), a papyrus umbel (41183), and a bundle of reeds wrapped in cloth and tied with a necklace of faience beads (43214) from this site. The material from the Timna temple includes a few nuts, date seeds and olive kernels, and over 700 grape pips (Kislev in Rothenberg 1988.240).

Even if some of the models were offered in place of real fruit and flowers, this need not diminish their symbolic value. Derchain has suggested that the fact that

the persea fruits ripened just before the inundation led to their being associated
with the life-giving flood waters. He points out that a link with rebirth is implied in
the extensive use of the persea in mummy garlands and during the Beautiful
Festival of the Wadi (1975a.72; 1976.8). Both these factors might make the persea a
suitable offering to Hathor. Vine arbours are also associated with the Beautiful
Festival of the Wadi and are painted on the ceilings of some 18th dynasty tombs
(Schott 1953.91–2, pl. 12). Grapes, which were mainly grown in the Delta, are not
common in offering scenes, but they are shown being brought to Hathor on some
votive textiles from Deir el-Bahri (2.2.5). On these cloths, a grapevine can be
combined with the 'cow and mountain' (Cat.3.3) or 'cow and marsh' motifs
(Pl. 22a). The offering of grapes may have evoked Hathor in her aspect as Lady of
Drunkenness, in which she seems to have mediated between the realms of the living
and the dead (2.4.6). Towards the end of the 18th dynasty, faience bunches of
grapes were in general use as jewellery elements and ceiling decorations (e.g. Hayes
1959.254, 278; Samson 1978.87), so the association with funerary rites cannot be
given too much weight.

    Like the persea, the lotus plant seems to have been a general symbol of
fecundity. The flower of the blue lotus was a symbol of rebirth (Hornung &
Staehelin 1976.164). Lotus buds and flowers decorate many of the votive offerings
including scaraboids (e.g. Fig. 3, top left); faience bowls (e.g. Pls. 7, 39, 63); menit
counterpoises (e.g. Pls. 4–5, 58); and Hathor mask and cow plaques (e.g. Pls. 2,
centre, 31). Some scholars link the blue lotus specifically with Hathor in her role as
mother of the Divine Child (Barguet 1953.104; Strauss 1974.79). Lotuses could
also have been offered to evoke the suckling of Horus in Chemmis (2.4.6). The
same is true of the papyrus amulets and miniature papyriform columns. Tall faience
lamps in the form of papyrus stems were found among the votive offerings at
Dendara (Fig. 6.12–3; van Siclen 1985.71, fig. 4), and in the sanctuary of Sekhmet
at Abusir (Borchardt 1910.133–4, fig. 184). Petrie proposed that such lamps were
used at Dendara to form a papyrus thicket around a statue of Hathor in cow form
(1900.28). 'Shaking Papyrus for Hathor' was an ancient rite (2.2.5). The bundle of
reeds from Deir el-Bahri (London BM 43214) could suggest that any type of marsh
flora was a suitable offering to Hathor. It is possible that this bundle should be
interpreted as the remains of a magical rite (see 3.3), but there could still be a
symbolic link with the protection of Horus in Chemmis.

2 Shells (Fig. 2;, Pl. 8)

A few cowrie and conus shells and a piece of Red Sea coral were found among the
votive offerings at Deir el-Bahri (e.g. London BM 41475–80; Hall in Naville
1913.18). Some pierced cowrie and conus shells were recovered from Faras (Oxford
PR unnumbered), and one pierced conus shell from Mirgissa (Karlin in Vercoutter
1970.340, no. 7a). Cowries and other common types of Red Sea shell, along with
coral and dried sea-urchins, were discovered in the temple at Timna (Rothenberg
1972.176, pl. 108; 1988.208–9, 260–6, pl. 153). Red Sea shells are among the small
objects found at Gebel Zeit. Most of them seem to come from the domestic area
close to the shrine (Castel & Soukiassian 1989a.165; Castel et al. 1986.100), but

cowrie and latirus (?) shells were found inside the shrine (Castel *et al.* 1984.48, 50, fig. 3). Intact mussel shells seem to have served as dishes, while fragments were used to make necklaces for fertility figurines (Castel *et al.* 1985.19). Shells were also found in the small Second Intermediate Period shrines at Site 2 (Posener-Kriéger 1986.381–2).

Many of the Timna shells were pierced for stringing. D. Reese suggests that the larger unpierced specimens might have been used as clappers, offering plates, or incense burners (in Rothenberg 1988.265). Kertesz believes that shell necklaces were the votive gifts of 'non-Egyptian workers from Midian and local inhabitants from the Arabah and the Negeb' (1988.209), but the occurrence of pierced shells at sites in Egypt and Nubia shows that they need not be classed as an un-Egyptian type of offering.

Most of these shells were probably prized for their shape and colour and, in southern Egypt and Nubia, for their scarcity, rather than for any specific symbolic value. However, the cowrie shell's resemblance to the vulva may have led to its being a symbol of female sexuality, of fecundity and, perhaps as an extension of this, of rebirth (Hornung & Staehelin 1976.122). A few faience cowries were found at Deir el-Bahri (*e.g.* London BM 41474; Fig. 2, bottom left) and Faras (London BM 51535; Oxford PR Unnumbered). Until recently, cowrie shell girdles were worn by women in many parts of Africa to ward off sterility inflicted by the evil eye. Some scholars have suggested that the same idea was current in ancient Egypt (*e.g.* Petrie 1914.27; Aldred 1971.15–6). This would link the cowrie with Hathor's sphere of fertility, birth, and rebirth (2.6.1.1, 2.6.3).

3 *Animals* (Pls. 8, 59c)

The cow and cat figurines have been discussed in 2.4.1 and 2.5.1. No other animals are common among the offerings. The largest group is formed by baboons and monkeys. Naville found two small baboon pendants in blue faience (London BM 47505; Oxford PR unnumbered = Pl. 59c, top left) and a faience baboon figurine, 5.3 cm high (Brussels MR E 733), at Deir el-Bahri. The British Museum has a crude phallic baboon figurine, 8 cm high (47682), and the head of another baboon (43153), both in pottery, from these excavations. A pottery phallic figurine from Winlock's excavations at Deir el-Bahri (Cairo JE 58765) may also represent a baboon. Griffith illustrated a small baboon pendant and the upper half of a faience figurine of a baboon (Pl. 8.32, 18 = London BM 51358; Oxford Ash. 1912.948). A faience cosmetic jar decorated with four monkeys (Karlin in Vercoutter 1970.351, no. 148, fig. 39), two fragments from rather cruder faience baboon figurines (1970.351, nos. 152–3), and a baboon pendant (1970.344, no. 70) were found at Mirgissa. There were also the baboon rings noted in 2.9.3.2. Three faience baboon pendants (London UC 35379–81) and a kohl tube held by a single monkey (Manchester 914) were excavated at Serabit el-Khadim, as well as several small sandstone statues of baboons (Petrie 1906.123–4, pl. 127; Černý 1955 nos. 217, 285). The offerings at Gebel Zeit included a number of crude pottery baboon figurines, some ithyphallic (Mey *et al.* 1980 fig. 5.2; Castel *et al.* 1984.52, fig. 52; Castel *et al.* 1985.20, fig. 11; 1986.104, pl. 5.11). There was also a New Kingdom baboon pendant in blue faience (1980.306, no. 10, fig. 1.2; Castel *et al.* 1985.17, fig. 3), as well as a green jasper baboon which may date to the Middle Kingdom or the Second Intermediate Period (Mey *et al.* 1980.306, no. 11, fig. 1.2).

Other species are rare. Three faience pendants in the form of recumbent animals, one from Faras (London 51357; Karkowski 1981.111, no. 20), one from Mirgissa (Karlin in Vercoutter 1970.344, no. 72), and one from Serabit el-Khadim (London UC 35376) might be lions or lionesses. Three amulets of a lioness-headed deity were excavated at Timna (Rothenberg 1988.140, fig. 48.4, 7–8). Carter stated that he found faience sphinxes at Deir el-Bahri (1912.32), but I have not traced any examples. The glazed steatite scaraboids from Faras included single, well carved, gazelle, hedgehog (Pl. 8.40, 58, location unknown), and hare-backed (Pl. 8.42 = Oxford Ash. 1912.957) examples.

These three animals are all thought to be symbols of rebirth (Wallert 1970.127; Hornung & Staehelin 1976.115, 138–40), while the leonine pendants might be representations of Hathor in her lioness form. However, these pieces, which are of common early or mid 18th dynasty types, were probably items of personal jewellery and may have had no individual significance as votive offerings. Baboon pendants are common; baboon figurines more unusual. Bruyère suggested that the monkey and baboon figurines which he found in houses at Deir el-Medina were fertility charms (1939.102). The baboon is also one of the protective animals which feature on apotropaic wands of the late Middle Kingdom and Second Intermediate Period (Bourriau 1988.116, 156). Monkeys often appear in scenes with erotic connotations (Manniche 1987.43–4), while the phallic nature of the baboon god Baba shows that baboons were linked to male sexuality (Derchain 1952; 2.7.2). As votive offerings, the pottery baboons may therefore be grouped with the phallic objects and the sphere of fertility. It is also possible that some should be identified with Thoth, who was worshipped in baboon form at Serabit el-Khadim (Petrie 1906.122–4). Thoth in ape form travelled to Nubia to pacify the 'Distant Goddess' (2.5.5). This association of Thoth with the transformation of Hathor from a fierce to a gentle deity would make representations of baboons a suitable offering to the goddess.

4 *Birds* (Fig. 3; Pl. 8)

One duck-backed scaraboid was among the objects from Deir el-Bahri drawn by Miss Carhew (Fig. 3). Griffith illustrated two small faience ducks (Pl. 8.39–40, location unknown) and a well carved duck-backed scaraboid in glazed steatite (1921 pl. 18.12 = Oxford Ash. 1912.959). This scaraboid is 1.4 cm long and has the cartouche of an Amonhotpe, probably Amonhotpe I, on its base. One fragment of a faience duck and two intact ducks in blue glass, each pierced for suspension, were found at Mirgissa (Karlin in Vercoutter 1970.341, no. 34, 344, nos. 75–6). At least one duck scaraboid was recovered from Gebel Zeit (Castel *et al.* 1985.19, fig. 8). All these ducks have their heads twisted round to face their tails. A tiny glazed steatite hawk was excavated at Faras (Pl. 8.25 = London BM 51356) and two similar pieces at Serabit el-Khadim (London UC 35377–8). An ostracon with a crowned falcon, perhaps representing Montu, was found at Mirgissa (Karlin in Vercoutter 1970.253, no. 183, fig. 36). A faience fragment from Timna has been identified as part of a falcon pendant (Kertesz in Rothenberg 1988.21–11, fig.84.122). Two broken wooden figurines, one of a crowned falcon and one of a crowned anthropomorphic god with a falcon head, were recovered from Gebel Zeit (Castel *et al.* 1984.52, fig. 2; Castel & Soukiassian 1985.286; Posener-Kriéger 1985 pl. 66b). Falcon amulets are said to have been excavated there (Castel *et al.* 1984.52), and an unusual Tell el-Yahudiya ware jug in the form of a hawk was found in the temple area (Posener-Kriéger 1985.298, pl. 66a).

Ducks, especially with their heads facing their tails, are thought to have had an erotic significance in New Kingdom art (Hermann 1932; Derchain 1976.6–7). They may have served as fertility charms. The faience falcons could represent Horus as the son or consort of Hathor. At Gebel Zeit, Horus *nb ḫ;swt* appears on two of the stelae from the shine and seems to have been a 'co-templar' deity with Hathor (Castel & Soukiassian 1985.290–1, pls. 62, 64; 1.6). The falcon-headed statuette may have been a cult image. However, the range of votive falcon figurines and plaques found at Giza (1.7) does not occur at Gebel Zeit. The duck scaraboids and the duck and falcon pendants are more likely to have been personal jewellery than specially made votive offerings.

5 *Fish* (Fig. 3; Pls. 3, 8, 42a)

Two 'blue glaze fish' are mentioned in the EEF distribution lists for Deir el-Bahri. One of these is a fragment 5.5 cm long (Ilkley CC 8425/23); the other is 2 cm long and pierced for suspension (London BM 41159). Miss Carhew drew a fish-backed scaraboid from the site (Fig. 3). One *wadjet* eye scaraboid from Deir el-Bahri has a fish and lotus motif on its base (Boston MFA 06 2499; D'Auria *et al.* 1988 no 69).Griffith illustrated three fish-backed scaraboids from Faras (1921 pl. 18.5, 14 = Oxford Ash. 1912.960b–c, pl. 18.54 = Oxford Ash. 1912.960a). These are in glazed steatite. Two are intricately carved; one having the cartouche of an Amonhotpe, probably Amonhotpe I, on its base and the other a fish holding a lotus in its mouth. The Pitt-Rivers has two smaller and cruder steatite fish, both pierced for suspension, from this site (unnumbered), and the Royal Scottish Museum has a small faience 'fish-shaped plaque' (1912.562; Karkowski 1981.111). A detailed faience fish figurine which, when intact, would have measured about 12 × 8.5 cm, was excavated at Serabit el-Khadim (Pl. 42a, bottom right = Manchester 909).

All these objects represent *Tilapia Nilotica*, which also occurs as a motif on bowls from Deir el-Bahri, Faras, Serabit el-Khadim, and Timna (*e.g.* Pl. 3, bottom right; see 2.11.3). This fish was a symbol of fecundity and rebirth, and may have been associated with the renewal of sexual potency in the afterlife (Dambach and Wallert 1966; Wallert 1970.283–94; Staehelin 1976.76–84). It has even been suggested that the *tilapia* can be a form of Hathor, in her role as mother of the sun god (Chappaz 1983.13).

A quantity of desiccated fish was found in the sanctuary at Mirgissa (1.3.3). Most fish were ritually impure and so, in theory at least, they were not offered in state temples (Yoyotte in Posener 1962.91–2). The excavators of the Mirgissa shrine do not state what species of fish were found. If they were all *tilapia*, then there probably was a specific symbolic link with Hathor. It could be that the fish had to act as a substitute for the standard offering of haunches of meat, which a community shrine probably could not obtain or afford on a regular basis. The bones of several types of fresh and seawater fish were found inside the temple at Timna (Rothenberg 1988.241–5, pls. 143–5). None is from species particularly associated with Hathor. The fish had clearly been eaten in the temple and may have been ritually offered to the goddess first. This is an example of the way in which special circumstances could cause deviations from standard religious practices. There is evidence that fish and shell-fish were cooked in the domestic area just behind the New Kingdom shrine at Gebel Zeit (Castel *et al.* 1984.53), so fish may have been offered to the goddess there too.

6 *Amphibians and reptiles* (Pl. 8)

Griffith illustrated two small faience or glazed steatite frogs from Faras (Pl. 8.23–4 = location unknown). The British Museum has a fine example from this site in blue frit (51354; Karkowski 1981.109). It is 1.5 cm high, pierced for suspension, and bears the prenomen of Kamose. A similar, frog scaraboid of the early 18th dynasty was found at Gebel Zeit (Castel *et al.* 1985.19, fig. 9). One fragmentary faience plaque from Faras is incised with crocodiles (Oxford Ash.942a; Karkowski 1981.109–10, pl. 12.2) and a small faience pendant in the form of a crocodile was found at Mirgissa (Karlin in Vercoutter 1970.344, no. 71). At some sites, such as Sumenu (Rizeiqat) and Kom Ombo, Hathor was regarded as the consort of Sobek, the crocodile god.

One faience uraeus, only 1.3 cm high, was excavated at Faras (Pl. 8.25 = London BM 51355). Seven small faience uraei, mostly with sun discs, were recovered from Mirgissa (Karlin in Vercoutter 1970.344, nos. 26–33). These are are all of different sizes, and so are unlikely to have come from a single necklace. Only one uraeus amulet was found at Serabit el-Khadim (London UC 35384), but the uraeus serpent is said to have been one of the most common types of amulet at Gebel Zeit (Castel *et al.* 1984.50). A wooden uraeus from this site may have formed part of a shrine (Posener-Kriéger 1986.381, pl. 71b).

Frogs were associated with birth and rebirth (Altenmüller 1965.170; Hornung & Staehelin 1976.111), but not specifically with Hathor. In the context of the relatively small number of offerings in the Mirgissa shrine, the seven uraei form a significant group, as do the uraeus amulets at Gebel Zeit. They probably represent Hathor in serpent form in her Solar Eye aspect (2.5.5).

7 *Insects, including scarabs* (Fig. 4; Pls. 2, 6, 8, 57d)

One locust pendant in black faience was found at Deir el-Bahri (London V&A 1200.1909), and a glazed steatite pendant from Faras may also represent a locust (Oxford PR unnumbered = Fig. 206, bottom right). Griffith illustrated three fly pendants from Faras (Pl. 8.51–2 = London BM 51352–3, 53, location unknown). The examples in the British Museum are made of glazed steatite and pierced for suspension. The Pitt-Rivers Museum has two similar, but cruder fly pendants from this site (unnumbered). One specimen was found at Mirgissa (Karlin in Vercoutter 1970.340, fig. 44e) and another at Gebel Zeit (Mey *et al.* 1980.308–9, no. 25, fig. 2.1). These pieces were probably items of personal jewellery. The same will have been true of many of the scarabs found at the five sites. Due to the very large amount of material involved, only a brief description of the range of scarabs at each site can be given.

The EEF distribution lists for Deir el-Bahri do not give the number of scarabs sent to each museum and Hall and Currelly did not indicate the quantity found. Miss Carhew drew about 20 scarabs and scaraboids from the 1892–4 excavations (Figs. 3–4; EES Archives). Forty-three scarabs or scaraboids are illustrated in the report on the excavations of 1903–7 (Naville 1913 pl. 25). One Middle Kingdom or Second Intermediate Period scarab bears the name of Senwosret III (1913.14, 26); the remainder date to the New Kingdom. I have examined about 200 specimens from these excavations. The royal names range from Ahmose to Amonhotpe II, with Hatshepsut being the most frequent (Hall in Naville 1913.14; Hall 1913.51–2, 54–5, 66; Fig. 4). Some of the scarabs are very small, have plain bases, and are made in brilliant blue faience (2.9.1). On the more elaborate examples, the bases are incised with floral designs, single devices such as a scorpion or a dancing man, royal names, mottoes, or jumbled hieroglyphs (*e.g.* Figs. 3–4; Pl. 2, bottom row). Animal-backed scaraboids are rare at. Although similar in type, few of the scarabs found among the offerings can compare in quality with those recovered from the foundation deposits of Hatshepsut's temple (*e.g.* Hayes 1959.87–8, fig. 48). Carter mentioned finding 'scarabs, scarab shaped and cowroid beads' at Deir el-Bahri (1912.32). Six of these are included in one of his photographs (Pl. 6F-G). Winlock stated that he recovered 'innumerable' scarabs bearing royal names from Ahmose to Amonhotpe III, though 'mostly of Thutmose III' (1923.28). He also found 'between three and four thousand' plain scarabs (2.9.1).

Griffith noted that 'About two hundred engraved scarabs and scaraboids were found' at Faras; 28 were illustrated in his report (1921.86, pl. 18). He also stated that 'plain scarabs' occurred 'in profusion' (1921.86). Karkowski publishes 57 scarabs and scaraboids from Faras which are are now in the Khartoum Museum, the British Museum, the Ashmolean Museum, and the Royal Scottish Museum (1981.92–108, 111–2, pls. 6–7). These include royal name scarabs of Kamose, Amonhotpe I, Thutmose I, and Thutmose III. Almost all the remaining scarabs have bases inscribed with mottoes or jumbled hieroglyphs. The Pitt-Rivers Museum has a further 90 scarabs from Faras. Thirty have bases decorated with mottoes or jumbled hieroglyphs, and 50 have floral or geometrical designs. A few have a single device such as a bound prisoner or a gazelle. Many of the scarabs are of fine workmanship. This museum also has 12 small, plain scarabs (in Box 18). The date range of the Faras scarabs covers the Second Intermediate Period and the early and mid 18th dynasty.

Only 14 scarabs and one glazed steatite button seal were recovered from the Hathor sanctuary at Mirgissa (Karlin in Vercoutter 1970.341, 352–3). The two most elaborate examples bear the prenomen of Amonhotpe III (1970 nos. 164, 167). Six of the scarabs, one in carnelian, one in red and four in blue faience, have plain bases. The remainder are incised with mottoes or jumbled hieroglyphs. Scarabs were also fairly scarce at Serabit el-Khadim. Petrie mentioned excavating 'imitation scarabs of blue pottery' (1906.152) and illustrated 22 strung together (1906 pl. 159, fifth row). In his table of royal name objects, Petrie listed one scarab each of Thutmose I, Thutmose III, and Amonhotpe III (Manchester 961, 964, 966), two of Seti I, and one of Merenptah (location unknown; 1906.149). A group of 17 scarabs from these excavations (Manchester 956–73), mainly with floral or geometrical designs on the bases, ranges in date from the 13th to the 19th dynasty. The Petrie Collection has ten scarabs from Serabit el-Khadim (London UC 15798, 35444–52), ranging in date from the Second Intermediate Period to the 19th dynasty. It includes a cattle-hunt scarab of Amenhotpe III (15798 = Petrie 1906 pl. 155.7).

Scarabs were also scarce at Timna. Rothenberg states that:—

> A number of scarabs and seals were found, bearing animal representations, geometrical designs and hieroglyphs. (1972.166)

Seven scarabs, five small plaques, and two seals are published in the final report (Rothenberg 1988.137–9, fig. 46). None of these objects definitely bears a royal name. Schulman believes that most of the inscriptions should be read as cryptograms on the name of Amon-Reᶜ (1988.137).

Only a few scarabs from Gebel Zeit have so far been published. They include two Second Intermediate Period (Castel *et al.* 1984.49; Castel *et al.* 1985.28, fig. 28) and five early New Kingdom examples (Mey *et al.* 1980.308–10, fig. 2.1). Apparently, numerous scarabs bearing the names of 18th dynasty kings have been recovered (Posener-Kriéger 1985.298). Examples dating to Amonhotpe I and Amonhotpe III have been published (Castel *et al.* 1984.49). As well as the duck and frog-backed scaraboids (2.11.4, 6), this site produced an unusual piece with the back in the form of a prostrate man or ape (1984.51, fig. 8). Small scarabs were among the jewellery worn by fertility figurines found at the site (2.6.1.2–3; 2.9.2.1); the excavators suggest that old scarabs were used for this purpose (Castel *et al.* 1985.19).

As an amulet, the scarab beetle is primarily associated with rebirth (Hornung & Staehelin 1976.13–7), but it was in such common use that its specific symbolic value may have become almost irrelevant. The plain scarabs should probably be regarded as beads (2.9.1). The huge quantities of these scarabs found at Deir el-Bahri suggest that they were locally made, especially for votive necklaces, and that such necklaces were the most common offering to Hathor at this site. The plain scarabs from Faras and Serabit el-Khadim are also likely to have been made for votive purposes. Of the inscribed or decorated scarabs, some may have been made for stringing on votive necklaces (*e.g.* Pl. 57d), some may have been used as seals in the temples, and others, particularly the animal-backed scaraboids, may have been worn as amulets before being dedicated to Hathor.

8 *Bes* (Fig. 2, Pls. 1, 8, 60a)

Apart from Hathor herself, Bes and Taweret are the only deities who represented in significant numbers among the votive offerings. In the case of Bes, a term such as 'spirit' or 'supernatural being' might be more appropriate than 'deity'. The name Bes is used here to cover a whole group of supernatural dwarf figures, who are sometimes identified as Bes, sometimes as Aha or Hity. The female form of Bes does not appear to be represented among the offerings.

A few Bes amulets were found at all six sites. Three 'blue glaze' figures of Bes and a 'necklace of Hathor heads and Bes pendants' are mentioned in the EEF distribution lists for Deir el-Bahri. A plaque from the 1892–4 excavations drawn by Miss Carhew shows what looks like a Bes figure holding a club (Fig. 2, second row). The 'club' might be a wand, a knife, or even a snake, as all of these can be held by the Bes figures which appear on apotropaic wands (*e.g.* Altenmüller 1965 figs. 9, 13). Winlock found one faience Bes figure, along with Hathor masks and beads, in a foundation deposit of Djeser-Djeseru (Hayes 1959.88). The leather hanging from Deir el-Bahri which probably depicts a Bes dancer (Pl. 54) has been described in 2.7.2. A pottery face illustrated by Naville (Pl. 1, bottom right) may come from a Bes jug or vase.

Griffith illustrated one faience Bes amulet (Pls. 8.36, 60a, top left = London BM 51360). It is 1.3 cm high and depicts Bes in a squatting position with the head shown frontally. Four faience amulets showing Bes in this pose were excavated at Mirgissa (Karlin in Vercoutter 1970.340–4, nos. 17–20). These range in height from 1–3.5 cm. One wears a feather crown (1970 no. 18). Six small, indistinct figures in green, blue, or violet faience may represent Bes, with head in profile, playing a tambourine (1970.344, nos. 21–6). Bes amulets of this type are characteristic of the late 18th dynasty and the Amarna period (Bosse-Griffiths 1977.99–101).

The Petrie Collection has six faience Bes amulets from Serabit el-Khadim, two showing him playing a tambourine, and four with him in a squatting position (London UC 35372, GN 35419). Petrie illustrated a hollow faience head of Bes wearing a feather crown which probably formed the neck of a small vase (1906.150, pl. 155.18). He also excavated fragments of at least two Ramessid alabaster vases in the form of Bes (1906 pl. 144.11; Leeds 1922 pl. 2, upper). One intact faience Bes amulet, 2.8 cm. high, was found at Timna (Rothenberg 1988.140, fig. 48.9). Two headless fragments are likely to have come from similar amulets (1988 fig. 48.4, 10). Schulman identifies these and three tiny intact amulets (1988 fig. 48.1–3) as Pataikos (1988.139–40), but all these pieces have the typical bandy-legged, hands on hips posture of Bes amulets. On the two headless examples a tail is visible, which supports an identification with Bes. Bes playing the tambourine is one of the three most common types of amulet found at Gebel Zeit (Castel *et al.* 1984.50). Four examples from this site have been published so far. One is of the squatting type (Mey *et al.* 1980.305, no. 22, fig. 1.3), while the other three show Bes dancing and playing the tambourine (1980.305–9, nos. 9, 27, figs. 1.2, 2.1, pls. 80d–e).

Faience Bes figurines were among the offerings at the Temple of the Obelisks at Byblos (Dunand 1950 pl. 180). These figurines are similar to examples from Middle Kingdom burials (*e.g.* Bourriau 1988.112–13, no. 99). Jewellery incorporating Bes amulets is occasionally found in New Kingdom burials (*e.g.* Peet & Loat 1913 pl. 16; Brunton & Engelbach 1927 pl. 42; Hayes 1959.134, 180). Seven Bes pendants are thought to come from the Royal Tomb at el-ʿAmarna (Martin 1974.79–80, pl. 50). Bes amulets are common in 18th and 19th dynasty domestic contexts (*e.g.* Peet & Pendlebury 1933.41, pls. 28–9; Bruyère 1939.103; Hayes 1959.252, 254; Borchardt and Ricke 1980.18, 26, 31–2, 41, 44, 46–53, 61, 64, 66, etc.; Herrmann 1990.29–30). The Bes amulets among the offerings might therefore be items of personal jewellery, but the occurrence of a small Bes pendant in a foundation deposit at Deir el-Bahri suggests that such pendants might be made as votive offerings (see 3.1). Alabaster unguent vases in the shape of Bes were found in the tomb of Tutankhamon (2.11.1.2), and Bes is a common motif on containers for cosmetics (Bruyère 1939.99, 102–3). The Bes vases at Serabit el-Khadim might be explained simply by his association with perfume and cosmetics, but two other reasons for offering figures of Bes to Hathor can be proposed.

First, there is Bes's link with conception, childbirth, and the protection of mothers and young children (Pinch 1983.412–3). This may be particularly relevant at Deir el-Bahri, where Bes and Taweret are shown in one of the royal birth scenes in Djeser-Djeseru (Naville [1894] pl. 51). Bes amulets could therefore belong to the group of offerings, consisting of fertility figurines, phalli, model vulvae and breasts, and Taweret amulets (2.10.1.9), which were dedicated to Hathor to ensure the conception and/or the safe birth and rearing of children. Second, there is the role of Bes in the myth of the 'Distant Goddess' (Junker 1911.86). Columns in the Hathor temple at Philae have carvings depicting dancing Bes figures playing musical instruments while escorting the pacified goddess back to Egypt (Daumas 1969.9–10, 17, pls. 1–2). Figures of Bes might then have been offered to placate Hathor in her dangerous aspect, especially at Serabit el-Khadim and Timna.

9 *Taweret* (Figs. 6, 13b; Pls. 2, 8, 57d, 59c–61,)

The name Taweret is often given to a composite lion/crocodile/hippopotamus deity, although other names for this being appear in ancient texts. The EEF distribution lists for Deir el-Bahri mention one 'Taweret mould', one 'blue glaze Taweret' (Kyoto UM 577), and a group of 'Taweret beads'. The piece in Kyoto is about 6 cm high, worked on one side only, and finely detailed. Six 'Taweret beads' from these excavations are now in the Pitt-Rivers Museum. The term 'Taweret bead' can be applied to highly stylized figures which are vertically pierced for stringing. The examples in the Pitt-Rivers are 3–8 cm high and in shades of dark and light blue faience. The museum also has an intact necklace from Deir el-Bahri which is strung with two small Taweret beads, two scarabs, and a leaf(?) pendant (Oxford PR 1904.35.87 = Pl. 57d). Hall illustrated one ordinary Taweret bead as well as an object which might be a double bead, showing two figures of the goddess standing back to back (Pl. 2, bottom left, location unknown). A mould for a double Taweret amulet was found at el-ʿAmarna (Samson 1978 pl. 50), and the British Museum has an unprovenanced wooden figure of this type (London BM 11480).

The details of the composite figure of Taweret are visible on a well made faience amulet from Faras (Pl. 61 = London BM 51258). This flat-backed piece is 4.1 cm high and pierced for suspension. The British Museum also has a smaller Taweret amulet from this site (Pls. 8.33, 60, top right = BM 51359), which appears to be carved in bone (Karkowski 1982.109). In addition, at least seven crude faience Taweret beads were recovered from Faras (Oxford Ash. 1912.944; Oxford PR 1912.211–17 = Pl. 59c). Two very similar beads were discovered at Mirgissa (Karlin in Vercoutter 1970.343, nos. 14–5) and nine at Serabit el-Khadim (London UC 35373–4, GN 35418–9; Oxford Ash. E 4468). The Petrie Collection and the Ashmolean Museum also have more finely executed Taweret figures from the latter site (UC 35375; Ash. Group No. E 4487). The example in the Ashmolean Museum is 2.5 cm high, made in green faience, and pierced through the stomach. One blue faience Taweret amulet from Gebel Zeit has so far been published (Mey *et al.* 1980.308–9, no. 26, fig. 2.1). At least two Taweret beads were among the 18th dynasty votive offerings at Dendara (Fig. 6.15, 17). A large group of faience hippopotami and three Taweret figurines were among the offerings in the Temple of the Obelisks at Byblos (Dunand 1950 nos. 15124–40, 15153–6).

Taweret beads and amulets are sometimes found in New Kingdom burials (*e.g.* Peet & Loat 1914 pl. 10; Brunton & Engelbach 1927 pl. 42.9; Winlock 1948.23, 33, pl. 14; Hayes 1959.13), but they are more common in domestic contexts (*e.g.* Peet & Pendlebury 1933.41, pls. 28–9; Bruyère 1939.107; Hayes 1959.252, 278, 322, 398). Gold Taweret beads occasionally form part of the jewellery of royal ladies (*e.g.* Pelizaeus Museum 1985 no. 121), and moulds for making Taweret amulets were found at the palace of Malqata (Bosse-Griffiths 1977.100). As with the Bes figures, it is possible that the Taweret beads and amulets among the offerings were items of personal jewellery. However, the mould found at Deir el-Bahri suggests that some Taweret figures were made for votive purposes.

As amulets, Taweret figures were probably worn during pregnancy and childbirth, and perhaps by nursing mothers. They are likely to have had a similar range of associations when used as votive offerings. Taweret's connection with childbirth is made explicit by her presence in royal birth scenes (Naville [1894] pl. 51; Brunner 1964.92, pl. 9) and by her title of 'Mistress of the Birth House' in the Graeco-Roman Period (Daumas 1958.29). Texts on Middle Kingdom apotropaic wands identify human mothers and babies with the infant sun god and his mother, and invoke the protectors of the Divine Child, among whom Bes and Taweret are prominent (Altenmüller 1965.66–9; Bosse-Griffiths 1977.102, fig. 1). Kemp notes that wall-paintings in houses at Deir el-Medina and in the craftsmen's village at el-ʿAmarna illustrate 'either a successful termination to childbirth and its ensuing period of uncleanliness or the deities who would ensure this (Bes and Thoëris)' (1979.53).

New Kingdom stone vases in the form of Taweret, or of women depicted with some of her characteristics, are thought to have held oil for anointing pregnant women (Brunner-Traut 1970a.38–48). The pendulous breasts of Taweret have been interpreted as those of a nursing mother (Bruyère 1939.98). Faience vases in the form of Taweret with pierced breasts, one of which was found among the votive offerings in the Sekhmet sanctuary at Abusir (Borchardt 1910.129–30, fig. 177), have been identified as milk containers (Darby *et al.* 1977.763–4, fig. 193; Doll in Brovarski 1982.293). Taweret in human form is shown suckling the king in the speos of Horemheb at Gebel el-Silsila (Desroches Noblecourt & Kuentz 1968.209), but many goddesses in human form appear in such scenes. There is no specific evidence to link the composite form of Taweret with suckling. The pendulous breasts and the paunch of her composite form resemble those of the so-called Nile deities, now known as fecundity figures (Baines 1985.127–8). Some scholars have therefore seen Taweret as a symbol of general fecundity (George 1977.40) or of the fecundating powers of the inundation (Altenmüller 1965.149; Desroches Noblecourt & Kuentz 1968.113, 212).

On bowls and vases from Deir el-Medina, Taweret is given the epithet ⟨hieroglyphs⟩, which seems to identify her with 'The Pure Water', although this is also a name for Gebel el-Silsila, a cult place of Taweret and a source of the inundation (Bruyère 1930.20–3; 1952.76–8). Since the inundation was thought to have its ultimate source in the waters of the Nun, Bruyère argued that the Middle Kingdom faience hippopotami painted with marsh flowers showed Taweret as a personification of the Nun (1952.76). Others have suggested that such hippopotami, which may be male, embody marsh hunting scenes (Bourriau 1988.119–20). In some vignettes to chapter 186 of the Book of the Dead, which combine the 'cow and marsh' and 'cow and mountain' motifs, a 'Taweret' figure is shown standing in front of the cow (*e.g.* Fig. 13b; Naville 1888 pl. 212). The spell itself refers to adoring Hathor and Mehet-Weret; the name Taweret is not mentioned in the available variants (Allen 1974.209–10). Bruyère used this linking of Taweret with the 'Great Flood' in the funerary context of the Western Mountain to support his theory that Taweret helped the deceased to be reborn, and purified his *ka* in preparation for his new life (1952.81). Others have seen Taweret as a symbol of regeneration in the primeval waters (Hornung & Staehelin 1976.127–9).

Bruyère stated that in his opinion Taweret 'n'est qu'un doublet populaire très caricatural d'Hathor' (1939.108). This may be too extreme a view, but it does appear that Taweret could be identified with Hathor in some of her aspects. In the funerary vignettes, the 'Taweret' figure and the cow seem to be two manifestations of a single deity. The votive basins and jars from Deir el-Medina name Taweret in their texts, but are usually decorated with Hathor masks (Bruyère 1952.72–6; Desroches Noblecourt & Kuentz 1968.112; see also 2.11.1.1). The 'cow and marsh' motif can be paralleled by scenes showing a hippopotamus in a papyrus thicket (*e.g.* Brunton *et al.* 1930 pl. 33; Hope 1987.50, fig. 67). Another iconographic link between the two goddesses is provided by the double Taweret figures. Like the bifrontal Hathor masks, these could express either a dual nature or a mediating role (2.3.4).

On a stela found at Deir el-Bahri in the temple of Thutmose III (Lipińska 1968.165, pl. 11.18), a priest and his wife adore an unnamed 'Taweret' figure which may, in this particular case, be a representation of Hathor. The Taweret beads and amulets among the votive offerings could be associated with general fecundity, with regeneration, or with protection in pregnancy and childbirth. A concern for the coming of the inundation and agricultural fertility might apply at Faras, but not at the other sites. The hope for regeneration would be shared by the donors at all the sites, but there is not very much evidence for Taweret's funerary aspect outside the Theban area. In the sphere of fertility, Taweret is distinguished from Hathor by not being definitely linked with conception or with suckling. In magical texts, the woman in labour may be identified with Hathor (2.6.4), but Taweret is invoked only as a protector of the mother and baby. It is probably in this capacity that she appears on a few fertility figurines (*e.g.* London BM 23071; D'Auria *et al.* 1988 no.74). The prominence of Taweret in the purification ritual which seems to have marked the end of a mother's period of isolation in the 'birth arbour' with her newborn baby (Brunner-Traut 1955.24; Kemp 1979.53) is presumably due to her 'Pure Water' aspect. A desire by, or on behalf of, female donors for protection during pregnancy and childbirth is a motive which could certainly apply at Deir el-Bahri, Faras and Mirgissa. The presence of numerous fertility figurines at Gebel Zeit and of a few examples at Serabit el-Khadim (2.6.1) shows that it need not be ruled out at desert mining sites.

10 *Throwsticks* (Fig. 6; Pl. 62)

Naville found at least two fragments from model throwsticks in faience at Deir el-Bahri (London BM 41081; Toronto ROM 907.18.148). An intact example with the cartouches of Hatshepsut was recovered from one of the foundation deposits of Djeser-Djeseru (Cairo JE 47715; PM II, 369). A faience fragment from Mirgissa might be the rounded end of a type of throwstick current from the end of the 18th dynasty (Karlin in Vercoutter 1970.339, no. 6). MacDonald brought back six throwstick fragments from Serabit el-Khadim (London BM 14945–7, 14953–5). Petrie found pieces of about 60 throwsticks at this site (Pl. 62; 1906.144–5, pl. 150), of which I have been able to examine 47. Five throwstick fragments were excavated at Timna (Rothenberg 1972.166, 169, pl. 90; 1988.135–6, fig. 45.2, 4–7).

All the throwsticks are made in blue or green faience with decorations and inscriptions in dark blue or purplish-black. When intact, they would have varied in length from 25–50 cm. Their shape underwent a change during the Amarna Period (Loeben 1987.147). This can be seen by comparing an example dating to Thutmose I (Petrie 1906 pl. 150.1 = Brussels MR E 2051) to one of Ramesses II (Petrie 1906 pl. 150.5 = Brussels MR E 2055). Most of the throwsticks are decorated and inscribed on both sides. These decorations consist of three kinds, parallel lines – which Hayes suggested imitated the lashings on functional wooden throwsticks (1959.149), lotus or papyrus patterns, and *wadjet* eyes (Pl. 62). During the Ramessid period, the parallel lines were sometimes replaced by decorative 'collars', suggesting that the origins of the motif were ignored by this time. Up until the Amarna period, both ends of the throwstick were rounded and decorated with a lotus petal or papyrus calyx pattern. Thereafter, this type of decoration is confined to a single rounded end, while the undecorated end has a squared-off handle shape (Loeben 1987.147–8, fig. 3). Early and mid 18th dynasty examples tend to have a *wadjet* eye on each side of a cartouche, either in the middle (*e.g.* Pl. 62, top) or near the tapered end (Daressy 1902 pl. 27). From the Amarna period onwards, there is usually a single *wadjet* eye next to the cartouche on the broadest part of the throwstick (*e.g.* Pl. 62, lower; Petrie 1906 pl. 150.5, 7, 9 = Brussels MR E 2057, 2059; 212b). On two Ramessid fragments, one from Serabit el-Khadim (London BM 41817) and two from Timna (Rothenberg 1988 fig. 45.5, 7) this broad part has a 'simple' eye and a line that looks like a mouth. This gives the impression of a snake's head. Since some wooden throwsticks do have snake form (*e.g.* Daressy 1902 pl. 27, nos. 21332–3), the possibility that these, or indeed all, the faience throwsticks represent snakes cannot be ruled out.

The inscriptions on the votive throwsticks consist of titularies in which the king is occasionally named as 'beloved of Hathor' (*e.g.* Brussels MR E 2000). The Ramessid titularies are more verbose than the 18th dynasty ones. The date range covers most of the New Kingdom. The rulers named on the throwsticks from

Serabit el-Khadim are Thutmose I (Petrie 1906 pl. 150.1), Thutmose III (London BM 14947), Amonhotpe III (Pl. 62, second row = Bolton 68.05.8; Brussels MR E 2052; Manchester 876), Ramesses I (Brussels MR E 2053), Seti I (Pl. 62, third row = Brussels MR E 2054; Bolton 68.05.15; Manchester 870; Oxford Ash. E 3320), Ramesses II (Petrie 1906 pl. 150.4–5 = Brussels MR E 2055, 2056; 6, location unknown; Liverpool 49.05.4; London BM 41816; UC 35242–3; V&A 703–4.1905; Oxford Ash. E 3321; Toronto ROM 906.16.44), Merenptah (Pl. 62, bottom left; Manchester 873), Ramesses III (Pl. 62 bottom right = Brussels MR E 2058; London BM 14953; Manchester 874), and Ramesses IV (Petrie 1906 pl. 150.9 = Brussels MR E 2059).

Eighteenth dynasty comparative material is quite plentiful. A faience throwstick fragment with the cartouche of Amonhotpe I was recovered from the Northern Temple at Buhen (Randall-MacIver & Woolley 1911.93, pl. 43). Throwsticks were among the 18th dynasty offerings at Dendara (Fig. 6.2–3) and Abusir (Borchardt 1910.133–4, fig. 184). Groups of inscribed faience throwsticks have been found in or near the tombs of Thutmose III (Daressy 1902.283), Amonhotpe II (1902.115–8, pl. 27), Thutmose IV (Carter & Newberry 1904.110–3, pl. 25), Amonhotpe III (Höhr-Grenzhausen 1978 no. 319), Tutankhamon (Hall 1928.74–5, pl. 9.4; van Wijngaarden 1936.1–2, pl. 1.2), and the Royal Tomb at el-ʿAmarna (Martin 1974.81, pl. 51). Fourteen uninscribed examples were recovered from Valley of the Kings Tomb 55 (Davis 1910.38–9, pl. 5).

Wooden throwsticks are found in private tombs (George 1980.10–11, 15, n.20) but faience examples do not seem to be. I know of only a few faience examples from a domestic context: a fragment from the palace of Amonhotpe III at Malqata (Hayes 1959.252) and throwsticks with the names of Amarna princesses found in the city of el-ʿAmarna (Pendlebury 1951.70–1; Martin 1987a.151–2). The Medelhavsmuseet has three unprovenanced Ramessid throwstick fragments (GN 10 089; George 1980.8, fig. 1), but the pieces from Serabit el-Khadim and Timna are the only provenanced Ramessid examples. As with the inscribed bracelets (2.9.3.1), this distribution must be due mainly to the fact that so little of the contents of the Ramessid royal tombs has survived. Hayes noted three unprovenanced faience throwstick fragments in the Metropolitan Museum of Art:–

> ... decorated with *wedjat*-eyes, floral designs, and, in one case, a dwarflike figure (the demigod Bes?) holding in either hand a large rabbit [hare?], grasped by the ears. (1959.215)

Petrie believed that these objects were wands used in ceremonial music and dancing (1906.144). They bear little resemblance to the 'clappers' used in Hathor dances (*e.g.* Ziegler 1979.19–30), but they have features in common with the snake wands and the ivory or faience 'apotropaic wands' of the Middle Kingdom (Bourriau 1988.113–116). Most scholars have identified the objects described in this section as model throwsticks (*e.g.* Carter & Newberry 1904.110; Davis 1910.38; Hall 1928.74; Martin 1974.81; George 1980.9–10; Loeben 1987.149). They have sometimes been found with wooden throwsticks (*e.g.* Daressy 1902.115–20). G.T. Martin refers to faience throwsticks as being 'pre-eminently funerary objects' (1974.81), but the votive examples outnumber the funerary ones.

B. George suggests four possible symbolic values for model throwsticks in general (1980.7–14). Throwsticks seem to have been used principally for hunting birds in the marshes. Scenes of such bird-hunts occur in tombs from the Old Kingdom onwards and it is possible that real or model throwsticks in burials allowed the tomb owner to enjoy such hunts in the afterlife (George 1980.12). Hunting and fishing are related to Sekhet, the personification of the marshes (1980.12–3). This connection might make faience throwsticks a suitable offering to Sekhet, or to other marsh goddesses such as Hathor, but a direct association between the votive throwsticks and the hunting of birds in the marshes is unlikely at any of the Hathor shrines.

George points out that in the Coffin Texts the deceased defends him or herself against demons, particularly demons in serpent shape, with a throwstick (1980.13; *CT* VI, 316*e*). Their magical role is confirmed by captions to paintings of throwsticks on Middle Kingdom coffins which call them *wr ḥkʒw* (Eaton-Krauss & Graefe 1985.38). The throwsticks in burials could then be amulets to protect the deceased during his dangerous journey to the place of judgement. Schulman identifies the Timna examples as 'apotropaic wands' (in Rothenberg 1988.135–6, 146). The faience throwstick fragment decorated with Bes holding up two rabbits or hares (Hayes 1959.215) strongly suggests a link between the throwsticks and the Middle Kingdom ivory 'apotropaic wands', since Bes frequently appears on the latter (Altenmüller 1965.66–9). Model throwsticks were probably thought to have protective powers against demons and other dangers in daily life, which would explain the presence of such a throwstick in the palace at Malqata. Since the 'apotropaic wands' are boomerang shaped, they too could be classed as model throwsticks. The New Kingdom faience throwsticks may have developed from the same prototype as the Middle Kingdom ivory wands.

George notes that the bird-hunt can be seen as a metaphor for the king destroying his enemies and, on a cosmic level, for order subduing chaos (1980.13). This may explain the prominence of throwsticks among royal burial equipment and could provide a reason for their being dedicated to Hathor. In her Solar Eye aspect, Hathor assisted and protected Re𐄂 against his enemies, the forces of chaos, and in particular against the chaos serpents (2.5.5). The forms of Hathor associated with this aspect are the uraeus, the lioness, the cat, and either a 'simple' or a *wadjet* eye. Eyes occur on all the votive throwsticks and some have serpent form. An inscription on a wooden throwstick fragment from Gurob mentions Weret-Hekau (Thomas 1981.84, pl. 38), a cobra goddess who personified magic power, particularly the power associated with the Solar Eye (Troy 1986.71–2). This raises the possibility that the throwsticks might symbolize Hathor in her aspect as Solar Eye. It may be significant that throwsticks were also dedicated to Sekhmet (Borchardt 1910.133–4), who could personify the fiercest aspect of the Solar Eye. It is surely no coincidence that they were standard offerings at the sites where cats are also prominent among the votive objects. In bird-hunting scenes, cats are sometimes shown retrieving the birds killed or stunned by throwsticks (*e.g.* George 1980.12, fig. 8). Cats wielding knives appear on the apotropaic wands (*e.g.* Altenmüller 1965 fig. 9; Bourriau 1988.115), and a 'Solar Cat' beheaded the great chaos serpent Apophis (2.5.5). The association of the cat form of Hathor with the slaying of demons would make it appropriate to desert sites, where the forces of chaos were close at hand. The same argument could apply to votive throwsticks. The throwsticks might have been offered to acknowledge or evoke Hathor in her fierce but protective Solar Eye aspect.

C. Loeben notes that an object which looks like a throwstick is shown under the bed on which the dead Osiris lies in a relief at Abydos and suggests that it is there to protect Osiris against the Sethian forces of chaos (1987.149). This may be so, but the relief shows the conception of Horus (Calverley 1938 pl. 62), which suggests that is the act of procreation that is being specifically protected by the throwstick. This was one of the purposes of the 'apotropaic wands' (2.6.3.3), which are thought to have been placed under beds. The fourth symbolic value listed by George allots a phallic symbolism to throwsticks (1980.14). Derchain argues for an erotic interpretation of marsh bird-hunting scenes (1976.8–9) and Westendorf points out that *ḳmꜣ* can mean both 'to throw', as of a throwstick, and 'to create/beget' (1967.142). Derchain comments that:–

> The erotic allusion is regulated by funerary preoccupations, and the deceased's sexual activity must be a promise of rebirth, of the constant regeneration of life... (1976.10)

In view of Hathor's funerary aspect, model throwsticks could have been offered as symbols of the regeneration that it was hoped she would grant to the donor. However, as with the votive menit counterpoises, a strictly funerary interpretation does not seem very appropriate for something that was a standard category of offering at Serabit el-Khadim and Timna. The Solar Eye aspect of Hathor still seems to provide the best explanation for throwsticks as votive objects.

11 *Cartouche and royal name plaques* (Fig. 4; Pl. 7)

Small, cartouche-shaped plaques bearing royal names were found among the offerings at Deir el-Bahri, Faras, Serabit el-Khadim, and Timna. Hall mentioned excavating cartouche plaques of Hatshepsut at Deir el-Bahri (in Naville 1913.14; 1913.51–2). I have traced 14 cartouche plaques from these excavations, one of Ahmose (Toronto ROM unnumbered), one of Amonhotpe I (London BM 41729), six of Hatshepsut (Edinburgh RSM 1904.134.18; London BM 41140–2, 41730–1 = Naville 1913 pl. 25.5, second row; New York MMA 05.4.96; Reading unnumbered), four of Thutmose III (London BM 41691, 43209; V&A 670.1905; Pittsburgh CM GN 4920.12), and one of Horemheb (London BM 41145). Miss Carhew illustrated two cartouche plaques, one of Hatshepsut, and one of Thutmose III (Fig. 4).

Two cartouche plaques of Thutmose III were excavated at Faras (Khartoum 926; London BM 51333; Karkowski 1981.41). Petrie illustrated a cartouche-shaped pendant from Serabit el-Khadim which bears the prenomen of Seti I and is surmounted by a double plume (1906 pl. 155.5 = London UC 35350). The Ashmolean Museum has two similar cartouche plaques of Seti I (E 3334–5) and the Petrie Collection 24 fragmentary Ramessid cartouche plaques from these excavations (London UC 353349, 35435a–f, 35436a–d, 35437–9, 35440a–b, 35441a–c, 35442a–e). A fragmentary cartouche plaque of Seti I or II was found in the temple at Timna (Rothenberg 1972.163–4; 1988.139, fig. 47.8). Glazed steatite cartouche plaques of Senwosret II, Amenemhet II, Senwosret III and Amenemhet III (Leclant & Clerc 1986 fig. 68) and a faience cartouche plaque of Ramesses II were recovered from Gebel Zeit (Mey *et al.* 1980.308–9, no. 28, fig. 2.1). Royal names were credited with apotropaic powers (Hornung & Staehelin 1976.41–2), so the cartouche plaques, like many of the royal name scarabs, could have been worn or carried as protective amulets before being dedicated.

At Deir el-Bahri, Naville excavated fragments from plain and inscribed rectangular faience plaques in bright blue faience. One of these, which now measures 5 × 5.5 cm, is inscribed in dark blue with the name and titles of Hatshepsut (Bolton 48.04.13). Carter found at least one royal name plaque of this type at Deir el-Bahri (Pl. 7, fourth row, right). Similar fragments from the EES excavations are inscribed with the name and epithets of Hathor (*e.g.* Bolton 48.04.7; Brussels MR E 29034; Ilkley CC 7002; Liverpool 2, now destroyed). The Victoria and Albert Museum has several plain fragments from such plaques (1216.1904a–b, 1225.1904a–b). Hayes noted that Winlock had discovered 'two rectangular plaques of blue faience, a little over three inches in width' inscribed with the name of Hatshepsut in the forecourt of Djeser-Djeseru (1959.86). No objects of this type were found in any of the foundation deposits which have been excavated at Deir el-Bahri, so they do not seem to be foundation tablets. Most of the plaques are glazed on both sides, so they cannot be tiles. They may have been token royal offerings, a possibility that cannot be entirely ruled out in the case of the cartouche-shaped plaques.

12 *Miscellaneous* (Fig. 6; Pl. 8)

A small number of common amulets were found at each of the five sites. Hall remarked that the amulets at Deir el-Bahri were:–

> … exclusively Hathoric, or have a possible connection with Amen, amulets exclusively connected with other deities, such as the ⏚ of Osiris, never occur …
>
> (in Naville 1913.16)

Although one *ḏd* amulet appears in the EEF distribution lists for these excavations, Hall was essentially correct. The only other amulets listed are a *waḏ* sceptre and two *ankhs*. Hall mentioned finding 'tiny ostrich-feather fans' (in Naville 1913.17), but I have not been able to trace any examples. Carter noted the presence of votive faience *ankhs* at Deir el-Bahri (1912.32). Large model *ankhs* in blue faience, similar to those found in 18th dynasty royal tombs (*e.g.* Daressy 1902 pls. 28–9; Carter & Newberry 1904.pl. 27), were among the offerings at Dendara (*e.g.* Fig. 6.7).

Griffith illustrated one amulet in the form of the feather of Shu (Pl. 8.25) and the Pitt-Rivers Museum has two green faience *nfr* amulets from Faras (unnumbered). An ankh, a *ḏd*, a *nfr*, and an Isis-knot pendant, all in faience, were recovered at Mirgissa (Karlin in Vercoutter 1970.342, fig. 35). At the latter site, there were also two Divine Child pendants (1970.340, nos. 16–7), two tiny dwarf amulets (1970.340, nos. 11–3), and two fragments showing the lower part of standing figures (1970.341, nos. 35–6). The Royal Ontario Museum has a small faience *ʿnḫ* and *wʒs* plaque from Serabit el-Khadim (906.16.26). Among the faience objects from this site in the Petrie Collection are two Divine Child amulets (Petrie 1906 pl. 155.2–3 = UC 35370), three Isis-knot pendants (UC 35400a–C), two fragmentary *ḥḥ* plaques (UC 35387), six *ḥs* vase amulets (UC 35404a–f), two ankhs (UC GN 35421), and seven *dd* pillars (UC 35415, 35388a–f). The amulets from Timna include the head and shoulders of a king wearing a double crown (Rothenberg 1972.166; 1988.140, fig. 48.11), at least two Divine Child amulets (1988.140, fig. 48.5–6), and two headless mummiform amulets (1988.140–1, fig. 47.3a–b). Two Isis-knot pendants were excavated at Gebel Zeit (Mey *et al.* 1980.304–5, fig. 1.2).

Summary

A narrow range of amulets occurs at each of the six sites. Most of those found can be associated directly with Hathor or with one of her spheres of influence, such as fertility or rebirth. Among the more common amulets were lotus flowers or buds, bunches of grapes, baboons, ducks, *tilapia* fish, and uraei. Royal name scarabs, scaraboids or plaques were found at all the Hathor sites. The finest decorative scarabs and scaraboids were from Faras. Objects depicting Bes or Taweret were found at most of the sites. The faience throwsticks form the most significant group of amuletic objects. These may be related to the Middle Kingdom 'apotropaic wands'. In the New Kingdom, they seem to be associated with Hathor's Solar Eye aspect.

Individual amulets, or jewellery incorporating amulets, may sometimes have been offered to Hathor by their owners after being worn, but if this had been a common practice one would expect to find a far greater number and range of amulets. The limited range suggests that most of the amulets were acquired at the shrines as votive offerings. Because so few intact necklaces survive, it is difficult to know how much significance can be attached to the combinations in which the amulets were strung. Some may have been chosen for their decorative value as ornaments for Hathor, rather than for any specific symbolic significance.

2.11 Vessels

Numerous fragments of vessels, in stone, pottery, glass or faience, were found among the offerings at the five sites. Since most of these vessels will have been used for the presentation or storage of perishable offerings, they should probably be regarded as 'ritual objects' rather than as votive offerings in their own right. For this reason, only those vessels whose form or decoration includes Hathor symbolism are described in detail.

2.11.1 Stone

1 *Stone basins* (Fig. 5)

At Deir el-Bahri, Naville excavated a fragment from a limestone basin inscribed with an offering formula (Brussels MR E 4411; Speelers 1923.60) and a 'Portion of stone bowl with rudely cut couchant jackal or cow on the edge' (1913.25 pl. 24.6, location unknown). The animal, which is too crudely carved for a definite identification, does not have the long ears of a jackal, but could be either a cow or a cat. Pieces of two sandstone basins inscribed with prayers to Hathor were found in Djeser-Akhet (Lipińska 1966.72, pl. 5.2; 1968.169, pl. 13.22; 1984.56, nos. 79–80). These basins, one of which is carved with a Hathor mask, have already been described (2.3.3.1).

Fragments from two basins, one in limestone and one in sandstone, were recovered from the Hathor temple at Faras (Griffith 1921.86, pl. 24.8–10; Karkowski 1981.83–4, 89–90). Two large fragments of the limestone basin survive (Fig. 5.8–9 = Khartoum 4450). When intact, it would have been about 18 cm high and 55 cm in diameter. The bowl is decorated on the outside with a lotus flower pattern. On the inside is part of a scene showing two women, facing in opposite directions, who stand on each side of a stand of three jars. One of the women, who is named as Tai, holds up a small bowl. Only the upper part of the other woman is preserved, but her arm position suggests that she too was offering something. There are traces of an inscription to the right of the figures. Three pieces of the rim of the sandstone basin have survived (Fig. 5.10 = Khartoum 4449). This basin would have been about 58 cm in diameter. The fragments are not decorated, but there is a band of inscription on the outside, just under the rim, which consists of an offering formula for the wife of the Viceroy Huy (for Huy see 1.2.1).

At Serabit el-Khadim MacDonald found a fragment, 6.3 × 6.4 cm, from a schist bowl with a lotus petal pattern on the exterior (London BM 14388). The bowl would originally have been about 15 cm in diameter. At both Serabit el-Khadim and Timna, large undecorated stone bowls were a major feature of the temple furnishings.

Stone bowls with three-dimensional figures on the rim are rare, but the pottery bowls with cows or cats provide comparative material (*e.g.* Fig. 1.32, 34; 2.4.3.1; 2.5.3). Most New Kingdom stone basins carved with Hathor masks come from votive or funerary chapels at Deir el-Medina (*e.g.* Bruyère 1927 pl. 30.4; 1930.21, fig. 2; 1934.63–5, fig. 46; 1952.144, figs. 139–40; 1952a.126). Undecorated stone basins inscribed with offering formulae were also common there (Bruyère 1939.210). As with the examples from Djeser-Akhet, donors are sometimes shown kneeling in adoration on the exterior of the basins, but the limestone basin from Faras appears to be unique in having a scene of donors making offerings on the interior. Among the pieces from Deir el-Medina, the only type of decoration found on the inside of stone basins is marsh flora and fauna (1939.210). This links them with the faience 'marsh bowls' (2.11.3), as do the lotus flower patterns on the exteriors of the limestone bowl from Faras and the schist bowl from Serabit el-Khadim.

One of the basins from Deir el-Bahri is inscribed with a fragmentary *ḥtp di nsw* formula addressed to Hathor, Lady of Djeser (Lipińska 1968.169; 1984.56). The similar basins from Deir el-Medina are usually inscribed with *ḥtp di nsw* formulae naming Hathor, or Taweret 'The Pure Water', and requesting standard life and funerary benefits for the donors (Bruyère 1930.21; 1934.64; 1939.198, fig. 89). The basins found in public areas of tombs, shrines and temples were presumably intended to continue in use long after the donor's death. There are two possible functions for such basins. On the basis of the frequent mention of Taweret 'The Pure Water', Bruyère suggested that they held water for lustration rituals (1934.63–5; 1939.210). The basins might have placed in the outer areas of shrines or tombs so that visitors could use them as lustration vessels. The donors probably hoped that the visitors would then pray for them. Alternatively, the function of the basins may have been to receive libations, either from priests, or from temple visitors. Some 'sistrophorus' statues have texts which appeal to priests and temple visitors for offerings and libations (see 3.2.4). One such statue incorporates a lotus shaped basin (Vandier 1958 pl. 174.3). The decoration of the limestone basin from Faras links it with libations rather than lustration. The jar stand could indicate that the basin was for offerings of wine. Although it might be argued that because the donors are shown on the interior, the basin must have held a clear liquid, such as water (see further 2.11.3.2).

2 *Calcite vessels* (Pl. 8)

Vessels made in calcite (Egyptian alabaster) were found at all six sites, but they were most common at Serabit el-Khadim. Naville found a calcite lid inscribed with the cartouches of Hatshepsut in the 11th dynasty temple at Deir el-Bahri (London BM 43142). This comes from an unguent container of the common beaker shape. Seventeen examples of this type of jar were discovered in the foundation deposits of Djeser-Djeseru (Hayes 1959.85, fig. 47). Griffith excavated one calcite kohl pot, and a possible lid from another, at Faras (Pl. 8.67; 1921.86; Oxford Ash. 1912.938; Karkowski 1981 no. 17). The neck of an calcite 'perfume flask' was recovered from the sanctuary at Mirgissa (Karlin in Vercoutter 1970.355, no. 199).

MacDonald brought back three calcite vase fragments from Serabit el-Khadim (London BM ER 221–3). Petrie stated that at this site:–

The alabaster vases had been plentiful in the temple, but all were reduced to fragments. Their forms were tall cylinders, cups and globular vases with loop handles on either side ... There were also many vases in the form of figures of the god Bes or of the cow of Hat.hor. (1906.137)

Petrie illustrated 18 vase fragments (1906 pls. 144–5). These, with about a hundred other calcite fragments, were sent to the Ashmolean Museum (Box E 4454), where it proved possible to reconstruct several vessels (Leeds 1922.1–3, pls. 1–2).

As well as the types of vessel mentioned by Petrie, there are pieces of kohl pots, narrow-shouldered jars, and openwork jar-stands. Twenty-two fragments are inscribed with royal titularies; these are incised and inlaid with red, blue, or black pigments. The rulers named are Ahmose-Nefertary, Thutmose I, Amonhotpe III, Ramesses II, and Merenptah (Petrie 1906 pl. 144; Černý 1955, nos. 171.1, 174.1, 222, 251, 265). Fragments from two fine lotiform chalices bear both the cartouches of Amonhotpe III and the name of the expedition leader Panehsi (Petrie 1906 pl. 145.1 = Oxford Ash. 1911.410, 414). In addition to the cow (1906 pl. 144.2–3, 8, 10) and Bes vases (1906.144.11, 216) noted in (2.4.3.1 and 2.10.1.8), there are fragments of other types of figure vase, including male and female heads, and a kneeling figure in flowing drapery (1906 pl. 145; Oxford Ash. Box E 4454). One set of fragments has been fitted together to form a pot-bellied dwarf carrying a jar on his shoulders (Leeds 1922 pl. 2 = Oxford Ash. 1911.407). Fragments from three calcite vessels, a vase, a cup, and a bowl were found at Timna (Rothenberg 1972.166, fig. 53.2; 1988.132, fig. 22). One limestone jar lid from this site is 'beautifully decorated with an open waterlily design' (Schulman in Rothenberg 1988.142, fig. 49.2). Crude vessels made from local calcite, including cups, vases, and kohl pots, were found in the shrine area at Gebel Zeit (Castel *et al.* 1984.49, 52–4, fig. 4; 1986.100).

Examples from Byblos suggest that simple calcite vessels and figure vases inscribed with royal names were presented to temples from the Old Kingdom onwards (Montet 1928.68–79; 1929 pl. 29). Calcite vessels have been found in 18th dynasty royal tombs (*e.g.* Davis 1906.109–11; Hayes 1959.45, 80, 130, 148, figs. 21, 43). Parallels for the lotiform chalices can be found in a piece with the cartouches of Akhenaten and Nefertiti (1959.293–4, fig. 181) and a more elaborate chalice from the tomb of Tutankhamon (Edwards 1972 no. 7, pl. 7). This tomb contained complex calcite animal and figure vases (*e.g.* Desroches Noblecourt 1963 pls. 24, 43–4) comparable to the cow and Bes vases from Serabit el-Khadim. Twelve elaborate calcite vessels were found near the tomb of Merenptah and may have been used during the embalming or anointing of the king's body (Hayes 1959.354, fig. 221; Reeves 1990a.97, 101). Small calcite vessels (*e.g.* 1959.67, 207, 317, figs. 35, 122, 199), and vases in the form of dwarfs (*e.g.* 1959.315, fig. 198; Vandier d'Abbadie 1972.103) and gross female figures (*e.g.* Brunner-Traut 1970 pls. 1–7; Doll in Brovarski 1982.293) seem to have been in quite common use among wealthier Egyptians during the New Kingdom (Bourriau in Brovarski 1982.126–32).

The lotiform chalices were probably used for libations (Brovarski 1982.146), but most of the calcite vessels will have served as containers for cosmetics and perfumes of various kinds. Several of the calcite figure vases from the tomb of Tutankhamon contained unguents (Edwards 1972 nos. 3–4). The more elaborate specimens from Serabit el-Khadim probably held unguents to be offered to, or used to anoint, the cult image. Since only one kohl pot was found at Faras, and only one calcite 'perfume flask' and a single faience kohl pot were excavated at Mirgissa, these pieces may have formed part of the equipment of these shrines.

The calcite objects found at Serabit el-Khadim and Timna were almost certainly brought there from Egypt. There are no calcite quarries close to these sites and the standard of workmanship is often far higher than that of the locally made stelae, statues, or small objects. On a stela of Amenemhet III, a calcite pot is listed among the offerings to Hathor (Černý 1952 pl. 37, no. 112; 1955.114). These offerings are described as being made to the goddess by the expedition leader on behalf of the king. During the New Kingdom, expedition leaders often had themselves depicted or named on royal stelae set up at Serabit el-Khadim. The inscriptions added by Panehsi to the chalices of Amonhotpe III may be seen as analogous to this practice. On one of these chalices, the king is named as 'beloved of Hathor, Lady of Mefkat' (Petrie 1906 pl. 145.1), indicating that the piece was specifically made, or at least inscribed, for presentation at Serabit el-Khadim. It is most likely that the calcite vessels with royal inscriptions were 'official' gifts for use in the temple, dedicated on behalf of the king by the expedition leader, who hoped to share in the blessings bestowed by the goddess in return for offerings. The uninscribed pieces could have been official offerings or the gifts of individual expedition members. In either case, the contents could have been of greater importance than the vessels.

2.11.2 Faience vessels (Figs. 1, 6; Pls. 6, 30b, 64)

Large quantities of faience bowl fragments were found at Deir el-Bahri (2.11.3). There were also a few pieces from other types of faience vessel. Hall illustrated a fragment from a 'moustache cup' (in Naville 1913 pl. 27.4 = London BM 47687) and a small, intact bottle with a 'collar' of stylised petals (1913 pl. 27.1, centre, location unknown). Part of a similar, but more elaborately decorated, bottle was found by Carter (Pl. 6e). From the EES excavations, the Ashmolean Museum has fragments from four 'bottles' with geometric decoration (E 2751, 2753-4, 2757; 1913 Pl. 26.2, upper) and part of a small vase in turquoise blue with a pattern inlaid in dark blue (E 2755). This inlay ware seems to be unique to Deir el-Bahri (Hall & Currelly in Naville 1913.18, 29 pl. 26.3; Fig. 1.11, 18). Other fragments of it come from large vases (e.g. Bolton 48.04.18; Edinburgh 1905.279.4; London BM 41023-4, 41032) or from bowls (e.g. London BM 43164). Also from the EES excavations are the upper part of a narrow-shouldered jar decorated with wavy lines (Bolton 48.04.17), the foot of a vessel, perhaps a ḥs vase (London BM 41681), and part of a narrow-shouldered jar decorated with spirals and hanging buds (London BM 43164 = Naville 1913 pl. 26.1, right). The smaller pieces could have held perfumes and the larger ones may have been used as libation vessels.

Griffith mentioned finding a 'fragment of vase in blue paste' at Faras (1921.86), which might be the blue frit dish now in the Ashmolean Museum (1912.951). This shallow dish, which has been reconstructed from several fragments, is 9.7 cm in diameter. Two faience fragments from Mirgissa are described by the excavators as

'Fragment d'un pied de coupe' and 'Fond de coupe' (Karlin in Vercoutter 1970.355, nos. 203–4). They also recovered 'Différents tessons de coupe' (1970.355, no. 202), but the example illustrated looks like a typical 'marsh bowl' fragment (see 2.11.3).

A far greater range of faience vessels was discovered at Serabit el-Khadim than at any of the other five sites. Many are of unusual or unique type, but they have received little attention from scholars. Among the faience brought back by MacDonald were 22 pieces of vessels inscribed with royal names and titles (London BM 13201–2, 13219–20, 13238, 13244, 13268, 13296 ER 224–5, 233, 243–4, 253–4, 260–1, 272–5, 283). Petrie also found royal name vases at Serabit el-Khadim:–

> The forms are pear-shaped vases with necks from Tahutmes I to Amonhotep III, tubular vases of Sety I and Ramessu II, and cups from Merenptah to Ramessu III. The forms of cup with and without stems were made at the same time. In all, parts of 73 vases were found with inscriptions ... (1906.140)

Most of these vessels are in pale blue or green faience with the inscriptions, and sometimes bands of stylized floral decoration, in black or dark blue. Petrie illustrated fragments of 14 such vessels (1906 pl. 146). Contrary to his account, surviving fragments show that 'pear-shaped' vases were dedicated under Ramesses III (e.g. Bolton 68.05.33) and 'tubular' vases under Merenptah (e.g. London BM 13231).

The faience from Timna included fragments of bowls, cups, jars, jugs, and juglets (Rothenberg 1988.127–135, figs. 49–44). Some of the fragments bear Ramessid royal names. One has cartouches of Merenptah (1988.128, fig. 28.3). A lotiform chalice from Timna has a cartouche which may be that of Ramesses IV (1972.163, 165–6, fig. 49.1–3, pl. 85; 1988.128, fig. 40.7). Petrie also found fragments from faience lotiform chalices, some bearing the cartouches of Ramesses II, at Serabit el-Khadim (1906 pl. 156.5 = Manchester 880). On several of the vessels from this site, the king is named as 'beloved of Hathor Lady/Mistress of Mefkat' (1906 pl. 146.3, 12–3), indicating that they were made, or at least inscribed, specifically for presentation at one of the mining temples.

As with much of the votive faience from Serabit el-Khadim and Timna, royal funerary equipment provides comparative material. Inscribed faience 'pear-shaped' vases and cups were recovered from the tombs of Amonhotpe II and Thutmose IV (Daressy 1902 pl. 46; Carter & Newberry 1904.92–4, figs. 41–3, pl. 23). Some faience cups with the cartouches of Ramesses VII were discovered in debris near the cache of royal mummies at Deir el-Bahri (Hayes 1959.375–6, fig. 235). At Deir el-Medina, large and elaborate faience vessels bearing 18th dynasty royal names have been found preserved in Ramessid votive and funerary chapels (Bruyère 1934.76–8, fig. 52).

Three other noteworthy types of 'royal' vessel were discovered at Serabit el-Khadim. Petrie illustrated several fragments with the cartouches of Amonhotpe III in fine green faience with the pale violet inlay characteristic of this reign (1906.140, pl. 146.4–5, location unknown). He also excavated pieces of a globular vessel with lotus petal and rosette patterns in violet inlay (1906 pl. 147.18 = Oxford Ash. E 2656). MacDonald brought back two small fragments with parts of the titulary of Amonhotpe III in the same sort of inlay (London BM 13268, 13296).

Similar vessel fragments have been recovered from the palace of Amonhotpe III at Malqata (Hayes 1951.231, 235, fig. 35).

The other two types of vessel are Ramessid. Petrie noted that:–

> Fragments were found, widely scattered, of two remarkable vases of cylindrical form, with scenes in relief modelled around them. In pl. 157 the upper group of fragments is of dark grey-green and light green. The subject was the king seated, with a girl standing before him holding a bouquet of flowers. On the other side of the vase were conventional figures of two tall bouquets and garlands between them, with a duck flying above the garlands ... The lower vase is more elaborate. The figures are not only in relief but brightly coloured, yellow on a violet ground; the petals at the base are green, violet and white. The same subject is repeated on opposite sides of the vase. King Ramessu III is seated, holding the *dad*, his cartouches before him, while a girl stands offering two bouquets to him. (1906.151)

Some fragments from these vases are now in the Victoria and Albert Museum (*e.g.* Pl. 30b, left). MacDonald found a fragment in green and violet faience with the lower part of a seated figure in relief (London BM 13297), indicating that there was a third vessel of this kind at Serabit el-Khadim. The closest parallels to the technique of these vessels are provided by an elaborate votive bowl, probably dating to the end of the 18th dynasty, from the shrine of Sekhmet at Abusir (Borchardt 1910.130–1, fig. 178, pl. 14), and by tiles from palaces of Ramesses II at Qantir (Hayes 1937.8–10, pls. 2, 4, 6–13), and of Ramesses III at Tell el-Yahudiya (Hayes 1959.367–8, fig. 232) and Medinet Habu (Hölscher 1951.42–7, pls. 30–8).

Petrie described and illustrated fragments from 'large cylindrical glazed vases with painted scenes and patterns' which he also dated to Ramesses III (1906.152, pl. 158). One of these pieces shows a girl in a transparent dress offering flowers to a seated king in an arbour entwined with convolvulus (Pl. 64, centre = London V&A 717.1905). The remaining pieces are decorated in black, purple, or green on a pale yellow ground, with feather and floral patterns or with *ḥḥ* figures holding year signs (1906 pl. 158 = Brussels MR E 2458; London V&A 713.1905, 716a–e.1905, 719.1905). MacDonald recovered fragments of similar vessels (London BM 13215, 13306). When intact, these cylindrical vases probably stood 40–50 cm high. The complex workmanship and fine white body of these two types of vessel suggest that they were made in Egypt, perhaps in the same workshop that produced the tiles for the palace at Tell el-Yahudiya. The scenes of the girls offering flowers to the king are reminiscent of those on the small gold shrine of Tutankhamon (Edwards 1972 no. 25, pl. 25), and of reliefs on the High Gate at Medinet Habu (Hölscher 1970 pls. 630–42). Westendorf has proposed an erotic interpretation of the imagery on the shrine, linking the queen with the role of Hathor (1967; 2.3.4). It has been suggested that young women in the royal 'harim', like those shown at Medinet Habu, were active in the cult of Hathor (Drenkhahn 1976.64; Troy 1986.77–9, fig. 51). The vases from Serabit el-Khadim seem to confirm these ideas.

Among the more unusual fragments brought back from Serabit el-Khadim by MacDonald were part of an undecorated dish in 'Egyptian blue' (London BM 13216; Cooney 1976.38, no. 336), a piece from an openwork faience cup decorated with stems of papyrus (London BM 13287), and a circular lid in dark blue and light violet faience with a design of running antelopes (London BM 13214). Cooney described this lid as a 'minor masterpiece of Egyptian ceramic art' (1972.284, pl. 45). Petrie excavated four fragments of a faience vessel with a lively frieze showing hunting dogs chasing wild animals (1906 pl. 156.1–3 = Oxford Ash. E 3337–9) and a piece of a cup with a leaping calf above a lotus petal design (1906 pl. 156.4 = Oxford Ash. E 3336). Like the lid found by MacDonald, these pieces probably date to the late 18th dynasty (Cooney 1972.284).

Petrie also noted the presence of circular faience stands, about 6 cm high, which were used to hold pointed-bottomed vessels or to support faience bowls (1906.145–6). He stated that:-

> Many of these glazed ring-stands are plain; others have a few bands with spots ... the commonest pattern is with a fringe of lotus petals. (1906.145 pl. 150.14–5; location unknown)

Some specimens are decorated with lotus petals on either side of a central band (*e.g.* Starr & Butin 1936 fig. 29.117), with wavy lines (*e.g.* London BM 41767–70), with wavy lines and dots (*e.g.* London UC 35345), or with a band of black triangles (*e.g.* London BM 41771). The examples which have Hathor masks or Hathor masks flanked by cats have been described in 2.3.3.1; 2.5.4; (Pls. 32d, 45). Some of the ring-stands are inscribed with the name and titles of a king, who is sometimes described as 'beloved of Hathor, Mistress of Mefkat' (*e.g.* Brussels MR E 2172, 2176; London BM 41772–3, 41775). The rulers named are Ramesses II (*e.g.* Bolton 68.05.25; Brussels MR E 2172; London BM 41774), Merenptah (*e.g.* Bolton 68.05.27; Brussels MR E 2174; London BM 41775), (Seti II (*e.g.* Brussels MR E 2175) and Tawosret (*e.g.* Brussels MR E 2173). Pieces from six faience ring stands were found at Timna (Rothenberg 1972.163; 1988.127, figs. 31, 39). Three are inscribed, one definitely bearing the name of Ramesses III (Schulman in Rothenberg 1988.127, fig. 31.5, pl. 119.3).

Pottery ring-stands were used in Egypt at all periods (Bourriau in Brovarski 1982.79). New Kingdom faience examples, sometimes decorated with lotus petals or simple geometrical patterns, are fairly common (*e.g.* Bruyère 1937.88; Hayes 1959.207–8, fig. 122). Inscribed stands are rare, but Petrie found at least one among the offerings at Dendara (Fig. 6.19). A stand with the cartouches of Horemheb was recovered from the sanctuary of Sekhmet at Abusir (Borchardt 1910.132). Ring-stands decorated with Hathor masks and cats appear to be unique to Serabit el-Khadim (2.5.4).

Cooney proposed that the faience vessels from Serabit el-Khadim were originally 'filled with scented ointments' (1972.284). This may well be true of the smaller vessels. The larger pieces could have been used for the temporary storage of other kinds of perishable offerings, or to hold liquids for libations or lustration rituals. It cannot be assumed that a particular type of vessel invariably had a single purpose. For example, lotiform chalices are shown in scenes of private individuals offering to Hathor being used both for libations and as containers for vegetables or flowers (*e.g.* Nagel 1938.199, figs. 174–8). The presence of fine faience vessels inscribed with royal names in private chapels at Deir el-Medina suggests that royal name vases need not always have been royal gifts. The use of cartouches on votive objects can be related to the concept of the king as intermediary with the gods.

However, the temples at Serabit el-Khadim and Timna were state foundations, visited by official expeditions. This fact, together with the splendour of some of the votive pieces, and the resemblance of others to vessels found in royal tombs, suggests that the royal name vessels at Serabit el-Khadim and Timna were royal gifts. According to Birch's record slips (see 1.4.3), a faience cup from Serabit el-Khadim once bore a dedication inscription of 'an officer' (London BM ER 349). This shows that some faience vessels were also dedicated on behalf of private individuals at this site.

2.11.3 Faience bowls

1 *Types of bowl* (Figs. 1, 6; Pls. 3, 7, 32, 39, 63)

Bowls were the most common kind of faience vessel at Deir el-Bahri, Faras, Serabit el-Khadim, and Timna. The size of the bowls varies considerably. Some specimens would have been no more than 10–12 cm in diameter when intact, while others would have been as large as 35–40 cm, with fabric 2–3 cm thick. The ground colour of the bowls is light blue or pale green and most have decoration in dark blue or purplish-black.

Miss Carhew illustrated several bowl fragments from the 1892–4 excavations at Deir el-Bahri (*e.g.* Pl. 3), and a large quantity was found during the 1903–7 excavations (Hall & Currelly in Naville 1913.17–8, 26, 29). Hall noted that:–

> Usually they were plain bowls of the same general type as the magnificent perfect specimen in the British Museum (no. 4790). Only fragments were found ... Beside the cows and Hathor-heads already mentioned, the designs consisted chiefly of representations of fish, papyrus-plants, spiral, zigzag and scale designs. The scales and zigzags in alternating dark and light blue inlay ... almost like *cloisonné* enamel, are very characteristic. (1913.18)

The reference to plain bowls is suprising, since I have not seen a single plain fragment among the 250 or so specimens from these excavations which I have been able to examine. Possibly the excavators did not preserve plain fragments for distribution.

Most of the surviving fragments come from light blue bowls with a simple lotus petal pattern on the exterior and a design of marsh flora radiating from a patterned rectangle or rosette on the interior. The top of the rim and the underside of the base are usually dark blue. One specimen has a rosette on the bottom of the base (Naville 1913 pl. 26.1). The most commonly depicted plants are blue lotus, papyrus, and potamogeton (pond weed). *Tilapia* fish, holding a lotus bud or other plant in their mouths, are occasionally shown (*e.g.* Pl. 3, bottom right; 1913 pl. 26.3, right = London 41685; Bolton 90,07.5; Brussels MR E 729; London V&A 663.1905). Two fragments preserve parts of some type of antelope or gazelle (Brussels MR E 731, 2438). The small numbers of pieces decorated with Hathor masks, cows, or cats have been described in 2.3.3.1 and 2.4.3.1; 2.5.3 (Pls. 3, 32a).

Bands of decoration are sometimes found on the exterior or interior of these bowls just below the rim. The patterns used include single or double spirals (*e.g.* Fig. 1.12 = Oxford Ash. E 2749; 7–8; locations unknown; Naville 1913 pl. 26.2, right = Oxford Ash. E 2747; Bolton 48.04.5, 144.06.4d; Brussels MR E 719, 729; London BM 41688; Oxford Ash. E 2746, 2748), triangles (*e.g.* Oxford Ash. E 2750, 2752; London BM 41018, 41025, 43148), diamonds (*e.g.* Fig. 1.11, location unknown; Bolton 144.06.4e), and bands of stylized, hanging buds (London BM 41018; Oxford Ash. E 2750). On one fragment the rim is pierced with deep vertical holes, perhaps for the insertion of model flowers or other ornaments (Glasgow K 07.790). Several bowls have wavy rims (*e.g.* London BM 41025; Oxford Ash. E 2749 = Naville 1913 pl. 26.4). Some bowls are inscribed on the inside with royal names and titles. Two pieces have cartouches of Hatshepsut 'beloved of Hathor' (Kyoto UM GN561; Toronto ROM 907.18.207) and one preserves part of a queen's titles (Pl. 3, bottom left = London BM 41020). The faience bowl fragment inscribed with a *ḥtp di nsw* formula for a donor who is shown adoring (Naville 1913 pl. 26.5), and the fragment with a Hathor mask on the exterior (Pl. 32c) have been described in 2.3.3.1.

Carter excavated faience bowl fragments at Deir el-Bahri similar to those found by Naville (Pl. 7). One large fragment has vertical holes pierced in the rim. Another bears the cartouche of Hatshepsut. All the inscribed 'marsh bowl' fragments mention queens or princesses rather than kings. A bowl fragment with the cartouche of Satamon, said to come from Deir el-Bahri, provides another example (Munich ÄS 2930; Strauss 1974.48–9, pl. 92). This could be Satamon I, who was sometimes worshipped with her mother Ahmose-Nefertary (Troy 1986.112, 162, fig. 76), rather than the eldest daughter of Amonhotpe III. Winlock noted that during his excavations of temple refuse heaps at Deir el-Bahri 'bits of broken blue faience platters … were uncountable' (1923.38), but the only piece he published was a fine bowl with a central rosette and lotus flower and bud decoration (1922 fig. 25).

Under the heading of 'Glazed Pottery', Griffith mentioned finding 'fragments of decorated bowls in great abundance' at Faras and he illustrated nine 'marsh bowl' fragments (1921.86, pl. 19a). In addition to the usual marsh flora, eight of the fragments show *tilapia* (Karkowski 1981 pl. 11.c–d; location unknown, b.f–j = Oxford Ash. GN 1912.941, k = London BM 51253). One has the head of a bird, and two have parts of animals, possibly antelopes (1981 pl. 11.e, l, m; location unknown). The examples with Hathor masks (Pl. 32b) have been described in 2.3.3.1. One bowl fragment from this site has a wavy rim (Oxford Ash. GN 1912.941). The few fragments from Mirgissa which may come from a 'marsh bowl' have been noted in 2.11.2.

MacDonald brought back a few 'marsh bowl' fragments from Serabit el-Khadim (London BM 13213, 13221–2, 13230, 13232–7, 13255, 13305). Petrie found numerous pieces of at least three types of bowl at the site. There were shallow bowls, 15–20 cm in diameter, plain on the exterior but inscribed on the interior with royal and/or divine names and titles (1906 pl. 147.1–7). Petrie stated that the royal names occurring on faience bowls from this site were Ahmose-Nefertary, a Thutmose, Ramesses II, Merenptah, Seti II, and Ramesses III (1906.141–2). Since he did not illustrate the piece with Ahmose-Nefertary's name it is possible that this came from a 'marsh bowl'. The cartouches on the royal name bowls are sometimes flanked by palm fronds (*e.g.* 1906 pl. 147.5). On the Ramessid specimens, the top of the rims are decorated with dots. The Royal Ontario Museum has a bowl fragment with an inscription reading 'Hathor, Mistress . . . ' (906.16.70). 132 plain fragments from Serabit el-Khadim in the Ashmolean Museum (in Box E 4457) may come either from plain bowls or from royal name bowls.

Petrie illustrated only a few pieces of 'marsh bowls' (1906 pls. 155–6) and gave no indication of the quantity found. The Ashmolean Museum has about 670 'marsh bowl' fragments from these excavations (mainly in Box E 4457). At a very conservative estimate, this must represent at least 35 bowls. Most of the fragments have the standard lotus and/or papyrus decoration. Petrie illustrated some which he described as having 'Rare pieces of plant decoration of natural style, which seems as if inspired by the Cretan school' (1906.151, pl. 156.6–7 = London BM 41789; Oxford Ash. E 4474). One fragment preserves part of a bird in flight (1906 pl. 155.22; location unknown). Twenty-four show *tilapia*, often with lotus plants in their mouths and seven have parts of animals, probably of antelopes or gazelles (all Oxford Ash. Box E 4457). Nine fragments form a bowl showing a spotted gazelle suckling its young in a papyrus thicket (Oxford Ash. 1912.57). The two fragments with Hathor masks and the two with cows have been described in 2.3.3.1 and 2.4.3.1. There are no inscribed examples among the pieces in the Ashmolean Museum.

Petrie also illustrated two bowls decorated on the interior with a large, stylized flower (1906 pls. 147.17; 155.25), a fragment with a band of hanging flowers on the exterior (1906 pl. 155.26), and another with a dot and circle pattern below the rim on the interior (1906 pl. 155.23). He again thought that some small fragments with geometrical designs on the exterior showed Aegean influence (1906.141; Pl. 39, top row, location unknown). Examples with simple spiral patterns could come from the upper part of 'marsh bowls'. At least one bowl from this site combined a band of geometric decoration with a lotus and water motif in the centre (Pl. 63). This design is very similar to that on a 13th dynasty 'marsh bowl' from Hu (Bourriau 1988 no. 126), raising the possibility that this might be a Second Intermediate Period object. The third Harvard Expedition also found 'marsh bowl' fragments at Serabit el-Khadim, including one piece with a band of hanging flowers on the exterior (Starr & Butin 1936 pl. 13).

Rothenberg notes that at Timna:–

> Among the uninscribed faience offerings were fragments of vases and bowls, some beautifully decorated with spirals, wave patterns and lotus flowers. A very fine bowl shows a fish amid lotus flowers and plants and there were other fragments of fish bowls. (1972.166)

Fragments from about 15 'marsh bowls' are published in the full report (1988.129–31, 134, figs. 41–4). One of these has lotus flower decoration and a spiral pattern on the exterior (Rothenberg 1988.143, fig. 41.6). Fish appear on several fragments (1988. nos. 113–116, 119; Figs. 42–4). There were also fragments from two bowls with a single large flower and an inscription on the interior (1988.129, figs. 40.8, 41.8), and pieces from bowls with geometric patterns (1988.135, figs. 41.7, 43.6, 8). No bowl fragments have yet been reported from Gebel Zeit.

Comparative material may be cited for almost all the kinds of faience bowl excavated at the Hathor sites. Undecorated bowls with cartouches are rare, but a few examples have been recovered from 18th dynasty burials (*e.g.* Hayes and Lansing 1935.34, fig. 42). Specimens with Ramessid cartouches were found in the sanctuary of Sekhmet at Abusir (Borchardt 1910.131). Bowls decorated with a single stylized flower were made in the 18th dynasty (*e.g.* Strauss 1974.14–5, figs. 2–5) and the Ramessid Period (*e.g.* Milward in Brovarski 1982 no. 142). The 'marsh bowls' are 'hardly ever found in a domestic context but come from tombs and temples' (Milward in Brovarski 1982.141). Such bowls were among the offerings at Dendara (*e.g.* Fig. 6.6) and Abusir (Borchardt 1910.129–30, figs. 179–80), and fragments were found in the terraced temple built by Ahmose at Abydos (Ayrton *et al.* 1904.15–6, pl. 58). They have not been recovered from royal tombs, but they occur in private burials in Egypt and Nubia from the late Middle Kingdom to the end of the 18th dynasty (Krönig 1934.144–50; Bourriau 1988.128–9, 131–3; for examples, see Garstang 1901 fig. 140, pl. 12; Carter and Carnarvon 1912 pl. 44.5; Brunton & Engelbach 1927 pl. 23; Bruyère 1927.53, fig. 41; 1937.87–9, figs. 43–5; Hayes & Lansing 1935.30, fig. 14; 1936.34, fig. 42; Steindorff 1937 pls. 91–2; Dunham 1967 fig. 3; 1978 pl. 58). Bowls from tombs are more often intact than those from temples, but when all the fragments are added up, it is clear that New Kingdom bowls from temples outnumber those from tombs.

Among this comparative material, and among unprovenanced examples, bowls decorated only with stylized marsh flora are the most common. The motif of the *tilapia* holding a lotus plant is by no means rare (*e.g.* Krönig 1934 pls. 26–7; Strauss 1974 figs. 9–15; Milward in Brovarski 1982 no. 139). Birds are sometimes depicted along with fish and flowers (*e.g.* Strauss 1974.22, 83, fig. 19; Milward in Brovarski 1982 no. 138; Bourriau 1988 no. 126), and wild animals are occasionally shown among the marsh flora (*e.g.* Strauss 1974.62–3, fig. 67). A bowl found in a tomb probably dating to Thutmose IV is decorated with marsh flora, fish, and a spotted gazelle suckling its young (KV 36; Cairo CG 24058; Daressy 1902.24, pl. 11; Reeves 1990.146–7, 159). Comparative material for the bowls with Hathor mask and cow motifs has been cited in 2.3.3.1 and 2.4.3.1. With the exception of the inlaid diamond shapes, which are unique to Deir el-Bahri (Strauss 1974.40–1), all the decorative borders used on the bowls from the five Hathor sites are also found on specimens from elsewhere. Wavy-edged bowls are depicted in reliefs from the Old Kingdom onwards (Winlock 1936.153–4, figs. 7–8). Carter found a faience example with lotus decoration and an inscription naming Hathor in a late Second Intermediate Period burial in the Asasif (1912.52, pl. 13.5).

Most of the 'marsh bowls' from the five sites date to the 18th dynasty, although a few (*e.g.* Pl. 63) could conceivably be as early as the late Middle Kingdom. Their date range is not thought to extend beyond the end of the 18th dynasty (Strauss 1974.65–6; Milward in Brovarski 1982.141–2). During the Ramessid Period new types of faience bowl were produced (Rogers 1948.154–60). Ramessid bowls tend to be deeper and more rounded, and to have a dot pattern on top of the rim but no external decoration. A. Milward notes that at this period:–

The designs on the inside change completely; the white lotus now appears more often than the blue, and instead of pond life, humans and animals are depicted – playing the lute or double flute, dancing, punting in the papyrus marshes, and bearing offerings. (in Brovarski 1982.141)

Bowls with motifs of this type have been found in both domestic and funerary contexts (1982.142). A bowl from the sanctuary of Sekhmet at Abusir, which has a single scene of a Hathor cow standing in a naturalistic papyrus thicket (Borchardt 1910 pl. 180), may be Ramessid. There is nothing comparable among the material from the Hathor sites. By using examples from tomb groups, it should be possible to date many of the bowls quite closely. This cannot be done here and Milward has been working on a dating system for this material.

2   The functions of the 'marsh bowls'

Were the bowls offered as decorative objects or were they used in rites of some kind by the donors, or by priests or priestesses of Hathor? If they were used as containers, how important were the contents in relation to the bowls? The 'marsh bowls' from temple contexts are all from sanctuaries of Hathor, or of goddesses who can be identified with her. 'Apart from Bastet, with whom she is identified, she [Hathor] is the only deity mentioned by name on these bowls' (Milward in Brovarski 1982.141). This indicates a close association between Hathor and the 'marsh bowls'. This association could be due solely to the symbolism of their decorative schemes or to a combination of the decoration of the bowls and the uses to which they were put.

In *Die Nunschale* (1974.70–3), E. Strauss argues that the decorative scheme of the bowls represents the Nun and that their symbolism is chiefly concerned with the birth of Reʿ from the primeval lotus and the waters of the Nun. She takes the *tilapia* as a form of Reʿ, as well as a symbol of regeneration (1974.81), and suggests that the Hathor masks, cows, and, more controversially, the stems of papyrus, represent Hathor directly (1974.77). She links Hathor and Reʿ through the idea of Mehet-weret giving birth to Reʿ, and concludes that the bowls can be associated with the concept of the deceased sharing in the rebirth of the Sun God from the life-giving waters of the Nun (1974.89).

While Strauss's proposed association of the bowls with rebirth is plausible, there is no definite evidence that they represent the emergence of Reʿ from the Nun. Probably due to its habit of incubating its young in its mouth and expelling them fully formed, the *tilapia* seems to have been regarded as a symbol of regeneration (Dambach & Wallert 1966.283–94). Its occurrence on the disc of menit counterpoises, suggests that it might also be a symbol of Hathor (Chappaz 1983.13). This fish also features in the erotic symbolism of New Kingdom love poetry (Derchain 1976.6).

The gazelle, which sometimes appears on the 'marsh bowls' in close association with the *tilapia* (*e.g.* Strauss 1974.22, fig. 20), may also have erotic connotations, since gazelle-head diadems seem to have been 'associated with women of subordinate ranking in the harem' (Troy 1986.130). An erotic element is very marked in the decoration of Ramessid faience bowls, which sometimes depict nude girls grouped with monkeys or punting in the marshes (*e.g.* Rogers 1948.155–60;

Milward in Brovarski 1982 no. 143). The gazelle and the *tilapia* are shown together on sacred barks in scenes depicting funerary festivals at Saqqara (Wallert 1970 pl. 14.3), suggesting that both were symbols of regeneration. The gazelle can be associated with Isis or Anukis, but some of the royal ladies shown wearing gazelle diadems were priestesses or singers of Hathor (A. Wilkinson 1971.116–8; Troy 1986.77, fig. 50, 87, fig. 59). In the Contendings of Horus and Seth, Hathor milks a gazelle and uses its milk to heal Horus (Gardiner 1932.51; 2.9.6). This might mean that the motif found on some bowls of a gazelle suckling its young in a marsh setting is equivalent to that of the divine cow suckling the infant Horus in the marshes of Chemmis. The image of Hathor in cow form as the mother or nurse of Horus is celebrated more often than the rather elusive concept of Hathor as the mother of Re⁽ (2.4.5). The marsh flora and fauna on the bowls could evoke Chemmis.

The presence of animals on some of the 'marsh bowls' could suggest that the decoration represents the life-giving properties of the inundation, whose ultimate source was in the Nun, rather than the primeval waters themselves. Hathor can be associated with the coming of the inundation (2.5.5), and this might explain her place in the decoration. There are relevant inscriptions, not cited by Strauss, on stone basins from Deir el-Medina which have marsh flora on the interior and Hathor masks on the exterior (2.11.1). The texts are prayers for standard life and funerary benefits addressed to Hathor or to Taweret 'The Pure Water' (Bruyère 1930.21; 1934.63–5). This indicates that bowls with marsh flora can be linked with the 'Pure Water' of the inundation flowing out of the Nun. In symbolism related to water, Hathor and Taweret are to some extent interchangeable (2.10.1.9). Desroches Noblecourt and Kuentz argue that both Chemmis and the Nun are the aquatic medium of birth and rebirth, ultimately to be equated with the womb of the Divine Mother (1968.111). This is an extreme view – Chemmis is not exactly equivalent to the Nun – but it expresses a general truth about the association of marshes with fecundity, birth, and rebirth. Rather than calling these objects Nun, Chemmis, or inundation bowls, it seems preferable to use the more neutral term 'marsh bowl'.

Milward believes that the importance of the 'marsh bowls' 'lay more in the decoration, with its theme of regeneration and transformation, than in any specific contents' (in Brovarski 1982.141). However, a link with a specific myth or mythical setting may sometimes have been formed by the contents of individual bowls. Winlock proposed that most of the 'marsh bowls' he excavated at Deir el-Bahri had originally held food offerings (1923.38). This cannot be disproved, but their aquatic decoration suggests that the bowls contained liquids. He did, however, make a good case for the wavy rimmed specimens having been used as flower bowls by reference to reliefs which show blue lotuses arranged in such vessels (1936.153–4, figs. 7–8). The decoration of the wavy rimmed bowls could then be seen as duplicating their original contents – water and marsh flora – and could have been a substitute for daily offerings of fresh flowers. Winlock compared these faience bowls with three metal ones, each with a cow figurine at their centre, which may come from Deir el-Bahri (1936.147–8, 155, figs. 1–4). These objects were probably used as flower bowls (1936.154–6, figs. 9–10) and would have provided a three-dimensional realization of the 'cow and marsh' motif which occurs on some faience bowls (2.4.3.1). Another metal bowl of this type has an inscription naming Hathor (G. Spalinger in Brovarski 1982 no. 108). Hayes suggested that such bowls specifically evoked Hathor suckling and protecting Horus in Chemmis (1959.206).

It is unlikely that all the 'marsh bowls' were used for holding flowers. Most of them are too shallow to make good flower bowls. Some are too small to take even a single lotus, although it could still be argued that they acted as substitutes for offerings of marsh flora at desert sites such as Serabit el-Khadim and Timna. Alternatively, the main purpose of the bowls could have been to hold water for lustration rituals or libations. The former is suggested by the inscriptions on the stone basins decorated with marsh flora. To wash in water from a 'marsh bowl' could have symbolised cleansing in the 'Pure Water' which flowed out of the Nun. One argument against this hypothesis is the size range of the bowls, many of which are small enough to be classified as cups and are therefore not likely to have been used in lustration rituals. The largest ones would have been too heavy to lift up to make a libation, but some libation scenes show liquid being poured from a small vessel into a large one before a deity (e.g. Nagel 1938.199, figs. 174–6). In a scene of this type on a small faience plaque from Deir el-Bahri, the vessel into which the libation is being poured might be a bowl on a stand (Pl. 37a, bottom left). Water was commonly used in libations, but water presented in a 'marsh bowl' could have evoked the benevolence of Hathor as the life-giving cow in the marshes.

Another liquid used in libations was wine. Schulman classes all the faience bowls from Timna as 'wine bowls' (in Rothenberg 1988.129). Ramessid faience bowls are sometimes referred to as 'wine bowls' and a few include grape vines in their decoration (e.g. Rogers 1948.154–5, fig. 1; Milward in Brovarski 1982 no. 143). Although grapes and dates do not appear on the marsh bowls, the idea that they held wine cannot be ruled out. Desroches Noblecourt and Kuentz suggest that wine could be used to represent the red waters of the inundation and point out that a grape vine can be substituted for a papyrus thicket in the 'cow and mountain' motif (1968.112–3; 2.10.1.1). Grape wine, which was mainly made in the Delta, was not incompatible with marsh symbolism. Metal bowls whose rims were decorated with lotus flowers, cows, cats, and Hathor masks may have been used to present intoxicating liquids as part of the ritual of pacifying the 'Distant Goddess' (2.5.5).

The third liquid which may have been presented in the 'marsh bowls' is milk. There is some definite evidence for this, since a 'marsh bowl' in a tomb at Deir el-Medina was found to contain a solid white substance which must once have been milk (Bruyère 1937.89–90; Strauss 1974.66). Strauss illustrates a scene on the 11th dynasty sarcophagus of Kawit from Deir el-Bahri which shows the royal lady drinking from a shallow bowl (1974 pl. 15). She suggests that the bowl contained milk from the cows depicted elsewhere on the sarcophagus and that this liquid could represent the revitalizing milk of the divine cow (1974.67).

On bowls that were used for milk, the marsh decoration is more likely to evoke Chemmis than the Nun or the inundation. The hypothesis that some privileged persons shared with the king the right to drink the milk of the sacred Hathor cows has been discussed in 2.4.4–5. It is possible that ordinary milk placed in a 'marsh bowl' and dedicated to Hathor was thought to take on some of the properties of divine milk. This milk could then have been used as a funerary offering to assure rebirth or nourishment for the deceased, or drunk by the donor in the hope of acquiring the life and vigour promised by the divine cow to her nursling. In the latter case, the bowl would presumably have been left behind as an offering. Cow's milk is unlikely to have been available at Serabit el-Khadim and Timna, but it could be argued that any liquid placed in a 'marsh bowl' could stand for the milk of the divine cow. However, it must again be stressed that many of the bowls are too big to be drinking vessels.

Another possibility is that the smaller bowls held perfumed fats or oils during anointing ceremonies (Strauss 1974.68). The blue lotus was used in perfumes and Hathor has a general association with perfumed substances.

The only thing that seems certain is that the 'marsh bowls' had no single function. The same is probably true of the other kinds of faience bowl, which could have contained any of the liquids listed above or have held food offerings.

Milward states of the 'marsh bowls' that 'the main theme of [their] decoration was rebirth' (in Brovarski 1982.141). This is likely for bowls found in tombs, but is not necessarily the case for those recovered from temples. The marsh symbolism can be associated with fecundity, and therefore with human fertility, and with revitalization of the living as well as the regeneration and purification of the dead. In other words, the 'marsh bowls' probably had much the same range of symbolic values as Hathor in cow form. Desroches Noblecourt sees marsh symbolism as specifically feminine. It is tempting to suggest that this is why only queens, who can be identified with Hathor in roles of mother, consort or daughter of the Sun God, are named on the 'marsh bowls'. Kings, however, do appear in a filial role in some 'cow and marsh' scenes (2.4.5), so their absence from the surviving bowls may be coincidental. The presence of numerous 'marsh bowls' at Serabit el-Khadim and Timna is a firm indication that they were not offered only by women. Some bowls have been found in male burials (*e.g.* Daressy 1902 pl. 11).

A large 'marsh bowl' bearing the cartouches of Ahmose-Nefertary was recovered from a private burial at Abydos (Petrie 1925.13; Strauss 1974 fig. 18 = Glasgow Hunterian Museum D. 1922.23). This shows that royal-name bowls could be in private ownership, though it might have been a royal gift. The royal-name bowls and some of the large and beautifully decorated marsh bowls, particularly at Serabit el-Khadim and Timna, may have been royal offerings. However, the presence of 'marsh bowls' in wealthier non-royal burials shows that these could have been the gifts of private individuals. The scarcity of such bowls at Mirgissa and Gebel Zeit may be an indication of the comparative poverty of the worshippers at these shrines.

2.11.4 Glass

No glass vessels seem to have been discovered at Deir el-Bahri or Faras. One vase fragment in black glass with bands of yellow and white was recovered from the sanctuary at Mirgissa (Karlin in Vercoutter 1970.355, no.200). MacDonald brought back 66 fragments of glass vessels from Serabit el-Khadim (London BM

17992–18059, 67797–800; Cooney 1976.54–7, nos. 508–72). These include mono-
chrome green, blue, and white fragments, and pieces in green, dark blue or light
blue, decorated with white and/or yellow. The forms comprise kohl tubes,
amphorae, lentoid flasks, and bowls. Some must have been exceptionally large for
glass vessels (1976.56). Cooney suggested that this group ranged in date from the
late 18th to the 19th dynasty and that all of them were made in Egypt. He proposed
that one vessel (London BM 18053) might have come from the glass factory at
Medinet Ghurab (1976.54). Petrie did not mention finding glass at Serabit
el-Khadim, but the Ashmolean has at least 700 small fragments of glass vessels from
his excavations there (E 4486–4494). These are dark blue or dark green with bands
of white, yellow, or light blue. The Petrie Collection has five fragments of blue
glass vessels from these excavations (London UC 35478–82).

Rothenberg excavated fragments of 50–60 glass vessels at Timna (1972.171,
pls. 14–5; 1988.212–23, figs. 85–6). He notes that:–

> The following types could be identified: krateriskoi, lentoid and globular flasks,
> vessels with elongated body and rounded base (amphoriskoi?) and bowls. With the
> exception of four fragments of green glass, all the vessels have a background of light
> blue, mainly an opaque sky-blue, or of dark blue in shades of cobalt or dark turquoise.
> The thread decorations of garlands or festoons, zig-zags and feather patterns are
> white, yellow and dark blue on the light blue backgrounds and white, yellow and light
> blue on the dark blue backgrounds ... Fragments of green glass include a rounded
> base, part of a vessel with the double cartouche of Ramesses II, part of bracelet with
> traces of an impressed pattern and a fragment possibly from the rim of a pomegranate
> bottle. This whole group belongs, from the point of view of typology and decoration,
> to the end of the XVIIIth and to the XIXth Dynasties. (1972.171)

In the full excavation report, G. Lehrer-Jacobson notes comparative material
from Lachish and Medinet Ghurab (in Rothenberg 1988.212–16). Most of this
material has a date range from Tutankhamon to Ramesses II. Chemical analyses of
the Timna glass revealed that it was 'virtually indistinguishable' from late 18th
dynasty glass from Amarna and Malqata, except for the type of lead ore used (Brill
and Barnes in Rothenberg 1988.217–23).

Cooney said of the glass from Serabit el-Khadim that:–

> The vessels could have served as containers of costly ointments to be presented to the
> goddess for use in her ritual. It is equally possible that they were intended for private
> use among the officials posted to this harsh duty. (1976.54)

The first proposal is the more likely, although it cannot be proved that the glass
brought back by MacDonald and Petrie came from inside the temple. The vessels
found at Serabit el-Khadim and Timna could have been the personal offerings of
wealthy donors, such as the expedition leaders. They might also have been royal
gifts, since similar pieces have been found in 18th dynasty royal tombs (*e.g.* Daressy
1902 pls. 43–5; Carter & Newberry 1904 pl. 27; Romer 1974.120). The one
specimen at Mirgissa may have been a prized component of the furnishings of the
shrine and/or the gift of a single rich donor – perhaps the official in charge of the
community. The absence of glass vessels from Deir el-Bahri and Faras is consistent
with the general scarcity of late 18th dynasty or Ramessid objects at these sites.

2.11.5 Pottery (Fig. 1; Pls. 1, 8, 33a–b, 38, 52c)

A wider range of pottery seems to have been found at Deir el-Bahri than at any of the other five sites. Hall noted that:-

> Fragments of unglazed painted ware vases were found, often decorated with polychrome plant-designs recalling, *non longo intervallo*, the contemporary naturalistic plant designs of the Cretan pottery of the first Late Minoan Period. (in Naville 1913.18)

He illustrated one such piece (1913 pl. 27.5 = Brussels MR E 738). I know of two similar sherds with floral designs from this site (Glasgow K 04.164.n; Oxford Ash. E 849). At least four sherds of the blue-painted ware, made from the late 18th to the 20th dynasty (Bourriau 1981.79; Hope in Brovarski 1982.88–94), were excavated at Deir el-Bahri (Brussels MR E 740–2; Ilkley 7011). Three, which probably came from large wine or storage jars, are decorated with garlands, and the fourth (E 742) with part of a papyrus thicket.

Much more common were the small 'rough double or triple vases ... joined together at the neck and base' (Hall in Naville 1913.15, pl. 23.1). These red vases are rarely more than 12 cm high. They may have served as miniature libation vessels. Equally characteristic of this site are the taller vessels:-

> ... decorated with painted knobs and button-like rosettes representing flowers, projecting from the edges of the pot..This pottery is very interesting in its evident imitation of the great gold vases, with flowers springing from them, which we see depicted on the walls of XVIIIth Dynasty tombs; the yellow paint with which it is plentifully besmeared is sufficient evidence of what it was intended to represent ... (1913.15)

Some of these vases seem to have been decorated with projecting Hathor masks as well as flowers (*e.g.* Pl. 33b, left; 2.3.3.1). They were probably libation vessels. Pottery vessels from the foundation deposit of Thutmose III at Koptos provide the closest comparative material (1.6; 2.4.3.1).

The elaborate painted pottery *kernoi* and ring vases whose rims are decorated with miniature pots, cow and cat figurines have already been mentioned (2.4.3.1; 2.5.3; Fig. 1.16). In some cases, the *kernoi* consist of bowls with incised wavy line decoration on the exterior, while the miniature pots are reduced to hollow knobs projecting from the rim (Naville 1913.25, pl. 23.6 = London BM 40984). Pottery ring vases or jars with miniature pots have been found in burials ranging in date from the Middle Kingdom to the early 18th dynasty (*e.g.* Garstang 1907 fig. 212; Petrie & Brunton 1924.40, pl. 30; Bourriau 1988.134, no. 132). They are thought to have held water offerings for the dead (Bourriau 1981.60; 1988.134). Vessels of this type were among the Second Intermediate Period pottery from Gebel Zeit (Castel *et al.* 1986.104). *Kernoi* with miniature pots, but no cows, have been recovered from Middle Kingdom tombs (*e.g.* Hope 1987 fig. 34) and from New Kingdom tombs and tomb chapels at Deir Rifa and Deir el-Medina (Nagel 1938.210–12, fig. 183). Rather similar vessels were used in temples in Palestine during the New Kingdom (Yeivin 1976.110–5, fig. 2). They may also be compared with the New Kingdom metal cups and bowls which had rims decorated with miniature pots, lotuses, cows, cats, etc. (2.5.4).

The ring vases may have been used to combine the rites of censing and libating which seem to have been standard parts of visits to a temple (3.2). They usually have two types of miniature pot (*e.g.* Fig. 1.16): narrow-necked vases which probably held water, and wide-necked vessels whose blackened interiors suggested that they were used for burning incense (Hall in Naville 1913.15). With the *kernoi*, water might have been placed in the central bowl while incense was burned in the miniature pots. However, on the *kernoi* fragments which I have been able to examine (Brussels MR E 1801; London BM 40984–5, 40988, 47671; Oxford Ash. E 908), the miniature pots, which are smaller than those on the ring vases, are not blackened. It is possible that the *kernoi* were used as flower bowls, with the pots on the rim holding small individual flowers, as on some Middle Kingdom flower vases (*e.g.* Bourriau 1981.67, no. 120).

Since they are so unusual, the vases with the projecting flowers and Hathor masks, and the ring vases and *kernoi* with cats or cows, may all be the products of a single workshop which concentrated on making pieces for the temples at Deir el-Bahri. Hall believed that these types of vessel all imitated metal objects and were 'the best imitation of the offerings of the great which the poor *fellah* could afford to buy' (in Naville 1913.15). Even these pottery vessels may have been beyond the means of the poorest strata of Egyptian society. The incense which seems to have been burnt in some of the vessels was a luxury product. In any case, it is not necessary to assume that one material was substituted for another purely for reasons of cost. Bourriau points out that pottery which imitates stone vases is found in rich, not poor, burials (1981.117). She suggests that the New Kingdom pottery vessels with projecting ibex heads, which seem be copied from metal vessels, were made only in royal workshops (1981.39). Two complex but crude pottery vessels decorated with cows and Hathor masks from a foundation deposit of Thutmose III at Koptos (2.4.3.1) demonstrate that such objects might be produced as royal, or at least official, gifts to temples. They probably served as magical substitutes for vessels in precious metals.

The pottery jars decorated with Hathor masks in relief have been described in 2.3.3.1. Some of these pieces, which have breasts, or arms and breasts, modelled on the body of the jar (*e.g.* Figs. 3.2, 6.2) might be counted as figure vases. On a few vessels of this type from other sites, the hands squeeze the breasts (*e.g.* Chicago OI 21044; Oxford Ash. 1892.1066; Hope 1987.48, fig. 62). Some specimens are painted with Hathor in cow form (*e.g.* Princeton 52.87). This has led to suggestions that they could be containers for milk, used medicinally or in temple rites (Bourriau 1981.37–8; in Brovarski 1982.78; Hope in Brovarski 1982.86–7). Such an interpretation would be particularly appropriate at Deir el-Bahri. Some vessels in Taweret-form with hands squeezing the breasts may have held water (2.10.9). A calcite vase with modelled Hathor mask and breasts from the tomb of Tutankhamon contained an unguent (Edwards 1972 no. 3). The blue-painted vessels with Hathor masks, common towards the end of the 18th dynasty, seem to have been wine jars (Hayes 1959.247–9, fig. 150; Hope in Brovarski 1982.87). As with the 'marsh bowls', it seems safest to say that Hathor mask jars could hold any of the liquids associated with the goddess. The same is probably true of the figure vases in cow form, one example of which was found at Deir el-Bahri (Pl. 38c; 2.4.3.1).

Hathor seems to have been specifically associated with grape, rather than date, wine. The former was a costly commodity. Some unguents were very precious. A humble-looking vessel which had once contained such commodities could be the remains of a valuable gift from a person of high status.

Undecorated sherds are unlikely to have been retained or recorded by Naville and his team. All the pottery published by Hall is elaborately decorated, and much of it is of types not found in domestic contexts. This was not the case with the pottery excavated by Carter and Carnarvon at Deir el-Bahri. Carter stated that among the refuse heaps to the north and north-west of Djeser-Djeseru, were 'dishes and bowls of pottery, some of which are of very large dimensions' and he illustrated 'a series of this votive pottery' (1912.32, pl. 23.2). Although almost all the pottery found by the EEF was in small fragments, the cups, dishes, and jars illustrated by Carter are intact. None of them resembles closely the types published by Hall. They are, however, quite similar to the crude vessels Carter and Carnarvon found in one of the foundation deposits of Djeser-Djeseru (1912 pl. 22.1). They may represent the type of pottery which was in daily use in the temple complex. Winlock did not mention finding any votive pottery in the course of his excavations at Deir el-Bahri, but it is improbable that none was recovered. One of his excavation photographs shows a series of 37 plain pottery jars beside the south postern gate of Akh-isut. Arnold suggests that these must have come from the 'Hathor dump' at this site (1981.29, pl. 8a).

Griffith noted finding fragments of 'numerous vessels' in 'plain pottery' at Faras (1921.86). He gave no further details and none of this plain pottery seems to have been distributed to museums. He illustrated one cream sherd with a projecting cow's head (Pls. 8.20, 38b; 2.4.3.1). The apparent scarcity of such decorated pieces suggests that there was no local workshop producing elaborate votive vessels. This sherd may have been part of a vase imported from Egypt. Again, the closest parallel is the Koptos foundation deposit material dating to Thutmose III (1.7).

The pottery vessels recovered from the Hathor sanctuary at Mirgissa are of simple and common types and were probably made locally. Most of the material was found together between the door and a granite slab which served as a base for the cult image (Karlin in Vercoutter 1970.322). This group included two cups in a dark ochre ware, each with a self slip and a band of maroon paint (1970.356, fig. 49c–d), part of a 'portable altar' (1970.356, fig. 49k), a fragment from a pot stand (1970.356, fig. 49h), and three-footed cups in what the excavators refer to as 'chamois' ware (1970.355–6, fig. 49b, e, f). There were also two shallow dishes, one in ochre and one in chamois ware (1970.356, figs. 49a, 50j), fragments from two similar dishes, and about a dozen sherds of ochre or chamois ware (1970.355–6).

The portable altar and one of the shallow dishes were blackened on their interiors (1970.323). Such altars, which could be made in one piece or consist of a shallow dish on a tall stand, were common in household shrines at Deir el-Medina (Nagel 1938.176–81). They have also been found in shrines at the 'workman's village' at el-ʿAmarna (Rose in Kemp et al. 1984.140). They were used for burning incense and food offerings. Most of the remaining vessels were bleached on the interior by contact with liquids and were probably used for libations (Karlin in Vercoutter 1970.321; 1.3.3). It seems that visitors to the shrines at Deir el-Bahri left behind the special vessels which they used for censing and libating, but this may not have been the practice at Mirgissa. No pottery was found in the forecourt. The vessels in the sanctuary were probably used by the officiating priest or priestess. In the north-east corner of the sanctuary stood a chamois ware jar, intact to a height of 25 cm, which contained a variety of small votive objects (Karlin in Vercoutter 1970.323, 356, fig. 22; 1.3.3). This demonstrates another use for pottery found in temple contexts.

The only pottery fragments which Petrie mentioned finding in the temple area at Serabit el-Khadim were plain, 12th dynasty sherds from the bed of ashes lying beneath rooms O to E (1906.99–100). Ten fragments said to be of 'Mycenean?' or 'Cypriot?' pottery vessels from these excavations are now in Brussels (MR E 3093–7). I was not able to examine this material. The Ashmolean Museum has the head of a pottery cow figure vase from Serabit el-Khadim (Pl. 38d; 2.4.3.1). These fragments are sufficient to indicate that decorated pottery was present at this site. In addition, the Petrie Collection has a red ware amphora handle stamped with the words ḥmt nṯr (London UC 35495) which is thought to come from the temple at Serabit el-Khadim. This amphora may once have held wine from the estate of a queen, perhaps Ahmose-Nefertary.

A large amount of pottery was excavated in or near the Hathor temple at Timna (Rothenberg 1972.153–62, figs. 45–7; 1988.92–114, pl. 106, figs. 4–21). The excavators divide this material into Midianite ware, local hand-made pottery, local wheel-made pottery, undecorated Egyptian pottery, and painted Egyptian or Negev ware. The Midianite ware, which made up about 25% of the total, consists of bowls, goblets, and jugs, all with elaborate painted decoration (1988.93–4, figs. 4–13). The main motifs on this pottery are 'geometric designs, birds and human figures' (1988.93). There appears to be no Egyptian influence on this material. This pottery was clearly votive or ritual but it is uncertain how much of it was present during the Egyptian phases of the temple (1.5.3).

The local hand-made pottery includes sherds from a few rough bowls and juglets, and from one goblet, one jar, and two pilgrim flasks (1988.94, Figs. 14–15). Two sherds have raised decoration which may represent snakes (1988.95, fig. 16.1–3). The local wheel-made pottery comprises sherds from *kraters*, cooking pots, storage jars and their ring bases, and from one goblet, one carinated bowl, and one incense burner (1988.94–5, figs. 16–20). There were a few sherds from undecorated bowls, jugs, jars and *kraters* of Egyptian types (1988.95, fig. 20). Some of this pottery may have been used at the meals which seem to have been prepared and eaten in the temple court (1.5.2), rather than in the service of the goddess in the sanctuary. A number of small vessels were painted red and decorated with black or brown bands (1988.95). Some of these seem to have been manufactured in the Nile Valley, and the excavators suggest that they were 'connected with ritual or votive functions' (1988.95–100, fig. 21).

Gebel Zeit produced a range of pottery including 'vases du type "Tell el-Yahoûdiyeh", piriformes et globulaires, en terre cuite noire ou ocre-rouge, vernissés, avec décors géométriques incisés' (Castel *et al.* 1986.104, pl. 5.12). There were also sherds of Pan Grave pottery (Castel *et al.* 1984.49–50; 1985.28) and 'vases à coupelles multiples, dits "à fleur", en terre cuite' (1986.104). All these were probably used in the first Hathor shrine. Tell el-Yahudiya ware was also found in the small shrines at Site 2 (Posener-Kriéger 1986.381–2). The New Kingdom pottery from Gebel Zeit published so far (Mey *et al.* 314–5, fig. 6) may have come from domestic areas of Site 1 rather than from the shrines.

2.11.6 Basketware

Both Carter (1912.32, pl. 79.1) and Winlock (see Arnold 1979 pl. 51) recovered baskets from the temple dumps at Deir el-Bahri. The baskets found by Carter were described by him as 'fig baskets'. They were wide and shallow with tall handles. The baskets excavated by Winlock seem to have been similar (Arnold 1979 pl. 51). Since Naville does not appear to have found any examples among the offerings in or close to the 11th dynasty temple, it is possible that the baskets recovered by Carter and Winlock were simply used to carry objects to the dumps. At Mirgissa, however, small offerings seem to have been presented on, or stored in, shallow reed baskets or circular reed platters (Karlin in Vercoutter 1970.323–4, figs. 19, 23–4; 1.3.3). This raises the possibility that votive offerings might have been presented in baskets at other sites.

No baskets survive from Faras, Serabit el-Khadim, or Timna. There may have been finds of baskets at Faras which Griffth did not record. Conditions at Serabit el-Khadim would not have favoured the survival of baskets, but some traces might have remained at Timna if baskets had been used in the temple there. The excavators of Gebel Zeit note 'petits paniers ronds avec couvercles, en folioles de palmier-dattier, utilisés pour transporter les offrandes dans le sanctuaire' (Castel *et al.* 1986.104; see Mey *et al.* 1980 pl. 81d). One small basket with a lid from this site has blue faience beads woven into it (Cairo JE 98138), which suggests that it was made to hold votive objects.

Summary

Many of the vessels and containers described in this chapter were probably ritual rather than votive objects. This distinction is not absolute, since vessels presented for use in the temple, or dedicated after being used in the temple by the donor, can count as votive gifts. Many of the more elaborate stone, faience and glass vessels may have been royal or official gifts. The range of calcite vases at Serabit el-Khadim can be matched only by objects from royal tombs. The unusual size and magnificence of some of the faience vases from this site, and the difficulty of transporting them intact from Egypt to Sinai, attest to the great importance that was attached to making offerings to Hathor at Serabit el-Khadim.

Decorated stone basins were dedicated at Deir el-Bahri and Faras. These have iconographic links with the faience 'marsh bowls' which were a popular offering to Hathor. Examples of 'marsh bowls' from temples outnumber those from tombs. The decoration of these bowls can be associated with the myth of Hathor in Chemmis, as well as with the emergence of the Divine Child from the Nun. The bowls from the Hathor sites vary greatly in size and must have had a variety of uses.

Some may have held flowers, while others will have contained water, milk, or wine.

Serabit el-Khadim and Timna produced two of the largest surviving groups of New Kingdom glass. Deir el-Bahri had by far the greatest range of votive pottery, including elaborate vessels decorated with Hathor masks or cows. Some of these vessels, and some of the simpler pottery from Mirgissa, were used for libations and/or the burning of incense. The range of pottery at Gebel Zeit reflects the mixture of ethnic groups in Second Intermediate Period Egypt. Basketware was used to contain or present the votive offerings at Mirgissa and Gebel Zeit and perhaps at other sites.

3

The place of votive offerings
in popular religion

In this general discussion of the votive offerings, standard terms relating to religion in daily life are used in accordance with the following definitions:–

Personal piety – Individual rather than corporate piety, but centred on one or more of the deities of the state cults.

Folk religion – Religious or magical beliefs and practices of the populace, independent of the state cults and centred on the home and family.

Popular religion – The religious beliefs and practices, whether corporate or individual, of ordinary Egyptians in daily life.

3.1 The manufacture and distribution of votive objects

How far can the votive offerings be seen as manifestations of popular religion? What evidence do they provide of the extent to which popular religion might be integrated with the official routine of state-run temples? Both these questions would be easier to answer if more were known about who manufactured the votive objects and how they were distributed.

Some stelae, textiles, and stone basins were clearly commissioned specially as offerings. Others were acquired ready-made and then 'personalized' by the addition of the donor's name. Commissioned objects can usually be distinguished by their quality and by the way in which the text is inscribed. The commissioned stelae and cloths may show family groups with each person carefully named in the inscription, although they display few apparent concessions to individual taste or circumstances. Uninscribed Type A stelae, Type 1 ear stelae, and stelae on which the names have been left out, or carelessly scratched in, are all examples of objects probably acquired from stock. On one cloth from Deir el-Bahri, there are several empty columns for text and space for more than the two donors shown (2.2. Cat.3.3; Capart 1942 pl. 591). On another, the last in a line of donors is painted over the striped border of the cloth (Cat.1.5; Fig.11.3). This suggests that these textiles were prepared with the goddess already painted in and a standard amount of space left for the donors to be added. There are no examples of fragments of old reliefs or statues re-used as votive pieces, such as have been found at Memphis (Schulman 1967; Schulman in A. Zivie 1988.84–5, 88), among the offerings from the six Hathor sites.

J. J. Janssen has shown that the craftsmen of Deir el-Medina accepted private commissions, for objects such as stelae and coffins, which they executed in their spare time (1975.510–11, 542–3; 1980.135). A 19th dynasty document from Deir el-Medina records a woman commissioning stelae for Hathor and Amon (Demarée in Demarée & Janssen 1982.104). Commissioning a piece was presumably more expensive than buying one ready-made. The donor's expenses are unlikely to have been confined to the cost of the object itself. There may have been a fee for the 'Opening of the Mouth' ceremony, which seems to have been performed on private statues (Morenz 1973.155; Yoyotte in Posener *et al.* 1962.270), and perhaps on figures in stelae and textiles. Agreements are likely to have been drawn up for endowing the cult of *ka* statues in temples, but a substantial 'donation' may have been necessary to secure a permanent place in a temple for any large votive object.

It was probably much cheaper to set up a stela in a community shrine like Mirgissa than in a shrine attached to a prestigious state temple, like those at Deir el-Bahri. At the former, the question of permission may not have arisen. The same could have been true, for different reasons, at Serabit el-Khadim and Timna. Expedition leaders had themselves depicted in reliefs and on royal commemorative stelae at Serabit el-Khadim in a manner which would not have been permissible in Egypt, but which can be paralleled in Nubian temples (*e.g.* Caminos 1974 pls. 16, 21, 23–6, 29–33, 40, 42–3 etc.).

The sites also differed in the numbers of craftsmen available in their vicinity. In the Theban area, there were numerous state-employed craftsmen who could have accepted private commissions or kept a stock of votive statues, stelae, or textiles. In theory, the offerings found at Deir el-Bahri could have come from workshops all over Thebes. This may be so in the case of commissioned objects, but the iconography of many of the stelae and textiles suggests that they were made specifically for Hathor at Deir el-Bahri. They may have come from workshops which specialized in making offerings for the deities worshipped at this site. Such workshops could have been part of the temple complex. Evidence was found at Deir el-Bahri for the mass-production of beads (Hall in Naville 1913.13, 17), and an inscription of Senenmut mentions the donation of one man and one woman to a workshop that was part of Djeser-Djeseru (Brovarski 1976.67; Dorman 1990.29–30). Perhaps the female slave was a textile worker.

The Hathor temple at Faras is unlikely to have had a large range of temple workshops, but it probably drew on craftsmen from Buhen. The shrine at Mirgissa will not have had any craftsmen officially attached to it. However, the community who worshipped at the shrine may have included craftsmen. There would also have been Egyptian craftsmen temporarily working on government projects in Nubia who might have accepted commissions. The stelae at Mirgissa are hardly of the best quality, but they are clearly not the work of amateurs (Vercoutter 1970 pls. 38–9).

At Serabit el-Khadim almost all the stelae are in local sandstone and must have been made at or near this site. Mining expeditions included among their personnel sculptors to work on the temple and on the royal commemorative stelae. Such sculptors set up stelae for themselves and must have accepted commissions from other expedition members. The poor quality of some of the private stelae (Figs. 8–9, Pls. 13–14a) shows that they were not all the work of the very competent craftsmen who carved the royal stelae and the temple reliefs. These may have been made by men whose main job was supervising or carrying out the work of cutting shafts and galleries in the turquoise mines.

The temple at Timna was not continuously added to like the one at Serabit el-Khadim and some of the mining at Timna was open-cast. Sculptors were probably not among the regular personnel of expeditions to this site and this would help to explain the scarcity of stelae and private statues there. Nor do highly skilled craftsmen seem ever to have been sent to Gebel Zeit. No decorated or inscribed masonry has been found there and the few royal stelae, which are small and not of local materials, must have been brought out with the expeditions (Mey *et al.* 1980 pl. 80a; Castel & Soukiassian 1985.288–93 pls. 61–4). The only offerings which seem to have been manufactured at the site were calcite vessels, and small, crude stelae in local stones (1985.293; Castel *et al.* 1984.53–4; 1985.23). This is enough to show that some of the galena miners had been trained as craftsmen.

Many of the small offerings from Serabit el-Khadim and Timna, such as the glass and the calcite vessels, will have been manufactured in Egypt. Rothenberg proposes that the strong similarity between the votive faience from Serabit el-Khadim and Timna indicates 'a central organization for the preparation and supply of the Egyptian mining expeditions into the desert' (1972.171). Such an organization would presumably have been based in the eastern Delta. Much of the 18th dynasty faience may have come from Egypt, but the composition of the Ramessid faience from Serabit el-Khadim suggests that it was made in Sinai (Kaczmarczyk & Hedges 1983.200–1). This faience has a distinctive crumbly red body and a glaze that is more green than blue. No evidence for faience production has been found on the plateau at Serabit el-Khadim, but some Egyptian faience was discovered among slag heaps at Bir Nasib, a site which had sources of water and fuel (Giveon 1978a.72; Rothenberg 1979.166). Small objects could have been produced there for dedication at Serabit el-Khadim and perhaps at other Egyptian foundations such as Timna. An overland route from Sinai to the Arabah is known to have been used by Egyptian caravans (Rothenberg 1972.201).

At sites such as Deir el-Bahri, the question arises of whether the acquisition of large votive objects was a private transaction between buyer and temple craftsman, or whether the temple was involved and took some kind of commission. There is evidence that temples were involved in the mass-production of votive stone plaques during the Late Period (Bianchi 1979.20). In the New Kingdom, it may have been possible to order a votive statue or stela from the temple in which it was to be set up. The temple might then have commissioned a craftsman or have produced a piece from a stock made in its own workshops, or in another workshop within the state system to which it had access. In the absence of records of such transactions, all this must remain conjectural.

The manner in which the small votive offerings were acquired by their donors is even more problematical. There has been very little discussion of this question. Concerning Deir el-Bahri Hall wrote that:–

> The presence of unfinished objects may possibly point to the existence of a regular factory of votive offerings close by: even glazed faience seems to have been fabricated within the sacred precincts. We can imagine a town of booths for the sale of these offerings crowding round the famous sanctuary, as, for instance, they crowd round such a modern holy place as the Austrian Mariazell. (in Naville 1913.13)

This seems an attractive picture, and parallels could be cited from the Roman world (*e.g.* Goodchild & Kirk 1954.27), but there are several difficulties.

Comparatively little is known about the extent to which private enterprise flourished on the fringes of the state-run economy of New Kingdom Egypt (Janssen 1975a.158–61). A representation in an 18th dynasty tomb of quay-side booths selling sandals, textiles, and cakes (Davies & Faulkner 1947.45–6, pl. 8) provides evidence for the existence of small traders, some of them women. Whether such traders would have been allowed to set up booths in or near a temple precinct is another matter. Nor is it certain how, in a barter economy, individuals would have paid the traders for inexpensive votive offerings. At Deir el-Medina, payments were sometimes made in small measures of grain or oil, or with cheap objects such as sandals (Janssen 1975.526). Similar payments could have been made for small votive objects, but it is difficult to see how the traders could have set more than approximate prices for their goods.

If small traders were involved at Deir el-Bahri, they are likely to have been regulated by the temple administration. In some south Indian Hindu temples, a range of votive objects is sold within the precincts by licensed traders. The type of goods sold is dictated by the priesthood, who bless each object and take a substantial share of the traders' profits (Hein 1978.441–2). A similar, semi-commercial arrangement might be envisaged at Deir el-Bahri. It is a possibility at Faras, but is unlikely for the small community shrine at Mirgissa and out of the question at the remote desert sites of Serabit el-Khadim and Timna. The situation at Gebel Zeit is more complicated, since most of the offerings found there were probably made at Koptos or Thebes (Castel *et al*.1984.49, 57; 1985.28). Some of them may have been acquired from temples or temple craftsmen at these sites.

Given the degree of uniformity between the Hathor offerings, it seems safest to assume that most New Kingdom small votive objects were made in temple or other state workshops and, at Deir el-Bahri and perhaps at Faras, sold directly by the priesthood. The problem of payment still remains. The temple economy could perhaps have 'recycled' sundry commodities received in return for votive objects more easily than private traders could. There might have been a system of donations according to means, in return for which the visitor received an object to dedicate in the temple. Presumably, the donors chose their offering from the fairly limited range of votive objects available. The marked variation in quality visible in objects such as pottery and faience cows does suggest some sort of scale of payments. Votive pottery from a shrine at Athribis, which functioned during the Late and Graeco-Roman Periods, shows a similar variation in quality, even though all the pottery is thought to have been made in a workshop attached to the shrine (K. Myśliwiec, lecture 1992).

The resemblance of much of the votive faience to pieces from royal tombs suggests an 'official' origin for this material. The faience pieces with royal names from Deir el-Bahri, such as bowls, plaques, and menit counterpoises, are obvious candidates for being made in state workshops. The same applies to the faience objects which occur only in temple contexts, such as the Hathor cow figurines and plaques. The royal-name objects may point to royal patronage of the Hathor shrines, although this does not necessarily mean that they were offered on behalf of the king. The use of royal names on votive objects might simply be a sign that they were produced in state workshops. It could imply that the king had an intermediary role and/or it could stress the king's role in making such offerings possible.

Objects in common use as amulets, such as small Bes figures and unifrontal Hathor masks, appear less likely to come from state workshops, but the discovery of four faience Hathor masks and a Bes pendant in one of the foundation deposits of Djeser-Djeseru (Hayes 1959.88) indicates that these were part of the official repertory, and probably officially manufactured. It also seems implausible that fertility figurines, which belong to the sphere of folk religion, would have been made in temple workshops. Yet the presence of Type 5 figurines in temple foundation deposits at Koptos and el-Kab (1.7; 2.6.1.5) confirms that they too had some official status.

The crudity of many of the pottery cows, Hathor masks, and fertility figurines could be used to suggest that they were made by poor donors or by not very skilful craftsmen from the donors' own communities. Artistic crudity is not, however, always a good criterion for judging the social status of the donors (2.6.4). There are also arguments against the donors' having manufactured their own offerings. First, there is the striking uniformity of some classes of votive object. For example, the Type 3 fertility figurines, though very crude, are obviously made to a standard pattern (Pls. 46d–48). More variation might be expected if the donors made such objects. Given the general Egyptian tendency to standardization, it is likely that most communities had a craftsman who knew the standard forms for fertility figurines and was able to reproduce them. Moulds for making fertility figurines have been excavated at Deir el-Medina (Bruyère 1939.214), and one Type 6a figurine has been found in a potter's workshop in the workmans' village at el-ʿAmarna (Rose in Kemp 1989.90).

As in similar contexts in other cultures (see 3.2.2), religious ritual was probably involved in the manufacture of votive objects. If such rituals could only be carried out by a priest, lay donors could not have made their own offerings. At Deir el-Medina at least, many craftsmen were also *waab* priests (Černý 1965.22) and some held the titles of *bȝk* or *is* of Hathor (Valbelle 1985.328). Thus some communities did have craftsmen who could carry out the appropriate rituals for making sacred objects. Indeed, such artisan-priests are likely to have formed a high proportion of the donors at several of the Hathor sites (3.2.3). Some of the offerings may then have been made by local craftsmen, on behalf of themselves or others, and taken to the chosen shrine.

One reason for thinking that most of the votive objects found at Deir el-Bahri were manufactured there is the comparatively limited period during which such offerings were made at the site. The royal-name faience ranges in date from Ahmose to Amonhotpe III, with Hatshepsut and Thutmose III the most frequently named rulers. The other small votive objects almost all fall into the same date range, reflecting a decline in the late 18th dynasty and a failure to revive after the Amarna period. It might be argued that shrines which were a focus for popular devotion were subject to sudden rises and falls in popularity according to the number of 'miracles' occurring at them, as was certainly the case with Christian shrines in the Middle Ages (Merrifield 1987.87–8). However, intermediary texts on 19th dynasty statues (3.2), and the 20th dynasty graffiti (1.1.2.4) at the site, indicate that people continued to come to Deir el-Bahri to pray to Hathor throughout the New Kingdom. If donors were accustomed to provide their own offerings and could dedicate them without any supervision or assistance from the temple priesthood, it would be difficult to account for the absence at Deir el-Bahri of small offerings from the end of the 18th dynasty and the Ramessid period. If, however, the shrines at Deir el-Bahri produced votive offerings on a large scale and provided the staff to deal with visitors dedicating such offerings (3.2.3) only during the reigns of those rulers who actively supported the cult of Hathor at the site, the decline is more explicable.

These comments about the manufacture of votive objects at Deir el-Bahri are largely applicable to the state-run Hathor temple at Faras. Apart from the absence of royal-name vessels or menit counterpoises, the range of offerings at Faras is remarkably similar to that found at Deir el-Bahri. In theory, votive objects could have been manufactured in some central workshop, probably in Thebes, and distributed to temples all over Egypt and its empire. However, since much of the votive faience found at Serabit el-Khadim is now known to be locally made, if anything was sent from Egypt to Faras it was probably the moulds for making votive faience. With such moulds, a small temple workshop with a kiln could have turned out a range of 'officially approved' votive offerings. Visitors to the Faras temple probably acquired objects such as ears, eyes, unifrontal Hathor masks, and Type 5 fertility figurines from a stock kept by the priesthood. Anything more elaborate would have had to be commissioned from such craftsmen as were locally available or imported from Egypt.

Few facilities for the manufacture of votive offerings seem to have existed at Mirgissa. In contrast to the other sites, only a small number of examples of the standard types of votive faience were recovered and a high proportion of the offerings may have been personal items of jewellery before being dedicated. Apart from two scarabs (2.10.1.7), which could also have been personal possessions, no royal-name faience was found. The presence of a small group of Type 5 fertility figurines suggests that someone in Mirgissa once had moulds for such objects, but this community shrine is unlikely to have had its own kiln.

Royal-name faience dominates the offerings at Serabit el-Khadim and Timna. At the former site, its date range covers almost all of the New Kingdom (1.4.3). As long as Egypt gave a high priority to exploiting the mineral resources of Sinai and the Negev, royal patronage of these two temples was bound to continue. Each expedition seems to have dedicated a range of standard royal-name objects in order to ensure its success, but the same objects may also have functioned as private offerings. The small, crude sandstone Hathor mask stelae from Serabit el-Khadim which name and depict private individuals (Pls. 13–14a) suggest that the very similar faience Hathor mask plaques which sometimes bear royal names (Pl. 31) could also have been private offerings. The same is likely to be true of the analogous cat plaques, and probably of the cat figurines and some of the model Hathor masks. Expedition members may have been supplied with suitable votive offerings as part of their equipment and a degree of choice could have been involved. Some of the jewellery and amulets found at Serabit el-Khadim and Timna could have been the personal possessions of the donors. A few objects, such as the small number of fertility figurines (e.g. Pl. 51d), may have been brought out from Egypt by expedition members with special requests to make of the goddess.

This proportion of 'official' to 'private' objects is reversed at Gebel Zeit. The excavators comment that:—

En quittant la Vallée du Nil, on emportait les objets destinés à être offerts dans le sanctuaire de la mine et, s'il s'y ajoutait sur place des offrandes locales – coquillages ou vases de calcite -, la plupart des objets à déposer étaient fabriqués en Egypte et devaient correspondre à une sorte de lot défini et nécessaire, composé avec soin selon des exigences précises, comme tout équipement qui doit rendre un service efficace. (Castel *et al.* 1984.49)

Nevertheless, the royal name faience so characteristic of Timna and Serabit el-Khadim is largely absent from Gebel Zeit. Among the Second Intermediate Period offerings it is represented only by scarabs and small faience stelae (1.6.3). Probably very little such faience was manufactured during this period. More suprisingly, royal name faience is also scarce among the New Kingdom offerings, suggesting that, in this period too, royal workshops did not supply expeditions to Gebel Zeit. The excavators remark that 'Dies war aber kein Hindernis, da man persönliche Exvoten zu den Bergwerken des Gebel Zeit mitnahmen' (Castel *et al.* 1985.21). The range of objects at Gebel Zeit is more like that of a community shrine than of a state foundaton (1.6.3). Expedition leaders will have brought some gifts and furnishings for the shrine, but many of the small offerings, particularly the fertility figurines and related objects, were probably privately acquired and taken to Gebel Zeit by individual miners.

Summary

Some of the votive stelae and textiles must have been commissioned, while others were bought from stock. In both cases, workshops attached to the temple where the stelae and textiles were to be dedicated are the most likely source. This is also true for most of the votive faience from Deir el-Bahri and Faras. There is evidence that even faience fertility figurines and Bes and Taweret amulets were made by temples. It is not clear whether or in what way, temples would have charged for such objects, or what range of choice was available. Some offerings, such as pottery fertility figurines, may have been made by craftsmen in the donors' communities who knew the appropriate forms and rituals.

Almost all the votive stelae from Serabit el-Khadim were made at the site by the craftsmen who came out with the mining expeditions. The 18th dynasty small votive offerings were brought out to Serabit el-Khadim from Egypt, probably from a depot in the eastern Delta. In the Ramessid period, some votive faience for Serabit el-Khadim and Timna seems to have been made in Sinai, possibly at Bir Nasib. Most of the offerings at these sites were part of the official equipment of the expeditions, but in the New Kingdom the small objects were probably shared out among the miners and artisans to give to the goddess. At Gebel Zeit, most of the offerings were the personal gifts of the miners, and were probably acquired at Koptos or Thebes.

3.2 The presentation of votive offerings

The actions of visitors to a temple may be divided into three categories: prayer, sacrifice, and the dedication of votive offerings. For the first and second there is textual and pictorial evidence, but for the third there is little evidence apart from the objects themselves.

Prayer could be subdivided into adoration and supplication. A visitor adoring a deity probably began with a low bow ('kissing the ground') and then knelt, or stood with arms raised, to praise the deity, almost certainly speaking aloud. Adoration dominates the votive inscriptions. Supplication, embodied in such actions as making requests of a deity, is represented only by very formal and generalized prayers. However, 20th dynasty private letters provide evidence that supplication could include personal and urgent requests (3.3). Another valuable source of information is the inscriptions of 'intermediary statues' in which the statue owner promises to pass the petitions of temple visitors on to the deity in return for offerings (Otto 1948.462–6; Yoyotte 1960.42–4; Clère 1968.143–4; 1969.1–4; for statues with intermediary texts see: Benson & Gourlay 1899.331–3; Legrain 1914.17–26; *Urk.* IV, 1832–5; Moret 1919.164–5; Borchardt 1930.173–5; 1934.103–5; Bruyère 1952.58–9, 68; Björkman 1971.29–32; Strasbourg Cat. 1973.37).

Three intermediary statues have been found at Deir el-Bahri. The block statue of the Royal Butler Tjau from Akh-isut (London BM 1459; Pl. 40) is inscribed with a hymn to Hathor (Naville 1913.7; Barucq & Daumas 1980.437–8) and with funerary prayers (Naville 1913.8, pl. 9). On the front of the statue, beside and below the cow's head, is a slightly damaged text (Pl. 40; Naville 1913 pl. 9.A = Fig. 17):–

> The Royal Butler, Tjau, he says 'I am the *iḥy*[1] [. . . . .] of Hathor, who listens to the petitions of every young girl who weeps and who trusts in Hathor[2]. Place perfumed oil upon my forehead[3], and beer for my mouth, bread and beer from what you offer, place offerings in front of (me); then I shall speak to Hathor, (for) she has listened[4] to what is repeated. For his *ka*, who is pure (?), the priest of the living royal *ka* [. . .].

[1] This can be translated as 'sistrum-player', or 'musician' (Schott 1950.81f; Barucq & Daumas 1980.438), but it is a specific priestly title whose bearers could be of high rank. It occurs on another intermediary statue of a Royal Butler (Moret 1919.164–5; Vandier 1958 pl. 148).

[2] Schott gave the more literal translation 'und auf Hathor baut' (1950.81f).

[3] [hieroglyphs] can mean 'tallow' (Faulkner 1962.252), but in this context it seems to be some kind of perfumed oil or fat. The same commodity is requested in the inscriptions of some other intermediary statues (*e.g.* Moret 1935.201; Bruyère 1952.68). Examination of the statue shows that Naville's [hieroglyph] should be emended to [hieroglyph].

[4] One would expect 'who listens' or 'who will listen' here.

A similar, but more elaborate, intermediary text is inscribed on the 'sistrophorous' statue of Amoneminet from Djeser-Akhet (Luxor J 141; Romano 1979 figs. 120–1; Lipińska 1984.21–2, figs. 66–8), which also has a biographical inscription describing his career as as army commander, Chief of Medjay, and Overseer of Works during the building of the Ramesseum (Lipińska 1969.41–9; 1969a.28–30; 1984.22). The intermediary text is written on the right side of the statue (Fig. 18). After a column listing the titles of Amoneminet, the inscription continues in the first person:–

> I am the *is*[1] of the goddess, the messenger[2] of his mistress. Anyone with petitions, speak [...] to my ear; then I will repeat them to my mistress in exchange for[3] offerings. Give to me *ḥnqt*-beer upon my hand and *srmt*-beer for my mouth, sweet and pleasant oil for my shaven head,[4] fresh garlands for my neck. Pour out for me with wine and beer, (for) I am the *is* of the Golden One. If there is no beer, give to me cool water because the mistress loves an *is*. Be prudent[5], pour out freely for me on to the ground. I am one who prospered (?), I did not knowingly speak falsely, (I) did not act twice,[6] I reached here [...] doing right, I am in the place of a just one.

[1] Statue owners are described as an ⸲ *is* of a goddess on five other intermediary statues (*HT* 1914.11, pl. 40; Borchardt 1934.103–5; Moret 1935.201; Björkman 1971.29–32; Strasbourg Cat. 1973.37). This title is related to the word for 'baldness'; when the head is preserved the statue owners are shown with their hair long at the back but with the crown of the head shaven (Romano 1979 fig. 121). This unusual hairstyle is best known from the statues of the 25th dynasty Mayor of Thebes, Mentuemhat, who also bore the title of '*is* of the Golden One' (Quaegebeur 1982.197–8).

[2] The title *wḥmw*, which may be translated as 'messenger, herald, reporter' or even 'mediator' (Kees 1960.138–9) and occurs in six other intermediary texts (Benson & Gourlay 1899.331–3; Legrain 1914.17–26; Moret 1919.164–5; Borchardt 1934.103–5).

[3] Lit. 'as the price of' (*swnt*). One might expect *m isw* here.

[4] Lit.'for my baldness'. See note 1.

[5] Or possibly 'Satisfy (me)'. Lipińska suggests the translation ' ... let me have cold water, because the Mistress loves that a *bald* is satiated, and pour for me ... ' (1984.22).

[6] Meaning 'I was not a double-dealer' (I was lacking in duplicity)?

A block statue fragment from Akh-isut has the remains of a similar text written across the knees (London BM 41645; Naville 1913.8, pl. 9b = Fig. 17; *HT* 1914.11, pl. 40). The ends of the seven remaining horizontal lines of inscription are missing, so a continuous translation is not possible:–

> 1 [. . . . .] her son Watjwatj [. . . . .] 2 [. . . . .] all people who enter the temple of the Golden One, fill my mouth with what you give, give [. . . . .] 3 [. . . . .] her *is*, who is satisfied. I am an *is* and I speak to the Golden One [. . . . .] 4 [. . . . .] you say.[1] O people of Thebes, noble ladies as well as poor girls, all women who come at (any) time[2] to Djeseret [. . . . . .] 5 [. . . . . .] to speak your petitions to the Cow of Gold, the Lady of the Good Lifetime,[3] the Mistress

of the Shaven Priests (?)[4], the Lady [... ...] 6 [... ... ...] chamber, door-keeper,[5] that she may give you a good child[6] (of) this house, happiness, and a good husband, bringing (?) [...] 7 [...........] she rest (her) feet (?). If (you) give to him offerings in his presence,[7] she will not be angry [......].

[1] After examining the statue, I read this group as ⌐⌐. To judge by parallels in other intermediary texts, this phrase ran something like 'I speak to the Golden One and repeat to her what you say'.

[2] Or possibly 'from time to time'.

[3] Probably meaning that the goddess bestows a good long life-span.

[4] I can find no parallel for the epithet ⌐⌐. It might be read as ⌐⌐ 'shaven priests', which could be an alternative term for an *is*. Another possibility is ⌐⌐, the title of a type of priest who seems to have danced before Hathor with menit necklaces (Quaegebeur 1982.198, 204–5).

[5] The title ⌐⌐ occurs on two other intermediary statues (Moret 1935.201; Björkman 1971.31–2).

[6] This seems to be a word for child unknown from other texts, unless it is a conflation of ⌐⌐ and ⌐⌐.

[7] That is, the statue owner's presence. As in the inscription of Tjau, the text switches from first to third person at the end.

Most votive stelae and textiles depict – whether realistically or not – donors in an act of worship which includes both prayer and sacrifice. In his book on Greek votive offerings, W. H. Rouse defined sacrifices as offerings of perishable commodities, and votive objects as permanent memorials of a prayer to a deity (1902.1). This distinction can be useful in an Egyptian context. Forms of sacrifice commonly depicted on large votive objects are the making of libations with wine, beer, milk, or water; the burning of incense or of foodstuffs, and the presentation of bread, fruit, and flowers. The intermediary texts make it plain that most temple visitors brought with them, or acquired at the temple, bread and beer or other foodstuffs and scented fats or oils. The inscription of Amoneminet, which asks for wine or beer or, failing them, water, suggests the presence of visitors who could not afford the more expensive beverages.

All these forms of sacrifice closely parallel components of the daily temple cult carried out by priests (*e.g.* Fairman 1954.178–81; Morenz 1973.87–8). Some of the pottery vessels from among the offerings at Deir el-Bahri seem to have been modelled and painted to resemble the elaborate metal vessels used in Djeser-Djeseru and other New Kingdom temples (*e.g.* Naville [1904] pl. 90; Wreszinski 1935 pl. 34a–b; Keimer 1956.226–7, fig. 12). At Mirgissa, stains on the granite pedestal of the cult image, and the state of the floor immediately in front of it, showed that libations had frequently been poured onto this area (Karlin in Vercoutter 1970.313, 324, fig. 7). North of the door to the sanctuary, beside an area of rough paving, was a dense concentration of broken pottery (1970 figs. 12, 21). Some of these vessels appear to have been used to hold foodstuffs and liquids, including milk, and others for burning incense (1970.322–3). Small vessels in faience, calcite and glass may have held cosmetics and perfumes for adorning and anointing the cult image (1970.328). So the surviving evidence suggests that the daily ritual of this community shrine followed on a small scale the cult practices of the great state temples.

Most of the votive objects are never shown being offered on stelae or textiles. There are probably three main reasons for this. Firstly, there was a general reluctance to depict new categories of object in a religious context, although exceptions are found, such as the introduction of the loop sistrum. Secondly, the act of dedicating votive objects did not correspond exactly with anything in the daily cult. Thirdly, such dedications never seem to have become a standard practice like prayer or sacrifice. Comparable constraints apply to religious texts (3.3). The dedication of votive objects is not mentioned in New Kingdom temple or private inscriptions from any of the five sites. One might expect the practice to be referred to in the late Ramessid private letters which allude to temple visits (Černý 1939; Wente 1967; 3.3). Its absence in these sources may be due to the fact that by the 20th dynasty small votive objects were being dedicated only at a very few sites, such as Serabit el-Khadim and Timna.

For these reasons, little that is definite can be said about the rituals attendant on the making and the dedication of votive offerings. It may be helpful to present what is known, and what can be conjectured, in a framework similar to that used by some anthropologists to describe and interpret ritual behaviour. J. Collins suggested that ritual specifics (components) should be divided into the following five basic categories:– material, ideological, human, supernatural, and mythological (1978.41–2).

3.2.1 Material components: the setting and the objects to be manipulated

Although the objects survive in the form of the votive offerings, there is some difficulty in identifying the setting. On the votive stelae and textiles, the donors are shown praying and sacrificing in front of a deity, or perhaps, a cult image of the deity. This is an abstract presentation based on the conventions of temple iconography, rather than a depiction of the actual context of private worship. Temple texts make it clear that the inner areas of temples, particularly the sanctuary, were accessible only to priests in a state of ritual purity (Fairman 1954.177, 201; Morenz 1973.99–100). Both an intermediary text (Borchardt 1930.174, pl. 115) and 20th dynasty private letters (*LRL* nos. 2–3, 14, 16, 50; Wente 1967.20–1, 47, 50, 83) refer to temple visitors praying and sacrificing in the ⟨hieroglyphs⟩. *Wbꜣ* has generally been translated as 'open forecourt', but P. Spencer argues that 'temple precincts' is more accurate, and that the word usually refers to all of a temple's land, but can occasionally have the specific sense of the area in front of the main entrance (1984.4–13). This meaning would fit with the evidence of intermediary statues being placed outside temple gateways, such as the 10th pylon at Karnak (Legrain 1914.15–7, pls. 1–2); with the model temple enclosures with divine ears carved on the outside of the walls (2.8.3.2); and with the popular cults of colossal statues flanking temple gateways, and of deities in reliefs on pylons (Yoyotte 1960.42–4).

However, some of the donors depicted on stelae and textiles were priests or priestesses. When they were in a state of ritual purity, they would have been able to enter a temple, though they are still not likely to have made private offerings in the sanctuary itself. At a community shrine such as Mirgissa, it is likely that any visitor could enter the open forecourt, while at Gebel Zeit any expedition member could probably have entered the sacred enclosure. At sites such as Serabit el-Khadim, Timna, and perhaps Faras, the normal rules of temple administration and iconography do not always seem to have been followed, and visitors may have penetrated deeper than they would have done at state temples in Egypt itself.

Even in Egypt, some shrines, such as that of Amon of the Hearing Ear at Karnak (2.8.3), seem to have been designed to be accessible to the lay visitor. The Hathor shrines at Deir el-Bahri probably fall into this category. The separate entrance constructed for the Hathor shrine of Djeser-Djeseru (1.1.2.3) may have been to allow visitors access to one or both of its transverse halls (Plan 1). It is also probable that many temples allowed access to their outer areas during festivals (3.2.3). By the 20th dynasty, when the Deir el-Bahri temples were in decline, visitors were entering and writing their graffiti in the hypostyle hall of Djeser-Akhet (1.1.2.4). This suggests that the temple areas accessible to the lay visitor, and what they were permitted to do there, could vary from period to period within the New Kingdom.

Apart from the prohibition on entering the innermost part of a temple, the main constraint on worshippers may often have been one of space. For example, all the rooms of the Hathor shrine of Djeser-Akhet are very small and quite unsuited to crowds of supplicants (1.1.2.4). Possibly visitors to this shrine prayed and made offerings in the nearby north upper colonnade or north court of Akh-isut or in the middle colonnade of Djeser-Akhet (Plans 1–2). The plan of the Faras temple is not well enough preserved for it to be possible to suggest a specific 'offering place'. At Mirgissa, Timna, and Gebel Zeit, the donors almost certainly worshipped in the open forecourts (Plans 4, 6; 1.6.2). At Serabit el-Khadim, the open court (P) and the 'sanctuary' (Q) seem the most likely places (Plan 5; 1.4.2).

In many ancient Greek temples, votive objects were piled up on altars in the open forecourt, with only the most valuable items being stored in a treasury (Rouse 1902.197). In Indian temples, the offerings frequently were and are heaped or lined up in the forecourt and left to disintegrate (Whitehead 1921.33; O'Malley 1935.100; Shah in Anand et al. 1982.51). In these cases, the purpose was or is to display the temple's popularity and to attract more offerings. This motive may have been absent from Egypt, where most temples were state-supported and not in fierce competition to attract worshippers. It seems clear from the presence of offerings inside the temples at Deir el-Bahri and from the example of Mirgissa, where the sanctuary was full of offerings but not a single one was found in the forecourt, that small votive objects were not intended to be left in open temple courts. Nor are there traces at any of the six sites of altars on which private offerings might have been placed in the open courts.

It seems probable nonetheless that these courts served as collection points for offerings, which were then taken into the inner part of the temple and dedicated there by priests. Thus, two settings should probably be envisaged, an outer area of a temple where the donor made his prayers, sacrifices and offerings, and an inner area in which the offerings were subsequently placed before the deity. The textile which shows the donor apparently standing in the open and the Hathor cow inside the sanctuary of Djeser-Akhet, without any of the intervening structures (Pl. 21a; Fig. 10.2), suggests a concentration on these two areas.

Very little is known about how the offerings were originally displayed inside the temples. At Giza, votive stelae were set into specially built mudbrick walls close to the Sphinx (Sadek 1988.25), but there is no evidence for this practice at any of the Hathor sites. Many of the small votive objects at Deir el-Bahri were originally strung together on cords (2.9.2.1), but it is not clear whether they were hung up in the Hathor shrines, as medieval votive offerings were hung from saints' tombs (e.g. Finucane 1977 pl. 13), or simply presented as heaps of necklaces.

At Mirgissa, apart from the pottery, the only categories of object which seemed to be grouped together in definite areas of the shrine were the stelae and the beads. The former were all in prominent positions, standing almost against the rear wall of the sanctuary on either side of the cult image (Karlin in Vercoutter 1970.320–1, fig. 8). A group of female-shaped pebbles was clustered at the base of the largest of the stelae (1970 fig. 17) – an interesting juxtaposition of the most sophisticated and the most primitive objects in the shrine that is repeated at Gebel Zeit (Castel & Soukiassian 1985 pl. 40). The numerous beads which had once formed votive necklaces were concentrated in four main areas: on either side of the cult image, and in the south-east and north-east corners of the sanctuary (Plan 4; 1970.324–5, fig. 24). Beneath these areas of beads, partially embedded in the floor, were the remains of shallow baskets or basketwork platters which Karlin suggests were used to present or contain small offerings (1970.323–4, figs. 19, 23–4). If groups of jewellery were presented in these baskets, this suggests that a number of people made offerings at the same time. One might envisage a priest or priestess collecting a basketful of offerings from worshippers in the court on a festival day. Alternatively, individual pieces could have been placed before the cult image and then tidied away into baskets when new gifts took their place.

Some baskets lay under a group of stelae found *in situ* just to the north of the base of the cult image. Reluctant to believe that the priests would have failed to remove objects which were no longer serving their proper functions, Karlin suggests that the stelae themselves were presented on basketwork platters (1970.321). It seems more likely that the platters, which still contained a few beads (1970 fig. 18), originally held jewellery and were used as props for the stelae after they became embedded in the floor. It is probably a mistake to assume that the Mirgissa shrine was kept immaculately neat and clean; instead, it should be imagined as dark and cluttered and smelling of incense, stale libations, and dried fish. While this picture applies primarily to community shrines, it may not be entirely inappropriate for the Hathor shrines of state temples.

Nothing was found in the rock-cut sanctuary of the Middle Kingdom/Second Intermediate Period Hathor shrine at Gebel Zeit and little was left of the sanctuary of the New Kingdom shrine, but one group of offerings was found *in situ* (1.6.3; Castel & Soukiassian 1985). The votive deposit in a stretch of the enclosure wall of the New Kingdom shrine (1985.288–9, fig. 2) demonstrates how stelae were displayed and protected at this site. The small objects in this deposit, and the pebbles at Mirgissa, may perhaps have been offered to the divine and royal images on the stelae. This could also have happened at other sites, the royal stelae in front of the temple at Serabit el-Khadim being likely candidates for such treatment. The placing of small votive objects in the the enclosure wall at Gebel Zeit is a custom not attested elsewhere. This could have been a reverent way of disposing of old offerings and/or a magical means of protecting the temple and continuing its rites between expeditions. The custom might also be linked to the role of temple enclosure walls as the place of prayer for ordinary visitors (2.8.3).

3.2.2 Ideological components: non-material components: actions and words

In many religions, the making and dedication of votive objects were or are accompanied by ritual words and gestures. In southern India, for example, sacrificial vessels and figurines to be used as votive offerings were made in clay taken from sacred ground by a special caste of 'priest-potters' who maintained a state of ritual purity and recited standard prayers at each stage of the work (Whitehead 1921.34). Among the 'tribal' peoples of north-west India:–

> Terracotta offerings are made individually or collectively on many different occasions: for the well-being of an individual or the village; for protection against ill-health or to avert evil; as offerings to ancestors; for the birth of a child; for the fertility of animals; to recover property if there has been a theft; when cows or buffaloes do not give milk; and when evoking the spirits of the dead ... During the ritual celebrations, the *patel*, the village headman.. the priest and the *dholi*, the drummer, go to get the terracotta figures from the potter. The priest ties red threads around the necks of five [votive] horses, makes a red spot on the forehead of Ganesh first, and then worships all the objects. There is much singing and dancing ... When making small offerings, the tribals take their terracottas to the sanctuary along with live chickens, incense, flags, rice, coins, wine and coconuts. But for more important occasions, the ritual begins with invitations to relatives and friends. People then get together at one place and dance and sing as they carry their offerings to the sanctuary ... First flags are offered and a lamp is lit. Then the *bhuva*, or priest, goes into a trance and offers rice, the wine and the chicken and to the accompaniment of chanting and singing calls all the gods ... Feasting and dancing completes the ritual. (Shah in Anand *et al.* 1982.51)

It is salutary to bear in mind that none of this could have been deduced from the objects themselves *in situ*. A votive offering is not simply an artifact, it is the surviving part of an act of worship.

Evidence for the ideological component of Egyptian votive offerings is usually lacking, but some suggestions can be made. Ritual purity was very important in Egyptian religion. A state of purity might have been required of anyone making votive objects, particularly those in the form of a deity. In the case of offerings such as miniature Hathor mask columns and cow figurines, some kind of 'Opening of the Mouth' ceremony may have been performed. The almost complete absence of small offerings directly representing Hathor at Mirgissa might be due to there rarely being a person of sufficient priestly rank attached to this shrine who could perform the proper ceremonies over such objects. At the very least, some priestly blessing was surely required. It is unlikely that the making of any divine image, however humble, could be a purely secular matter. Obviously offerings of these types were not regarded as vehicles for the goddess in the same way as her cult statues, but they could still have enjoyed a status not very much below that of other representations of deities within temples. The fact that some offerings were eventually dumped just outside temple precincts does not necessarily argue against this. There could have been some kind of 'deconsecration' ceremony for old votive offerings. Ancient sacred objects and buildings were not always treated respectfully in Egypt. The striking thing is that the Hathor offerings remained in the shrines for as long as they did.

As in other cultures, the acquisition of votive offerings probably had its attendant ceremonies. Rituals to link a votive object with its donor could have been carried out before, during, or after its manufacture. The inscribing of a name is the most obvious method of making an object personal to the donor, but inscribed offerings are comparatively rare. Simple formulae incorporating donors' names may have been recited over uninscribed offerings. In medieval Europe, candles burnt in churches to accompany prayers for the sick had special wicks which were made to the exact length of the sick person, or the affected part of their body, and then folded over and over (Merrifield 1987.90–1). This type of 'personalization' would not be obvious from any exterior view of the candle. Similar hidden links between donor and object may exist among Egyptian votive material. Pottery fertility figurines might, for example, have incorporated drops of menstrual blood from a female donor and/or semen from a male donor or the spittle or hair of donors of either sex.

The dedication of votive objects in a temple could have been marked not just by spoken prayers, but by chanted invocations to the deity, singing, dancing, and the playing of musical instruments. All of this would require space, again making an open court the most likely place for such rituals. In the case of votive offerings in the form of the deity, the objects themselves could have been the focus for the donors' devotions, as Hall suggested about the ring vases and *kernoi* decorated with cows (in Naville 1913.15). Some kind of dedication ·feast may also have been involved, and there is evidence from Mirgissa, Timna, and Gebel Zeit for the preparation and consumption of food inside or very close to the temple enclosure (1.3.2; 1.5.3; 1.6.3).

In other cultures two types of ritual are commonly associated with the dedication of votive objects. The first type may be described as a 'sacralization ritual', in which possessions of the donor, such as clothes, jewellery, weapons or tools, or newly made amulets or figurines, are transformed from mundane to sacred objects, fit for dedication to a deity (Tambiah 1984.243–57). Except at Mirgissa and Gebel Zeit, only a few of the offerings to Hathor are likely to have been personal possessions. This seems to be true of Egyptian votive offerings as a whole. The presentation of personal items of jewellery may have involved a special prayer by the donor to ask the goddess to accept them, or have required a priest to rule on whether they were acceptable or to pronounce a formula over them to make them so. In his study of Buddhist amulets, S.J.Tambiah notes that 'it is a common practice that when a Buddha statue is being sacralized..the laity (and monks) will bring small statues newly purchased or cast and their favourite amulets, so that they too can undergo the rite' (1984.243). It is possible that something similar may have happened at the consecration of cult images and other royal or divine statues in Egyptian temples.

The second type of ritual may be described as a 'substitution ritual'. Here, votive objects are substituted for more valuable commodities, or for a regular offering of some commodity. In Japan, for example, a painting of a horse could be substituted for the expensive gift of a real horse; and was then treated in the dedication ritual as if it was a real horse (Hauge & Hauge 1978.231, pl. 28). Although the concept of substitution is common in Egyptian funerary religion, it seems to be rare among votive material. Cow figurines or plaques are unlikely to be substitutes for live cows, or cat figurines and plaques substitutes for live cats. There may be some exceptions. The model lotuses and bunches of grapes (2.10.1.1) might have been substitutes for daily offerings of flowers and fruit. The yellow painted pottery vessels with projecting decoration have been seen as substitutes for costly metal vessels (2.11.5). With the latter, the fact that they copy the form of the cult vessels may have been more important than the imitation of the metal. There seems to be little emphasis on intrinsic value in New Kingdom votive offerings (3.3), and this could explain why there are few definite examples of substitution.

The question of whether some categories of votive object were supplicative or manipulative is discussed in 3.3, but it has some relevance here too. If, for example, the ear models, plaques and stelae were supplicative – symbolizing a plea to the deity to hear the donor's petition – then a prayer from the donor could have been all that was necessary to accomplish their dedication. However, if these objects were manipulative – laying some kind of compulsion on the deity to hear the donor – a spell might have been an essential component of the dedication. Spells are normally the province of specialists in magic but in Egypt such specialists were often priests, rather than secular magicians. Spells had a place in daily life, particularly in medicine (*e.g.* Borghouts 1971; 1978) and were prominent in funerary religion. It does not seem very likely that spells pronounced for the benefit of an individual would have been acceptable in the context of a state temple. However, magical rites could have been performed in the donor's home and the object that embodied the magic then dedicated in a temple in order to strengthen the spell (3.3).

Another type of ritual that can sometimes be associated with votive offerings may be described as a 'nullification ritual'. In this, objects are broken in order to prevent their reuse or to emphasize that they are passing into the ownership of the deity (Merrifield 1987.29–30, 110–12, 190–2). On the evidence of the Timna material, Kertesz (1976) suggested that most votive offerings to Hathor were ritually broken in this fashion (Kertesz 1976). Examples of ritual breakage do occur in a funerary context (Garstang 1907.121, 158–60; Borchardt 1930), but they are not very common. The way in which most of the votive objects from the six sites are broken suggests accidental damage. Many intact objects survive, especially from the relatively undisturbed shrine of Mirgissa, and at Gebel Zeit. Ritual breakage cannot be entirely ruled out – it is a strong possibility for vessels used in sacrifice – but it was not standard practice.

I have reviewed only a few of the rituals which could have been associated with the dedication of votive offerings. It is impossible to reconstruct this extra dimension with any certainty, but its existence should be borne in mind constantly.

3.2.3 Human components: the human participants

The most obvious human participants in the dedication of votive offerings are the donors themselves. The Deir el-Bahri shrines were close to one of the largest urban areas in the country and must have had the widest range of visitors. The Faras Hathor temple was in one of the more densely populated parts of Nubia and its 'catchment area' probably included Buhen. Trading and gold-mining expeditions may have visited Faras. If the local ethnic Nubians worshipped in the temple, they did so in Egyptian fashion. As elsewhere in Nubia, the population of the Faras area seems to have declined or to have become impoverished during the Ramessid Period (Trigger 1976.131–4), but officials travelling up and down the Nile are likely to have visited this temple throughout the New Kingdom. At Mirgissa the donors appear to have been a small Egyptian or Egyptianized community, perhaps living in the 'Open Town' (1.3.1). The Mirgissa shrine does not seem to have attracted travelling officials.

At Serabit el-Khadim and Timna the donors were members of Egyptian mining expeditions. In both these temples, some offerings were dedicated by local people working with the Egyptians. There is no definite evidence for this at Gebel Zeit. The Tell el-Yahudiya wares from this site were probably the gifts of Egyptians, but the presence of Pan Grave pottery in both shrines and burials and the mention of a Medjay on at least one stela (Posener-Kriéger 1986.381–2) suggests that some of the expedition members were Nubian nomads. They probably served as huntsmen and guards. It is possible that women sometimes accompanied the miners to Gebel Zeit (see below).

To judge from the evidence of intermediary texts and private letters, there seem to have been no restrictions on the age or sex of visitors to the outer areas of temples. Admittedly, most of this evidence comes from the Ramessid Period and the rules could have been different in the 18th dynasty. In one letter, the late 20th dynasty scribe Thutmose urges a group of male and female relatives and friends to visit Amon of the Thrones of the Two Lands at Medinet Habu 'taking the children along with you' (LRL no.1; Wente 1967.18). Family groups occur on some 18th dynasty stelae and textiles from Deir el-Bahri, and on one stela from Mirgissa. Not everyone shown in such groups had necessarily visited the temple in person. The donors will also have included groups of unrelated people, associated by their work or place of domicile. Such groups are found among the 20th dynasty graffiti in Djeser-Akhet (Marciniak 1971) and are shown on stelae from Serabit el-Khadim (2.1.4; Figs. 8–9). In the case of small votive objects, the expense may also sometimes have been shared by groups of relatives, friends, or associates.

Some of the textiles from Deir el-Bahri apparently show groups of unrelated women (2.2.5; e.g. Pl. 18b). The high proportion of female donors on stelae from Deir el-Bahri and Mirgissa has been emphasized in 2.1.4. Two of the intermediary texts at Deir el-Bahri are addressed chiefly to women (3.2), as is a text on a similar statue from the temple of Mehyt at Thinis (Clère in Björkman 1971.31). It could be argued that the women shown on the stelae and textiles are all priestesses of Hathor (2.2.5), but while appeals to the living inscribed on temple statues often specifically address priests (*e.g.* Borchardt 1925.109–10, pl.95; Page 1976.57, fig.63), the intermediary texts at Deir el-Bahri refer not to priestesses but to 'young girls' or to 'noble ladies as well as poor girls'. The Thinis statue simply addresses the women of the town of Pi-Mehyt (Björkman 1971.31). This indicates that women of all kinds were expected to visit these temples, not just those who served the goddess on a regular basis.

In India, women seem always to have visited local shrines and gone on pilgrimage more often than men (O'Malley 1935.100; Bhardwaj 1973.29–30). The male bread-earners were not at leisure to go on lengthy piligrimages more than once in a lifetime, or to visit a local shrine every day. For Hindu women religion provided, and provides, an acceptable reason for leaving the seclusion of their homes and unparalleled opportunities for meeting people. This social factor should not be discounted for ancient Egypt, where a similar situation may have existed. Since most women were not in state employment, their time may have been more flexible than that of their male relatives. Women probably performed religious duties on behalf of their families, in the home, at family and community shrines, and on visits to state temples. There is much more evidence for the presence of women at some temples, such as Deir el-Bahri, than at others, such as the temple of the Great Sphinx at Giza (2.1.4). This may be because women chiefly visited the temples of deities such as Hathor who had relevance to family life. In describing the cults at Deir el-Medina, where the women ran the village much of the time while the men were away working, D. Valbelle points out that 'Hathor, dame de l'Occident, a incontestablement la première place' (1985.313).

The cult of Hathor dominates the priestly titles borne by high-status women during the Old and Middle Kingdoms (Galvin 1984). In the New Kingdom, such women usually had titles relating to the cult of Amon. There were still numerous priestesses of Hathor, and many of the women at Deir el-Medina were singers of Hathor (Valbelle 1985.328), but in this period they seem to be lower down the social scale. Some of the women shown on the stelae from Deir el-Bahri and Mirgissa and on the textiles from Deir el-Bahri may represent this more 'middle class' Hathor clergy.

G. Robins has pointed out that in the New Kingdom, apart from participation in men's funerals, the religious activities of women are scarcely ever shown in the tombs decorated for their husbands or sons (in B. Lesko 1989.107–8). The votive material from Deir el-Bahri is particularly important as evidence for women's participation in religion because it includes objects which not only depict women but which were presumably commissioned by them. Several stelae and textiles show a woman as the principal donor making the sacrifice to the deity, while men take the passive secondary role usually allotted to women (*e.g.* Pls. 9, top left; Pl. 21b). This reversal of roles may have been considered proper at certain Hathor festivals. The textiles showing groups of women before the goddess may commemorate rituals or festivals from which men were excluded.

Except in a crisis (3.3), men who were not part-time priests may have tended to visit temples only on major religious holidays. In the Instruction of Ani, which may have been composed in the 18th dynasty (Lichtheim 1976.135), the son is told to celebrate the annual festival of his god, but he is not exhorted to visit the god as often as possible (Gardiner 1959.12–15). Personal festivals of Hathor, at which individuals seem to have celebrated their dedication to the goddess, are frequently mentioned in texts from Deir el-Medina (Valbelle 1985.323–5; Sadek 1988.114–18; 1989.365–6). Some of the votive objects at Deir el-Bahri, and perhaps at other sites, may have been offered on the occasion of such festivals.

Although officials often took the opportunity to visit temples while travelling on government business (see 3.3), Yoyotte argues that the majority of inscribed votive objects found in Egyptian temples can be shown to have been dedicated by local people (1960.140–1). Certainly at Deir el-Bahri many of the male donors of statues and stelae, and some of the men on the cloths, are known to have been attached to the staff of one of the temples or to have supervised building or restoration work in one of them. Temple statues, including those inscribed with prayers to Hathor, were often dedicated by, or on behalf of, important people such as Senenmut (Marciniak 1965) or the Vizier Paser (Borchardt 1925.109–10, pl. 95). The officials so favoured usually had some definite connection with the temples in which their statues were set up.

The donors depicted on the stelae and textiles belong mainly to what might be termed a 'middle class' of minor officials, priests, and chief artisans. The intermediary text which refers to 'noble ladies as well as poor girls' (Fig. 17) suggests a wider social range of visitors. The intermediary texts on the statues placed in front of the 10th pylon at Karnak specifically refer to poor (*nmḥ*) petitioners to the deity (*e.g.* Legrain 1914.18; *Urk.* IV, 1832–5), although it could be that in this context 'poor' just means ordinary citizen, or someone who was humble in the religious sense.

The social and economic status of the donors can be difficult to determine from the evidence of the small offerings. In China, people of all classes used to burn cheap paper models as offerings to the god at New Year (Day 1975.13–29). In medieval England, votive objects in wax were hung in the shrines of popular saints by donors ranging from kings and nobles to apprentices and housewives (Radford 1949.164–6, pl. 21; Finucane 1977.96–9, pl. 13; Merrifield 1987.88–91, figs. 27–8). In many Roman Catholic churches, the practice of buying and lighting a candle is still observed by all, irrespective of social and economic status. These examples warn against reading too much into the intrinsic value of a votive object; crude offerings in cheap materials are not necessarily the gifts of the very poor.

The 20th dynasty graffiti in Djeser-Ahket were written by or on behalf of soldiers, sailors, minor priests and officials, and their families (Marciniak 1964.167–70). One mention of a slave (1964.140) is the sole indication of visitors from the lowest stratum of society. Even this is doubtful, as the slave of a rich man may have been in a more favourable economic position than a peasant. Hall's theory that most of the small 18th dynasty offerings at Deir el-Bahri were 'dedicated by the ancient *fellaḥin*' (in Naville 1907.17) is untenable. Some of the types of offering found there also occur in domestic or funerary contexts where they belonged to artisans, priests, and minor officials (*e.g.* 2.6. Lists 3–7; 2.9.1; 2.10.1–9; 2.11.5). At Deir el-Bahri,

Faras, and Mirgissa, the temple visitors may have included the poorest classes of Egyptian society, but the offerings cannot be seen as peculiar to these classes, or as proving their participation. The Hathor offerings should probably be associated with the existence of a prosperous 'middle class' in the 18th dynasty.

If it is difficult to form a clear picture of the donors of the votive objects, it is even harder to make definite statements about the other 'human component' – the temple personnel. As noted in 3.2.2, both temple craftsmen and priests may have been involved in making votive objects. Priests might have been necessary to perform rituals over some of the offerings on behalf of the donors. The question also arises of who read the inscriptions on intermediary statues to illiterate visitors and who wrote graffiti for them. The services of temple scribes may have been available. Priests would have been necessary to place the votive offerings in the inner areas of the shrines, and the temple staff must have been in charge of their care and subsequent disposal.

For much of the 18th dynasty, each of the temples at Deir el-Bahri will have had quite a large full and part-time staff, including musicians and dancers for Hathor (Otto 1952.62, 108). The stela of Senenu, who was High Priest of Amon and Hathor in Djeser-Djeseru under Hatshepsut, shows four phyles of clergy (Brovarski 1976.60, pl. 11). In the early and mid 18th dynasty, the Hathor temple at Faras may have had its own full or part-time priesthood. If, however, the temple was used only for festivals of the goddess, rather than on a daily basis, it could have been run by clergy from Buhen. Later in the New Kingdom, the temple at the 'Hathor rock' was probably served by priests from Tutankhamon's temple complex (1.2.1). At Mirgissa, the shrine was presumably served by a rota of part-time priests and priestesses, possibly members of a particular family. At Serabit el-Khadim and Timna expedition leaders seem to have served as chief priests. At the former site, there may at some periods have been a small resident staff. There is even one possible Middle Kingdom reference to a woman attached as a 'Sealer' to the temple at Serabit el-Khadim (Ward in B. Lesko 1989.36–7). At Gebel Zeit, the expedition leader presumably acted as chief priest, with some of the miners serving as *bakw* or *waab* priests. The discovery in the shrine area of hand-shaped clappers of a type commonly used by women (Castel *et al.* 1985.20) raises the possibility that Hathor priestesses or *ḥnr* dancers may have visited this shrine.

Were the activities associated with the dedication of votive offerings carried out by temple staff as a part of their official duties, or on the basis of private arrangements between priests and donors? The huge quantity of small offerings recovered from Deir el-Bahri argues against the 'private arrangement' hypothesis. When votive objects were being manufactured and dedicated on this scale, the practice can scarcely have been unofficial. The inscriptions on the two intermediary statues of Amonhotpe son of Hapu which were set up in front of the 10th pylon at Karnak state that it was the king (Amonhotpe III) who appointed Amonhotpe 'to hear the words of the poor' (Legrain 1914.18; *Urk.* IV, 1833.18, 1835.6–7). The shrine of Amon of the Hearing Ear at Karnak contained a statue of Thutmose III 'who listens to prayers', and later statues of Ramesses II and Ptolemy VIII Euergetes II bear the same epithet (2.8.3). These examples demonstrate that special facilities for ordinary visitors might be provided in the king's name at certain temples (see further 3.3). Where these facilities included provision for the dedication of small votive offerings, some of the temple staff would necessarily have participated. This participation may have been subject to limitations, such as being available only during certain festivals. A gratuity or a donation to the temple may still have been expected from the donor.

The next question is whether such duties can be associated with any particular priestly titles. The intermediary texts may help here. Two of the most common titles in them are *wḥmw* 'messenger' or 'herald' and *iri-ꜥ* 'door-keeper'. The idea of a messenger to a deity is based on the messengers who reported, at least nominally, to the king. In the New Kingdom, *wḥmw* became a priestly title, whose holders seem to have acted as intermediaries between men and deities, particularly in the context of oracles (Kees 1960.140; Morenz 1960.103).

A door-keeper may have been in charge of the whole outer area of a temple as well as the main gate (Jelínková-Reymond 1970.39–59). His duties probably included the reception and supervision of visitors. The shrine of Amon of the Hearing Ear at Karnak had its own door-keeper (Labib Habachi 1972), and a 'Door-Keeper of Hathor of Henketankh' is known from the joint reign of Hatshepsut and Thutmose III (Quirke 1990.172). There must have been a similar post for each of the Hathor shrines at Deir el-Bahri. One could draw up a list of temple personnel who might have been involved with the dedication of votive offerings: lector-priests to perform some of the more specialized rituals, 'inventory-scribes' to record the gifts (Gardiner 1959.15), and so on. There is, however, no direct evidence for their involvement, and only Deir el-Bahri would have possessed large hierarchies of clergy and administrators. The priestly half of the 'human component' cannot therefore be examined in detail.

3.2.4 Supernatural components: supernatural beings and powers

By far the most important supernatural component in the dedication of the votive offerings was Hathor herself, or any of the goddesses who can be identified with her. On some of the stelae, Hathor is shown or named with one or more other deities (2.1.3). Joint dedications are common on temple statues found at Deir el-Bahri (*e.g.* Figs. 7, 17). In contrast, there is very little evidence for the joint dedication of small offerings. This is particularly striking at Deir el-Bahri where, although in the New Kingdom Amon-Reꜥ was nominally the principal deity of each of the temples, not a single small votive object can be proved to have been solely or jointly dedicated to him. Amon-Reꜥ was not a focus for popular devotion there, although he was the focus in the shrine of the Hearing Ear at Karnak. This is one indication that the integration of popular and state religion in temples was carefully organized (see further 3.3).

The deities of the state cults were not the only supernatural component involved in the dedication of votive offerings. First, there were also beings of ambiguous status, such as Bes and Taweret, who were closely associated with Hathor (2.10.1.8–9). Secondly, there were living and dead kings, or the statue cults of such kings, who were worshipped in their own right or served as intermediaries (2.1.3; 2.2.4). Thirdly, there were the *ka*s of the owners of the intermediary statues. It is not clear whether these statues began to function as intermediaries before their owners' deaths. In the texts from Deir el-Bahri, the *ka*s of the statue owners offer to act as intermediaries between temple visitors and the goddess, or perhaps more specifically, the goddess as manifest in certain cult images. Libations and gifts of food and perfumed oil are requested in return for the passing of petitions to Hathor. These statues seem to provide a counterpart in the official cult, for the role of the dead in popular religion, as manifested in letters to the dead, *akh iķr* stelae and ancestor busts (Demarée 1983; Friedman 1985). There is no evidence that votive objects were dedicated to such statues, although they could have been left in front of them to be collected up by priests. Votive offerings may sometimes have been made by visitors with a specific petition to the goddess. In such cases an intermediary statue could have been asked both to 'forward' the petition and to secure the acceptance of the gift. However, the intermediary statues at Deir el-Bahri date to the 19th dynasty, a time when few small votive objects were being dedicated in the Hathor shrines (see further 3.4).

3.2.5 Mythical components: mythical underpinning or legitimation of a ritual or its components

Mythical legitimation can be identified in some ritual components of the dedication of votive objects to Hathor. Among the material components, everything from the plan of the temple to the design of an offering may have mythical underpinning. To what extent the donors were aware of this is another matter. Possible examples which have been discussed in this book include the 'cow and marsh' scenes on stelae, textiles, plaques and bowls, which were underpinned by the myth of 'Horus in Chemmis' (2.4.5); the cat plaques and figurines, underpinned by the myth of the 'Distant Goddess' (2.5.5), and the phalli underpinned by the creation myth of the 'Hand of Atum' (2.7.3).

In many cases, it is impossible to point to a specific story which gives meaning to a votive object; the underpinning is more in the nature of a mythic image than a myth. This is particularly true of offerings which can also be associated with funerary religion. For example, the nightly progress of the sun god through the underworld is conveyed by a series of complex but essentially static images rather than by a coherent myth. These images are utilized in royal funerary religion. By the New Kingdom, they acquired relevance for the dead in general. Some of the votive offerings appear to be oblique expressions of the ordinary Egyptian's desire to identify himself with the dead king and therefore, at one remove, with the sun god himself (2.4.6–7). An object with a 'cow and mountain' motif has several layers of mythical underpinning, with the king, as the representative of mankind, playing a pivotal role.

Some of this underpinning may have been expressed in the ideological component of the dedication of votive objects. This is an area in which the general lack of information on the words and gestures which may have been used in dedication rituals is particularly frustrating. Medical texts in which appropriate formulae and gestures are given for identifying the officiant, the patient, the medicine, and the instruments with persons and objects from myths (*e.g.* Erman 1901; Borghouts 1971; 1978) may provide a clue as to how such rituals could be reconstructed. This analogy suggests that the human component not only might have formulated and expressed the mythical underpinning, but could also have been perceived as participants in it; playing, or seeing themselves as assimilated to, mythical roles (3.3).

Summary

Visitors to temples prayed, sacrificed, and sometimes made votive offerings to a deity. Texts on 'intermediary statues' provide evidence for the type of people who visited temples, the sacrifices they made, and the content of their prayers. Most visitors performed their devotions in the open forecourt. The votive offerings were then taken by priests to be displayed in or near the sanctuary. Many rituals are likely to have been involved in the making and presentation of votive objects. In Egypt and Egyptianized Nubia, women were probably the most frequent temple visitors. Most donors of votive objects were artisans, priests, or officials, together with their female relatives. At Serabit el-Khadim and Timna, the donors were the Egyptian mining expedition members, as well as 'Asiatics' who worked with them. At Gebel Zeit, the mining expeditions included Nubians and, possibly, women. Priests or priestesses must have been involved in the making and presentation of votive objects. The supernatural element included Hathor and goddesses associated with her, semi-divine beings such as Bes, deified kings, and the *ka*s resident in temple statues. The presentation of votive offerings could be underpinned by mythical images or the enacting of mythical roles.

3.3 Deity and donors

There is ample evidence for widespread personal piety in the Ramessid period. Private individuals, at least of the artisan class and above, clearly considered themselves capable of experiencing a direct relationship with a deity (Černý 1952a.68–70; Nims 1954.79; Morenz 1973.101–9; Assmann 1979; Brunner 1982. 951–63). The deities of the state cults came to be regarded as taking an interest in the welfare not just of the world as a whole, or the human world as embodied by the king, but of ordinary individuals. They could be appealed to for help, not only in the afterlife, but in personal matters in daily life. This idea, which should by no means be taken for granted, is expressed in a few Middle Kingdom (Vernus 1983.115–7) and 18th dynasty (Posener 1975) texts, and in many Ramessid hymns and prayers (Gunn 1916; Fecht 1965; Assmann 1975.349–420; Baines in Shafer 1991).

Among the offerings to Hathor, the change from corporate to personal piety is best illustrated by the differences between the Middle and New Kingdom stelae at Serabit el-Khadim. Only royal stelae survive from the Middle Kingdom. These are inscribed with prayers offered to Hathor on behalf of each expedition as a body. In the New Kingdom, scribes and artisans set up their own stelae at Serabit el-Khadim showing themselves before the goddess (2.1.4). The change represented by such stelae is cognitive, social and economic, but it is difficult to say which of these aspects was the most important. In the less formal context of the cliffs at Maghara, there are some Middle Kingdom religious graffiti of private individuals (Černý 1952 pls. 13–4; 1955.72–4). The formulae they contain, or the prayers which they address to Hathor or Thoth, are purely funerary, unlike those on the New Kingdom votive stelae at Serabit el-Khadim, which mainly ask for life benefits (2.1.5). The Gebel Zeit material adds to the small number of Second Intermediate Period stelae from Egypt which show non-royal individuals before statues of deities (e.g. Simpson 1974 pls. 25.2; 71.2; Baines 1986.51–3, pl. 8).

The majority of the large votive objects from the Hathor sites can be regarded as the products of personal piety, but some of them seem to display a certain lack of confidence in the relationship between deity and donor. There was a strong tendency to pray to deities as manifest in their cult images or sacred animals and to treat these manifestations as if they were separate entities. Among votive offerings from temples in Egypt itself, animal forms are more commonly depicted than the human or semi-human forms which dominate temple iconography. This may be due to constraints on the design of votive objects, in line with constraints on what could be depicted in various areas of a temple (Baines 1976.14). It might also be symptomatic of a reluctance to encounter deities in their more sacred and awesome human forms, and of a concomitant preference for worshipping divinity at one remove.

The intermediary texts suggest that, although the epithet 'the one who listens to prayers' was given to deities from at least the mid 18th dynasty onwards (2.8.3), not every temple visitor was confident that the deity would hear their unaided prayer. The standardization of the offerings also suggests a rather more formal and impersonal relationship between individual and deity than that described in the Ramessid hymns and prayers cited above. It could be argued that the 18th dynasty offerings represent a transitional stage between corporate and personal piety, but it may also be that personal piety never did or could develop real freedom of expression in the context of a state-run temple. Nevertheless, some shrines within state temples were visited by numerous individuals, who will have approached the deities with a variety of needs and expectations. The circumstances in which such visitors came to the Hathor shrines obviously varied from site to site. Since Serabit el-Khadim, Timna, and Gebel Zeit were special cases, being visited only by mining expeditions, they will mainly be disregarded in the discussion which follows.

In the New Kingdom, deities could be worshipped at household altars, in private votive chapels, and in shrines built and run by the local community. As already argued, Mirgissa should be classed as a 'community shrine', comparable to some of those in the workmen's villages at el-ᶜAmarna and Deir el-Medina (1.3.2). The Hathor temple complex at Deir el-Medina should probably be counted as a state foundation (Valbelle 1985.168–9, 326–7), and when the artisans' community moved down to Medinet Habu in the late 20th dynasty they appear regularly to have used the temple of Ramesses III to worship a wide range of deities (Wente 1961.255–6). Other state temples which were very close to settlements may have been used in the same way. The Faras Hathor temple could have functioned as a 'community shrine' as well as a state temple. In the case of Deir el-Bahri, where the strictly local population was small, the question arises as to why individuals or groups chose to visit one of these temples rather than worshipping in their homes or in their nearest 'community shrine'.

It is clear from stelae, graffiti, and private letters that officials travelling on government business visited temples on their route. Three main motives for such visits are discernible in late New Kingdom letters (Černý 1939; Wente 1967). First, there is a desire to honour or propitiate local deities in order to obtain a kind of 'safe-conduct' through their territory. Second, it was felt that that the more deities or hypostases of deities one prayed to the better – a feeling reflected in the standard formulae for beginning letters. Third, there is a love of sight-seeing, with an element of status-seeking attached. The second and third of these motives might have encouraged people, especially women, to go on pilgrimages to famous state temples outside their own districts, but the New Kingdom evidence for such pilgrimages is not extensive.

There is evidence that individuals and families visited nearby state temples during religious festivals and played a part in the celebrations, particularly during the 'appearance' of the deity (Morenz 1973.88–90; Altenmüller 1977.171). Some caution is necessary when mentioning the role of the 'people' in festivals, since it has been argued that participation in the more important events within the temple enclosure was restricted to men and women who made up a kind of religious association with semi-lay, semi-priestly status (Fairman 1954.202; Gardiner 1959.15). Some of the votive textiles from Deir el-Bahri may commemorate participation in festivals by such an elite (2.2.8). Twentieth dynasty graffiti in Djeser-Akhet show that artisans, officials, priests, and priestesses visited the temple during the Beautiful Festival of the Wadi and took the opportunity to pray and sacrifice to Hathor (Marciniak 1971; 1974.35). Many of the 18th dynasty votive objects at this site may have been dedicated by visitors during this festival.

The Instruction of Ani implies that a festival visit could be viewed in terms of renewal of an annual 'contract' with a deity (Gardiner 1959.14–5). Several other types of temple visit can be suggested. Particularly pious individuals may have made frequent journeys to the temples of their special deities as acts of devotion. Supplication was also a pious act, since it expressed human dependence on the gods. It may have been felt that prayers relating to important stages in a person's life, such as the birth of a child, were best made to the prestigious hypostases of deities in the state temples instead of, or as well as, to the deities manifest in community and household shrines. This is suggested by the offerings linked to fertility found at Deir el-Bahri and Faras (2.6.4). It is notoriously difficult to find traces of 'rites of passage' in Egypt, except for those connected with death, and, to a lesser extent, birth. Such rites probably belonged to the sphere of folk religion and had little or nothing to do with the state cults. It has, however, been suggested that Hathor, Bes, and Taweret played a role in such rites of passage as circumcision (2.7.2), and the purification of mothers and newborn babies (2.6.3–4). It is possible that in the New Kingdom some rites of passage involved a visit to a state temple, probably during an appropriate festival.

Individuals may also have visited state temples to ask for help in a personal or family crisis and to give thanks when the crisis was over. In India, the practice of visiting temples or shrines to ask for such help was and is so widespread that some Hindu deities have been described as 'problem-solving mechanisms' (Bhardwaj 1973.128). This could not be the principal characterization of any Egyptian deity, but some, particularly Amon-Reʿ, Hathor, Ptah, and Thoth, do appear to have 'solved problems' in addition to their functions in state and funerary religion. New Kingdom instruction texts, hymns, and prayers exhort individuals to pray to deities about their personal needs and problems, but it is not usually clear whether a visit to any sort of shrine was involved in such prayers. The intermediary statue from Thinis mentions Mehyt granting good health to a woman's child (Clère in Björkman 1971.31), which could mean either a conventional request for continuing good health or a plea for a sick child. Twentieth dynasty private letters provide evidence for regular visits to temples during and after family crises – such as the absence of the head of the family on a dangerous mission to Nubia (Černý 1939; Wente 1967). The purpose of some of these visits was to pray and sacrifice (LRL nos. 1–2, 5, 9, 15–6), and of others to consult divine oracles (LRL 14, 31). During the Ramessid period, oracles seem to have been the main way in which deities solved problems and resolved conflicts (Černý in Parker 1962.35–48; Kákosy 1982.600–6). Some inscriptions at Serabit el-Khadim could be interpreted as saying that Hathor, Lady of Mefkat, gave oracles about where to dig for the best turquoise (Lake et al. 1928.39; Černý 1952 nos. 53, 136, 182, 200). It seems likely that Hathor gave oracles at Deir el-Bahri during festivals, but there is no direct evidence for this.

Marciniak's theory that there may have been some sort of sanatorium at Deir el-Bahri as early as the Ramessid period would imply that the goddess sent dreams to the sick (1981.289–91). However, A. K. Philips (1986) has convincingly challenged Marciniak's reading of the relevant graffito. The only piece of evidence that might possibly support Marciniak's theory, is a stela inscription of the 19th dynasty Deir el-Medina scribe, Qenherkhepshef. This relates various pious deeds of Qenherkhepshef, including sleeping in the forecourts of several shrines and setting up stelae at Deir Bahri; S. Quirke points out that this scribe is known to have owned a book of dream interpretations (1992.71). The wording of the inscription does not make it clear whether Qenherkhepshef spent a night at Deir el-Bahri, as well as sleeping in shrines at Deir el-Medina.

At none of the six sites does the inscription on any New Kingdom votive object refer to a personal crisis of the donor. This should probably be regarded as symptomatic of the inflexibility of conventional religious language rather than as proof that personal problems were never brought before the goddess. The *sprw* 'petitions' mentioned on intermediary statues at Deir el-Bahri and elsewhere may often have been urgent personal prayers, equivalent to petitioning a high official for justice. New Kingdom love poetry may be taken as very general evidence that people looked to Hathor for help in affairs of the heart (Hermann 1959.108–10). A reference in one of the intermediary texts from Deir el-Bahri to 'young girls who weep' (Fig. 17) might imply prayers to Hathor in a personal crisis, even though its language is conventional. Another intermediary text from this site seems to refer to prayers for a husband or a child (Fig. 17) – though whether such prayers should be classified as 'critical' is open to doubt. Some manifestations of Hathor, whether in cult images, reliefs, or sacred animals, may have achieved a particular reputation, for example for helping childless women to conceive. It would require only a few successes for such a reputation to build up and become self-sustaining. The deity might then draw worshippers from a wider area than normal to pray, sacrifice, and perhaps make votive offerings at their shrine.

Rouse defined the three main motives for the dedication of votive objects in ancient Greek temples as propitiation, intercession, and thanksgiving (1902.350–2). In the context of Egyptian religion it can be difficult to distinguish between propitiation and adoration. The gesture of 'kissing the ground' before a deity might be taken as propitiation or adoration, or a fusion of the two. Although in general the Egyptians seem to have viewed the gods as well disposed towards humanity, this did not rule out an element of fear – especially in the case of Hathor with her dual nature. Some aspects of Hathor did evoke fear (2.5.5). Propitiation was a necessary part of worshipping Hathor and some of the votive offerings, such as the sistra, may symbolize acts of propitiation (2.3.4). None of the votive inscriptions from the six sites refers to propitiating the goddess after specific transgressions against her, whereas a few texts of this type relating to other deities are known from Deir el-Medina (Gunn 1916.83–7; Assmann 1975.351–67). Propitiation of Hathor may have been a standard part of a temple visit, sometimes commemorated or reinforced by a votive offering, rather than being occasioned by a specific manifestation of her anger.

The importance of intercession or supplication has already been stressed. Some large votive objects are inscribed with formal prayers of intercession. Many of the small offerings, particularly the ears and eyes, could be seen as records of acts of intercession. Temple visits to give thanks to a deity after receiving the specific favour of a safe return home are mentioned in some 20th dynasty letters (*LRL* nos. 14, 50), but none of the inscribed votive objects expresses gratitude for favours already received. Nor do any of the inscriptions state that votive objects were given in fulfilment of a vow to make an offering if the goddess granted a petitionary prayer. New Kingdom inscriptions of this type are very rare, although the well-known stela of the draughtsman Nebamon provides one example (Gunn 1916.83–5; Erman 1924.158–62; Assmann 1975 no. 148). In Egypt, thank-offerings seem usually to have been made in anticipation of the granting of prayers and were thus an expression of faith in the deity.

Many of the offerings might be seen as embodying an automatic sequence of propitiation, intercession, and thanksgiving. This could be challenged on the grounds that some practices that may be associated with the dedication of votive objects seem to be at odds with the humble and reverent attitude of donor to deity implied by those terms. First, there is the notion of identification between the donor and a deity (2.4.5–6; 2.6.4; 2.7.3). In the Coffin Texts, the deceased is identified in different spells with Hathor herself, with Ihy her son, with her sacred cattle, and with servants in her train, such as her scribe (see Drioton 1958.188–90). The number and variety of these identifications demonstrate that such religious role-playing was not meant to signify any lasting mystic union between individual and deity (Wente 1982). The language and imagery of identification is adapted from royal funerary religion (2.4.6). In spite of the king's being identified with the sun god and other deities, in life his attitude towards the gods was expected to be one of relative deference (Posener 1960.77–89). If this was so with the king, it must have applied all the more to private individuals.

There is nothing inconsistent with piety in a donor's wishing to claim a filial relationship to Hathor. The practice of identifying moments or events in an individual's life with moments or events in myth, such as the woman in childbirth identifying with the Divine Mother giving birth to Horus, might be compared with the way in which Christians are urged to identify with the passion of Christ, without in any way claiming equality with him. Such a comparison could be misleading, because it assumes a spiritual content in what might have been regarded as a practical exercise. Identification occurs primarily in funerary and medical/magical texts, where it forms part of a technical vocabulary devised and applied by specialists. It would not always have had much relevance to the beliefs and attitudes of ordinary people.

There remains the question of whether any of the votive objects should be classed as manipulative rather than supplicative, and therefore, according to Frazer's classic definition (1922.13–4), as belonging to the sphere of magic rather than religion. Some types of offering, such as the ears and eyes, could be regarded as instruments of 'sympathetic magic' (2.8.3.4; 2.8.6.3), but it is difficult here to see magic and religion as opposites. These ears and eyes were dedicated in state temples and any ritual involved would probably have been carried out by priests, who might themselves have been magical practitioners, rather than by 'secular' magicians. Possible exceptions to this are types of votive object that are known or thought to be instruments of protective magic in other contexts. There is, for example, evidence for fertility figurines being involved in magical rites in the late Middle Kingdom and Second Intermediate Periods (2.6.3.3; Bourriau 1988.110–11; Pinch, forthcoming). Some of the figurines from the six sites could have been deposited in Hathor shrines after being used in such rites in order to strengthen or perpetuate their effect. The curious find at Deir el-Bahri of a bundle of reeds wrapped in linen and tied with faience beads (2.10.1.1) might also be the relic of some magical rite, since several spells for the curing of women's ailments specify that they are to be spoken over reeds (*e.g.* Borghouts 1978 no. 64). Much Egyptian magic was based on a knowledge of the true identity of beings and things, which is not in itself impious. This knowledge is referred to in the Instruction for Merikare˹ as a gift from the gods to mankind (*cf.* Morenz 1973.231; Hornung 1982a.209–10). The use of practices which might be classified as magical need not imply an irreverent or arrogant attitude toward the gods.

Even apart from this question of magic, it might be asked whether the dedication of votive objects was thought to lay any kind of obligation on the deity. The formulae used in private inscriptions sometimes give the impression that if the donor goes through the correct sequence of prayer and sacrifice the deity will automatically grant the requested blessings. This could be seen as a facet of what H. Frankfort termed 'attunement' – the process of living in harmony with Maat (1948.72). By prayer, sacrifice, and offerings the donor placed him or herself in the correct relationship with a deity, acknowledging indebtedness. When that relationship was established, the deity would automatically respond with blessing, in accordance with the divine order. In this sense it might be possible to speak of a contract between deity and donor, although the term 'covenant' would be more appropriate.

The description of the deity's response as automatic needs qualification. Presumably, the proper ritual sequence and the appropriate sacrifices were not in theory considered enough, although in practice many must have hoped that they were. Sincerity in the adoration of the deity, grounded in a good conscience, will also have been required. The Instruction of Ani states that it is necessary to pray 'with a loving heart' in order to have a prayer granted (Lichtheim 1976.137). Some prayers and sacrifices could be judged unacceptable because the donor was wrongly disposed towards the deity. Fear of such a rejection may sometimes have been the motivation behind reinforcing a prayer with a votive offering.

If private individuals interpreted the covenant with the gods in a mechanistic, fashion one might expect to find an emphasis on the intrinsic value of the sacrifices and offerings made, but, in the New Kingdom at least, this seems to be lacking. In ancient Greece, objects of all kinds were used as votive offerings on the basis of their rarity or intrinsic value. It was common for donors to dedicate precious personal possessions or to commission luxury goods which had no religious symbolism as gifts for the gods (Rouse 1902.318–21). All this is in contrast to the offerings to Hathor. Individuals did donate expensive objects such as statues and stelae, but the point of these gifts did not lie in their intrinsic value. Shells and coral are the only examples of things which might have been offered for their rarity value

(2.10.1.2). The dedication of personal possessions, whether valuable or cheap, does not seem to have been very common.

There is also a notable scarcity of objects in precious materials, such as votive mirrors. The small gold plaques from Faras (2.4.2.1; 2.6.2.2), and the bronze Hathor cow bowls which probably come from Deir el-Bahri (2.4.3.1) provide some examples. It is possible that the larger metal objects were periodically melted down, or were removed or stolen when the Hathor shrines fell into disuse. There is, however, no evidence for the kind of competitive approach to the donation of votive objects which seems to have prevailed in Greece (Rouse 1902.333–4). Neither New Kingdom instruction texts nor the intermediary texts advise giving precious gifts to deities. When the scribe Thutmose was anxious about returning safely from Nubia, he asked his family to make regular libations of water to Amon-Re^c (*LRL* nos. 1, 2, 3, 16). No mention is made of trying to gain the god's favour with gifts. In acts of supplication, the emphasis seems to have been on prayer accompanied by standard sacrifices, rather than on valuable offerings. There are degrees of quality, but it is the symbolic value of the votive offerings which seems to be the dominant factor. This suggests a theological awareness and a certain familiarity with temple iconography among the donors.

Summary

From the Second Intermediate Period onwards, the deities of the state cults came to be regarded as taking an interest in the affairs of ordinary individuals. In the New Kingdom, people visited state temples when travelling, during major festivals, to renew a annual 'contract' with their particular deity, and at times of personal crisis. Cult images in prestigious state-run shrines were probably thought to be more powerful than the deities of household and community shrines.

The symbolic identification of donors with deities and the possible involvement in magical rites of some of the votive objects, do not imply an impious attitude on the part of the donors. If the donor placed him or herself in the correct relationship with the goddess, she would respond with a blessing. The dedication of expensive objects was not considered necessary. The emphasis was on the symbolic, rather than the intrinsic value of the votive offerings. The dedication of small votive objects was an optional practice, subsidiary to prayer and sacrifice. The majority were intended to reinforce or perpetuate prayers. Many must relate to general prayers for the well-being of the donor and his or her family. Other offerings seem to have reinforced more specific prayers by symbolizing aspects of the goddess which were relevant to areas of special concern, such as fertility or rebirth.

3.4 Votive offerings and the state cults

Most of the New Kingdom votive objects, large and small, conform to the strict conventions of Egyptian religious art and language. Their imagery is mainly derived from temple iconography and royal funerary religion. The artistic treatment of the figures of the donors shows some flexibility, responding to fashions in costume and hairstyles, but the representation of deities, and the position of the donors in relation to deities, developed comparatively little after the mid 18th dynasty. Such innovations as are found usually appeared earlier in a funerary sphere. There seems to have been greater freedom of expression and potential for development in private funerary religion than in personal piety in the context of state temples.

The conventions of religious language were a factor constricting the development of personal piety, especially as those conventions had been framed to express the needs of king and state rather than those of the individual. The most personal and specific New Kingdom religious texts are probably the 'penitential prayers' from the Theban area (Posener 1975; Assmann 1975.351–68), but even these ostraca and stelae express similar sentiments in a similar way. If one considers that most Deir el-Medina stelae were made by the craftsmen themselves and placed in houses, tomb chapels, votive chapels, or community shrines, rather than state temples, the general adherence to the conventions of religious art and language seems more noteworthy than the occasional departures from them.

There is nothing comparable with the 'penitential prayers' among the votive inscriptions to Hathor. A few of the stelae and textiles are inscribed with brief conventional texts praising the goddess (2.1.5; 2.2.6). A Ramessid 'intermediary' statue from Akh-isut is inscribed with a hymn to her (3.2; Fig. 17Aa), but this consists simply of a string of divine epithets linked, like the brief praises on the stelae and textiles, to an offering formula. Some of these pieces may have been offered out of deep personal devotion to the goddess, or as the result of the kind of religious experience described in a tomb inscription about Hathor appearing to a man in a dream (Assmann 1978), but nothing of the personality of individual donors, and little of their feelings towards the goddess, can be deduced from these texts.

In other cultures it has been possible for votive objects dedicated in major temples to be inscribed with specific and personal requests phrased in colloquial language (e.g. Rouse 1902.333; Hauge & Hauge 1978.232). This could happen in Graeco-Roman Egypt, as witnessed by a Ptolemaic graffito at Deir el-Bahri which consists of a letter written by a woman to Amonhotpe son of Hapu asking him to cure her sterility (Karkowski & Winnicki 1983.102). In contrast, requests to Hathor in the New Kingdom votive inscriptions from the six sites are confined to a standard list of benefits and are generally expressed in formulae adapted from funerary inscriptions. One might expect to find more individuality and greater freedom of expression in graffiti, but the late New Kingdom examples at Deir el-Bahri simply employ another set of formulae, of which the vague ⟨glyph⟩ ⟨glyph⟩ 'do good, do good for' is the most common (Marciniak 1968; 1974.20). Even the graffiti in the grotto in the cliffs behind the temple are largely made up of standard formulae (Marciniak 1981; 1981a). Specific or urgent personal needs could not easily be expressed in a language formulated to convey the general and the timeless. The benefits named in the inscriptions are those which were relevant to the cycle of life, death, and rebirth of any Egyptian in any age.

It would be wrong to try to make a rigid distinction between benefits relating to life and those relating to the afterlife. The Egyptians viewed life and the afterlife as a continuum. This is something which distinguishes Egyptian votive offerings from those of many other cultures. A good burial or a safe passage through the underworld was of benefit only to the individual involved, but the life benefits tend to be those which equipped an individual to contribute to society. The *spd ḥr* 'skill/alertness' often requested of the goddess, was one of the principal qualities expected of a good official. 'Favour and love' were bestowed by the king on a good subject, as well as by the goddess on her worshippers. The ideal relationships between deity and donor and between king and subject are presented in much the same terms.

There is no definite evidence that the beliefs or practices associated with personal piety, or with popular religion in general, were disapproved of by the priesthood of the state cults. The way in which temple visitors were encouraged to use royal and private statues as intermediaries might suggest that the state wished to play down the idea of direct contact between individual and deity or to control that contact. Some New Kingdom texts which stem from personal piety, such as the prayers to Amon as judge or vizier of the poor (Gardiner 1937.2, 16–7; Caminos 1954.9–10, 44–5; Fecht 1965.39–41, 44–5; Posener 1971), could be regarded as 'subversive', but they are critical of corrupt individuals rather than of the office of judge or vizier. By speaking of Amon in these terms, they reinforced the idea that Egyptian society was modelled on the order of gods and king and so perpetuated its hierarchical character. Moreover, the king's frequent intermediary role in popular religion (2.1.3; 2.8.3; 3.2.4) must have increased reverence for the office of kingship and the prestige of individual kings. New Kingdom popular religion can be seen as an example of religion supporting social integration.

In a discussion of the deification of Ramesses II, Labib Habachi suggested that some kings were worshipped in their own life-times because they had made 'great contributions to the prosperity of the country in general or to a certain part of it' (1969.46). This may be so, but such kings appear to have established their own cults and took pains to popularize them, particularly by setting up royal statues to 'listen to prayers' (2.8.3). By providing facilities for popular devotion in the Hathor shrines at Deir el-Bahri or at the shrine of Amon of the Hearing Ear at Karnak, Hatshepsut and Thutmose III not only earned the gratitude of the Theban populace, but also publicized their own roles as the offspring of Hathor or Amon. For a ruler such as Hatshepsut, whose claim to the throne was questionable, the popularity and prestige gained by such moves may have been of some importance. Both Hatshepsut and Thutmose III were probably genuinely devoted to Hathor and Amon-Re', but this would not have stopped them exploiting that devotion to their own advantage.

The provision of facilities for popular religion within state temples involved building or adapting a shrine that was accessible to the lay public, appointing staff to deal with visitors and, in some cases, manufacturing suitable votive objects for those visitors to donate. I believe that mass-produced votive faience, particularly royal-name faience, was probably confined to sites under direct royal patronage. Kings may sometimes have preferred to set up their own 'popular shrines' rather than to continue high levels of patronage at shrines established by their immediate ancestors. For example, comparatively few objects bearing the name of Amonhotpe II were found at Deir el-Bahri. That could be because Amonhotpe II diverted resources to build and endow a temple by the Great Sphinx at Giza which was a focus for popular devotion (Selim Hassan 1953.77; 1.7) and a temple of Nekhbet at el-Kab which may have had a similar function (1.7).

There seems to have been something of a revival at Deir el-Bahri under Amonhotpe III, but the dedication of small faience objects did not resume there after the Amarna period (1.1.3.5). Yet at the comparable shrine of Sekhmet at Abusir votive faience, and other types of small offering, were dedicated again from Horemheb to Ramesses II (Borchardt 1910.131-2). This pattern may relate to royal patronage of a limited number of popular shrines. In general, provision for the dedication of votive objects seems to have been rare in the Ramessid Period. It may have been replaced by other types of royal patronage of popular religion, such as statue cults and, perhaps, the provision of facilities for consulting oracles. One might expect votive offerings to be part of an alternative system of beliefs and practices, but in the New Kingdom they provide further evidence for the centralizing character of Egyptian society and religion and for the involvement of the king and state in every facet of life.

All this is not to say that the state invented small votive offerings in the 18th dynasty. Votive faience was dedicated in cult temples during the Early Dynastic Period (1.7). The scarcity or absence of late 3rd dynasty and of 4th dynasty examples could be a consequence of the major diversion of resources and craftsmen towards royal rather than cult temples at this period. The increasing scarcity of pottery figurines of women, children, and dwarfs might reflect the continuing development of the state religion away from the fertility magic which forms the most ancient stratum of many religions. After a revival at provincial sites such as Abydos and Aswan during the late Old Kingdom (1.7), votive faience seems to disappear from Egyptian temples in the Middle Kingdom. This could, however, be due to the scarcity of well-preserved temples from these periods. The late Middle Kingdom votive faience at Byblos (1.7) is the first, indirect, indication of the practice's being resumed.

Some of the New Kingdom votive offerings, such as the sistra and the menit necklaces, are based on cult objects used in state temples. They could be seen as imitations of the type of gift that the king would give to a temple. Others, such as the fertility figurines, the phalli, and the Bes and Taweret figures, ultimately stem from folk religion and magic. Fertility figurines and Bes and Beset figures and masks were recovered from Middle Kingdom houses at Kahun (Petrie 1890.30,

pl. 8; Bosse-Griffiths 1977.103–4, figs. 103–4; Bourriau 1988.110–11). Hippopotamus figurines and Bes figures were discovered on altars in Second Intermediate
Period houses at Lisht (Lansing 1921.6, fig. 3). Numerous fertility figurines and Bes
and Taweret figures and paintings have been discovered in association with
household altars at Deir el-Medina and el-ʿAmarna (Bruyère 1939.93–108; Kemp
1979; 2.10.1.8–9). This evidence strongly suggests a continuity in the kind of
religion practised in the home between the Middle and New Kingdoms.

The same type of religion dominates the Middle Kingdom/Second Intermediate
Period shrine at Gebel Zeit, in which pottery fertility figurines and ithyphallic
baboons were the most characteristic offerings (1.6.3). The contents of the Middle
Kingdom or Second Intermediate Period Hathor shrine at Faras seem to have been
similar (1.2.3). Nothing of this kind was found among the Middle Kingdom material
at Serabit el-Khadim. This may be because lay-people were not granted access to state
temples to make offerings at this period. During the Middle Kingdom, ordinary
people may have resorted to magic and ancestor cults and visited local community
shrines and the sanctuaries of the deified dead, such as that of Heqaib at Aswan
(Habachi 1985), rather than divine images in state-run temples. Since few, if any
expeditions, seem to have gone to Serabit el-Khadim during the Second Intermediate
Period, we cannot know whether religious practices would have changed there at this
time. It is possible that during 'intermediate periods' even state-run temples reverted
to something which was closer to the religion of the people.

There appears to have been a dramatic change in the 18th dynasty, when the
dedication of votive objects, including those linked with fertility, seems to have
been encouraged at certain shrines within prestigious state temples. The way in
which the Middle Kingdom types of fertility figurine, some of which do not
conform to the conventions of Egyptian art (e.g. Pls. 46b–48), were replaced by the
middle of the 18th dynasty with types which do conform (e.g. Pls. 50–1), suggests an
increasing influence of state religion on practices that originated in folk religion.
The excavators at Gebel Zeit remark on the gradual evolution of the offerings at
this site (Castel et al. 1984.52); the late 18th dynasty and early Ramessid material,
like the majority of the objects from the community shrine at Mirgissa, conforms to
standard Egyptian iconography and is much less like the contents of household
shrines than the Second Intermediate Period offerings. However, the presence of
Bes and Taweret in 18th dynasty royal birth scenes (2.10.1.8–9) and on New
Kingdom palace furniture (e.g. Baker 1966.104, figs. 134–5, pl. 5; Bosse-Griffiths
1977.100–1) suggests that folk beliefs relating to fertility were to be found at the
highest levels of Egyptian society and were integrated with the state religion, even
though they did not occupy a central position in it.

Hathor might almost be seen as the symbol of a continuity of belief between all
levels of society. She had a pivotal position between popular and state religion,
which may be why far more votive offerings were made to her in the New
Kingdom than to any other deity. In her fertility aspect, Hathor played an
important part in folk religion. She was one of the deities 'who listen to prayers'
and was a focus for personal piety. She was a prominent deity of the state cult and
played a major role in royal and private funerary religion. All these aspects are
reflected in the votive objects from the six sites.

Summary

Personal piety could not develop freedom of expression in the context of state temples. It was constrained by the rigid conventions of religious language and iconography. This is why urgent personal requests are not found among the votive inscriptions. The 'life benefits' requested in these inscriptions are those which made people into good citizens. In the New Kingdom, the state partially controlled popular religion by providing shrines for the people within state-run temples. The king's prestige was strengthened by royal statue cults in such shrines and by the distribution of royal-name faience.

Throughout Egyptian history, votive faience is likely to have been mass-produced only at or for shrines under direct royal patronage. Votive objects associated with fertility belong to the sphere of folk religion and are found in household and community shrines of the Middle Kingdom and Second Intermediate Periods. In the New Kingdom, these objects were re-integrated with the state religion and came under the influence of the conventions of official Egyptian art. The goddess Hathor forms a link between folk religion, personal piety, and the state cults. Her numerous aspects are richly displayed in the objects from the six sites.

Abbreviations and Bibliography

1   Abbreviations: Museums

Ash.	The Ashmolean Museum, Oxford
BM	The British Museum, London
CC	Cliffe Castle Museum, Ilkley
CM	Carnegie Museum, Pittsburgh
Fitz.	The Fitzwilliam Museum, Cambridge
K	The City Museum and Art Gallery (Kelvingrove), Glasgow
MMA	The Metropolitan Museum of Art, New York
MFA	Museum of Fine Arts, Boston
MR	Les Musées Royaux d'Art et d'Histoire, Brussels
NM	The National Museum, Dublin
PR	The Pitt-Rivers Museum, Oxford
ROM	The Royal Ontario Museum, Toronto
RSM	The Royal Scottish Museum, Edinburgh
UC	The Petrie Museum, University College, London
UM	The University Museum, Kyoto
V&A	The Victoria and Albert Museum, London

2   Abbreviations: Periodicals and Series

AAA	*Annals of Archaeology and Anthropology, Liverpool University*
ASAE	*Annales du Service des Antiquités de l'Egypte*
ADAIK	*Abhandlung des Deutschen Archäologischen Instituts, Abteilung Kairo*
AfO	*Archiv für Orientforschung*
AH	Aegyptiaca Helvetica
ARCE	American Research Center in Egypt
ASE	Archaeological Survey of Egypt
AV	Archäologische Veröffentlichungen des Deutschen Archäologischen Instituts, Abteilung Kairo
BÄBA	Beiträge zur Ägyptischen Bauforschung und Altertumskunde
BASOR	*Bulletin of the American Schools of Oriental Research*
BIE	*Bulletin de l'Institut d'Egypte*
BIFAO	*Bulletin de l'Institut Français d'Archéologie Orientale du Caire*
BMH	*Bulletin of the Museum Haaretz*
BMMA	*Bulletin of the Metropolitan Museum of Art, New York*
BSE	British School of Archaeology in Egypt (and Egyptian Research Account)

CAH   *Cahiers d'Histoire Egyptienne*
Cat. Cairo   Catalogue général des antiquités égyptiennes du Musée du Caire
CdE   *Chronique d'Egypte*
CRIPEL   *Cahiers de Recherches de l'Institut de Papyrologie et d'Egyptologie de Lille*
CT   *Coffin Texts*
EEF/EES Mem. Egypt Exploration Fund/Society Excavation Memoirs
EEF Arch. Rep. Archaeological Report of the Egypt Exploration Fund
ET   *Etudes et Travaux*, Warsaw
FIFAO   Fouilles de l'Institut Français d'Archéologie Orientale du Caire
GM   *Göttinger Miszellen. Beiträge zur ägyptologischen Diskussion*
HT   *Hieroglyphic Texts from Egyptian Stelae, etc., in the British Museum*
IFAO Doc.   Institut Français d'Archaeologie Orientale du Caire: Documents de Fouilles
IFAO Mem.   Mémoires de l'Institut Français d'Archéologie Orientale du Caire
JAOS   *Journal of the American Oriental Society*
JARCE   *Journal of the American Research Center in Egypt*
JEA   *Journal of Egyptian Archaeology*
JEOL   *Jaarbericht van het Voorasiatisch-Egyptisch Genootschap "Ex Oriente Lux"*
JNES   *Journal of Near Eastern Studies*
LÄ   *Lexikon der Ägyptologie*. Wiesbaden
LD   Lepsius, C. R. *Denkmäler* ... see Lepsius
MÄS   Münchner Ägyptologische Studien
MB   *Medelhavsmuseet Bulletin*
MDAIK   *Mitteilungen des Deutschen Archäologischen Instituts, Abteilung Kairo*
MIO   *Mitteilungen des Instituts für Orientforschung*
OBO   Orbis Biblicus et Orientalis
PM   Porter & Moss, *Topographical Bibliography of Ancient Egyptian Hieroglyphic Texts, Reliefs, and Paintings I–VII*
PT   *Pyramid Texts*
RAIN   *Royal Anthropological Institute News*
RdE   *Revue d'Egyptologie*
RT   *Recueil de Travaux Rélatifs à la Philologie et a l'Archéologie Égyptiennes et Assyriennes*
SAK   *Studien zur Altägyptischen Kultur*
SAOC   *The Oriental Institute of the University of Chicago, Studies in Ancient Oriental Civilizations*
SHR   Studies in the History of Religions (Supplements to *Numen*)
UGAÄ   Untersuchungen zur Geschichte und Altertumskunde Ägyptens
Urk. IV   *Urkunden der 18. Dynastie*. See under Helck and Sethe
ZÄS   *Zeitschrift für Ägyptische Sprache und Altertumskunde*

3 Bibliography

Abdalla, A. 1988, 'A Group of Osiris Cloths of the Twenty-First Dynasty in the Cairo Museum.' *JEA* 74.157–64.

Abou–Ghazi, Dia⁣ꜥ 1963, 'Die Katze in Religion und Leben im alten Ägypten.' *Das Altertum* 9.7–16.

Adams, B. 1974, *Ancient Hierakonpolis*. Warminster.

—— 1975, 'Petrie's Manuscript Notes on the Koptos Foundation Deposits of Tuthmosis III.' *JEA* 61.102–13.

—— 1977, *Egyptian Objects in the Victoria and Albert Museum*. Warminster.

Adams, W. Y. 1961, 'Archaeological Survey of Sudanese Nubia. Introduction.' *Kush* 9.7–10.

—— 1964–5, 'Post-Pharaonic Nubia in the Light of Archaeology.' *JEA* 50.102–20, 51.160–78.

—— 1977, *Nubia: Corridor to Africa*. London.

Adams, W. Y.–Nordström, H. 1963, 'The Archaeological Survey on the West Bank of the Nile. Third Season, 1961–2.' *Kush* 11.10–46.

Albright, W. F. 1939, 'Astarte Plaques and Figurines from Tell Beit Mirsim.' *Mélanges Syriens offerts à Monsieur René Dussaud* 107–20. Paris.

Aldred, C. 1971, *Jewels of the Pharaohs*. London.

—— 1961, *New Kingdom Art in Ancient Egypt*. (2nd ed.), London.

Allam, S. 1963, *Beiträge zum Hathorkult*. MÄS 4.

Allen, T. G. 1923, *A Handbook of the Egyptian Collection*. Art Institute of Chicago, Chicago.

—— 1936, 'Types of Rubric in the Egyptian Book of the Dead.' *JAOS* 56.145–54.

—— 1974, *The Book of the Dead or Going Forth by Day*. SAOC 37, Chicago.

Alliot, M. 1933/1935, *Rapport sur les fouilles de Tell Edfou 1932/1933*. FIFAO 9.2, 10.2, Cairo.

—— 1949/1954, *Le Culte d'Horus à Edfou au Temps des Ptolémées*. Cairo.

Altenmüller, H. 1965, *Die Apotropaia und die Götter Mittelägyptens*. Dissertation, University of Munich.

—— 1975, 'Bes.' *LÄ* 1.720–4.

—— 1977, 'Festen.' *LÄ* 2.171–91.

—— 1978, 'Zur Bedeutung der Harfnerlieder des Alten Reiches.' *SAK* 6.1–24.

—— 1981, 'Amenophis I. als Mittler.' *MDAIK* 37.1–7.

Amer, H. I. 1986, 'L'offrande spécifique des bracelets-ḥꜣdrt à Dendara et Edfou.' In Daumas 1986.17–24.

Anand, U. *et al.* 1982, *Gods of the Byways*. Oxford.

Anderson, R. D. 1976, *Musical Instruments*. Catalogue of the Egyptian Antiquities in the British Museum 3, London.

Anthes, R. 1943, 'Die deutschen Grabungen auf der Westseite von Theben in den Jahren 1911 und 1913.' *MDAIK* 12.1–68.

—— 1959, *Mit Rahineh 1955*. Philadelphia .

—— 1965, *Mit Rahineh 1956*. Philadelphia.

Arkell, A. J. 1950, 'Varia Sudanica.' *JEA* 36.24–40.

—— 1961, *A History of the Sudan from the Earliest Times to 1821*. (2nd. ed.), London.

—— 1962, 'An Early Pet Cat.' *JEA* 48.158.

Arnold, D. 1974/1974a/1981, *Der Tempel des Königs Mentuhotep von Deir el-Bahari*:
—— 1. *Architektur und Deutung*. AV 8.
—— 2. *Die Wandreliefs des Sanktuares*. AV 11.
—— 3. *Die königlichen Beigaben*. AV 23.
—— 1979, *The Temple of Mentuhotep at Deir el-Bahari: From the Notes of Herbert Winlock*. Publications of the MMA Egyptian Expedition, 21.

Arnold, D.–Settgast, J. 1965/1966/1967, 'Erster/Zweiter/Dritter Vorbericht über die vom Deutschen Archäologischen Institut Kairo in Asasif unternommenen Arbeiten . . .' *MDAIK* 20.47–61, 21.72–94, 22.19–26.

Assmann, J. 1969, *Liturgische Lieder an den Sonnengott. Untersuchungen zur altägyptischen Hymnik* I. MÄS 19.
—— 1975, *Ägyptische Hymnen und Gebete*. Zurich.
—— 1978, 'Eine Traumoffenbarung der Göttin Hathor.' *RdE* 30.22–50.
—— 1979, 'Weisheit, Loyalismus und Frömmigkeit.' In *Studien zu altägyptischen Lebenslehren,* ed. E. Hornung & O. Keel, OBO 28.11–72. Freiburg, Switzerland.

Ayrton, E. R. *et al*. 1904, *Abydos* III. EEF Mem. 25, London.

Badawy, A. 1968, *A History of Egyptian Architecture: The Empire*. Berkeley.

Baines, J. 1970, '*Bnbn*: Mythological and Linguistic Notes.' *Orientalia* 39.389–40.,.
—— 1973, 'The Destruction of the Pyramid Temple of Saḥureʿ.' *GM* 4.9–14.
—— 1976, 'Temple Symbolism.' *RAIN* 15 (August).10–15.
—— 1976a, 'The Sebekḥotpe VIII Inundation Stela: An Additional Fragment.' *Acta Orientalia* (Copenhagen) 37.11–20.
—— 1985, *Fecundity Figures: Egyptian Personification and the Iconology of a Genre*. Warminster.
—— 1986, 'The Stela of Emhab: Innovation, Tradition, Hierarchy.' *JEA* 72.41–53.

Baines, J.–Málek, J. 1980, *Atlas of Ancient Egypt*. Oxford.

Baker, H. S. 1966, *Furniture in the Ancient World: Origins and Evolution 3100–475 B.C.* London.

Bakry, H. S. K. 1971, 'The Discovery of a Temple of Sobk in Upper Egypt.' *MDAIK* 27.131–46.

Baldwin, J. A. 1975, 'Notes and Speculations on the Domestication of the Cat in Egypt.' *Anthropos* 70.428–48.

Ballod, F. 1913, *Prolegomena zur Geschichte der zwerghaften Götter in Ägypten*. Moscow.

Baraize, E. 1914, 'Compte rendu des travaux exécutés à Déîr el-Médinéh.' *ASAE* 13.19–42.

Barguet, P. 1953, 'L'origine de la signification du contrepoids de collier-menat.' *BIFAO* 52.103–111.
—— 1962, *Le temple d'Amon-Rê à Karnak*. IFAO Recherches d'archéologie, de philologie, et d'histoire 21, Cairo.

Barguet, P.–Leclant, J. 1954, *Karnak-Nord* IV *(1949-1951)*. FIFAO 25, Cairo.

Barns, J. W. B. 1954, 'Four Khartoum Stelae.' *Kush* 2.19–25.

Barta, W. 1968, *Aufbau und Bedeutung der altägyptischen Opferformel*. Ägyptologische Forschungen 24, Glückstadt.

—— 1985, 'Bemerkungen zur Existenz der Rituale für Geburt und Krönung.' *ZÄS* 112.1–13.

Barucq, A.–Daumas, F. 1980, *Hymnes et prières de l'Egypte ancienne*. Littératures anciennes du Proche-Orient 10, Paris.

Behrens, P. 1982, 'Phallus.' *LÄ* 4.1018–20.

Beit-Arieh, I. 1980, 'A Chalcolithic Site near Serâbît el-Khâdim.' *Tel Aviv* 7.1–2.45–64.

Bell, H. 1948, 'Popular Religion in Graeco-Roman Egypt I. The Pagan Period.' *JEA* 34.82–97.

Bénédite, G. 1907, *Miroirs*. Cat. Cairo.

Benson, M.–Gourlay, J. 1899, *The Temple of Mut in Asher*. London.

Berlandini, J. 1982, 'Meret.' *LÄ* 4.80–88.

Berlin Cat. 1967, *Ägyptisches Museum, Berlin*. Staatliche Museen Preussischer Kulturbesitz, Berlin.

Bhardwaj, A. 1973, *Hindu Places of Pilgrimage in India: A Study in Cultural Geography*. Berkeley.

Bianchi, R. S. 1979, 'Ex-Votos of Dynasty XXVI.' *MDAIK* 35.15–22.

Bietak, M. 1972, *Theben-West (Luqsor): Vorbericht über die ersten vier Grabungskampagnen (1969–71)*. Österreichische Akademie der Wissenschaften, Phil.–hist. Klasse, Sitzungsberichte 278.4.

—— 1973, 'Theben West–Asâsîf.' *AfO* 24.230–9.

Bietak, M.–Reiser-Haslauer, E. 1978, *Das Grab des ʿAnkh-Hor* I. Österreichische Akademie der Wissenschaften, Denkschriften der Gesamtakademie VI.

Birch, S. 1880, *Catalogue of the Collection of Egyptian Antiquities at Alnwick Castle*. London.

Björkman, G. 1971, *A Selection of the Objects in the Smith Collection of Egyptian Antiquities at the Linköping Museum, Sweden*. Bibliotheca Ekmaniana 65, Stockholm.

Black, J.–Green, A. 1992, *Gods, Demons and Symbols of Ancient Mesopotamia*. London

Blackman, A. M. 1914–5, *The Rock Tombs of Meir* I–III. ASE 22–4, London.

—— 1918, 'The Funerary Papyrus of Nespeḥerʿan (Pap. Skrine, no. 2).' *JEA* 5.24–35.

—— 1953, with Apted, M. R. *The Rock Tombs of Meir* VI. ASE 29, London.

Blackman, W. S. 1927, *The Fellāḥīn of Upper Egypt*. London.

Bleeker, C. J. 1973, *Hathor and Thoth*. SHR 26, Leiden.

—— 1973a, 'Der religiöse Gehalt einiger Hathor-Lieder.' *ZÄS* 99.82–8.

Blok, H. P. 1928, 'Remarques sur quelques stèles dites "à oreilles".' *Kêmi* 1.123–35.

Boeser, P. A. A. 1918, *Mummiekisten van het Nieuwe Rijk*. Beschrijving van de Egyptische Verzameling in het Rijksmuseum van Oudheden te Leiden X. The Hague.

Bomann, A. H. 1991, *The Private Chapel in Ancient Egypt*. London & New York.

Bonnet, H. 1952, *Reallexikon der ägyptischen Religionsgeschichte*. Berlin.

—— 1961, 'Herkunft und Bedeutung der naophoren Statue.' *MDAIK* 17.91–8.

Borchardt, L. 1897, *Die aegyptische Pflanzensäule*. Berlin.

—— 1909, *Das Grabdenkmal des Königs Nefer-ir-keʒ-Reʿ*. Ausgrabungen der Deutschen Orient-Gesellschaft in Abusir 1902–1908, 1. Leipzig.

—— 1910, *Das Grabdenkmal des Königs Saʒḥu-Reʿ* I: *Der Bau*. Ausgrabungen ... 1902–1908, 6. Leipzig.

—— 1913, *Das Grabdenkmal des Königs Saʒḥu-Reʿ* II: *Die Wandbilder*. Ausgrabungen ... 1902–1908, 7. Leipzig.

—— 1911/1925/1930/1934, *Statuen und Statuetten von Königen und Privatleuten*. Cat. Cairo.

—— 1923, *Altägyptische Festungen an der zweiten Nilschnelle*. Leipzig.

—— 1930, 'Bilder des "Zerbrechens der Krüge".' *ZÄS* 64.12–16.

Borchardt, L.–Ricke, H. 1938, *Ägyptische Tempel mit Umgang*. BÄBA 2.

—— 1980, *Die Wohnhäuser in Tell el-Amarna*. Berlin.

Boreux, C. 1932, *Musée National du Louvre, Département des antiquités égyptiénnes. Guide catalogue sommaire*. Paris.

Borghouts, J. F. 1971, *The Magical Texts of Papyrus Leiden I 348*. = *Oudheidkundige Mededelingen uit het Rijksmuseum van Oudeheden te Leiden* (n.s.) 51, Leiden.

—— 1978, *Ancient Egyptian Magical Texts*. Nisaba 9, Leiden.

Bosse-Griffiths, K. 1973, 'The Great Enchantress in the Little Golden Shrine of Tutʿankhamūn.' *JEA* 59.100–108.

—— 1977, 'A Beset Amulet from the Amarna Period.' *JEA* 63.98–106.

Bosticco, S. 1965, *Le stele egiziane del Nuovo Regno (Museo Archeologico di Firenze)*. Florence.

Boulos, T. 1906, 'Report on Excavation at Nag el-Kelebat.' *ASAE* 7.1–3.

Bourriau, J. 1981, *Umm el-Gaʿab. Pottery from the Nile Valley before the Arab Conquest*. Cambridge.

—— 1988, *Pharaohs and Mortals. Egyptian Art in the Middle Kingdom*. Cambridge.

Bourriau, J.–Millard, A. 1971, 'The Excavation of Sawâma in 1914 by G. A. Wainwright and T. Whittemore.' *JEA* 57.28–57.

Boyaval, B. 1981, 'Quelque remarques démographiques sur les nécropoles de Mirgissa.' *CRIPEL* 6.191–206.

de Bragança, M. 1978, *Ancient Egypt: God, King and Man: A Guide to the Exhibition ... Peabody Museum of Natural History, Yale University*. New Haven.

Breasted, J. H. Jnr 1948, *Egyptian Servant Statues*. Bollingen Series 13, New York.

Bresciani, E. 1975, *La collezione egizia nel Museo Civico di Bologna*. Ravenna.

Brovarski, E. 1976, 'Senenu, High Priest of Amun at Deir el-Baḥri.' *JEA* 62.57–73.

Brovarski, E. *et al*. 1982, *Egypt's Golden Age: The Art of Living in the New Kingdom 1558–1085 B.C.* Boston.

Brunner, H. 1954, 'Die theologische Bedeutung der Trunkenheit.' *ZÄS* 79.81–3.

—— 1955, 'Das Besänftigungslied im Sinuhe (B 269–279).' *ZÄS* 80.5–11.

—— 1964, *Die Geburt des Gottkönigs: Studien zur Überlieferung eines altägyptischen Mythos*. Ägyptologische Abhandlungen 10, Wiesbaden.

—— 1975, 'Blindheit.' *LÄ* 1.830–1.

—— 1982, 'Persönliche Frömmigkeit.' *LÄ* 4.951–63.

—— 1988, *Das hörende Herz. Kleine Schiften zur Religions- und Geistesgeschichte Ägyptens*, ed. W. Röllig. OBO 80, Freiburg.

Brunner, H.–Brunner-Traut, E. 1982, *Die ägyptische Sammlung der Universität Tübingen*. Mainz.

Brunner-Traut, E. 1938, *Der Tanz im Alten Aegypten*. Glückstadt.

—— 1955, 'Die Wochenlaube.' *MIFO* 3.11–30.

—— 1956, *Die altägyptischen Scherbenbilder*. Wiesbaden.

—— 1970, 'Gravidenflasche. Das Salben des Mutterleibes.' In *Archäologie und Altes Testament: Festschrift für Kurt Galling* 35–48. Tübingen.

—— 1970a, 'Das Muttermilchkrüglein. Ammen mit Stillumhang und Mondamulett.' *Die Welt des Orients* 5.145–64.

Brunton, G. 1927–8/1930, *Qau and Badari* I–III. BSE 44–5, 50, London.

Brunton, G.–Engelbach, R. 1927, *Gurob*. BSE 41, London.

Bruyère, B. 1924–53, *Rapport sur les fouilles de Deir el-Médineh*. FIFAO, Cairo:

1.1 *1922–3* (1924).

2.2 *1923–4* (1925).

3.3 *1924–5* (1926).

4.3 *1926* (1927).

5.2 *1927* (1928).

6.2 *1928* (1929).

7.2 *1929* (1930).

10.1 *1931–2* (1934).

14 *1933–4* (1937).

15 *1934–5* (1937a).

16 *1934–5* (1939).

20.1 *1935–40* (1948).

20.2 *1935–40* (1952a).

20.3 *1935–40* (1952).

21 *1945–7* (1952b).

26 *1948–51* (1953).

—— 1925, 'Quelques stèles trouvées par M. E. Baraize à Deir el Médineh.' *ASAE* 25.76–96.

—— 1930, *Mert Seger à Deir el Médineh*. IFAO Mem. 58, Cairo.

Bruyère, B. *et al.* 1937, *Tell Edfou 1937*. Fouilles Franco-Polonaises 1, Cairo.

Buchberger, H. 1983, 'Sexualität und Harfenspiel.' *GM* 66.11–43.

Budge, E. A. W. 1899, *Egyptian Magic*. London.

—— 1909, *A Guide to the Egyptian Collections in the British Museum*. London.

—— 1914, *Egyptian Sculptures in the British Museum*. London.

Buhl, M.-L. 1974, *A Hundred Masterpieces from the Ancient Near East in the National Museum of Denmark*. Copenhagen.

Burckhardt, J. L. 1822, *Travels in Nubia*. (2nd. ed.), London.

Burlington Cat. 1922, *Burlington Fine Arts Club: Catalogue of an Exhibition of Ancient Egyptian Art*. London.

Calverley, A. M.–Broome, M. F. 1933/1935/1938, *The Temple of King Sethos I at Abydos* I–III. London and Chicago.

Caminos, R. A. 1954, *Late-Egyptian Miscellanies*. Brown Egyptological Studies 1.

—— 1968, *The Shrines and Rock-Inscriptions of Ibrim*. ASE 32, London.

—— 1974, *The New-Kingdom Temples of Buhen*. ASE 33–4, London.

Caminos, R. A.–James, T. G. H. 1963, *Gebel El-Silsilah* I: *The Shrines*. ASE 31, London.

Campbell Thompson, R. 1905, 'A Note on Sinaitic Antiquities' and 'Note on the Antiquities of Sinai.' *Man* 5 nos. 54, 73, pp. 87–91, 131–3.

Capart, J. 1905, *Primitive Art in Egypt*. London.

—— 1931, 'Note sur un fragment de bas-relief au British Museum.' *BIFAO* 30.73–5.

—— 1942, *L'art égyptien; choix de documents* . . . : III. *Les arts graphiques*. Brussels.

—— 1946, *Fouilles en Egypte: El Kab*. Brussels.

Carter, H. 1901, 'Report on the Tomb of Mentuhotep Ist at Deir el-Bahari, known as Bab el-Hoçan.' *ASAE* 2.201–5.

—— 1927/1933 *The Tomb of Tut·ankh·Amen* II–III. London.

Carter, H.–Carnarvon, Lord 1912, *Five Years' Explorations at Thebes . . . 1907–11*. London.

Carter, H.–Mace, A. C. 1923, *The Tomb of Tut·ankh·Amen* I. London.

Castel, G.–Soukiassian, G. 1985, 'Dépôt de stèles dans le sanctuaire du Nouvel Empire au Gebel Zeit.' *BIFAO* 85.285–93.

—— 1989, *Gebel el-Zeit* I: *Les mines de galène*. FIFAO 35, Cairo.

—— 1989a, 'Les mines de galène du Gebel Zeit.' *SAK* Beiheft 2.161–70.

Castel, G.–Gout, J.-F.–Soukiassian, G. 1984, 'Découverte de mines pharaoniques au bord de la Mer Rouge.' *Archéologia* 192–3, July/August.44–57.

—— 1985, 'Gebel Zeit. Pharaonische Bergwerke an den Ufern des Roten Meeres.' *Antike Welt* 16, 3.15–28.

—— 1985, 'Fouilles de Gebel Zeit (Mer Rouge): Première et deuxième campagnes (1982–83).' *ASAE* 70.99–105.

Cecil, Lady W. 1903, 'Report on the Work done at Aswân.' *ASAE* 4.51–73.

Černý, J. 1927, 'Le culte d'Amenophis Ier chez les ouvriers de la nécropole thébaine.' *BIFAO* 27.159–203.

—— 1935, 'Questions adressées aux oracles.' *BIFAO* 35.41–58.

—— 1939, *Late Ramesside Letters*. Bibliotheca Aegyptiaca IX, Brussels.

—— 1942, 'Nouvelle série de questions adressées aux oracles.' *BIFAO* 41.13–24.

—— 1945, 'The Will of Naunakhte and the Related Documents.' *JEA* 31.29–53.

—— 1949, *Répertoire onomastique de Deir el-Médineh*. IFAO Doc. 12, Cairo.

—— 1952/1955, *The Inscriptions of Sinai* I–II. EES Mem. 45, London.

—— 1952a, *Ancient Egyptian Religion*. London.

—— 1958, *Egyptian Stelae in the Bankes Collection*. Oxford.

—— 1965, 'Egypt from the Death of Ramesses III to the End of the Twenty-First Dynasty.' *Cambridge Ancient History* II, 2nd. ed., Chap. 35.

—— 1972, 'Troisième série de questions adressées aux oracles.' *BIFAO* 72.49–69.

—— 1973, *A Community of Workmen at Thebes in the Ramesside Period*. IFAO Bibliothéque d'Etude 50, Cairo.

Champollion, J. F. 1845, *Monuments de l'Egypte et de la Nubie* III. Paris.

Chappaz, J. L. 1983, 'Un contrepoids de collier "Menat" au Musée d'Art et d'Histoire.' *Geneva* 31.9–16.

Champollion, J. F. 1845, *Monuments de l'Egypte et de la Nubie* III. Paris.

Chappaz, J. L. 1983, 'Un contrepoids de collier "Menat" au Musée d'Art et d'Histoire.' *Geneva* 31.9–16.

Chassinat, E. 1934–5, *Le temple de Dendara* I– III. Cairo.

Christophe, L. A. 1955, 'Les fêtes agraires du calendrier d'Hathor à Edfou.' *Cahiers d'Histoire Egyptienne* 7. 35-42

—— 1965, *Abou-Simbel et l'épopée de sa découverte*. Brussels.

Clark, R. T. R. 1959, *Myth and Symbol in Ancient Egypt*. London.

Clarke, S. 1898, 'The Temple of Deir el Bahari.' EEF Arch. Rep [7].3.

—— 1916, 'Ancient Egyptian Frontier Fortresses.' *JEA* 3.155–79.

Clédat, J. 1919, 'Notes sur l'isthme de Suez,' *BIFAO* 16.201–28.

Clère, J. J. 1968, 'Deux statues 'Gardiennes de Porte' d'époque ramesside.' *JEA* 54.135–48.

—— 1969, 'Propos sur un corpus des statues sistrophores égyptiennes.' *ZÄS* 96.1–4.

Coffin Texts 1935–61, A. de Buck, *The Egyptian Coffin Texts* I–VII. (ed. A. de Buck and A. H. Gardiner) Oriental Institute Publications, 34, 49, 64, 67, 73, 81, 87. Chicago.

Collins, J. J. 1978, *Primitive Religion*. Totowa, New Jersey.

Cooney, J. D. 1972, 'Major Macdonald, a Victorian Romantic.' *JEA* 58.280–5.

—— 1975, 'Three Minor Masterpieces of Egyptian Art.' *Bulletin of the Cleveland Museum of Art* 62.11–16.

—— 1976, *Glass*. Catalogue of Egyptian Antiquities in the British Museum: IV. London.

Curto, S. 1970, *Il tempio di Ellesija*. Turin.

Dąbrowska-Smektała, E. 1968, 'List of Objects Found at Der el-Bahari in the Area of the Tuthmosis III's Temple: Season 1962–63 and 1963–64.' *ASAE* 60.95–130.

Dąbrowski, L. 1964, 'Preliminary Report on the Reconstruction Works of the Hatshepsut Temple at Deir el-Bahari during 1961–1962 Season.' *ASAE* 58.37–60.

—— 1968, 'Preliminary Report on the Reconstruction Works of Hatshepsut's Temple at Deir el-Bahari During the Seasons 1962/3 and 1963/4.' *ASAE* 60.131–7.

Dambach, M.–Wallert, I. 1966, 'Das Tilapia-Motiv in der altägyptischen Kunst.' *CdE* 41.273–94.

Darby, W. J. *et al.* 1977, *Food: The Gift of Osiris*. 2 vols. London and New York.

Daressy, G. 1893, 'Notes et remarques.' *RT* 14.165–85.

—— 1902, *Fouilles de la Vallée des Rois (1898–1899)*. Cat. Cairo.

—— 1905–6, *Statues de divinités*. Cat. Cairo.

Dasen, V. 1988, 'Dwarfism in Egypt and Classical Antiquity: Iconography and Medical History.' *Medical History* 32.253–276.

Daumas, F. 1958, *Les mammisis des temples égyptiens*. Paris.

—— 1959, *Les mammisis de Dendara*. Cairo.

—— 1969, 'Les propylées du temple d'Hathor à Philae et le culte de la déesse.'

ZÄS 95.1–17.

—— 1970, 'Les objets sacrés de la déesse Hathor à Dendara.' *RdE* 22.63–78.

—— 1977, 'Hathor.' *LÄ* 2.1024–33.

—— 1986, *Hommages à François Daumas* I. Montpellier.

D'Auria, S. 1983, 'The Princess Baketamun.' *JEA* 69.161–2.

D'Auria, S.–Lacovara, P.–Roehrig, C. 1988, *Mummies and Magic: The Funerary Arts of Ancient Egypt*. Boston.

Davies, N. de G. 1902, *The Rock Tombs of Deir El Gebrâwi* I–II. ASE 11–12, London.

—— 1913, *Five Theban Tombs*. ASE 21, London.

—— 1920, 'An Alabaster Sistrum Dedicated by King Teta.' *JEA* 6.69–72.

—— 1920a, *The Tomb of Antefiḳer*. Theban Tomb Series 2, London.

—— 1922–3, *The Tomb of Puyemrê at Thebes*. MMA Egyptian Expedition. Robb de Peyster Tytus Memorial Series 2–3, New York.

—— 1925, 'The Tomb of Tetaky at Thebes (No.15).' *JEA* 11.10–18.

—— 1925a, *The Tomb of Two Sculptors at Thebes*. MMA Egyptian Expedition. Robb de Peyster Tytus Memorial Series 4, New York.

—— 1927, *Two Ramesside Tombs at Thebes*. MMA Egyptian Expedition. Robb de Peyster Tytus Memorial Series 5, New York.

—— 1930, *The Tomb of Ḳen-Amūn at Thebes*. MMA Egyptian Expedition Publications 5, New York.

—— 1933, *The Tomb of Nefer-ḥotep at Thebes*. MMA Egyptian Expedition Publications 9, New York.

—— 1943, *The Tomb of Rekh-mi-Rēʿ at Thebes*. MMA Egyptian Expedition Publications 11, New York.

—— 1948, *Seven Private Tombs at Ḳurnah*. Mond Excavations at Thebes 2, London.

—— 1953, *The Temple of Hibis in el Khargeh Oasis* III: *The Decoration*. MMA Egyptian Expedition Publications 17, New York.

Davies, N. de G.–Faulkner, R. O. 1947, 'A Syrian Trading Venture to Egypt.' *JEA* 33.40–6.

Davies, Nina de. G. 1944, 'A Scene of Worshipping Sacred Cows.' *JEA* 30.64.

—— 1963, *Scenes from Some Theban Tombs*. Oxford.

Davies, Nina de G.–Gardiner, A. H. 1915, *The Tomb of Amenemḥēt (No. 82)*. Theban Tombs Series 1, London.

—— 1920, *The Tomb of Antefoḳer and his wife Senet (No. 60)*. Theban Tombs Series 2, London.

—— 1926, *The Tomb of Ḥuy, Viceroy of Nubia in the Reign of Tutʿankh-amūn (No. 40)*. Theban Tombs Series 4, London.

Davis, T. 1910, *The Tomb of Queen Tîyi*. London.

Day, C. K. 1975, *Popular Religion in Pre-communist China*. San Francisco.

Demarée, R. J. 1983, *The ꜣḫ iḳr n Rʿ-stelae: On Ancestor Worship in Ancient Egypt*. Egyptologische Uitgaven 3, Leiden.

Demarée, R. J.–Janssen, J. J. (eds.) 1982, *Gleanings from Deir el-Medina*. Egyptologische Uitgaven 1, Leiden.

Derchain, P. 1952, 'Bébon, le dieu et les mythes.' *RdE* 9.23–47.

—— 1970, 'La réception de Sinouhé à la cour de Sésostris Ier.' *RdE* 22.79–83.

—— 1972, *Hathor Quadrifrons.* Uitgaven van het Nederlandsch Historisch Archaeo-logisch Instituut te Istanbul 28.

—— 1975, 'La perruque et le cristal.' *SAK* 2.55–74.

—— 1975a, 'Le lotus, la mandragore et le perséa.' *CdE* 50.65–86.

—— 1976, 'Symbols and Metaphors in Literature and Representations of Private Life.' (trans. J. Baines) *RAIN* 15.7–10.

Desroches-Noblecourt, C. 1952, 'Pots anthropomorphes et recettes magico-médicales dans l'Egypte ancienne.' *RdE* 9.49–67.

—— 1953, '"Concubines du Mort" et mères de famille au Moyen Empire.' *BIFAO* 53.7–47.

—— 1963, *Tutankhamen.* London.

Desroches-Noblecourt, C.–Kuentz, C. 1968, *Le petit temple d'Abou Simbel.* Cairo.

Devéria, T. 1896, 'Des oreilles et des yeux dans le symbolisme de l'ancienne Egypte.' In Devéria, *Mémoires et fragments* I, Bibliothèque égyptologique 4.147-57. Paris.

Dewachter, M. 1971, 'Notes diverses, 1 à 5.' *BIFAO* 70.83–117.

van Dijk, J. 1979–80, 'The Birth of Horus According to the Ebers Papyrus.' *JEOL* VIII no. 26.10–25.

—— 1986, 'ʿAnath, Seth and the Seed of Prēʿ.' in *Scripta signa vocis* 31–51. ed. H. L. J. Vanstiphout *et al.* Groningen.

Donadoni, A. M. (ed.) 1988, *Egyptian Civilization: Daily Life.* Turin.

Dorman, P. 1988, *The Monuments of Senenmut.* London and New York.

Downes, D. 1974, *The Excavations at Esna 1905–1906.* Warminster.

Drenkhahn, R. 1975, 'Eine Privatstiftung des Vizekönigs Setau in Elkab.' *SAK* 3.43–48.

—— 1976, 'Bemerkungen zu dem Titel *ḫkr.t nswt.' SAK* 4.59–67.

Dreyer, G. 1986, *Elephantine* VIII: *Der Tempel der Satet. Die Funde der Frühzeit und des Alten Reiches.* AV 39, Mainz.

Drioton, E. 1958, Review of *The Egyptian Coffin Texts* VI. In *Bibliotheca Orientalis* 15.187–90.

Dunand, M. 1954/1958, *Fouilles de Byblos* II: *1933–38. Texte.* Etudes et Documents d'Archéologie 3, Paris.

Dunbar, J. H. 1929, 'Betwixt Egypt and Nubia.' *Ancient Egypt* 14.108–117.

Dunham, D. 1978, *Zawiyet el-Aryan.* Boston.

Dunham, D. *et al.* 1960, *Second Cataract Forts* I: *Semna, Kumma.* Boston.

—— 1967, *Second Cataract Forts* II: *Uronarti, Shalfak, Mirgissa.* Boston.

Dyke, P. J.–Uphill, E. P. 1983, 'Major Charles Kerr MacDonald 1806–67.' *JEA* 69.165–6.

Eaton-Krauss, M.–Graefe, E. 1985, *The Small Golden Shrine from the Tomb of Tutankhamun.* Oxford.

Eckenstein, L. 1914, 'The Moon-Cult in Sinai on the Egyptian Monuments.' *Ancient Egypt* 1.9–13.

—— 1921, *A History of Sinai.* London.

EEF Cat. 1904, *Catalogue of Egyptian Antiquities … Exhibited at University College July 4th – 30th.* London.

—— n.d. [1906], *Catalogue of an Exhibition of Antiquities and Papyri . . . King's College, Strand. July 10th – August 4th.* London.

—— 1907, *Catalogue of an Exhibition of Antiquities . . . King's College, Strand. July 9th–July 30th.* London.

—— n.d. [1922], *Catalogue of Egyptian Antiquities Found by Professor Flinders Petrie and Students at Lahun and Sedement 1920–1.* (W. M. F. Petrie,) London.

Edwards, I. E. S. 1955, 'A Relief of Qudshu-Astarte-Anath in the Winchester College Collection.' *JNES* 14.49–51.

—— 1965, 'Lord Dufferin's Excavations at Deir el-Baḥri and the Clandeboye Collection.' *JEA* 51.16–28.

[Edwards, I. E. S.] 1972, *Treasures of Tutankhamun.* London.

Edwards, I. E. S. *et al.* 1964, *A General Introductory Guide to the Egyptian Collections in the British Museum.* London

Emery, W. B. 1970, 'Preliminary Report on the Excavations at North Saqqâra 1968–9.' *JEA* 56.5–11.

—— 1979, *The Fortress of Buhen: The Archaeological Report.* EES Mem. 49, London.

Engelbach, R. 1915, *Riqqeh and Memphis* VI. BSE 26, London.

Erman, A. 1901, *Zaubersprüche für Mütter und Kind aus dem Papyrus 3027 . . . .* Abhandlungen der Königl. Preuss. Akademie der Wissenschaften zu Berlin 1901, Berlin.

—— 1911, 'Denksteine aus der thebanischen Gräberstadt.' *Sitzungsberichte der Königl. Preussischen Akademie der Wissenschaften, phil.–hist. Klasse* 1911.49, Berlin.

—— 1934, *Die Religion der Ägypter.* Berlin and Leipzig.

Fairman, H. W. 1954, 'Worship and Festivals in an Egyptian Temple.' *Bulletin of the John Rylands Library* 37.165–203.

Fakhry, A. 1942, 'A Note on the Tomb of Kheruef at Thebes.' *ASAE* 42.447–532.

Faulkner, R. O. 1962, *A Concise Dictionary of Middle Egyptian.* Oxford.

—— 1969, *The Ancient Egyptian Pyramid Texts.* Oxford.

—— 1973/1977–1978, *The Ancient Egyptian Coffin Texts* I–III. Oxford.

Fayolle, B. 1958, *Le livre du Musée Guimet de Lyon.* Lyon.

Fecht, G. 1965, *Literarische Zeugnisse zur "Persönlichen Frömmigkeit" in Ägypten.* Abhandlungen der Heidelberger Akademie der Wissenschaften, Phil.-hist. Klasse 1965.1.

Finucane, R. C. 1977, *Miracles and Pilgrims: Popular Beliefs in Medieval England.* London.

Firth, C. M. 1927, *The Archaeological Survey of Nubia: Report for 1910–11.* Cairo.

Fischer, H. G. 1962, 'The Cult and Nome of the Goddess Bat.' *JARCE* 1.7–23.

—— 1968, *Dendera in the Third Millennium B.C.* New York.

—— 1974, 'The Mark of a Second Hand on Egyptian Antiquities.' *Metropolitan Museum Journal* 9.5–34.

Foucart, G. 1924, 'La Belle Fête de la Vallée.' *BIFAO* 24.1–209.

Frank, F. 1934, 'Aus der ʿAraba.' *Zeitschrift des Deutschen Palästina-Vereins* 57.191–280.

Franke, D. 1983, *Altägyptische Verwandschaftsbezeichnungen im Mittleren Reich.* Hamburger Ägyptologische Studien 3, Hamburg.

Frankfort, H. 1958, *Ancient Egyptian Religion*. New York.

Fraser, P. M. 1956, 'A Temple of Ḥathōr at Kusae.' *JEA* 42.97–8.

Frazer, J. G. 1922, *The Golden Bough*. (abridged ed.) London.

Friedman, F. 1985, 'On the Meaning of Some Anthropoid Busts from Deir el-Medîna.' *JEA* 71.82–97.

Gaballa, G. A. 1977, *The Memphite Tomb-Chapel of Mose*. Warminster.

Gabra, G. 1977, 'The Site of Hager Edfu and the New Kingdom Cemetery of Edfu.' *CdE* 52.207–222.

Galvin, M. 1984, 'The Hereditary Status of the Titles of the Cult of Hathor.' *JEA* 70.42–9.

Gardiner, A. H. 1908, Gardiner Mss. AHG/23.65 (Nubian inscriptions). Griffith Institute.

—— 1912, 'Notes on the Story of Sinuhe (Fourth Article).' *RT* 34.52–77.

—— 1916, 'An Ancient List of the Fortresses of Nubia.' *JEA* 3.184–92.

—— 1930, 'A New Letter to the Dead.' *JEA* 16.19–22.

—— 1931, *The Library of A. Chester Beatty ... The Chester Beatty Papyri, No. 1*. London.

—— 1932, *Late-Egyptian Stories*. Bibliotheca Aegyptiaca 1, Brussels.

—— 1937, *Late-Egyptian Miscellanies*. Bibliotheca Aegyptiaca 7, Brussels.

—— 1959, 'A Didactic Passage Re-examined.' *JEA* 45.12–15.

Gardiner, A. H.–Sethe, K. 1928, *Egyptian Letters to the Dead: Mainly from the Old and Middle Kingdoms*. London.

Garstang, J. 1901, *El-Arábah*. ERA 6, London.

—— 1907, *The Burial Customs of Ancient Egypt*. London.

Gauthier, H. 1907–17, *Le livre des rois d'Egypte: recueil de titres et protocoles royaux*. IFAO Mem.17–21, Cairo.

—— 1912, *Le temple de Ouadi es Sebouâ*. Cairo.

—— 1913, *Le temple d'Amada*. Cairo.

—— 1931, *Les fêtes du dieu Min*. IFAO Recherches d'Archéologie, de Philologie, et d'Histoire 2, Cairo.

—— 1936, 'Une fondation pieuse en Nubie.' *ASAE* 36.49–71.

Gayet, A. 1894, *Le temple de Louxor*. Mémoires publiés par les membres de la Mission Archéologique Française au Caire 15.

George, B. 1977, 'Eine löwenköpfige Nilpferdgöttin in Stockholm.' *MB* 12.38–44.

—— 1978, 'Hathor, Herrin der Sistren.' *MB* 13.25–31.

—— 1980, 'Drei altägyptische Wurfhölzer.' *MB* 15.7–15.

Germer, R. 1985, *Flora des pharaonischen Ägypten*. Sonderschrift des Deutschen Archäologischen Instituts Abteilung Kairo 14, Mainz.

Germond, P. 1981, *Sekhmet et la Protection du Monde*. AH 9, Geneva.

Gestermann, L. 1984, 'Hathor, Harsomtus und Mntw-ḥtp.w II.' *Studien zu Sprache und Religion Ägyptens* 2 [Fs. Westendorf]. 763–76. Göttingen.

Ghalioungui, P. 1963, *Magic and Medical Science in Ancient Egypt*. London.

Gilbert, P. 1953, 'Le sens des portraits intacts d'Hatshepsout à Deir el-Bahari.' *CdE* 28.219–22.

Giorgini, M. S. *et al.* 1965/1971, *Soleb* I–II. Florence.

Gitton, M. 1975, *L'Epouse du dieu Ahmes Néfertary*. Paris.

Giveon, R. 1971, 'Egyptian Inscriptions and Finds from a Temple in the Timna Area.' *Proceedings of the Fifth World Congress of Jewish Studies, Jerusalem* 50–3. Jerusalem.

—— 1972, 'Le Temple d'Hathor à Serabit el-Khadem.' *Archeologia* 44.64–9.

—— 1974, 'Investigations in the Egyptian Mining Centres in Sinai: Preliminary Report.' *Tel Aviv* 1.100–8.

—— 1975, 'Egyptian Objects from Sinai in the Australian Museum.' *Australian Journal of Biblical Archaeology* 2 no. 3.29–47.

—— 1976, 'Two Critical Notes Concerning Sinai.' *GM* 20.23–5.

—— 1977, 'Inscriptions of Sahurēᶜ and Sesostris I from Wadi Khariğ.' *BASOR* 226.61–3.

—— 1978, *The Impact of Egypt on Canaan*. OBO 20, Freiburg.

—— 1978a, *The Stones of Sinai Speak*. Tokyo.

—— 1981, 'A New Kingdom Stela from Sinai.' *Israel Exploration Journal* 31.168–71.

—— 1982, 'A God who Hears.' in *Studies in Egyptian Religion Dedicated to Professor Jan Zandee*, ed. M. Heerma van Voss *et al.* 38–42. Leiden.

Giveon, R. *et al.* 1978, 'Explorations at Serâbît el-Khâdim – 1977.' *Tel Aviv* 5.170–87.

Glueck, N. 1935, 'Explorations in Eastern Palestine II.' *Annual of the American Schools of Oriental Research* 15.

Glodlewski, W. 1972, 'Faras à l'époque méroïtique.' *ET* 6.185–93.

Godron, G. 1971, 'Recherches sur quelques inscriptions hiéroglyphiques de la XVIIIe dynastie découvertes à Faras.' *Orientalia* 40.373–85.

—— 1974, 'L'Elephantine-du-Sud.' *CdE* 49.238–53.

Goedicke, H. 1970, 'The Story of a Herdsman.' *CdE* 45.244–66.

Goff, B. 1979, *Symbols of Ancient Egypt in the Late Period*. The Hague.

Golénischeff, V. S. 1891, *Ermitage Impérial - Inventaire de la collection égyptienne*. [St. Petersburg].

Goodchild, R.–Kirk, J. R. 1954, 'The Romano-Celtic Temple at Woodeaton.' *Oxoniensia* 19.15–37.

Goodenough, E. R. 1956/1958, *Jewish Symbols in the Greco-Roman Period* 6–7. Bollingen Series 37, New York.

Gray, J. 1964, *The Canaanites*. London.

Grdseloff, B. 1940, 'L'insigne du Grand Juge égyptien.' *ASAE* 40.185–202.

Grébaut, E. 1900, *Le Musée Egyptien: Recueil de monuments et de notices sur les fouilles d'Egypte* I. Cairo.

Grenfell, A. 1910, 'The Rarer Scarabs, etc., of the New Kingdom.' *RT* 32.113–36.

Grieshammer, R. 1975, 'Briefe an Tote.' *LÄ* 1.863–70.

Griffith, F. Ll. 1900, *Stories of the High Priests of Memphis*. Oxford.

—— 1921, 'Oxford Excavations in Nubia.' *AAA* 8.1–18, 65–124.

—— 1924, 'Oxford Excavations in Nubia.' *AAA* 11.141–80.

—— 1925, 'Pakhoras-Bakharâs-Faras in Geography and History.' *JEA* 11.259–68.

—— 1926, 'Oxford Excavations in Nubia.' *AAA* 13.17–37.

Griffith, F. Ll.–Newberry, P. E. 1895, *El Bersheh* II. ASE 4, London.

Griffiths, J. G. 1970, *Plutarch's De Iside et Osiride*. Cambridge.
—— 1982, 'Pamylien.' *LÄ* 4.659–60.
Grinsell, L. V. 1972, *Guide to the Collections from Ancient Egypt*. The Bristol Museum. Bristol.
Guidotti, M. C. 1978, 'A proposito dei vasi con decorazione hathorica.' *Egitto e Vicino Oriente* 1.105–118.
Gunn, B. 1916, 'The Religion of the Poor in Ancient Egypt.' *JEA* 3.81–94.
Gutbub, A. 1962, 'Remarques sur les dieux du nome tanitique à la Basse Epoque.' *Kêmi* 16.42–75.

Habachi, Labib, 1954, 'Khatâ'nâ–Qantir: Importance.' *ASAE* 52.443–562.
—— 1959, 'The First Two Viceroys of Kush and their Family.' *Kush* 7.45–62.
—— 1963, 'King Nebhepetre' Mentuhotp: His Monuments, Place in History, Deification, and Unusual Representations in the Form of Gods.' *MDAIK* 19.16–52.
—— 1969, *Features of the Deification of Ramesses II*. ADAIK 5, Glückstadt.
—— 1972, 'Nia, the *wʿb*-Priest and Doorkeeper of Amun-of-the-Hearing-Ear.' *BIFAO* 71.67–85.
—— 1985, *Elephantine* IV: *The Sanctuary of Heqaib*. AV 33, Mainz.
Haeny, G. 1977, 'Hathor-Kapitell.' *LÄ* 2.1039–41.
Hall, H.R. 1913, *Catalogue of Egyptian Scarabs, Etc., in the British Museum* I. *Royal Scarabs*. London.
—— 1925, 'An Egyptian Stela from Deir al-Bahri.' *The Connoisseur* 73.237.
—— 1928, 'Objects of Tut'ankhamūn in the British Museum.' *JEA* 14.74–7.
Hall, R. 1985, '"The Cast-Off Garment of Yesterday": Dresses Reversed in Life and Death.' *BIFAO* 85.235–43.
—— 1986, *Egyptian Textiles*. Aylesbury.
Hani, J. 1976, *La religion égyptienne dans la pensée de Plutarque*. Paris.
Harpur, Y. 1980, 'Zšš wꜣḏ Scenes of the Old Kingdom.' *GM* 38.53–61.
Harris, J. 1961, *Lexicographical Studies in Ancient Egyptian Minerals*. Deutsche Akademie der Wissenschaften zu Berlin, Institut für Orientforschung Veröffentlichung 54, Berlin.
Hassan, Selim. 1943, *Excavations at Gîza* IV: *(1932–33)*. Cairo.
—— 1953, *The Great Sphinx and its Secrets*. [*Excavations at Gîza* VIII.] Cairo.
Hastings, J. (ed.) 1908–21, *Encyclopaedia of Religion and Ethics*. Edinburgh.
Hauge, V.–Hauge, T. 1978, *Folk Traditions in Japanese Art*. Tokyo and New York.
Hayes, W. C. 1936, 'The Tomb of Nefer-khewet and His Family.' *BMMA* 30.17–36.
—— 1937, *Glazed Tiles from a Palace of Ramesses II at Ḳantir*. MMA Papers 3, New York.
—— 1951, 'Inscriptions from the Palace of Amenhotep III.' *JNES* 10.231–42.
—— 1953/1959, *The Scepter of Egypt* I–II. New York.
—— 1957, 'Varia from the Time of Hatshepsut.' *MDAIK* 15.78–90.
—— 1960, 'A Selection of Tuthmoside Ostraca from Dēr El-Baḥri.' *JEA* 46.29–52.
Hein, E. 1978, *Temple, Town and Hinterland in the Cult of Jaganath*. Manokar.
Helck, W. 1958, *Urkunden der 18. Dynastie*, Heft 19. Berlin.

—— 1971, *Betrachtungen zur Grossen Göttin und den ihr verbundenen Göttheiten.* Munich.

—— 1975, 'Die grosse Stele des Viziekönigs *Stw* aus Wadi es-Sabua.' *SAK* 3.85–112.

—— 1975a, 'Beischläferin.' *LÄ* 1.684–6.

—— 1977, 'Hathoren, sieben.' *LÄ* 2.1033.

Henne, H. 1924–5, *Rapport sur les fouilles de Tell Edfou 1921–2; 1923–4.* FIFAO 1.2, 2.3, Cairo.

Hermann, A. 1936, 'Das Grab eines Nachtmin in Unternubien.' *MDAIK* 6.1–40.

—— 1932, 'Das Motiv der Ente mit zurückgewendetem Kopfe im ägyptischen Kunstgewerbe.' *ZÄS* 68.86–105.

—— 1937, 'Die Katze im Fenster über der Tür.' *ZÄS* 73.68–74.

—— 1959, *Altägyptische Liebesdichtung.* Wiesbaden.

Hermsen, E. 1981, *Lebensbaumsymbolik im alten Ägypten.* Bonn.

Herodotus 1954, *The Histories.* (trans. A. de Sélincourt), London.

Herrmann, C. 1985, *Formen für ägyptische Fayencen.* OBO 60, Freiburg.

—— 1990, 'Weitere Formen für ägyptische Fayencen aus der Ramsesstadt.' *Ägypten und Levante* 1.17–74.

Hickmann, H. 1949, *Les instruments de musique.* Cat. Cairo.

—— 1954, 'La Menat.' *Kêmi* 13.99–102.

—— 1954a, 'Die altägyptische Rassel.' *ZÄS* 79.116–125.

—— 1956, *Musicologie pharaonique.* Kehl, France.

Hieroglyphic Texts, 1911–82, *Hieroglyphic Texts from Egyptian Stelae, Etc., in the British Museum.* London:

—— 1914, 5.

—— 1922, 6.

—— 1925, 7.

—— 1970, 9.

—— 1982, 10.

Hildesheim Cat. 1985, *Nofret–die Schöne. Die Frau im alten Ägypten.* Exhibition Catalogue, Hildesheim.

Hilton-Price Cat. 1911, *A Catalogue of Egyptian Antiquities, the Property of the Late F. G. Hilton-Price.* Sotheby's, London.

Hinkel, F. 1965, 'Progress Report on the Dismantling and Removal of Endangered Monuments in Sudanese Nubia.' *Kush* 13.96–101.

Hodjash, S. I.–Berlev, O. 1982, *The Egyptian Reliefs and Stelae in the Pushkin Museum of Fine Art, Moscow.* Leningrad.

Höhr-Grenzhausen Cat. 1978, *Meisterwerke altägyptischer Keramik . . . .* Exhibition catalogue, Höhr-Grenzhausen Rastal-Haus. Hachenberg.

Hölscher, U. 1951, *The Mortuary Temple of Ramesses III* II: *The Excavation of Medinet Habu* IV. Chicago.

—— 1954, *Post-Ramessid Remains: The Excavation of Medinet Habu* V. Chicago.

Hoenes, S.-E. 1976, *Untersuchungen zu Wesen und Kult der Göttin Sachmet.* Habelts Dissertationsdrucke Ägyptologie 1, Bonn.

Hofmann, I. 1985, 'Die Löwen auf dem Fenstersims.' *Varia Aegyptiaca* 1.99–105.

Honroth, W. *et al.* 1910, 'Bericht über die Ausgrabungen auf Elephantine in den Jahren 1906–1908.' *ZÄS* 46.14–61.

Hope, C. 1987, *Egyptian Pottery*. Aylesbury.

Hopfner, T. 1913, *Der Tierkult der alten Ägypter*. Vienna.

Hornblower, G. D. 1922, 'Some Hyksos Plaques and Scarabs.' *JEA* 8.201–6.

—— 1926, 'Phallic Offerings to Hat-hor.' *Man* 26.81–2.

—— 1927, 'Further Notes on Phallicism in Ancient Egypt.' *Man* 27.150–3.

—— 1929, 'Predynastic Figures of Women and their Successors.' *JEA* 15.29–47.

Hornemann, B. 1951–69, *Types of Ancient Egyptian Statuary*. 7 parts. Copenhagen.

Hornung, E. 1976, *Das Buch der Anbetung des Re im Westen (Sonnenlitanei)* II. AH 3, Geneva.

—— 1977, 'Verfall und Regeneration der Schöpfung.' *Eranos Jahrbuch* 46.411–49.

—— 1979, 'Die Tragweite der Bilder: Altägyptische Bildaussagen.' *Eranos Jahrbuch* 48.183–237.

—— 1981, 'Auf den Spuren der Sonne: Gang durch ein ägyptisches Königsgrab.' *Eranos Jahrbuch* 50.431–75.

—— 1982, *Der ägyptische Mythos von der Himmelskuh*. OBO 46, Freiburg.

—— 1982b, *Conceptions of God in Ancient Egypt*. (trans. J. Baines), Ithaca, New York and London.

Hornung, E.–Staehelin, E. 1976, *Skarabäen und andere Siegelamulette aus Basler Sammlungen*. Ägyptische Denkmäler in der Schweiz 1, Mainz.

IFAO Cat. 1981, *Un siècle de fouilles françaises en Egypte 1880–1980*. Paris.

Irby, C. L.–Mangles, J. 1823, *Travels in Egypt and Nubia, Syria and Asia Minor 1817–1818*. London.

Jacoby, A.–Spiegelberg, W. 1903, 'Der Frosch als Symbol der Auferstehung bei den Aegyptern.' *Sphinx* 7.215–9.

Jacquet, J. 1958, 'Un bassin de libation du Nouvel Empire dédié à Ptah. 1. L'architecture.' *MDAIK* 16.161–67.

Jakobielski, S. 1972, *Faras III: A History of the Bishopric of Pachoras on the Basis of Coptic Inscriptions*. Warsaw.

James, T. G. H. 1965, 'Egypt: from the Expulsion of the Hyksos to Amenophis I.' *Cambridge Ancient History* II, 2nd. ed., Chap.8.

—— 1974, *Corpus of Hieroglyphic Inscriptions in the Brooklyn Museum* I: *From Dynasty I to the End of Dynasty XVIII*. Brooklyn.

James, T. G. H. (ed.) 1982, *Excavating in Egypt: The Egypt Exploration Society 1882–1982*. London.

Janssen, J. J. 1975, *Commodity Prices from the Ramessid Period*. Leiden.

—— 1975a, 'Prolegomena to the Study of Egypt's Economic History during the New Kingdom.' *SAK* 3.127–85.

—— 1976, 'The Economic System of a Single Village.' *RAIN* 15.17–9.

—— 1980, 'Absence from Work by the Necropolis Workmen of Thebes.' *SAK* 8.127–52.

Janssen, J. J.–Janssen, R. 1990, *Growing up in Ancient Egypt*. London.

Jeffreys, D. G.–Malek, J. 1988, 'Memphis 1986, 1987.' *JEA* 74.15–29.

Jeffreys, D. G.–Malek, J.–Smith, H. S. 1986, 'Memphis 1984.' *JEA* 72.1–14.

Jelínková-Reymond, E. 1953, 'Recherches sur le rôle des "gardiens des portes" (*iry-ꜥ;*) dans l'administration générale des temples égyptiens.' *CdE* 28.39–59.

Jéquier, G. 1922, *Matériaux pour servir à l'établissement d'un Dictionnaire d'Archéologie Egyptienne*. = *BIFAO* 19.

—— 1924, *L'architecture et la décoration dans l'ancienne Egypte* III: *Les temples ptolémaïques et romains*. Paris.

Jesi, F. 1958, 'Observationes prosographicae ad Sacerdotes Eponymos Lagidarum pertinentes.' *Aegyptus* 38.159–83.

Jidejian, N. 1968, *Byblos through the Ages*. Beirut.

Johns, C. 1982, *Sex or Symbol? Erotic Images of Greece and Rome*. London.

Junker, H. 1911, *Der Auszug der Hathor-Tefnut aus Nubien*. Abhandlungen der Königl. Preuss. Akademie der Wissenschaften zu Berlin 1911, Berlin.

—— 1917, *Die Onurislegende*. Kaiserliche Akademie der Wissenschaften in Wien, phil.–hist. Klasse, Denkschriften 59:1, Vienna.

—— 1940, *Gîza* IV. Akademie der Wissenschaften in Wien, phil.–hist. Klasse, Denkschriften 71:1, Vienna.

Kaczmarczyk, A.–Hedges, R. E. M. 1983, *Ancient Egyptian Faience*. Warminster.

Kaiser, W. *et al*. 1988, 'Stadt und Tempel von Elephantine. 15./16. Grabungsbericht.' *MDAIK* 44.135–182.

Kákosy, L. 1982, 'Orakel.' *LÄ* 4.600–6.

Kamal, A. B. 1910, 'Rapport sur les fouilles du comte de Galarza.' *ASAE* 10.116–21.

Karkowski, J. 1972, 'The Problem of the Origin of the Tuthmoside Blocks Found in Faras.' *ET* 6.83–92.

—— 1975, 'A note on the 'Hathor Rock' at Faras.' *ET* 8.117–24.

—— 1981, *Faras V: The Pharaonic Inscriptions from Faras*. Warsaw.

Karkowski, J.–Winnicki, J. K. 1983, 'Amenhotep, Son of Hapu and Imhotep at Deir el-Bahari–Some Reconsiderations.' *MDAIK* 39.93–105.

Keel, O. 1980, *Das Böcklein in der Milch seiner Mutter und Verwandtes*. OBO 33, Freiburg.

Kees, H. 1926, *Totenglauben und Jenseitsvorstellungen der alten Ägypter*. Leipzig.

—— 1933, *Ägypten*. Kulturgeschichte des alten Orients 1, Munich.

—— 1960, 'Der berichtende Gottesdiener (𓁐𓏏).' *ZÄS* 85.138–43.

—— 1961, *Ancient Egypt: A Cultural Topography*. (ed. T. G. H. James, trans. I. F. D. Morrow), London.

Keimer, L. 1924, *Die Gartenpflanzen im alten Ägypten* I. Berlin.

—— 1940, 'Jeux de la nature retouchés par la main de l'homme, provenant de Deir el-Médineh (Thèbes) et remontant au nouvel-empire.' In L. Keimer, *Etudes d'égyptologie* 2.1–21. Cairo.

—— 1943, 'Un Bes tatoué (?).' *ASAE* 42.159–61.

—— 1948, *Remarques sur le tatouage dans l'Egypte ancienne*. Mémoires présentés à L'Institut d'Egypte 53, Cairo.

—— 1956, 'La vache et le cobra dans les marécages de papyrus de Thèbes.' *BIE* 37.215–257.

Kemp, B. J. 1979, 'Wall Paintings from the Workmen's Village at El-ʿAmarna.' *JEA* 65.47–53.

—— 1989, *Ancient Egypt. Anatomy of a Civilization*. Cambridge.

Kemp, B. J. (ed.), 1985/1986/1987/1989, *Amarna Reports* II–V. Egypt Exploration Society Occasional Publications 2, 4, 5, 6. London.

Kemp. B.–Merrillees, R. S.–Edel, E. 1980, *Minoan Pottery in Second Millennium Egypt*. Mainz.

Kertesz, T. 1976, 'The Breaking of Offerings in the Cult of Hathor.' *Tel Aviv* 3.134–6.

Kestner Cat. n.d. (c. 1970) *Ägyptische Abteilung*. Loose leaf museum guide. Hannover.

Kitchen, K. A. 1976, 'A Pre-Ramesside Cartouche at Timna.' *Orientalia* 45.262–4.

—— 1976a, 'Two Notes on Ramesside History.' *Oriens Antiquus* 15.311–15.

Klebs, L. 1931, 'Die verschiedenen Formen des Sistrums.' *ZÄS* 67.60–3.

Koefoed-Petersen, O. 1948, *Les stèles égyptiennes*. Publications de la Glyptothègue Ny Carlsburg 1, Copenhagen.

Krönig, W. 1934, 'Ägyptische Fayence-Schalen des Neuen Reiches.' *MDAIK* 5.144–66.

Kuentz, C. 1969, 'Stèle aux crocodiles.' *Mélanges de l'Université Saint-Joseph* 45 [Fs. Dunand I].185–94.

Lacau, P. 1909, *Stèles du Nouvel Empire*. Cat. Cairo.

Lacovara, P. 1980, 'Archaeological Survey of Deir el-Ballas.' *ARCE Newsletter* 113.3–11.

Lacovara, P. (ed.) 1990, *Deir el-Ballas: Preliminary Report on the Deir el-Ballas Expedition 1980–1986*. American Research Centre in Egypt Reports 12, Winona Lake, Indiana.

Lake, K. *et al.* 1928, 'The Serabît Inscriptions.' *Harvard Theological Review* 21.1–67.

—— 1932, 'The Serabit Expedition of 1930.' *Harvard Theological Review* 25.95–203.

Lange, H. O. 1927, *Der magische Papyrus Harris*. Det Kgl. Danske Videnskabernes Selskab. Historisk-filogiske Meddelelser XIV.2, Copenhagen.

Lange, H.–Schäfer, H. 1908/1923/1925, *Grab- und Denksteine des Mittleren Reiches*. Cat. Cairo.

Langton, N. 1936, 'Notes on Some Small Egyptian Figures of Cats.' *JEA* 22.115–20.

—— 1938, 'Further Notes on Some Egyptian Figures of Cats.' *JEA* 24.54–68.

Langton, N.–Langton, B. 1940, *The Cat in Ancient Egypt*. Cambridge.

Lansing, A. 1917, 'Excavations in the Assasîf at Thebes.' *BMMA* 12, May Supplement.7–26.

—— 1920, 'Excavations in the Asasif at Thebes, Season of 1918–19.' *BMMA* 15, July Supplement.11–24; December Supplement.4–12.

—— 1934, 'The Excavations at Lisht.' *BMMA* 29, November II.4–41.

—— 1935, 'The Museum's Excavations at Thebes.' *BMMA* 30, November II.4–16.

—— 1945, 'An Egyptian Painting on Linen.' *BMMA* (n.s.) 3.201–3.

Lansing, A.–Hayes, W. C. 1937, 'The Museum's Excavations at Thebes.' *BMMA* 32, January II.4–39.

Lanzone, R. V. [1881]–1975, *Dizionario di mitologia egizia* I–IV. Turin.

Laskowska-Kusztal, E. 1984, *Deir el-Bahari* III: *Le sanctuaire ptolémaïque*. Warsaw.

Leahy, A. 1981, 'Saite Lamp Donations.' *GM* 49.37–46.

Leca, A.-P. 1971, *La médécine égyptienne au temps des Pharaons*. Paris.

Leclant, J. 1957, 'Tefnout et les Divines Adoratrices thébaines.' *MDAIK* 15.166–71.

—— 1959, 'Le rôle de l'allaitement dans le cérémonial pharaonique du couronnement.' *Akten des Vierundzwanzigsten Internationalen Orientalisten Kongresses München, 1957*, 69–71. Wiesbaden.

—— 1961, 'Sur un contrepoids de menat au nom de Taharqa.' *Mélanges Mariette* 251–284. IFAO Bibliothèque d'Etudes 32, Cairo.

—— 1984, 'Fouilles et travaux en Egypte et au Soudan 1982–1983.' *Orientalia* 53.350–416.

Leclant, J.,–Clerc, G., 1985/1986/1987, 'Fouilles et travaux en Egypte et au Soudan ... .' *Orientalia* 54.337–415; 55.236–319; 56.292–389.

Leeds, E. T. 1922, 'Alabaster Vases of the New Kingdom from Sinai.' *JEA* 8.1–4.

Legrain, G. 1906/1909/1914, *Statues et statuettes de rois et de particuliers*. Cat. Cairo.

—— 1914, 'Au pylône d'Harmhabi à Karnak (X^e pylône).' *ASAE* 14.13–44.

Leibovitch, J. 1934, *Les inscriptions protosinaïtiques*. IFAO Mem. 24, Cairo.

Leiden Cat. 1981, *National Museum of Antiquities*. Dutch Museums VI, Harlem.

van Lepp, J. 1988, 'The Role of Dance in Funerary Ritual in the Old Kingdom.' *SAK* Beiheft 3.385–94.

Lepsius, C. R. [1849–59], *Denkmaeler aus Aegypten und Aethiopien*. Abtheilungen 1–6, vols. I–XII. Berlin. [Cited by Abtheilung.]

Lesko, B. (ed.) 1989, *Women's Earliest Records from Ancient Egypt and Western Asia*. Atlanta.

Lesko, L. (ed.) 1986, *Egyptological Studies in Honor of Richard A. Parker*. Hanover, New Hampshire and London.

Lichtheim, M. 1973/1976/1980, *Ancient Egyptian Literature* I–III. Berkeley.

Lilyquist, C. 1979, *Ancient Egyptian Mirrors from the Earliest Times through the Middle Kingdom*. MÄS 27, Munich.

Lipińska, J. 1966, 'List of the Objects Found at Deir el-Bahari Temple of Tuthmosis III, Season 1961/1962.' *ASAE* 59.63–98.

—— 1967, 'Names and History of the Sanctuaries Built by Tuthmosis III at Deir el-Baḥri.' *JEA* 53.25–33.

—— 1968, 'List of Objects Found at Deir el-Bahari in the Temple of Tuthmosis III.' *ASAE* 60.153–204, 205–212.

—— 1969, 'Amenemone, Builder of the Ramesseum.' *ET* 3.41–9.

—— 1969a, 'Inscriptions of Amenemone from the Temple of Tuthmosis III at Deir el-Bahari.' *ZÄS* 96.28–30.

—— 1977, *Deir el-Bahari* II: *The Temple of Tuthmosis III: Architecture*. Warsaw.

—— 1984, *Deir el-Bahari* IV: *The Temple of Tuthmosis III: Statuary and Votive Monuments*. Warsaw.

Lipiński, E. (ed.) 1979, *State and Temple Economy in the Ancient Near East*. Orientalia Lovaniensia Analecta 5–6, Louvain.

Liverpool Cat. 1932, *Handbook and Guide to the Egyptian Collection on Exhibition in The Public Museums, Liverpool*. Liverpool.

Loat, L. 1904, *Gurob*. Egyptian Research Account 10th Year, London.

Loeben, C. 1987, 'A Throwstick of Princess *Nfr-Nfrw-Rˁ*, with Additional Notes on Throwsticks of Faience.' *ASAE* 71.143–59.

Lucas, A. (revised by J. R. Harris) 1962, *Ancient Egyptian Materials and Industries*. (4th ed.), London.

Lyons, H. G. 1916, 'The Temple at Mirgisse.' *JEA* 3.182–3.

Mace, A. C. 1921, 'Excavations at Lisht.' *BMMA* 16, November II.5–19.

Mahmud, Abdulla el-Sayed 1978, *A New Temple for Hathor at Memphis*. Warminster.

Malaise, M. 1976, 'Histoire et signification de la coiffure hathoriques à plumes.' *SAK* 4.215–36.

—— 1981, 'Inventaire des stèles égyptiennes du Moyen Empire porteuses de représentations divines.' *SAK* 9.259–83.

Malek, J.–Miles, E. 1989, 'Early Squeezes Made in the Tomb of Khaemhet (TT57).' *JEA* 75.227–9.

Manniche, L. 1977, 'Some Aspects of Ancient Egyptian Sexual Life.' *Acta Orientalia* (Copenhagen) 38.11–23.

—— 1978, 'Symbolic Blindness.' *CdE* 53.13–21.

—— 1987, *Sexual Life in Ancient Egypt*. London.

—— 1989, *An Ancient Egyptian Herbal*. London.

Marciniak, M. 1965, 'Une nouvelle statue de Senenmout récemment découverte à Deir el-Bahari.' *BIFAO* 63.201–7.

—— 1968, 'Quelques remarques sur la formule *ir nfr, ir nfr*.' *ET* 2.25–31.

—— 1971, 'Encore sur la Belle Fête de la Vallée.' *ET* 5.53–64.

—— 1974, *Deir el-Bahari* I: *Les inscriptions hiératiques du temple de Thoutmosis III*. Warsaw.

—— 1981, 'Un texte inédit de Deir el-Bahari.' *BIFAO* 81 (*Bulletin du Centenaire*) 283–91.

—— 1981a, 'Une inscription commémorative de Deir el-Bahari.' *MDAIK* 37.299–305.

Mariette, A. 1877, *Deir el-Bahari: Documents topographiques, historiques, et ethnographiques recueillis dans ce temple*. Leipzig.

Marseilles Cat. 1978, *Catalogue des antiquités égyptiennes: Collection des Musées d'Archéologie de Marseille*. Marseille.

Martin, G. T. 1974, *The Royal Tomb at el-ˁAmarna* I: *The Objects*. ASE 35, London.

—— 1981, *The Sacred Animal Necropolis at North Saqqâra*. EES Mem. 50, London.

—— 1987, '"Erotic" Figurines I: The Cairo Museum Material.' *GM* 96.71–84.

—— 1987a, 'A Throwstick of Nefertiti in Manchester.' *ASAE* 71.151–2.

Maspero, G. 1880, 'Rapport sur une mission en Italie.' *RT* 2.159–99.

—— 1881, *La trouvaille de Deir el-Bahari*. Cairo.

Matouk, F. S. 1977, *Corpus du scarabée égyptien* II. [Beirut.]

Maxwell–Hyslop, K. 1971, *Western Asiatic Jewellery, c. 3000 – 612 B.C.* London.

Mercer, S. A. B. 1952, *The Pyramid Texts in Translation and Commentary* I–IV. New York.

von Mercklin, E. 1962, *Antike Figuralkapitelle*. Berlin.

de Meulenaere, H. 1953, 'La légende de Phéros d'après Hérodote.' *CdE* 28.248–60.

Mey, P.– Castel, G.– Goyon, J. C. 1980, 'Installations rupestres du Moyen et du Nouvel Empire au Gebel Zeit (près de Râs Dib) sur la Mer Rouge.' *MDAIK* 36.299–318.

Meyer, C. 1982, *Senenmut: Eine prosopographische Untersuchung*. Hamburger Ägyptologische Studien 2, Hamburg.

Michałowski, K. *et al.* 1938, 1950, *Tell Edfou 1938–9*. Fouilles Franco-Polonaises II–III, Cairo.

—— 1961, 1965 *Faras* I–II. Warsaw.

—— 1962–5, 'Polish Excavations at Faras … ' *Kush* 10.220–44, 11.235–56, 12.195–207, 13.177–89.

Michels, A. K. 1953, 'The Topography and Interpretation of the Lupercalia.' *Transactions and Proceedings of the American Philological Association* 84.35–59.

Mileham, G. S. 1910, *Churches in Lower Nubia*. Eckley B. Coxe Junior Expedition to Nubia 2, Philadelphia.

Miller, R. L. 1991, 'Palaeoepidemiology, Literacy, and Medical Tradition Among Necropolis Workmen in New Kingdom Egypt.' *Medical History* 35.1–24.

Moftah, R. 1965, 'Die uralte Sykomore und andere Erscheinungen der Hathor.' *ZÄS* 92.40–7.

Mogensen, M. 1930, *La collection égyptienne de la Glyptothèque Ny Carlsberg*. Copenhagen.

Mond, R.–Myers, O. H. 1940, *Temples of Armant*. EES Mem.43, London.

Montet, P. 1928–9, *Byblos et l'Egypte. Quatres campagnes de fouilles à Gebeil, 1921–4*. Paris.

—— 1957, 'Hathor et les papyrus.' *Kêmi* 14.102–8.

de Morant, H. 1937, 'Le chat dans l'art d'égyptien.' *CdE* 12.29–40.

Morenz, S. 1958, 'Eine Wöchnerin mit Siegelring.' *ZÄS* 83.138–41.

—— 1973, *Egyptian Religion*. (trans. A. E. Keep), London and Ithaca.

Moret, A. 1913, 'Monuments égyptiens du Musée Calvet à Avignon.' *RT* 35.193–206.

—— 1919, 'Monuments égyptiens de la collection du Comte de Saint-Ferriol.' *Revue Egyptologique* (n.s.) 1.1–27.

Müller, H. W. 1964, *Ägyptische Kunstwerke, Kleinfunde und Glas in der Sammlung E. & M. Kofler-Truniger, Luzern*. MÄS 5, Berlin.

Munich Cat. 1976, *Staatliche Sammlung ägyptischer Kunst* (2nd. ed.), Munich.

Munro, P. 1962, 'Einige Votivstellen an *Wp wꜣwt*.' *ZÄS* 88.48–58.

—— 1969, 'Eine Gruppe spätägyptischer Bronzespiegel.' *ZÄS* 95.92–109.

Murray, M. A. 1910, *National Museum of Science and Art, Dublin. General Guide to the Art Collections* III: *Egyptian Antiquities*. Dublin.

—— 1956, 'Burial Customs and Beliefs in the Hereafter in Predynastic Egypt.' *JEA* 42.86–96.

Muscarella, O. W. 1974, *Ancient Art. The Norbert Schimmel Collection*. Mainz.

Myśliwiec, K. 1972, 'A propos des signes hieroglyphiques "ḥr" et "tp".' *ZÄS* 98.85–99.

—— 1988, 'Remains of a Ptolemaic villa at Athribis.' *MDAIK* 44.183–97.

Nagel, G. 1938, *La céramique du Nouvel Empire à Deir el-Médineh*. IFAO Doc. 10, Cairo.

Nagy, E. 1977, 'Fragments de sistres au Musée des Beaux Arts.' *Bulletin du Musée Hongrois des Beaux Arts* 48–9.49–70.

Naville, E. 1886, *Das aegyptische Todtenbuch der XVIII. bis XX. Dynastie*. Berlin.

—— 1893–6, 'Work at the Temple of Deir el-Bahari.' *EEF Archaeological Report* 1893–4.1–7; 1894–5.33–7; 1895–6.1–6.

—— 1894, *The Temple of Deir el-Bahari: Its Plan, its Founders and its First Explorers*. EEF Mem. 12, London.

—— n.d. [1895]–1908, *The Temple of Deir el-Bahari* I–VI. EEF Mem. 13, 14, 16, 19, 27, 29, London.

—— 1907, 1910, 1913, *The XIth Dynasty Temple at Deir el-Bahari* I–III. EEF Mem. 28, 30, 32, London.

—— 1907a, 'Excavations at Deir el-Bahari.' *EEF Archaeological Report* 1906-1907.1–7.

Naville, E.–Hall, H.R. 1904–6, 'Excavations at Deir el-Bahari.' *EEF Archaeological Report* 1903–4.1–12; 1904–5.1–10; 1905–6.1–7.

Negbi, O. 1976, *Canaanite Gods in Metal: An Archaeological Study of Ancient Syro-Palestinian Figurines*. Tel Aviv University Institute of Archaeology Publications 5.

Newberry, P. [1895], *El Bersheh* I. ASE [3], London.

—— 1907, *Scarab-shaped Seals*. Cat. Cairo, London.

—— 1933, 'A Statue and a Scarab.' *JEA* 19.53–4.

Nims, C. [1956?], 'Popular Religion in Ancient Egyptian Temples.' *Proceedings of the 23rd International Congress of Orientalists, Cambridge 1954*, 79–80. London.

—— 1955, 'Places about Thebes.' *JNES* 14.110–23.

—— 1969, 'Thutmosis III's Benefactions to Amon.' In *Studies in Honour of John A. Wilson*, 69–74. SAOC 35, Chicago.

—— 1970, 'A Scene on the South Wall of a Court in the Temple of Khonsu.' *ARCE Newsletter* April. 5–7.

—— 1971, 'The Eastern Temple at Karnak.' In *Aufsätze zum 70. Geburtstag von Herbert Ricke*. BÄBA 12, 107–11. Wiesbaden.

Niwiński, A. 1985, 'Miscellanea de Deir el-Bahari.' *MDAIK* 41.197–227.

Nord, D. 1981, 'The Term ḫnr: "Harem" or "Musical Performers"?' In Simpson and Davis 1981.137–45.

Nordström, H.-A. 1962, 'Excavations and Survey in Faras, Argin and Gezira Dabarosa.' *Kush* 10.34–58.

Northampton, Marquis of et al. 1908, *Report on Some Excavations in the Theban Necropolis during the Winter of 1898–9*. London.

O'Malley, L. 1935, *Popular Hinduism*. Cambridge.

Omlin, J.A. 1975, *Der Papyrus 55001 und seine satirisch-erotischen Zeichnungen und Inschriften*. Catalogo del Museo Egizio di Torino. 1st series 3, Turin.

Oppenheimer Cat. 1936, *Catalogue of the Collection of Egyptian, Greek and Roman Antiquities ... Formed by the late Henry Oppenheimer ....* Christie's, London.

Otto, E. 1948, 'Zur Bedeutung der ägyptischen Tempelstatue seit dem Neuen Reich.' *Orientalia* 17.448–66.
—— 1952, *Topographie des thebanischen Gaues.* UGAÄ 16, Berlin.

Page, A. 1976, *Egyptian Sculpture: Archaic to Saite. From the Petrie Collection.* Warminster.
—— 1983, *Ancient Egyptian Figured Ostraca in the Petrie Collection.* Warminster.
Palmer, C. H. *et al.* 1869, *Ordnance Survey of the Peninsula of Sinai* I–II. Southampton.
Patch, D. C. 1990, *Reflections of Greatness: Ancient Egypt at the Carnegie Museum of Natural History.* Pittsburgh.
Parker, R. A. 1962, *A Saite Oracle Papyrus from Thebes in the Brooklyn Museum.* Brown Egyptological Studies 4, Providence.
Parlasca, K. 1966, *Mumienporträts und verwandte Denkmäler.* Wiesbaden.
Pavlov, V. V. 1949, *Egipetskaya skul'ptura v Gosudarstvennom Muzee Izobrazitelnykh Iskusstv im A. S. Pushkina: Malaya plastika.* Moscow.
Pawlicki, F. 1974, 'Egipskie Sistra.' *Rocznik Muzeum Narodowego w Warszawie* 18.7–21.
Peck, W. H. 1978, *Drawings from Ancient Egypt.* London.
Peet, T. E. 1914, *The Cemeteries of Abydos* II: *1911–1912.* EEF Mem. 34, London.
Peet, T. E.–Loat, W. L. S. 1913, *The Cemeteries of Abydos* III: *1912–1913.* EEF Mem. 35, London.
Peet, T. E.–Woolley, C. L. 1923, *The City of Akhenaten* I: *Excavations of 1921 and 1922 at El-ʿAmarneh.* EEF Mem. 38, London.
Pendlebury, J. D. S. 1951, *The City of Akhenaten* III: *The Central City and the Official Quarters.* EES Mem. 44, London.
Pendlebury, J. D. S.–Frankfort, H. 1933, *The City of Akhenaten* II: *The North Suburb and the Desert Altars.* EES Mem. 40, London.
Perdrizet, P. 1911, *Bronzes grecs d'Egypte de la Collection Fouquet.* Paris.
Peterson, B. E. J. 1973, *Zeichnungen aus einer Totenstadt: Bildostraka aus Theben West* ... . = MB 7–8.
Peterson, B. J,–George, B. 1982, 'Egypten.' In *Medelhavsmuseet: En Introduktion* 9–116. Stockholm.
Petrie, W. M. F. 1890, *Kahun, Gurob and Hawara.* London.
—— 1896, *Koptos.* London.
—— 1897, *Six Temples at Thebes, 1896.* London.
—— 1898, *Religion and Conscience in Ancient Egypt.* London.
—— 1900, *Dendereh (1898).* EEF Mem.17, London.
—— 1901, *Diospolis Parva. The Cemeteries of Abadiyeh and Hu.* EEF Mem. 20, London.
—— 1902–3, *Abydos* I–II. EEF Mem. 22, 24, London.
—— 1905, *Ehnasya.* EEF Mem. 26, London.
—— 1905a, 'The Sinai Expedition.' *EEF Archaeological Report* 1904–1905.10–12.
—— 1906, *Researches in Sinai.* London.
—— 1907, *Gizeh and Rifeh, 1907.* BSE 13, London.
—— 1909, *Memphis I, 1908.* BSE 15, London.

—— 1909a, *The Palace of Apries (Memphis II), 1909*. BSE 17, London.

—— 1909b, *Qurneh, 1909*. BSE 16, London.

—— 1912, *The Labyrinth, Gerzeh and Mazghuneh, 1911*. BSE 21, London.

—— 1914, *Amulets*. London.

—— 1925, *Tombs of the Courtiers and Oxyrhynkhos*. BSE 37, London.

—— 1927, *Objects of Daily Use*. BSE 42, London.

—— 1934, *Ancient Gaza* IV. BSE 56, London.

—— 1937, *The Funeral Furniture of Egypt*. BSE 59, London

Petrie, W. M. F. *et al.* 1891, *Illahun, Kahun and Gurob*. London.

—— 1910, *Meydum and Memphis* (III). BSE 18, London.

—— 1923, *Lahun* II. BSE 33, London.

Petrie, W. M. F.–Brunton, G. 1924, *Sedment* I–II. BSE 34–5, London.

Philips, A. K. 1986, 'Observation on the Alleged New Kingdom Sanatorium at Deir el-Bahari.' *GM* 89. 77–83.

Piankoff, A. 1954, *The Tomb of Ramesses VI*. Bollingen Series 40.1, New York.

—— 1955, *The Shrines of Tut-ankh-Amon*. Bollingen Series 40.2, New York.

—— 1964, *The Litany of Re*. Bollingen Series 40.4, New York.

Pinch, G. 1983, 'Childbirth and Female Figurines at Deir el-Medina and el-ʿAmarna.' *Orientalia* 52.405–14.

—— forthcoming, 'Fertility Magic.' In *Studies in Egyptian Magic,* ed. J. Bourriau and M. Collier.

Polaczek-Zdanowicz, K. 1975, 'The Genesis and Evolution of the Orant Statuettes against a Background of Developing Coptic Art.' *ET* 8.135–49.

Posener, G. 1956, *Littérature et politique dans l'Egypte de la XIIe dynastie*. Paris.

—— 1960, *De la divinité du Pharaon*. Cahiers de la Société Asiatique 15, Paris.

—— 1971, 'Amon juge du pauvre.' In *Aufsätze zum 70 Geburtstag von Herbert Ricke*. BÄBA 12, 59–63.

—— 1975, 'La piété personelle avant l'âge amarnien.' *RdE* 27.195–210.

—— 1986, 'La légende de la tresse d'Hathor.' in L. Lesko 1986.111–7.

Posener, G. *et al.* 1962, *A Dictionary of Egyptian Civilization*. (trans. A. MacFarlane), Paris.

Posener-Kriéger, P. 1983, 'Les travaux de l'Institut Français d'Archéologie Orientale en 1982–1983.' *BIFAO* 83.343–63.

—— 1984, 'Les Travaux ... 1983–1984.' *BIFAO* 84.347–65.

—— 1985, 'Les Travaux ... 1984–1985.' *BIFAO* 85.295–320.

—— 1986, 'Les Travaux ... 1985–1986.' *BIFAO* 86.367–97.

Pritchard, J. B. 1943, *Palestinian Figurines in Relation to Certain Goddesses Known through Literature*. New Haven.

Pyramid Texts 1969, *The Ancient Egyptian Pyramid Texts,* trans. R. O. Faulkner. Oxford.

Quaegebeur, J.–Rammant-Peeters, A. 1982, 'Le pyramidion d'un "danseur en chef" de Bastet.' *Studia Paulo Naster Oblata* II, 179–205. Louvain.

Quibell, J. E. 1898, *The Ramesseum* (with *The Tomb of Ptah-hetep*). ERA 2, 1896. London.

—— 1898a, *El Kab*. ERA 3, London.

—— 1900, *Hierakonpolis* I. ERA 4, London.

—— 1907, *Excavations at Saqqâra (1905–1906)*. Cairo.

—— 1908, *The Tomb of Yuaa and Thuiu*. Cat. Cairo.

Quirke, S. 1990, 'Kerem in the Fitzwilliam Museum.' *JEA* 76.170–4.

—— 1992, *Ancient Egyptian Religion*. London.

de Rachewiltz, B. 1964, *Black Eros*. London.

Radford, U. M. 1949, 'The Wax Images Found in Exeter Cathedral.' *The Antiquaries Journal* 29.164–8.

Rainey, A. F. (ed.) 1987, *Egypt, Israel, Sinai: Archaeological and Historical Relationships in the Biblical Period*. Tel Aviv.

Ramsès le Grand Cat. 1976, *Ramsès le Grand: Galeries Nationales du Grand Palais*. Paris.

Randall-MacIver, D. – Mace, A. C. 1902, *El Amrah and Abydos 1899–1901*. EEF Mem. 23, London.

Randall-MacIver, D. – Woolley, C. L. 1911, *Buhen*. Eckley B. Coxe Junior Expedition to Nubia 7–8, Philadelphia.

Ranke, H. 1935/1952/1977, *Die ägyptischen Personennamen*. 3 vols. Glückstadt.

—— 1936, *The Art of Ancient Egypt*. Vienna.

—— 1943, 'Eine spätsaïtische Statue in Philadelphia.' *MDAIK* 12.107–138.

—— 1950, 'The Egyptian Collections of the University Museum.' *Bulletin of the University Museum* (Pennsylvania) 15, nos. 2–3.

Ratié, S. 1984, 'Quelques réflexions sur l'aspect de l'oeil et sur les transpositions dans l'ancienne Egypte.' In *Mélanges Adolphe Gutbub* 177–82. Montpellier.

Reeves, C. N. 1986, 'Two Name-Beads of Hatshepsut and Senenmut from the Mortuary Temple of Queen Hatshepsut at Deir el-Bahri.' *The Antiquaries Journal* 66.387–8.

—— 1990, *The Complete Tutankhamun*. London and New York.

—— 1990a, *Valley of the Kings: The Decline of a Royal Necropolis*. London and New York.

Reid, R. W. 1912, *Illustrated Catalogue of the Anthropological Museum, University of Aberdeen*. Aberdeen.

Reisner, G. A. 1907/1958, *Amulets*. Cat. Cairo.

Ricke, H. 1939, *Der Totentempel Thutmoses' III*. BÄBA 3.1, Cairo.

—— 1954, *Das Kamutef-Heiligtum Hatschepsuts und Thutmoses' III. In Karnak*. BÄBA 3.2, Cairo.

—— 1965/1969, *Das Sonnenheiligtum des Königs Userkaf*. BÄBA 7–8, Cairo.

Riefstahl, E. 1944, *Patterned Textiles in Pharaonic Egypt*. Brooklyn.

—— 1968, *Ancient Egyptian Glass and Glazes in the Brooklyn Museum*. Wilbour Monographs 1, Brooklyn.

—— 1972, 'An Enigmatic Faience Figure.' *Miscellanea Wilbouriana* 1.137–43.

Robins, G. 1989, 'Some Images of Women in New Kingdom Art and Literature.' In B. Lesko 1989.105–116.

Robins, G. (ed.) 1990, *Beyond the Pyramids: Egyptian Regional Art from the Museo Egizio, Turin*. Atlanta.

Roeder, G. 1913/1924, *Ägyptische Inschriften aus den Königlichen/Staatlichen Museen zu Berlin*. 2 vols. Leipzig.

—— [1931], *Vorläufiger Bericht über die Ausgrabungen in Hermopolis 1929–30*. Hildesheim.

—— 1938, *Der Felsentempel von Bet el-Wali*. Cairo.

—— 1956, *Ägyptische Bronzefiguren*. Berlin.

—— 1959, *Hermopolis 1929–1939*. Hildesheim.

Rössler-Köhler, U. 1980, 'Löwe, Löwen-Köpfe, Löwen-Statuen.' *LÄ* 3.1080–90.

Rogers, E. 1948, 'An Egyptian Wine Bowl of the XIX Dynasty.' *BMMA* (n.s.) 6.154–60.

Romano, J. 1979, *The Luxor Museum of Ancient Egyptian Art*. Cairo.

—— 1980, 'The Origin of the Bes-Image.' *Bulletin of the Egyptological Seminar* 2.39–56.

Romer, J. 1979, *A History of Floods in the Valley of the Kings*. San Francisco.

—— 1981, *Valley of the Kings*. London.

Rothenberg, B. 1969 'An Archaeological Survey of South Sinai.' *BMH* 11.22–38.

—— 1970, 'An Egyptian Temple of Hathor discovered in the Southern ʿArabah (Israel).' *BMH* 12.28–35.

—— [1971], *Midianite Timna. Valley of the Biblical Copper Mines*. British Museum Exhibition Catalogue. [London].

—— 1972, *Timna. Valley of the Biblical Copper Mines*. London.

—— 1972a, 'Sinai Explorations 1967–72.' *BMH* 14.31–42.

—— 1973, *Timna. Tal Des Biblichen Kupfers . . . .* Bergbau Museum Catalogue. Bochum.

—— 1979, *Sinai: Pharaohs, Miners, Pilgrims and Soldiers*. Washington.

—— 1988, *The Egyptian Mining Temple at Timna*. London.

Rouse, W. H. D. 1901, *Greek Votive Offerings. An Essay in the History of Greek Religion*. London.

Rowe, A. 1930/1940, *The Four Canaanite Temples of Beth-Shan* I–II. Philadelphia.

Russmann, E. R. 1973, 'The Statue of Amenemope-em-hat.' *Metropolitan Museum Journal* 8.33–46.

de Rustafjaell, R. 1906, 'The Earliest Known Paintings on Cloth.' *The Connoisseur* 14.56.239–42.

—— 1909, *The Light of Egypt: From Recently Discovered Predynastic and Early Christian Records*. London.

de Rustafjaell Cat. 1913, *Catalogue of the Remaining Part of the Valuable Collection of Egyptian Antiquities Formed by R. de Rustafjaell*. Sotheby's, London.

Sadek, A. I. 1984, 'An Attempt to Translate the Corpus of the Deir El-Bahri Hieratic Inscriptions.' *GM* 71.67–91; 72.65–86.

—— 1987, *Popular Religion in Egypt during the New Kingdom*. Hildesheimer Ägyptologische Beiträge 27, Hildesheim.

—— 1988a, 'Les fêtes personelles au Nouvel Empire.' *SAK* Beiheft 3.353–368.

Säve-Söderbergh, T. 1941, *Ägypten und Nubien*. Lund.

—— 1949, 'A Buhen Stela from the Second Intermediate Period (Kharṭūm No. 18).' *JEA* 35.50–8.

—— 1957, *Private Tombs at Thebes* I: *Four Eighteenth Dynasty Tombs*. Oxford.

—— 1960, 'The Paintings in the Tomb of Djehuty-Hetep at Debeira.' *Kush* 8.25–44.

—— 1962/1968 'Preliminary Report of the Scandinavian Joint Expedition.' 'Archaeological Survey between Faras and Gamai, January–March 1961,' and 'Archaeological Investigations between Faras and Gamai, November 1963–March 1964.' *Kush* 10.76–105; 15.211–50.

Saleh, A. A. 1981/1983, *Excavations at Heliopolis: Ancient Egyptian Ounû* I–II. Cairo.

Saleh, M.–Sourouzian, H. 1987, *Official Catalogue of the Egyptian Museum Cairo.* Mainz.

Samson, J. 1978, *Amarna, City of Akhenaten and Nefertiti.* (2nd ed.), London.

Sandman Holmberg, M. 1946, *The God Ptah.* Lund.

Sauneron, S. 1969, *The Priests of Ancient Egypt.* (trans. A. Morrissett), New York.

el-Sayed, Ramadan. 1979, 'Stèles de particuliers relatives au culte rendu aux statues royales de la XVIIIe dynastie à la XXe dynastie.' *BIFAO* 79.155–66.

—— 1980, 'Les sept vaches célèstes, leur taureau et les quatre gouvernails.' *MDAIK* 36.357–90.

Scamuzzi, E. 1964, *Egyptian Art in the Egyptian Museum of Turin.* Turin.

Schäfer, H. *et al.* 1910, *Ägyptische Goldschmiedearbeiten.* Königliche Museen zu Berlin, Mitteilungen aus der Ägyptischen Sammlung 1, Berlin.

Scharff, A. 1923, *Götter Ägyptens.* Berlin.

—— 1926, *Die archäologischen Ergebnisse des vorgeschichtlichen Gräberfeldes von Abusir el-Meleq.* Leipzig.

Schiaparelli, E. 1887, *Catalogo generale de Museo Egizio di Firenze.* Florence.

Schlögl, H. 1977, *Der Sonnengott auf der Blüte.* AH 5, Geneva.

Schott, S. 1930, 'Die Bitte um ein Kind auf einer Grabfigur des frühen Mittleren Reiches.' *JEA* 16.23.

—— 1950, *Altägyptische Liebeslieder mit Marchen und Liebesgeschichten.* Zurich.

—— [1953], *Das schöne Fest vom Wüstentale.* Akademie der Wissenschaften und der Literatur, Abh., Geistes- und socialwiss. Klasse 1952.11, Mainz.

Schulman, A. R. 1963, 'Memphite Stelae: Documents Pertaining to Popular Religion in Ancient Memphis during the Egyptian New Kingdom and Later.' *Year Book of the American Philosophical Society*, 595–8.

—— 1964, 'The God *Nḥj*.' *JNES* 23.275–9.

—— 1967, 'Ex-Votos of the Poor.' *JARCE* 6.153–6.

—— 1976, 'The Royal Butler Ramessesemperrē.' *JARCE* 13.117–30.

—— 1981, 'Reshep Times Two.' In Simpson and Davis 1981.157–66.

—— 1985, 'The Cult Statue "Reshep, He Who Hears Prayers".' *Bulletin of the Egyptological Seminar* 6.89–97.

—— 1988, *Ceremonial Execution and Public Rewards. Some Historical Scenes on New Kingdom Private Stelae.* OBO 75, Freiburg.

—— 1988a 'Memphis 1915–1923: The Trivia of an Excavation.' In Zivie 1988.81–91.

Scott, N. E. 1958, 'The Cat of Bastet.' *BMMA* (n.s.) 17.1–7.

Seipel, W. 1983, *Bilder für die Ewigkeit. 3000 Jahre ägyptische Kunst.* Konstanz.

Sethe, K. 1906-9, *Urkunden der 18. Dynastie.* Leipzig.

Shafer, B. E. (ed.) 1991, *Religion in Ancient Egypt: Gods, Myths, and Personal Practice*. London.

Shorter, A. W. 1930, 'A Phallic Figure in the British Museum.' *JEA* 16.236.

—— 1931, *An Introduction to Egyptian Religion: An Account of Religion in Egypt During the 18th Dynasty*. London.

van Siclen, C. C. 1981, *Wall Scenes from the Tomb of Amenhotep (Huy), Governor of Bahria Oasis*. San Antonio.

—— 1985, 'Amenhotep II at Dendera (Iunet).' *Varia Aegyptiaca* 1.69–73.

Simpson, W. K. 1974, *The Terrace of the Great God at Abydos: The Offering Chapels of Dynasties 12 and 13*. New Haven.

Simpson, W. K.–Davis, W. M. 1981, *Studies in Ancient Egypt, the Aegean, and the Sudan. Essays in Honor of Dows Dunham*. Boston.

Smith, H. S. 1976, *The Fortress of Buhen: The Inscriptions*. EES Mem. 48, London.

Smith, W. S. 1946, *A History of Egyptian Sculpture and Painting in the Old Kingdom*. London.

—— 1965, *The Art and Architecture of Ancient Egypt*. (2nd. ed.), London.

Smither, P. C. 1939, 'The Writing of *Ḥtp-di-nsw* in the Middle and New Kingdoms.' *JEA* 25.34–7.

Sourouzian, H. 1983, 'Une chapelle rupestre de Merenptah dédiée à la déesse Hathor, maîtresse d'ʿAkhouy.' *MDAIK* 39.207–23.

Speleers, L. 1923, *Recueil des inscriptions égyptiennes des Musées Royaux du Cinquantenaire à Bruxelles*. Brussels.

Spencer, A. J. 1979, *Brick Architecture in Ancient Egypt*. Warminster.

Spencer, P. 1984, *The Egyptian Temple: A Lexicographical Study*. London.

Spiegelberg, W. 1898, *Zwei Beiträge zur Geschichte und Topographie der thebanischen Nekropolis im Neuen Reich*. Strasbourg.

—— 1903, 'Der Stabkultus bei den Aegyptern.' *RT* 25.184–90.

—— 1904, 'Demotische Miscellen: Der Gott Μεστασύτμις.' *RT* 26.56–7.

—— 1906, 'Varia.' *RT* 28.161–87.

—— 1917, *Der Ägyptische Mythus vom Sonnenauge*. Strasbourg.

—— 1929, 'Die Weihstatuette einer Wöchnerin.' *ASAE* 29.162–5.

Stadelmann, R. 1985, 'Votivbetten mit Darstellungen der Qadesch aus Theben.' *MDAIK* 41.265–8.

Staehelin, E. 1978, 'Zur Hathorsymbolik in der ägyptischen Kleinkunst.' *ZÄS* 105.76–84.

—— 1982, 'Menit.' *LÄ* 4.52–3.

Starck, S. 1977, *Introductory Guide to the Victoria Museum of Egyptian Antiquities at Uppsala University*. Uppsala.

Starr, R. F. S.–Butin, R. F. 1936, *Excavations and Protosinaitic Inscriptions at Serabit el Khadem*. Studies and Documents 6, London.

Steindorff, G. 1935/1937, *Aniba* I–II. Glückstadt.

Stewart, H. M. 1976, *Egyptian Stelae, Reliefs and Paintings from the Petrie Collection* I: *The New Kingdom*. Warminster.

—— 1983, *Egyptian Stelae, Reliefs and Paintings from the Petrie Collection* III: *The Late Period*. Warminster.

Strasbourg Cat. 1973, *Antiquités égyptiennes. Exposition à l'Ancienne Douane* .... Strasbourg.

Strauss, E.-C. 1974, *Die Nunschale: Eine Gefässgruppe des Neuen Reiches.* MÄS 30, Berlin.

Stricker, B. H. 1956, 'Bes de danser.' *Oudheidkundige Mededelingen uit het Rijksmuseum van Oudheden te Leiden* 37.35–48.

Szafrański, Z. E. 1985, 'Buried Statues of Mentuhotep II Nebhepetre and Amenophis I at Deir el-Bahari.' *MDAIK* 41.257–263.

Tambiah, S. J. 1984, *The Buddhist Saints of the Forest and the Cult of Amulets.* Cambridge Studies in Social Anthropology 49, Cambridge.

Tait, W. J. 1974, 'A Duplicate Version of the Demotic *Kufi* Text.' *Acta Orientalia* (Copenhagen) 36.23–37.

Tefnin, R. 1975, 'La chapelle d'Hathor du temple d'Hatshepsut à Deir el-Bahari.' *CdE* 50.136–50.

Thomas, A. P. 1981, *Gurob: A New Kingdom Town.* Egyptology Today 5, Warminster.

Thomas, E. 1980, 'The Tomb of Queen Ahmose (?) Merytamen. Theban Tomb 320.' *Serapis* 6.171–181.

Thompson, D. J. 1988, *Memphis under the Ptolemies.* Princeton.

Thompson, T. 1975, *The Settlement of Sinai and the Negev in the Bronze Age.* Beihefte zum Tübinger Atlas des Vorderen Orients B 8, Wiesbaden.

Tosi, M.–Roccati, A. 1972, *Stele e altre epigrafi di Deir el Medina.* Catalogo del Museo Egizio di Torino 2.1, Turin.

Trigger, B. G. 1965, *History and Settlement in Lower Nubia.* Yale Publications in Anthropology 69, New Haven.

—— [1976], *Nubia under the Pharaohs.* [London].

Troy, L. 1986, *Patterns of Queenship in Ancient Egyptian Myth and History.* Boreas 14, Uppsala.

Tutundjian, C. 1986, 'A Wooden Sistrum Handle.' *Varia Aegyptiaca* 2.73–8.

Uphill, E. P. 1961, 'A Joint Sed-Festival of Thutmose III and Queen Hatshepsut.' *JNES* 20.248–51.

Valbelle, D. 1972, 'Le naos de Kasa au Musée de Turin.' *BIFAO* 72.179–94.

—— 1981, *Satis et Anoukis.* Mainz.

—— 1985, *"Les Ouvriers de la Tombe." Deir el-Médineh à l'époque ramesside.* IFAO Bibliothèque d'Etude 96, Cairo.

Valbelle, D.–Bonnet, C. 1975–6, 'Le village de Deir el-Médineh. Reprise de l'étude archéologique.' *BIFAO* 75.429–46; 76.317–42.

Vandier, J. 1958, *Les grandes époques. La statuaire.* Manuel d'Archéologie Egyptienne 3, Paris.

—— 1964–6, 'Iousâas et (Hathor)–Nébet-Hétépet.' *RdE* 16.55–146; 17.89–176; 18.67–142.

—— 1969, 'Un groupe du Louvre représentant la déesse Hathor sous quatre de ses aspects.' *Mélanges de l'Université Saint-Joseph* 45.159–83.

—— 1973, *Musée du Louvre. Le Département des antiquités égyptiennes. Guide sommaire.* (5th ed.), Paris.

Vandier d'Abbadie, J. 1937/1959, *Catalogue des ostraca figurés de Deir el Médineh.* IFAO Doc. 2, Cairo.

—— 1938, 'Une fresque civile de Deir el Médineh.' *RdE* 3.27–35.

—— 1940, 'Deux nouveaux ostraca figurés.' *ASAE* 40.467–88.

—— 1946, 'A propos des bustes de laraires.' *RdE* 5.133–5.

—— 1957, 'Deux ostraca figurés.' *BIFAO* 56.21–34.

—— 1972, *Catalogue des objets de toilette égyptiens au Musée du Louvre.* Paris.

Varille, A. 1956, 'La grande porte du temple d'Apet à Karnak.' *ASAE* 53.79–118.

te Velde, H. 1982, 'The Cat as Sacred Animal of the Goddess Mut.' In *Studies in Egyptian Religion Dedicated to Professor Jan Zandee,* ed. M. Heerma van Voss *et al.* 127–37.

—— 1988, 'Mut, the Eye of Re.' *SAK* Beiheft 3.395–404.

Venot, C. 1974, 'Le cimetière MX TD de Mirgissa.' *CRIPEL* 2.27–49.

Ventura, R. 1974, 'An Egyptian Rock Stela in Timna.' *Tel Aviv* 1.60–3.

Vercoutter, J. 1963, 'Fouilles à Mirgissa (Octobre–Novembre 1962).' *RdE* 15.69–75.

—— 1964, 'La stèle de Mirgissa IM. 209 et la localisation d'Iken (Kor ou Mirgissa?).' *RdE* 16.179–91.

—— 1964a–1965, 'Excavations at Mirgissa I–II.' *Kush* 12.57–62; 13.62–73.

—— 1970–6, *Mirgissa* I–III. Paris.

Vergnieux, R. 1982, 'Karnak 1908: Fouilles à l'est du lac sacré (manuscrit inédit du Docteur Lortet).' *Cahiers de Karnak* VII, 387–94. Cairo.

Vernier, E. 1907, *La bijouterie et la joaillerie égyptiennes.* IFAO Mem. 2, Cairo.

Vernus, P. 1983, 'Etudes de philologie et de linquistique (II).' *RdE* 34.115–28.

Verwers, G. J. 1961, 'Trial Excavations in the Faras Region.' *Kush* 9.15–29.

—— 1962, 'The Survey from Faras to Gezira Dabarosa.' *Kush* 10.19–33.

Wagner, G.–Quaegebeur, J. 1973, 'Une dédicace grecque au dieu égyptien Mestasytmis de la part de son synode.' *BIFAO* 73.41–60.

Wainwright, G. A. 1920, *Balabish.* EEF Mem. 37, London.

Wallert, I. Gamer- 1970, *Fische und Fischkulte im alten Ägypten.* Ägyptologische Abhandlungen 21, Wiesbaden.

Wall-Gordon, H. 1958, 'A New Kingdom Libation Basin Dedicated to Ptah. Second Part. The Inscriptions.' *MDAIK* 16.168–75.

Wallis, H. 1900, *Egyptian Ceramic Art.* [London].

Ward, W. A. 1986, *Essays on Feminine Titles of the Middle Kingdom and Related Subjects.* Beirut.

—— 1989, 'Non-Royal Women and their Occupations in the Middle Kingdom.' In B. Lesko 1989.33–43.

Watson, P.–Eastwood, G. 1983, *A Brief Guide to the Cataloguing of Archaeological Textiles.* York.

Weber, W. 1914, *Die ägyptisch-griechischen Terrakotten.* Königliche Museen zu Berlin, Mitteilungen aus der Ägyptischen Sammlung 2, Berlin.

Weigall, A. E. P. 1906, 'A Report on the Excavation of the Funeral Temple of Thoutmosis III at Gurneh.' *ASAE* 7.121–41.

—— 1907, 'Some Inscriptions in Prof. Petrie's Collection of Egyptian Antiquities.' *RT* 29.216–22.

Weill, R. 1904, *Recueil des inscriptions égyptiennes du Sinai.* Paris.

—— 1908, *La presqu'île du Sinai.* Paris.

Wein, E. J. 1963, *7000 Jahre Byblos.* Nüremberg.

Weinstein, J. M. 1973, *Foundation Deposits in Ancient Egypt.* Doctoral dissertation, University of Pennsylvania.

Wenig, S. 1967, *Die Frau im alten Ägypten.* Leipzig.

Wente, E. F. 1961, 'A Letter of Complaint to the Vizier To.' *JNES* 20.252–7.

—— 1967, *Late Ramesside Letters.* SAOC 33, Chicago.

—— 1969, 'Hathor at the Jubilee.' In Wilson 1969.83–91.

—— 1982, 'Mysticism in Pharaonic Egypt?' *JNES* 41.161–79.

Werbrouck, M. 1933, 'A propos du dieu Bes.' *Egyptian Religion* 1.28–32.

—— 1949, *Le temple d'Hatshepsout à Deir el Bahari.* Brussels.

—— 1953, 'Ostraca à figures.' *Bulletin de Musées Royaux d'Art et d'Histoire* 25.93–111.

West, S. 1969, 'The Greek Version of the Legend of Tefnut.' *JEA* 55.161–83.

Westendorf, W. 1966, *Altägyptische Darstellungen des Sonnenlaufes auf der abschüssigen Himmelsbahn.* MÄS 10, Berlin.

—— 1967, 'Bemerkungen zur "Kammer der Wiedergeburt" in Tutanchamungrab.' *ZÄS* 94.139–50.

—— 1977, 'Noch einmal: Die "Wiedergeburt" des heimgekehrten Sinuhe.' *SAK* 5.293–304.

Wheeler, N. F. 1961, 'Diary of the Excavation of Mirgissa Fort. 14 November 1931 to 3 February 1932.' *Kush* 9.87–179.

Whitehead, H. 1921, *The Village Gods of Southern India.* London.

Wiedemann, A. [1915], 'Varia XVIII.' *Sphinx* 18.167–72.

Wild, H. 1963, 'Les danses sacrées de l'Egypte ancienne.' In *Les danses sacrées.* Sources Orientales 6, 33–118. Paris.

Wildung, D. 1974, 'Zwei Stelen aus Hatschepsuts Frühzeit.' *Festschrift zum 150jährigen Bestehen des Berliner Ägyptischen Museums* 255–68. Berlin (East).

—— 1977, 'Felstempel.' *LÄ* 2.161–7.

Wildung, D. (ed.) 1985, *Entdeckungen. Ägyptische Kunst in Süddeutschland.* Mainz.

Wilkinson, A. 1971, *Ancient Egyptian Jewellery.* London.

Wilkinson, J. G. 1835, *Topography of Thebes and General View of Egypt.* London.

—— 1843, *Modern Egypt and Thebes.* London.

—— 1878, *The Manners and Customs of the Ancient Egyptians.* (new ed., revised by S. Birch), London.

Williams, C. R. 1924, *Gold and Silver Jewelry and Related Objects. Catalogue of Egyptian Antiquities Numbers 1–160.* New York Historical Society, New York.

Wilson, J. A. 1969, *Studies in Honor of John A. Wilson.* SAOC 35, Chicago.

Wilson, V. 1975, 'The Iconography of Bes.' *Levant* 7.77–103.

van Wijngaarden, W. D. 1936, 'Objects of Tutʿankhamūn in the Rijksmuseum of Antiquities at Leiden.' *JEA* 22.1–2.

Winlock, H. E. 1921, 'Excavations at Thebes.' *BMMA* 16, November II.29–53.

—— 1922, 'Excavations at Thebes.' *BMMA* 17, December II.19–49.

—— 1923, 'The Museum's Excavations at Thebes.' *BMMA* 18, December II.11–39.

—— 1924, 'The Museum's Excavations at Thebes.' *BMMA* 19, December II.5–33.

—— 1926, 'The Museum's Excavations at Thebes.' *BMMA* 21, March II.5–32.

—— 1928, 'The Museum's Excavations at Thebes.' *BMMA* 23, February II.3–58; December II.3–28.

—— 1929, 'The Museum's Excavations at Thebes.' *BMMA* 24, November II.3–34.

—— 1930, 'The Museum's Excavations at Thebes.' *BMMA* 25, December II.3–28.

—— 1932, 'The Museum's Excavations at Thebes.' *BMMA* 27, March II.4–37.

—— 1936, 'An Egyptian Flower Bowl.' *Metropolitan Museum Studies* 5.147–56.

—— 1942, *Excavations at Deir el Baḥri 1911–1931*. New York.

—— 1948, *The Treasure of Three Egyptian Princesses*. New York.

de Wit, C. 1951, *Le rôle et le sens du lion dans l'Egypte ancienne*. Leiden.

Woldering, I. 1955, *Ausgewählte Werke der aegyptischen Sammlung*. Bildkataloge des Kestner-Museums, Hannover I. Hannover.

Wreszinski, W. 1923–1942, *Atlas zur altägyptischen Kulturgeschichte* I–III. Leipzig.

Wysocki, Z. 1985, 'The Temple of Queen Hatshepsut at Deir el Bahari.' *MDAIK* 41.293–307.

—— 1986, 'The Temple of Queen Hatshepsut at Deir el Bahari: Its Original Form.' *MDAIK* 42.213–28.

Yeivin, S. 1976, 'Canaanite Ritual Vessels in Egyptian Cultic Practices.' *JEA* 62.110–4.

Yoyotte, J. 1960, 'Les pèlerinages dans l'Egypte ancienne.' In *Les pèlerinages*. Sources Orientales 3, 19–74. Paris.

Žába, Z. 1974, *The Rock Inscriptions of Lower Nubia (Czechoslovak Concession)*. Czechoslovak Institute of Egyptology in Prague and in Cairo, Publications I, Prague.

Zayed, Abdel Hamid 1962, 'Some Notes on a Statuette of a Cow.' *ASAE* 57.137–42.

Ziegler, C. 1979, *Catalogue des instruments de musique égyptiens au Musée du Louvre*. Paris.

—— 1984, 'Sistrum.' *LÄ* 5.959–63.

Zivie, A. P. (ed.) 1988, *Memphis et ses nécropoles au Nouvel Empire*. Paris.

Zivie, C. [1976], *Giza au deuxième millénaire*. IFAO Bibliothèque d'Etude 70, Cairo.

Index

Museums are indexed under the names of the cities in which they are situated. Museum inventory numbers are not included. Archaeological expeditions are listed under 'expedition'. Only scholars who excavated at the principal cites discussed or who produced relevant primary publications are included in the index. 'Hathor', 'shrine', 'temple', and the 18th and 19th dynasties are not indexed.

PLANS

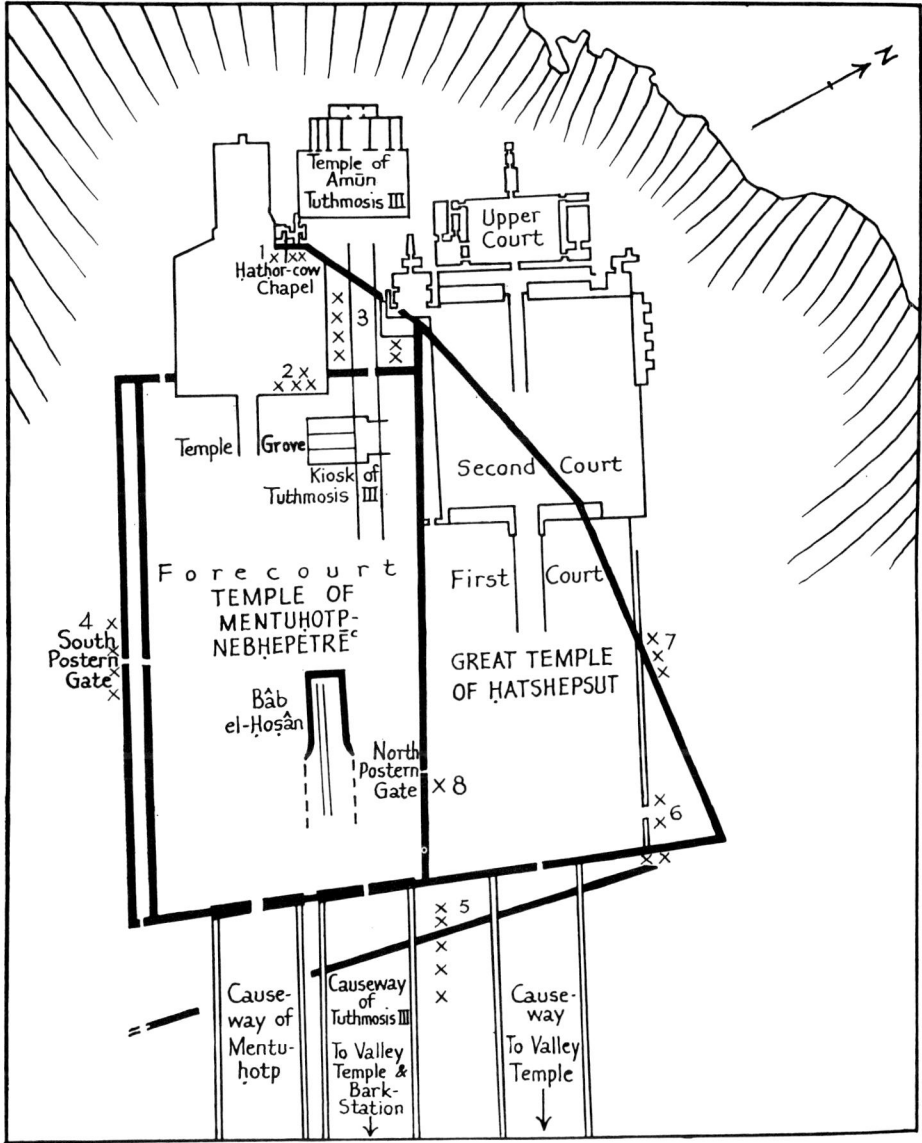

Plan of the three main temples at Deir el-Bahri showing the main deposits of votive offerings

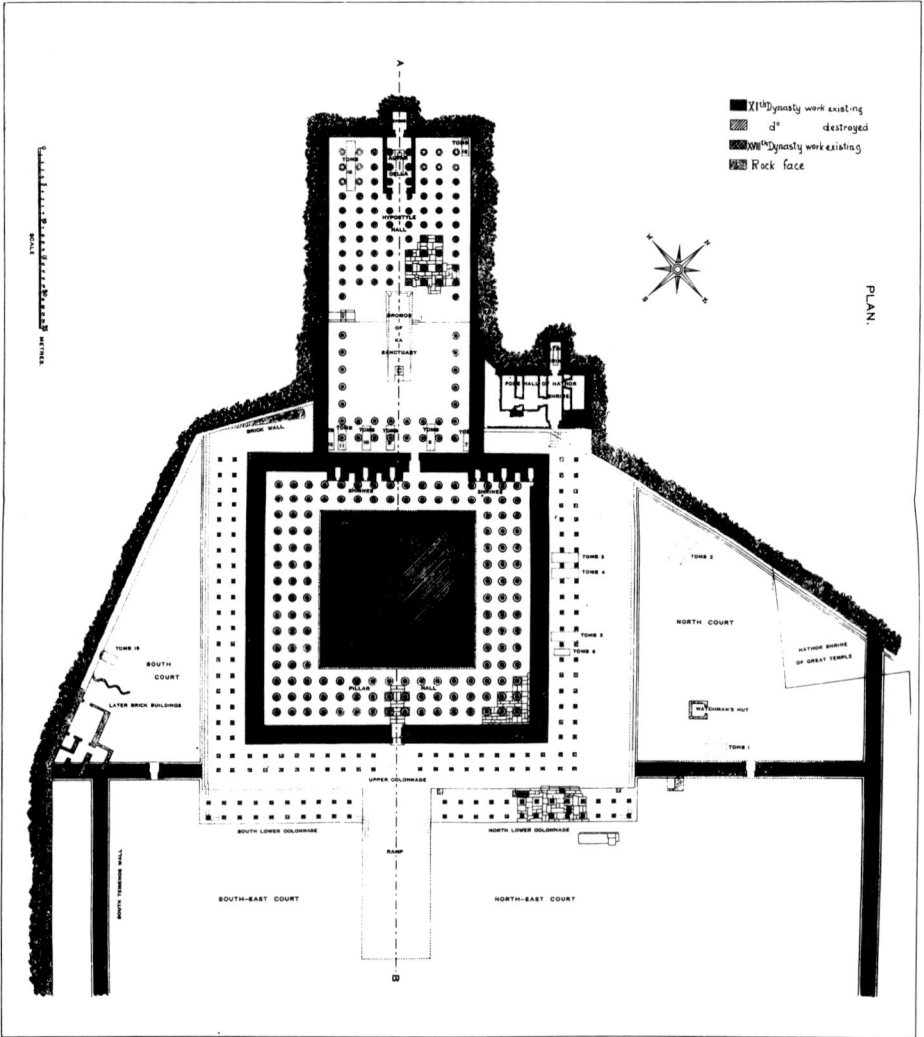

Plan of Akh-isut, the 11th dynasty temple at Deir el-Bahri

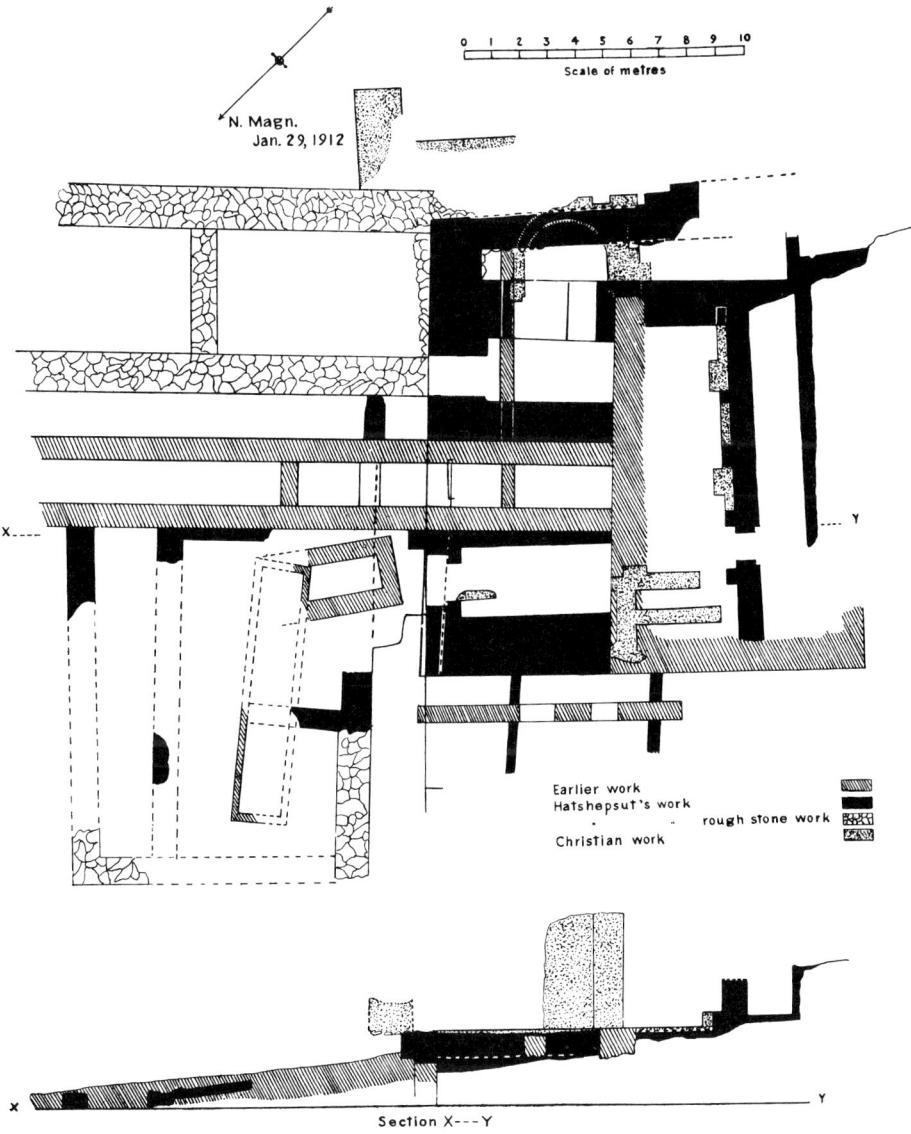

N. Magn.
Jan. 29, 1912

0 1 2 3 4 5 6 7 8 9 10
Scale of metres

Earlier work
Hatshepsut's work
Christian work
rough stone work

Section X---Y

Plan of the Hathor temple at Faras

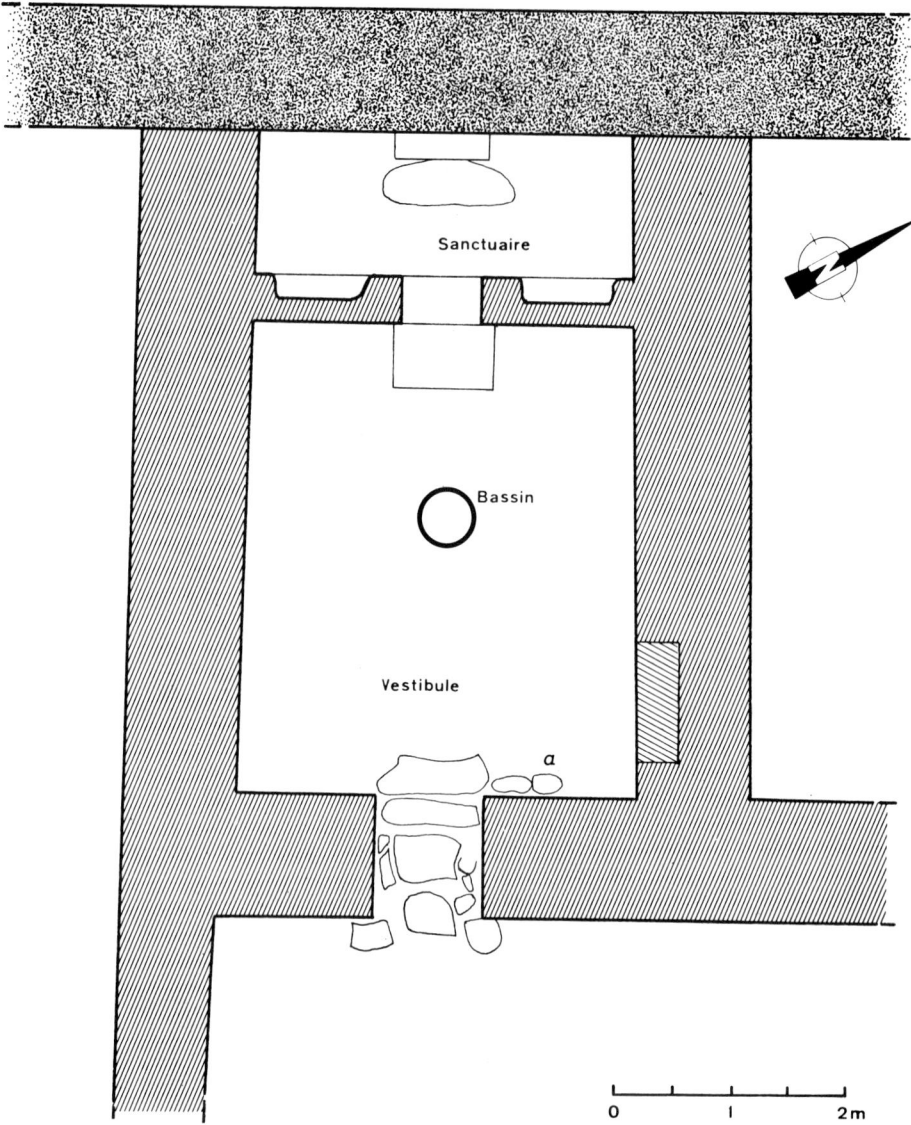

Sanctuaire

Bassin

Vestibule

a

0   1   2m

Plan of the Hathor shrine at Mirgissa

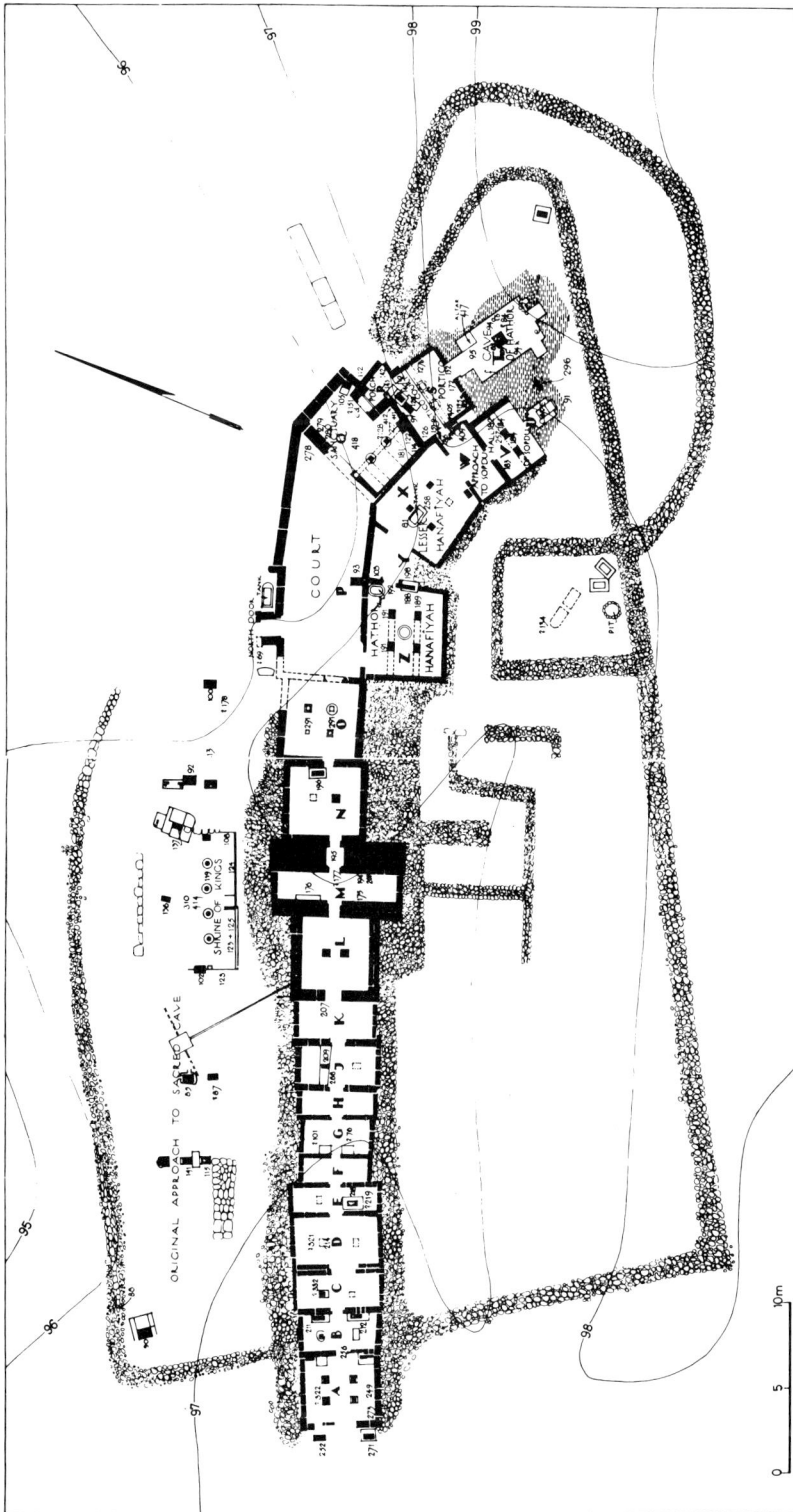

PLAN 5

Plan of the Hathor temple at Serabit el-Khadim

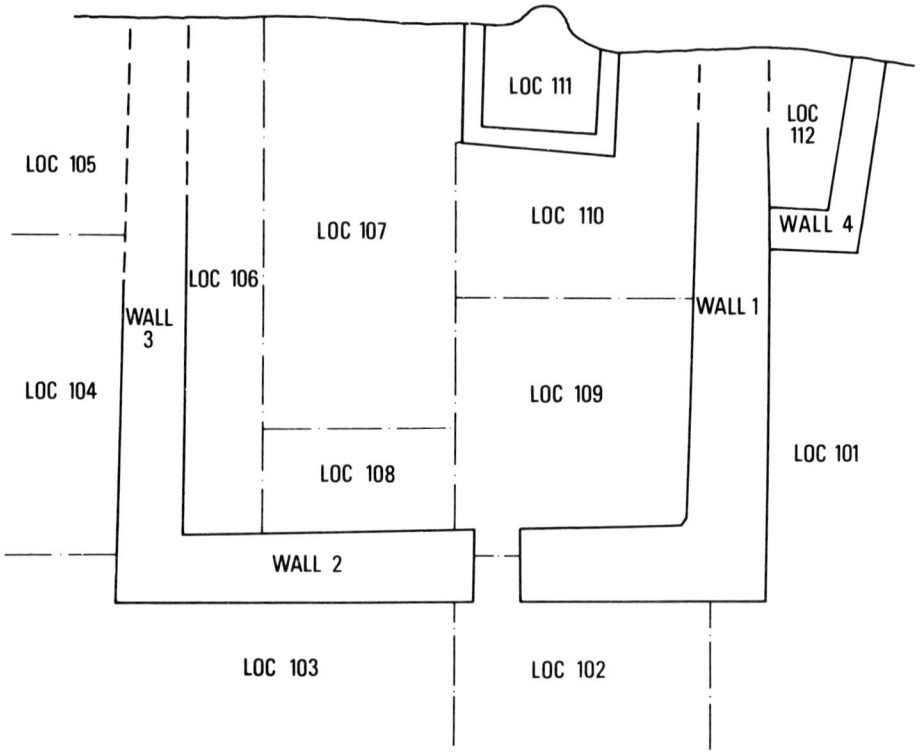

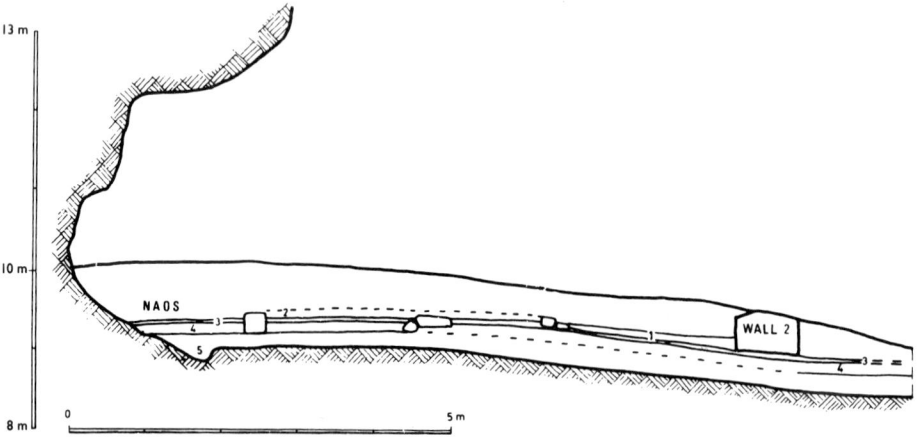

Plan of the Hathor shrine at Timna

FIGURES

FIGURE I

Votive objects from the 1903–7 EEF excavations at Deir el-Bahri

FIGURE 2

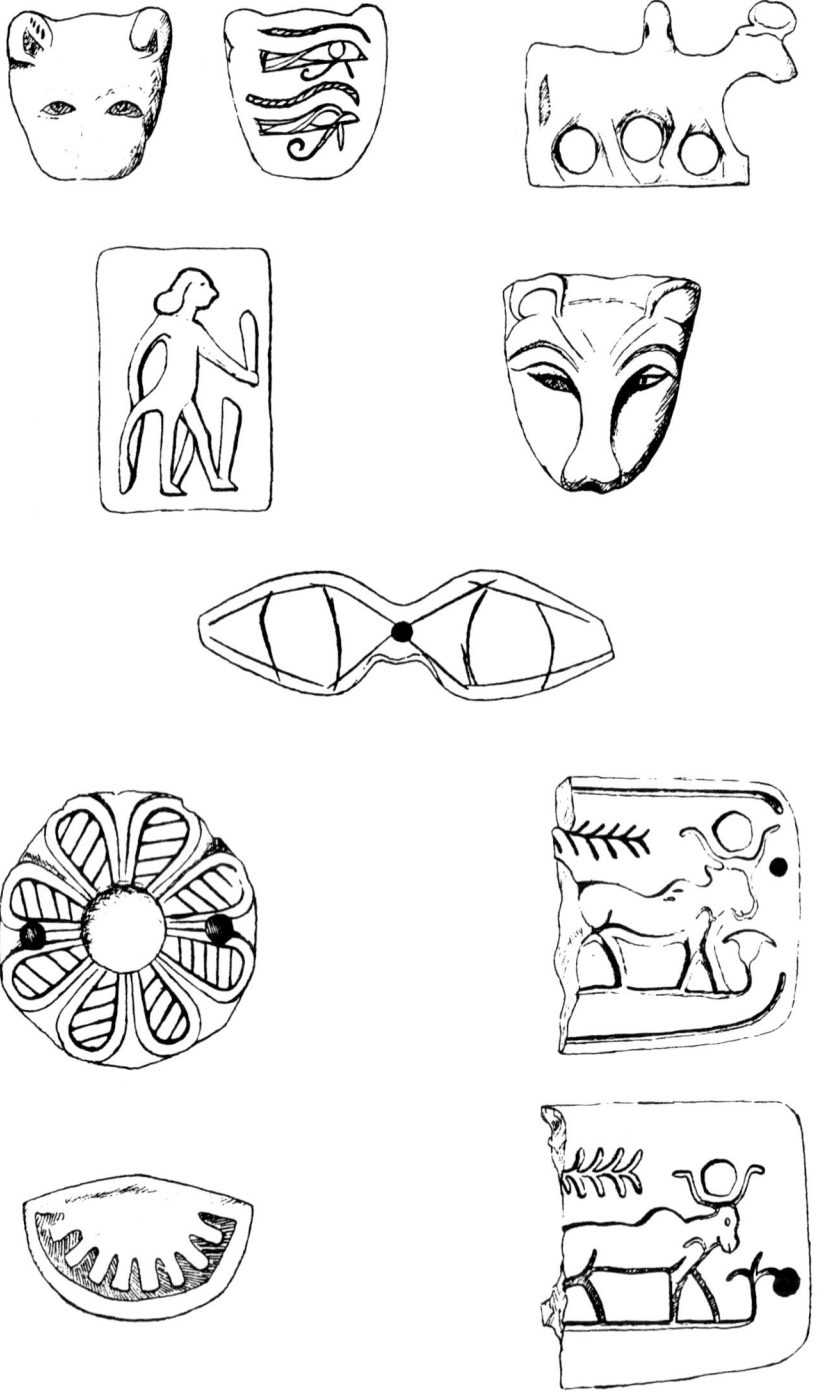

Drawings of votive objects from the EEF excavations at Deir el-Bahri

FIGURE 3

Drawings of scarabs and scaraboids from the EEF excavations at Deir el-Bahri

FIGURE 4

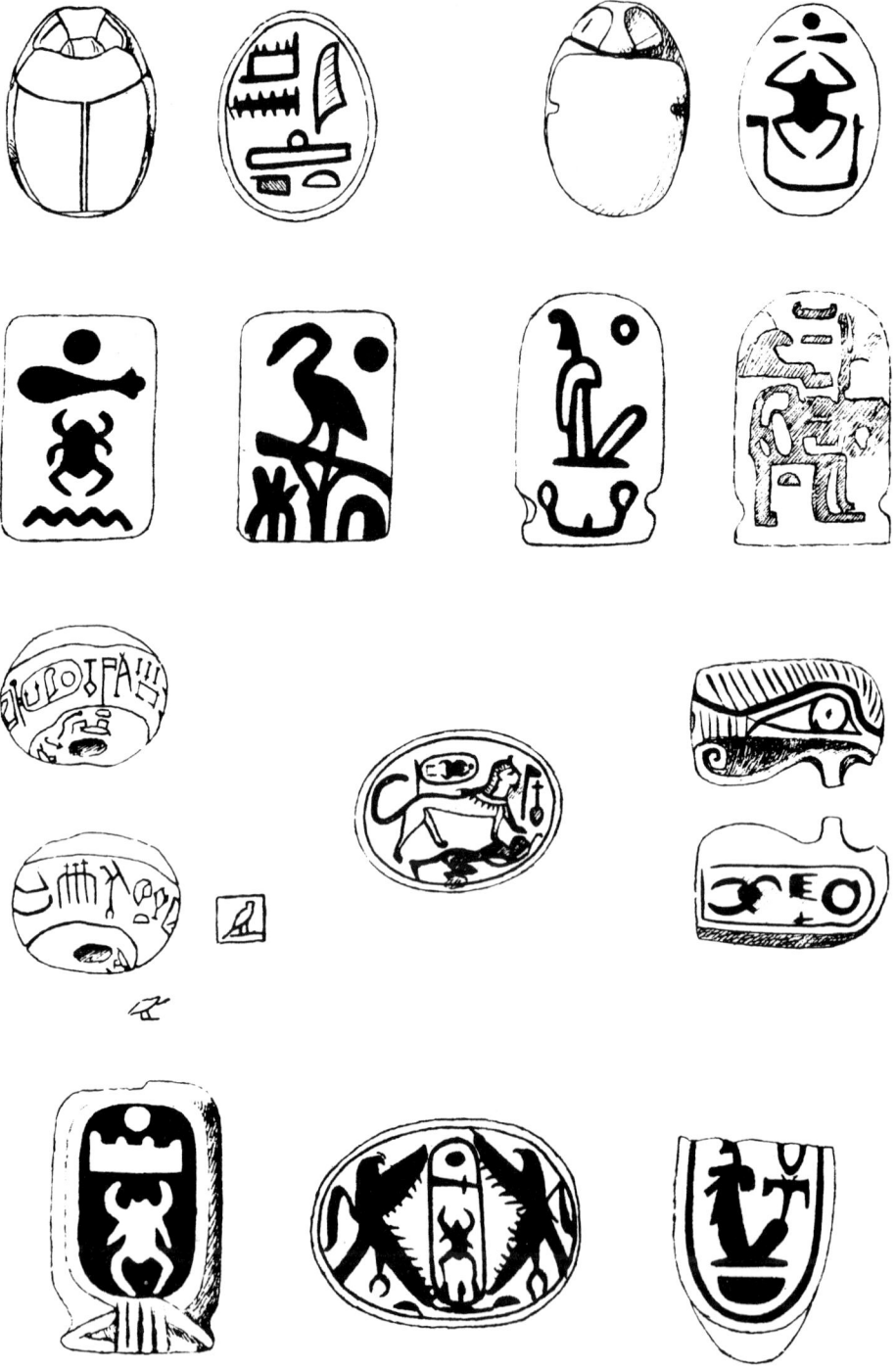

Drawings of objects with royal names from the EEF excavations at Deir el-Bahri

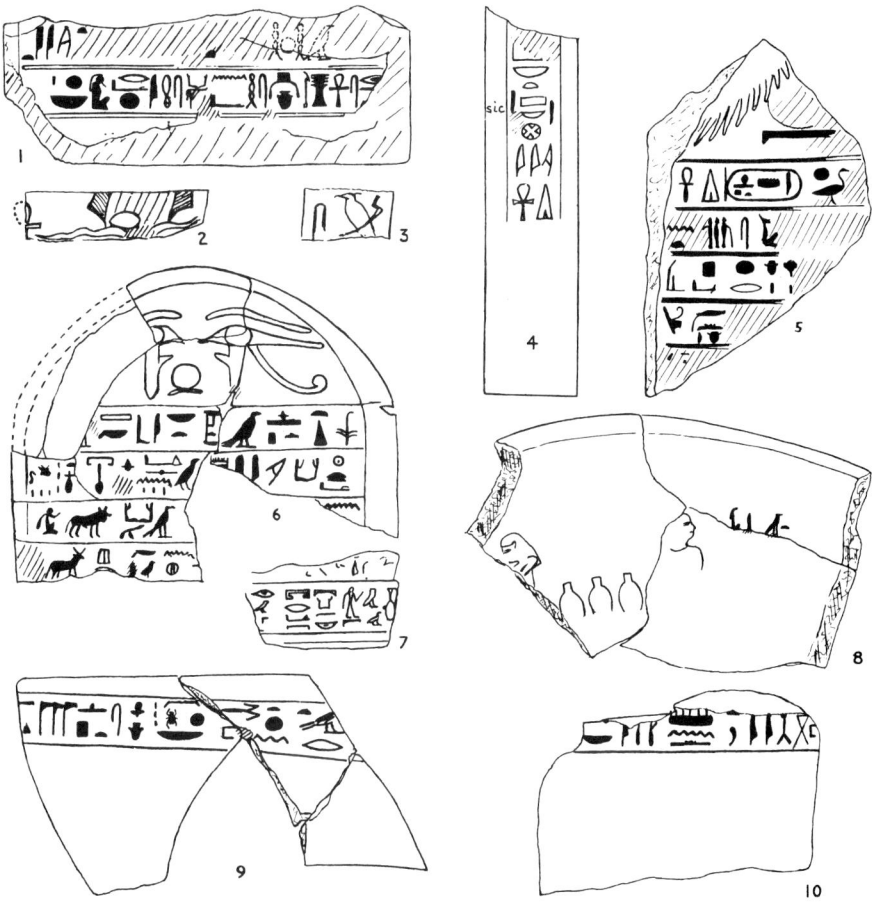

FIGURE 5

Temple

Speos

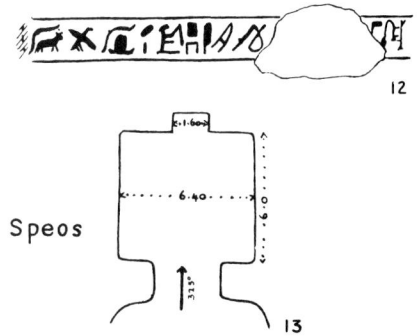

Inscribed pieces from the Hathor temple and grotto at Faras

FIGURE 6

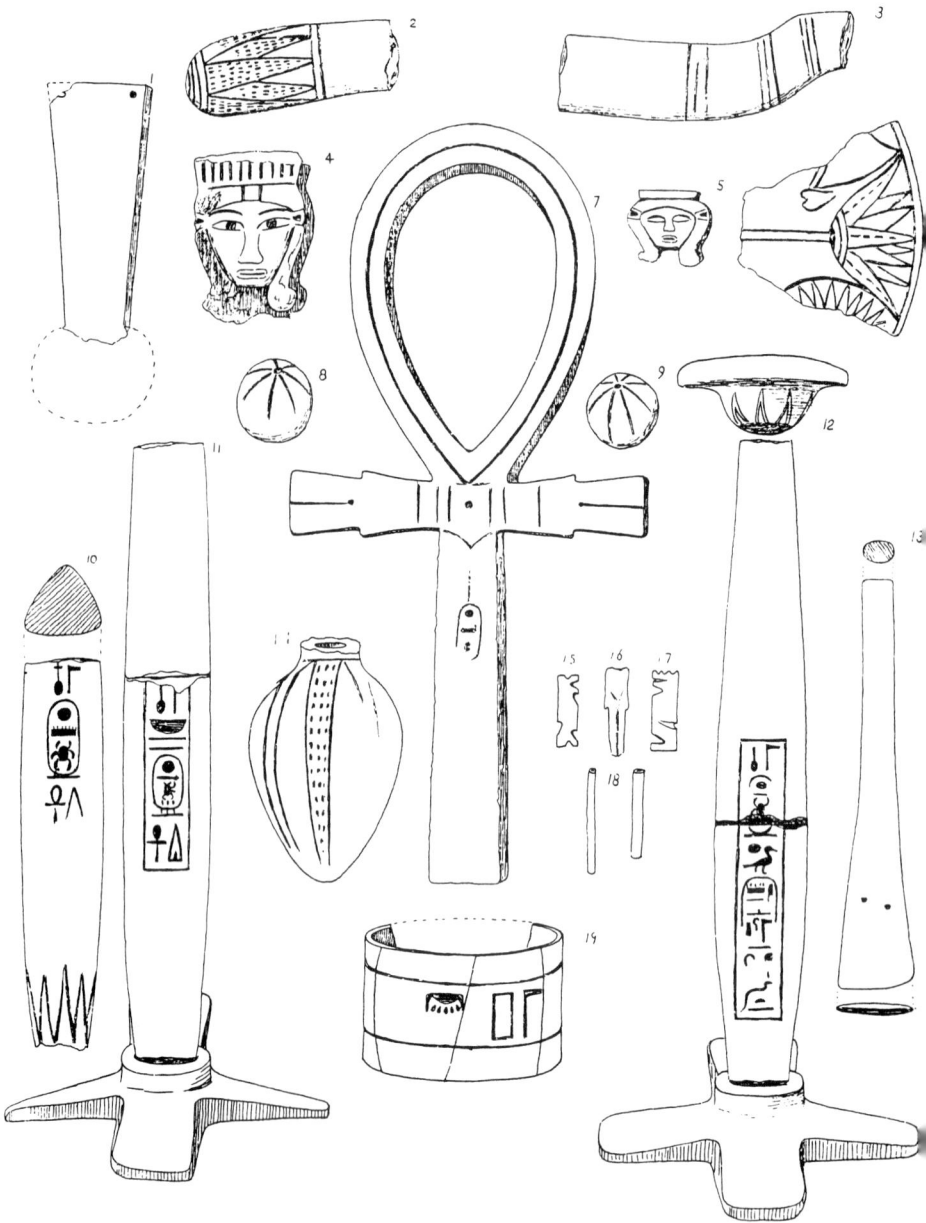

Votive offerings from Dendara

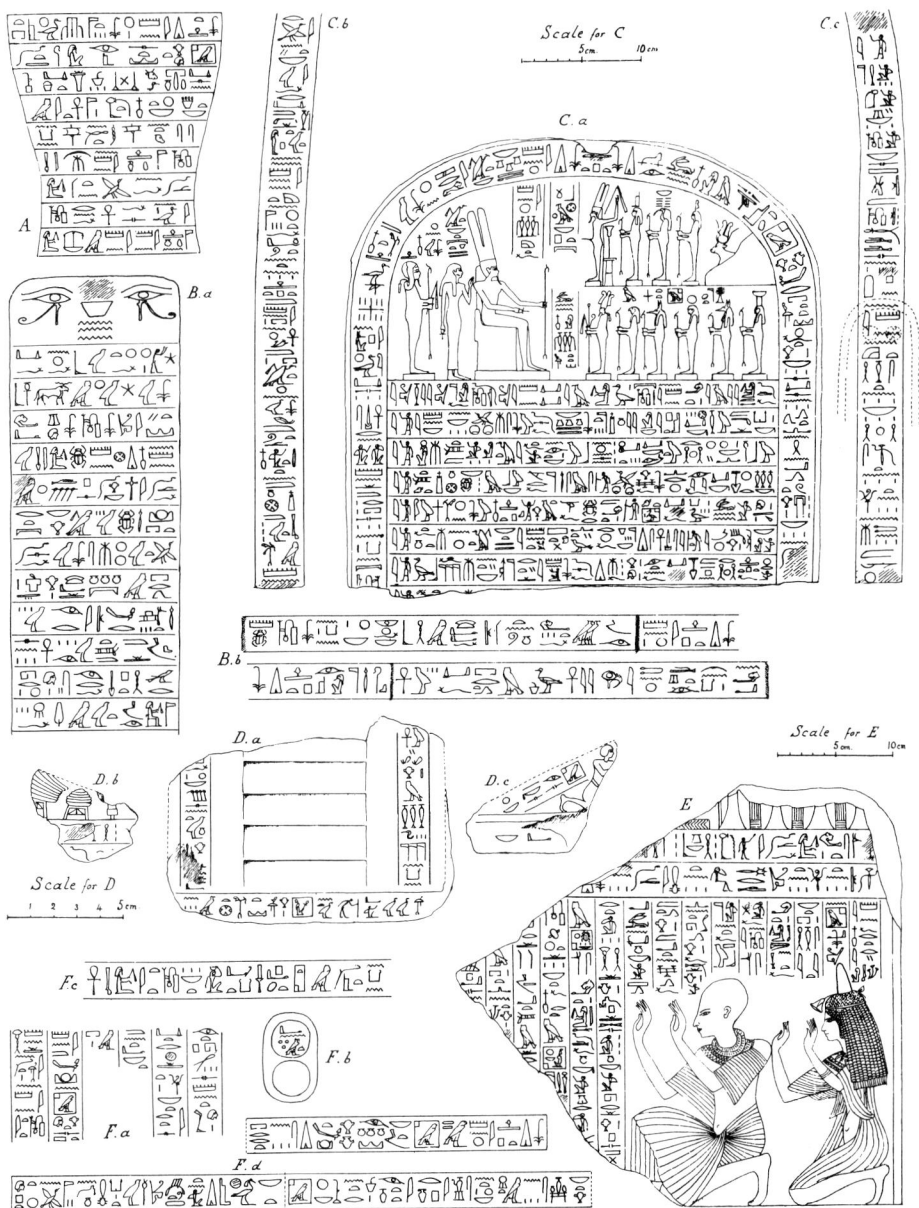

FIGURE 7

Inscribed stelae and statues from the 11th dynasty temple at Deir el-Bahri

FIGURE 8

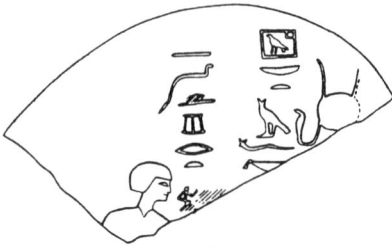

226

233

234

235

Votive stelae from Serabit el-Khadim

FIGURE 9

236

239

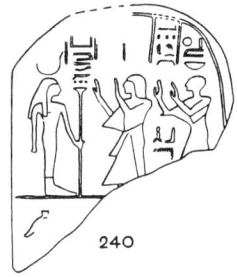

240

242

243

306

Votive stelae from Serabit el-Khadim

FIGURE 10

A) Votive cloth from Deir el-Bahri, Toronto ROM 910.16.1

B) Votive cloth from Deir el-Bahri

FIGURE 11

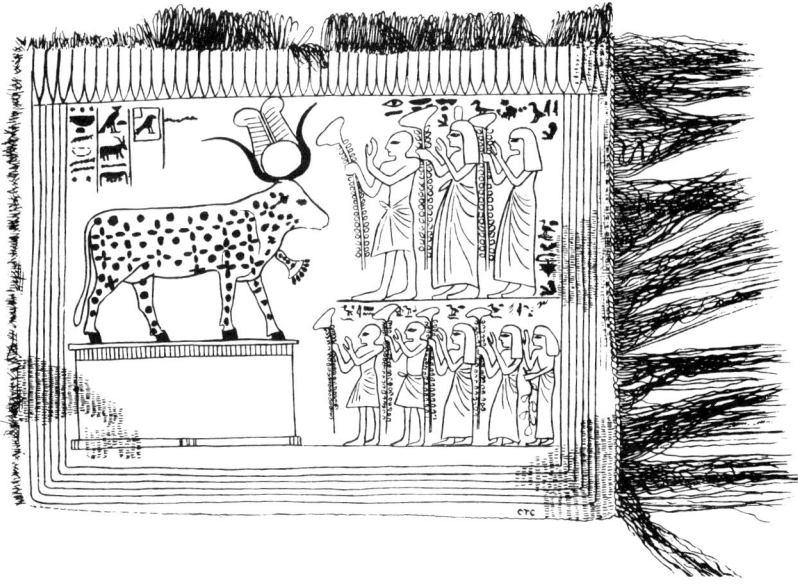

A) Votive cloth from Deir el-Bahri

B) Votive cloth from Deir el-Bahri

FIGURE 12

Votive cloth from the 11th dynasty temple at Deir el-Bahri, Boston MFA E 42. 81

FIGURE 13

A) Scene from Theban Tomb 68 showing sacred cows

B) Vignette from Chapter 186 of 'The Book of the Dead'

FIGURE 14

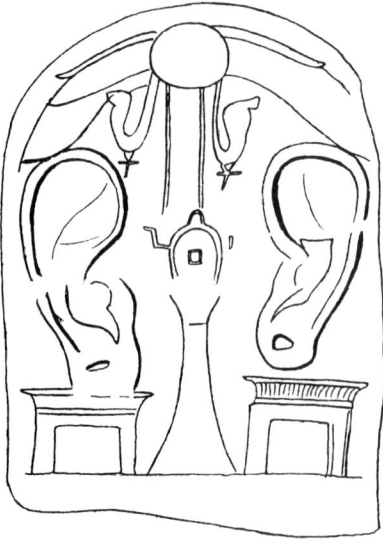

A) Type 1 ear stela from the temple of Ptah at Memphis

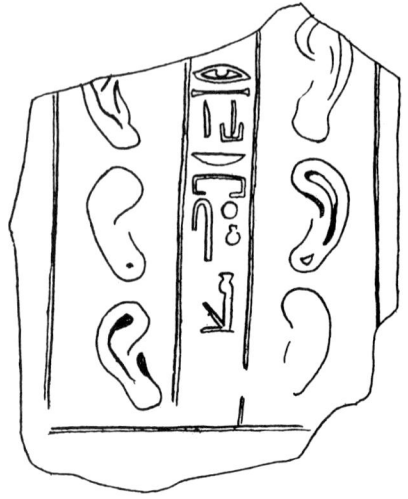

B) Type 1 ear stela from the temple of Ptah at Memphis

C) Type 2 ear stela from near the temple of Ptah at Memphis

D) Type 3 ear stela from the temple of Ptah at Memphis

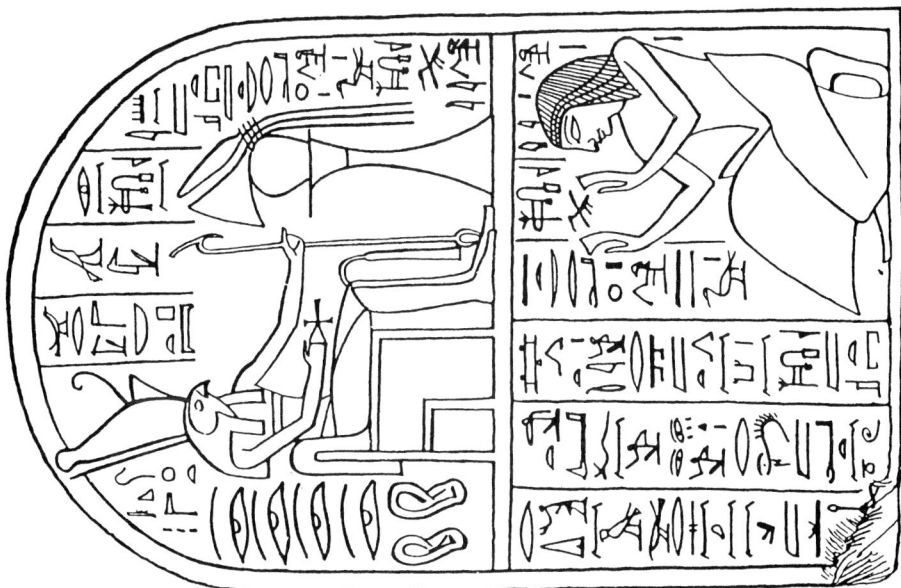

FIGURE 15

B) Type 4 ear and eye stela from Deir el-Medina

A) Type 4 ear stela from the temple of Ptah at Memphis

FIGURE 16

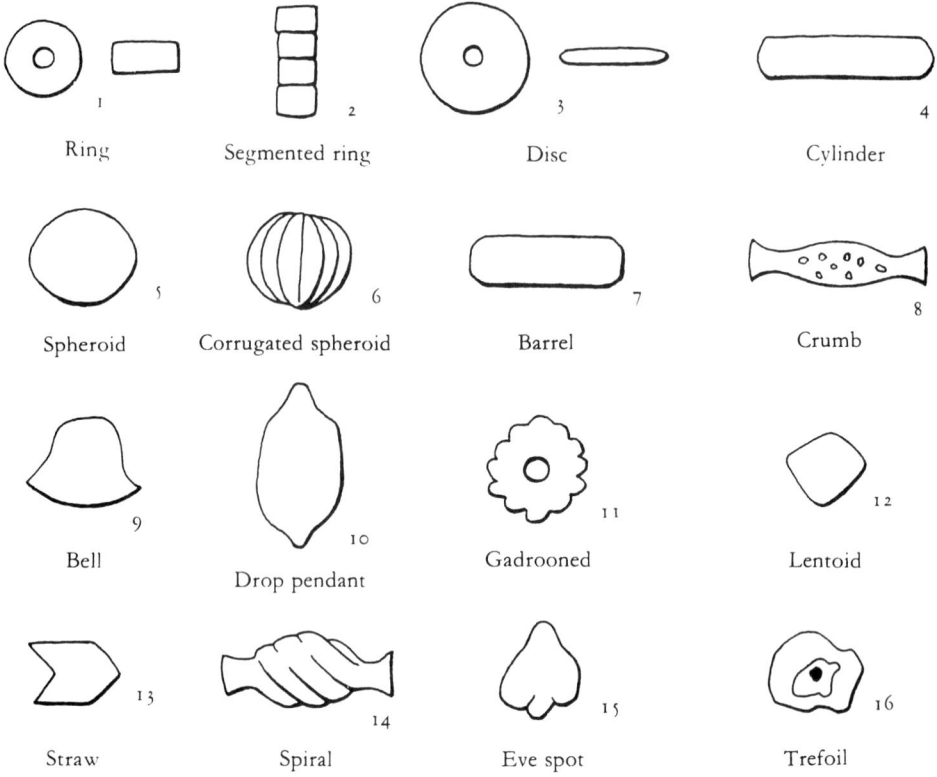

Drawings of Bead Types

FIGURE 17

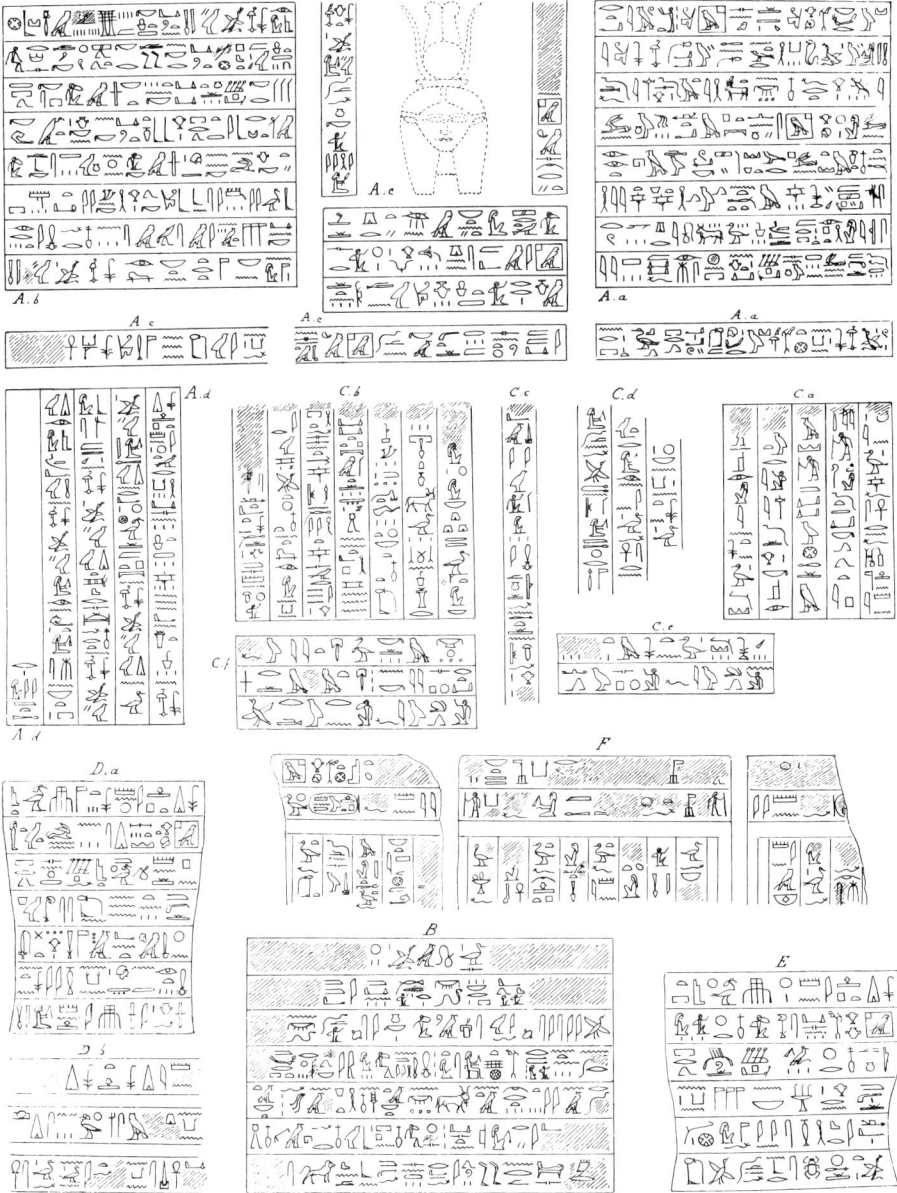

Statue texts from the 11th dynasty temple at Deir el-Bahri

FIGURE 18

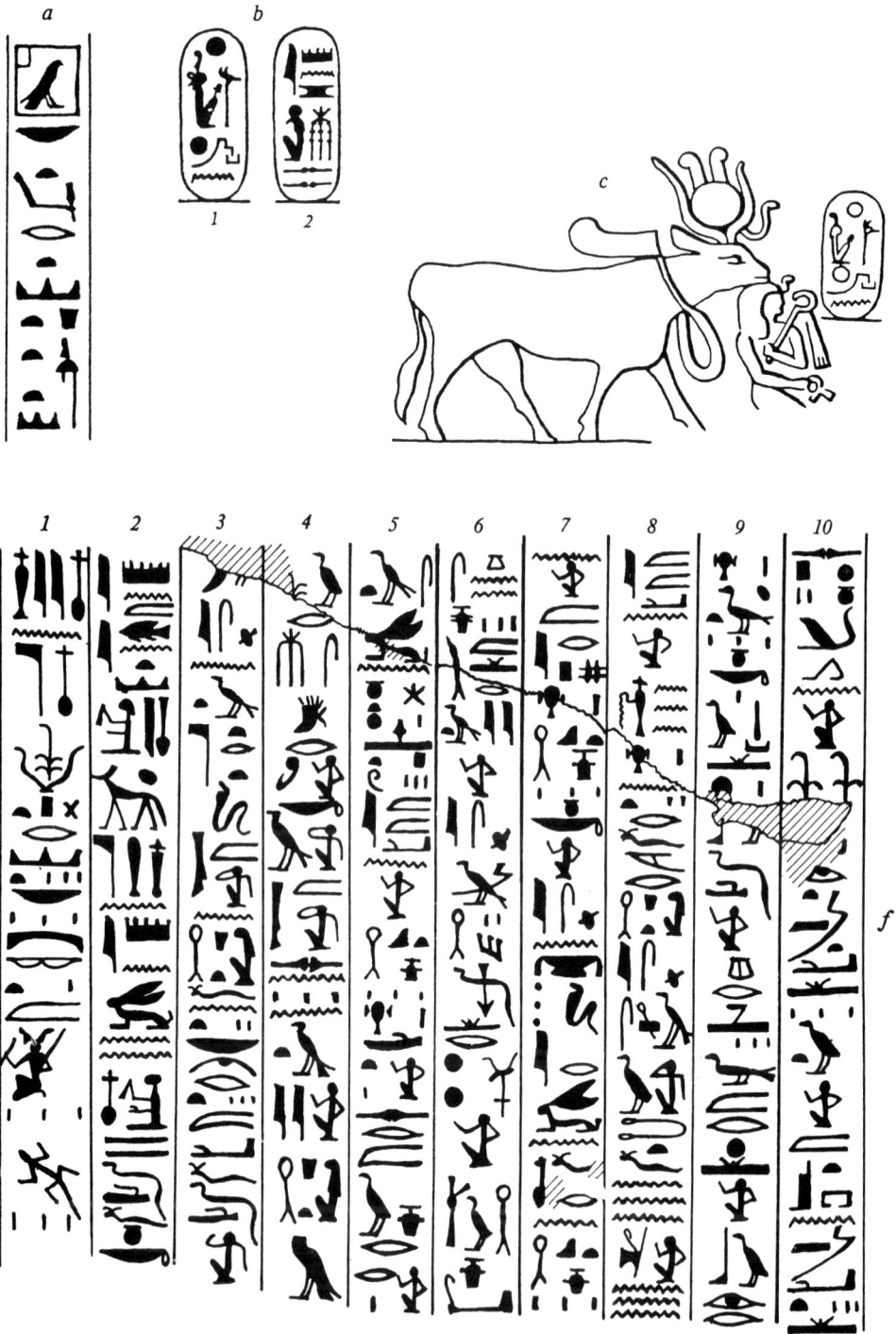

Detail of incised Hathor cow and texts from the 'intermediary statue' of Amoneminet from the temple of Thutmose III at Deir el-Bahri

PLATES

PLATE I

Votive objects from the EEF excavations of the 11th dynasty temple at Deir el-Bahri

PLATE 2

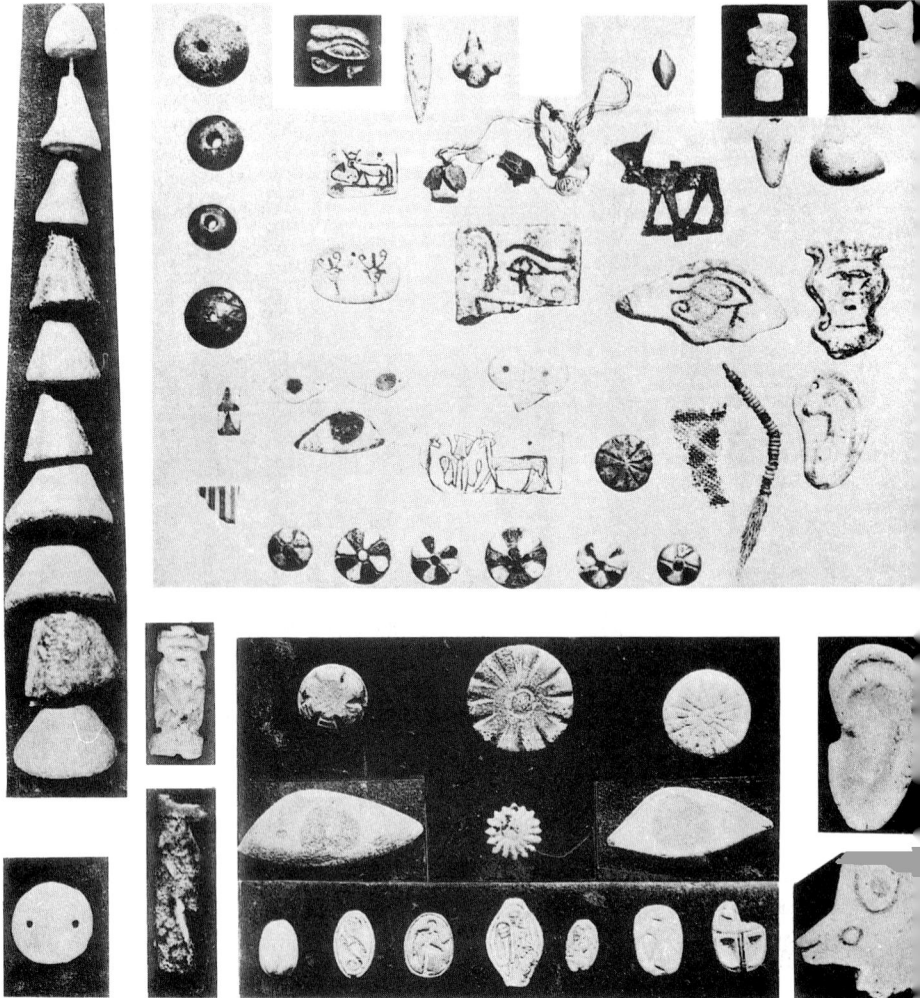

Votive objects from the EEF excavations of the 11th dynasty temple at Deir el-Bahri

PLATE 3

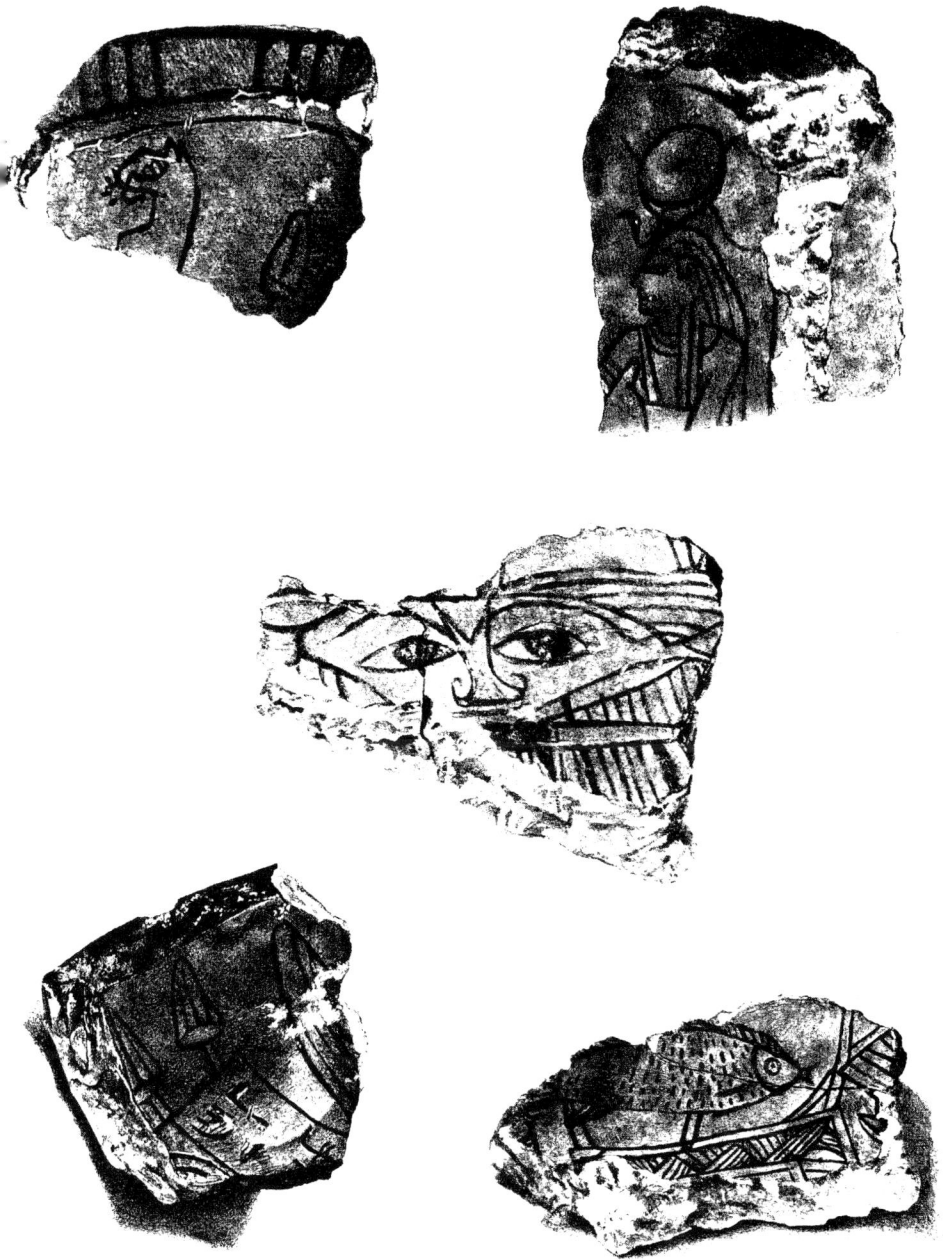

aintings of votive faience from the EEF excavations at Deir el-Bahri

PLATE 4

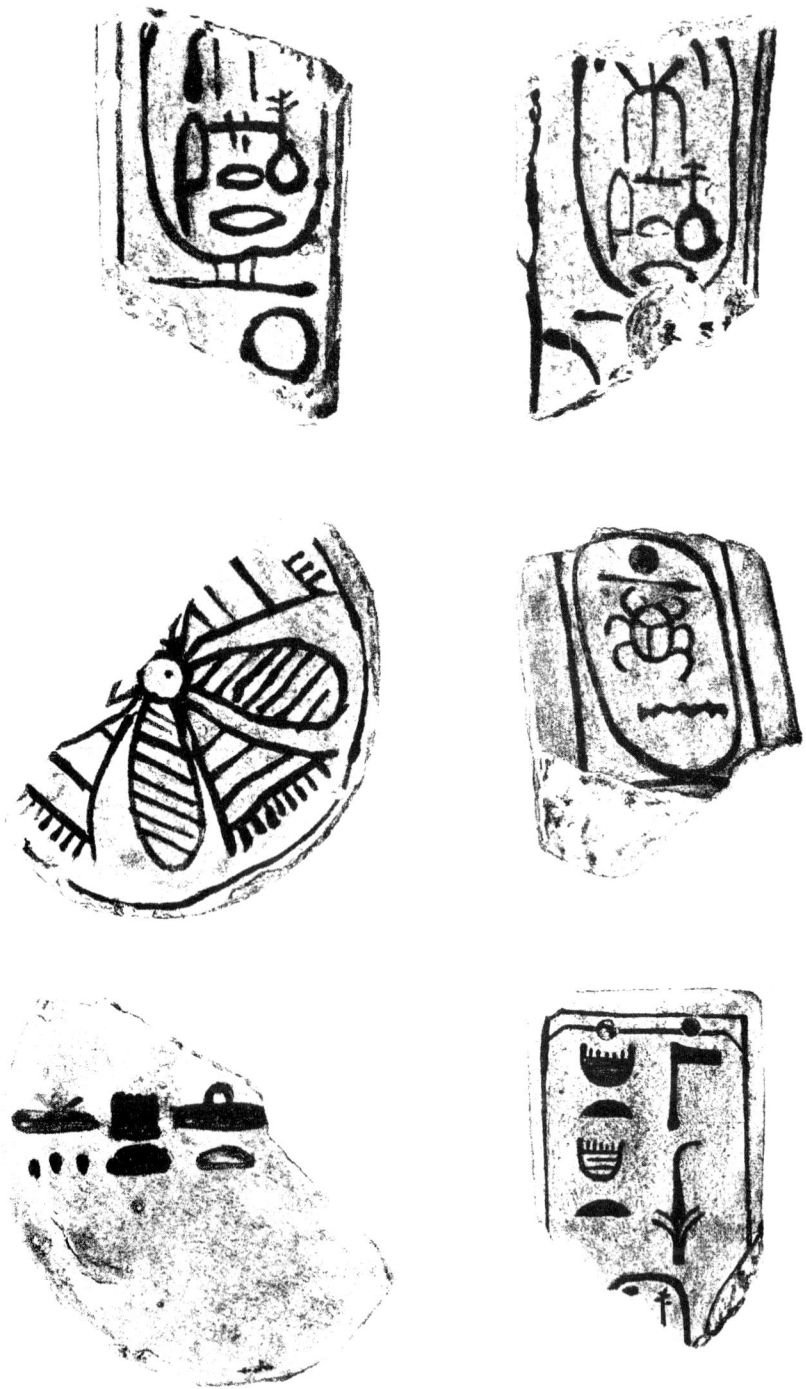

Paintings of menit counterpoises from the EEF excavations at Deir el-Bahri

PLATE 5

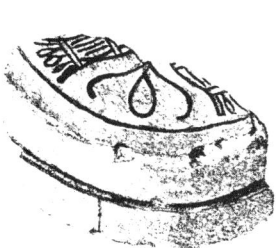

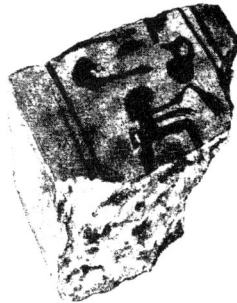

Paintings of menit counterpoises from the EEF excavations at Deir el-Bahri

PLATE 6

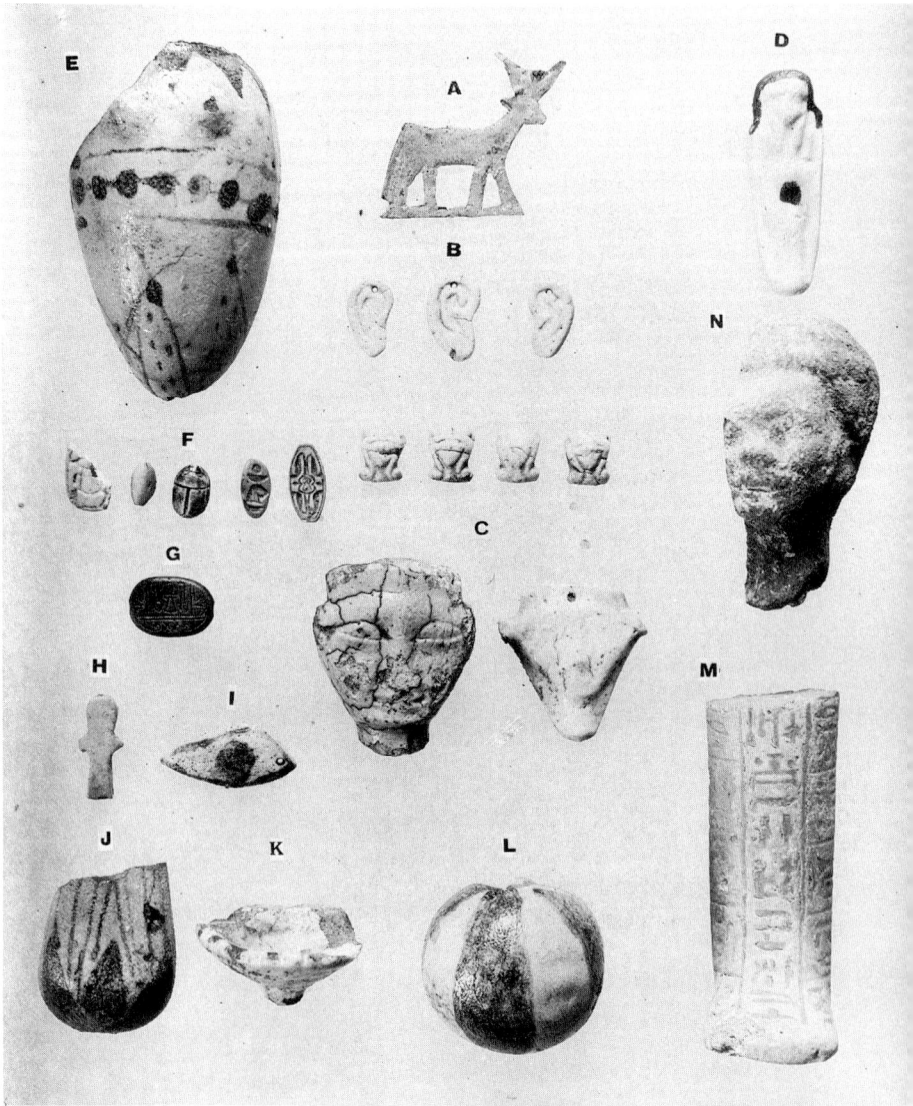

Votive objects found by Carter and Carnarvon at Deir el-Bahri

PLATE 7

Votive objects found by Carter and Carnarvon at Deir el-Bahri

PLATE 8

Votive objects found by Griffith at the Faras Hathor temple

PLATE 9

Votive stelae with Hathor cows and an alabaster cow's head from the 11th dynasty temple at Deir el-Bahri

PLATE 10

Wooden stela from the 11th dynasty temple at Deir el-Bahri, Manchester 4404

PLATE 11

Painted stone stela from the 11th dynasty temple at Deir el-Bahri, Bristol H 520

PLATE 12

Stela fragments from the 11th dynasty temple at Deir el-Bahri
A) Bolton 48.04.26
B) Ilkley CC 7145

PLATE 13

A–B) Double sided stela from Serabit el-Khadim, Brussels MR E 2474

PLATE 14

A) Stela from Serabit el-Khadim, Brussels MR E 3084

B) Votive shirt, probably from Deir el-Bahri, Berlin E 17568

PLATE 15

Votive cloth from the 11th dynasty temple at Deir el-Bahri, London BM 43216

PLATE 16

A) Votive cloth from Deir el-Bahri, London BM 65348

B) Votive cloth from Deir el-Bahri

PLATE 17

Votive shirt, probably from Deir el-Bahri, Boston MFA E 52.28

PLATE 18

A) Fragmentary votive cloth from the 11th dynasty temple at Deir el-Bahri, London V & A 468.190

B) Votive cloth from Deir el-Bahri, London BM 43215

PLATE 19

Votive shirt, probably from Deir el-Bahri, Boston MFA 52.29

PLATE 20

Votive shirt, probably from Deir el-Bahri, London BM 43071

PLATE 21

A) Votive cloth from the 11th dynasty temple at Deir el-Bahri, Toronto ROM 910.16.5

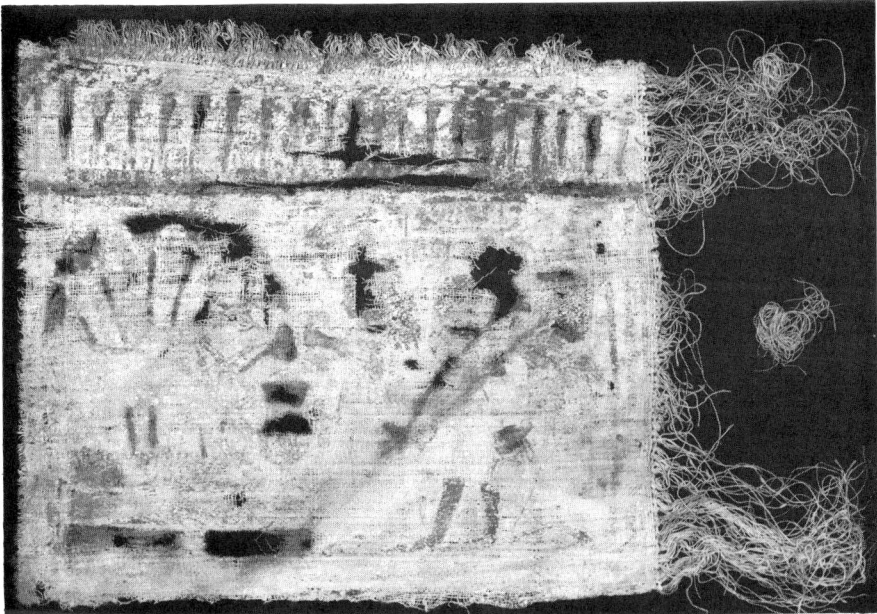

B) Votive cloth from the 11th dynasty temple at Deir el-Bahri, Toronto ROM 910.16.6

PLATE 22

A) Votive cloth from the 11th dynasty temple at Deir el-Bahri, Berlin E 17579

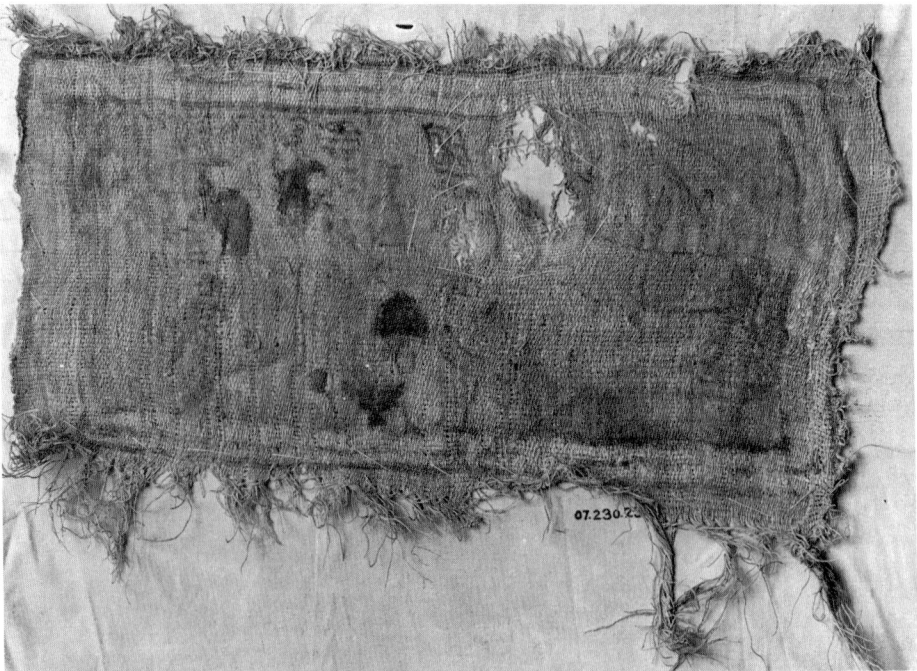

B) Votive cloth from the 11th dynasty temple at Deir el-Bahri, New York MMA 07.230.23

PLATE 23

Votive cloth from the 11th dynasty temple at Deir el-Bahri, London BM 47805

PLATE 24

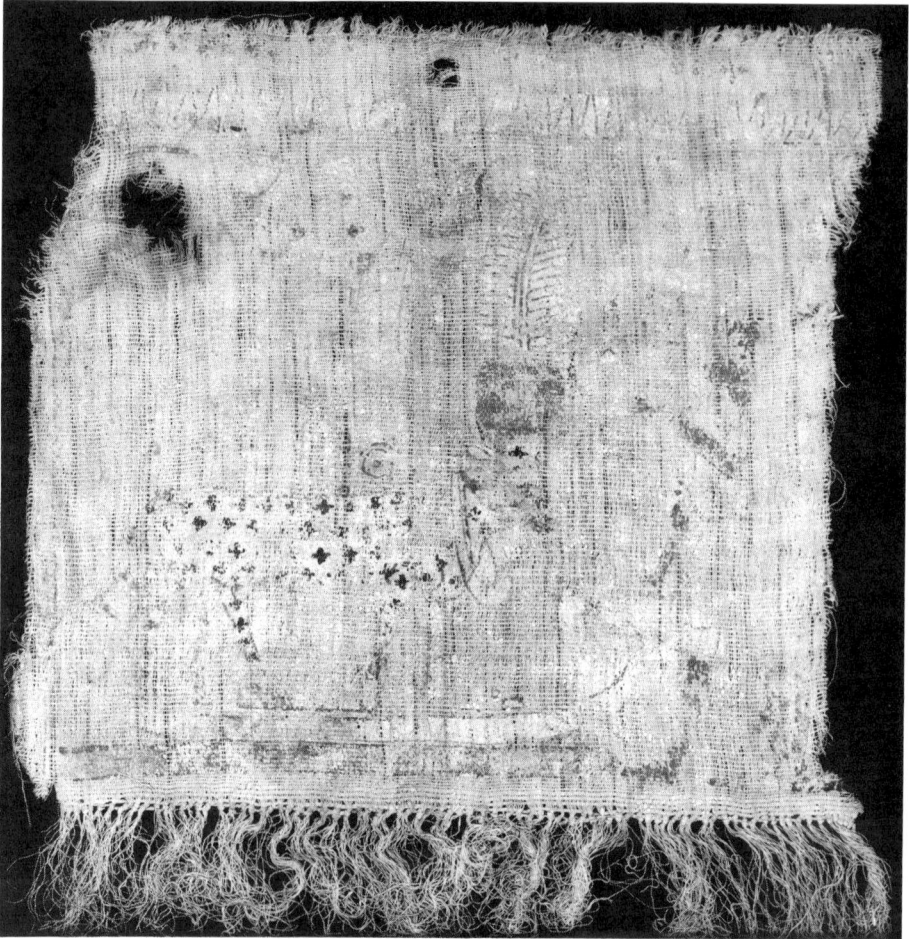

Votive cloth from the 11th dynasty temple at Deir el-Bahri, Toronto ROM 910.16.2

PLATE 25

A) Votive cloth from Deir el-Bahri, Leningrad H 2400

B) Votive cloth from Deir el-Bahri, Huntingdon, Long Island, HM 59.294

PLATE 26

A) Votive cloth from the 11th dynasty temple at Deir el-Bahri, Toronto ROM 910.16.4

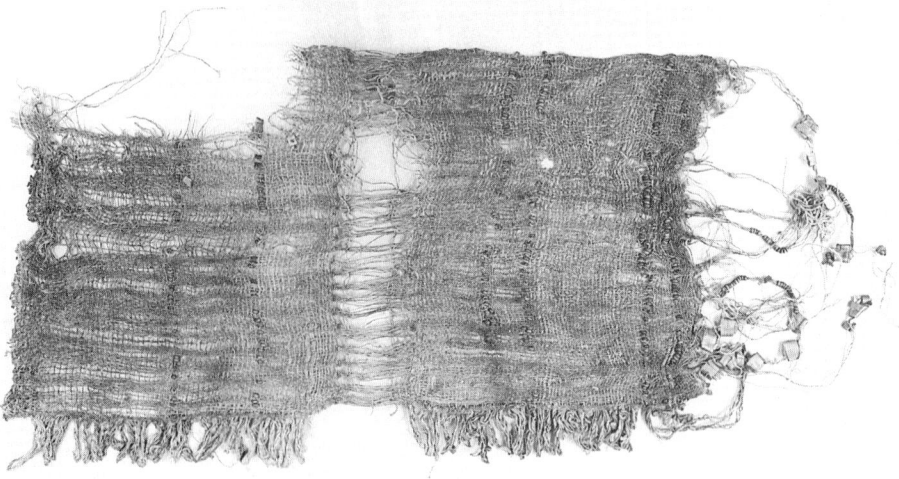

B) Votive cloth from the 11th dynasty temple at Deir el-Bahri, London V&A 1907.730

PLATE 27

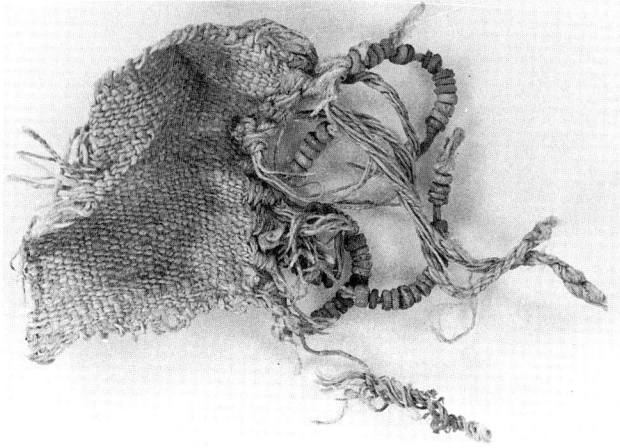

A) Fragment of votive textile from the 11th dynasty temple at Deir el-Bahri, Oxford PR 1904.35.84

B) Fragment of votive textile from the 11th dynasty temple at Deir el-Bahri, London V&A 1907.729

C) Stone Hathor mask from miniature column from Deir el-Bahri, London BM 4100

D) Faience Hathor mask from Deir el-Bahri, Toronto ROM 907.18.169

PLATE 28

A) Top row: unifrontal faience Hathor masks from
   Deir el-Bahri, Oxford PR 1906.45.15, 14
   Bottom row: unifrontal faience Hathor masks
   from Deir el-Bahri, London BM 41091, 41088

B) Faience bifrontal Hathor mask from Deir el-
   Bahri, Toronto ROM 907.18.168

PLATE 29

Faience Hathor masks, miniature columns and sistra from Serabit el-Khadim

PLATE 30

A) Part of a faience Hathor mask loop sistrum from Deir el-Bahri, London BM 43145

B) Fragments of a faience loop sistrum from Serabit el-Khadim, London V&A 720.1905

C) Flat faience Hathor mask from Serabit el-Khadim, London BM 41839

D) Flat faience Hathor mask from Serabit el-Khadim, Toronto ROM 906.16.99

PLATE 31

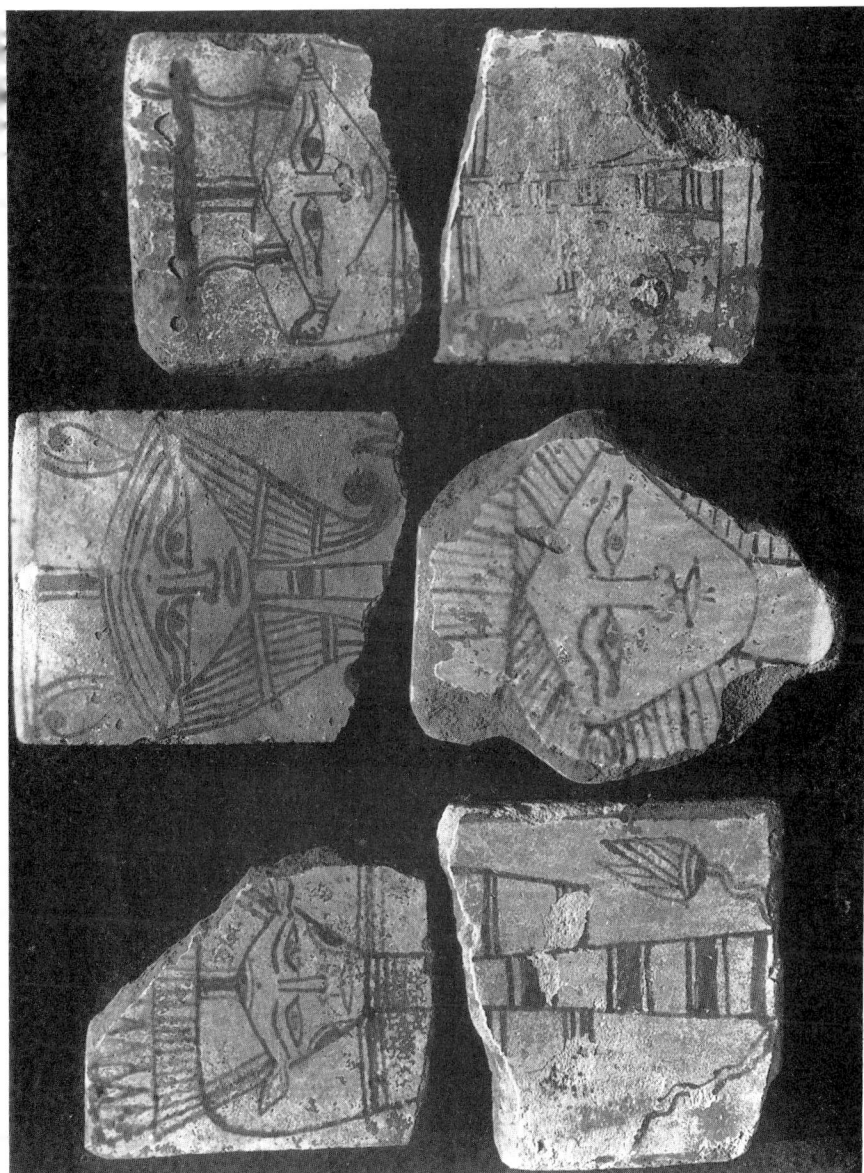

Faience Hathor mask plaques from Serabit el-Khadim

PLATE 32

A) Faience bowl fragment with
   Hathor mask from Deir
   el-Bahri, Brussels MR E 718

B) Faience bowl fragments with Hathor masks from Faras
   London BM 51254, 51252.

C) Faience bowl fragment from Deir
   el-Bahri with Hathor mask on exterior,
   Toronto ROM 907.18.217

D) Faience ring-stand fragment from Serabit
   el-Khadim, Bolton 68.05.22.6

PLATE 33

A) Sherd with Hathor mask from a pottery jar from Deir el-Bahri, London BM 49250

B) Projecting Hathor mask from pottery vessel from Deir el-Bahri, London BM 47680, and blue frit plaque with pair of breasts from the same site, London BM 41100

C) Faience Hathor mask rings from Serabit el-Khadim, London UC 30064–6

PLATE 34

A) Stone cow from Deir el-Bahri, Brussels MR E 2517

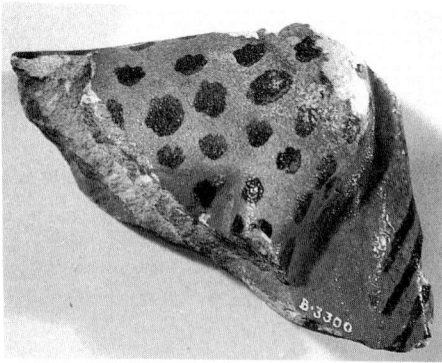

B) Rear end of faience cow from Deir el-Bahri, Toronto ROM 907.18.164

C) Body of faience cow from Deir el-Bahri, Toronto ROM 907.18.162

PLATE 35

A) Head of a faience cow from Deir el-Bahri, London BM 48908

B) Head of a faience cow from Deir el-Bahri, Toronto ROM 907.18.158

C) Faience plaque with cow from Deir el-Bahri, Brussels MR E 722

D) Fragment from faience plaque with cow, Toronto ROM 907.18.257

PLATE 36

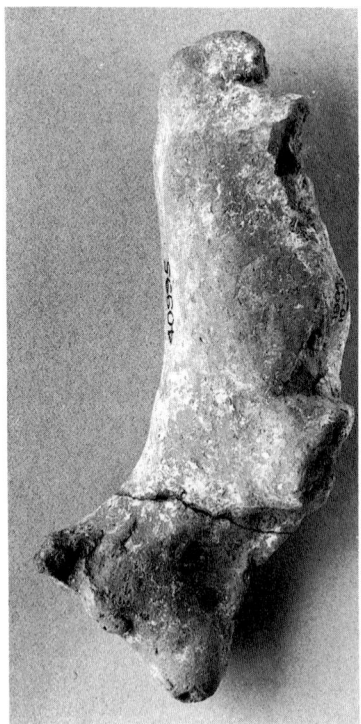

A) Pottery cow from Deir el-Bahri, London BM 40995

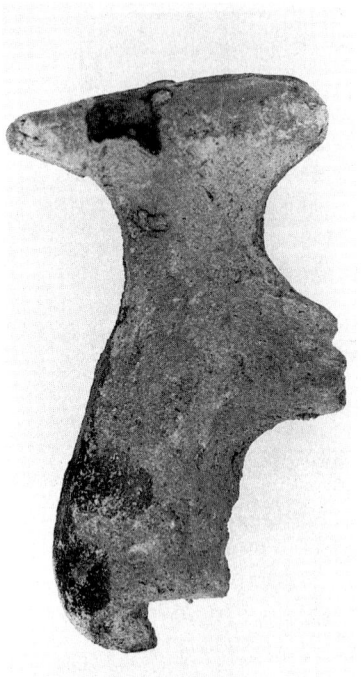

B) Pottery cow from Deir el-Bahri, Oxford PR 1906.45.7

C) Double pottery cow from Deir el-Bahri, Oxford Ash. E 866

D) Pottery cow from Faras, London BM 51268

PLATE 37

A) Faience and metal cow plaques and pendants from Deir el-Bahri.
Top left London BM 41062, top right, London BM 41054, bottom left London
BM 41732, bottom right London BM 41061

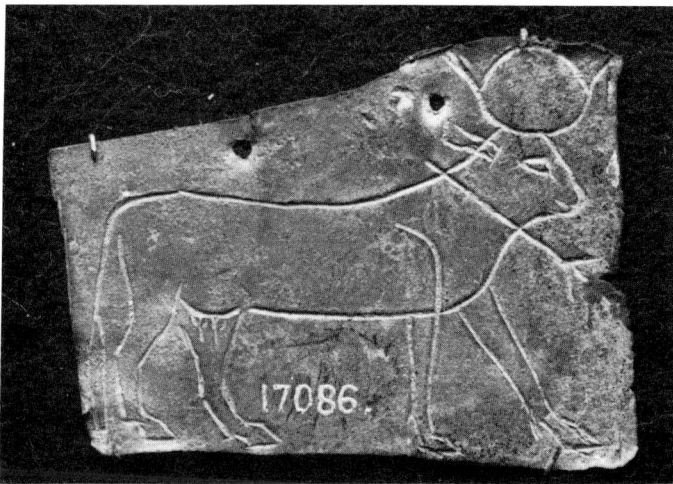

B) Metal cow plaque from Deir el-Bahri, London BM 17086

PLATE 38

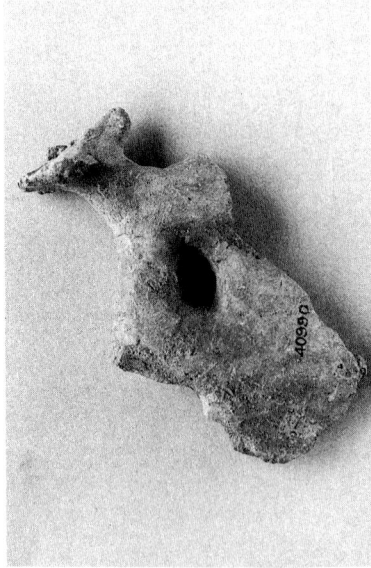

A) Rim of pot with cow from Deir el-Bahri, London BM 40990

B) Sherd with projecting cow's head from Faras, Oxford Ash. 1912.950

C) Part of cow-shaped pottery vase from Deir el-Bahri, Oxford Ash. E.8.

D) Part of cow-shaped pottery vase from Serabit el-Khadim, Oxford Ash. E.3444

PLATE 39

Faience bowl fragments from Serabit el-Khadim

PLATE 40

'Intermediary statue' with cow's head from the 11th dynasty temple at Deir el-Bahri, London BM 145

PLATE 41

A) Ostracon with cow-headed Hathor from Deir el-Bahri, Toronto ROM 907.18.15

B) The cow statue from the speos of the Hathor shrine of Djeser-Akhet

PLATE 42

A) Faience figurines from Serabit el-Khadim

B) Body of faience cat from Deir el-Bahri, London V & A 674.1905.

C) Head of faience cat from Deir el-Bahri, Toronto ROM 907.18.151.

PLATE 43

Faience cat plaques from Serabit el-Khadim

PLATE 44

Faience cat plaques from Serabit el-Khadim

PLATE 45

B) Faience ring-stand fragment with cat from Serabit el-Khadim, Toronto ROM 906.16.91

D) Faience ring-stand fragment with Hathor mask and cat from Serabit el-Khadim, Toronto ROM 906.16.103

A) Faience ring-stand fragment with cat from Serabit el-Khadim, Bolton 68.05.22.7

C) Faience ring-stand fragment with Hathor mask and cat from Serabit el-Khadim, Toronto ROM 906.16.90

PLATE 46

A) Type 1 faience fertility figurines from Kahun, London UC 16723-4

B) Type 6c pottery fertility figurine, London BM 20982

C) Type 2 pottery fertility figurine from Gebel Zeit

D) Head of Type 3 pottery fertility figurine from Gebel Zeit

PLATE 47

B) Type 3 pottery fertility figurine with child, London BM 23424

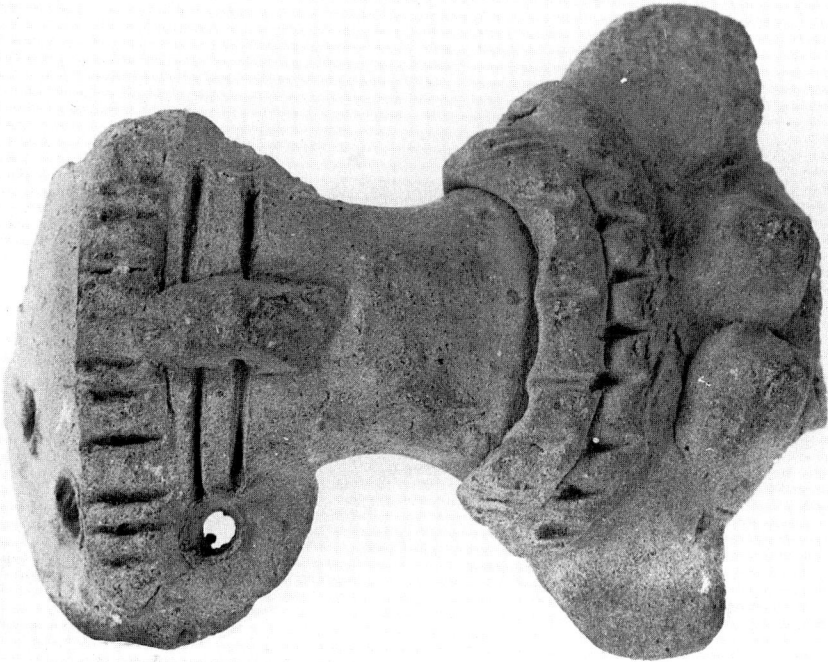

A) Head of Type 3 pottery fertility figurine from Deir el-Bahri, Oxford PR 1906.45.15

PLATE 48

A) Heads of Type 3 pottery fertility figurines, upper from Faras, London BM 51269–70; lower from Deir el-Bahri, London BM 41105

B) Fragmentary pottery fertility figurines from Faras, including Type 3 with child, Oxford Ash. GN 1912.949

PLATE 49

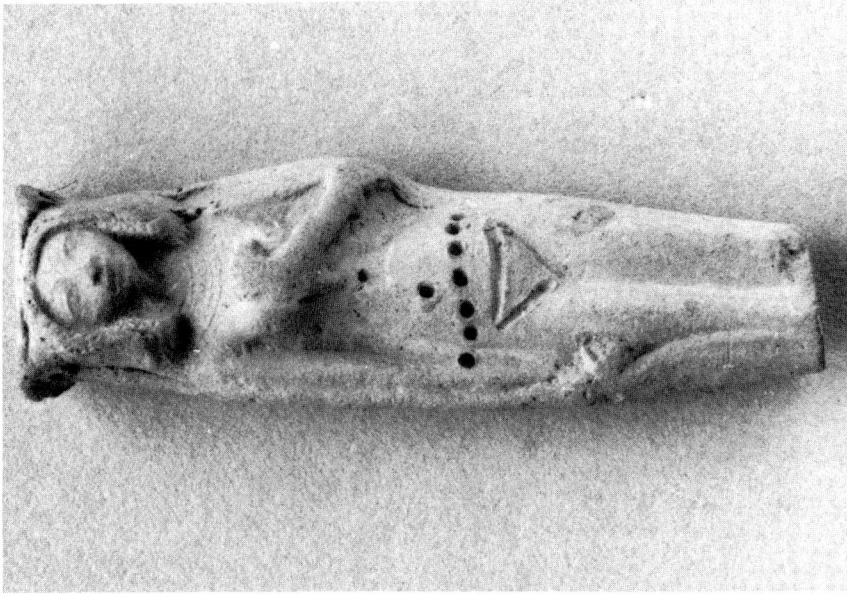

B) Type 4 pottery fertility figurine from Faras, London BM 51263

A) Left, Type 4 pottery fertility figurine from Deir el-Bahri, London BM 41107; right body of Type 3 figurine from the same site, London BM 41108

PLATE 50

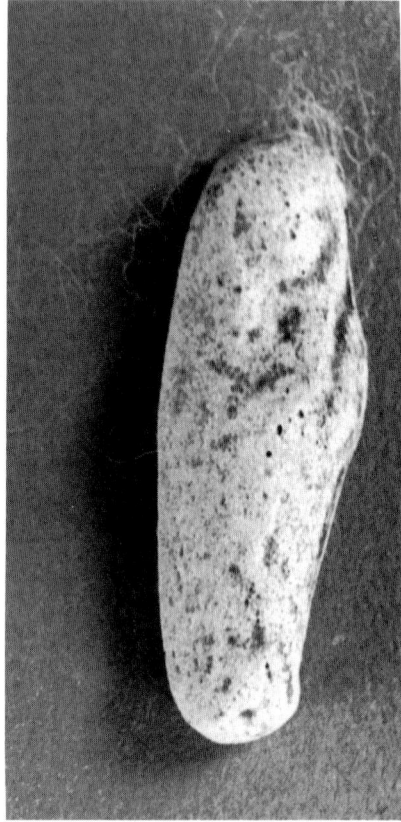

A) Two Type 5 faience fertility figurines from Faras, Oxford PR 1912.89.218–9

B) Five Type 5 faience fertility figurines from Faras, London BM 51259–62, 51361.

PLATE 51

) Type 4 pottery fertility
figurine from Deir el-Bahri,
Oxford PR 1906.45.13

B) Type 4 pottery fertility figurine from Deir el-Bahri,
Oxford Ash.E 871, and Type 5 faience figurine
from Faras, Oxford Ash. 1912.943.

Type 5 faience fertility figurine
from Deir el-Bahri, Oxford
PR 1906.45.11

D) Type 6b faience fertility
figurine from Serabit
el-Khadim, Cambridge
Fitz. E FG 10

PLATE 52

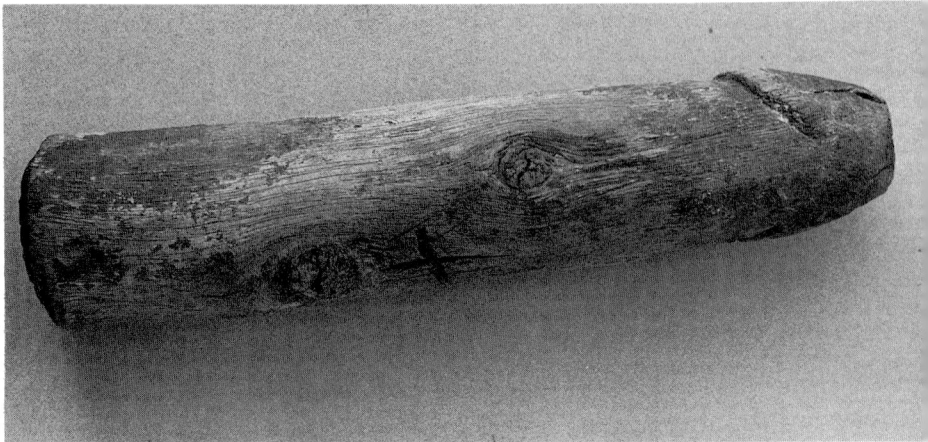

A) Wooden phallus from Deir el-Bahri, Oxford Ash. 1926.401

B) Faience vulva and phallus from Deir el-Bahri, London BM 47766, 47768

C) Pottery sherd with breasts from Deir el-Bahri, London BM E 2722

PLATE 53

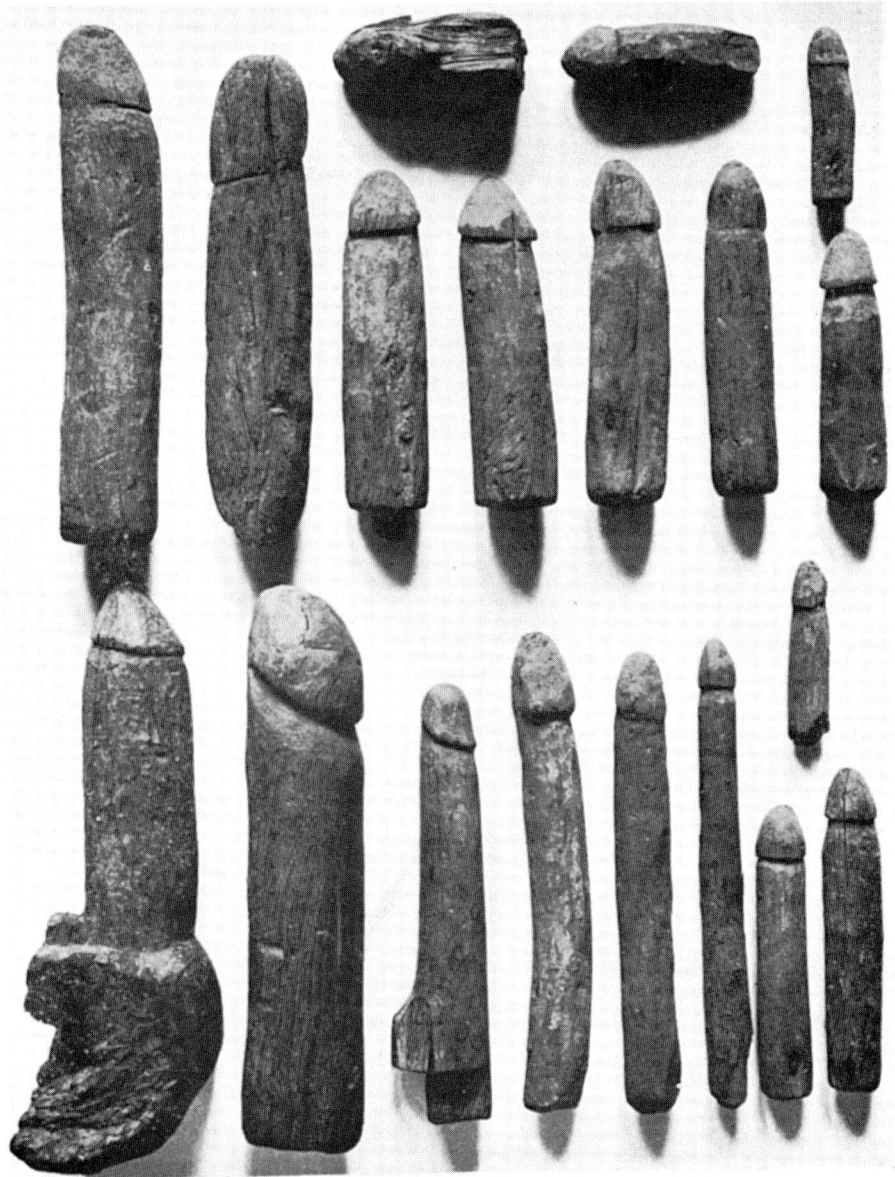

Wooden phalli from the Hathor shrine of Djeser-Akhet

PLATE 54

Fragment of a painted leather hanging from Deir el-Bahri, New York MMA 31.3.98

PLATE 55

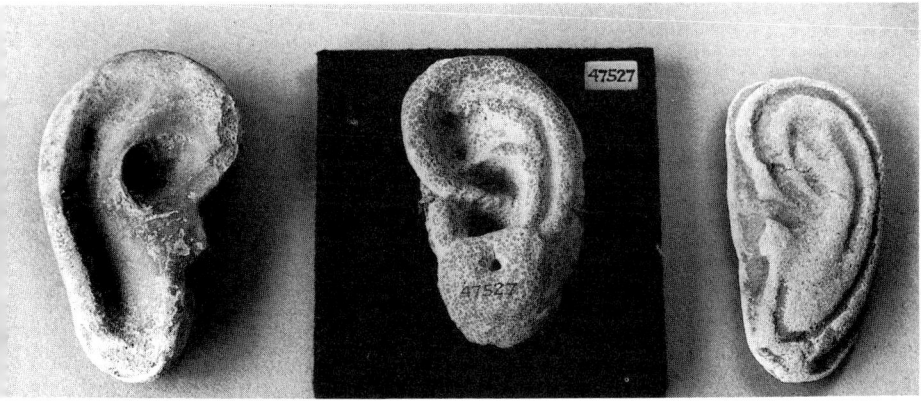

A) Left, stone ear from Faras, London BM 51257; centre, stone ear from Deir el-Bahri, London BM 47527; right, faience ear from Faras, London BM 51256

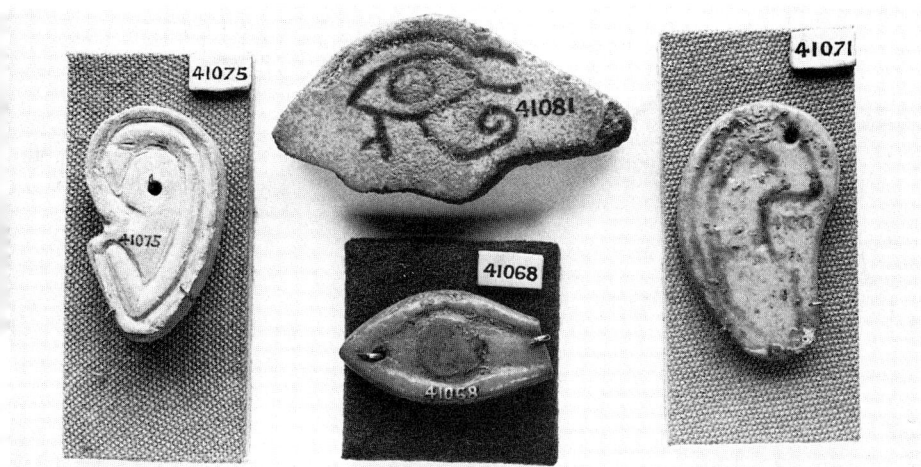

B) Faience ears and eyes from Deir el-Bahri, London BM 41075, 41081, 41068, 41071

C) Fragmentary metal *wadjet* eye plaque from Deir el-Bahri, Oxford PR 1904.35.104

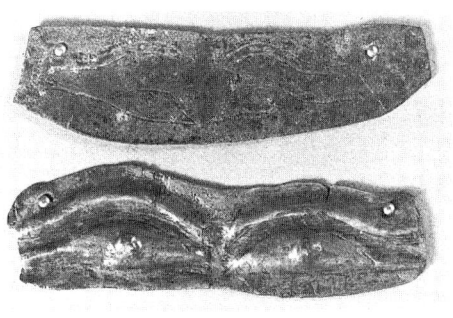

D) Two metal eye plaques from Deir el-Bahri, Oxford PR 1906.45.3-4

PLATE 56

A) Wooden ear stela from Deir
   el-Bahri, Brussels MR E 2440

B) Wooden *wadjet* eye stela
   from Deir el-Bahri,
   Oxford PR 1904.35.107

C) Wooden ear from Deir el-Bahri,
   London BM 41077

D) Faience eye plaque from Deir el-Bahri,
   Oxford PR 1906.45.5

PLATE 57

A) Faience persea fruits and segmented ball
from Faras, London BM 51261–2, 51255

B) Faience disc beads from Deir el-Bahri, Oxford PR 1904.35.82

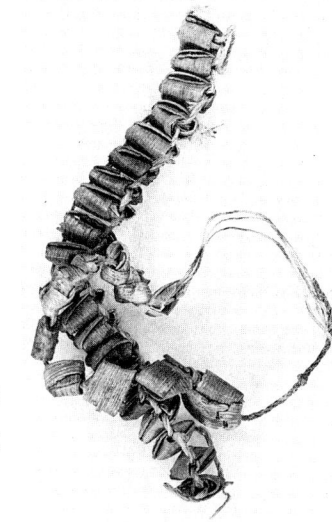

C) Necklace of reed packet beads from Deir
el-Bahri, Oxford PR 1904.35.83

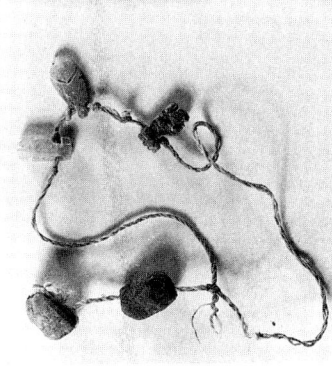

D) Intact votive necklace
from Deir el-Bahri,
Oxford PR 1904.35.87

PLATE 58

Faience menit counterpoises from Serabit el-Khadim

PLATE 59

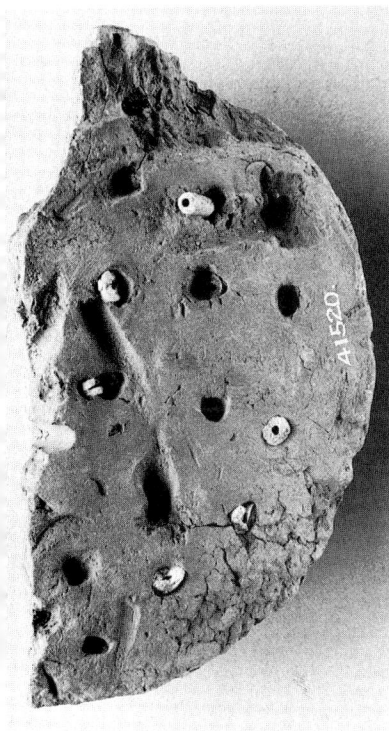

A) 'Bead loaf' from Deir el-Bahri, London BM 41520a

C) Faience Taweret beads from Faras, Oxford PR 1912.89.211–17

B) Wooden and faience menit counterpoises from Deir el-Bahri, Brussels MR E 711, 2470

PLATE 60

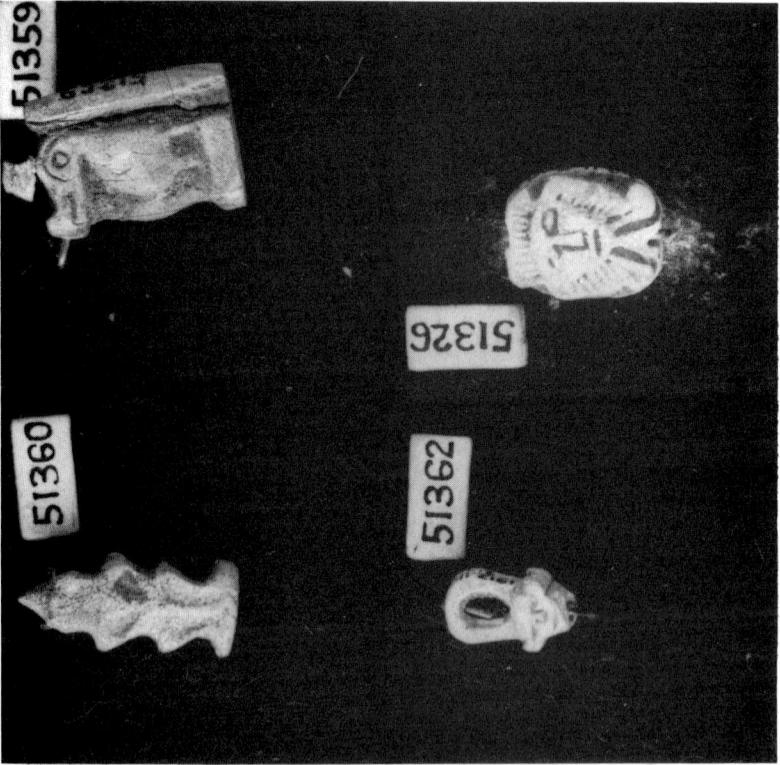

B) Faience Taweret amulet from Faras, London BM 51258

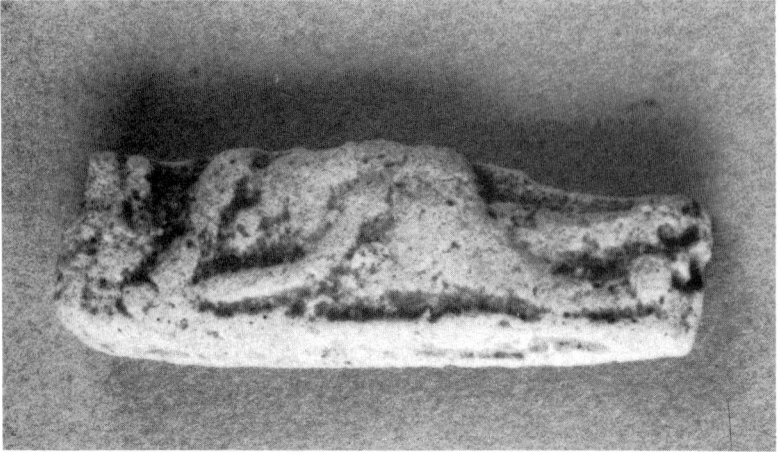

A) Faience or steatite amulets from Faras: top left Bes, London BM 51360, top right Taweret, London BM 51359, bottom left loop sistrum, London BM 51362, bottom right Hathor mask, London BM 51326.

PLATE 61

Faience bracelets from Serabit el-Khadim

PLATE 62

Faience throwsticks from Serabit el-Khadim

PLATE 63

Fragmentary faience bowl from Serabit el-Khadim

PLATE 64

Detail of faience vase fragments, showing girl presenting flowers to king, London V & A 717 1905